ISBN 978-1-5285-4847-2
PIBN 10922250

English
Français
Deutsche
Italiano
Español
Português

www.forgottenbooks.com

Mythology Photography **Fiction**
Fishing Christianity **Art** Cooking
Essays Buddhism Freemasonry
Medicine **Biology** Music **Ancient
Egypt** Evolution Carpentry Physics
Dance Geology **Mathematics** Fitness
Shakespeare **Folklore** Yoga Marketing
Confidence Immortality Biographies
Poetry **Psychology** Witchcraft
Electronics Chemistry History **Law**
Accounting **Philosophy** Anthropology
Alchemy Drama Quantum Mechanics
Atheism Sexual Health **Ancient History**
Entrepreneurship Languages Sport
Paleontology Needlework Islam
Metaphysics Investment Archaeology
Parenting Statistics Criminology
Motivational

REPORTS

OF

CASES DETERMINED

BY THE

SUPREME COURT

OF THE

STATE OF MISSOURI

Between February 15, 1916, and May 31, 1916.

PERRY S. RADER,

REPORTER.

VOL. 267.

COLUMBIA, MO.:
E. W. STEPHENS PUBLISHING CO.
1916

NOV 1   1916

(ii)   [267 Mo.

JUDGES OF THE SUPREME COURT

DURING THE TIME OF THESE REPORTS

JUDGES OF THE SUPREME COURT

BY DIVISIONS

DIVISION ONE.

HON. WALLER W. GRAVES, Presiding Judge.

HON. ARCHELAUS M. WOODSON, Judge.

HON. HENRY W. BOND, Judge.

HON. JAMES T. BLAIR, Judge.

HON. STEPHEN S. BROWN, Commissioner.

HON. ROBERT T. RAILEY, Commissioner.

DIVISION TWO.

HON. CHARLES B. FARIS, Presiding Judge.

HON. ROBERT FRANKLIN WALKER, Judge.

HON. CHARLES G. REVELLE, Judge.

HON. REUBEN F. ROY, Commissioner.

HON. FRED L. WILLIAMS, Commissioner.

TABLE OF CASES REPORTED

IN THIS VOLUME.

CASES OVERRULED OR DISAP-
PROVED.

TABLE OF CASES CITED

IN THIS VOLUME.

IN MEMORIAM.

In compliance with a previous order, Court in Banc met on April 12, 1916, to receive suitable memorials prepared by committees appointed by the Missouri Bar Association in memory of Hon. John Chilton Brown, who had died while a member of the court, on September 4, 1915, and of Hon. Elijah H. Norton and Hon. Warwick Hough, both of whom had in former years been Judges of the Court and had shortly prior thereto departed this life.

The memorial to Hon. John C. Brown was presented by Hon. Henry Lamm, on behalf of the committee, composed of himself, Hon. Sanford B. Ladd, Hon. M. E. Rhodes and Judge David H. Harris.

The memorial to Hon. Elijah H. Norton was presented by Hon. DeWitt Clinton Allen, on behalf of the committee, composed of himself, Hon. R. P. C. Wilson and Hon. Willard P. Hall.

The memorial to Hon. Warwick Hough was presented by Hon. Frederick N. Judson on behalf of the committee, composed of himself, Hon. William M. Williams and Hon. Charles W. Bates. These memorials follow:

HON. JOHN CHILTON BROWN.

The day will come when the pious hand of some scholarly friend, delving here and there for the facts, will laboriously collect the material for a history of this Court, now nearing its century mark. That history if written in true proportion and with a discriminating pen, will tell the life stories of the Judges of this bench. Already the material for a suitable estimate of their tastes and predilections in the law, their mastery of accurate reasoning and of legal literature and style, their wisdom, intellectual grasp and serenity of judgment, their learning in the law and its philosophies and the whole range of the quality of their judicial work is now at hand; for it is imperishably preserved for the use of your future historian in their decisions and judgments. The portraits hanging on your walls will aid that historian; for unless nature is a lie the soul of a man somewhat speaks from his face. It is of few men it can be said that you can "read their history in a nation's eyes." It is of all men it may be said that you can read somewhat of the immortal part of them in their own. But the basic facts, the manner of men they were as they lived, moved and had their being among their fellows, the actual men themselves, is another matter.

It was the quaint yet shrewd conceit of a delightful Boston philosopher and poet that every man was made up of three men, each distinct and differing. There, for example, was the man stripped of all disguise, the actual man as the eye of God sees him. There was also the man as he sees himself—another person altogether. Then there was the man the public see—a man differing essentially from either of the other two. God deals with the first, autobiography with the second, biography with the last.

Much of the material for the lives of the early Judges is covered by the steadily down-sifting dust of oblivion and is either irretrievably lost, or exists only in the faintest and barest outline of memory and tradition—a memory but a leaking cup, a tradition out dimmer and dimmer with each passing year. Much of it is not only fragmentary but is scattered and hid out in this and that publication and can only be assembled, digested and arranged with infinite patience and labor. Accordingly it is not only a labor of love but it is in order to preserve in your own records something of substance in the details of their lives and something worth while in a contemporaneous estimate of the characters of your dead brethren, to aid your future historian, that the Missouri Bar Association reverently arranges and presents at your bar Memorials like this.

Judge John Chilton Brown, youngest of three sons, was born March 22, 1860, in Aldrich Valley, Carter County, Missouri, a year after its organization, dying at St. Luke's Hospital in St. Louis on September 4, 1915, aged fifty-five. An uncommonly reticent man, he talked little of himself and little of his ancestry. A favorite theory of his was that ancestry was of value if a man, under the glow of its stimulus, lived up to a good name and thus made a record for himself, otherwise it counted but little in measuring the man. He considered himself a distant relative of B. Gratz Brown and had assembled a family record, presently destroyed by fire. The scanty facts at hand touching his ancestry were got at by correspondence. It is known that James Brown, his father, was a Virginian presumably of Scotch or English blood and descended from a colonial family. Relatives of Judge Brown (Shadrach Chilton and Judge F. M. Carter) hazard the suggestion that there was a strain of Indian blood in James Brown, but this must be taken with a grain of salt because of the other fact that a strain of Indian ancestry is a poetical and romantic notion prevalent in Virginia, orginating in colonial history and taking root in the pleasing legends of Pocahontas. James Brown at an early and unknown date migrated from Virginia (it is likely by way of Tennessee, sojourning there a spell), and pushing on West finally settled in what is now Carter County, opening a small farm in Aldrich Valley, now the site of the present town of Chilton and near the Current River, a noble stream on whose banks his children were born. He there presently married Adaline Chilton, whose family name lives in that of her distinguished son. That son always fondly spoke of her as a tender and devoted mother, and it is said he resembled her to a marked degree, possessing her affectionate and retiring disposition. There is a faint tradition that an ancestor of the American Chiltons took ship and crossed the seas in the Mayflower, a pilgrim, and landed at Plymouth Rock with Brewster, Carver, Bradford, Alden, Priscilla, Standish and the rest. But this tradition is without substance. The Chiltons were Welch, coming from Wales to Virginia before the Revolution and settling on the Potomac. Then some of them migrated to East Tennessee, and in 1818 or 1820 some of these, in turn, moved to the wilderness of Southern Missouri and settled in Carter County, veritable pioneers and frontiersmen. The name, Chilton, is mentioned by Houck in his scholarly history of early Missouri, is respectably connected with the legislative annals of the State, is preserved in the geography of the region, and is now borne by good citizens. On the mother's side Judge Brown was also related to the Carter family—a family long, well and honorably known to the judiciary, the bar and banking circles of Missouri. Zimri Carter, the family's head, settled in Carter County in 1820, became its chief citizen, is mentioned by Houck as a pioneer and was honored by the county's taking his name on its organization in 1859. It has been said that in 1860 Zimri Carter and James Brown were the only two men who owned slaves in Carter County, that they owned one each and that these slaves inter-married when freed.

A word more of James Brown: When the civil war broke and Missourians were stirred mightily, he listened to the call of Governor Jackson for the organization of State Guards. With the ready fealty of a backwoodsman to his principles, he espoused the cause of the South with all his heart, riding double on that war summons with his eldest son to Greenville to enlist in Col. Aden Low's regiment, then forming there, as a private, taking the son along to bring his horse back for family use, and leaving his youngest son an infant in arms. It is a pathetic incident of his leave taking that in bidding farewell to his wife he told her he would never return until the war was over and the South victorious. The phrase of that promise made his farewell final; for he never returned. He was elected captain of a company in Low's regiment, bore himself well as a soldier under Price and perished of sickness in the Confederate service before the battle of Fredericktown at which his colonel was killed. After the war, when John was nine years old, his mother married Timothy Reeves, a Baptist preacher, who also had been a captain in Price's army. This man of God was a genuine backwoodsman and a renowned bear hunter, a kindly, happy-go-lucky person, shy of the knack of getting on in the world. At any rate the small estate left by Captain Brown was soon exhausted and at the age of thirteen young John, without a penny, was cast on his own resources to win his bread and get on in the world as the master of his own fate. To rightly estimate a man his environment must be sharply reckoned with; for it is the immutable law of our being that not only is the child father to the man, but the man himself is part of all he saw, thought and did. Let us glance, then, at the scene of his childhood. Time has worked wonders there, but fifty years ago Carter County was (as were Reynolds, Wayne, Oregon, Shannon, Ripley and Butler, bounding it) a wild, secluded and almost inaccessible region of hills and valleys. Its hills were covered with primeval pine and its valleys with soft and hard woods, the home of game and clawed animals. Its settlements were scattered. Its people were sturdy but primitive mountaineers of Virginia, Kentucky and Tennessee. The region was cut off from traffic on the Mississippi River by the then swamps and sloughs of Southeast Missouri. To the North and West were the virgin Ozarks. The only outlet for its small commerce was by streams flowing south into Arkansas. The roads were trails, the streams bridgeless—of railroads there were none. In all that country in 1860 the population was so sparse that (counting the towns, villages, hamlets and lone settlers) the average was a human soul to, say, three hundred acres of land. To add to it all, the Civil War smote Carter County sorely. Its so-called school-houses were abandoned dwellings, log cabins, without blackboards, furnished with rough benches and the only school apparatus was the master's rod.

Congreve makes a character in one of his plays say: "I came upstairs into the world for I was born in a cellar." John Chilton Brown was not born in a cellar but he was born in what would now be called unkindly surroundings, his early life was that of a barefoot, backwoods boy and he literally "came upstairs into the world." It is no fanciful flight to say that his College was the log school-house of Carter County, his University the school of a harsh master, Experience. His learning, which was considerable, he pluckily acquired by study by his own tallow dip and his hero was Abraham Lincoln, whose remarkable life was his Mentor and inspiration. Fortunately for him and us he belonged not to the class of whom it is written:

> "Chill penury repress'd their noble rage
> And froze the genial current of the soul."

Your Honors, his life was so modest, so sincere, so brave, so plain that we know he would wish its story told simply and without varnish. He was not ashamed of it and neither should we be, for the primary virtues of courage determination, perseverence in persistent effort, temperance, calmness, good-nature, sincerity, forthright honesty so shaped themselves in him that he made his own "place in the sun," by innate grit and the divine gift of plodding effort, a resolute self-determination that knew no turning back when his hand was once put to the plow. The lesson to be learned from his life is that Fortune at the end had a smile for the courageous soul. At thirteen, coming to Van Buren his county town, he went into a newspaper office, that of the Van Buren Times or Vidette, and was taught to set type. Later, and while still a lad, he was its joint proprietor and editor. It was the estimate of his associate, his Honor Judge Walker, that he there acquired his direct, unadorned and simple style of writing. Later the "Gold fever" seized him and with his eldest brother he prospected in the Gunnison County in Colorado. Unsuccessful and returning to his home county, he opened a set of abstract books and (there being activity in pine lands) he became a land agent before he was of age, had large interests intrusted to his hands, meanwhile serving his people as justice of the peace—an humble sort of service to one's neighbors having illustrious examples in kind in John Quincy Adams' and Thomas Jefferson's service as "pathmasters" or "road-overseers."

We say large interests were intrusted to him while he was yet under age and we say so on the authority of a fine lumberman, J. B. White of Kansas City, who vouches for the fact and gave him his first case after his admission to the bar. Brown's gratitude was so keen and abiding for White's confidence and aid that long after-wards it made him fear his friendship would disturb his judicial judgment and for that reason alone he declined to sit in a trust case involving heavy interests of his old-time friend, and once pending in this court—an incident not without value in estimating his delicacy of mind and exquisite faithfulness to duty.

In 1887, when twenty-seven, he married Miss Sarah E. Pool, an estimable lady who survives him. Of this happy union two children were born, a son, Lasker, dying in infancy and a daughter, Nina, who was indeed the apple of his eye sharing with her mother his self-sacrificing devotion. In 1888, wholly self-taught in the law, he was admitted to the Carter bar. His estimate of himself at this time was so modest that he doubted his ability to be a lawyer of the class he aspired to and his hesitancy to pursue his studies and enroll was overcome by his wife and his partial friends. Presently, in the same year he was elected prosecuting attorney. There were turbulent men and times in Carter County in those days, his life was threatened by desperate criminals, his papers were destroyed by incendiary fires and he made a record for himself as a man of personal courage and a lawyer of efficiency. Afterwards, his health breaking, he regained it in Arizona. Returning he sought larger opportunities and in 1892-4 located west of Carter at Willow Springs, in Howell. Here he steadily grew in his profession and in public esteem, was mayor and was nominated in 1902 for Circuit Judge of the 20th District by the Republicans, failing of election (in a memorable contest against a veteran Judge in a circuit politically hostile) by six votes. In 1896 he changed his party affiliations. He was born and reared a Democrat of the strictest school. His people and region were of that faith and it speaks well for him as a man that contrary to the usual fact, neither the party he left or that to which he came ever questioned his disinterested sincerity or his sturdy independence in the change. In that change he acted on principle, as he saw it, and men honored him for it. Feeling himself handicapped because of that race, in 1903 he removed to Fredericktown in another circuit. In 1909 he served on the legislative committee to revise the Statutes and a year later was elected to this honorable bench for a ten-year term, served half of it and died of an insidious disease which, baffling human skill, fastened a clutch upon him he could not shake off.

If the court please, this committee voices the universal regret of the bar and bench that death by its untimely stroke in the prime of his life in the midway of his term forever ended his judicial labors; for of him it may be said that adversity had sweetened not soured him, that there was in him a great reservoir of that rare thing, "saving common-sense," and a cluster, as we have already said, of such primal virtues as love of humanity, honesty, calmness, patience, temperance, courage, simplicity, sincerity, straightforwardness, industry, kindness, charity, modesty. He was a comfortable man to know if one cared to know him well and he had a homely and dry wit rarely used but startling through its unexpectedness when employed. "Is there," said he to counsel who argued against enforcing a statute in the instant case for that it had fallen into disuse,—"is there such a thing as repealing a statute by refusing to enforce it?" It is believed by the bar that on a time a learned counsel for an hour had inadvertently muddled his case by lack of clarity. That the bench, save Judge Brown, had in turn plied counsel with question after question. That thereat Judge Brown took a hand in this wise: "I wish to perform my full duty on this bench and it seems I can only do so by asking questions. Will counsel inform the court what the case is about and which side he is on?" But this view of him counts for little along side of matters of more substance.

He was sensible and brave enough to recognize his own limitations and feared not to mention them. He moved among us of full size with the stooped shoulders and earnest face of the thinker and philosopher he was—plain in mien, manners, apparel, speech and thought, devoid of ostentation of pretense and with none of that artificial effusiveness often allied to insincerity. He had in him a tang of the soil and the vernacular of his region, and, loving streams, hills, and valleys and communion with nature in the open air, the confinement and intense application to his labors in chambers sapped his constitution and induced the malady that closed his life.

In justice to him and to the truth of history it should be said that for a year or two after he came to this bench he was under a cloud of singular embarrassment and labored under a strain. Not only was the title to his office held in judgment in pending litigation in his own court (of which he could not complain and which disturbed the serenity of a sensitive man like him) but he keenly realized that the vicissitudes of an election had, in his behalf, defeated a man whose interesting career as a soldier under Lee and whose charm of manner and established fame as a jurist had made him a figure of which the State was proud. No man could be more keenly alive than he was to the fact that he was an unknown and untried judicial factor and that he faced a critical bar. From his cloud of embarrassment he gently and steadily but surely emerged as the quality of his work shows. He loved his work and it was a cruel decree of fate that ordained that he was not to be allowed to round out a public career, more and more promising well.

It is too early to finally estimate his labors as a judge. It may be safely said, however, that his was a growing judicial mind, that he more and more supplied his lack of early advantages by patience and assiduous toil and that he corrected a native lack of mental quickness and brilliancy by meditation and study. He formed his conclusions slowly but when formed wrote with clarity and simple directness, and announcing his judgments without overdress of adornment and without elaborate reasoning, No one can read his opinions sympathetically without seeing he had a true passion for justice. He was glad if precedents were found to fortify his conclusions but believed the day of making them was not over and he turned his back on old ones without regret if they interfered with his own settled view of the very right of the matter. Whether that course be wise or unwise as tending to settle or unsettle the law may be passed by; but is must be admitted to be an inseparable incident to independent and original thinking on the bench—a quality Judge Brown had. He had the master virtue in a just judge of being blind in his judgments to the mere adventitious trappings of social rank, power and wealth. A great soul once said: "God must love common people or he would not have made so many of them." That saying fell from the lips of Judge Brown's hero and he held to that doctrine himself.

Yours Honors, lawyers prone to controversy and argumentation write with a feeble pen in calm biography. This tribute is therefore inadequate. It is respectfully submitted as sincere.

HON. ELIJAH HISE NORTON.

At his home near Platte City, Missouri, on August 6, 1914, died Elijah Hise Norton, a man distinguished alike in the political and judicial annals of this State.

Judge Norton—so he was called by the people and his friends—was born in Russellville, Logan County, Kentucky, on November 21, 1821. He was of Pennsylvanian strain. His father, William Norton, and his mother were natives of the Keystone state. They had emigrated thence and settled in Kentucky—the former near the year 1806 and the latter near 1802. They were married in Russellville on April 11, 1813. The mother's maiden name was Mary Hise. In their son were united the bloods of England and Germany.

He received a classical education, and his taste for the classics remained during his life. He chose the law for his profession, and graduated in the Law Department of Transylvania University,

Lexington, Kentucky, in 1843. During his attendance there, Judge George Robertson was at the head of the Law Department. The vast learning and massive intellect of that great jurist impressed all who came under their influence.

At the completion of his preparation for legal practice, for the home of his life, he was attracted to the "Platte Purchase" in Missouri, and, of its subdivisions, to Platte County. At this distant day, it is difficult to fully realize and appreciate all of the causes, including opportunities for individual effort, which, seventy years ago and beyond, drew settlers to the "Platte. Purchase" from all over the Union. It was the "paradise of lawyers," nor was there then, anywhere in the Union, perhaps, a county where, in proportion to population and wealth, there was a greater amount of valuable litigation than in Platte County. There were then in it thirty-five attorneys.

He arrived in Platte City—and made it the home of his life— on January 8, 1845. He found the people of the town and vicinity engaged in celebrating the battle of New Orleans. This was in harmony with his feelings and of those of the people among whom he had been born and reared. The day was to him auspicious. At once he opened his law office, and on the 15th day of April following was enrolled a member of the Platte County Bar. From the outset his practive was lucrative. The people of Platte County admired and loved him.

The year 1845 was, assuredly, in a period of great lawyers in Western Missouri. Of those who then practiced in the Platte Circuit Court may be mentioned the following: Alexander W. Doniphan, Amos Rees, John Wilson, Willard P. Hall, Henry M. Vories, Richard R. Rees, James H. Baldwin, Robert P. Clark, Lorenzo D. Bird, Bela M. Hughes, Gen. David R. Archison, James Craig, William B. Almond, William M. Paxton, Solomon P. McCurdy, and, later, Gen. Ben. F. Stringfellow and James N. Burnes. These gentlemen constituted an aggregation of intellectual power and eloquence not surpassed, if equalled, by any bar in the Union.

These great attorneys, as well as Judge Norton, had acquired their legal training under the old system—delving long and well into the legal text-books. The late Washington Adams—who, in his day, graced our Supreme Bench—had read Chitty on Pleading fourteen times. The late Amos Rees was required by his legal preceptor to read Bacon's Abridgement through, beginning with the first article. And this he did.

The year 1845, it will be remembered, was prior to the revolution in practice caused by the adoption in Missouri in 1849 of the "code" system of pleading. Then the authorities in pleading were Chitty, Stephen and Story,—the highest science,—and in evidence old Starkie and Peake. The "code" was spoken of as "Wells's Code." In its first form, it allowed such broad pleas that a plea, tendering an issue, was jocularly called by the lawyers the "prairie plea." The years mentioned above indicate that Judge Norton's legal training was under the old system. Thrown into contact with the great lawyers just mentioned, he absorbed their mental overflow and rose to an equality with them.

His "roll of honor" is long and distinguished. In 1850 he was appointed attorney for Platte County. Shortly following this, he was elected judge of the circuit of which Platte County was a part. It was then the 12th. At the end of his term, he was again elected judge of the circuit. At re-election he had no opposition. During his second term as circuit judge, he was elected to Congress. On February 18, 1861' he was elected a delegate from the 13th Senatorial District to the State Convention called to take such action as the interest and welfare of the State might require. His colleagues from that district were Cols. Alexander W. Doniphan and James H. Moss. At the November election, 1874, he was chosen from the Senatorial District, composed of the counties of Platte, Clay and Clinton, a delegate to the State Convention called to revise and amend the State Constitution adopted in 1865. It assembled in May, 1875. On September 12, 1876, he was appointed a member of the Supreme Court of our State, to fill the unexpired term of the Hon. Henry M. Vories. At the November election, 1878, he was elected to the Supreme Bench for the term of ten years. His first opinion on the Supreme Bench was rendered in Ellis v. Railroad Co., 63 Mo. 131.

At the conclusion of his twelve years on our Supreme Bench he returned to his elegant home near Platte City and gave the remainder of his life to his family and friends, the peace and comfort of his church affiliations, and the advancement of charitable and educational matters. In 1871 he was chosen a member of the Board of Trustees of William Jewell College. He continued a trustee of that institution during the remainder of his life, rendering it essential service in many ways. In 1882 that institution conferred on him the honorary degree of L.L.D.

Judge Norton was twice married. His first wife was Miss Melinda Clark Wilson, a daughter of John Wilson, the great lawyer already mentioned, and who was familiarly known througnout Missouri as John Wilson of Platte. He and she were married on May 28, 1850. She died on May 15, 1873. Of that union seven children were born. On September 17, 1877, he was married to Mrs. Missouri A. Marshall, who survives him.

His admirable preparation for life by study and investigation, upon the basis of a clear, balanced intellect, enabled him to maintain himself with ease and dignity in every position wherein he was called to act. He was in Congress in "stormy and tempestuous times, when the Government was unsettled." He discharged his duties there with firmness, courage and fidelity to his constituents. The same condition was true of the time when he was a delegate to the State Convention called in 1861. Time has much obscured conditions and motives in Missouri during the continuance of that convention. It may truly be said of the action of Judge Norton and his associates therein that it was a mighty factor in securing peace and good government in Missouri.

His ability as a legislator was conspicuously shown in the Constitutional Convention held in 1875. As all know that convention formulated our existing organic law. No one in it was more thoroughly equipped for the work of such a body. There was no better constitutional lawyer in it. His general information, familiarity with the decisions of the courts and statutory law (with his mental poise, calmness, urbanity and fairness), were of high value at every stage of its proceedings. His influence pervades every portion, almost, of the Constitution which that body formulated.

Perhaps, all things considered, he was more nearly in his true element on the bench, and shone there with a clearer, brighter light. The judicial quality was predominant in his mental and moral composition. Though near fifty-five years have elapsed since he quitted the circuit bench, yet the elders—those citizens of Northwest Missouri, whose heads have on them the silver of time,—will occasionally refer to his quick, clear, accurate decisions and firm government of his court while on the circuit bench.

Repute won on the circuit bench will pass away with those who saw and heard. Not so with fame achieved on our Supreme Court bench. The terse, clear, logical opinions of Judge Norton rendered while on that bench— instinct, as they are, with common sense and reasoned with the sure touch of a balanced intellect—are a part of our judicial history and will remain while our great State shall have records to preserve.

In physique, he was rather small—something below the middle size—but he was unusually active and strong. His manners were easy, unrestrained, and affable. His eyes were striking and beamed with good will on meeting with acquaintances and friends. They had a quick and searching glance. His convictions as to principles and duties were very strong. In politics, he was ever an unflinching Jeffersonian Democrat, and in religion, and ardent Baptist.

In all of the relations of life growing out of citizenship and the headship of a family, the conduct of few or none could have more safely or honorably undergone the "critical dissection" mentioned by Robert Burns.

He had no angles—no eccentricities—but was soundly and perfectly balanced. This completeness could not be better expressed than in the condensed and powerful Latin of the Roman Horace— whom Judge Norton greatly admired—to be found in one of his satires:

Et in seipso totus teres atque rotundus.

HON. WARWICK HOUGH

HONORABLE WARWICK HOUGH, member of this court from January 1, 1875, to December 31, 1884, was born in Loudoun County, Virginia, on January 26, 1836, and died in the city of St. Louis, Missouri, October 28, 1915.

His parents removed to Missouri in 1838, and his father, George W. Hough, for many years a merchant in Jefferson City, was prominent and influential in the political controversies of the Benton and anti-Benton factions immediately preceding the outbreak of the Civil War.

Warwick Hough was reared in Jefferson City, receiving his primary and preparatory education in the schools of the city, graduating from the State University in the class of 1854. He was exceptionally distinguished in his college career, not only in his love for the classics, but in his scientific attainments, particularly in the sciences of geology and astronomy; and after his graduation he was appointed by Governor Sterling Price as Assistant State Geologist. He found time to study law, and in 1859 was admitted to the bar. In 1860 he formed a law partnership with J. Proctor Knott, then Attorney-General of Missouri, which continued until January, 1861, when he was appointed Adjutant-General by Governor Claiborne F. Jackson.

Before he attained his majority he was clerk in the office of the Secretary of State, and he was Secretary of the State Senate during the sessions of 1858-59, 1859-60, and during the critical and eventful sessions of 1860-61.

As Adjutant-General he issued the general order of April 22, 1861, calling the military organizations of the State into encampment; and this was the order which brought together the State troops at Camp Jackson in St. Louis, resulting in the armed conflict which began the Civil War in Missouri.

During the Civil War he adhered to the Confederate cause, serving as Adjutant-General with the rank of Brigadier General until the death of Governor Jackson, when he was appointed Secretary of State by the Confederate Governor, Thomas C. Reynolds. He resigned this office in 1863 to enter the Confederate military service, wherein he continued through the Civil War, serving successively on the staffs of Lieutenant-General Leonidas M. Polk, General Stephen D. Lee, and later on that of General Dick Taylor, with whom he surrendered at the close of the war, on May 10, 1865.

The proscriptive provisions of the Drake constitution prevented his return at once to the practice of his profession in Missouri, and until 1867 he practiced law at Memphis, Tennessee. On the abolition of the test oath for attorneys he removed to Kansas City, and soon attained a prominent position at the bar, and in November, 1874, was elected Judge of this court for a term of ten years. The Constitution of 1865 was then in force, though the court had been increased from three judges to five by the amendment adopted in 1872.

While the Constitution in 1875 went into operation on November 30th of that year, it was not amended in relation to the judiciary department until after Judge Hough's term had expired; so the court remained during the entire period of his service as one court composed of five judges. The intermediate appellate system established by the Constitution in 1875 remained in effect during that period, that is, with the St. Louis Court of Appeals, including the City of St. Louis and the counties of St. Louis, St. Charles, Lincoln, and Warren, with the appellate jurisdiction in the Supreme Court as defined in the Constitution.

Judge Hough was first associated during his term as judge with Judges David Wagner, H. M. Vories, T. A. Sherwood, and W. B. Napton. On the retirement of Judges Wagner and Vories, Judge John W. Henry and Elijah H. Norton succeeded; and in 1880 Judge Napton retired and was succeeded by Judge Robert D. Ray. The only survivor of the judges of this period is Judge Thomas A. Sherwood. In the last two years of this term the State made its first trial of commissioners to assist the court; and the first commissioners serving in 1883 and 1884 were Honorable John F. Phillips, Alexander Martin, and Charles A. Winslow, the latter of whom on his death was succeeded by the Honorable H. Clay Ewing. Of these commissioners the only survivor is the Honorable John F. Phillips. The ten year term during which Judge Hough served as judge, from January, 1875, to December, 1884, was an exceptionally interesting period in the political and judicial history of the State. In 1875 the Constitution of 1866 was still in force. The distractions of the Civil War and reconstruction period had ended with the repeal of the proscriptive legislation of that period. The Constitution of 1875, which went into force in November, 1875, with its abolition of special legislation and its restriction upon the exercise of the taxing power by counties and municipalities, reflected the public opinion of that time, but largely increased the volume of litigation and presented novel questions both of constitutional and statutory construction for the determination of the court.

The opinions of Judge Hough are found in twenty-six volumes of the Supreme Court, 58 to 83, inclusive. They rank high in judicial learning, in clearness and scholarly finish, and, as a rule, had the supreme merit of brevity. It would extend too much the limits of this memorial to view in detail these four hundred or more opinions contributed by Judge Hough during his term of office.

The judicial independence of Judge Hough and his firm stand in upholding the integrity of public obligations were shown in his concurring with Judge Napton in dissenting from the judgment in Webb v. Lafayette County, 67 Mo. 353, which declared invalid the bonds issued in aid of railroads under the Township Aid Act of 1868; also in his separate concurring opinion in State ex rel. Woodson v. Brassfield, 67 Mo. 331; and also in State ex rel. Wilson v. Rainey, 74 Mo. 29, in concurring in the opinion of the court delivered by Judge Norton, upholding the validity of the tax levied under a mandamus from the Federal court for the payment of a judgment on county bonds which had been adjudged valid by the Federal court, but had been held invalid by the State courts. These cases and opinions recall the conflict, happily ended many years since, between the State and Federal courts in Missouri.

His opinions in the Sharp and Johnson cases, 59 Mo. 557, 76 Mo. 660, are leading cases on the law of malicious prosecution; and the law of disputed boundary established by long acquiescence, is lucidly declared in Turner v. Baker, 64 Mo. 218.

The statute of limitations and the proof of ancient deeds, where title is based upon Spanish land titles, were set forth in an exhaustive and scholarly opinion in Smith v. Madison, 67 Mo. 694.

Jurists have differed on the subject of dissenting opinions. Some think that the custom is more honored in the breach than in the observance; but it is true that dissenting opinions are at times a necessary feature in the development of the law through judicial precedent, which is the essential basis of our jurisprudence. The dissenting opinions of Judge Hough are not numerous; in fact, they are comparatively few. But it is interesting to recall that in several important cases these dissenting opinions have been declared to be the law, even after his retirement from the bench.

Thus, in Valle v. Obenhause, 62 Mo. 81, it was held by a majority of the court that where a husband during coverture is a tenant by the courtesy initiate, the Statute of Limitations begins to run against the wife from the disseizen; and her right of action is therefore barred if she fails to sue within twenty-four years after the disseizen. Judge Hough in his dissenting opinion contended that the Statute of Limitations did not begin to run against a married woman on account of disseizen of her fee simple land until the determination of the tenancy of her husband by the courtesy initiate. Just before his retirement from the bench in 1884 in the case of Campbell v. Laclede Gas Light Company, 84 Mo. 352, three of the five judges concurred in declaring that his dissenting opinion in Valle v. Obenhause stated the correct view of the law; and after Judge Hough's retirement from the bench in 1886, in Dyer v. Witler, 89 Mo. 81, the case of Valle v. Obenhause was definitely overruled and the view expressed by Judge Hough in his dissenting opinion was adopted as the law of the court.

In Noell v. Gaines, 68 Mo. 649, Judge Hough dissented in a learned opinion from the rulings of the court that where a deed of trust provided that the two promissory notes secured thereby should both become due on the failure to pay one, the demand and notice to an endorser at the final maturity of the second note, came too late, as such demand should have been made immediately upon the declaration that the notes were due for foreclosure. Judge Hough insisted that the rule in relation to reading several cotemperaneous instruments together was not applicable to mortgages and notes secured thereby; and this view was adopted by the court several years after he left the bench in Owens v. McKenzie, 133 Mo. 323, so that in this case his dissenting opinion again became the law of the State.

In one of the last cases during his term, Abbott v. Kansas City, St. Joseph & Council Bluffs Railroad Co., 83 Mo. 271, Judge Hough had the satisfaction of noting in his concurring opinion that the rule declared by him in his dissenting opinion in Shane v. K. C. & St. J. & C. B. Ry. Co., 71 Mo. 237, that the rule of the common law, and not the civil law, as to surface water, should prevail in the State, had been adopted by the court and declared the law of the State.

The State University of Missouri conferred upon him the degree of Doctor of Laws in 1883.

On his retirement from the bench in December, 1884, he removed to the city of St. Louis and formed a partnership with John H. Overall and Frederick N. Judson in the name of Hough, Overall & Judson, which continued until December, 1889. Thereafter he was associated with his son, Warwick M. Hough; and also for a time with Hon. Robert F. Walker.

In November, 1900, he was elected to the circuit bench of the city of St. Louis and served with eminent distinction for the full term of six years. It is interesting to note that his associate on the Supreme Bench, John W. Henry, in like manner served in the circuit court of Jackson County for several years after his retirement. After the expiration of this term, Judge Hough was again associated with his son Warwick M. Hough—for a time also with Ex-judge Jacob Klein until the latter's death—and in this association he continued until his death on October 28, 1915. Judge Hough was married in 1861 to Nina E. Massey, the daughter of the Honorable Benjamin F. Massey, then Secretary of State, and she survives him, with five children born of the marriage, two sons and three daughters. The elder son, Warwick M. Hough, is now practicing in St. Louis and is a well known and successful member of the bar of this court.

Politically Judge Hough always adhered to the views which he inherited as to the nature and limited powers of the Federal Government and the reserve rights of the States and always affiliated with the Democratic party. He was widely known to the Masonic Fraternity as a thirty-second degree Scottish-Rite Mason.

Memorializing this distinguished public career of Judge Hough, we can only briefly allude to the exceptional interesting personality of the man. His dignified courtesy and native independence of character, with his wide range of reading and the unusual combination of literary and scientific tastes, gave him a rare personal charm and his interesting and varied experiences in life, and broad human sympathetic philosophy of life made him always welcome in cultured and refined circles, and endeared him to those who were privileged to enjoy an intimate association.

Judge Hough was fortunate in preserving to the last the appreciative enjoyment of those literary and cultured tastes which had distinguished him through life. He was still more fortunate in having to the end of his life the ministrations of the wife of his youth and of his children and "all that should accompany old age—love, honor, obedience, and troops of friends."

As to the closing scene of the drama of this eventful life, we quote the eloquent words of Judge Hough in presenting in the United States Court a few years since, a memorial on a deceased brother of the Bar:

"He has entered upon the impenetrable mystery of the great unknown, athwart whose vast expanse the feeble taper of earthly wisdom sheds no light, and in whose depths the plummet of the profoundest philosophy finds no resting place, and in the contemplation of which the anxious soul finds no consolation, or relief, save in the rainbow of hope, cast upon the sky of the future, by the Son of Righteousness, shining through our tears."

Requiescat in pace.

CASES DETERMINED

BY THE

SUPREME COURT

THE

STATE OF MISSOURI

AT THE

OCTOBER TERM, 1915.

(Continued from Volume 266.)

SAMUEL M. KENNARD et al., Appellants, v. GOTT-LIEB EYERMANN et al.

Division Two, February 15, 1916.

1. **PUBLIC STREET: Park Carriage Drive.** A conveyance to a city of a strip of ground fifty feet wide along an established park to be used as a "carriage avenue" of the park "for all such carriages and teams as by regulations and rules governing the park may be allowed to run in same," was a dedication of the strip for highway purposes; and a further clause in the grant subjecting it to the "immediate government of the park commissioners" means such regulation as may be exercised by them in the control of a public street, and nothing more; and being dedicated to street purposes, and being accepted and since uniformly regarded by the city as a street, the strip's status as a street is fixed.

2. ———: ———: **Evidence of Dedication.** The establishment by the city of public improvements on such "carriage avenue," such as pavements, lights, sewers and water mains, constitutes evidence of its permanent public character as a street, as do also the knowledge of and acquiescence in such improvements on the part of the dedicator.

3. ———: ———: **For Use as Boundary of Benefit District.**
At any rate, such "carriage avenue" has been so dedicated as a
street as to authorize the city to so consider it in fixing the
boundary of a benefit district for special taxation, in pursuance
to a charter provision which declared the boundary line of such
district should be midway between the street to be improved
and the next parallel street.   •

Appeal from St. Louis City Circuit Court.—*Hon. D. D. Fisher*, Judge.

AFFIRMED.

Barclay, Orthwein & Wallace and *Smith & Pearcy* for appellants.

(1) (a) In a dedication to the public of property by an individual, the law construes the grant strictly as against the public. Spires v. Los Angeles, 150 Cal. 64; Hopkinsville v. Jarrett, 156 Ky. 777, 50 L. R. A. (N. S.) 465; Riverside v. MacLean, 210 Ill. 308, 66 L. R. A. 288; Jones v. Jackson, 104 Miss. 449. (b) The public under a dedication acquires only a right to use the property given to it for the purpose specified in the dedication. Cummings v. St. Louis, 90 Mo. 264; Refining Co. v. Elevator Co., 82 Mo. 125; Williams v. Plank Road Co., 21 Mo. 582; Ferrenbach v. Turner, 86 Mo. 419; Gaskins v. Williams, 235 Mo. 563; Board of Regents v. Painter, 102 Mo. 471; Goode v. St. Louis, 113 Mo. 257; Jones v. Jackson, 104 Miss. 449; Park Comrs. v. Ward, 248 Ill. 309; Young v. Landis, 73 N. J. L. 266; Poole v. Rehoboth, 9 Del. Ch. 201. The public has no right to change a specified, limited and defined purpose specified in a grant so as to subject the property to a use for a different purpose. Mulvey v. Wangeheim, 23 Cal. App. 271; Price v. Thompson, 48 Mo. 361; Riverside v. Mac-Lean, 210 Ill. 308, 66 L. R. A. 288; Seward v. Orange, 59 N. J. L. 331; Hopkinsville v. Jarrett, 156 Ky. 777, 50 L. R. A. (N. S.) 467. (2) (a) A park and park use

have been defined in the following cases: State ex
rel. v. Schweikerdt, 109 Mo. 496; Bennett v. Seibert,
10 Ind. App. 369; Ehmen v. Gothenburg, 50 Neb. 715;
People ex rel. v. Green, 52 How. Pr. 440. It is a place
of amusement, and roadways are necessary therein.
Driveways in a public park are common and, like
walks and bridle paths, are not only not inconsistent
with the use of a park as such, but are a part of the
common and ordinary means by which a park is used
by the public. In the case of a large park, such as
Forest Park, paths and driveways are essential to
their satisfactory use. The ordinary use by the public of paths and driveways through a public park is
consistent with and incidental to the purpose of a park
and is a park use and not a use as a street or public
highway. A park road is such a park use. Buffalo
Co. v. Hoyer, 214 N. Y. 247. (b) The county of St.
Louis acquired this strip of land from Griswold in
1876 under a grant which was accepted by the county.
By the terms thereof the board of control (the commissioners of Forest Park) had control of the strip,
and these two and one-half acres were by the grant incorporated into and became a part of Forest Park.
The grantor reserved, however, an easement which
attached to the property on the north of the road, giving it access, light and air and outlet and inlet to such
property and right of temporary stoppage in front
thereof, but such rights were under the regulations
and rules governing the park, as promulgated by the
commissioners of Forest Park. This was the only
limit placed upon the use of the strip as a park road
by the grantor. Lands may be dedicated for park
purposes subject to a private easement of access,
light, and air, and such easements are not antagonis-
tic to the rights of the public in such lands for park
purposes. Buffalo v. Hoyer, 214 N. Y. 246. A street
is a public highway and is open for unrestricted use
to the public. A street is open to public traffic of all

kinds. Every person has a right to pass over the same. No one can be excluded. This is not the case here. Even the travel to and from the houses fronting on the north of the road can be regulated, and any kind or all other kinds of traffic can be excluded. By ordinance and by the regulations of the Park Commissioner the travel is now regulated and has been so regulated for many years. A street use and a park use are distinct uses. Bennett v. Seibert, 10 Ind. App. 379; Pickett v. Mercer, 106 Mo. App. 696; Riverside v. MacLean, 210 Ill. 325; Board of Education v. Detroit, 30 Mich. 505. (3) This road is not a street, but a park road, and cannot be used as a street. It cannot be used to fix the south boundary of the assessment district for improving McPherson avenue. Art. 6, sec. 14, City Charter; Collier v. Paving Co., 180 Mo. 390; Buffalo Co. v. Hoyer, 214 N. Y. 236; Commonwealth v. Boston, 135 Mass. 551. (4) The strip of land having been acquired by the county of St. Louis as and for a park road and having been incorporated into the boundaries of Forest Park as a part thereof, and the city having acquired the rights of the county under the scheme of separation, no amount of user by the public of this park road could divest the city as trustee for the public of its right acquired for park purposes and make it a street. Limitation does not . run against the city in this way. Sec. 1886, R. S. 1909 (G. S. 1865, sec. 7, p. 746); Laclede-Christy Co. v. St. Louis, 246 Mo. 460; State ex rel. v. Doniphan, 169 Mo. 615. Use of a park road by the public for any length of time does not change the character of the use or title. Such use is permissive. Cohn v. Parcels, 72 Cal. 367, 370; Hamilton v. Morris, 18 Upper Canada Common Pleas 245, 249; Collier v. Paving Co., 180 Mo. 362. No length of use of a private road will make it a public highway. Bradford v. Fultz, 149 N. W. 929; Princeton v. Gustavson, 241 Ill. 566; Weldon v. Prescott, 187 Mass. 415.

Schnurmacher & Rassieur for respondents.

(1) "A street is a road or public way in a city, town or village. A way over land set apart for travel in a town or city is a street, no matter by what name it may be called. It is the purpose for which it was laid out and the use made of it that determines its character." Elliott on Roads and Streets, sec. 19. (2) The word "street" is a generic term and is broad enough to include boulevards and other restricted public ways and streets like Lindell avenue, which, though a part of the park, are nevertheless used for public street purposes. Paige & Jones on Taxation by Assessment, secs. 307, 401; Park Comrs. v. Farber, 49 N. E. (Ill.) 433; Bancroft v. Bancroft, 61 Atl. (Del.) 689. (3) Lindell avenue was dedicated and has always been used as a "street" within the meaning of section 14, article 6, of the charter of St. Louis. Steinacher v. Gast, 89 S. W. (Ky.) 481; Collier v. Pav. & Supply Co., 180 Mo. 387. (4) It is part of the Forest Park, but, nevertheless, a street in the park and it must always be used as a street. The city may regulate its use as part of the park, just as the city may regulate the use of all streets; but the regulations must be reasonable; the city cannot regulate away the rights of adjoining owners or of the public in this strip as a street. (5) The use of the sub-soil at the request of adjoining owners, for general municipal purposes, is a strong circumstance, showing that the strip has been used as a street, even though it is part of the park. Elliott on Roads and Streets, sec. 20. (6) The improvement of the street by adjoining owners under permit from the Board of Public Improvements, their conveyances naming Lindell avenue as the street on which their lots front, and their use of it for general street purposes, estop the Forest Park Improvement Association and its

grantees from questioning that it is a street. People
v. Underhill, 39 N. E. (N. Y.) 333; Hannibal v. Draper,
15 Mo. 634; Rutherford v. Taylor, 38 Mo. 315.·

WALKER, J.—This is a proceeding to enjoin the
collection of special tax bills issued by the city of St.
Louis to the defendant G. Eyermann & Bro., contractors, who reconstructed Waterman Avenue between Kingshighway and Union Boulevard, public
streets of said city.

The charter of the city of St. Louis provides how
the benefit district which shall bear a portion of the
cost of such improvements shall be fixed; section 14,
article 6, of the charter in relation thereto being as
follows:

"The districts herein referred to shall be established as follows: a line shall be drawn midway between the street to be improved and the next parallel
or converging street on each side of the street to be
improved, which line shall be the boundary of the
district," etc.

Waterman Avenue, on which the work was done,
runs from east to west and is parallel with and quite a
distance north of Forest Park.

Plaintiffs, who were the owners of property fronting on Portland Place (a private "Place" within the
benefit district), attack the validity of the tax bills and
claim that the Board of Public Improvements, in determining the amount of tax required to be paid by the
respective lots in the benefit district, failed to include
the entire area legally subject to the tax, and therefore
the bills against their lots are for excessive amounts.

On the north the board drew the line midway between Waterman Avenue and the next street north.
This plaintiffs concede. On the south the board drew
the line midway between Waterman Avenue and Lindell Avenue, claimed by the board to be the next street

south. But plaintiffs claim that Lindell Avenue is not
a street within the meaning of the charter, and that
the board should have drawn the line midway between
Waterman Avenue and Berthold Avenue, or possibly
Clayton Avenue, a street running through the park,
and that the district should thus have included a large
part of Forest Park.

Plaintiffs concede that the contract was properly
let and the bills were otherwise properly issued. The
only ground urged by them is as to the validity of the
board's action in fixing the taxing district.

The contract for the work was let and the special
tax bills were issued in 1910 and the status of Lindell
Avenue as of that date must be determined. Its history is as follows:

William D. Griswold was the owner of a tract of
eighty acres lying immediately north of Forest Park,
bounded on the east by Kingshighway and on the west
by Union Avenue. In 1876 Griswold conveyed to the
county of St. Louis a strip of fifty feet wide off the
south side of said eighty acres, adjoining the north
line of Forest Park and extending from Kingshighway to the St. L. K. C. & N. railroad. This strip now
is Lindell Avenue, the street in question.

The deed to the county was for the following uses
and purposes: "To have and to hold the same to said
St. Louis County for the uses and purposes following,
viz.: That same shall be incorporated into and be
held, improved, used and controlled as a part of Forest Park and shall be subject to the jurisdiction and
government of the commissioners of Forest Park in
same manner and to same extent as pertains to the
general territory and property of same. That said
board of commissioners shall cause to be constructed
a carriage avenue over the premises described, embracing part of the present north line of the said park
adjoining the land hereby conveyed, such carriageway
to be not less than fifty feet in width extending from

Kingshighway to the line of said railroad, the same
for the width of fifteen feet to be completed after the
best manner of the other carriage avenues of said
park, and for the balance of width to be graded in conformity with the said fifteen feet of width so as to
form in connection with same a common avenue, that
they shall grade a foot walk along the north side of
said avenue corresponding with the level or elevation
of same and fronting the said tract of eighty acres,
and during the current winter or coming spring, plant
shade trees along the curbing or border of said foot
walk of such kind and in such distances as to the said
commissioners may seem expedient and in harmony
with the general improvement of the park. . . .
And also said Griswold and persons holding under
him, owners or occupiers of the land and lots fronting
upon said avenue and foot walk, shall have outlet and
inlet from and into their premises and right of temporary stoppage in front thereof, for all such carriages and teams as by the regulations and rules governing the park may be allowed to run in the same,
and that the streets which may be laid out upon the
said eighty acres may enter and be connected with
said avenue, and that said streets shall be accessible
through the same for all such carriages and teams.''

Upon the separation of the city and county, the
strip passed to the city.

Griswold owned the tract until May, 1887, when
he conveyed it to the Forest Park Improvement Association; the deed specifies the metes and bounds of the
entire eighty-acre tract. In May, 1888, the grantee
platted the tract and laid it out in blocks and lots. The
association also dedicated to the city, for the same
uses, a short strip fifty feet wide, adjoining the railroad tracks, and extending the strip dedicated by
Griswold through to Union Boulevard—thus making
a continuous strip from Kingshighway to Union Boulevard. This fifty-foot strip from Kingshighway to

Union Boulevard is designated on the city plat as the "Park Road." The part dedicated parallels the railroad tracks and runs diagonally into Union Avenue. Subsequently the city condemned as a street a strip fifty feet wide, extending the Griswold strip on a straight line from its western terminus to Union Boulevard, and the strip west of Union Boulevard was also acquired for uses similar to the uses created by Griswold, and the same was similarly improved and now makes one continuous straight street from Kingshighway to Skinker Road, although the diagonal piece connecting Union Boulevard with Lindell Avenue is also used as a street.

Soon after the improvement was completed the property was placed on the market and the association disposed of the lots for residence purposes, and all lots fronting on this strip were described as having so many feet fronting on Park Road. In 1903 the name of the street was changed, by ordinance, from Park Road to Lindell Avenue, and since the plat was filed, in all conveyances of lots fronting on this street, they were described as fronting on Park Road (prior to the change of name), and thereafter as fronting on Lindell Avenue.

After the association acquired the property, under permit from the Board of Public Improvements it installed a main sewer, water and gas mains therein. The street was also paved, and from time to time, as lots were sold, residences were erected and the owners were granted permits by the sewer department to connect with this main sewer, and by the street department to connect with the water and gas mains and to construct granitoid sidewalks in front of their premises.

In 1889 the city refunded to the association the amount expended by it for the water main and took it over as part of its system, and also the sewer main as part of the district sewer and relieved the property from special taxation for district sewer purposes.

The city also installed lamp posts for street lighting and fire plugs for fire protection. The lots have all been sold and improved with residences. The houses are numbered, as on other streets.

In the plat-books in the Assessor's office, in the Street Department and in the Special Tax Department, the strip has always been carried and treated as a public street.

When Union Boulevard was reconstructed, Lindell Avenue was treated as a public street and the special taxes were issued on that basis. When Kingshighway, extending north of Lindell Avenue, was widened, Lindell Avenue was again treated as a public street and the tax bills were issued on that basis. At no time in any of these departments has Lindell Avenue been treated otherwise than as a public street.

The Police Department patrols this street as any other, although the park itself is patrolled only by employees of the Park Department. There was evidence that Lindell Avenue was kept in repair only by the Street Department, but there also was evidence that the Street Department did so only at times when the Park Department was short of funds and that the Park Department at other times also made repairs.

Lindell Avenue has always been sprinkled by the city, as other streets; the advertisements and contracts call for its sprinkling, and the property fronting on the street has always been charged therefor by special taxation, the same as other property fronting on streets in the city of St. Louis. For a number of . years the street has been oiled, which eliminates sprinkling, but the sprinkling taxes are levied as before to pay for the oiling instead of sprinkling.

The street has at all times been used for every purpose for which a public street may be used, except that after 1907 or 1908 the Park Commissioner ordered that no heavy traffic be permitted on the street, and since that time an effort is made to keep off heavy traffic, except such as is necessary to supply the residences on the street with coal, ice, building material, etc. Such heavy traffic is now and has always been permitted. There was evidence also that only heavy traffic intended for the residences on the street was permitted prior to 1907, except during the World's Fair period.

Lindell Avenue is a continuation of Lindell Boulevard, an established street, long in use before Lindell Avenue was dedicated, and excepting a slight jog at Kingshighway) it makes one continuous street from Grand Avenue to Skinker Road—a distance of three or four miles.

Upon the facts above set forth the circuit court found that Lindell Avenue is a street within the meaning of the charter and that the Board of Public Improvements was right in fixing the midway line between Lindell Avenue and Waterman Avenue as the southern boundary line of the benefit district. From the judgment dismissing the petition, plaintiffs appealed to this court.

Is Lindell Avenue a Public Street?—The sole matter at issue is whether Lindell Avenue, between Kingshighway and Union Boulevard, is a street within the meaning of the charter; if so, then the judgment of the trial court which denied the right of relators to the injunctive process herein prayed for, should be affirmed; otherwise, reversed.

The title to the strip of ground now designated as Lindell Avenue, between the limits stated, was conveyed to St. Louis County (now city) by William D. Griswold in 1876 with stipulations as to the use to which the ground was to be put by the grantee, viz., in general terms, that it was always to be used as a "carriage avenue." While it was to be a part of Forest Park, it was to be constructed and maintained as

a carriage avenue, by which the grantor meant, not
merely a passageway for carriages, but such a highway as would afford the occupiers of lots fronting on
said avenue egress and ingress to and from their
premises "for all such carriages and teams as by the
regulations and rules governing the park may be allowed to run in same." This, as well as other terms in
the grant, is indicative of a purpose to dedicate for a
public use. [Hannibal v. Draper, 15 Mo. 634.]
There is no claim that the city, which became invested
with the control of the street as a successor to the
county upon the adoption of the Scheme and Charter,
has ever attempted to divert the use of same to other
purposes than those designated by the grantor, but
on the contrary, all the official acts of the municipality, in whatever department exercised, have been in
recognition of and in conformity to the terms of the
deed of grant. These are set forth in detail in the
statement and their repetition would serve no useful
purpose. The fact that the strip granted is by the
terms of the deed subjected to the "immediate government of the commissioners of Forest Park" means
such regulation as may be exercised by the commissioners in the control of a public street—nothing more.
For such purpose was the grant made, and an attempt
to exercise other control by the park commissioners
would defeat the very purpose of the dedication. In
short, the street, or as now designated, Lindell Avenue,
must always be open to the public as a highway under
the limitations stated; and the fact that it remains a
part of the park detracts in nowise from its use as a
street, nor is it in any manner inconsistent with its
defined character as such. It is too well established
to admit of argument that land dedicated for street
purposes cannot thereafter be diverted for park purposes. Under any reasonable construction of the
grant, therefore, the strip must remain a highway,
and it was so accepted and has uniformly been so re-

garded by the city. This fixes its status so far as
municipal affairs are concerned. [Collier Est. v. Paving & Supply Co., 180 Mo. l. c. 387.] Lindell Avenue is
not the only instance of the establishment of a public
street in Forest Park. There are others, not necessary to be enumerated, which, upon their dedication,
became permanent in their nature, free from change
by the park commissioners, but to an extent subject to
their control, as is that part of Lindell Avenue in question, but nevertheless subject to the general control of
the city; and unlike drives or roads, which may be
abolished or changed as the judgment or taste of the
commissioners may dictate.

It was contended that the city had used the avenue
for general street purposes; this, if true, and in violation of the terms of the grant, would avail appellants
nothing, because evidence in support of this contention would simply serve to show a further dedication
by the city to public use. The establishment of permanent improvements on said street by the city in
accordance with the demands of modern municipal life,
such as paving, lighting, sewering and placing water
mains therein, in nowise conflicts with the terms of
the grant, but constitutes further evidence of the permanent public character of the street. The knowledge and acquiescence of the grantor in this work is
further proof of his intention to dedicate this street
for public use in all that the term implies. It is established that the intention of the owner to dedicate for
a public use may be shown in various ways, and his
approval of the city's action in this case may well be
classified as one of same. [Brinck v. Collier, 56 Mo.
l. c. 165; Price v. Thompson, 48 Mo. l. c. 365.]

After all, the real question is not what is seemingly admitted, viz., has Lindell Avenue been established and dedicated as a public street; but has it been
so dedicated as to authorize the Board of Public Improvements to designate it as a boundary in the deter-

mination of a special taxing district. That it has
been established as a public street for general purposes, both by private deed and public recognition,
the facts sufficiently show. This character having
been established, the Board of Public Improvements,
under the fourth paragraph of section 14 of article 6
of the former charter of the city of St. Louis, is authorized to designate it as a boundary determinative
of a district for special taxation.

Arguments as to strict construction of a grant
and what technically constitutes a dedication; what is
"park use;" or the extent of the separate government of the Forest Park commissioners, as contradis-
tinguished from the general control of the city of St.
Louis; and the claim that the grantees under the Griswold deed must be confined literally to the terms of
same, have but little substantial weight in the face of
the many cogent facts to establish the dedication of
the strip as a street and its recognition and adoption
as such by the city.

We have reviewed the numerous cases cited and
discussed by counsel for appellants as sustaining their
contention, but find no substantial merit in them. We
therefore hold that the judgment of the trial court
denying the right of appellants to the injunctive relief prayed for should be affirmed, and it is so ordered.
All concur.

THE STATE v. JAMES COFF, Appellant.

Division Two, February 15, 1916.

1. **INSTRUCTIONS: No Assignment in Motion.** Whether or not
   it was error to give an instruction on murder in the second
   degree, or to fail to give an instruction on involuntary manslaughter in the fourth degree, or to give an instruction concerning the bad feeling existing between defendant's and de-

cedent's families, or to give an instruction on manslaughter
in the fourth degree, will not be reviewed on appeal, where none
of these matters was assigned as error in the motion for a
new trial.

2. **ACCIDENTAL HOMICIDE: Instruction Required.** Where the
evidence for defendant tended to show that his participation
in the combat was merely that of a person defending himself,
and that he was, therefore, engaged in a lawful act; that while
in the act of defending himself, the deceased grabbed him by
the throat, and in order to protect himself he shoved deceased
away, causing him to stagger and fall; and that in the fall deceased's head struck the curb-stone and received the fatal
wound, the statute (Sec. 4452, R. S. 1909) declaring that homicide shall be excusable when committed "upon sudden combat,
without any undue advantage being taken and without any
dangerous weapon being used, and not done in a cruel and
unusual manner" required the court to give an instruction on
accidental homicide; and a failure to do so, where the point
was properly raised at the trial and preserved for review, was
reversible error.

Appeal from St. Louis City Circuit Court.—*Hon. William T. Jones*, Judge.

REVERSED AND REMANDED.

Thomas J. Rowe, Jr., and *Henry Rowe* for appellant.

(1) The court erred in failing to instruct the
jury on the theory that deceased may have gone to his
death by accident or misfortune, and on the evidence
in the case defendant was entitled to such instruction.
State v. Reed, 154 Mo. 122; French v. Commonwealth,
88 S. W. 1070; Sec. 4452, R. S. 1909; State v. Cook,
3 L. R. A. (N. S.) 1152. (2) The court erred in failing to instruct the jury on the law applicable to the
evidence of the combat between defendant and William
Conway, son of deceased, and the subsequent participation of deceased therein.

John T. Barker, Attorney-General, and *Lewis H. Cook* for the State.

(1) It is well established that the defendant is required to call the court's attention particularly in the motion for a new trial to the question upon which it failed to instruct the jury, in order to entitle him to a new trial upon such ground. That was not done in this case. No instruction was asked on this proposition. Neither was the attention of the court called specifically in the motion for a new trial to its failure to so instruct. This court has recently ruled that a general specification in the motion is insufficient, in that it fails to call the attention of that court to the particular point omitted in the instructions. State v. Conway, 241 Mo. 271; State v. Walls, 262 Mo. 113; State v. Douglas, 258 Mo. 281; State v. Sydnor, 253 Mo. 380; State v. Wellman, 253 Mo. 316; State v. Sykes, 248 Mo. 712; State v. Horton, 247 Mo. 663; State v. Chissell, 245 Mo. 555; State v. Connors, 245 Mo. 482; State v. Bostwick, 245 Mo. 483; State v. Harris, 245 Mo. 450; State v. Perrigan, 258 Mo. 237; State v. Dockery, 243 Mo. 592. (2) It is conceded that defendant is entitled to clear and explicit instructions as to excusable and justifiable homicide, where there is any evidence in the case to support the theory, but where it plainly appears that in no view of the case is the law of excusable or justifiable homicide applicable, a refusal or omission to give instructions on those points is not error. In the case at bar every witness, including the defendant, testified that defendant struck deceased one or more blows under circumstances that would preclude any instructions on justifiable homicide.

WILLIAMS, C.—Under an indictment charging him with murder in the second degree, defendant was tried in the circuit court of the city of St. Louis, found guilty of manslaughter in the fourth degree, and his punishment assessed at two years in the penitentiary. Defendant duly perfected an appeal.

There was evidence tending to establish the following facts:

At the time of the tragedy, it appears that defendant, a blacksmith, twenty-eight years of age, resided with his parents at No. 3909 Kennerly Avenue, in St. Louis, Missouri. W. A. Conway, together with his wife and fourteen-year-old sister, were tenants of the second story of the house next door to the east, being No. 3907 Kennerly Avenue; the lower portion of that house being occupied by a family by the name of Hazlit.

About a week before this tragedy, Benjamin F. Conway, the father of W. A. Conway, came from his home in Kentucky to make his son a visit. Benjamin F. Conway is the deceased.

The Conway family had been living in this house about four and one-half months and it appears that, during that time, considerable ill feeling had grown up between the women of the two households, the nature of which is not disclosed. About two months prior to the tragedy, the Coffs had caused to be erected at the rear of their premises, and on the side next to the house occupied by the Conways, a high brick wall so as to prevent persons in the Conway house from seeing persons to the rear of the Coff house. A sheet-iron shutter or shield was also erected on the Coff premises, immediately in front of one of the windows in the Conway house.

The killing occurred on September 4, 1914. The owner of the Conway house had employed a painter to paint the same. The space between the two houses was about two and one-half feet. The day before the tragedy, the painter had placed the bottom of his ladder over on the Coff premises and, in doing so, had slightly injured a hedge belonging to the Coffs. Mrs. Coff called a policeman and had the painter remove the ladder.

The next day, about 11 a. m., W. A. Conway and the owner of the house in which he lived were out in the front yard looking at the painting. The painter was painting on the front porch, but was not using a ladder. Mrs. Coff was sitting on her front porch. She exhibited a revolver and stated to W. A. Conway that if they came over on her premises, they would be killed. W. A. Conway replied that he would have her arrested. A policeman was called and after a short conversation, W. A. Conway and his wife and the owner of the building proceeded down to the Municipal Courts Building for the purpose of having a warrant issued. It appears that the defendant returned to his home just about the time that the Conways started down town and while the Conways were waiting for a street car they saw the defendant coming toward them and they moved down the street two or three blocks to catch a car.

That same evening, about six o'clock, W. A. Conway and his wife started out for a little walk. In a few minutes, Benjamin F. Conway (the deceased) and his fourteen-year-old daughter started down the street to mail a letter. They overtook W. A. Conway and his wife, who had stopped to observe a show window, and asked them to wait while they went down the street and mailed a letter. The deceased and his daughter proceeded about a half block, and, at this time, the defendant, on his way home from work, passed W. A. Conway and his wife on the street. (In order that the testimony may be better understood, we will refer to W. A. Conway as Conway, Jr., and Benjamin F. Conway, the deceased, as Conway, Sr.). Defendant as he approached Conway, Jr., said, "You G— d— s— of a b—, I am going to kill you for insulting my mother." Conway, Jr., started to say, "I didn't insult your mother,'' but before he could say it, defendant knocked him down. Conway, Jr., then got up and defendant again knocked him down and was on top of Conway, beating him, when Conway's wife called for Conway, Sr., who was then about a haif-block away. Conway, Sr., ran over to the scene of the fight, carrying the letter in his hand, and threw something which appeared to some of the witnesses to be a paper and called out to the two men to stop. Defendant then turned upon Conway, Sr., and struck him a blow which felled him to his knees. Conway, Sr., arose and defendant struck him another blow which knocked him down and as he fell his head struck the curb-stone. Defendant then kicked Conway, Sr., several times, and he rolled into the gutter unconscious. He never regained consciousness and died the following day at a hospital.

The evidence upon the part of the State tends to show that neither Conway, Jr., nor Conway, Sr., struck at the defendant. Conway, Jr.'s, testimony was corroborated by the following eye-witnesses to the fight, to-wit: Alex Campbell, Catherine M. Conway, Frank D. Williams and Elizabeth Conway.

The deputy physician to the coroner testified that he made an examination of the body of the deceased and described the deceased as being a white male, about fifty years of age. He found a fracture of the skull, about three inches long, on the left side of the head, extending down into the base of the skull.

The evidence upon the part of the defense tends to establish the following facts:

Defendant, testifying in his own behalf, said that he was going home from work about six o'clock and that Conway, Jr., stopped him at the corner of Maffitt Street and accused him of using vulgar language in the presence of Mrs. Conway. Defendant attempted to reply by telling Conway that he had insulted defendant's mother, but, before he could do so,

Conway, Jr., struck him a blow in the mouth. Defendant then struck Conway, Jr., and knocked him down. Mrs. Conway then grappled with the defendant and. defendant heard someone say, "Look out." Defendant then broke Mrs. Conway's hold and turned just in time to see Conway, Sr., rush up with an old broom with which he tried to strike defendant, but the broom slipped from Conway, Sr.'s, hand and missed the defendant. Conway, Sr., then grabbed defendant by the throat, but defendant shoved Conway, Sr., and he staggered out into the gutter and fell.

On cross-examination of the defendant, the following occurred:

"Q. Then you knocked him (Conway, Sr.) down? A. No, sir, not until he choked me."

Later in his cross-examination, the following questions and answers were given:

"Q. Did the old man get hold of your throat? A. Yes, sir, both hands around my throat.

"Q. And then you pushed him off, at that time, is that so, pushed him off and struck him? A. No, sir, I didn't strike him; I just pushed him away from me and he staggered and fell.

"Q. You pushed him away and he staggered and fell. You didn't hit him at all then? A. Why you can call it hitting if you want; I just stuck my arm out.

"Q. You just pushed him off and he staggered and fell, is that your story? A. Yes, sir, that is my story.

"Q. Then your story to the jury is you didn't hit the old man at all, but you pushed him off as he grabbed your throat, and you pushed him off and he fell? A. Yes, sir, I pushed him off and he fell.

"Q, Then you didn't hit him in the face or anywhere else? A. No, I pushed him; maybe that marked his face."

Defendant testified that after the fight his lip was swollen and his neck was scratched in many places and his shirt was torn to shreds.

Albert Smith testified for the defendant that Conway, Sr., threw a broom at the defendant and then caught the defendant by the throat and that defendant broke loose and hit the deceased, causing him to fall to the sidewalk and roll into the gutter. Four other witnesses corroborate the testimony of witness Smith, some of them saying that deceased's head struck the curb as he fell.

Several witnesses testified that the general reputation of defendant for peace and quietude, prior to this controversy, was good.

I. Appellant contends that the court erred (1) in giving an instruction on murder in the second degree, (2) in failing to give an instruction on involuntary manslaughter in the fourth degree, *Instructions.* (3) in giving the instruction concerning the bad feeling existing between the two families, and (4) in giving the instruction on manslaughter in the fourth degree.

Concerning each and every one of the above points, it is sufficient to say that these matters were not assigned as errors in the motion for a new trial, and we are, therefore, precluded from a review of the same.

II. It is further contended that the court erred in failing to instruct the jury on the theory of an accidental homicide. This point is properly raised and preserved for our review, and we have reached the conclusion that the same is well taken.

Accidental or excusable homicide is defined by section 4452, Revised Statutes 1909, as follows:

"Homicide shall be deemed excusable when committed by accident or misfortune, in either of the following cases: First, in lawfully correcting a child, apprentice or servant, or in doing any other lawful act by lawful means, with usual and ordinary caution, and without unlawful intent; or second, in heat of passion, upon any sudden or sufficient provocation, or upon sudden combat, without any undue advantage being taken, and without any dangerous weapon being used, and not done in a cruel and unusual manner."

It will be noted that the evidence of defendant tends to show that his participation in the combat was merely that of a person defending himself, and that he was, therefore, engaged in a lawful act; that while in the act of defending himself, the deceased grabbed him by the throat, and in order to protect himself he shoved deceased away, causing him to stagger and fall. In the fall deceased's head struck the curb and received the fatal wound. If, therefore, defendant's evidence be true, the death occurred by accident or misfortune "upon sudden combat, without any undue advantage being taken, and without any dangerous weapon being used, and [the killing was] not done in a cruel and unusual manner." Such evidence was sufficient to justify an instruction on the theory of an accidental killing and the court, therefore, erred in failing to so instruct.

The Wisconsin statute is almost identical with the above quoted Missouri statute, and the Supreme Court of Wisconsin in two cases, where the evidence was not so favorable to defendant as is the evidence in the case at bar, held that the court erred in failing to instruct the jury on accidental homicide as defined by said statute. [Campbell v. State, 111 Wis. 152; Ryan v. State, 115 Wis. 488.]

It follows that the judgment should be reversed and the cause remanded. It is so ordered. *Roy, C.,* concurs.

· PER CURIAM.—The foregoing opinion by WILLIAMS, C., is adopted as the opinion of the court. All of the judges concur.

THE STATE v. CHARLIE PFEIFER, alias CHARLES N. PETERS, Appellant.

Division Two, Febuary 15, 1916.

1. **SODOMY: Covered by Statutes, Etc.** Notwithstanding section 4725, Revised Statutes 1909, was repealed and re-enacted, with an amendment, in 1911, the crime of sodomy may be committed by a man by inserting his sexual organ in the mouth of a woman.

2. **EVIDENCE OF OTHER CRIMES: Res Gestae.** Where the information charges sodomy *per os* it is not error to admit evidence tending to show sodomy *per anum* where the proof shows both acts were so connected as to show both were parts of the *res gestae*.

3. ————: ————: **Restricted by Instruction: No Exception.** Nor can an assignment that an instruction should have been given at the trial restricting the evidence of the crime not charged be considered on appeal where no exception was sayed to the giving or refusal of any instruction, or to the giving of the whole instructions.

4. ————: ————: ————: **Not Required.** And where the two crimes are parts of the *res gestae*, and testimony tending to prove that one not charged is therefore admissible, no instruction as to the evidentiary weight of the testimony or the purpose for which it may be considered is required.

5. **DEFENDANT: Cross-Examination.** In view of the plain wording of the statute (Sec. 5242, R. S. 1909) forbidding them, questions asked defendant in cross-examination upon matters neither touched upon nor growing out of his examination in chief, are presumed to be prejudicial error, unless the contrary is made to appear; and where he is compelled to state all his movements the night of the crime, his acquaintanceship with two other persons who had committed a crime against the same woman two hours before he and they are charged with having committed a similar crime against her, and whether or not he and they had been companions since their school days and frequenters of the same saloon—all matters not touched upon in his examination in chief and brought out for the purpose of corroborating a police officer—the questions were not only unwarranted but were prejudicial.

6. ————: ————: **One Law for Innocent and Guilty.** There can be but one law for the trial of the innocent and guilty; and

notwithstanding the court may be of the opinion that the evidence is sufficient to warrant a verdict of guilty, a plain statute forbidding the cross-examination of a defendant concerning matters wholly outside his examination in chief must be applied to all defendants alike. The Constitution has not ordained that apparent guilt is the sole condition of affirmance by the Supreme Court of a verdict of guilty.

Appeal from St. Louis City Circuit Court.—*Hon. W. T. Jones*, Judge.

REVERSED AND REMANDED.

Paeben & Friday for appellant.

(1) Section 4725, R. S. 1909, was repealed and re-enacted by the General Assembly in 1911 (see Laws 1911, p. 198). The amendment of 1911 does not make the act set out in the information, nor testified to in the evidence, a crime. The act charged did not constitute an offense at common law nor does it constitute an offense under the statute. Since the statutes of Missouri do not undertake to define the meaning of the phrase, "The abominable and detestable crime against nature," but merely prescribe a punishment, we must go to the common law to ascertain the meaning of the words used. 12 Cyc. 141; State v. Rader, 262 Mo. 129; 8 Am. & Eng. Ency. Law, 276; Brandon v. Carter, 119 Mo. 572; State v. Hartley, 185 Mo. 669; Sec. 8047, R. S. 1909; United States v. Freight Assn., 58 Fed. 58; Ex parte Vincent, 26 Ala. 145; Commonwealth v. Chapman, 13 Metcf. (Mass.) 68; State v. Cowley, 67 Vt. 322. (2) At common law the phrase "The abominable and detestable crime against nature" was clearly defined. It was sodomy when committed with mankind and buggery or bestiality when committed with an animal. The act described in the information and referred to in the testimony in the case was neither of these offenses. The use of the mouth does not constitute sodomy. The act must be *per anum*. Bishop's Crim. Law, secs. 1191-

1196; Ausman v. Veal, 10 Ind. 356; People v. Boyle, 116
Cal. 658; Prindle v. State, 31 Tex. Crim. 551; Wharton
on Crimes, secs. 575-579; Russell on Crimes, 937; Commonwealth v. Poindexter, 133 Ky. 720; McLean's Crim.
Law, 1153; Davis v. Brown, 29 Ohio St. 326; Estes v.
Carter, 10 Iowa, 400; Kinnan v. State, 125 N. W. (Neb.)
594. (3) The testimony of Dr. A. C. Vickery over the
repeated objections of the defendant as to the physical
condition of the rectum and vagina of the prosecuting
witness was clearly inadmissible and could serve no
other purpose than the purpose of inflaming the minds
of the jury against the defendant. Evidence of other
crimes committed by the defendant are clearly inadmissible. Here we have testimony of a crime not committed by the defendant, but by some other person with
which the defendant is not in the remotest manner connected by participation, conspiracy or otherwise. Even
the attorney for the State said that the purpose of this
testimony should be covered by an instruction which the
court failed to give. State v. Hyde, 234 Mo. 200; State
v. Myers, 174 Mo. 352; State v. Weaver, 165 Mo. 1;
State v. Faulkner, 175 Mo. 546; State v. Spray, 174 Mo.
569; R. S. 1909, sec. 5231; State v. Taylor, 118 Mo. 171.
(4) The State was permitted on cross-examination, in
spite of repeated objection thereto, to examine the defendant touching matters not brought out on the examination in chief. R. S. 1909, sec. 5242; State v. Mc-
Graw, 74 Mo. 573; State v. Porter, 75 Mo. 171; State v.
Palmer, 88 Mo. 568; State v. Graves, 95 Mo. 510; State
v. James, 216 Mo. 404. (5) The State's attorney was
allowed over the objection of the defendant to comment
in his address to the jury on matters regarding which
the defendant did not testify, and in regard to the flight
of the defendant regarding which there was no testimony. State v. James, 216 Mo. 405; State v. Fairlamb,
121 Mo. 150.

John T. Barker, Attorney-General, and *Lee B. Ewing*, Assistant Attorney-General, for the State.

(1) The information charges a felony under the statute (Laws 1911, p. 198) and is sufficient. State v. Katz, 266 Mo. 493; State v. Wellman, 253 Mo. 311; State v. Kelly, 192 Ill. 119; State v. Honsleman, 168 Ill. 172; State v. Means, 125 Wis. 650. (2) No objection was made to the instructions given. No instructions were refused. Therefore, the only question, relative to the instructions, that this court will review is whether or not they cover all the law of the case. State v. Douglas, 258 Mo. 281. The given instructions fully cover every issue in the case. (3) There was no reversible error in the trial court's rulings upon the admission of testimony. The testimony as to the physical condition of prosecutrix, as shown by the examination of the dispensary physician, Dr. Vickery, was admissible. Kelly's Crim. L. & Pr., sec. 541; State v. Scott, 172 Mo. 536; State v. Murphy, 118 Mo. 7; State v. Reed, 237 Mo. 224; State v. Mathews, 98 Mo. 128; State v. Fields, 234 Mo. 626; State v. McKinney, 254 Mo. 453. In the cross-examination of accused, there was no prejudicial error. (a) It was legal cross-examination. State v. Keener, 225 Mo. 500; State v. Donnington, 246 Mo. 354; State v. Eisenhour, 132 Mo. 148; State v. Harvey, 131 Mo. 345; State v. Benning, 91 Mo. 85; State v. Cunningham, 154 Mo. 174; State v. Foley, 247 Mo. 638; State v. Myers, 221 Mo. 598; State v. Miller, 156 Mo. 76. (b) Even if held to be erroneous, this cross-examination was not prejudicial to accused, and, therefore, not reversible error. State v. Baldwin, 247 Mo. 635; State v. Corrigan, 262 Mo. 209; State v. Barrington, 198 Mo. 81; State v. Brooks, 92 Mo. 582.

FARIS, P. J.—Defendant appeals from a conviction in the circuit court of the city of St. Louis on the charge of sodomy, and a resulting sentence in accordance with the verdict to imprisonment in the penitentiary for a term of two years.

The case is a companion case to that of State v. Katz, decided at this term, and officially reported in 266 Mo. 493. The facts and the acts of defendant here were the same as the facts and the acts of defendant Katz in the case supra. They transpired at the same time and place and were perpetrated upon the identical victim, one Mary Emmenegger. The only difference in the cases is that defendant here did not appear upon the scene or take part in the commission of the acts alleged till after Mary Emmenegger had been in the hands of Katz and his confederates for some two hours or more, and until she had been taken to the rear of a certain building mentioned in the Katz case and called the old Cherokee Brewery. Thereupon and at that place defendant appeared and said to her that he was the head of these detectives, the boss over them, and that she would have to submit to the same things from him that she had submitted to from the others. Then the four of them, to-wit, Katz, Long, Gausmann and this defendant took her to a point in the rear of the old brewery where defendant assaulted her and thrust his private male organ into her mouth; the latter act constituting the phase of alleged sodomy charged and here relied on.

The facts are inexpressibly filthy, and since they have been set out already, another cumbering of the books with their abysmal obscenity would subserve no useful purpose. The more so, since regard being had to the nature of the errors urged, it is obvious that a solution of them is to no substantial extent dependent upon the intimate details of defendant's attack upon the prosecuting witness. If, however, these details be found necessary to an understanding of the points, they may be read in the Katz case.

I. The point is made that neither the information charges, nor the facts show, that defendant committed any crime known to the laws of this State. These con-

Sodomy. tentions are both bottomed on the assumption that since section 4726, Revised Statutes 1909 (which was repealed and re-enacted in 1911, with an amendment, Laws 1911, p. 198), *dehors* such amendment, refers us to the common law for a definition of sodomy, the amendment in question added nothing to it, and was in fact utterly nugatory. In short, that it is yet legally impossible, the statute to the contrary notwithstanding, to commit the crime of sodomy in the manner charged and proved in this case. These contentions have been ruled against defendant in the case of State v. Katz, supra, and with the holding on this point in that case we are content.

II. It is also strenuously urged that by the testimony of Dr. Vickery incompetent and hurtful evidence touching the physical condition of the prosecuting witness's private parts came into the

Evidence of Other Crimes. case. This upon the theory that since the charge here is sodomy perpetrated *per os*, testimony showing, or tending to show a rape and sodomy *per anum*, showed other crimes and was therefore prejudicial and inadmissible. In this contention learned counsel loses sight of the fact that while the testimony so bitterly complained of may have tended to show rape, and other acts of sodomy, *ergo*, another sodomitical crime, yet the proof also showed that all of these acts and things were parts of the *res gestae* and admissible as such, regardless of the fact that defendant may have been hurt by testimony concerning them. [State v. Anderson, 252 Mo. 83.] This was his misfortune, for which he and not the State is at fault. He should see to it that he commits but one felony at a time. We disallow this contention so far as regards the phase of it set forth above.

Upon the alleged error bottomed upon the contention that an instruction ought to have been given restricting the purposes of this evidence of other crimes, it is sufficient to say that under the condition of this record we are not permitted to review any error based upon the instructions, since no exception is anywhere taken or saved to the giving of or refusal to give any instructions in the case, or to the giving of the whole of the instructions. [State v. Vinso, 171 Mo. 576; State v. Eaton, 191 Mo. 151; State v. Urspruch, 191 Mo. 43; State v. Welch, 191 Mo. 179; State v. Dilts, 191 Mo. 665; State v. King, 194 Mo. 474; State v. McCarver, 194 Mo. 717; State v. Maupin, 196 Mo. 164; State v. Delcore, 199 Mo. 228; State v. Beverly, 201 Mo. 550; State v. Yandell, 201 Mo. 646; State v. Chenault, 212 Mo. 132; State v. George, 214 Mo. 262; State v. Sassaman, 214 Mo. 695; State v. Rhodes, 220 Mo. 9; State v. Nelson, 225 Mo. 551; State v. Kretschmar, 232 Mo. 29; State v. Stevens, 242 Mo. 439; State v. Sykes, 248 Mo. 708; State v. Patrick, 107 Mo. 147; State v. Gordon, 196 Mo. 185; State v. Tucker, 232 Mo. 1; State v. Morgan, 196 Mo. 177; State v. Harris, 199 Mo. 716.] Another answer is that heretofore given, viz., that the evidence was a part of the *res gestae*, and for this reason, and since it fell naturally among the facts, no instruction as to its evidentiary weight or purpose was required to be given. If it had not been a part of the *res gestae* its admission would have been an error in this sort of case, which no instruction could have cured, present proper preservation of the point. What we here say as to lack of exceptions, also disposes of all assignments of error bottomed in any wise upon the instructions given, or which the court failed or refused to give.

III.   Complaint is made that, over the objections of defendant, counsel for the State was permitted to comment upon the fact that defendant did not testify **Comment on Defendant's Failure to Testify.** touching certain mentioned matters while he was on the stand. This assignment is not borne out by the record. An objection, it is true, was made by counsel for defendant to a part of the argument of the State before the jury, on this alleged ground, but the trial court then ruled—correctly as is plain upon the record—that what was said by counsel for the State did not have reference in any wise to any failure of the defendant to cover any fact in his testimony. So we need not now consider whether the cases cited to us by the defendant were, or were not, correctly overruled in State v. Larkin, 250 Mo. 218.

IV. Which brings us to a consideration of the one serious point in the case, to-wit, whether the court erred in permitting the State, over the objections of defend-
Cross-Examination of Defendant. ant, repeatedly to ask defendant questions on cross-examination upon matters not touched upon in, or growing out of, his examination in chief. The record bears out this complaint of defendant fully, and discloses a cross-examination of defendant which, standing alone, is utterly inexcusable.

The examination of defendant in chief consisted of three questions: He was asked his name, his age and whether he had committed the specific offense charged in the information. Answering, he gave his name as Charles H. Pfeifer, his age at 29 years and he denied he had committed the crime charged. This was all. In cross-examination the State asked him forty-six questions outside of his examination in chief, among others, for example, (a) where he was on the night the assault was made on the prosecuting witness, (b) where he was at four o'clock of the morning following that assault, (c) where and when he went to bed, (d) at what places he had been and with whom, and whom he saw that night, (e) whether he knew Katz, Gaussman and Long, (f) how long he had known them, and (g) whether he had seen them on the night in question, and (h) whether he was not known by the name of Charles H. Peters (the *alias* contained in the information) and also whether he was not known by the name of ''Cockey.''

It is not contended that any of this cross-examination was directly responsive to anything defendant said in his examination in chief. It is urged in excuse of it that the State is not to be confined in its cross-examination of an accused person on trial to a mere categorical reiteration of the examination in chief, and besides, regardless of the violation of the statutory rule forbidding such cross-examination (Sec. 5242, R. S. 1909), defendant was not hurt by any part of it in the case at bar. On these two propositions we are cited to the cases of State v. Keener, 225 Mo. l. c. 500; State v. Corrigan, 262 Mo. 195; State v. Barrington, 198 Mo. l. c. 81; State v. Brooks, 92 Mo. l. c. 582; State v. Miller, 156 Mo. 76; State v. Myers, 221 Mo. 598; State v. Foley, 247 Mo. l. c. 638; State v. Cunningham, 154 Mo. l. c. 174; State v. Berning, 91 Mo. l. c. 85; State v. Harvey, 131 Mo. l. c. 345; State v. Eisenhour, 132 Mo. l. c. 148; and State v. Donnington, 246 Mo. l. c. 354. These cases furnish, it may be, under the facts existing here, ample authority to excuse the asking of all questions except those having reference to whether he knew Katz and Gaussman, how long he had known them, and *seriatim* as to his movements after defendant left his own witness, Smitters. If the statute is to be regarded, these questions are inexcusable and are reversible error. [State v. Grant, 144 Mo. 56; State v. Hathhorn, 166 Mo. 239; State v. Hudspeth, 150 Mo. l. c. 31; State v. Bell, 212 Mo. 111; State v. Cook, 112 S. W. l. c. 712; State v. Sharp, 233 Mo. l. c. 284.] It is impossible to say upon the facts that these questions and answers did not hurt defendant. The other forty-three may be excused by the authorities cited above and by others not cited; at least we may so concede for the purposes of this case. But where a plain statute forbids such cross-examination, hurtful error is to be presumed, from a failure to observe that statute, unless the contrary clearly appears. Under the facts here, *when it had been shown by the testimony and not denied*, that for some two

hours or more said Katz, Gaussman and Long had
held prosecutrix in custody and brutally assaulted,
maltreated and mistreated her in the precise way defendant is here charged with doing, and when other
testimony in the case put defendant within less than
four hundred feet of the place of the occurrence of the
said acts done by Katz and others about the time these
acts were happening, it cannot be excused as harmless error, that defendant, *dehors* his examination
in chief, is forced to corroborate Officer McCullough
and to admit his meeting McCullough at the point
the latter had already testified to having met him.
Neither can it be called innocuous error that he was
compelled to admit an acquaintance with said Katz and
Gaussman extending over a period which began in their
school-days, and that the three were all frequenters of his father's saloon, in the light of the
heinous acts of these parties as this record then
showed these acts without a syllable of contradiction. So, not only does it not clearly appear
that these unwarranted questions and answers did not
hurt defendant, but *per contra*, it clearly appears that
they did prejudice him.

It is urged that defendant may not simply deny
his acts and then refuse to go into details to contradict
his denial when the State cross-examines him, and that
that is what is meant in State v. Miller, supra, where it
is substantially said that the State is not to be confined
to a categorical reiteration of defendant's examination in chief. But, even a departure from categorical
reiteration does not comport a latitude as broad as the
entire case, as was here present. Morever, such an argument palpably begs the question and assumes the
guilt of defendant, instead of proving his guilt, as the
object of a trial is. For, if defendant were perchance
innocent, the moment he says he did not commit the offense with which he is charged, and the moment he says
he did not see the prosecutrix at all that night, he has

told all he knows about the case. To assume that he is falsifying and that he does know more, is to assume his guilt and beg the question, and to an extent compel him to convict himself. Such procedure and such assumption, aside from the statute supra, may be logically excusable in trying a guilty man, but not even excusable in logic in trying an innocent one. There can be but one law, if we are to hold fast to and retain any stable rules of law at all, by which to try both the guilty and the innocent. Defendant may be guilty; we think the record shows he is, and that the evidence is amply sufficient to warrant the verdict of the jury. But notwithstanding this the law guarantees to him the same kind of a trial an innocent person gets, and till such time as the Legislature and those who make State Constitutions shall see fit to ordain that apparent guilt is the sole condition precedent to an affirmance here, it will continue to be our duty to see to it that he and others similarly situated get this kind of a trial.

For the manifold errors in going outside of the statutory prohibition in cross-examining defendant, this case must be reversed and remanded for a new trial. Let this be done. All concur.

THE STATE v. JAMES L. ARNOLD, Appellant.

Division Two, February 15, 1916.

1. **CARNAL KNOWLEDGE: Evidence of Prosecutrix's Age.** Where the statute requires the prosecutrix to be under fifteen years of age in order to constitute sexual intercourse with her rape, proof that she was not fifteen at the time should be satisfactory and if possible her testimony thereto should be corroborated.

2. ———: ———: **Family Record.** Where the prosecutrix has testified that she was at the time of the carnal knowledge under fifteen years of age, and that her knowledge of her age was obtained from her parents and a family record, and the book being produced testified that it had been changed, the record, showing the date of birth of herself and brothers and sisters, should be admitted in evidence, and it was error to reject it, for three reasons: first, it was evidence of her true age; second, it was competent as tending to show that her statement of her age, based as she said, on said record, was false; and, third, it would tend to contradict her statement that the record, which, admittedly, for sometime had been in defendant's possession, had been changed.

3. ———: **Pregnancy; Year After Offense.** Where the trial for rape occurs more than twelve months after the prosecutrix was fifteen years of age, testimony by her and her physician that at the trial she was pregnant, and by her that her pregnancy was due to sexual intercourse with defendant, is incompetent, and if admitted is reversible error.

4. ———: **Continuance: Age of Prosecutrix.** Ordinarily in a prosecution for carnal knowledge of a female under fifteen years of age, where her age is a vital issue, an application for a continuance, based on the absence of her grandmother, sick and unable to attend the trial, who, if present, would testify that at the time of the offense she was over fifteen, should not be denied.

5. **REMARKS OF COUNSEL: Not Preserved for Review.** An assignment that the State's counsel was guilty of improper conduct in resorting to unwarranted argument cannot be reviewed if such matters are not preserved in the bill of exceptions.

Appeal from New Madrid Circuit Court.—*Hon. Frank Kelly*, Judge.

REVERSED AND REMANDED.

Riley & Riley, Thomas Gallivan and *E. F. Sharp* for appellant.

(1) The court erred in overruling the application for a continuance filed by the defendant on the ground of the sickness of Mrs. Baum, a most important witness. State v. Hesterly, 182 Mo. 32; State v. Maddox, 117 Mo. 667; State v. Dewitt, 152 Mo. 85;

State v. Warden, 94 Mo. 650; State v. Bradley, 90 Mo. 160. (2) The court erred in permitting the prosecuting witness to state on the stand, over the objection of the defendant, that she was pregnant and that the defendant was responsible for her condition. State v. Palmberg, 199 Mo. 233; State v. Scott, 172 Mo. 536; State v. Houx, 109 Mo. 654; State v. Evans, 138 Mo. 125; People v. Clark, 33 Mich. 112. (3) The court erred in permitting Dr. E. E. Jones to testify that he had made an examination of the prosecutrix a short time before the trial and that he found from such examination that she was pregnant. In the case at bar the court admitted Dr. Jones to testify as to her physical condition fourteen months after the date of the alleged act and over a year after the time when, according to her statement, she became fifteen years of age, and capable of consent under the law. State v. Evans, 138 Mo. 125; State v. Houx, 109 Mo. 662; State v. Scott, 172 Mo. 541. (4) The court erred in refusing to admit the family record as kept in the family of the prosecuting witness and which record would have shown her to have been over fifteen years of age at the time of the alleged intercourse. State v. Houx, 109 Mo. 664. The book was not a Bible, but was an "agricultural" report book. What kind of a book it was is immaterial. State v. Neasby, 188 Mo. 471; Beckham v. Nacke, 56 Mo. 546; Wigmore on Evidence, 1495; McKelvy on Evidence, secs. 153-160.

John T. Barker, Attorney-General, and *W. T. Rutherford,* Assistant Attorney-General, for the State.

(1) Absent a motive for a false accusation, a conviction may be sustained for statutory rape upon the uncorroborated testimony of the prosecutrix. State v. Manuel, 263 Mo. 674; State v. Stockhouse, 242 Mo. 449; State v. Tevis, 234 Mo. 276; State v. Goodale, 210 Mo. 282; State v. Brown, 209 Mo. 413;

State v. Donnington, 246 Mo. 343. (2) The evidence is sufficient to sustain the verdict. State v. Manuel, 263 Mo. 273; State v. Bowen, 247 Mo. 584; State v. Stockhouse, 242 Mo. 444; State v. Miner, 263 Mo. 275; State v. Swain, 239 Mo. 727; State v. Lovitt, 243 Mo. 510; State v. Skillman, 228 Mo. 436; State v. Devorss, 221 Mo. 473; State v. Pipkin, 221 Mo. 464; State v. George, 214 Mo. 271; State v. Campbell, 210 Mo. 234. (3) An application for a continuance is addressed to the sound discretion of the court, with the exercise of which an appellate court will not interfere, unless it clearly appears from all the facts and circumstances that such discretion has been abused to the prejudice of appellant. State v. Sassaman, 214 Mo. 735; State v. Cummings, 189 Mo. 640; State v. Sublett, 191 Mo. 171; State v. Richardson, 194 Mo. 335; State v. Temple, 194 Mo. 250; State v. McKenzie, 228 Mo. 397; State v. Cain, 247 Mo. 704. (4) It is not error to refuse a continuance because of an absent witness when the testimony of such witness would be merely cumulative. State v. Horn, 209 Mo. 462; State v. Temple, 194 Mo. 252; State v. Crane, 202 Mo. 74; State v. Riddle, 179 Mo. 295. (5) When diligence is not shown it is not error to deny a continuance. (6) Prosecutrix was competent to testify to her own age subject to cross-examination. State v. Marshall, 137 Mo. 466; State v. Evans, 138 Mo. 121; State v. Congat, 121 Mo. 463. (7) United States census reports and certified copies thereof, containing the name, age, sex, color and occupation of inhabitants of this country, being public official records, required by law to be kept, and made by sworn public officials, are competent evidence to show the age and date of birth of such inhabitants. Priddy v. Boice, 201 Mo. 333, 9 L. R. A. (N. S.) 733.

REVELLE, J.—This is a prosecution by information charging rape upon a female child under the age of fifteen years. Trial resulted in a verdict of guilty, and assessment of punishment at imprisonment in the penitentiary for a term of five years.

On the part of the State; Mabel Stuart, the prosecutrix, testified that about June 1, 1913, she was employed by defendant as a domestic in his home, and so continued until August 3rd of that year. During the first three weeks of her employment the defendant's family was absent, and from the first night of her stay in his home, on until she left, he had sexual intercourse with her about each night, this continuing even after the return of his family. She testified that at that time she was not fifteen years old, her statement being that she did not reach that age until the following September. She stated that her information and knowledge relative to her age was obtained from her parents, and an entry in a book which had been treated as a family record. This book was produced and identified by her, but she stated that same had been changed. She was unable, however, to specify or point out any changes that had been made . therein, and finally admitted that she could neither read nor write. Her statement as to her age is not corroborated by any substantial testimony. Over the objections of defendant, she and one Doctor Jones were permitted to state that she was then, at the time of the trial, pregnant.

The record discloses that the trial was had more than a year after she had arrived at the age of fifteen years, even according to her own statement of her age. She further testified that defendant was responsible for her pregnant condition, and that this was the result of his acts of intercourse with her.

On the part of the defendant the mother of prosecutrix testified that the girl was born on the 1st day of September, 1897, and that at the time of the alleged acts of intercourse she was over fifteen years of age. She further testified that she had recorded the age of

prosecutrix in the record, to which reference has heretofore been made, and that this correctly disclosed her
age.

One Lewis, a neighbor of the Stuart family, testified that he knew the age of the prosecutrix by reason of his knowledge of the date of the birth of one
of his own children, and that she was born in the year
1897, and was, as testified to by the mother, over the
age of fifteen years at the time of the alleged assault.

An application for a continuance, which was made
by defendant, and overruled by the court, sets up that
the grandmother of prosecutrix, then sick and unable
to attend the trial, would testify that the girl was born
in 1897.

Upon objections by the State, the court refused
to admit in evidence the family record which both the
prosecutrix and her mother had identified.

The views which we entertain on certain legal
questions presented by this record make unnecessary
a more extensive statement of the facts.

OPINION

I. The overshadowing issue in this case was the
age of the prosecutrix. In the law it is written that
the assaulted girl must be under the age of fifteen
years, and establishment of this fact
is just as essential to a conviction as is
the fact of sexual intercourse, and the
same satisfactory proof thereof is
required. Proof of lascivious or reprehensible conduct alone does not make out the charge of statutory
rape, and a defendant charged with the latter crime
can, as in all criminal cases, take issue with the State
on any of the material and essential elements.

Rape: Age of
Prosecutrix:
Family Record.

We have heretofore held that, absent an evident
motive for a false accusation, a conviction for statutory rape may be sustained upon the uncorroborated
testimony of the prosecutrix, but when we so declared

we were dealing principally with cases where the question went to the act of sexual intercourse, and we there recognized the commonly known fact that such acts are usually committed under circumstances which render corroborative proof unavailing. In the cases where we have held that corroboration of the prosecutrix's testimony as to her age was unnecessary her statements have been clear and positive, and not based upon a hypothesis which defendant showed to be false.

In the instant case the prosecutrix is not only not corroborated, but is contradicted by her mother and others by whom such a fact is generally and most satisfactorily proven. She says her information as to her age comes from her parents and a family record. The mother repudiates her statements as to the information coming from her, and the court refused to admit in evidence proof of the other source from which she says her information is derived. This was offered by the defendant and excluded upon the State's objection. The defendant's offer, however, discloses that it too would have contradicted her. For the present we leave as open the question as to whether, under such circumstances, her uncorroborated and contradicted statement of her age would be sufficient to sustain a conviction.

Upon what theory the court excluded the family record, which had been duly identified, we are unable to perceive. The date of the birth of the prosecutrix and of her brothers and sisters had been duly and timely recorded therein, and prosecutrix based her knowledge of her age largely thereon. This document had been prepared and preserved as a family record and was a matter of pedigree. It was competent for three purposes: (1) It was evidence of her true age (State v. Neasby, 188 Mo. 467); (2) it was competent and all important as tending to show that her statement as to her age, based, as she said, upon this record, was false; and (3) it would tend to contradict her statement that the record, which, admittedly for sometime had been in the possession of defendant, had been changed. If an examination thereof by the jury disclosed no evidence of a change therein, after she had sworn it had been changed, would this not tend to affect her credibility as a witness; and it must be remembered that it is upon her testimony alone that this defendant stands convicted. [State v. Shouse, 188 Mo. l. c. 479.] We again repeat what we have, in one form or another, so frequently said, that while corroboration in certain cases may not be legally required, prosecutions on a charge for which there is a human abhorrence must be conducted with scrupulous fairness, so as to avoid adding other prejudice than that which the charge itself frequently produces. The trained legal mind owes this not only to the accused, but to the honest, and sometimes mistaken, juror who, by reason of human sentiment, is led amiss.

II. This record discloses another equally grievous error. The trial occurred more than twelve months after the prosecutrix was, according to her own statements, fifteen years of age, and a similar length of time after the acts of intercourse upon which the State relies were committed.

Pregnancy Long After Deflowering. Over the objections of defendant the State was permitted to prove that at the time of the trial, prosecutrix was pregnant. If we indulge the presumption that we are no more ignorant than the rest of mankind, we must judicially notice that the acts of sexual intercourse upon which this prosecution is based, occurred at a time which rendered it physically impossible for this pregnancy to result therefrom, and yet the prosecutrix testified that her pregnant condition was due to her intercourse with defendant. This, of course, was but proof that defendant had intercourse with her subsequent to the acts relied upon, and this court has held, and, in my opinion, properly so, that such evidence is incompetent, and, when introduced, is sufficient to warrant a reversal. [State v. Palmberg, 199 Mo. 233.] Particularly is this true when the subsequent acts are as remote in time as this record discloses. [State v. Evans, 138 Mo. 116; State v. Scott, 172 Mo. l. c. 541.]

III. Complaint is also made that error was committed in overruling defendant's application for a continuance. While we probably would not reverse the judgment for this reason alone, we are of the opinion that, under the peculiar circumstances of this case, the State should not have insisted, and the court should not have ordered, that the trial proceed in the face of this application, it seemingly possessing real merit.

Continuance.

IV. The objection that State's counsel was guilty of improper conduct in resorting to unwarranted argument is not open to review, since no such matters are preserved in the bill of exceptions.

Improper Argument.

For the errors heretofore pointed out the judgment is reversed and the cause remanded. *Faris, P. J.,* and *Walker, J.,* concur.

THE STATE v. DANIEL TAYLOR, Appellant.

Division Two, February 15, 1916.

1. **CARNAL KNOWLEDGE: Evidence of Good Reputation.** In a prosecution for carnal knowledge of a female of previous chaste character, testimony to the effect that her general reputation for chastity in the community in which she lived, prior to the alleged occurrence, was good, is admissible. [Refusing to follow *dictum* in State v. Kelley, 191 Mo. l. c. 691.]

2. **SPECIFIC ASSIGNMENT: All Law of Case.** An assignment in the motion for a new trial that the court failed to instruct the jury as to all the law arising upon the issues in the case, which does not specify upon what point the court failed to instruct, does not raise a point for appellate review.

3. **CARNAL KNOWLEDGE: Issuable Matters.** In a prosecution for carnal knowledge of an unmarried female of previous chaste character between the ages of fifteen and eighteen years, the question of whether or not she consented to the acts of sexual intercourse is not material to the issue, and even though her testimony tending to show that she did not consent seems unbelievable, that does not affect a verdict of guilty. The material issues are (a) that she was an unmarried female between the ages of fifteen and eighteen years, that (b) defendant had sexual intercourse with her and (c) that prior to the act charged she was of chaste character.

Appeal from Nodaway Circuit Court.—*Hon. William C. Ellison*, Judge.

AFFIRMED.

Shinnabarger, Blagg & Ellison for appellant.

John T. Barker, Attorney-General, and *Kenneth C. Sears* for the State.

(1) Prosecutrix's character for chastity was in issue. It could be established by her general reputation regardless of any nice distinction between "character" and "reputation." 2 Wigmore on Evidence, section 1620; Carroll v. State, 74 Miss. 690; In re Vandiver, 4 Cal. App. 654; State v. Connor, 142 N. C. 705; State v. Kelley, 191 Mo. 691. In the following cases the evidence was admitted but the question was not discussed. State v. Schenk, 238 Mo. 440; State v. Pipkin, 221 Mo. 458; State v. DeWitt, 186 Mo. 63. (2) The defendant did not properly object to a failure to instruct upon all the law; and since the fourth point in the motion for a new trial is not specific, the omission of the court, if any, is not open for review. State v. Conway, 241 Mo. 271; State v. Douglas, 258 Mo. 281.

WILLIAMS, C.—Upon an information charging him with the carnal knowledge of an unmarried female of previous chaste character between the ages of fifteen and eighteen years, defendant was tried, in the circuit court of Nodaway County, found guilty, and his punishment assessed at two years' imprisonment in the penitentiary.

The evidence upon the part of the State tends to establish the following facts:

In July, 1913, the date of the alleged crime, prosecutrix, fifteen years and six months of age, and unmarried, resided, with her parents, on a farm in Nodaway county. At that time, the defendant, a young man, nineteen years of age, was in the employ of the father of the prosecutrix as a farm hand and resided at the home of prosecutrix's father very much the same as if he were a member of the family. One afternoon, about the middle of July, 1913, the father and mother of prosecutrix went to the town of Graham, on an errand, leaving at the house the defendant, the prosecutrix and four other younger children. A short time after the parents left, prosecutrix was in one of the bedrooms doing some house work, when she heard defendant enter the house. He immediately came into the bedroom where she was. Upon coming into the bedroom, he locked the door, pulled down the blinds, threw her down on the bed, overcame her resistance and had intercourse with her. While this was occurring, three of the other children, including a fourteen-year-old girl, were out doors, at play. The youngest child, one year old, was in some other portion of the house.

After the transaction, defendant left the house and prosecutrix did not see him again until after her father and mother returned about four or five o'clock that afternoon. She did not tell her father and mother for the reason that she states the defendant had told her she would always regret it if she did. Prosecutrix

was in good health and weighed about one hundred
and thirty pounds and stated that she used all the
force possible; that she was not bruised or scratched
nor was there any laceration of the parts. She stated
that she did not scream because defendant told her not
to and she was afraid of him.

Defendant continued, after the occurrence, to reside at the farm until August 6, 1913, upon which date
he and the mother of prosecutrix had some disagree-
ment, and defendant left. He again returned to work
on the farm, December 1, 1913, and remained until
some time in January, 1914.

Defendant had never offered prosecutrix any in-
dignities prior to the occurrence in July, 1913, and
never made any further advances except about Christmas time, 1913, at which time she refused him.

Sometime in January, 1914, the mother and sister
of defendant visited the home of prosecutrix. It does
not appear what was said by the parties on that occasion but, on the following day, the family physician
was summoned and, after an examination, the physician thought that prosecutrix was pregnant. Later,
on March 17, 1914, prosecutrix was taken to a mater-
nity hospital in Kansas City and there, on April 17,
1914, she gave birth to a child.

Prosecutrix testified that she had never had intercourse with anyone prior to the above-mentioned time.

Evidence was introduced to show that the reputation of prosecutrix for chastity in that community,
prior to the alleged offense, was good. It further appears that she had not kept company with other boys.

George Herron, a neighbor of the prosecutrix,
testified that, sometime in the winter following the
alleged occurrence in the summer, defendant asked
him what would be the penalty "if a fellow that wasn't
of age would get a girl in a fix that wasn't of age;"

and asked what would be the consequences if he would marry her. The witness told defendant that if the girl was not of age, he would have to get the consent of her parents before he could get a license to marry her. The defendant then said, "I guess I have a move coming." Later, in another conversation, the defendant admitted that it was. the prosecutrix who was in trouble.

The evidence upon the part of the defendant tended to establish the following facts. Defendant, testifying in his own behalf, stated that there was nothing improper between prosecutrix and himself in the year 1912, but that about the first of May, 1913, he and prosecutrix were in the kitchen while he was making a prepartion for a sick horse and that "she kept hanging around me, standing up close to me and I put my arms around her and kissed her." That a short time thereafter they met in the cellar while putting away the milk and defendant there hugged and kissed the prosecutrix. The prosecutrix then said, "If you are going to do anything, hurry up and do it or the folks will catch us." That he then proceeded to have intercourse with the prosecutrix. Defendant denied the story related by prosecutrix concerning his having intercourse with her on the day that her parents went to town, but stated that, after the occurrence in the cellar, in May, he continued to have intercourse with the prosecutrix once or twice a week until he left the place in August, 1913; that prosecutrix would come to his room at night after her father and mother had retired. A few days after defendant quit working at the farm, he returned a buggy belonging to the father of prosecutrix and, at that time, he had a conversation with the prosecutrix in which he reminded her that she had told him that he was the only one with whom she had been intimate and then told her that "Curly" Deacon had told him that Clyde Goodpasture had told Deacon that he had been intimate with the prosecutrix, prior to the time that defendant had had intercourse with her. Defendant testified that thereupon, prosecutrix admitted to him that the accusation was true.

Five witnesses testified that defendant's reputation for morality and chastity was good in that community, prior to the time of his arrest.

In rebuttal, the prosecuting witness denied that she had admitted to the defendant that she had been intimate with Clyde Goodpasture. Goodpasture testified denying that he had ever had improper relations with the prosecutrix and also denied that he had so stated to Deacon. Deacon testified that he did not remember of telling the defendant of this occurrence and stated that Clyde Goodpasture had never told him that he had had intercourse with the prosecutrix.

Two of the attorneys, representing the defendant, then testified that, a short time before the trial, Deacon was in their office and had told them that he had told the defendant of the alleged Goodpasture incident.

We have not been favored by appellant with a brief, but pursuant to our statutory duty in the premises, we will review the record and discuss the points raised in the motion for a new trial.

OPINION.

I. The first two grounds in the motion for a new trial assign error in the admission and exclusion of evidence. The only matter coming within either of these two grounds and of sufficient importance to merit discussion is the matter of

Reputation.

introducing, over the objection and exception of defendant, the testimony to the effect that the general reputation of prosecutrix for chastity, in the community where she lived, prior to the alleged occurrence, was good.

One of the requirements of the statute under which defendant stands charged is the requirement that prosecutrix must be of *previous chaste character*.

While it is true that reputation and character are not synonymous, yet the former is always some evidence from which the latter may be inferred and is, therefore, admissible. The correct rule in this regard is stated in 2 Wigmore on Evidence, section 1620 (1), as follows:

"As to *chastity* or its opposite, no doubt has ever arisen, except in a single and peculiar action. In the statutory action or prosecution for seduction of a woman of 'previously chaste character,' the question first arises whether this 'character' is actual character or reputation. Assuming the former view to be taken, then, although actual character is the fact in issue, there is no reason why reptuation should not be admissible, as in all other issues, to prove the chaste or unchaste character. But in some jurisdictions the court's adoption of the view that the actual character is the fact in issue has led it erroneously to exclude reputation as evidence of that character."

To the same effect are the following authorities: Carroll v. State, 74 Miss. 688, l. c. 690; State v. Lockerby, 50 Minn. 363; In re Vandiveer, 4 Cal. App. 650, l. c. 654; State v. Connor, 142 N. C. 700, l. c. 705.

In State v. Kelley, 191 Mo. 680, l. c. 691, there appears to be a mere *dictum* to the contrary, which should not be followed.

II. The third ground of the motion attacks instructions numbered 1, 2 and 3. It would serve no

Instructions. useful purpose to copy these instructions into the opinion. We have carefully examined the same and find them to be in proper form and free from error.

III. The fourth ground complains because the court failed to instruct the jury as to all the law arising upon the issues in the case. Since

Specific Assignment. the above does not *specify* upon what point the court failed to instruct, it does not raise a point for appellate review.

IV. The remaining grounds of the motion raise the question as to the sufficiency of evidence to support the verdict. The evidence is suffi-

Sufficiency of Evidence. ciently stated in the foregoing statement. While some of the story of the prosecutrix appears to be very unusual and unbelievable, yet the unusual portion of her testimony refers to matters not necessary to be proven to sustain a conviction, towit, her testimony tending to show that she did not consent to the act of intercourse. The question of whether or not she consented to the act of intercourse was not material to the issues. The material issues were whether she, as an unmarried female, between the ages of fifteen and eighteen years, had intercourse with defendant, as charged and submitted to the jury, and, if so, was she of previous chaste character?

We are of the opinion that the evidence was amply sufficient to sustain the verdict.

The judgment is affirmed. *Roy C.,* concurs.

PER CURIAM.—The foregoing opinion by WIL-LIAMS, C., is adopted as the opinion of the court. All the judges concur.

THE STATE v. W. F. ALLEN, Appellant.

Division Two, February 15, 1916.

1. **ARRAIGNMENT: Appeal.** The failure of the record to show either an arraignment or a plea will not, of itself, entitle defendant to a reversal, the record also failing to show that any objection was made at any time to a lack of arraignment or plea until the case reached the appellate court. .

2. **INFORMATION: Amendment of Statute After Crime: Substantial Rights of Defendant.** It is error for the information to charge that the age of the prosecutrix was under fifteen years and that of defendant above seventeen years, in the language of the amendment of the statute which raised the age of consent from fourteen to fifteen years and that of defendant from sixteen to seventeen years, where the act of carnal knowledge was committed before the amendment went into effect; but under the Statute of Jeofails the error is not reversible, unless it tends to the prejudice of the substantial rights of the defendant on the merits; and it does not so prejudice those rights, where the evidence clearly establishes that the prosecutrix was at the time of the alleged crime above fifteen years of age and the defendant above seventeen.

3. **CHANGE OF VENUE: Trial With Application Pending.** Where the record fails to show anything on the subject except the bare fact that an application for a change of venue was filed, it will not be held on appeal that the case was tried while a formal and sufficient application was pending.

4. ———: ———: **Matter of Exception.** Complaint that the case was tried while an application for a change of venue was pending is a matter of exception, to be saved for review in the bill of exceptions.

5. ———: **Jurisdiction of Another Judge: Agreement upon Special Judge.** Where the record shows that an application for a change of venue was filed and that a judge of another circuit was called by the regular judge to sit in the case and "was on the bench" and tried the case without objection, it will be presumed, in the absence of a record showing to the contrary, that both the State and defendant waived the privilege of selecting a special judge; and, aided by the presumption of right action on the part of a court of general jurisdiction, it will be *held* that the judge so called in had authority to try the case.

267 Mo. 4

6 **EVIDENCE: Impeachment: Carnal Knowledge: Offer to Settle For Money.** Evidence in a prosecution for carnal knowledge of a female under the age of consent that the prosecutrix proposed to defendant or his attorney, to leave the State and not appear at the trial if money were paid to her, and that her uncle after a conference with her and her mother and in pursuance to an understanding with them hunted up defendant and proposed to him, and later proposed to defendant's attorney, that if money were paid to him he would take prosecutrix out of the State and see to it that she did not appear at the trial, is competent for the purpose of impeaching both the prosecutrix and her mother as witnesses to the main fact of sexual intercourse, and the exclusion of such testimony is reversible error.

Appeal from Stoddard Circuit Court.—*Hon. E. M. Dearing,* Judge.

REVERSED AND REMANDED.

Mozley & Woody and *J. W. Farris* for appellant.

(1) The record in this case discloses that, on the first day of the March term, 1914, of the circuit court of Stoddard county, the same being the return term of the information, defendant filed his application for a change of venue under R. S. 1909, sec. 5198. That application has never been disposed of, but is still pending. The application being in due form, it became mandatory upon the court to grant the change, and make such disposition of the case as required by statute. R. S. 1909, secs. 5198, 5199; State v. Spivey, 191 Mo. 87; State v. Shipman, 93 Mo. 147. (2) The cause was not set down for trial by Hon. W. S. C. Walker, the judge of said court, and there is nothing to show that Judge Dearing was called in by Judge Walker. R. S. 1909, sec. 5201; State v. Gillham, 174 Mo. 671. (3) Defendant was charged with violating section 2, page 219, Laws 1913. The offense, if committed at all, was committed during either the month of March or the month of April, 1913. Said section 2

did not become a law until June 23, 1913, hence defendant could not have violated said law in March or April, 1913. Constitution, art. 4, sec. 36; State v. McMahon, 234 Mo. 611; State v. Schenk, 238 Mo. 429; State v. Howard, 175 S. W. 58; Neef v. McGuire, 52 Mo. 493; Ex parte Smith, 135 Mo. 223; State v. Finley, 187 Mo. App. 72. (4) Under all the facts and circumstances detailed in evidence in this case, the character of the parties, the time and place where this offense is, according to the testimony of the prosecuting witness, alleged to have been committed, the conduct of the parties after the alleged commission, the time which elapsed, between the alleged commission and the date when prosecuting witness told her mother, the means used by her mother to compel her to make the charge, all go to show that the story of the prosecuting witness is an unreasonable one. The testimony is not sufficient to prove the guilt of defendant beyond a reasonable doubt, and his instruction in the nature of a demurrer to the evidence should have been given. State v. Jaeger, 66 Mo. 173; State v. Primm, 98 Mo. 368; State v. Burgdorf, 53 Mo. 65; Harper v. Railroad, 186 Mo. App. 296. (5) Defendant was not arraigned, therefore, his motion in arrest of judgment should have been sustained. R. S. 1909, sec. 5165; 12 Cyc. 344; 2 Ency. Pl. & Pr. 787; State v. Williams, 117 Mo. 379; Shelp v. U. S., 81 Fed. 694; Crain v. U. S., 162 U. S. 625; State v. Cisco, 186 Mo. 49; Secs. 22 and 30, art. 2, Constitution.

John T. Barker, Attorney-General, and *Lee B. Ewing,* Assistant Attorney-General, for the State.

(1) The information is good. State v. Salts, 263 Mo. 308; Kelly's Crim. Law & Practice, sec. 535; State v. Clark, 158 Mo. App. 489; State v. Nave, 185 Mo. 125; Sec. 4472, R. S. 1909. (2) Appellant was not ar-

raigned, but he was present at the trial and made no objection or exception thereto. He offered evidence in his defense and also testified himself. By going to trial without objection, he waiyed arraignment. State v. O'Kelley, 258 Mo. 345; State v. Gould, 261 Mo. 694. (3) Appellant filed application for change of venue. The transcript does not disclose the grounds for the application, nor whether or not the trial court ruled thereon. Neither does it show that appellant made any objection or exception to the ruling of the court, or his failure to rule thereon. It does disclose that Judge Walker, the regular judge of the circuit, called in Judge E. M. Dearing of the Twenty-first Circuit and appellant went to trial without objection before the latter judge. Nor did appellant present the question to the trial court for review, either in his motion for a new trial or in arrest of judgment. This record does not convict the trial court of error in this regard. Drainage District v. Richardson, 227 Mo. 252; Leslie v. Chase, 200 Mo. 263; Wolff v. Ward, 104 Mo. 127. (4) There was no reversible error in the trial court's rulings upon admission and rejection of testimony.

FARIS, P. J.—Defendant, convicted in the circuit court of Stoddard County for a violation of the provisions of section 4472, Revised Statutes 1909, for that he had carnal knowledge of a female under the age of consent, after the usual motions for a new trial and in arrest of judgment, has appealed.

The information upon which this prosecution is bottomed was filed on the 5th day of February, 1914. It charges the defendant with committing the alleged offense in March, 1913. Except in the behalf discussed in the opinion, the information is conventional and we need not cumber the record with the whole of

it, but we mention in passing that as to the ages of
the persons involved it follows the amendment of 1913,
which amendment went into effect subsequent to the
date of the commission of the alleged offense.

The facts in brief, so far as they are pertinent
and so far as we do not set them out in our opinion,
run thus:

Defendant is a physician and surgeon now practicing in the city of St. Louis, but at the time of the
alleged commission of the offense charged, engaged,
a portion of his time at least, in practicing his profession in Stoddard County, Missouri, and having offices
at one time or another both in Dexter and in Bloomfield
in that county. Defendant while practicing in Stoddard County seems to have specialized in the treatment
of diseases of the eye and was thus brought profes-
sionally into contact with the prosecuting witness, one
Hattie Allard, aged at the time set out in the information, sixteen years, lacking a few days. Having been
treated by defendant for an affection of the eyes while
he was in Dexter, she followed him to Bloomfield for
the purpose, as the record shows, of having the treatment continued. She remained in Bloomfield for
some five weeks taking such treatment, and while thus
under the care of defendant the first sexual act of
defendant with her took place in the latter part of
March or the first days of April, 1913. From that time
on, until November, 1913, as occasion offered, other
acts of sexual intercourse occurred between defendant
and the prosecuting witness, the last act occurring in
the room of defendant at a hotel in Dexter on Thanksgiving Day, 1913. While the prosecuting witness and
defendant were in this room, the mother of the former,
suspecting the relations existing, slipped into an adjoining room and overheard suspicious noises which
she deemed to indicate that defendant and her daugh-

ter were engaged in illicit intercourse. Going into this room the moment defendant unlocked the door, she found, she tells us, prosecutrix sitting in defendant's lap. Soon thereafter this prosecution was commenced. Other elements necessary to be proven are sufficiently shown by the record. The State showed a telephone conversation between defendant and the prosecutrix, and likewise a conversation between defendant and a Mrs. Kimbell, which to an extent corroborates the testimony of the prosecutrix.

On cross-examination of the prosecutrix and likewise of her mother, who testified for the State, it was shown that for some five days after the mother had, as she says, caught her daughter and defendant in the compromising position mentioned, prosecutrix had continued to deny any illicit relations with defendant, and that it was not until the mother had slapped prosecutrix's face repeatedly and otherwise physically maltreated her, that she confessed these relations.

The defense was not guilty in the broadest sense of the word, in this, that defendant denied ever having been intimate with prosecutrix and averred that the sole relation existing was that of physician and patient. The age of defendant is not definitely shown, but it is shown that he attended medical school four years prior to the year 1897 and that he graduated as a physician and surgeon in that year. His general reputation for morality and chastity is shown by the record to be good and in no wise is this denied or controverted by the State.

Such further facts as may be required to make clear the points discussed will be found set out in our opinion, at which place they may appositely serve to make clear our discussion of the questions mooted.

I. Defendant by his learned counsel contends that inasmuch as the record fails to disclose either an arraignment or a plea, he is for this **Arraignment.** entitled to a reversal out of hand. The record also shows that no objection was lodged anywhere touching the lack of an arraignment and plea till the case got here, and that defendant was tried in all respects just as if a formal arraignment and plea had been had—as they doubtless were, if we were permitted, *as we are not*, to speculate upon facts on which the record is silent.

Defendant's learned counsel concede that the cases of State v. O'Kelley, 258 Mo. 345, and State v. Gould, 261 Mo. 694, are against this contention, but they cite and quote at some length from Crain v. United States, 162 U. S. 625, and largely upon the authority of the latter case, insist that we were wrong in the O'Kelley and Gould cases, and urge us to overrule the latter cases and get back to the good old technical rule of other days. We are not disposed to overrule the holding made in the O'Kelley case for the reason so ably urged upon us by counsel, or for any other reason; especially since about the time the O'Kelley case was ruled, the Supreme Court of the United States in an opinion in which all concurred, overruled the case of Crain v. United States, supra, cited to us and relied on by counsel. [Garland v. State of Washington, 232 U. S. 642; see, also, State v. Garland, 65 Wash. 666.] Hence, we disallow this contention.

II. There is no doubt that an error occurs in the information, in that, while it was filed subsequent to the taking effect of the amendment of **Amendment of Statute After Crime.** 1913, Laws 1913, p. 219, it charged an offense committed in March, 1913, prior to the taking effect of said amendment. When the alleged offense occurred, the statute forbade carnal knowledge between males of sixteen years and upwards and unmarried females of previous chaste character between the ages of fourteen years and eighteen years. Pending the alleged commission of the crime and the filing of the information at bar, the amendment was passed and took effect, raising the age of the male from sixteen to seventeen years and that of the female from fourteen years as a minimum to fifteen years, to conform to the age of consent statute defining statutory rape amended by the same bill. In the information herein these ages are set out as *seventeen* years and *fifteen* years respectively, instead of *sixteen* and *fourteen,* as the law and the time of the facts required. The error conceded, the inquiry arises, is it reversible error? Clearly not, unless this error tends "to the prejudice of the substantial rights of the defendant upon the merits." [Sec. 5115, R. S. 1909.] The above provision of our Statute of Jeofails is obviously in point here. Since it is impossible to see wherein defendant was prejudiced by this error, the point should be disallowed. For we judicially notice from the facts in proof that defendant was over seventeen years of age in March, 1913; because he says he was in medical school four years and that he graduated therefrom in 1897, and that he is married and had a son sixteen years of age at the time of trial. At the time of the carnal intercourse alleged the female was, as the proof likewise shows, a few days less than sixteen years of age. So since defendant was over seventeen years and prosecutrix was under eighteen years of age, an erroneous averment as to the statutory minimum which serves to differentiate statutory rape from carnal knowledge does not, in our view, prejudice defendant in any wise.

III. Complaint is made that the case was tried while a sufficient and formal application for a change of venue was pending. This complaint is **Change of Venue.** not borne out by the record; for the record fails to show aught except the bare fact that an application for a change of venue was filed. Neither the application itself, nor any record of any action thereon, appears in the record, nor is any exception to the action of the court, nor any exception to the failure of the court to act thereon, shown by the bill of exceptions. For aught that appears, except by fairly plain inference, defendant waived action thereon after filing the application for a change of venue. The inference referred to is that he got the identical change of venue he asked for; because the case was tried by Judge Dearing of the Twenty-First Circuit, and not by the regular judge of the Stoddard Circuit Court, whom we judically know to be Judge W. S. C. Walker. But be this as may be, matters of this sort are matters of pure exception to be saved for review in the bill of exceptions, and since the point is not so saved, we cannot review it. [Drainage District v. Richardson, 227 Mo. 252.]

Cognate to this complaint, is the contention likewise urged that Judge Dearing had no authority to **Calling in Another Judge.** try this case because the record is bare of averments making for jurisdiction in him. The contention touching the record is true, save and except the meagre entries (a) that an application for a change of venue was filed, and (b) that Hon. E. M. Dearing, "who was called by the Hon. W. S. C. Walker, regular judge of this court, and requested to sit in the following cases: State of Mo. v. W. F. Allen . . . was on the bench." While these entries are meagre in averment and the last one does not appear till after one mis-trial (errors in which we are not here called on to review), we are of opinion that, aided by the presumptions we are permitted to entertain, of the right and proper action of a court of general jurisdiction, they are sufficient to show that Judge Dearing was for a sufficient reason called in by the regular judge to sit in this case. While the record here does not show any effort of defendant and the prosecuting attorney to elect, or rather agree on, a special judge before Judge Dearing was called in (Sec. 5199, R. S. 1909), yet in the absence of a record showing the contrary it will be presumed that both the defendant and the State waived the privilege of selecting a special judge. [State v. Wear, 145 Mo. 162; State v. Gillham, 174 Mo. 671; State v. Hunter, 171 Mo. l. c. 439.] Since, as forecast, a circuit court is a court of general jurisdiction, every presumption will be entertained touching the rightness and orderliness of its proceedings, naught else appearing, and since the record shows that the regular judge did call in Judge Dearing to try this case and that he tried it without objection from any source, it was not fatal to Judge Dearing's jurisdiction that the record failed to show affirmatively the reasons moving Judge Walker in such behalf. [State v. Hunter, 171 Mo. l. c. 440; State v. Gilmore, 110 Mo. 1; State v. Gamble, 108 Mo. 500; State ex rel. v. Wear, 129 Mo. l. c. 625.] As seen, however, the inference is obvious that Judge Dearing was called in because Judge Walker had been theretofore "sworn off the bench," as the local vernacular would designate it, by the application for a change of venue. The conclusion follows that this contention should be disallowed.

IV. In the course of the cross-examination of the prosecuting witness she stated in answer to a question

Compounding Felony: Impeachment

by counsel for defendant, that her uncle, one Franklin Fowler, had talked with her and her mother about going to St. Louis. Thereupon defendant's counsel asked her this question: "What was the discussion between your uncle, your mother and yourself about his going to St. Louis to see Dr. Allen?" An objection by the State was interposed and sustained to this question for that it had no tendency to prove any issue in the case and defendant excepted. Whereupon the jury and the prosecuting witness were both removed and defendant made his formal offer of proof thus:

"The purpose of this offer is to show that, as the witness has testified, her uncle came down there to Dexter and had a conference with her mother and her, respecting this case, with a view of her uncle going to St. Louis and getting a thousand dollars to settle the case. I expect to show that in pursuance to that conference, he did go to St. Louis and hunted up Doctor Allen, that he demanded a thousand dollars from him, and Doctor Allen told him that he would have to see Mr. Mozley, his attorney at Bloomfield, and that he couldn't discuss the matter with him. I expect to show that he came directly from St. Louis to my office and made the same demand on me; that he stated to me that if we would pay a thousand dollars, he would see that Miss Allard was not here for the trial; that if we would pay him a thousand dollars, he would take Miss Allard and go to Illinois and not appear at the trial of this case. I expect to show that I declined to do it and ordered him out of my office."

Upon this offer the court again ruled that since "the State could not be bound by such conduct on the part of the uncle or anybody else," and the offering "had no tendency to prove or disprove any of the allegations charged in the information," objection by the State to the offering would be sustained, and defendant again saved his exception. In this refusal to allow the defendant to investigate the alleged connection of prosecutrix and her mother, who was also a very damaging witness in the case, with the alleged acts of the uncle, we think the learned court *nisi* erred. This offer of proof could, indeed, neither bind nor estop the State, nor did it tend to prove or disprove any of the component elements of the offense charged, but it would have served to impeach both the prosecuting witness and her mother, from whom alone came practically all of the evidence of defendant's guilt. There was an entire lack of physical corroborating facts. Prosecutrix was never examined by a physician or by any one else, neither did she become pregnant from the alleged intercourse. In short, the proof of her deflowering rests upon the oral averments of her mother and herself, diminished as to herself in probative weight by the fact that she first confessed defendant's behavior with her under stress of a face-slapping and hair-pulling from her maternal parent.

The sole defense was that defendant had never had sexual intercourse with her. Upon this alleged truth and his good character he relied for acquittal; so, an inquiry into the motives if any, of those who appeared against him was peculiarly important in his defense. If prosecutrix's uncle went to St. Louis and offered to compound this felony of his own accord and without the consent and concurrence of witnesses who appeared against the defendant, then it follows of course that his acts—unless to impeach him should he become a witness in the case—are inadmissible for any purpose. But if he went to see defendant to make this offer with the consent and concurrence of prosecutrix and her mother, he became their agent on the ground, to mention no other, that all became co-conspirators and they are to be impeached by what he said or offered to do while endeavoring to carry through the common enterprise, just as though they had made the offer themselves. If the rule were otherwise compounders of felony and blackmailers need only to employ an intermediary in order to go unwhipt of justice. There are old cases which seem to hold that even the prosecutrix would not be impeached for that she offered to compromise the case. Doubting the logic of such a view, but distinguishing these cases if they are right, from a case wherein an offer is made by one representing the chief witnesses in the case, that if the sum of one thousand dollars be paid by the defendant the prosecutrix will leave the State and not appear at the trial, we are impelled to say that if such proof would not be meet for impeachment, it is difficult to imagine conduct which would be admissible for that purpose. In analogous cases in this State, and squarely in point elsewhere, it has been so held. [Barkly v. Copeland, 86 Cal. 483; Alward v. Oakes, 63 Minn. 190; Bessette v. State, 101 Ind. 85; Jenkins v. State, 34 Tex. Cr. App. 201; Richards v. State, 34 Tex. Cr. App. 277; Comm. v. Bell, 4 Pa. Superior Ct. 187; Pleasant v. State, 13 Ark. l. c. 377; State v. McKinstry, 100 Iowa, 82.] Upon the facts here this case is to be clearly distinguished from that of State v. Caudle, 174 Mo. l. c. 393.

The point is made that the evidence is not sufficient to take the case to the jury. This point is not well taken. There was substantial evidence of guilt, and since the weight and credibility of the evidence is for the jury and not for us, we are not disposed, nor have we the legal right to interfere. For the error noted let the case be reversed and remanded for a new trial. It is so ordered. All concur.

THE STATE v. JOHN R. BURTON, Appellant.

Division Two, February 15, 1916.

1. **FAILURE TO SUPPORT WIFE: No Element of Vagrancy.** Section 4789, Revised Statutes 1909, declaring, among other things, that "every able-bodied married man who shall neglect or refuse to provide for the support of his family . . . shall be deemed a vagrant" and upon conviction punished by imprisonment or fine, is a statute defining vagrancy, and cannot be used to enforce a civil liability; nor is a husband who

honestly tries to obtain work and is unable to procure sufficiently remunerative employment to properly support his
family, a criminal or a vagrant, nor can he be punished under
said statute. [Disapproving Marolf, v. Marolf, 191 Mo. App. 239,
so far, if at all, as it conflicts with this holding.]

2. ————: ————: **Placing Wife With Sister to Board.** A
husband who at a time when he was receiving sixty dollars
per month put his wife and child with her sister under an
agreement to pay her twenty dollars per month for their
board and lodging, and paid the amount regularly for three
months, and who, having lost his position, after two or three
weeks' effort to secure employment obtained a position at a
hotel at five dollars a week, cannot be convicted for failure
during the next three months to pay to his wife or her sister
any part of the five dollars, his purpose being to discharge his
obligation to his wife's sister as soon as he was able.

3. ————: ————: **Wife With Money.** The gift of one thous-
and dollars by the wife to her sister within the time her husband was unable to obtain remunerative employment simply
has a tendency to show the wife was not in destitute circumstances.

Appeal from St. Louis Court of Criminal Correction.
—*Hon. Benjamin F. Clark*, Judge.

REVERSED AND DEFENDANT DISCHARGED.

Fish & Fish for appellant.

John T. Barker, Attorney-General, and *Kenneth
C. Sears* for the State.

REVELLE, J.—This cause was originally appealed to and decided by the St. Louis Court of Appeals, and certified to us for final determination because one member of that court deemed the majority
opinion to be in conflict with the decision of the Kansas City Court of Appeals in the case of Marolf v.
Marolf, 191 Mo. App. 239.

The case involves the correct construction of section 4789, Revised Statutes 1909, and its application
to the facts here disclosed. The substantive part of

the charge is that defendant, being an able-bodied
married man, did wilfully neglect and refuse to provide for the support of his lawful wife and child, in
that he neglected to provide the necessary food and
clothing for their maintenance and support, and left
them wholly destitute of the same and in a condition of
suffering and want.   The information is predicated
upon that clause of the following section (Sec. 4789,
R. S. 1909) italicized:

"Every person who may be found loitering around
houses of ill-fame, gambling houses, or places where
liquors are sold or drank, without any visible means of
support, or shall attend or operate any gambling device or apparatus, or be engaged in practicing any
trick or device to procure money or other thing of
value, or shall be engaged in any unlawful calling
whatever, and *every able-bodied married man who
shall neglect or refuse to provide for the support of
his family,* and every person found tramping or wan-
dering around from place to place without any visible
means of support, *shall be deemed a vagrant,* and
upon conviction thereof, shall be punished by imprisonment in the county jail not less than twenty days, or
by fine not less than twenty dollars, or by both such
fine and imprisonment."

The evidence tends to prove that defendant is an
able-bodied man and with his wife lived at the home of
his parents from April, 1912, the time of his marriage,
until the latter part of January, 1913, at which time
his parents changed their residence, and defendant
thereupon made arrangements with his wife's sister
to furnish his wife, as well as his recently born child,
with board, lodging and necessary care.   In consideration of this, he agreed to pay the sister the sum
of twenty dollars per month, the understanding being
that this arrangement should continue until such time

as defendant could earn money sufficient to enable him "to take her to a flat of some kind." At that time he was in the employ of the American Car Company, and was receiving sixty dollars per month. This plan and arrangement seemed entirely satisfactory to all parties concerned at the time of its adoption, and, in pursuance thereof, the wife and child received from the sister proper care and maintenance, and the defendant, up to March 25, 1913, paid the sister the aggregate amount of twenty-five dollars. In the meantime defendant lost his position with the car company, and, after two or three weeks' effort (honest effort, so far as the record here discloses), he procured work at a hotel at a wage of five dollars per week, and in this capacity, and at this remuneration, he served to the time of his trial, to-wit, July, 1913. After March 25th he made no payments to the wife's sister, and did not otherwise contribute to the support and maintenance of his wife or child. His explanation of this was that he had an invalid father for whom he was also trying to care; that he knew his wife and child were being well provided for by relatives with whom he had contracted, and that his hire had not been sufficient to enable him to fully carry out his part of the contract with his wife's sister, although he recognized his legal liability to the sister and expressed his desire to discharge same when able.

It also appears from the record that the wife had personal property of her own amounting to something over a thousand dollars, but her brother and sister explained that this the wife *gave* to the sister.

The defendant also stated that his inability to procure more remunerative employment was due in part to the action of his wife's brother (chief witness for the State) in refusing to endorse and recommend him for certain positions when called upon to so do.

I. There is no evidence that the sister with whom the contract was made, or anyone for her, at any time notified the defendant that, because of his breach and failure to promptly pay, the wife and child were not receiving, and would not receive, the care and necessaries for which he had contracted, and which, seemingly, were adequate to their wants and station in life. On the other hand, the record discloses that they did, in point of fact, receive such, and were not, as the information alleges, "left wholly destitute of food and clothing, and in a condition of suffering and want." They were not cast upon the charity and mercy of the world, and, so long as the sister saw fit to continue her part of the agreement, as she had done up to the time of the trial, and take her chances on collecting the debt, there was no likelihood of defendant's family becoming destitute or in want or a burden upon the State; nor is there evidence that had she refused to further care for them, in pursuance of her contract, the defendant would not, to the extent of his ability, have made other arrangements for their care and support. What is the distinction between this case and that of the man who, upon his credit and by his agreement to pay, induces the butcher, grocer and merchant to furnish supplies and life's necessities to his family, and then refuses to pay therefor? The defendant's conduct in this case evinces, at least, a solicitude for his family, even though it shows not the same concern about the payment of his debts. This case smacks too strongly of an effort to use the criminal laws for the purpose of enforcing a civil liability. This statute was not enacted to protect creditors, or make the liberty of men security for their debts; it is not so nominated in the bond, and we have rather ancient and long-standing authority for refusing to extend the terms of such a bond; neither was it enacted to add further

Failure to Support Wife.

pangs to the "wretched soul already bruis'd with adversity." It is a statute defining *vagrancy*, and by its very terms excludes the man who is not able-bodied. Why this express exemption, except upon the theory that a man shall not be denounced and punished as a criminal when nature or earthly misfortune has rendered him physically unable to fulfill his marital and paternal obligations; and if this is the spirit of the act why hold responsible the man to whom misfortune has come in *other* forms? Poverty brings its suffering and adversity its sorrow, but neither, in themselves, is disgraceful, and until the properly constituted authority so expressly ordains, I am unwilling to brand them criminal. Why should the man who, because of business depression, or peculiar misfortune, is unable to procure sufficiently remunerative employment to properly support his family be branded as a vagrant and a criminal?

In the case at hand the evidence does not disclose that the defendant was not at all times willing and anxious to, and in point of fact, did work, and was earning such compensation as his employment and efforts permitted. Should he then be placed in the class denounced by this statute—the class of the vagrant and vagabond and among those who loiter around houses of ill-fame, gambling houses, etc.? In Gallemore v. Gallemore, 115 Mo. App. l. c. 191-2, Nortoni, J., in discussing this section, said: "Indeed, such a construction in times of commercial depression and paralyzed industry, might prove ruinous to the peace and repose of society. Men theretofore honest, seeking employment, would be. in many instances driven to pillage and plunder to render the support required, rather than render themselves liable to prosecution and subject to divorce proceedings upon their failure to provide such support. No such unjust and unreasonable construction of the statute should be had or even contemplated for a moment. It therefore must necessarily follow that the Legislature intended, when it provided that an able-bodied man should be deemed a vagrant when he either neglects or refuses to support his family, that it was leveling the penalty of the law only at the *vagabond husband* who had the means or ability to render such support and neglected or refused, and that it was not intended to level such penalty at the husband who was willing to do so and whose neglect or failure in that respect arose solely from his inability to find employment. It seems quite clear that such a case was not contemplated as being within the spirit of the act. Indeed, the employment of the words 'neglect' or 'refuse' by the Legislature is demonstrative of the intent. 'Neglect' arises from an inattentive state of mind, want of care for and an utter disregard of, in this connection, the obligation resting upon the husband to support his family; whereas, the word 'refuse' imports a wilful disavowal of or disregard for such obligation. It is therefore obvious that the husband who is denounced as a vagrant, is one who neglects or refuses the support from his want of proper regard for the social duties and obligations of life, his total or partial disregard of the ties of filial affection, and his insensibility to and want of respect for the family relation upon which the whole superstructure of civilized society rests.''   :

The evidence also discloses that the wife had personal property of the value of more than one thousand dollars, and that she *gave* this to her sister. Comment on this is unnecessary, further than to observe that it only emphasizes the notion that she was not in a destitute or suffering condition, and that this prosecution is for purposes other than that contemplated by the law.

The majority opinion of the Court of Appeals in this case is in accord with Dwyer v. Dwyer, 26 Mo. App. 647, Gallemore v. Gallemore, 115 Mo. App. 179, and State v. Burton, 171 Mo. App. 345, and we see no substantial conflict between it and the case of Marolf v. Marolf, 191 Mo. App. 239, but to the extent that minds may differ as to these respective holdings the latter is disapproved.

The judgment of the court of criminal correction is therefore reversed, and the defendant discharged. *Faris, P. J.,* and *Walker, J.,* concur.

JAMES F. CASHION and AUDREY BELL RAY, Appellants, v. J. W. GARGUS et al.

Division Two, Febuary 15, 1916.

1. **ADMISSION: By Pleading.** A litigant cannot challenge a finding of facts by the court which stand admitted by his own pleading.

2. **TIMELY ANSWER: Must Be Shown By Record.** Allegations in a motion for judgment on the pleadings, that defendant failed to file his answer within the time given him by the court, do not prove themselves, but must be established by record entries; and in the absence of any record entries in the abstract tending to show them to be true, the motion cannot be considered on appeal.

3. **AMENDED PETITION: Departure: Description of Land.** An amendment of a petition in a suit for the specific performance of a contract to purchase land by changing the erroneous description of the land to a correct description, made before judgment, by leave of court, is permissible, and is not such a departure as to change the cause of action.

4. ——: ——: ——: **Minors: No New Summons.** And although the defendants are minors, if they have been properly brought into court, a guardian *ad litem* appointed and his acceptance filed, the filing thereafter of an amended petition by which an erroneous description of the land contained in the original petition is corrected, is as binding on them as upon adult defendants, and they have no greater right to an additional summons and service; and a judgment against them without such additional summons is not void or voidable.

Appeal from Dunklin Circuit Court.—*Hon. C. B. Faris,*
Judge.

AFFIRMED.

Bradley & McKay for appellants.

(1) The original petition upon which said.judg-
ment was rendered, failed to state any facts sufficient to
constitute a cause of action against defendants in that
cause: 1st, because the petition, being based upon a
verbal contract for the sale of real estate, failed to
plead facts which would take it out of the Statute of
Frauds, and no proof of facts could be offered which
would take it out of the statute without being pleaded;
2nd, because the petition failed to describe the land;
and 3rd, because the petition showed on its face that
it was barred by laches. Therefore, no valid judgment
could be rendered against these minor defendants on
said petition. Chambers v. LeCompte, 9 Mo. 575; Wild-
bahn v. Robidoux, 11 Mo. 659; Walker v. Ray, 111 Ill.
315; Lloyd v. Kirkwood, 112 Ill. 229; Meyer v. Mitchell,
77 Ala. 312; Price v. Bell, 91 Ala. 108; Askeer v. Carr,
81 Ga. 685; Northrob v. Boone, 66 Ill. 368; In re Ferguson, 124 Mo. 574; Anderson v. Scott, 94 Mo. 637. (2)
A demurrer ought to have been sustained to the evidence in the original cause of action, because the petition was based upon an oral contract for the sale of
real estate and O. B. Harris could not testify, the other
party to the alleged contract having been dead and
the burden was on plaintiff to establish his case
against these minors by proving all the material allegations. Veth v. Gierth, 92 Mo. 97; Foster v. Kimmons,
54 Mo. 488; Taylor v. Williams, 45 Mo. 80; Davis v.
Petty, 147 Mo. 374; Gibbs v. Whitwell, 164 Mo. 387;
Charpiot v. Sigerson, 25 Mo. 63; Strange v. Crowley,
91 Mo. 287; Taylor v. Von Schrader, 107 Mo. 206; Alex-

ander v. Alexander, 150 Mo. 579; Collins v. Trotter, 81 Mo. 275. (3) The judgment rendered on the 24th of January, 1896, against the minor heirs of James H. Cashion, is not binding because the petition was amended wholly changing the cause of action as alleged in the original petition filed, and the record fails to show any additional service upon the minors after the amendment, and fails to show the answer of the guardian *ad litem* to said amended petition and for that reason the judgment does not bind these plaintiffs. Cauthorn v. Berry, 69 Mo. App. 404; Powell v. Horrell, 92 Mo. App. 406; Liese v. Meyer, 143 Mo. 547; Pruett v. Warren, 71 Mo. App. 84; Grigsby v. Barton County, 169 Mo. 221; Finner v. Nichols, 158 Mo. App. 539; Bick v. Baughn, 140 Mo. App. 595. (4) The guardian *ad litem* must do for the minor what he could do for himself, and when the record fails to show that the guardian *ad litem* has performed his duties, a judgment rendered against minors will not bind them. Reineman v. Larkin, 222 Mo. 156. (5) All of the facts upon which one relies for judgment against an infant, answering by guardian *ad litem*, must be proved. And the guardian *ad litem* cannot omit anything, or waive anything which will sustain the adverse party's case. Collins v. Trotter, 81 Mo. 275; Revely v. Skinner, 33 Mo. 98. (6) The original judgment rendered on the 24th day of January, 1896, is, as to these minors, a default judgment, because the guardian *ad litem*, if any, appointed by the court, could not waive or admit anything, and the petition and judgment, must show jurisdiction in order to make a valid judgment against plaintiffs who were minors at the time the judgment was rendered, and the petition and judgment in that cause failed to show jurisdiction, upon the minor plaintiffs, and the judgment was void in a direct attack. Schneider v. Patton, 175 Mo. 684; Jewett v. Boardman, 181 Mo. 647; Wilson v. Dorrow, 223 Mo. 520.

T. R. R. Ely for respondent.

The minors in the original suit for specific performance were duly served with summons to appear at the January term of the Dunklin County Circuit Court and cause was continued to July term, 1894, and at July term,. 1894, a guardian *ad litem* was duly appointed, who filed his acceptance and answer. All the statutory requirements were complied with and the court had jurisdiction over said minors. Secs. 1745 and 1748, R. S. 1909. While the guardian could waive nothing or confess nothing for his wards, that did not affect plaintiffs' right to amend after service and the appointment of guardian *ad litem* and filing of his acceptance and answer, and he can then do for the minor what he could do for himself so far as pleading is concerned, and "he can act in regard to his ward's interest, just like an ordinary litigant," except he could not waive or confess anything for them, which he did not do in this case. Collins v. Trotter, 81 Mo. 284. There is nothing in this record to show that the guardian waived anything or admitted anything for his ward, but on the contrary appeared and required strict proof of all the allegations in the petition and the judgment was a valid one. Pevely v. Skinner, 33 Mo. 98; LeBourgeoise v. McNamar, 82 Mo. 189. The court having acquired jurisdiction it had the right to order or permit the pleadings to be amended upon such terms as were just. Sec. 1846, R. S. 1909. And there is no different rule provided by statute where the minor is represented by a guardian *ad litem*.

WILLIAMS, C.—This action was instituted in the circuit court of Dunklin County to set aside the decree rendered in a certain cause in said court on the 24th day of January, 1896, and to reinstate said original cause and to permit the plaintiffs in this case to answer and defend against the same. Trial was had resulting

in a judgment in favor of the defendants, and plaintiffs
duly perfected an appeal to this court. The decree
which this suit seeks to set aside was a decree entered
in a suit for specific performance of a contract to convey real estate. The original decree granted the relief prayed and vested the title to the real estate in the
plaintiff in said original suit. The two plaintiffs in the
present suit were minor defendants in the original
suit. O. B. Harris, one of the defendants in the present
suit, was the plaintiff in the original suit. Defendant
Gargus in the present suit is the grantee of said Harris.
Defendant Hardesty in the present suit is the tenant
of said Gargus.

The petition in the present suit was in two counts,
the first count seeking the relief above mentioned and
the second count being in ejectment. Plaintiffs, in
the first count of the petition, allege in substance that
the plaintiff in the original suit was not entitled to
recover therein, but that they have a good and sufficient
defense to his claim for specific performance of a contract to convey said land to him, and further alleged
that the day before the case was tried the plaintiff in
said original suit was permitted to amend his original
petition by changing the description of the land therein mentioned and that the amendment entirely changed
the cause of action, and that no additional service was
had upon said minor defendants after said amended
petition was filed, and that for that reason said original decree was null and void and had no binding force
or effect upon said minor defendants (these plaintiffs). The petition further alleged that the original
petition showed on its face that the cause of action
was barred by laches and failed to allege that any demand for performance had been made by the plaintiff
upon the person with whom he contracted for the purchase of said land.

The answer filed in the present suit was a general
denial. At the request of the plaintiffs in the present

suit, the trial court made a special finding of law and fact and upon examination we find that the same correctly and tersely states the facts shown by the evidence and necessary to be known for a proper review of the points presented upon this appeal. For that reason we copy this special finding of facts and law, together with the trial court's judgment, which was as follows:

"Come now plaintiffs herein in person and by counsel and the defendants in person and by counsel, and this case is taken up and submitted to the court, and the court proceeds to hear the evidence and to determine the rights of the parties in this case, and after hearing the evidence and a motion having been filed asking separate findings of law and facts, the court finds:

"That at the January term of the Dunklin County Circuit Court, 1894, in a certain case wherein O. B. Harris was plaintiff, and Mollie A. Shelton, formerly Mollie A. Cashion, widow of decedent Cashion, below mentioned, Charles E. Cashion, a minor, James F. Cashion, a minor, and Audrey Bell Cashion, a minor, heirs of James F. Cashion, were defendants, a certain bill in equity, the general nature of which was for specific performance of a contract to convey real estate and to divest title to the northwest quarter of the northwest quarter of section twenty-five, township eighteen north, of range nine east, in Dunklin County, Missouri, out of the defendants and to vest same in the plaintiff, came on to be heard, plaintiff alleging, among other things in his petition, that James F. Cashion, deceased, father of the minor defendants and former husband of said Mollie A. Shelton, had sold the land in dispute to O. B. Harris, during his (decedent's) lifetime, and had placed him, said Harris, in possession of said premises, and that full payment for said land had been made by said Harris, but that the said James F. Cashion departed this life in April, 1901, without making the said O. B. Harris a deed for said land.

"The court further finds that the defendants were properly summoned into court; that Hon. W. S. C. Walker was appointed guardian *ad litem* for all the minors, and that he filed his acceptance and answer in said cause; that the original petition misdescribed the land in question as the southeast frl. quarter of section thirty-four, township eighteen, range nine, Dunklin County, Missouri. That afterwards and prior to the submission of said cause and prior to the rendition of judgment thereon, the plaintiff, by leave of court, amended his petition correctly describing the lands in question as the northwest quarter of the northwest quarter of section twenty-five, township eighteen, range nine, Dunklin County, Missouri. The court further finds that the defendants were duly summoned into court and duly represented by W. S. C. Walker as guardian *ad litem*, that a judgment was regularly rendered at the January term of the Dunklin County Circuit Court, 1896, in said cause, which said judgment is as follows:

" 'O. B. Harris, Plaintiff, vs. Mollie A. Shelton et al., Defendants—No. 904.

· " 'Comes now O. B. Harris, plaintiff, in person as well as by attorney, and Mollie A. Shelton, widow of Jas. M. Cashion, deceased, Chas. E. Cashion, Jas. F. Cashion and Audrey Bell Cashion, minors, by attorney and guardian *ad litem* and this case is taken up for trial and the court proceeds to hear, try and determine the rights of this suit, and after hearing the evidence doth find that prior to the death of said Jas. M. Cashion, the plaintiff, O. B. Harris, did purchase and pay for the northwest quarter of the northwest quarter of section twenty-five, township eighteen north, of range nine, and the court further finds from the evidence that for and in consideration of the said sum of three hundred and forty dollars, which amount said plaintiff was to pay and did pay for the lands as herein described, the said Jas. M. Cashion was to make to the said O. B. Harris, plaintiff herein, a good and sufficient deed, and the court further finds from the evidence that the said Jas. M. Cashion did put the plaintiff, the said O. B. Harris, in possession of the land as herein described, but failed to make, execute and deliver to the said plaintiff the deed which the said Jas. M. Cashion promised to make, execute and deliver; therefore it is ordered and adjudged by the court that the rights, benefits and title in and to the land herein described, as against the party defendants or their assigns, are hereby decreed in plaintiff and that he have of and recover from the defendants his costs in this behalf expended.'

"The court further finds that in the obtaining of the judgment by plaintiff in said former action against the plaintiffs herein, there was no fraud or collusion, nor is any charged by the petition. The action is bottomed upon the alleged lack of jurisdiction in the Dunklin County Circuit Court to permit said amendment of the description of the said land involved.

"The court further finds that, prior to the death of plaintiffs' ancestor, James F. Cashion, and to-wit, about the month of January, 1889, said Harris entered into possession of the lands in controversy, and that said Harris or the defendant and his *mesne* grantors, who claim title to the land under the sale to said Harris and under the decree set out above herein, has been in possession of said land since about January, 1889, continuously, and that defendant is now in possession of the same.

"From the above facts, the court concludes, as a matter of law, that in the absence of fraud, or collusion (which neither is pleaded or relied upon) and in the absence of irregularities in summons or judgment or other jurisdictional fact, the mere fact that after infant defendants were duly in court, and being there represented by a duly appointed guardian *ad litem,* the court permitted an amendment to be made changing the description of the land touching which specific performance to convey was sought by the action, will not render the judgment void as to such infants, and that the same is valid and binding, and that the judgment and finding of the court should be for the defendants, upon both counts of the petition.

"It is therefore ordered, considered and adjudged by the court that plaintiffs take nothing by their suit, that defendants go hence without day; that the costs in this case be adjudged against the plaintiffs, and that execution may issue therefor."

OPINION.

I. Appellants contend that there was no evidence to justify the court in finding the fact to be that the defendant minors in the original suit

Admission in Pleading.

were properly summoned into court or that W. S. C. Walker was appointed guardian *ad litem* for all of said minors and filed his acceptance and answer in said cause.

Concerning this point, it is sufficient to say that appellants' petition alleged that said minors "were duly served to appear" in the original suit and that the court in said cause duly "appointed Hon. W. S. C. Walker as guardian *ad litem* for said minors" and that said W. S. C. Walker "filed his acceptance as guardian *ad litem*" and appeared in said cause and was by the court granted leave to plead on or before the first day of the next term of said court. Appellant should not be heard to challenge the court's finding of facts which stand admitted by their own pleading. Furthermore, the decree in the original suit recites that said minors, naming them, did appear by their guardian *ad litem,* upon the trial and at the hearing of the evidence in said cause.

II. It is further contended that the court erred in overruling their motion for judgment upon the pleadings. This motion was filed January 16, 1912.

The motion as set forth in the bill of exceptions alleges that the defendants failed to file their answer within the time given them by the court **Failure to File Answer.** and that up to the time of filing the motion no answer had been filed. We are unable to discuss this point, for the reason that there are no record entries set forth in the abstract upon which the facts alleged in the motion can be founded. The only record entry which, in any manner, has to do with the matters alleged in the motion is the record entry showing that defendants did file their answer on the 17th day of October, 1910, which was long before the motion was filed. The allegations in the motion do not prove the existence of the facts therein alleged, but such allegations in order to furnish a ground for review here, should have been supported by a proper showing, at the proper place, elsewhere in the record.

III. It is further contended that the decree rendered against said minors in the original suit, January 24, 1896, was not binding upon said minors, because the petition was so amended as to wholly change the cause **Amending Pleading: Departure.** of action alleged in the original petition, and that after the petition was so amended there was no additional service of summons upon said minors.

The amendment, to which reference is here made, consisted of correcting an error in the description of the land involved. The land was described erroneously in the first petition, and the plaintiff, by leave of court, made an amendment by changing the erroneous description to a correct description. This was not such an amendment as changed the cause of action and the amendment was properly permitted to be made. [Sec. 1848, R. S. 1909; Callaghan v. M'Mahan, 33 Mo. 111;

Blanchard v. Dorman, 236 Mo. 416, l. c. 443; Wright v. Groom, 246 Mo. 158, and cases therein cited.] The statute on amendments does not make any exception prohibiting amendments in pleadings where minors are parties to the suit and we are not aware of any reason calling for a distinction in that regard. If the court has acquired jurisdiction over the person of the minors, as was true in the case under discussion, any amendment, not a departure from the cause of action originally stated, should be permitted, the same as if all the parties were of legal age.

The amendment made being entirely permissible and not such as to amount to a departure from the cause of action originally stated, it was unnecessary that there should have been further service of summons upon the minor defendants. They had been duly served with summons, a guardian *ad litem* had been duly appointed and he had filed his written acceptance of his appointment and appeared in the case. The court was thereby given jurisdiction of the persons of said minors, and the judgment thereinafter rendered was binding upon them. The evidence fully supported the judgment of the trial court and it should be affirmed. It is so ordered. *Roy, C.,* concurs.

PER CURIAM.—The foregoing opinion by WIL-LIAMS, C., is adopted as the opinion of the court. All the judges concur, except *Faris, J.,* not sitting.

CHARLES A. PITMAN, Appellant, v. JOHN W. DRABELLE et al.

In Banc, February 21, 1916.

1. **CONSTITUTIONAL LAW: City Charter.** A municipal charter or a statute of the State will not be held to violate the Constitution if any other rational interpretation can be given it.

2. ———: ———: **Legislative Power of People.** Except as inhibited by the Federal or State Constitution the power of the people of a State to legislative is plenary, and they may exercise that power through the Legislature, or the Initiative, and the same principle applies to municipal corporations, which in their public capacity are but agents of the State.

3. ———: ———: **Legislation By Initiative: One House Legislature.** The clause of the new charter of St. Louis which provides that, upon the failure of the one house of the municipal legislature to act upon the certification to it of petitions showing the measure which the people request them to adopt, the measure may be enacted into law through the instrumentality of an initiative petition and the vote of the people, does not contravene that clause of the Constitution which declares that the charter of such a city "shall be in harmony with and subject to the Constitution and laws of the State, and shall provide, among other things, for a chief executive and at least one house of legislation to be elected by general ticket." Nor in conditioning initiative legislation upon the inaction of the one house is it so out of harmony with the constitutional amendment of 1908 applicable to the whole State, or with the statutes of 1913 which gave initiative powers to cities of the second and third class, as to render it invalid. Nor does the Constitution require a municipal legislature of more than one house.

4. ———: ———: **Arrest of Legislation: Election: Injunction.** An election called in pursuance to a provision of the city charter under a valid plan for initiative legislation and proper petitions, cannot be enjoined on the ground that the ordinances as proposed are unconstitutional. During the process of legislation in any mode the work of the lawmakers is not subject to judicial arrest, or control, or even open to judicial inquiry. It is only after the proposed legislation has become an accomplished fact that its constitutionality can be determined by the courts.

Appeal from St. Louis City Circuit Court.—*Hon. George H. Shields, Judge.*

Affirmed.

Henry S. Caulfield, Homer G. Phillips and *George L. Vaughn* for appellant.

(1)   There can be no doubt as to the right of a taxpayer, suing on behalf of himself and all other cit-

izens and taxpayers who are similarly interested with him, to have relief by injunction for the prevention of an illegal or unauthorized diversion of public funds belonging to the municipality. 2 High on Injunction (4 Ed.), 1237; Dillon, Municipal Corporations, sec. 1579 et seq.; Newmeyer v. Railroad, 52 Mo. 81; Rubey v. Shain, 54 Mo. 207; Black v. Cornell, 30 Mo. App. 641; Black v. Ross, 37 Mo. App. 250; Knapp v. Kansas City, 48 Mo. App. 485; Mayor of Baltimore v. Gill, 31 Md. 375; Savidge v. Spring Lake, 112 Mich. 91. And this right exists where the illegal or unauthorized diversion is for an election of the kind here involved, for which there is no warrant in law. 22 Cyc. 885; 2 High on Injunction (4 Ed.), 1237; Mayor of Macon v. Hughes, 110 Ga. 795; Layton v. Mayor, 50 La. Ann. 121; Railroad v. Board of Commissioners, 108 N. C. 56; Solomon v. Fleming, 34 Neb. 40; Connor v. Gray, 88 Miss. 489. (2) The city of St. Louis has no power or authority, under the Constitution, to provide by charter for any method or system of legislation independent of at least one house of legislation to be elected by general ticket. State ex inf. v. Railroad, 151 Mo. 162; St. Louis v. Telephone Co., 96 Mo. 628; St. Louis v. Eddy, 123 Mo. 557; Independence v. Cleveland, 167 Mo. 388; St. Louis v. Dreisoerner, 243 Mo. 223; St. Louis v. Quarry. Co., 244 Mo. 479; State ex rel. v. Skeggs, 154 Ala. 249; In re Dunn, o Mo. App. 255; State ex inf. v. Kansas City, 233 Mo. 162; St. Louis v. Dorr, 145 Mo. 466; Westport v. Kansas City, 103 Mo. 141; Cooley, Const. Limitations (7 Ed.), p. 98; Dield v. People, 3 Ill. 79; Graham v. Roberts, 200 Mass. 152; Mo. Constitution, art. 9, sec. 22, art. 4, sec. 57.

Benjamin H. Charles, Charles H. Daues and *Everett Paul Griffin* for respondents.

(1) The court had no jurisdiction of the subject-matter covered by the petition, and no jurisdiction to

grant the relief prayed for. (a) Because equity has no
jurisdiction to restrain, by injunction or otherwise,
the exercise of the political rights of the people. State
ex rel. v. Aloe, 152 Mo. 466; Fletcher v. Tuttle, 151
Ill. 51; Green v. Mills, 30 L. R. A. 90, 69 Fed. 852;
Morgan v. Wetzel, 53 W. Va. 372; Anthony v. Burrow,
129 Fed. 783; Giles v. Harris, 189 U. S. 475; Fisler
v. Brayton, 145 Ind. 71; McAlester v. Milwee, 31
Okla. 620; Walton v. Develing, 61 Ill. 201. (b) Because an equity court has no jurisdiction to restrain,
by injunction or otherwise, the exercise of the law-
making power, nor the process of legislation. Al-
bright v. Fisher, 164 Mo. 64; State ex rel. v. Gates,
190 Mo. 556; Kansas City v. Hyde, 196 Mo. 506;
Duggan v. Emporia, 84 Kan. 429; Pfeifer v. Graves,
104 N. E. 529. (c) Because an equity court has no jurisdiction to restrain or arrest, by injunction or otherwise, the official acts of public officials preparatory to,
or in the conduct of, public elections. Shoemaker v.
Des Moines, 129 Iowa, 244, 3 L. R. A. (N. S.) 382;
Duggan v. Emporia, 84 Kan. 429; People ex rel. v.
Galesburg, 48 Ill. 485; Weber v. Timlin, 37 Minn. 274;
Friendly v. Orcott, 61 Ore. 580. (d) Equity has no jurisdiction, because the complainant has a complete and
adequate remedy at law to test the validity of the proposed ordinances, in case they should be adopted.
(e) An allegation that the complainant is a taxpayer
is not an allegation that his property rights are about
to suffer injury. It is merely colorable; thrown in to
make a show of right to proceed in equity to an attack
on a charter provision. State ex rel. v. Aloe, 152 Mo.
466; State ex rel. v. Thorson, 9 S. D. 149; Libby v.
Olcott, 66 Ore. 134. (2) The initiative and referendum
provisions of the St. Louis charter are valid. Wagner's St. Louis Charter, arts. 5 and 6, pp. 40, 41. (a)
Because the Constitution contains no grants of power
to the city of St. Louis. It merely provides a method

of incorporation; and indicates a part of the form of
its government, namely, a chief executive, and at least
one house of legislation. Missouri Constitution, art.
9, secs. 20, 22, 23. "No limitation is placed upon the
character of the charter, save and except that it shall
always be in harmony with and subject to the Constitution and laws of the State." Kansas City v. Oil
Co., 140 Mo. 470; St. Louis v. Gleason, 15 Mo. App.
30, affirmed (on this point), 93 Mo. 38; State ex rel.
v. Stobie, 194 Mo. 14, 54; St. Louis v. Tel. Co., 149
U. S. 465. Powers conferred by this charter are of
equal dignity with powers conferred upon a municipal corporation by an act of the Legislature. Ex
parte Smith, 231 Mo. 122; Kansas City v. Bacon, 147
Mo. 272; State ex rel. v. Field, 99 Mo. 352; Kansas
City v. Oil Co., 140 Mo. 458; St. Louis v. Gleason, 15
Mo. App. 30. (b) The purpose disclosed in the Constitution was that a charter thus adopted might embrace
the entire subject of municipal government, and be a
complete and consistent whole, with such provisions
as to the powers conferred and the methods of exercise of such powers, as the people of the city might
adopt. State ex rel. v. Field, 99 Mo. 352; Kansas
City v. Bacon, 147 Mo. 272; Haag v. Ward, 186 Mo.
343. (c) If the initiative and referendum provisions
of the St. Louis charter are void, then the same provisions in charters of cities of the second and third
classes are void; because the St. Louis charter stands
on the same basis as any other legislative act of the
State. (d) The provisions are not repugnant to any
provision of the Constitution. The Constitution contains no prohibition against the adoption by the city of
St. Louis of these methods of legislation. (e) The provisions are in harmony with the Constitution and laws
of the State. To be in harmony with the Constitution
means merely in "substantial harmony" with the
principles of the Constitution. Kansas City v. Bacon,
147 Mo. 259; St. Louis v. De Lassus, 205 Mo. 585.

Legislation by the initiative and referendum are now
(since 1908) principles of the Constitution. And these
principles have been recognized by the Legislature in
its grant of charters to cities of the second and third
classes. Laws 1913, pp. 443, 530. (f) The new charter
of St. Louis shows on its face that the purpose of the
Board of Freeholders which framed it, was to confer
practically unlimited powers on the mayor and aldermen, with one check only. That check is the initiative
and referendum. Remove it, and the people of that
city are powerless, except at the polls, and then only
at long intervals. (g) The initiative and referendum
methods of legislation with respect to municipalities
as well as the State at large, have, in other jurisdictions, been sustained as constitutional, with scarcely a
dissent. Oregon v. Tel. Co., 53 Ore. 162, 223 U. S. 118;
Kadderly v. Portland, 44 Ore. 118; Kiernan v. Portland, 57 Ore. 459; In re Pfahler, 150 Cal. 71; Graham
v. Roberts, 200 Mass. 152; Hantig v. Seattle, 53 Wash.
432; Hindman v. Boyd, 84 Pac. (Wash.) 609; State
v. Paul, 151 Pac. (Wash.) 116. See, also, cases from
Ohio, Oklahoma, Texas, Kansas and other jurisdictions, cited under our point one.

OPINION.

I.

BOND, J.—Plaintiff, a taxpaying citizen, sued to
enjoin the holding of an election on the 29th of February, 1916, for the adoption of two ordinances proposed under article 5 of the charter of St. Louis, re-
serving to the people of that city the power "known
as the initiative."

The ordinances to be submitted to a ballot are referred to in the petition by number and title, and provide for "the use of separate blocks for residence by
white and colored races and for the gradual complete
occupancy of blocks by one of the two races to the exclusion of the other."

The ground of the petition is the alleged unconstitutionality of the provisions of the charter with reference to the exercise of the initiative in legislation, and the misappropriation of public money for the holding of the election. The defendants, the board of election commissioners, the city comptroller and the city treasurer, demurred, whereupon the petition was dismissed, and plaintiff appealed to this court where the cause was advanced for public reasons.

II.

The rule is apodeictical that the charter of a municipal corporation or a State statute will not be held to violate the Constitution if any other rational interpretation or construction can be given to it. [State ex rel. v. Kirby, 260 Mo. 1. c. 127; State ex rel. v. St. Louis, 241 Mo. 1. c. 247; State ex rel. v. McIntosh, 205 Mo. 1. c. 602; State ex rel. v. Warner, 197 Mo. 1. c. 656; Ex parte Loving, 178 Mo. 1. c. 203.]

Municipal Initiative Legislation.

This maxim is particularly applicable to the framework of our State government, for the Constitution of Missouri is only limitative of the plenary power to legislate reserved to the people of the State, who may exercise it through the law-making body, or its auxiliaries in government, or by the initiative except to the extent they have restrained themselves by the prohibitions of the Constitution. [Harris v. Bond Co., 244 Mo. 1. c. 687; McGrew v. Railroad, 230 Mo. 496; State ex rel. v. Warner, 197 Mo. 650; State ex rel. v. Sheppard, 192 Mo. 497.]

In that respect our State government differs from the Federal republic whose law-making body derives its only power to act from the grants contained in the Constitution of the United States; while the State Legislature may enact any laws not forbidden by the State or Federal Constitutions. It follows that the relation of the State Legislature to our Constitution is the antinomy of the relation of Congress to the Federal Constitution.

The same principle governs the action of a municipal corporation which in its public capacity as an agent of the State government, may amend its charter in any manner or enact ordinances for any purpose not in conflict with the Constitution and the laws, State and Federal.

The crux of this case is whether the inclusion in the amended charter of the provisions giving to the people the *additional* right to legislate by the initiative plan is prohibited by the language of the Constitution (Art. 9, sec. 22), which provides for the amendment of the charter of the city of St. Louis.

It is claimed that the amended charter, though otherwise regularly framed and adopted, contravened the Constitution by the inclusion therein of the power to legislate through an instrumentality different from the one referred to in the Constitution. The argument being that by referring to a "house of legislation" and requiring that any amendment of the charter should "provide at least" one of these, the Constitution *impliedly* prohibited any further provision for an additional mode of legislation. To determine this point, it is necessary to consider the language of the Constitution providing what shall be the character and the contents and the method of adoption of a new charter of the city of St. Louis. So much of the language as is pertinent to the inquiry is, to-wit:

"Which said charter shall be in harmony with and subject to the Constitution and laws of the State, and shall provide, among other things, for a chief executive and at least one house of legislation to be elected by general ticket." [Mo. Constitution, art. 9, sec. 22, Amendment adopted in 1902.]

It is not contended that the charter under review fails to meet the requirements of this language in any other respect than that it gives the people the right to legislate by ballot if the one ''house'' of legislation fails to act upon the certification to it of petitions showing the measures which the people request them to adopt. [New Charter of St. Louis, art. 5, page 45, sections 1 to 6 inclusive.]

The plan incorporated in the amended charter conditions the right to its exercise upon the inaction of the board of aldermen and in that respect it lacks the full faculty of legislation which was reserved to the people of the State in the amendment of the Constitution in 1908. [Constitution of Missouri, art. 4, sec. 57.] But with this exception and others necessary to make it workable and applicable to municipal purposes and limits, the plan is the same as that embodied in the State Constitution construed in State ex rel. v. Carter, 257 Mo. 52, and is practically identical with the powers given to cities of the second and third classes by the General Assembly in 1913. [Laws 1913, pp. 443-4, sec. 29; Laws 1913, p. 530, sec. 20 et seq.; Barnes v. Kirksville, 266 Mo. 270.]

Hence it is evident that the feature of the charter under review is completely congruous with the constitutional policy that the people of the State at large should enjoy the right of the initiative, and also with the declared policy of the State expressed in the above acts of the Legislature granting the same powers as to the local administration and providing for their inclusion in the charters of the cities of the State. In view of this declaration of the public policy of this State through the medium of the highest exponents thereof, the Constitution and the General Assembly, we may dismiss from view any consideration of the suggestion that the amended charter of the city of St. Louis is out of harmony with the Constitution or laws of the State in so far as it provides for the exercise by the people of that city of the power to legislate by the initiative.

III.

It only remains to inquire whether there is anything in the above language of the Constitution which prohibits expressly or by necessary implication

One House. the enactment of so much of the amended charter as secures to the people of St. Louis a qualified power to legislate in this mode? All that the Constitution contains in reference to any instrumentality of legislation is comprised in these words; to-wit, "shall provide among other things . . . at least one house of legislation." This requirement was completely provided in the new charter by creating a board of aldermen who were given legislative power subject to the limitations therein. [New Charter of St. Louis, art. 4, sec. 1.] Having prescribed that one house of legislation would be enough, the Constitution does not prohibit, but impliedly permits the addition of any other house or body with the capacity to legislate. The only restriction placed by it upon the framing of a new charter is that it must provide "at least one" of such legislative bodies. This necessarily left the people free to give legislative functions to another body, for it simply required that the number should not be less than one.

The use of the words "at least" *ex vi termini* are only a restriction against dispensing with one house of legislation, but does not forbid nor prohibit the use of *more* than one house of legislation. So, under the language of the Constitution it would have been entirely lawful for the new charter to have retained the bi-cameral body which was the earlier form of legislation in St. Louis. But is was one of the purposes of the subsequent constitutional amendment (containing the language under review) to enable the people of St. Louis to dispense with the ancient form or to readopt it, or to provide different methods of legislation with the single qualification that whatever mode should be devised it must include at least one house, or legislative body, after which the makers of the new charter were left free to provide, without restriction or prohibition, any mode of legislation in harmony with the Constitution and laws of the State. 'This provision of the Constitution was fully effectuated by the adoption of the scheme contained in the new charter which provides for one house of legislation and an auxiliary thereto, known as the Initiative.

A careful analysis of the sections of the present charter referring to the exercise of this auxiliary power to legislate, shows that it cannot be exercised at all unless the board of aldermen shall fail to adopt a proposed ordinance submitted to them by the people of the city. Plainly this contrivance does not deprive the board of aldermen of the power to originate and enact laws, for it leaves them with full authority so to do and merely guards against their refusal to enact a local law which is approved by a majority of the qualified voters of the city; for unless it is supported by a majority of the voters it could not carry at the election and would never become a law.

It is of the very essence of free government that the laws regulating a community should reflect the view and voice of a majority of its voters. Hence the plan (initiative) by which the people are empowered to do the business which their recalcitrant representatives have failed to perform, has met with full judicial sanction. [In re Pfahler, 150 Cal. 71; Pacific States T. & T. Co. v. Oregon, 223 U. S. 118.]

We are unable to find anything in the language of the Constitution under review which prohibits the people of St. Louis, after having provided in their charter for one house of legislation, to reserve to themselves the power to legislate in case of the refusal of that body to act. There being no restriction express or implied in the language of the Constitution of the State against the inclusion of this faculty in the

Pitman v. Drabelle.

charter, and it being plain to a demostration that the power thus reserved is not inconsistent with the laws of the State or nation, we hold that the petition framed on the theory of the unconstitutionality of the initiative provisions of the charter stated no cause of action and the demurrer thereto was well taken.

IV.

The record shows that the election to adopt or reject the ordinances proposed by the initiative method of legislation, has not yet been held. The question of the constitutionality of these laws is not, therefore, now presented for decision; for during the process of legislation in any mode, the work of the lawmakers is not subject to judicial arrest or control, nor open to judicial inquiry. [State ex rel. v. Meier, 72 Mo. App. l. c. 626; Dreyfus v. Lonergan, 73 Mo. App. l. c. 346; State ex rel. v. Gates, 190 Mo. l. c. 559 et seq.; Glasgow v. St. Louis, 107 Mo. l. c. 203.] But after the lawmaking department of the government in any of its forms or by any of its agencies has finished its work and the act of legislation in which it was engaged has become *fait accompli* and is clothed with the outward forms of law, the question of the constitutionality of the completed bill or ordinance becomes one for ultimate determination by the judiciary.

V.

Nor can it be doubted what judgment would be given if it were shown that a law had been enacted violative of the fundamental principle upon which the government of the State and nation is founded, or destructive of the legal rights of person or property of any citizen or class of citizens of the United States. [Constitution of the United States, Amendment 14.] For it must be borne in mind that no citizen of this State has any legal or political right which does not belong to every other who has not forfeited it by conviction of crime.

Pitman v. Drabelle.

Distinctions based on character, culture and leadership are inherent in progressive society and exclusively regulated by that association; but they find no recognition or enforcement in judicial tribunals when called upon to decide the natural rights of all persons "to life, liberty and enjoyment of the gains of their own industry," to secure which is the chief design of government. [Constitution of Missouri, art. 2, sec. 4.]

In upholding the rights of a *"ward"* of the nation (an Indian) to the equal protection of the law it was said:

"It is part of the American creed—expressed in the chart of our liberties—that all men are created equal before the law. In the administration of justice, neither race, rank, nor riches confers any advantage on its possessor over any other person. These accidents arc not permitted to mar the wisdom and purity of laws made for the equal protection of every human being. Upon this principle we have builded, on this continent, the fairest fabric of freedom which has met the eye of Time." [Whirlwind v. Von der Ahe, 67 Mo. App. l. c. 630.]

For the reasons given in the former paragraphs of this opinion the judgment in this case is affirmed. *Woodson, C. J.*, and *Graves, J.*, concur; *Faris, Blair* and *Revelle, JJ.*, concur to all except as to paragraph five, as to which they express no opinion.

MAUDE PARRISH et al. v. JOHN TREADWAY et al., Appellants.

Division One, February 29, 1916.

1. **MINOR: Conveyance of Real Estate.** The deed of a minor is not void, but only voidable; and to be avoided must be disaffirmed by him after reaching his majority.

2. ——: ——: **Limitations.** The deed of a minor conveying his interest in real estate, unless disaffirmed within ten years after he reaches his minority, is valid, and cannot be avoided by him.

3. ——: ——: ——: **Remainderman.** The act of disaffirmance of a conveyance of real estate by a minor goes to the instrument itself, and has no particular reference to the estate conveyed or attempted to be conveyed. If the deed conveyed the contingent reversion of a remainderman while he was yet a minor and while the life tenant was yet living, the remainderman's deed cannot be disaffirmed by him after the expiration of ten years after he reached his majority, it matters not how long the life tenant lived after the deed was executed.

4. ——: ——: ——: **Disability of Coverture.** And the deed of a minor who was a married woman at the time it was made, must be disaffirmed within ten years after she first became discovert, having then reached her majority, although she may have soon thereafter married a second time. The disability of a second coverture cannot avail her. And where the only act of disaffirmance is by bringing suit, the petition must be filed within ten years after she first became discovert.

5. **PARTITION: Attorney's Fee.** No allowance should be made counsel as general costs for services in contested matters between the parties in a partition suit. But an allowance to plaintiff's attorney should be taxed as costs for such work as counsel would do in an ordinary non-contested partition, although, after new plaintiffs were added, there were brought into the case contested matters between them and defendants because of a denial of the validity of the deeds previously made by some of them.

Appeal from Pike Circuit Court.—*Hon. B. H. Dyer,* Judge.

REVERSED AND REMANDED (*with directions*).

F. J. Duvall and *Pearson & Pearson* for appellants.

(1) Deeds of minors are not void but only voidable, at their election upon attaining their majority, respectively. Their respective deeds were operative, sufficient to pass, and did pass, to their respective grantees, and those claiming under them, whatever right, seizin, title and estate, said grantors respectively, though minors, may have had in the property described in the petition at the date thereof. Harris v. Ross, 86 Mo. 95; Huth v. Marine Ry. & Dock Co., 56 Mo. 209; Singer Mfg. Co. v. Lamb, 81 Mo. 225; Shafer v. Diete, 191 Mo. 389; Goodman v. Simmons, 113 Mo. 127. (2) Unless they disaffirmed their deeds, at some period within ten years from the date they, respectively, reached their majority, they were forever thereafter barred from any rights and powers to disaffirm. Harris v. Ross, 86 Mo. 95; Linville v. Greer, 165 Mo. 398; Huth v. Carondelet, 56 Mo. 209. (3) The right to disaffirm a contract or deed, made by an infant is a personal privilege, and must be exercised by him after he attains his majority, and within ten years from that date. It is not dependent in this case, upon the death of Phoebe E. Henderson, or her occupancy of the land described in the deed. But it depends solely on the will and pleasure of the minor exercised within ten years from the date of his majority. Huth v. Marine Ry. & Dock Co., 56 Mo. 209; Jackson v. Carpenter, 11 John. 541; Harris v. Ross, 86 Mo. 96; Linville v. Greer, 165 Mo. 398.

R. L. Sutton, D. A. Ball and *Hostetter & Haley* for respondents.

While the Statute of Limitations relative to real actions may be a guide as to the time within which a late minor may disaffirm his deed according to the holding of some of the courts, yet in the case at bar, that principle, if conceded to be sound, would not aid the appellants. Here the children of Phoebe E. Henderson during her lifetime made deeds. They were not her bodily heirs. The most that could be claimed for them was that they were her prospective bodily heirs. They had no vested interest in the land or in the trust fund at the time of the execution of their deeds. They were not entitled to any interest in the property until the death of their mother. Consequently the Statute of Limitations would not commence to run against them until the date of their mother's death. The Statute of Limitations does not run against any one who has no right of possession; and where there is an outstanding estate, all the authorities agree that during the continuance of such particular estate, the remainderman cannot maintain an action for possession. Littleton v. Patterson, 32 Mo. 357; Carr v. Dings, 54 Mo. 95; Miller v. Bledsoe, 61 Mo. 96; Dyer v. Brannock, 66 Mo. 422; Brown v. Moore, 74 Mo. 633; Linville v. Greer, 165 Mo. 380; Givens v. Ott, 222 Mo. 422. Mere silence, however long, or omission to act, is not an affirmance. Youse v. Norcum, 12 Mo. 549; Huth v. Carondelet, 56 Mo. 210; Linville v. Greer, 165 Mo. 380, 398; Stull v. Harris, 2 L. R. A. 742.

GRAVES, P. J.—This is a partition suit from Pike County. In 1870 Washington Treadway and wife, Elizabeth, deeded a certain tract of land in Pike County to John Treadway "for the use and benefit of Phoebe E. Henderson and the heirs of her body" as alleged in the petition. By his last will he devised to John Treadway another small tract for the same purpose. These two tracts constitute the subject of litigation here. Neither this deed nor will is in evidence. The trial court found in accordance with the petition thus:

"The court being fully advised in the premises doth find the defendant John Treadway held in trust for Phoebe E. Henderson, and her bodily heirs, the following described real estate situated in Pike county, Missouri, to-wit:''

This is not a disputed matter and details need not be given. Suffice it to say that where a child of Phoebe E. Henderson died before she did, and such child left heirs, counsel seem to have conceded that a prior deed from such child conveyed no interest as against the grandchildren. So much for the construction of these trust instruments.

Phoebe E. Henderson died March 20, 1912, leaving as her bodily heirs certain children and grandchildren. She had nine children, but only seven survived her. The two who died before she did left children. The seven children surviving the mother made deeds to their interest in the lands prior to the mother's death, except the deed of Hurley N. Henderson did not cover the nine-acre tract covered in the will mentioned. The plaintiff, Maude Parrish, daughter of a deceased son, had never conveyed, nor had her father. A daughter, Lizzie Henderson, who married first Rice and then Nelson, made a deed, but died before the mother. Appellants claim nothing under this deed. Three of the children who made deeds made them just prior to reaching their respective majorities, and the trial court found these deeds to be void. These three interests and a dispute over the attorney's fee allowed counsel for plaintiff are the only questions here.

The plaintiffs are all the heirs of the body of Phoebe E. Henderson, and the defendants are the parties purchasing from the children and John Treadway, the trustee in the instruments of trust. For the present this sufficiently states the case.

I. The finding of the court which is first challenged by counsel for appellant is:

"The court further finds Olin G. Henderson and Thomas S. Henderson and Anna N. Megowan, form-

Minor's Deed.   erly Anna N. Wells, were minors at the time they made their deeds pleaded in the answers, and the court further finds that nothing passed to the grantees in any of said deeds."

The following unchallenged statement appears in appellant's brief:

"The record shows, that this second amended petition, in which all of the plaintiffs, except Maude Parrish, were for the first time made plaintiffs, was filed July 15, 1912. That Thomas S. Henderson was born July 12, 1876; that he and his wife executed the deed in question, August 14, 1896; that he attained his majority, July 12, 1897, which was fifteen years before the institution of this suit. That Anna N. Megowan, nee Wells, was born February 10, 1879; that she and her husband executed the deed in question August 9, 1895; that she attained her majority February 10, 1897, which was fifteen years and four months before the institution of this suit. That Olin G. Henderson was born May 9, 1881; that he and his wife executed the deed in question October 4, 1901; that he reached his majority May 9, 1902; which was ten years and two months before the institution of this suit."

It appears that the consideration paid in each instance was about $200, and respondents claim that the conveyance not only covered their interest in the land, but their interest in a $2000 trust fund in addition. The matter of consideration is not material, because not an issue under the pleadings. Upon this branch of the case there are but two questions to be answered: (1) is the deed of a minor void or merely voidable, and (2) if voidable, within what time must he disaffirm? There is no act of disaffirmance shown except the petition, so that dates are easily calculated. Seemingly the case below was tried on the theory that these deeds were void, or on the theory that they did not have to disaffirm until after the death of the mother in 1912. When made, these deeds conveyed the contingent remainder of these parties in the lands involved. The grantees took the title subject to the contingency of the death of the grantor prior to the falling in of the life estate, or in other words prior to the death of the mother. The parties so construed these deeds in the course of the trial. In the record we find:

"Mr. Gene Pearson: I now offer in evidence 'Defendants' Exhibit Three,' being a warranty deed from Lizzie Rice to Benjamin G. Patton, dated the 29th day of August, 1895.

"Mr. Hostetter: We object to that being read in evidence, because Lizzie Rice, according to the testimony thus far adduced, died in 1903, and being a daughter of Phoebe Henderson and having died before Phoebe Henderson, nothing passed under the deed. Nothing could pass under the deed offered in evidence, and that's admitted by the counsel for the defendants. I think you practically state you didn't make any claims, is that right?

"Mr. Gene Pearson: Well, that's right."

The heirs of Lizzie Rice, *nee* Lizzie Henderson, recovered in the case and appellants do not challenge their recovery. We give this construction of the two trust instruments as given by counsel, because the two instruments are not before us for construction.

From an early day it has been held that a deed made by a minor is not void, but merely voidable. In the case of Singer Manufacturing Co. v. Lamb, 81 Mo. l. c. 225, this court through MARTIN, C., said:

"The deed of a minor is not void, but only voidable, after he reaches his majority. [Peterson v. Laik,

24 Mo. 541; Huth v. Marine Railway & Dock Co., 56 Mo. 202.] The right to disaffirm may be exercised by his heirs and representatives within the time permitted to him for doing the act. [Land & Loan Co. v. Bonner, 75 Ill. 315.] It requires no affirmative act to continue its validity, but only an absence of any disaffirming acts. It remains valid in all respects, like the deed of an adult, until it has been disaffirmed by the maker, after reachig his majority.''

LAMM, J., in Shaffer v. Detie, 191 Mo. l. c. 389, said:

''Now it may be conceded to appellant that the deed of a minor is not void, but only voidable; for such is the law. The policy of the law is to make the conveyance of a minor effective or non-effective, as a minor grantor may elect to affirm or disaffirm when he attains the mature judgment of full age; and all persons, whether innocent purchasers or not, must deal with the minor's title to real estate subject to this privilege, since his title passes lame and halt with an infirmity, of which the world at large at its peril must take notice. But this is a personal privilege to be exercised by him, or in case of his death, or being *non compos*, by his heirs or personal representatives; so that, the mantle of privilege to object to such deed does not fall upon the shoulders of strangers to the transaction, and least of all upon one holding and asserting a hostile title, as here.''

We shall not go further with authorities. The deed of a minor remains good and conveys title until such deed is disaffirmed. The minor is not required to act until he reaches his majority, but he must act to thwart the deed. Within what time he must act we take in the next paragraph.

II. These deeds being voidable merely the next question is, within what time must minors disaffirm their deeds? And we might add, from what date the time to disaffirm begins to run? Answering the last question first, we are forced to say that the minor is not required to act until he reaches his majority, and the time could not begin to run prior to that time.

Disaffirmance by Minor of Deed: Limitations.

The time allowed for disaffirmance is not statutory, but court-made law. This court has considered the question several times, and the rule established seems to be within ten years after the infant reaches his majority. The time fixed for disaffirmance by the court has been made analogous to the Statute of Limitations for real actions.

In the very early case of Peterson v. Laik, 24 Mo. l. c. 544, Scott, J., made use of this language:

"That a deed executed by one who has attained his majority, conveying lands, which he had alienated during his infancy, is a disaffirmance of the deed of alienation made during his infancy, is the well-settled doctrine of this court. The acquiescence of the infant, after his reaching his full age, for a period short of that which would secure a title by the Statutes of Limitations, does not destroy or take away the right which the law for wise purposes has conferred on infants of disaffirming their deeds. Whether the infant may not after attaining full age, within a shorter time, by his declarations, acts or conduct, restrain himself from a disaffirmance of his acts done during infancy, is a question not presented by any thing contained in this record."

The foregoing from Scott, J., it might be said, hardly formulates the rule, but it has been made the basis for the rule, for in Huth v. Railway & Dock Co., 56 Mo. l. c. 209, this court through Napton, J., said:

"There is no doubt, that a conveyance by an infant passes the title, subject to a right on the part of the infant when reaching full age, to disaffirm this contract and convey to some third person. What length of time will be allowed the infant after attaining majority, to disaffirm, is a question which has never been passed upon by this court so far as my examination has extended. There are loose *dicta* in text books, and perhaps a decision or more of respectable courts, that this disaffirmance must be made in a reasonable time, and that mere acquiescence beyond this reasonable period is equal to an affirmance. That is a very indefinite expression, 'and amounts to very little more than that the acquiescence of the adult, laboring under no disabilities, must be attended with such acts as to amount to a virtual recognition of the validity of his deed.

"I incline to think that Judge Scott's observation in Peterson v. Laik laid down the only practicable rule on the subject. That was, that, in general, the Statute of Limitations would be the guide—but that in cases where an infant does something totally inconsistent with an intention to disaffirm, as in receiving rent on a lease made in his infancy, after he becomes of age, an affirmance may be inferred.

"I do not find any authority for the doctrine, that mere silence or inaction, unless continued so long as to effect a bar under the Statute of Limitations, will prevent the infant from disaffirming."

This rule as to the time in which the infant must act, that is, within ten years after attaining majority, has been recognized later by this court. [Harris v. Ross, 86 Mo. 89; Linville v. Greer, 165 Mo. 380.]

The act of disaffirmance goes to and effects the deed. It does not necessarily mean a suit, although a suit to recover the land would be a disaffirmance of the deed. The time fixed for the disaffirmance of a deed by an infant is not a Statute of Limitations, but is a working rule of law established by the courts, and in reasoning out what the rule should be as to the time of disaffirmance, the courts have made it analogous to the Statute of Limitations for real actions. The date of the beginning is the advent of majority, and the time expires ten years after the advent of majority. The act of disaffirmance goes to the instrument itself, and has no particular reference to the estate conveyed or attempted to be conveyed. For this reason the date of the mother's death in 1912 cannot be taken as the beginning of the ten years in which disaffirmance of the deeds might be allowed under the law. Before her death they had a contingent remainder which they could convey, and this was a substantial right and interest. If they desired to avoid the conveyance of that interest or right, they should have done so by some act of disaffirmance within ten years from the advent of majority. This they did not do. The last positive expression of this court that we find is that of BLACK, P. J., in Lacy v. Pixler, 120 Mo. l. c. 388:

"There is a line of cases which hold that a minor must affirm his deed within a reasonable time after he attains majority. On the other hand many courts hold that he may exercise his right to disaffirm the deed at any time within the period of the Statute of Limitations, *after majority,* there being no ratification."

The italics are ours. That learned jurist then adds that he is saved further investigation by the holding of this court in Huth v. Carondelet Marine Ry. & Dock Co., 56 Mo. 202-209, which announces the ten-year rule.

The trial court erred in holding that the deeds of Thomas S. Henderson and Olin G. Henderson, passed no title.

The deed of Anna N. Megowan we take later, because of another question being involved therein.

III. Annie Henderson, now Annie Megowan, was married twice. She was born February 10, 1879.

Married Female Minor. She was married to Alburtus Wells on the 19th day of March, 1895, and was therefore just passed sixteen years of age at her marriage. She made the deed involved in this case on August 9, 1895, and was therefore just sixteen years and six months old at the making of the deed. She lived with the first husband, Wells, for seven years, and until his death. This would make her a *femme sole* in March, 1902, according to her testimony. The question was asked her: "Q. How long after your marriage did Mr. Wells live? A. I lived with him seven years." We quote her language because counsel for respondent claim that she did not become discovert until less than ten years before the petition was filed in this case. They say she was under double disability when the deed was made, i. e. both infancy and coverture. But under her own evidence she had recovered from both long before the filing of the second amended petition in this case, which is the first time she did any thing to disaffirm her deed. This second amended petition was filed July 15, 1912, and she became discovert March 19, 1902. Ten years and nearly four months expired after she became discovert before this suit was brought. When the time began to run, as it would at the latest in March, 1912, when she became discovert, it would continue to run even though she married again. This on the theory that this rule as to time for disaffirmance is analogous to statutes of limitation, and such is the view of this court.

The facts in the case as above indicated makes it unnecessary for us to discuss the question as to whether or not under the Married Woman's Act as it stood when this deed was made, coverture would have been a good excuse for not disaffirming the deed. We leave that mooted question to a case where it becomes vital. It therefore follows that the trial court was also in error when it held that Mrs. Megowan's deed conveyed no title.

IV. This leaves but one further question. Appellants claim that the allowance of $290.75 as attorney's fee to plaintiffs' counsel, to be fixed as costs, is wrong. They claim that the whole case was contested issues, and therefore no part of plaintiffs' counsel fees should be taxed as costs.

Attorney's Fees.

The suit was first brought by Maude Parrish, and all other parties were made defendants. Later, July 15, 1912, this second petition was filed, and the parties named as they now appear. This petition does state that none of the defendants have any interest in the property, and ask the court to so adjudicate. The answer set up the title of the defendants and asked for partition. The reply averred that the deeds made by the heirs conveyed nothing. The trial took the ordinary course of partition suits where there are contested issues, as well as non-contested issues, between the parties. The court heard evidence on this attorney's fee. It made the following finding thereon, which is justified by the evidence:

"The court finds in this case that prior to the institution of this suit, Mr. Robert L. Sutton was employed by plaintiff, Maude Parrish, as her attorney, to institute this suit under an agreement that he should have a reasonable attorney's fee for his services in this case, which fee should be fixed as to amount by the court and charged as general cost of the case. That Mr. Sutton is a resident of Troy, Lincoln county, Missouri, and a member of the Lincoln county bar, and that he had associated with him Mr. Hostetter, before the suit in partition was filed; that after the suit was filed Mr. Ball became associated with Mr. Sutton and Mr. Hostetter as attorneys for the plaintiffs in this case throughout the proceedings and up to the present time. The court finds that $290.75 is a reasonable fee for Mr. Sutton and his associates, Mr. Hostetter and Mr. Ball, for their services rendered in the matter of the partition and sale of the real estate in this case, that is, for the partition suit itself. The court awards them nothing for services rendered upon any issue that was contested as between any of the plaintiffs and the defendants, Lowell and Kenneth Patton and O. H. and M. W. Treadway.''

We concede it to be the law that no allowance should be made counsel for their services in contested matters between the parties in partition. The allowance which the statute contemplates may be taxed as costs is for such work as counsel would do in an ordinary non-contested partition suit. If the contest grows out of the construction of the deed or will of the ancestor, and not out of things done by the parties, the services in such a contest might be taxed as costs. In this case the evidence upon the allowance was confined to such class of service, and the court so finds as above indicated. After the new parties plaintiff were added there was a pleaded ''legal conclusion'' to the effect that defendants had no interest, but the whole trial shows that Maude Parrish, the original plaintiff, had no contest with any other party to the suit. We could, if necessary, eliminate from consideration all other plaintiffs, and allow this fee stand in favor of Maude Parrish. As to her there was a straight partition suit. The land sold for nearly $6,000 and the evidence is that five per cent of the sale value is a reasonable attorney's fee for doing the work required in ordinary partition suits, leaving out all services on contested matters. As to this matter the judgment *nisi* should be affirmed.

The judgment for the other reasons will be reversed and remanded, with directions to the trial court to enter up a new judgment in accordance with the views herein expressed. The data are all before the court, and there is no need for a retrial. Let the judgment be reversed and the cause remanded with the directions aforesaid.

It is so ordered. All concur; *Woodson, J.,* in separate opinion.

WOODSON, J. (concurring)—I understand the opinion of Brother GRAVES to hold that ten years is the limit of the period in which a minor may disaffirm his or her deed, regardless of the period in which the estate conveyed thereby is barred by the Statutes of Limitations, whether that be ten, twenty-four or thirty years; and with that understanding I concur therein.

In re Estate of MATHILDA A. LARGUE; MARTHA N. MARTIN et al., Appellants, v. W. B. THOMPSON et al.

Division One, February 29, 1916.

1. **SPECIFIC LEGACIES: Bank Stock: Use of Word My.** When a specific number of shares of stock in a named bank is by the will given to a named legatee, whether the word "stock" is or is not preceded by the word "my" or a similar expression, and the will upon its face fairly discloses an intention on the part of the testator to make a specific bequest, the legacy is specific, and not general.

2. ————: ————: **Manifestation of Intention: Gift to Trustee: Ademption.** And the testatrix's intention to make specific legacies is strengthened by the fact (1) that at the time she made her will and gave a certain number of shares of the stock of a named bank to each of a large number of legatees, she owned the aggregate number of shares in said bank, and (2) by the fact that she owned and was in possession of the same shares of stock at the time of her death, and (3) is made

manifest by the fact that by one item of the will she gave
46 shares of stock in said bank to a named trustee, to be kept
for the use of a named legatee during her life, and at her
death to go in equal parts to five other named persons, and
(4) by the fact that there is no intimation in the will that testatrix intended to adeem any portion of said stock, or to require her executors to go into the market and buy stock of any
kind.

3. ————: ————: **Identification.** If the shares of stock are
for the same amount in the same corporation, and all are alike
and all are owned by testatrix, they are as fully separated and
identified by being bequeathed in different amounts to each
of a large number of legatees, as they would be were the aggregate number given to one person, or were they given in common by one clause to all the legatees.

4. ————: **Dividends.** All dividends on corporate stock specifically bequeathed belong to the specific legatee, and not to the
residuary legatee.

Appeal from St. Louis City Circuit Court.—*Hon.
Daniel D. Fisher,* Judge.

REVERSED AND REMANDED (*with directions*).

J. Lionberger Davis for appellants.

(1) The intent of the testatrix must govern if
it clearly appears from the language of the will. Sec.
583, R. S. 1909; Finley v. King, 3 Pet. 346; Sanitarium
v. McCune, 112 Mo. App. 337. (2) The law was then
and is now that the bequests of shares of stock which
were owned by the testatrix are specific legacies.
Waters v. Hatch, 181 Mo. 262; Sanitarium v. McCune,
112 Mo. App. 332; White v. Winchester, 6 Pick.
(Mass.) 48; Drake v. True, 72 N. H. 322; Lewis v.
Sedgwick, 223 Ill. 213; Trust Co. v. Powell, 29 Ind.
App. 494. (3) All dividends declared on stock specifically bequeathed, i. e., on specific legacies, belong to
the specific legatees, and not to the residuary legatee.
This proposition of law was conceded, hence no authorities are cited.

Schnurmacher & Rassieur for respondent.

(1)   Since specific legacies interfere with a just and, uniform settlement of an estate as one whole, courts lean against pronouncing legacies specific, except in the clearest case; and in case of doubt, will construe a legacy as general rather than as specific. Schouler on Wills, p. 522; Dryden v. Owings, 49 Md. 356; Morton v. Murrell, 68 Ga. 141; Giddings v. Seward, 16 N. Y. 365; Balliet's Appeal, 14 Pa. St. 461; Cogdell v. Widow, 3 Desaus (S. C.), 373; Smith v. Lampton, 8 Dana (Ky.), 69.   (2)   The legacies to petitioners called for no particular shares or particular certificates of stock; each legacy could have been satisfied by the delivery of any shares or certificates of the requisite number; they were in no wise identified or distinguished from the other shares of the same stock and were therefore general, and not specific, legacies.   Woerner on Am. Law of Administration, sec. 444; Roper on Legacies, 157; Tifft v. Porter, 8 N. Y. 516; Sponsler's Appeal, 107 Pa. 95; In re Snyder, 217 Pa. St. 71; Johnson v. Goss, 128 Mass. 433; Re Eckfeldt's Est., 7 Wkly. Notes of Cases (Pa.) 19; Osborne v. McAlpine, 4 Redf. (N. Y. Surr.) 1; Davis v. Cain, 1 Ired. Eq. 304; Sibley v. Perry, 7 Ves. 524; Robinson v. Addison, 2 Beav. 515.   (3)   The mere fact that a testator owns, in the aggregate, exactly the number of shares of stock disposed of by his will, does not, of itself, make the legacies specific.   Woerner on Am. Law of Administration, sec. 444; Tifft v. Porter, 8 N. Y. 516; Evans v. Hunter, 86 Ia. 413; Gilmer v. Gilmer, 42 Ala. 9; Dryden v. Owings, 49 Md. 356; Shethar v. Sherman, 65 How. Pr. 9; Ives v. Camby, 48 Fed. 718; Townsend v. Martin, 7 Hare, 471; Davis v. Cain, 1 Ired. Eq. (N. C.) 304; Re Tyler, 65 L. T. N. S. 367.   (4)   Dividends on specific legacies of stock follow the stock; dividends on general legacies of stock, go to the residue.   Tifft v. Porter, 8 N. Y. 516;

Dryden v. Owings, 49 Md. 356; Re Eckfeldt's Estate, 7 Wkly. Notes of Cases (Pa.) 19.

RAILEY, C.—On January 11, 1912, appellants, Martha Norris Martin, Elizabeth Norris Nelson, Jennie Norris Angloch, Mary M. Norris, Mary M. May and Albert W. Wallace, filed in the probate court of the city of St. Louis their petition, against respondents, as executors of the estate of Mathilda A. Largue, deceased, reciting therein that they were the respective owners of the shares of stock mentioned in paragraphs three, four and seven of the will of Mrs. Largue, hereafter set out in full (318 shares), and alleging that since her death on October 12, 1909, all dividends declared by the National Bank of Commerce in St. Louis, Missouri, on said 318 shares of stock, have been paid to respondents as executors aforesaid, and that no part of same has been distributed to appellants; that said dividends amount to $27 on each and every share of said stock.

It is further alleged that said executors have on hand sufficient sums to pay all debts, legacies and expenses of administration, and the aggregate amount of dividends herein prayed for; that appellants have paid their collateral inheritance taxes and are entitled to the dividends aforesaid.

The petition asked the court to make an order on said executors, requiring them to pay over to appellants the dividends aforesaid.

Upon a hearing in the probate court, the latter found against appellants, and held that the bequests of the 318 shares of stock aforesaid were *general* and not *specific* bequests. Appellants appealed to the circuit court aforesaid, where the cause was tried anew. The will of Mathilda A. Largue was read in evidence, and is in words and figures following, to-wit:

"Know All Men by These Presents, That I, Mathilda A. Largue, of the city of Saint Louis, Missouri, being of sound and disposing mind, do hereby make, declare and publish this to be my last will and testament, hereby revoking all former wills.

"First. I direct my executors to pay all just debts against my estate.

"Second. I give and bequeath to my brother, William R. Anderson, of Denver, Colorado, 100 shares of stock of the National Bank of Commerce in Saint Louis.

"Third. I give and bequeath to my sister, Mary M. May, of Beaver Falls, Pa., 137 shares of stock of the National Bank of Commerce in Saint Louis.

"Fourth. I give and bequeath 136 shares of stock of the National Bank of Commerce in Saint Louis to Martha Norris Martin, Elizabeth Norris Nelson, Mary M. Norris, and Jennie Morris Angloch, daughters of my late sister, Katherine Norris, share and share alike.

"Fifth. I give and bequeath to William A. Brandenburger, trustee, 46 shares of stock of the National Bank of Commerce in Saint Louis, in trust, however, for the following uses and purposes: The said trustee or his successor in this trust shall keep said shares of stock and collect such dividends as may be paid thereon and pay the same as they are collected to Melinda Wallace during the term of her natural life, and at the death of Melinda Wallace I give and bequeath said 46 shares of stock to Linnie Brandenburger, Jessie Verdier, Edith Taylor, Blanch Taylor and Grace Mortland, share and share alike.

"Sixth. I give and bequeath 46 shares of stock of the National Bank of Commerce in Saint Louis to William Ramsey, Harry Ramsey, Sadie Ferree, Hallie Ramsey, Lynn Ramsey and George Ramsey of Pittsburgh, Pa., share and share alike.

"Seventh. I give and bequeath to Albert W. Wallace of Allegheny, Pa., 45 shares of stock of the National Bank of Commerce in Saint Louis.

"Eighth. I give and bequeath to Mrs. Sarah A. Walker of Philadelphia, Pa., one bond of the Merchants Bridge Company of Saint Louis of the face value of $1000.

"Ninth. I give and bequeath to Mrs. Alma E. Armstrong of Atlanta, Ga., one bond of the Merchants Bridge Company of Saint Louis of the face value of $1000.

"Tenth. All the rest and residue of my estate, real, personal and mixed, of whatever kind and wheresoever situate, including my residence, known as 3840 Lindell Boulevard, and contents, I give, devise and bequeath to my beloved niece, Mathilda A. Puller.

"Eleventh. I nominate and appoint Edwin S. Puller and William B. Thompson or survivor, executor of this will and request that they give bond equal to the value of my estate, excluding realty.

"Twelfth. In the event that any legatee, devisee or executor contests the validity of this will, either directly or indirectly, I do hereby revoke the legation, devise or appointment as executor of said legatee, devisee or executor so contesting this will.

"In Testimony Whereof, I, the said Mathilda A. Largue, have hereunto set my hand and seal this 6th day of July, 1909.

"Mathilda A. Largue. (seal)"

A written stipulation was entered into in the court below, which, without signatures, reads as follows:

"It is hereby stipulated by and between Martha Norris Martin, Elizabeth Norris Nelson, Jennie Norris Angloch, Mary M. Norris, Mary M. May and Albert W. Wallace, legatees under the will of Mathilda A. Largue, by their attorney, J. Lionberger Davis, William B. Thompson and Edwin S. Puller, executors of the estate of Mathilda A. Largue, and Mathilda A. Puller, by her attorneys, Schnurmacher & Rassieur,

that the said Mathilda A. Largue, at the time of the
execution of her said will, to-wit, on July 6, 1909, and
at the time of her death, was the owner of five hundred and ten shares of the capital stock of the National
Bank of Commerce in St. Louis.''

It was further stipulated by counsel, that the National Bank of Commerce of St. Louis, declared a
dividend of $27 per share, on each of the 318 shares
aforesaid; that the same was received by said executors, and that the aggregate amount of dividends
so declared on the shares belonging to plaintiffs was,
and is, $8586.

After argument, the case was taken under advise-
ment, and on March 17, 1913, the circuit court found
the issues in favor of defendants, and entered judgment generally against the plaintiffs.

Appellants in due time filed a motion for a new
trial, which was overruled, and the cause duly appealed to this court.

I. The question at issue involves the construction of Mrs. Largue's will heretofore set out. It is
dated July 6, 1909, and executed in St. Louis,
Specific   Missouri. It is conceded that, at the date of
Legacy.   its execution, the above testatrix was the
owner and in possession of 510 shares of the capital
stock of the National Bank of Commerce, St. Louis,
Missouri. It is conceded, that testatrix was the owner
and in possession of 510 shares of said stock at the
time of her death, on October 9, 1909. By the provisions of said will, testatrix bequeathed to the legatees
named therein 510 shares of stock in the National
Bank of Commerce aforesaid. She bequeathed to appellants 318 shares of stock in said bank, as shown in
paragraphs three, four and seven, of the will aforesaid. It does not appear from either the will, or the
record herein, that testatrix owned any more than 510
shares of stock in said bank.

It appears by stipulation "that the amount of dividends declared by the National Bank of Commerce in St. Louis on each and every share of the capital stock of said bank, which was bequeathed by the will of Mathilda A. Largue, was $27 per share, and that that amount was received by the defendants as executors of said will, and was and is retained by said executors and defendants; and that the aggregate amount of dividends so declared on the shares belonging to plaintiffs was and is $8586."

Counsel for respondents in their brief, with commendable frankness, state the issues involved, as follows:

"The testatrix did intend to dispose of the five hundred and ten shares of stock she owned; but the true question is, did she, by the language she used in expressing her last wishes, dispose of them in such a way that, as a matter of law, they amount to specific legacies or general legacies?"

As said by the New York Court of Appeals, in Cammann v. Bailey, 210 N. Y. l. c. 30:

"Rules for the construction of wills are for the sole purpose of ascertaining the intention of the testator, and if the intention is clear and manifest, it must control, regardless of all rules that have been formed for the purpose of determining their construction."

In Roper on Legacies (4 Ed.), chapter 3, section 1, page 190, a *specific* bequest is defined as follows:

" 'The bequest of a particular thing or money specified and distinguished from all others of the same kind, as of a horse, a piece of plate, money in a purse, stock in the public funds, a security for money, which would immediately vest with the assent of the executor.' "

The same author, on page 203 of the same volume, says:

"From the definition of a regular specific legacy
in the beginning of the chapter, it is obvious that *stock*
or *government annuities* or *shares* in public companies
may be specifically bequeathed; but in order to make
the bequests specific, the intention that they should be
so, must be clear, otherwise the bequests will be general."

It is insisted by respondents that the legacies to
appellants called for no particular shares or particular certificates of stock; that each legacy could have
been satisfied by the delivery of any shares or certificates of the requisite number; that they were in
nowise identified or distinguished from the other
shares of the same stock and were therefore general,
and not specific legacies. The following authorities
are relied upon, in support of the foregoing contention: Woerner on Am. Law of Administration, sec.
444; Roper on Legacies, 157, and cases cited; Tifft v.
Porter, 8 N. Y. 516; Sponsler's Appeal, 107 Pa. 95;
Snyder's Estate, 217 Pa. St. 71; Johnson v. Goss, 128
Mass. 433; Eckfeldt's Estate, 7 Weekly Notes of
Cases (Pa.), 19; Osborne v. McAlpine, 4 Redfield (N.
Y. Sur.), 1; Davis v. Cain's Exr., 1 Iredell Eq. (N. C.)
304; Sibley v. Perry, 7 Ves. 524; Robinson v. Addison,
2 Beavan's Reports, 515; Evans v. Hunter, 86 Iowa,
413; Gilmer's Legatees v. Gilmer's Executors, 42 Ala.
9; Dryden, Exr., v. Owings, 49 Md. 356; Palmer v.
Estate of Palmer, 106 Me. 25.

Tifft v. Porter, supra, seems to be the leading
authority relied upon, and follows the English rule
upon the question involved. In the Tifft case it is
said:

"In those cases in which legacies of stocks or
shares in public funds have been held to be specific,
some expression has been found from which an intention to make the bequest of the particular shares
of stock could be inferred. Where, for instance, the

testator has used such language as, 'my shares,' or any other equivalent designation, it has been held sufficient. But the mere possession by the testator at the date of his will of stock of equal or larger amount than the legacy, will not of itself make the bequest specific.''

It is practically conceded in all the authorities cited supra, that if the will in controversy had said "my stock," or "the stock which I own," or had used some similar expression, the legacies granted to appellants would have been *specific*. It is admitted in the stipulation on file "that the said Mathilda A. Largue, at the time of the execution of her said will, to-wit, on July 6, 1909, and at the time of her *death*, was the owner of five hundred and ten shares of the capital stock of the National Bank of Commerce in St. Louis." It is conceded by respondents' counsel in their brief, that: *"The testatrix did intend to dispose of the five hundred and ten shares of stock she owned."* It thus conclusively appears that she was disposing of her *own* stock, and not some other, which might be bought with her funds after her death.

The third paragraph of the will with the word "my" inserted in front of "stock," would have read as follows:

"Third. I give and bequeath to my sister, Mary M. May, of Beaver Falls, Pa., 137 shares of 'my' stock of the National Bank of Commerce in Saint Louis."

Under the authorities heretofore cited, if each of the bequests had been written as the above, by inserting "my" before the word "stock," it would have characterized the respective legacies of appellants, as *specific*, instead of general. If testator understood she was doing the very thing which the use of "my" before "stock" would imply, in framing said legacies, then her *intention*, if carried out, would convey to each of said legatees a specific bequest.

Many of the courts of last resort in this country have broken away from the arbitrary and iron-clad English rule aforesaid, and construe legacies as *specific,* when bank stock or other stock is disposed of, without the use of "my" or similar expressions, where the will upon its face, fairly discloses the intention of testator to make a specific bequest. · In support of this proposition, we call attention to the following authorities: Jewell v. Appolonio, 75 N. H. 317; Drake v. True, 72 N. H. 322; Ferreck's Estate, 241 Pa. St. 340; Lewis v. Sedgwick, 223 Ill. 213; Gardner v. Viall, 36 R. I. l. c. 440; In re Lyle, 85 N. Y. Supp. 290; Gordon v. James, 86 Miss. l. c. 746-748; In re Zeile, 74 Cal. l. c. 130; New Albany Trust Co. v. Powell, 29 Ind. App. 494; White v. Winchester, 6 Pick. (Mass.) 48; Metcalf v. Framingham Parish, 128 Mass. 370; Harvard Unitarian Society v. Tufts, 151 Mass. l. c. 78-9; Thayer v. Paulding, 200 Mass. 98; Kunkel v. Macgill, 56 Md. l. c. 126; Norris v. Exrs. of Thomson, 16 N. J. Eq. 542; School District No. 1 v. International Trust Co., 149 Pac. (Colo.) 620; Douglass v. Douglass, 13 D. C. App. l. c. 29; Waters v. Hatch, 181 Mo. 262.

In the foregoing cases, bank stock and other stock were disposed of by testators under facts similar to those in the case at bar, and the legacies were declared *specific* bequests, without the use of the word "my" or words of similar import.

Recurring to the provisions of the will under consideration, it appears from the fifth paragraph of same that testatrix was not only *intending* to dispose of her *own* stock, but created an active trust, by appointing Wm. A. Brandenburger, trustee, as to 46 shares of said bank stock, and devolved upon him the duty of holding said shares of stock. It required him to collect the dividends thereon and pay the same to Melinda Wallace, during her natural life. She then gave said 46 shares, at the death of Melinda Wallace, to those named, share and share alike.

There is nothing in the record to indicate that testatrix owned any other bank stock, aside from said 510 shares disposed of in the will. There is not the slightest intimation on the face of the will, that she intended to *adeem* any portion of said stock, or to have her executors go into the market and buy stock of *any* kind.

Keeping in mind the obligation resting upon us, to ascertain and carry out the intention of testatrix, we cannot escape the conviction, that Mrs. Largue fully intended that these appellants should have and hold as specific bequests, the bank stock left them by the will, as well as the dividends paid thereon to the executors of said estate.

II. It is suggested in the brief of respondents that, if all the stock mentioned in the will had been bequeathed to *one* legatee, or to *several* legatees *in common,* the bequest might be considered *specific,* under the ruling of this court in Waters v. Hatch, 181 Mo. 262. In the latter case, paragraph 2 of the will construed reads as follows:

Identification of Stock.

"'I give and bequeath to my daughter, Mrs. Sarah M. Vernon, of Des Moines, Iowa, sixty shares of stock of the Carthage National Bank of Carthage, Missouri.'"

Judge MARSHALL, speaking for this division in which all concurred, on page 288, said:

"The second clause of the will separates these shares from the balance of the estate and bequeaths them to Mrs. Vernon. It would be hard to conceive of a more specific legacy."

The conclusion reached in the Hatch case is fully sustained by many of the well considered cases heretofore cited.

We are at a loss to understand why the disposition of 60 shares of stock to one legatee, when testator had no more, is any more *specific* than if he had bequeathed 510 shares, being all he owned, to five or more persons, giving each a different number of shares from the other. In each instance, the testator bequeaths all the stock he owns. Each share of stock is of the same value as every other share of the same stock. The 60 shares in the Hatch case could no more be separated and identified than the 510 shares of stock in the case at bar. We see no reason for departing from the rule promulgated in the Hatch case, and hence hold that the principles there enunciated, in respect to foregoing matters, stamp the legacies aforesaid, of the will in controversy, as *specific,* rather than general bequests.

III. When testatrix executed the will under consideration in 1909, she was authorized by the ruling of this court in the Hatch case to dispose of her 510 shares of stock in the National Bank of Commerce, as she did in the several paragraphs of her will. She was dealing with her own bank stock, without any apparent intention of *adeeming* same or any portion thereof. It made no difference to her *which* particular shares of stock each legatee received, as they were all alike, and all of the same value.

Adomption.

If she had sold in her lifetime the 510 shares of stock in said bank to the legatees named in her will, and had received pay therefor, each purchaser under said sale, in case she refused to deliver his stock, could have maintained an action in replevin against her, for his aliquot part of the stock, as it was all alike, of the same value, and not separated. [Kaufmann v. Schilling, 58 Mo. 218; Groff v. Belche, 62 Mo. 400; Lead Co. v. White, 106 Mo. App. 1. c. 235; Hamilton v. Clark, 25 Mo. App. 1. c. 438; Chapman v. Shepard, 39 Conn. 413;

Rust Land & Lumber Co. v. Isom, 70 Ark. 99; Gardner
v. Dutch, 9 Mass. 407; Kimberly v. Patchin, 19 N. Y.
330; Pleasants v. Pendleton, 6 Randolph (Va.), 473.]

In view of the law upon this subject, it would be
illogical to hold that the bank stock given each legatee
under the will was not sufficiently described and identified, when the will in its entirety, in connection with
the clear intention of testatrix, is taken into consideration.

IV.   On the facts disclosed by the record, we hold
that the legacies given appellants in paragraphs three,
four and seven of the will in controversy, are specific
bequests, and that appellants are legally entitled to
$8586 received by the executors as dividends on the
318 shares of stock aforesaid.

The judgment below is accordingly reversed, and
the cause remanded with directions to the trial court
to dispose of the case in conformity to the views here
expressed.

Brown, C., concurs.

PER CURIAM.—The foregoing opinion of
RAILEY, C., is adopted as the opinion of the court. All
of the judges concur; *Blair, J.*, in the result.

JAMES POWELL, Appellant, v. J. E. POWELL.

Division One, February 29, 1916.

1. **VOLUNTARY PARTITION: Through Conduit.** The fact that
all the heirs of the owner of land, which they had inherited
from him, selected their mother as a mere conduit for the
purposes of partition, by deeding it to her, to be by her deeded
to them in severalty, did not affect the character of the voluntary partition, nor did the deed from her to them convey any title, but only designated the possessory boundary to
the land they already owned.

2. ———: **Deed to Husband and Wife.** And a deed in voluntary partition by a conduit to a daughter of the deceased owner and her husband, though seemingly a deed by the entirety, did not vest the husband with the title to the land described in the deed; but upon the daughter's death the entire title descended to her children or her other heirs, since, in spite of said deed, the entire title to the tract designated had been inherited by the daughter from said deceased owner.

3. ———: ———: **Money Paid to Equalize Interest.** A payment made by the husband of one of the coparceners to another coparcener for the purpose of equalizing the share of his wife, did not convert the deed to him and her into a deed by the entirety; at most it made them tenants in common, but it did not have even that effect if it conveyed only the .wife's share, for a deed in voluntary partition does not convey the title, but that was cast upon the wife by descent.

4. ———: ———: **Estoppel.** Even though the wife directed that her husband's name be placed in the deed as grantee made in the voluntary partition of land inherited by her and others from her father, and he improved it with her knowledge, neither she, nor her heirs after her death, are estopped to deny that he acquired any title by the partition deed.

5. ———: ———: **Limitation: Husband's Possession: Curtesy.** Prior to the amendment of the Married Woman's Act of 1889, the husband was entitled to the possession of the wife's land, and that amendment did not change his possessory right already accrued. His wife could not maintain an action to oust him of his possession begun prior to 1889, nor could his children after her death, because immediately upon her death he became a tenant by the curtesy for life; but that possession cannot avail to invest title in him by limitations.

6. **QUIETING TITLE: Limitation: Time to Bring Suit.** No limitation is fixed by the statute (Sec. 650, R. S. 1889; Sec. 2535, R. S. 1909) in which a suit to quiet title must be brought. The ten-year Statute of Limitations does not apply. [Following Armor v. Frey, 253 Mo. 1. c. 474.]

Appeal from Dallas Circuit Court.—*Hon. C. H. Skinker*, Judge.

REVERSED AND REMANDED (*with directions*).

O. H. Scott and *L. C. Mayfield* for appellant.

(1) The deed from Angeline Patterson to defendant and wife was made to partition her father's

estate and the husband took no title thereby. Propes
v. Propes, 171 Mo. 407. She took by descent from her
father. Palmer v. Alexander, 162 Mo. 127. Her directions to have the deed made to both her husband
and herself did not affect the title or estate. Propes
v. Propes, supra; Snyder v. Elliott, 171 Mo. 362;
Whitsett v. Wamack, 159 Mo. 14. (2) Although the
defendant may have paid $30 to equalize the shares
in the partition of the land (which we do not admit),
this would give him an interest at most as tenant in
common with his wife. There would be no survivor-
ship, and at her death, he would hold as a tenant in
common with his children and by curtesy. Harrison
v. McReynolds, 183 Mo. 533. And if only the wife's
interest in her father's estate was conveyed, as was the
fact, any payment made by the husband inured to the
wife's benefit. Hickman v. Link, 97 Mo. 493; Manning v. Coal Co., 181 Mo. 359. Improving the wife's
land and paying the taxes thereon does not give the
husband any title or interest therein. Curd v. Brown,
148 Mo. 83; Woodard v. Woodard, 148 Mo. 241;
Boynton v. Miller, 144 Mo. 687. (3) Neither the Statute
of Limitations nor estoppel apply to this case. The
deed under which the defendant took possession was
made before the amendment to the Married Woman's
Act of 1889 and the husband was entitled to the exclusive possession of the wife's land. Snyder v. Elliott,
171 Mo. 362; Manning v. Coal Co., 181 Mo. 359; Arnold v. Willis, 128 Mo. 149; Flesh v. Lindsey, 115 Mo.
1. The husband's possession was the wife's possession; and she could bring no action against him, absent fraud or deception. There is no charge of fraud,
and therefore no "right of action" accrued to the
wife during her lifetime. At the wife's death the
husband became tenant by curtesy; and was and is
entitled to the exclusive possession of the land during
his lifetime, and no action for possession can be
brought by the heir, unless the husband should claim

by hostile or adverse possession to the heir. This is not pleaded or proven in this case. Dyer v. Wittler, 14 Mo. App. 52; Miller v. Bledsoe, 61 Mo. 96; Manning v. Coal Co., 181 Mo. 359; Martin v. Castle, 193 Mo. 183.

John S. Haymes and *J. N. Miller* for respondent.

(1) Whether the deeds offered in evidence were executed to effect a voluntary partition of the land is to be determined by the testimony. (2) The evidence discloses a transaction amounting to more than the ordinary voluntary partition of land by co-tenants. At that time, husband and wife could deal with each other in equity, at least with respect to their properties. Tennison v. Tennison, 46 Mo. 77; Tillman v. Tillman, 50 Mo. 40; Chapman v. McIlwrath, 77 Mo. 46; Halferty v. Scearce, 135 Mo. 439; McBreen v. McBreen, 154 Mo. 330; Bower v. Daniel, 198 Mo. 320. The contract was made May 2, 1889, before the present married woman's law took effect. But a safer course still was followed in this case. The whole of the land was conveyed to a third party, who conveyed to defendant and his wife. Gibb v. Rose, 40 Md. 387. So the statute in reference to the husband and wife joining in the conveyance of the wife's land, was complied with. R. S. 1879, sec. 669. Both defendant and his wife intended that the deeds should convey title to defendant; and the intention controls. Perry on Trusts (2 Ed.), secs. 139, 140; Morris v. Clare, 132 Mo. 236; Higbee v. Higbee, 123 Mo. 287. A contract made between husband and wife in the friendly partitioning of the wife's, and other land, by which they are to become tenants by the entirety, will be enforced against the wife's heirs. Whittaker v. Lewis, 264 Mo. 208. In the pending case the contract was fully executed by the parties themselves. (3) If a cause of action ever existed, the Statute of Limitations is a complete bar thereto. All the facts were known to defend-

ant's wife, and his deed was of record, giving constructive notice (Hudson v. Cahoon, 193 Mo. 559), and if defendant occupied such relation to the land that he could have conveyed it to an "innocent purchaser," as plaintiff thinks he could, or otherwise wrongfully held title to it, although the wife of defendant, a cause of action arose in the wife's favor in 1886. Reed v. Pointer, 145 Mo. 341. The wife died in 1888, and there is no tacking of disabilities. Gray v. Yates, 67 Mo. 601; Robinson v. Allison, 192 Mo. 566. Plaintiff was barred in 1896, ten years after a cause of action accrued to the mother. R. S. 1909, secs. 1881, 1883; Reed v. Painter, supra; DeHatre v. Edmunds, 200 Mo. 246. This action was commenced July 13, 1912, and at that time any action accruing prior to July 13, 1888, was also barred by the twenty-four-year Statute of Limitations. DeHatre v. Edmunds, 200 Mo. 274. Again the statute under which the present action was brought, was enacted in 1897, and a cause of action accrued under it when it took effect. Garrison v. Fugate, 165 Mo. 40. Actions under this statute are barred in ten years. Haarstick v. Gabriel, 200 Mo. 244. But as plaintiff was a minor till May 30, 1905, and had three years free from disability in which to sue, the action was barred May 31, 1908. Plaintiff may have had no right of entry, but he had a right of action. Even if defendant did have a curtesy interest in the land, under the plain provisions of the statute (R. S. 1909, sec. 2535) under which the action was brought, "pending the life estate, the opportunity existed without any impediment whatever, of bringing suit." Hoester v. Sammelmann, 101 Mo. 624.

GRAVES, P. J.—Action by a son against the father to ascertain and determine title to eighty acres of land in Dallas County.

Counsel for appellant have made a very fair and a very succinct statement of the facts as follows:

"Thomas R. Patterson died on the 28th day of March, 1864, owning the real estate described in plaintiff's petition, with other lands. There survived him his widow, Angeline Patterson, and children, J. F. Patterson, T. B. Patterson, Sarah E. Patterson, Nancy A. Patterson and L. C. Patterson.

"L. C. Patterson died unmarried and without issue December 11, 1884, and the widow Angeline Patterson, died April 29, 1889.

"On the 18th day of February, 1886, all the heirs of Thomas R. Patterson, for the purpose of partitioning the land, deeded it all to their mother, who at once executed deeds to each heir.

"Nancy A. Patterson had married the defendant, J. E. Powell, and the deed from her mother was made to her and her husband.

"Nancy E. Powell died September 1, 1888; she left surviving, her husband, the defendant, and two children, the plaintiff and Ethel Powell, who died about a year afterward.

"The family were residing on the land at Nancy A. Powell's death and the defendant has ever' since resided thereon.

"It is conclusively shown that the deed to defendant and his wife was made at the time the several deeds were made in partition of the Thomas R. Patterson land; and if defendant secured any title other than through the marital relation, it was purchased at the time of the execution of the deed. He says he paid $30 to Thomas R. Patterson, but it is not clearly shown why this was paid to Patterson. The land conveyed, defendant admits, was his wife's interest in her father's estate. It was worth about $350 or $400.

"Defendant also claims title because his wife desired that he be protected in the possession in the event of her death; as he refused to go upon the land unless it was so arranged.

"Defendant also pleads the Statute of Limitations and estoppel.

"The judgment of the court found for defendant, and adjudged him vested with title in fee in the land."

Further details of the evidence can, if necessary, be stated in the opinion. Defendant claims the estate as the survivor under this deed by the entirety.

I. It is clear that the mother and widow, Angeline Patterson, was selected by the children and heirs as a mere conduit in their partitioning of the estate of the father. The fact of the deeds being executed contemporaneously makes this clear, as does the evidence. It is also clear that the land conveyed to defendant and his wife was the portion of her father's estate coming to her and no more. The fact that the heirs in making the partition selected a conduit rather than deeding to themselves does not differentiate the case. Both methods would reach but one result, i. e., a partition of the land.

Friendly Partition.

For the time being, leaving out of consideration the alleged payment of $30 by defendant at the execution of the deeds, the defendant's status as to this land has been firmly fixed ever since the very lucid and learned opinion of BRACE, P. J., in Whitsett v. Wamack, 159 Mo. 14. This case has been frequently reaffirmed since. In the Whitsett case it was held that the making of a deed to both husband and wife in the voluntary partition of lands in which the wife was a coparcener, conveyed no title to the husband. Such a deed it was held conveyed no title at all, but was a mere instrument of settling between the coparceners their respective possessions of land to which they already had the title. The title came to them by inheritance, and that title they always had. So, also, it is said that our statutory proceeding of partition conveys no title, when the land is divided and allotted to the coparceners. Such proceeding only. adjusts the different rights of the parties to the possession. Voluntary partition as is involved in this case has no greater effect. [Whitsett v. Wamack, 159 Mo. 1. c. 23; Palmer v. Alexander, 162 Mo. 127; Propes v. Propes, 171 Mo. 1. c. 416 et seq.]

In the Propes case, supra, it is said:

"The first point for consideration is, what is the legal effect of the partition deed from the other tenants in common to plaintiff, or to her and her husband for the land in question, conceding that it is a legal and valid instrument? Defendants insist that on its face it created in plaintiff and defendant Propes an estate by the entirety.

"A similiar question was before this court in the case of Whitsett v. Wamack, 159 Mo. 14, in which it was held that a deed of release or quitclaim made by two coparceners to a third and her husband in an effort at voluntary partition of their jointly-inherited estate conveys no title to the husband.

"In Palmer v. Alexander, 162 Mo. 127, the plaintiff and his sister made parol partition between themselves of the lands inherited from their father, but by mistake the deeds incorrectly described the lands. Thereafter she married, and to correct the mistake, new deeds were made, but in the deed to her, she and her husband were named as grantees, and on the theory that this deed created an estate by the entirety in them, after her death, plaintiff bought the land from the surviving husband, and it was held that the husband acquired no title to the land by the deed in partition, and therefore his deed to plaintiff conveyed none. That the lands were rightly the wife's by descent, having descended to her by operation of the statute, and the deed conveyed no title to her, but simply adjusted among the coparceners the right to several possession by metes and bounds.

"So in the recent case of Cottrell v. Griffiths, 108 Tenn. 191, the Tennessee Supreme Court held that a deed to the wife and husband as grantees, conveying her share of property in which she has an undivided interest, will vest in him no greater interest than if the deed were made to the wife alone. The same rule is announced in Davis v. Davis, 46 Pa. St. 342; Stehman v. Huber, 21 Pa. St. 260; Carson v. Carson, 122 N. C. 645.

"And this is so even if the deed in the case at bar was made to the plaintiff and her husband by her direction, as the grantors conveyed no part of their shares, and had no interest in the shares embraced in the deed to the grantees; it belonged to the wife by inheritance, and the title being already in her, the deed merely designated her share by metes and bounds in order that it might be held in severalty. [Harrison v. Ray, 108 N. C. 215; Yancey v. Radford, 86 Va. 638.]"

The direction of the wife to have the deed thus made to the husband as well as to herself does not change the situation. The statute relating to married women would require such a direction to be in writing at least. But the better reason is that the deed conveys no title and her direction to put his name therein does not change the character of deeds made in furtherance of voluntary partition. That her direction does not change the character of the deed has been expressly held in this State. [Propes v. Propes, 171 Mo. l. c. 417; Snyder v. Elliott, 171 Mo. 362; Whitsett v. Wamack, 159 Mo. 14.] So that if we leave out of consideration the alleged payment of thirty dollars by the husband at the time the deeds were executed, it must be held that he acquired no title by the deed from the elder Mrs. Patterson. He had full knowledge of the purposes of that deed. His position might be different from that of a stranger, but he knew and admits in this record that Mrs. Patterson was a mere conduit through which the voluntary partition was brought about. Unless sustainable upon some other ground the judgment *nisi* must be reversed.

II. We come now to the matter of the alleged payment of thirty dollars at the time of this voluntary partition. It is not claimed that the wife got more than her proportionate part of the estate. It is not clear for what reason this thirty dollars was paid, if paid at all. Defendant claims to have **Equalizing Wife's Share.** paid the thirty dollars to Thomas Patterson, and to have paid it upon this land, but the purpose or reason for such a payment is not given. Whether it was paid to equalize the share of his wife with that of Thomas Patterson no where appears.

But upon no theory can this matter justify the judgment below. He could only be entitled to all of the land upon the theory that the deed created an estate by the entirety. In such case the payment of the thirty dollars neither adds to nor takes from his case. If he paid it to equalize the shares of his wife and Thomas Patterson, and that is the only imaginable purpose, it still avails him not. In this case only the wife's share was conveyed to the twain. Thomas Patterson's share was not conveyed to them. If these deeds performed the function merely of a voluntary partition, then they conveyed no title, as we have held, supra, and his payment of thirty dollars brought him nothing. Had he by this payment acquired and the deed conveyed to him and his wife a part or all of the portion of Thomas Patterson we would have a diffrent case, but this record shows no such case. But even in that case he would become nothing more than a tenant in common with the wife and not a tenant by the entirety. The evidence of this thirty dollar payment and its purpose is after all too vague for much speculation here.

III. Defendant next relies upon the doctrine of estoppel. The wife was not estopped upon any theory of the law. If we are correct in holding that this deed to him and his wife conveyed no title, but merely served as the voluntary partition of the land, then **Estoppel.** even though she directed his name to be placed therein, the land was the wife's by inheritance from the father, and not by virtue of the deed. If the land was hers, then although he improved it with her knowledge, she is not estopped thereby to assert her title. This question we have gone over in the case of Holman v. Holman, 183 S. W. 623, at this term of court. The cases will be found collated in that case. In the brief the defendant does not seriously press the matter of estoppel. This should be said in fairness to them.

IV. Nor does the Statute of Limitation avail him. The deed under which defendant and his wife took possession of this particular portion of her father's **Limitations.** estate was made prior to the amendment of the Married Woman's Act of 1889. At that time he was entitled to the full possession of his wife's lands. [Flesh v. Lindsay, 115 Mo. 1; Arnold v. Willis, 128 Mo. l. c. 149.] The husband's possession having accrued prior to the amendment of 1889, that amendment did not change his right. [Arnold v. Willis, 128 Mo. l. c. 150; Leete v. Bank, 115 Mo. 184.]

Being so entitled, the wife had no action for possession against him, and the son none, at least until the death of the mother, and not then because defendant at once became a tenant by the curtesy. There is no evidence in this record tending to show that the possession of the land as the husband of plaintiff's mother, or the possession subsequently as tenant by the curtesy, was such as to indicate a claim of ownership of the full title as against the heir. So that if we hold that the father is now a mere tenant by the cur-

tesy, it is clear that no action for the possession has
ever accrued to the son, and none will accrue to the son
until the father's death. In the Arnold case, supra,
on page 149, it is said:

"Plaintiff's right to the possession of the interest
of his wife in the lots accrued at the death of her
mother, Mrs. Ricker, which terminated the lease from
her son, John W., to her. As to when this occurred
the evidence was very unsatisfactory, but some time,
it seems, about the year 1884. When it did transpire,
plaintiff, by virtue of his marital rights under the statute then in force, became entitled to the possession of
the lots, his wife having the title in fee simple, and not
as separate property, and he had the right to sue therefor in his own name. [Mueller v. Kaessmann, 84 Mo.
318, and authorities cited; Bledsoe v. Simms, 53 Mo.
305; Wilson v. Garaghty, 70 Mo. 517; Flesh v. Lindsay,
115 Mo. 1.]"

And on page 150 of the same case it is further
added:

"The Married Woman's Act as it now stands, in
so far as the marital rights of the husband to the possession of land belonging to the wife are concerned,
materially changed his common-law rights, and, in
legal contemplation, as completely deprived him of all
right to the possession or control of the increase and
profits, as if it belonged to some other person.

"But the fact that the right of plaintiff's wife to
sue in her own name for her separate property was
conferred upon her by the Revised Statutes of 1889,
did not deprive him of a right already vested, that is,
the right to the possession of the lots, from and after
the death of Mrs. Ricker, at which time the right accrued. [Leete v. Bank, 115 Mo. 184.]"

If, therefore, we are right in holding that this
deed made for the mere purpose of partition conveyed
no title to the husband, then his possession to the death
of the wife was one created by the marital relation,

but it was a legal right of the husband. His possession was not ousted by the amendment of 1889. The
wife never had a right of action against him, and of
course the son had none. Upon his death he became
entitled to the full possession as tenant by curtesy,
and this possession now continues.

V. Lastly it is claimed that the plaintiff is barred
because he did not bring his action under the Act of
1897, old section 650, now section 2535, Revised Statutes 1909, within proper time.

"Plaintiff was a minor till May 30, 1905," as
stated in respondent's brief. But we need not discuss
this minority, nor the question of a tolling of a statute of limitation. This court in Armor v. Frey, 253
Mo. l. c. 474 et seq., has held that there was no limitation fixed for the bringing of an action under the original Act of 1897. In this case Roy, C., goes at length
into the case law, and we are satisfied with his conclusion. What was said in Haarstick v. Gabriel, 200
Mo. l. c. 244, was not necessary to that case, and if the
language could be construed as a declaration of law
to the effect that the right to sue under old section
650 was barred in ten years it should be held to be
obiter. What was there said was said by VALLIANT,
J., *arguendo* upon a contention that the five-year statute applied. Our brothers in Division Two evidently
understood this language in promulgating the opinion in Brewster v. Land & Improvement Co., 247 Mo.
l. c. 226. But whatever has been the previous notions
of the court before, we are satisfied with the rulings
in Armor v. Frey, supra. Under that holding there
is nothing in this defense for the defendant. Under
the facts of this case the plaintiff has the fee to this
land subject only to the curtesy estate of the defendant. The court *nisi* should have so declared.

The judgment is reversed and the cause remanded
with directions to the circuit court to enter up such

a judgment as above indicated. It is so ordered. All concur.

ON MOTION TO MODIFY JUDGMENT.

GRAVES, P. J.—When this case was first written we adopted the statement of facts made by counsel for appellant, and in directing a decree we overlooked this statement of fact: "That Nancy E. Powell died September 1, 1888; that she left surviving, her husband, the defendant, and two children, the plaintiff and Ethel Powell, who died about a year afterward."

Considering this fact, when Nancy E. Powell died, the husband was possessed of a curtesy estate, and the fee passed to the two children. Upon the death of Ethel Powell her interest in the fee would pass to the brother and father in equal portions. We will, therefore, modify our original opinion so as to hold that the trial court should have found that the defendant had a curtesy estate in the whole of this land, and in addition thereto had one-fourth interest in the fee estate, and the plaintiff herein had a three-fourths interest in the fee estate, subject to the curtesy estate of the father.

The judgment is therefore reversed and the cause remanded with directions to the trial court to enter judgment as herein above indicated, rather than as indicated in the original opinion. All concur, except *Woodson, J.,* absent.

MARION D. RAY et al., Appellants, v. LOU WESTALL et al.,

Division One, February 29, 1916.

1. **WILL: General Incompetency of Witness: Husband of Legatee.** A will must stand or fall as a whole; and if the husband of the principal devisee is a competent witness for any person in a suit by which the validity of the will is being contested, his testimony would inure to her benefit.

2. ————: **Husband of Legatee: Competency as Witness.**
Property, both real and personal, devised to a married woman
by a will, is her separate property, and can be sold or mortgaged
without reference to her husband; and in a suit contesting the
validity of the will, by which she is made the principal legatee
and he is given nothing, he is competent to express his opinion,
as a non-professional witness, based upon what he observed
while in testatrix's presence, as to her sanity.

3. ————: **Instruction: Incapacity: Undue Influence: Submitted
In Alternative.** An instruction for the proponents of a will, telling the jury that if testatrix "was not of unsound mind and incapable of making a will, or that the said paper writing was
not procured to be made and executed by undue influence, then
you must find that said paper writing was the will" of said
testatrix, is palpably erroneous. The two grounds of contest
being charged, and there being testimony to sustain both, the
instruction required the jury to sustain the will if they found
either charge was not supported by the evidence, whatever they
might find as to the other charge.

4. ————: ————: **Incapacity: Monomania.** An instruction
telling the jury that if they find from the evidence that at
the time of making the will, the mind of testatrix "was unsound or impaired in any one or more particulars, yet practically sound and unimpaired in all others, still you will not
be warranted in finding that she was thereby mentally incapacitated from making a will," is misleading, since it authorized
the jury to sustain the will, even though her mental impairment had gone to the extent of rendering her incapable of understanding the nature and extent of her property.

Appeal from Jackson Circuit Court.—*Hon. O. A.
Lucas*, Judge.

REVERSED AND REMANDED.

Rees Turpin and *James E. Taylor* for appellants.

(1) The husband of the principal respondent was
erroneously permitted to testify. Paul v. Leavitt, 53
Mo. 595; Roberts v. Bartlett, 190 Mo. 680; Layson v.
Cooper, 174 Mo. 211; Haerle v. Kreihn, 65 Mo. 202;
Joice v. Branson, 73 Mo. 28; Wood v. Broadley, 76 Mo.
23; Norvell v. Cooper, 155 Mo. App. 445; Greenleaf on
Evidence (14 Ed.), sec. 335; Tomlinson v. Lynch, 32
Mo. 160; Cook v. Neely, 143 Mo. App. 632; Berst v.

Moxom, 157 Mo. App. 342; Henning v. Stevenson, 118
Ky. 318. (2) Defendants' instructions 7 and 9 contradict plaintiffs' instruction P-b and improperly declare
the law and are confusing and misleading. Ghio v.
Mercantile Co., 180 Mo. App. 686; Sheperd v. Transit
Co., 189 Mo. 362; Imp. Co. v. Ritchie, 143 Mo. 587; Ross
v. St. Ry. Co., 132 Mo. App. 472; Hovey & Brown v.
Aaron, 133 Mo. App. 573; Mining Co. v. Fidelity Co.,
161 Mo. App. 185; Spillane v. Railroad, 111 Mo. 555;
Baker v. Railroad, 122 Mo. 533; Morton v. Heidorn,
135 Mo. 608.

Calvin & Rea for respondents.

(1) Instruction 7 is a correct declaration of the
law under the issues joined by the pleadings and under
the testimony adduced. It properly submitted to the
jury the two, and the only, questions left for their
determination. Sayre v. Princeton University, 192 Mo.
120; Winn v. Grier, 217 Mo. 453; Cach v. Lusk, 142 Mo.
630; Sayre v. Lindeman, 153 Mo. 288; Cutler v. Zolin-
ger, 172 Mo. 92. (2) There was no error committed by
the court in permitting the witness, Westall, to detail
the facts which he gave in testimony, even though his
wife was a party defendant in the action. Denning v.
Butcher, 59 N. W. (Iowa) 69; Shanklin v. McCracken,
140 Mo. 348; Loder v. Whelpley, 111 N. Y. 239.

RAILEY, C.—This action was commenced in the
circuit court of Jackson County, Missouri, on January
30, 1909, to contest the last will and testament of Mrs.
Nona Ferguson, a widow, who died in said county on
January 6, 1909, possessed of real and personal property located in said county. She left no lineal descendants at the time of her death. It is charged in the
petition that no surviving kindred of Mrs. Ferguson, of
any degree, are known to plaintiffs; that the latter are
the only persons having any interest as heirs or devisees in Mrs. Ferguson's estate; that they claim their
respective interests under a will made by said testator

in 1905, and that the defendants herein are the only other persons known to plaintiffs who claim any interest in said estate.

It appears from the record that Mrs. Ferguson, on December 14, 1908, executed an instrument purporting to be her last will and testament. Defendant J. H. Martin, one of the legatees, is named as executor of said will. The principal legatee named therein is defendant Lou Westall—wife of Frank Westall—who is given the real estate and the bulk of testator's property.

Appellants charge in petition, and at the trial attempted to show, that the will aforesaid was procured through undue influence exercised by defendants over the mind of testator; and that the latter was mentally incompetent to make a will, etc.

The abstract of record contains the following:

"Defendants to sustain the issues upon their part further offered and introduced the testimony of James Cole and James H. Hawthorne, witnesses to the execution of said paper writing, Dr. Franklin E. Murphy, Dr. George C. Mosher, Mrs. Allen H. Draper, Allen H. Draper, James H. Martin, I. Schwartz, Sophie Johnson and Lou Westall, who, among other things, testified that in their opinion Nona Ferguson was sane, and related incidents of her conduct which defendants claimed tended to show that said Nona Ferguson was sane.

"Plaintiffs in order to sustain the issues upon their part offered and introduced the testimony of Mrs. Dora Webster, Dennis J. Stroub, Anna O. Stroub, Mrs. J. A, King, Dr. H. P. Hueyette, Mrs. Minnie M. Lord, Dr. James E. Trexler, Mrs. Hattie Shepherd and Regina Stroub, who testified that in their opinion Nona Ferguson was insane at the time said paper writing was executed, and related incidents of her conduct which the plaintiffs claimed tended to show that Nona Ferguson was insane."

The trial court gave to the jury instructions purporting to cover the two grounds of contest supra, and
hence we infer that there was evidence tending to show
want of mental capacity upon the part of testator to
make a will, as well as undue influence brought to bear
upon the mind of testator which induced the making
of same. The instructions given in the trial below will
be considered hereafter.

The jury returned a verdict for defendants, sustaining the will, on June 20, 1912, and judgment was
entered on said verdict in due form.

Plaintiffs filed motions for new trial and in arrest
of judgment. Both motions were overruled and the
cause duly appealed to this court.

I. Mrs. Lou Westall was one of the principal beneficiaries in Mrs. Nona Ferguson's alleged will. Her
husband, H. F. Westall, over the objection of plaintiffs, was permitted to testify in behalf of the defendants, other than his wife, as to the *sanity*
of testator. Appellants contend that said
witness was incompetent to testify, and
assign as error the action of the trial court in permitting him to do so.

We may say in passing, that if H. F. Westall was
a competent witness for *any* person, his testimony
would inure to the benefit of his wife as well as the
other legatees in the will, for the *latter* must stand or
fall as a *whole*. [Schierbaum v. Schemme, 157 Mo. l. c.
17 and following; Wood v. Carpenter, 166 Mo. l. c. 485;
King v. Gilson, 191 Mo. l. c. 333; Meier v. Buchter, 197
Mo. l. c. 92; Seibert v. Hatcher, 205 Mo. l. c. 101-2;
Teckenbrock v. McLaughlin, 209 Mo. l. c. 541-2.]

Mr. Westall is not a beneficiary in the will, nor is
he a party to this action. If the will is sustained, the
property acquired thereunder by his wife would become
at once her *separate* estate, and both the real and personal property bequeathed to her could be sold, or

encumbered by her without any reference to her husband.

It does not appear from the record that Mrs. Westall was present at any of the times referred to by her husband when he observed the acts and conduct of testator. He was not asked to state any *conversation* he had with testator, or any other person. He was simply called upon to express his *opinion* as a non-professional witness, based upon what he observed while in the presence of testator. We find nothing in our statutes, nor in the provisions of the common law construed in connection with the statutes, which would preclude Mr. Westall from testifying *as he did,* in behalf of all the defendants to this action.

The conclusion just reached is strongly supported by the following authorities in this State, and elsewhere: Lead & Zinc Inv. Co. v. Lead Co., 251 Mo. l. c. 741; Brown v. Patterson, 224 Mo. l. c. 651-2; Weiermueller v. Scullin, 203 Mo. l. c. 469 and following; Lynn v. Hockaday, 162 Mo. l. c. 121 and following; Shanklin v. McCracken, 140 Mo. l. c. 356 and following; Banking House v. Rood, 132 Mo. l. c. 258 and following; The First Nat. Bank of St. Charles v. Payne, 111 Mo. 297 and following; Bates v. Forcht, 89 Mo. l. c. 126 and following; German-American Bank v. Camery, 176 S. W. l. c. 1077; Denning v. Butcher, 91 Iowa, 432-3 and following; Kostelecky v. Scherhart, 99 Iowa, l. c. 124-5.

The Missouri authorities supra review the common law and our statutes in reference to the matter under consideration here, and in our opinion sustain the right of H. F. Westall to testify as he did in the trial below. Appellants contention, therefore, that Mr. Westall was an incompetent witness, is overruled.

II. Plaintiffs assign as error the action of the trial court in giving, at the instance of defendants, instruction numbered seven, which reads as follows:

"The jury are further instructed that if you find and believe from the evidence that at the time of the making of the paper writing propounded herein as the Defenses will of Nona Ferguson, that she, the said stated in Alternative. Nona Ferguson, was not of unsound mind and incapable of making a will, or that the said paper writing was not procured to be made and executed by undue influence, exercised with or upon her by the defendants herein, then you must find that said paper writing is the will of the said Nona Ferguson."

It is charged in the petition, and plaintiffs' evidence tends to show, that Mrs. Nona Ferguson was mentally incapable of making a will and that she was unduly influenced to execute the instrument offered as her last will and testament. This instruction is complete within itself, and authorized the jury to return a verdict sustaining the will, if they believed testator was mentally capacitated to make one, although the jury might believe from the evidence that she had been unduly influenced by defendants to do so. On the other hand, it authorized the jury to sustain the will, if testator was *not unduly influenced* by defendants to execute it, although they might have believed from the evidence, that she was *mentally incapacitated* to make a will. On the facts presented by the record, the jury should have been told in *substance*, that if testator was mentally capable of making a will, *and* that the instrument offered and read in evidence, as Mrs. Ferguson's last will and testament, was not procured through the undue influence of said defendants or either of them, then the jury should return a verdict sustaining said will.

The above instruction is palpably erroneous, and the giving of same necessitates the reversal of the cause.

III. Complaint is made of defendants' instruction numbered nine, which reads as follows:

"The jury are further instructed that should you find and believe from the evidence that, prior to or at the time of the making of the paper writing in evidence before you, the mind of the said Nona Ferguson was unsound or impaired in one or more par- **Monomania.** ticulars, yet practically sound and unimpaired in all others, if you so find, still you will not be warranted or justified in finding that by reason of such unsoundness, if any, or impaired condition, if any, she was thereby mentally incapacitated from making a will, but before you can find that said paper writing is not the will of the said Nona Ferguson, you must find and believe from the evidence that by reason of the unsound or impaired condition of her mind (if in fact you find such condition or conditions did exist), she was thereby rendered unable to transact her ordinary business and was thereby rendered incapable of understanding the nature and extent of her property and of appreciating the natural objects of her bounty."

This instruction informed the jury that if Mrs. Ferguson's mind was "unsound" in "one or more particulars," yet sound in all others, the jury would not be justified in finding, that by reason of *such* unsoundness, she was mentally incapacitated from making a will. In other words, if the jury believed she was unable to transact her *ordinary business* and *was incapable of understanding the nature and extent of her property* (both of which might have been included in the *one or more particulars* above mentioned), yet the jury would not be warranted in finding from the above, that testator was incapable of making a will. But this is not the only objection to said instruction. It concludes as follows:

"But before you can find that said paper writing is not the will of the said Nona Ferguson, you *must find* . . . that by reason of the *unsound* . . . *condition of her mind* . . . [a] *she was thereby rendered unable to transact her ordinary business, and*

[b] *was thereby rendered incapable of understanding
the nature and extent of her property and* [c] *of appreciating the natural objects of her bounty.''*

If testator, at the time of the execution of the
will, had possessed the qualifications negatived in paragraphs a, b, and c, supra, she would have been competent to make a will under the laws of this State. The
instruction, however, as it reads, imposed upon plaintiffs the burden of showing that testator was deficient
in respect to all the matters referred to in sub-propo-
sitions *a, b* and *c* when the jury might have concluded
from the evidenc that Mrs. Ferguson was incompetent
to transact her ordinary business, *and* was incapable
of understanding the nature and extent of her property.
If testator was mentally incompetent to transact her
ordinary business *and* was *incapable* of understanding
the nature and extent of her property, she was not qualified under the law to make a will, *although* she might
have appreciated the natural objects of her bounty, as
stated in said instruction.

The above charge is not only misleading, but does
not properly declare the law and should not have been
given in its present form.

IV.   On account of the errors heretofore pointed
out, the cause is reversed and remanded, in order that
it may be proceeded with in conformity to the views
here expressed.

Brown, C., concurs.

PER CURIAM:—The foregoing opinion of RAILEY,
C., is hereby adopted as the opinion of the court.
Graves, P. J., and *Woodson, J.,* concur; *Blair, J.,* concurs in paragraphs 2 and 3 and in the result; *Bond, J.,*
concurs in paragraphs 1 and 2 and result.

ELSBERRY DRAINAGE DISTRICT v. LOTTIE
PATTON HARRIS et al., Appellants.
ELSBERRY DRAINAGE DISTRICT, Appellant, v.
LOTTIE PATTON HARRIS, W. A. RICHARDS,
CARSON E. JAMISON et al.

Division One, February 29, 1916.

1. **DRAINAGE DISTRICT: Care in Procedure.** The statutes providing for the reclamation of waste lands necessarily involve such radical interference with the owner's control of his property and such a liberal exercise of the taxing power, as to call for the utmost care in their preparation and execution.

2. ———: **Jurisdiction: Notice: Personal Service.** The jurisdiction of the circuit court to extend the boundary lines of an existing drainage district, under the Act of 1913, is not dependent upon personal service upon resident owners of the land to be included. Neither the Constitution of Missouri nor of the United States requires a uniform method of obtaining jurisdiction of the persons of litigants, in either general or special proceedings. A notice by publication in the language of the statute "to all persons interested," is sufficient.

3. ———: **Right to Extend Boundaries: Must be Shown by Record: Judicial Notice.** The right of a drainage district to extend its boundaries so as to include other lands subject to overflow must be found in the record at the trial. Its mere corporate existence does not prove its cause of action in such case, The court cannot take judicial notice of its original plan of reclamation and all proceedings of the company connected therewith.

4. ———: **Inclusion of Other Lands Not Benefited.** The statutes do not authorize an organized drainage district to so extend its boundaries as to include within the district other lands which do not need reclamation and protection from water. Unless they are beneficially affected and there is some common interest between them and those of the existing district, they cannot be included against the will and protest of their owners. A drainage district can neither go outside the object of its organization to force upon owners of adjoining land an improvement in which they have no interest, nor compel such owners to improve the land without receiving some benefit to compensate them for the outlay.

5. ———: ———: **Lands Subject to Overflow.** Notwithstanding that at the time a drainage district was organized it could include only "swamp and overflowed lands," and subsequently the statute was so changed as to permit the inclusion also of lands "subject to overflow," an attempt by it, after the change in the law, by way of extending its boundaries, to surround sixty-five hundred acres of land, disconnected from that for the improvement of which it was organized, with a levee so high and strong as to render its own land immune from the effects of a repetition of a flood which occurred more than fifty-five years ago, when it last overflowed, and, by a complicated plan of drainage, to turn loose into its own ditches, to be enlarged for the purpose, all the surplus water which may accumulate in the vast area, and after it has been carried twelve miles through the ditch, to pump it into the Mississippi River, there being no showing that the land thus surrounded would be benefited and its owners exhibiting no desire to join in it, cannot be looked upon with judicial favor.

6. ———: **To Aid Private Enterprises.** A drainage district has no power to levy taxes to aid a purely private enterprise. Where the plan of reclamation of land which it is proposed to include in a drainage district by an extension of its boundaries, is the plan agreed upon by a contract between the district engineer and the owner of a part of the land, by which that part was to be admitted to the benefits of the improvement and the cost to be charged against it was to be limited to a designated amount, the balance and principal amount to be charged against the remaining lands to be included against the will of its owners, the extension instituted for the purpose of consummating that contract should not be allowed.

Appeal from Lincoln Circuit Court.—*Hon. E. B. Woolfolk*, Judge.

FOR JUDGMENT, SEE *post*, PAGE 162.

J. D. Hostetter and *Avery, Young, Dudley & Killam* for plaintiff.

(1) The Drainage Act of 1913 is constitutional notwithstanding it only provides for notice by publication. The proceeding is not one to take anybody's land or property, but is a proceeding to establish a public corporation for reclamation purposes, and no notice at all is necessary in order to constitute due pro-

cess of law. State ex rel. v. Blair, 245 Mo. 293; Drainage District v. Campbell, 154 Mo. 156; Land & Stock Co. v. Miller, 170 Mo. 259; Levee Co. v. Hardin, 27 Mo. 495; Levee Co. v. Meier, 39 Mo. 57; Drainage District v. Railroad, 236 Mo. 109; Barnes v. Construction Co., 257 Mo. 175. (2) The statute does not limit the extension of the boundaries to a single extension. There is no reason in the nature of the thing why there should be such limit and there is abundant reason why the benefits of reclamation should not be so restricted that one extension is all that can be had. Laws 1913, p. 254, sec. 40. Nor does the fact, if it were a fact, that the land owners in the territory did not initiate or ask for the extension, affect the power to extend the boundaries. The statute expressly confers power on the district, through its supervisors, to inaugurate the proceedings. (3) The assertion that the land is not wet, swamp or overflow land finds its overwhelming refutation in the evidence in the case. And further, by the fact that the right to include any particular tract or tracts of land does not depend, as a matter of law, entirely upon the character of the land. Little River Drainage District v. Railroad, 236 Mo. 107. (4) The Drainage Act very clearly provides that the thing that shall be tried is the "objections" of the defendant. On the objections of the defendant in this case, no issue arose as to the incorporation of the Elsberry Drainage District. The court takes judicial notice of its own records in these cases, in fact, in all cases. Besides, it is alleged in the petition that the defendant is a drainage corporation under the laws of this State, and there is no denial under oath as required by statute.

F. J. Duvall and *Pearson & Pearson* for defendants.

(1) Both the Constitution of the United States, and the Constitution of Missouri prohibits the de-

priving of any person of life, liberty or property without due process of law. Art. 2, sec. 30, Constitution. The notice by publication is not due process of law, within the meaning of either Constitution. In re Strom's Est., 134 Mo. App. 347; Gardner v. Robertson, 208 Mo. 610; Hunt v. Searcy, 167 Mo. 178; Dulaney v. K. C. Police Ct., 167 Mo. 678; Turner v. Gregory, 151 Mo. 103; Bardwell v. Collins, 20 Am. St. 547, 44 Minn. 97. It must be by personal service. It is not sufficient that the defendant has actual knowledge that the suit is pending; he is entitled to service of the writ in one or the other of the modes pointed out by the statutes. Bank v. Kingston, 204 Mo. 700; Blickensderfer v. Hanna, 231 Mo. 108; Ohlman v. Saw Mill Co., 222 Mo. 66; Shuck v. Moore, 232 Mo. 656; Stanton v. Thompson, 234 Mo. 11; Chilton v. Tamm, 235 Mo. 502; Walter v. Schofield, 167 Mo. 554; State ex. rel. v. Field, 107 Mo. 451. The law required personal service in all such drainage proceedings, until this enactment of 1913. Sec. 5500, R. S. 1909. (2) The petition does not state facts sufficient to constitute a cause of action, against these objectors. First: It nowhere states that the land of these objectors sought to be annexed, is a contiguous body of wet, swamp or overflowed lands. Sec. 2, p. 233, Laws 1913. Second: This being a petition for an extension of the boundaries of a district already incorporated and organized, to give petitioner the right to extend its boundaries, it must state in its petition some specific necessity for the annexation of the land sought to be annexed or incorporated in the district. There must be facts stated in the petition, showing what the necessity is. The law does not give a drainage district authority to extend its boundaries to take in lands for the sole purpose of improving those lands, according to the individual opinions of the supervisors of a district. Drainage District v. Turney, 235 Mo. 80. Third: The petition does not state, and there was no proof of the fact, that the Elsberry Drainage District was ever incorporated in Lincoln County, or anywhere else. This is not such a corporation, that the court can take judicial knowledge of its incorporation, or its existence. Fourth: The petition fails to state that it is seeking this extension, at the instance, or upon the request of any owners of lands, sought to be attached to the district. Fifth: The petition does not state facts sufficient to show, that no other extension of the boundaries has been sought by Elsberry Drainage District. Sec. 40, p. 254, Laws 1913, grants to a drainage district the privilege of making only one extension. Drainage District v. Turney, 235 Mo. 95. (3) There is absolutely no legal, competent, evidence upon which to base the finding and judgment of the court, as to objectors' land. (a) There is no evidence that objectors' land was a contiguous body of wet, swamp or overflowed lands. (b) There was no evidence, showing a necessity, or what that necessity is for extending these boundaries. (c) There was absolutely no testimony, that the completion of the district as contemplated, without the annexation of objectors' lands, would in any manner benefit the land of these objectors.

BROWN, C.—This is a proceeding begun August 26, 1913, in the Lincoln Circuit Court, under the Act of March 24, 1913, relating to the organization of drainage districts by the circuit courts. It was instituted by the supervisors of the Elsberry Drainage District for and in behalf of said district for the purpose of extending the boundaries so as to include lands of objectors who are appellants and respondents here, and to amend the "plan of reclamation" which had been adopted by the district. The petition states that it is necessary and desirable to include these additional lands, all of which are in Pike County, because the supervisors propose to amend the plan for reclamation already adopted so as to completely reclaim the lands in the northern end of the district by means of certain improvements, so that these lands would be greatly improved and benefited, and should be made to bear their just proportion of the burden. The main and controlling features of these improvements consist of the construction of a levee completely surrounding these lands with other lands in Pike County' lately annexed to the district and called in the record the "Annada Annex." The petition states that this levee was to extend five feet above high water mark of 1858, a flood in which the river attained a height never since equaled. All the lands then included in this annex had been annexed by order of the Lincoln Circuit Court made August 8, 1912, in a proceeding which was still pending on objection to the assessment of benefits to seventeen hundred acres of the land owned by one R. C. Jefferson. The petition in that case alleged, as required by the act then in force, that the land proposed to be annexed was "a contiguous body of swamp and overflowed land contiguous to the said Elsberry District," and "that it is necessary for the complete protection of the lands now embraced in the said Elsberry Drainage District that the lands herein sought to be added to said district be embraced in said district for the purpose of having not only the lands sought to be added to said Elsberry District but also the lands in said district contained fully reclaimed and protected from the effects of water. And if said extension of the said Elsberry Drainage District is made. as petitioned for herein, it will greatly increase the value of all of said lands for agricultural purposes and will largely add to the sanitary condition of the persons owning and residing on said lands."

The objectors who are here as appellants are owners of lands not included in the original Annada

Annex. Those who are respondents are the owners
of a large tract of land included in the petition for the
annex, and which was, upon issue joined, adjudged
not to be wet and overflowed land, and was, therefore,
not included.

The Act of March 30, 1911, under which the proceeding for the original Annada Annex had been instituted and conducted, provided only for the organization into drainage districts of swamp and overflowed
lands, from which class the lands of the objecting respondents were excluded by the order of August 8,
1912. At the next session of the Legislature an
amendment was enacted (Laws 1913, p. 233, sec. 2)
by which land "subject to overflow" was added.
This act was approved March 24, 1913, and on the
same day Mr. Jefferson entered into a written agreement with Harmon, chief engineer of the district on
behalf of the supervisors, to the effect that his objections to the assessment were to be withdrawn on condition that the supervisors adopt a plan agreed upon
for complete reclamation of the land in the annex by
levee against overflow and a system of drainage shown
in "plans on file." It also contained the following
paragraph:

"It is further agreed that if any reductions in
assessment be made between the supervisors and any
parties in the annex, the assessments shall be proportionately reduced on the Jefferson lands in said annex."

In pursuance of this stipulation the objections
of Jefferson were dismissed, the present proceeding
was instituted to carry it into effect, and Mr. Harmon
"found a buyer" for the entire tract, and also for a
Patton tract of some eleven hundred acres. Using
Mr. Harmon's own language: "Before those sales
were made, an agreement was made in this court, or

at the time that the Patton sale was made, an agreement was made in this court, with those that then owned this land that this should be done; it was a part of that stipulation or settlement with him on the other assessment. The Patton land was sold at the time and while court proceedings were pending, and the Jefferson land was sold afterwards, and it was agreed with Mr. Jefferson as a part of the settlement in this court of the previous assessments, that the entire area should be reclaimed.''

The Elsberry Drainage District was organized in the Lincoln Circuit Court on March 13, 1911, and included about twenty-five thousand acres of land, all being in Lincoln County with the exception of a strip a mile or two wide on the north end, which was in Pike County. Its north line ran westerly from a point on the west bank of the Mississippi River corresponding with the center of section 26, township 52, range 2 east, substantially along the present line of Bryant's Creek to the Chicago, Burlington & Quincy railroad near the village of Annada. About two and a half miles north of this, Ramsey Creek, another stream from the bluffs having a drainage area of about sixty square miles, flows east across the railroad into the Mississippi. It is between these streams that the land annexed, and that proposed in this proceeding to be annexed, is situated. The entire tract contains about sixty-five hundred acres and was, to a great extent, made of deposits from the overflow of Guinns Creek, a stream having a drainage area of about forty square miles, which ran all over it in an unstable channel until some twenty or thirty years ago, when it was confined to the south side of a levee built by the King's Lake Drainage & Levee District from the bluffs easterly across the railroad where it joins the present converted .channel of Bryant's Creek. The village of Annada as well as the adjacent lands to the north had been protected by this old levee, which was adopted as a part of the enclosing levee of the annex.

Mr. Harmon now states in his testimony that the district wants to take in the land of the respondent objectors to get a better, cheaper and safer place to build the levee and ditch necessary to carry out the Jefferson agreement.

His plan of reclamation of the original district contemplated a pumping plant near Apex, ten or twelve miles from its north line, and the new scheme involves a concrete culvert two hundred feet long, by which the water is expected to be transferred from the enclosed annex, under the bed of Bryant's Creek at a depth not stated, and released into the main ditch of the company on the other side, along which it would flow twelve or thirteen miles to the contemplated pumping plant, which together with the main ditch was to be enlarged to take care of it. He states that one or more of these pumping plants, under private ownership, was already at work in the annex at the time of the trial.

The court refused in this proceeding to include in the district the lands of the respondents, J. H. and W. F. Patton, Carson E. Jamison and W. A. Richards, which had been excluded in the former proceeding, on the ground that upon the facts the previous judgment was conclusive. From this the drainage district has appealed. All the appellants whose lands are annexed to the district by the terms of the judgment appealed from, are appealing on the ground (1) that the court by its publication, which was the only notice attempted to be given the landowners, acquired no jurisdiction to impose upon such lands the burdens consequent to their annexation to the district; and, (2) that the record does not disclose facts sufficient to authorize the annexation of these lands to the drainage district under the terms of the Act of 1913, even

though the notice was sufficient to confer jurisdiction
upon the court to act.

I. While statutes providing for the reclamation of
waste lands are, in some respects, highly remedial,
they necessarily involve such radical interference with
the control of property by the owner, and
such a liberal exercise of the taxing power,
as to call for the utmost care in their preparation and execution. There is no governmental function in the exercise of which the control
which ordinarily pertains to the management and
preservation of one's own must be more liberally surrendered in the interest of all. On the other hand the
great increase in values attending the redemption of
our swamps from pestilence, and clothing them with
fertility, has a tendency to excite the speculative instincts of those who wait upon opportunity to acquire
property without adequate investment. In avoiding
errors incident to these conditions it is frequently
found that we have committed errors even more serious than those we have escaped. In this way it has
happened that of late years the statutes relating to the
formation and powers of drainage and levee districts
by circuit courts have rarely survived, in their original
form, the biennial legislative period in which they
were enacted, and that the proceedings we are now
called upon to consider have progressed for three
years under as many different statutes. It is evident
that when their extraordinary powers are used in summary proceedings to place a pecuniary burden upon
the property of individuals, all the conditions precedent which they prescribe should and must be complied
with. [Nishnabotna Drainage District v. Campbell,
154 Mo. 151, 157.] This principle is clearly recognized
by the Legislature, in charging these powers and duties upon constitutional courts of general jurisdiction,

*Drainage
District
Statutes.*

which can only proceed upon inquiry, and condemn
after an opportunity to be heard. It is in pursuance of
the same legislative policy that this record is now before us upon appeal. Our duty is to determine whether the facts which there appear authorized the relief
granted by the circuit court, a question which seems to
be well put by the several objections of the appellant
landowners which are set out in it.

II. The appellants contend, as we understood
them, that because this jurisdiction is vested by the
act in the circuit court, a judicial tribunal established by the Constitution which
generally exercises its judicial functions
by procedure governed by the civil code, conformity
to this procedure will be implied as a prerequisite
to its jurisdiction over the persons of the litigants
in this case. We understand them to say that the
right of the court to try the issues of fact submitted to it in this case and to render judgment thereon
depends upon its judicial character conferred by the
Constitution, and that the provision of the act under
which it attempted to exercise that jurisdiction is
void because it does not require the issue of summons
to resident defendants, and does not therefore constitute due process of law within the meaning of the
State and Federal Constitution.

Sufficiency of Notice by Publication.

We cannot agree with this proposition in its application to this case. We find nothing in these constitutions which implies that a uniform method of
obtaining jurisdiction of the persons of litigants in
either general or special proceedings is necessary. The
Act of March 24, 1913, under which this proceeding
was instituted, prescribed a method by publication
which was followed, and the sufficiency of which constitutes the only question in this connection.

We said in Houck v. Little River Drainage District, 248 Mo. 373, 382, in connection with the citation of many Missouri authorities, that it was no longer open to question, ''that the State, by the Legislature, has the power to create corporations for the purpose of reclaiming or improving swamp and overflowed lands by ditches and drains and levees, in districts prescribed by it, or to be ascertained and fixed by such appropriate instrumentalities as it may provide.'' That this includes the right of the Legislature to clothe the constituted courts with jurisdiction to inquire of and determine such *judicial questions* as may arise in the course of the proceedings, and to prescribe the practice therefor is also plain. Having exercised this right by the terms of the Act of 1913; having submitted to the court all questions of law and fact involved in the determination of the question whether, under the terms of the act, the lands in question should be annexed to the Elsberry Drainage District, we will assume that a practice must be provided or made available which will enable the court to proceed in accordance with that fundamental principle of all judicial procedure which gives the parties interested in the subject of the inquiry a reasonable opportunity to be heard. The subject of this inquiry is the status of the land involved. The Legislature undertook to provide for notice to all parties interested in it by publication of notice of its pendency. We do not have to take into consideration the fact that they are all here, contending strenuously for what they conceive to be their rights, to enable us to determine that the notice provided by the act and given in this case was well calculated to the end, and we hold that it was sufficient.

III. There being actually no evidence in the record as to the plan of reclamation of the lands included in the plaintiff district other than a profile of its contemplated main ditch extending from its levee along the

south side of Bryant's Creek to its contemplated
pumping station ten or twelve miles

**Drainage District:
Judicial Notice
of Plan of
Reclamation.**
down the river, it suggests that the
court will take judicial notice of its
records, not only relating to the incorporation, but to all other proceedings of the company
which appeared therein, all such proceedings being "in
the same case." Were this true, the objectors could
only come to this court with their appeal by bringing
the whole mass of records accumulated from the conception of the district to the time of the trial, to show
that nothing has occurred during all that time to deliver them over to their adversary. The true rule
sits in sightly simplicity upon a well beaten road.
The act of incorporation can only be assailed by a
special plea verified as required by the code. When
it has entered upon its work as a *quasi*-municipal corporation it becomes immune against collateral attack.
With respect to the assertion of its legal rights, it
stands no higher than an individual, so that its mere
existence does not prove its causes of action against
strangers having no connection with its creation, but
it must prove them by competent evidence by which
its adversary is bound. We must find the right of the
plaintiff to have the relief it is seeking, in the record
of the trial before us.

IV. The objectors deny that there is any reason
why their lands should be made a part of the Elsberry
Drainage District, and say that the execution of its
plan of reclamation would in no way affect the lands
sought to be annexed, and that no scheme of drainage

**Extending District
to Include Lands
Not Benefited.**
proposed for such lands would affect
the Elsberry Drainage District. In
short, they plead, in substance, that
there is no connection whatever between the levee and
and drainage conditions affecting the Elsberry Drainage District and those affecting the lands sought to

be annexed to it, and that the owners of the former ought not to be permitted to meddle in the affairs of their neighbors in which they have no legitimate concern. In support of their position they point to the statute under which this district was organized, which fairly represents the general legislative policy of the State on the subject (article 1, chapter 41, R. S. 1909), and direct our attention to the fact that it required that the district to be organized should consist of a ''contiguous body of swamp or overflowed lands,'' and that a majority in interest of the owners should unite in its formation. [R. S. 1909, sec. 5496.] We find no suggestion in this or any of these laws that if the majority in interest in any such body of lands should fail to agree to the formation of a drainage district, a coterie of them might form a little district of their own, from which they could reach out and take in their recalcitrant neighbors, through the assistance of the courts, extended for the mere asking. This proposition is too absurd to be considered seriously. The submission of these questions to the courts implies that they are to be determined according to those fixed rules of construction and determination which are unfailing characteristics of all judicial action. In the recent case of Squaw Creek Drainage District v. Turney, 235 Mo. 80, 95 et seq., we examined this question at length, and arrived at the conclusion that while the policy of this statute was that schemes of this character must be inaugurated by the owners of the lands requiring the improvement, the right to extend the limits of the district so as to include other lands of like character was given to meet cases in which there is something in the character or situation of the lands to be annexed, or the nature of the contemplated improvement, which would enable them to share in the benefit of the work without contributing to the cost, or would otherwise make it inequitable to withhold their assistance. It is particularly noticeable that there is nothing in the law under which the plaintiff was organized, nor in the Act of 1913 under which this proceeding was brought, which authorized the inclusion, by extension, of any lands not of the character entitling them to be included in its organization. While the fullest authority was given (Laws 1911, p. 232, sec. 5704a) to construct and maintain ditches, canals, levees, dams, sluices, reservoirs, holding basins, flowways, pumping stations and any other improvements in or out of the district, necessary to the reclamation of the land within the district, it had no power to include in the district any lands for that purpose other than such as needed reclamation and protection from water. Its powers were ample to acquire lands for these purposes by purchase or condemnation, but not under pretense of subjecting it to any part of the burden of an improvement of which it was not susceptible and which it did not need.

It follows that the question before the circuit court in this case was whether, in accordance with the principles we have just stated, the Elsberry Drainage District was entitled, against the will and protest of the owners, to annex these lands; and we hold that unless there was some common interest between them, by reason of which the improvement of the district would affect beneficially those of the objectors, the right did not exist. We use the word beneficially because we can find nothing in these acts expressive of a legislative intent to provide for the annexation of other swamp or overflowed lands as a substitute for their appropriation by condemnation, and that such an act would be a taking of the land for the purpose of the improvement without compensation being first paid. Section 9 of the Act of 1913 (Laws 1913, p. 237) necessarily calls for this construction. It provides that immediately upon the appointment of the chief engineer he "shall make all necessary surveys of the lands within the boundary lines of said district, as described by the articles of association, *and of all lands adjacent thereto that may or will be improved or reclaimed in part or in whole by any system of drainage or levees that may be outlined and adopted*," and that his "report shall contain a plan for drainage, leveeing and reclaiming the lands and property described in the articles of association *or adjacent thereto from overflow or damage by water.*" The improvement or reclamation of these adjoining lands is the only purpose for which the district is authorized to meddle with them.

V. Although, as we have already said, statutes of this character should be liberally construed to the end that the public benefit contemplated by the Legislature be not defeated, it is equally important that this beneficent purpose should not, by construction, be made a vehicle of private greed or undue personal advantage. The facts of this case indicate that we should come to its consideration with both these suggestions well in mind.

Facts of Case.

The purpose of the plaintiff corporation seems to have been the reclamation from water of about twenty-five thousand acres of Mississippi River bottom lands lying between the Chicago, Burlington & Quincy Railroad and the river, and south of Bryant's Creek in Pike County. The record is obscure as to the particulars of its incorporation, and its subsequent proceedings, and we resort to the admission of counsel in printed argument, and such fragmentary evidence as bears upon these subjects, for the meager details of which we are able to avail ourselves. One thing, however, is made plain. The lands of the Elsberry Drainage District were isolated from the lands lying north of it by Bryant's Creek. It is also plain that its plan of reclamation involved the straightening of this stream and the construction of a levee along the south side of the converted channel, of such height and strength as to protect the district by turning back its flood waters upon these lands to the north. It does not plainly appear how any plan for the drainage and improvement of the district could benefit or improve the lands lying north of this stream, and the owners of the latter exhibited no desire to join in the enterprise. Notwithstanding this the new district, on May 4, 1912, presented its petition to the Lincoln Circuit Court to have about five thousand acres of this land attached to it, stating that it was necessary to the complete protection from the effects of water, of the lands already embraced in the district, as well as that sought to be added. Neither the plan for doing this nor the nature of the mutual interest requiring it was referred to. Among the lands involved in that proceeding was about seven hundred acres belonging to Carson E. Jamison, W. A. Richards and J. H. and F. W. Patton. J. H. Patton is now dead and his former interest is represented in this suit by Lottie Patton Harris, his sole heir. These owners objected to the inclusion of their lands, asserting that they were neither swamp nor overflowed. An issue was made upon this question, which was tried and found for said owners, and the court adjudged that the lands were not wet, or overflowed, and excluded them, and, on August 8, 1912, entered its decree annexing the other lands described in the petition. The owners of the lands so excluded are pleading that judgment as an adjudication of the same question in this case. This plea was sustained by the court, and its action in this respect affords the ground of plaintiff's appeal.

VI. About seventeen hundred acres, being more than one-third of all the lands annexed in the proceeding referred to in the last paragraph, were then owned by one R. C. Jefferson. That these were swamp and

overflowed lands badly in need of reclamation is evi-
Further dent. Proceedings were immediately tak-
Facts of Case. en to assess the benefits to the land included. Mr. Jefferson was dissatisfied with the assessment
as to his own land and formally objected thereto and
the cause was continued upon his objection until settled by the agreement to which we shall presently refer.

Upon the incorporation of the Elsberry Drainage
District Jacob A. Harmon of Peoria, Illinois, was appointed its chief engineer. He was a civil engineer of
twenty-five years experience, engaged in drainage
work, in which he was an expert, and in addition to
his professional employment sometimes found purchasers for lands of the character to which his activities were directed. In that character and during these
proceedings, he found purchasers for the seventeen
hundred acres owned by Mr. Jefferson and eleven hundred acres owned by one or more of the Pattons.
These tracts included the greater part of the land in
the annex.

The Elsberry peeple were not discouraged by
their failure to obtain all they wanted in the proceeding from which Jamison, Richards and the Pattons
had escaped. By a fortunate coincidence the next
Legislature enacted a new law on the subject (Laws
1913, p. 232). The law in force during the previous
proceedings had only provided for the organization into such districts of "swamp or overflowed lands."
The new act (Laws 1913, p. 233, sec. 2) added the
words "or lands subject to overflow," so that the
loophole through which they had escaped was closed.
The Elsberry people quickly took notice of this. The
bill contained an emergency clause (Laws 1913, p. 267,
sec. 63) and was approved March 24, 1913. On the
same day Mr. Jefferson entered into a written agreement with Mr. Harmon, representing the supervisors of
the Elsberry District, by the terms of which his objec-

tions were to be withdrawn on condition that assessments for the work should not cost more than thirty per cent. of the benefits assessed. It provided that the supervisors should adopt a plan for the complete reclamation of the lands in the annex by levee against overflow and a system of drainage constructed to an outlet into the system of drains to the pumping plant, and that if any reductions in assessment be made between the supervisors and any parties in the annex, the asessment should be proportionately reduced on the Jefferson lands. There were other stipulations which, in the view we take of its effect, need not be noticed. On August 22, 1913, the supervisors commenced this proceeding to extend the boundaries of the district and amend its "plan for reclamation."

Mr. Harmon, who seems to have been the moving spirit in the affairs of the Elsberry District and especially in those matters connected with the improvement of the Jefferson lands, as well as its principal witness in this case, states in his testimony that it was agreed with Mr. Jefferson as a part of the settlement of the assessment against his land "that the entire area should be reclaimed;" "that that would be a protection, a complete protection and reclamation of the Jefferson lands;" "that in accordance with the plan he had made these surveys for the Elsberry Drainage District to protect that land and that is the reason why it is being done." We have here an authoritative statement which can mean nothing less than that this proceeding was instituted under an agreement with a single owner to improve his lands upon the plan made by the agent who found a purchaser for them, and for a consideration moving entirely from that owner in the withdrawal of his objections to an assessment made against him. It is also in proof by the same witness, and like his other statements to which we have referred, undisputed, that the "plan of reclamation" made in accordance with the agreement could be accomplished more cheaply by the use of the lands excluded from the district in the former proceeding, excluded because they did not meet the description of "swamp or overflowed lands." It was here that the Act of 1913 played its part in the transaction. In 1858 there had occurred an overflow of waters of the Mississippi River which has never since been duplicated, but which overflowed these same lands. They were therefore "subject to overflow" so that the plan for reclamation adopted and set out in the petition contained the following statement: "The top or grade line of the levee will be five feet above high water of 1858." The petitioner is now insisting that in the former proceeding for the annexation of this land the question as to whether or not it was subject to overflow was not and could not have been tried, because the law making that a ground for including it in the drainage district had not yet been enacted.

In the plan of reclamation presented by the petition in this case the petitioner for the first time attempts to show how the lands north of Bryant's Creek will be benefited by attaching them to the Elsberry District. It presents a scheme by which the water that accumulates either from local rain or overflow, are to be gathered to the lowest point of the proposed levee on the north side of that stream, and then through a concrete culvert two hundred feet long passing under its bed, then up into the main ditch of the district which is to be enlarged to take care of it, to the proposed pumping station at Apex, which is in turn to be enlarged to raise it over the levee and into the river. This is an interesting plan, but we are not called upon to compare its utility with the more simple one of pumping it into the river from the land upon which it accumulates.

VII. We have already said in a preceding paragraph that to authorize a drainage district organized under these acts to extend its limits over other lands without the consent of the owners, the lands of the district and those to be annexed must bear such a relation to each other that the proposed improvement will be of mutual benefit. A district has no right, either to go outside the object of its organization to force upon its neighbor an improvement in which he has no interest, or to compel its neighbor to improve his own land without receiving some benefit to compensate him for the outlay.

Looking at this proceeding in the light of these principles we are confronted with the difficulties in finding a reason to support it. Its object is to surround sixty-five hundred acres of land disconnected from that for the improvement of which the petitioner was incorporated, with a levee so high and strong as to render it immune from the effects of a repetition of a flood which occurred more than fifty-five years ago, and, by the complicated arrangement described in its plan, to turn loose on its land all the surplus water which may accumulate in this vast enclosure, enlarging its own ditches and pumps to take care of it. We may realize, to some extent, the magnitude of this last work from the profile of its main ditch to be enlarged for that purpose. It shows this ditch to be more than twelve miles long from the pumping station near Apex to the place where it would catch this water as it emerges from the ground beneath the bed of the stream and the levee intended to confine it. We have nothing in the record showing the cost of this work of enlargement, but considered as a disinterested act of charity it would be considerable.

We are not unmindful of the fact that before the beginning of this proceeding the larger part of this territory had been annexed to the Elsberry District by a judgment of the court from which no appeal was taken. That this judgment is binding we do not question, so that for all the purposes of this case we must consider the boundaries of the district as affected by its terms and the mutual interest of the parties as founded upon the lines of division which it establishes. We have examined at length the rights of the parties to this controversy as they existed at the time of the incorporation of plaintiff, because we think the evidence tends to show that the subsequent proceedings for the annexation of territory were in pursuance of a general plan or motive which is the controlling factor of this case.

That Mr. Harmon had great influence in the affairs of the Elsberry District is shown conclusively in this record. That he was not averse, notwithstanding his official connection with the enterprise, to involving himself in its financial possibilities appears from the fact that during the progress of these proceedings he found purchasers for more than one-half the land included in the original annex, so that it is fair to say that in addition to his official compensation for the work done by him he shared in the first fruits of that enterprise. The largest item of this participation related to the sale of the Jefferson tract which comprised more than one-third of the land annexed in the first proceeding. This sale was made after the decree for the annexation of the land had been entered and in contemplation of all the resulting benefits and profits.

There is nothing in the record to indicate whether it was Mr. Harmon or Mr. Jefferson or both of them together, that first conceived the idea of the contract prepared and signed by both, which embodied the final word fixing the favorable terms upon which the Jefferson land was to be admitted to the benefits of the improvement, limiting the amount of the cost that was to be charged against it, and providing that the supervisor should adopt for its benefit a plan for complete reclamation of all the land in the annex by levee against overflow and a system of drains constructed to an outlet to the pumping plant. That the plan presented in this petition is the plan for reclamation referred to in the contract is evident and that this contract contemplated the bringing of this proceeding is equally evident. Both the contract and the petition described it with equal certainty, although with different degrees of particularity. That this proceeding was instituted solely for the performance of that contract is practically admitted in the evidence.

Whether under the Act of 1913, a drainage district may extend its limits for the purpose and under the circumstances we have stated is the question before us. The authors of the plan and the petitioner by its evidence frankly admit that the object of the extension is to carry out the terms of the Harmon-Jefferson agreement that the petitioner will reclaim the lands of the latter, principally at the cost of protesting neighbors, who are shown by the evidence to be amply able to take care of their own.

These corporations are clothed by the State with governmental functions, including taxation and eminent domain, because the development in productiveness of the lands of the State and the promotion of the health and comfort of the people are matters of governmental concern, which are to be exercised only for the benefit of the public. The drainage district in these respects are agencies of the State, and it is not necessary to say that they have no more power to levy a tax to aid a purely private enterprise than would the State itself. The very fact that they are clothed with these extraordinary powers imposes upon the courts in the exercise of their jurisdiction, the duty of watchfulness to see that such powers are not prostituted to the purposes of private speculation. By the terms of the act (section 17) the chief engineer was made superintendent of all the works and improvements, and the special adviser of the board, and while we do not think it necessary to condemn Mr. Harmon for his participation in the sale of lands that must depend largely for their value on his own advice, we think the court should take the fact into its consideration in determining whether the motive of this proceeding was a public or private one.

For the reasons stated in this paragraph we think the court erred in extending the limits of the plaintiff district to include the lands of the objectors upon the evidence before it. For this reason the judgment will be reversed so far as it includes in the Elsberry Drainage District the lands of the appellant objectors, and affirmed as to the respondent objectors, and the cause is remanded with directions to the circuit court to proceed to final judgment in accordance with the principles stated in this opinion.

Railey, C., concurs.

PER CURIAM.—The foregoing opinion of Brown, C., is adopted as the opinion of the court. All of the judges concur.

THE STATE v. HOMER EVANS, Appellant.

In Banc, March 1, 1916.

1. **REMARKS OF COUNSEL: Preserved for Review.** Where defendant's counsel, in his objection to argument made to the jury by the State's counsel, repeats the statement made by said counsel and states his reason therefor, and the court by his ruling, accepts the repetition as a true reiteration of what had been said, the ruling, being excepted to, is for review on appeal, without any further preservation in the bill of exceptions than the statement and objection of appellant's counsel and the ruling and remarks of the court, and the exception.

2. ————: **Weak Evidence.** Argument of counsel to the jury, assigned as prejudicial to appellant, is to be examined in the light of the facts of the particlular case. Where the evidence of defendant's guilt is weak, the offense charged is one which decent men abhor, and there is no testimony pertaining to a fact which reasonable men would expect to be developed, remarks of counsel for the State, either in their opening statement or in their argument to the jury, by which such lacking testimony is attempted to be supplied, may alone constitute reversible error.

3. ————: **Seduction: No Request for Fulfillment of Promise to Marry: Supplied by Attorney.** The fact that, after prosecutrix discovered her pregnancy as the result of an admitted sexual relationship, she frequently kept company with defendant in the presence of her and his relatives and requested him to marry her to shield her from its consequences, but at no time suggested or claimed a reparation on account of a promise to marry, there being no legal impediment or other obstacle in the way of such a marriage, tends to impeach her testimony that there had been such a promise, and in view of her unsatisfactory testimony. as to the fact of an engagement was a matter of grave importance for the jury in determining whether or not her testimony was true; and remarks made by the State's counsel, in his opening statement that "the young girl who was wronged by this young man has solicited and begged and importuned him to marry her and give this bright little baby a father and a name," and repeated in substance in the argument to the jury, the effect being, whether intended or not, to break the force of the significant omission, and to supply the lack of it, were reversible error.

Held, by REVELLE, J., dissenting, that it is but common knowledge and ordinary human experience that no juror will sit

through a trial of a seduction case without the thought
that the girl, whose shame and disgrace would be lessened
by marriage, was anxious to and did what she could to
bring about the marriage, and the statement of counsel
could only have hastened the thought; and, in this case,
it was not prejudicial, because the jury knew the defendant had not married her, and counsel's statement that
she begged him to do so and his refusal, if effective at all,
tended only to corroborate his testimony that he had never
promised to marry her at any time.

4. **SEDUCTION: Evidence: Conclusions and Opinions.** In a
prosecution for seduction under promise of marriage, the father
of prosecutrix should not be permitted to state his conclusions
and give his opinions as to the relations between her and defendant, such as, "He treated her like a sweetheart," "He
seemed to think a good deal of her."

Held, by REVELLE, J., dissenting, that the testimony was
not reversible error, since the father's knowledge and information upon which the conclusions were based were
completely developed, and the jury were fully capable of
determining whether or not the conclusions expressed were
warranted.

5. ———: ———: ———: **Estimates of Others.** A voluntary
conclusion of prosecutrix's father, drawn from a conversation
with some neighbors of defendant, that "from the way they
talked about him they had no use for him," is not competent
evidence.

Held, by REVELLE, J., dissenting, that, as the statement came
out in connection with his explanation of certain matters
concerning which he had been interrogated on cross-examination and no motion was made to strike it out, the trial
court cannot be convicted of error.

6. ———: ———: ———: ———: **No Motion to Strike Out.**
The usual rule is that a motion to strike out is prerequisite to
a review of a conclusion voluntarily injected into the case by
a witness; but where the trial court, upon an objection being
made, ruled on the point on its merits, without such motion, the
point is thereby preserved for review on appeal.

Held, by REVELLE, J., dissenting, that the trial court, on an
objection being made by simply directing attorneys to "go
ahead" did not rule on the merits, and it cannot be anticipated what his ruling would have been had a motion to
strike out been made.

7. ———: **Remarks of Court: No Objection.** Unless there is
an objection directed to an objectionable remark made by the
trial court, it cannot be reviewed on appeal.

8. ————: **Admission of Promise: Corroboration.** The promise of marriage must precede seduction; and while testimony of a witness that defendant, eight months after the alleged seduction, admitted that "he did promise to marry" prosecutrix, is competent and is evidence upon which an instruction on corroboration may be based, if the admission refers to a time preceding the alleged seduction, it is neither corroboration nor admissible if the admission fixes no time when the promise was made.

9. **INSTRUCTION: Weight to Be Given Defendant's Testimony:** *Held*, by BLAIR, J., with whom WOODSON, C. J., and GRAVES, J., concur, that, where the usual general instruction pertaining to the credibility of witnesses is given, it is error to give the usual cautionary instruction as to the weight and credibility to be given to defendant's testimony, telling them, among other things, to take into consideration the fact that he is the defendant and on trial, for several reasons: *first*, it is a palpable comment on the evidence; *second*, it is violative of the principle that the mere fact that defendant is charged with a crime is no evidence of his guilt; *third*, similar instructions have always been adjudged erroneous in civil cases, and for the reason that liberty or life is more valuable than property, it should be likewise held to be prejudicial in a prosecution for a crime; *fourth*, the statute (Sec. 5242, R. S. 1909) which is supposed to authorize it and which provides that when defendant offers himself as a witness, the fact that he is the defendant "may be shown for the purpose of affecting the credibility of such witness," merely lays down a rule of evidence and cannot be regarded as justifying the giving of an instruction which specifically singles out and designates the credence to be given any particular one among those the statute renders competent as witnesses; and, *fifth*, while there may be cases, such as upon a plea of guilty, in which such an instruction may be considered harmless, in most cases, especially where the State's case upon material issues is inherently weak, it does harm to give it. *Held*, by REVELLE, J., that, while the instruction should never be given, it does not constitute reversible error where there is, as in this case, no doubt of defendant's guilt. *Held*, by FARIS, J., dissenting, that, while conceding some of the reasons given for the impropriety of the instruction to be sound, and that the giving of it subserves no useful purpose, it is nevertheless buttressed by a solemn statute (Sec. 5242, R. S. 1909) and has for more than forty years been held not to be reversible error, and to now hold it to be such would (1) cause much uncertainty in the law, and (2) if it is to be eliminated that should be done by the Legislature; and (3) the instruction but expresses the law as declared by the statute, and it cannot of itself be reversible error to tell the jury by an instruction what the law is.

Appeal from Buchanan Circuit Court.—*Hon. Thomas F. Ryan,* Judge.

REVERSED AND REMANDED.

G. L. Zwick for appellant.

(1) The court erred in submitting the case to the jury and in failing to instruct the jury to find the defendant not guilty, which instruction was asked by defendant at the close of the State's case, because the evidence was not sufficient to establish the contract of marriage. State v. Heed, 57 Mo. 252; State v. Reeves, 97 Mo. 668; State v. Eckler, 106 Mo. 593; State v. Long, 238 Mo. 393; State v. Bruton, 253 Mo. 361. (2) The court erred in failing to fully cover all the law in the case in the instructions given for that the evidence of the defense as to previous acts of intercourse was entirely ignored. Clemons v. Seba, 131 Mo. App. 378; State v. Patterson, 88 Mo. 93; State v. Wheeler, 94 Mo. 252; State v. Fogg, 206 Mo. 712; State v. Long, 257 Mo. 225; Staples v. State, 175 S. W. (Tex.) 1056; Humphrey v. State, 143 S. W. (Tex.) 641. (3) The court erred in permitting the prosecuting attorney to make improper and prejudicial remarks in his opening address to the jury as to defendant's failure and refusal to marry prosecutrix after the alleged seduction and in allowing him to repeat such remarks during the argument at the close of the case. 35 Cyc. 1335; State v. Spivey, 191 Mo. 112; State v. Bobbst, 131 Mo. 338; State v. Upton, 130 Mo. App. 316; State v. Graves, 95 Mo. 510; State v. Leaver, 171 Mo. App. 376; State v. Wellman, 253 Mo. 302; State v. Schneiders, 259 Mo. 330; Cook v. People, 2 Thompson & C. 404; State v. Good, 46 Mo. App. 515; State v. Webb, 254 Mo. 434; State v. Hyde, 234 Mo. 256; State v. Clancy, 225 Mo. 654; State v. Elmer, 115 Mo. 401; State v. Fischer, 124 Mo. 464; State v. Ulrich, 110 Mo. 365; State v. Young,

99 Mo. 666; State v. Jackson, 95 Mo. 623. (4) Instruction number 2 should have required the jury to find that prosecutrix was of previous chaste character; or, at least, that she was honestly pursuing the path of virtue at the time instead of merely that she was "of good repute." State v. Howard, 175 S. W. 58; State v. Wheeler, 94 Mo. 252; State v. Marshall, 137 Mo. 467; People v. Weinstock, 140 N. Y. S. 453; State v. Primm, 98 Mo. 368. (5) Instruction number 3 is erroneous in not attempting to define what is meant by "corroboration," and, further, in being a comment upon the evidence by suggesting that defendant had admitted to other parties that he was engaged to prosecutrix, when there was no evidence of such an admission. State v. Reeves, 97 Mo. 674; State v. Chyo Chiagk, 92 Mo. 416. (6) The court erred in admitting incompetent, irrelevant and immaterial testimony offered on the part of the State and objected to by defendant.

John T. Barker, Attorney-General, and *Lewis H. Cook* for the State.

(1) The trial judge followed the approved instructions in the case of State v. Meals, 184 Mo. 244. The court did not fail to instruct the jury as to the meaning of corroborative evidence and the weight of corroborative evidence required under the law in cases of this character. State v. Meals, 184 Mo. 244; State v. Fogg, 206 Mo. 696. Instruction number 2, while it does not specifically tell the jury that previous acts of intercourse on part of prosecutrix with other persons would entitle the defendant to an acquittal, yet requires the jury to find prosecutrix of good repute in the neighborhood, and that is all that is required by the law and that is the only issue raised by the statute. State v. Walker, 232 Mo. 252. (2) Samuel Jeffries stated that the defendant "seemed to treat her as his

sweetheart and seemed to think lots of her," and at
another point in his testimony stated "she didn't seem
to care for anyone else," "she didn't seem to care for
any other company and didn't go with anyone else."
These utterances were made in connection with a detailed statement by him of the actions of prosecutrix
and defendant, and while it may be that such statements were mere conclusions of the witness, yet when
made in connection with a detailed statement of the
actions of the parties showing upon what he based
his conclusion, they could not have been prejudicial
to the defendant. Hunter v. Briggs, 254 Mo. 28; Lee
v. Lee, 258 Mo. 612. (3) The court should not have
sustained the demurrer to the evidence offered at the
close of the State's testimony, assigning as a reason
therefor that there was no corroborative evidence of
the engagement of marriage or promise of marriage as
testified to by prosecutrix. State v. Long, 257 Mo. 199;
State v. Sublett, 191 Mo. 163; State v. Salts, 263 Mo.
304. (4) Defendant complains that the court erred
in the argument of the case when he permitted Mr.
Sherman, the assistant prosecuting attorney, over the
objection of the defendant, to argue before the jury
that the prosecuting witness begged him to marry her.
Those remarks were not preserved in the record, and
if ever made, are not before this court. Mr. Sherman's
remarks were not preserved, nor were they later
proved in a manner that would place them properly in
the record. It is true defendant's attorney made affidavit that such remarks were made, and the State's
attorney also made an affidavit concerning said remarks, but such affidavits prove nothing. They accompany this bill of exceptions but are not a part thereof.
This assignment of error, therefore, is not bottomed on
anything that appears in the record; hence, on this
point, there is nothing before the court for review.
State v. Feeley, 194 Mo. 315; State v. McAfee, 148

Mo. 380; State v. Feeley, 194 Mo. 740; State v. Valle, 196 Mo. 34. In his opening statement the assistant prosecuting attorney told the jury that prosecutrix, after her conception, had begged the defendant to marry her. There was no evidence offered to prove the specific statements complained of. Were such remarks proper? If they were not proper, were they prejudicial? We have been unable to find a case in which the propriety of such remarks has been decided, and we therefore can only leave the question to this court. This court has been loath to reverse judgments on account of improper remarks of attorneys in the argument when the proof is clear, for the reason that in such cases a verdict of guilty would have been returned regardless of the improper remarks. State v. Dietz, 235 Mo. 332; State v. Harvey, 214 Mo. 403; State v. Church, 199 Mo. 605; State v. Hibler, 149 Mo. 478; State v. Summar, 143 Mo. 220; State v. Levy, 262 Mo. 193. "If the case was a close one, and the conviction rested upon testimony that was unsatisfactory, we might consider this point as worthy of serious consideration, for as we said in the cases of State v. Hess, 240 Mo. 160; State v. Horton, 247 Mo. 657; and State v. Baker, 246 Mo. 376, the misconduct of a public prosecutor will be weighed in connection with the facts of each case, and when the State's case is weak it will require less misconduct on the part of the prosecutor to work a reversal than where, as in this case, the evidence of defendant's guilt is very strong." State v. Helton, 255 Mo. 183. Courts of other jurisdiction have recognized that a misstatement of the evidence in the opening statement by the State's attorney is not as serious and as prejudicial to the defendant's rights as improper remarks in the closing argument. People v. Bleason, 127 Cal. 323; Reynolds v. State, 147 Ind. 3; State v. Todd, 110 Iowa, 631; State v. Carins, 124 Mich.

616; People v. Milks, 55 N. Y. App. Div. 372; People v. Chalmers, 5 Utah, 201; 12 Cyc. 568.

BLAIR, J.—In the circuit court of Buchanan County, Homer Evans was convicted of seducing Ruby Jeffries under promise of marriage, sentenced to three years in the penitentiary, and has appealed. Prosecutrix fixes the date of the first illicit act as November 24, 1912, and testifies the only other instance of the kind was upon December 14 of the same year. She was born November 6, 1892, and is one year younger than appellant. She lived with her parents, and, a quarter of a mile away, appellant lived with his sisters and widowed mother, near Saxton, Missouri. The two were reared thus near each other and attended the same public school for some time. Prosecutrix at the age of sixteen or seventeen began to attend the high school at St. Joseph, six miles from her home, and boarded there with her aunt. She attended school at St. Joseph three years.

There is no direct evidence tending to corroborate prosecutrix as to a promise of marriage, and she, herself, does not testify to a formal proposal of marriage and a like acceptance by her. She testified she attended school with appellant and "always went with him," but was not allowed to "keep company with him" until she was eighteen, which was November 6, 1910; that while she was in school in St. Joseph, appellant worked there and would meet her at the train when she came from home, and that he took her to church sometimes, but that she was not allowed to go to any other places because she was in school; that in 1910, at appellant's request, she promised to "go with him after she was eighteen" and "go with no one else" except when her father and mother wanted her to do so, "only when it was necessary." She testified concerning appellant, that "when we were going to school,

he said we would be married some day and how nice
it would be when I was old enough, and we would not
be married now, but go together and have a good time,
for when we were married we would have to settle
down and think of something else.'' This last was
prior to 1910. As to what occurred upon the occasion
on which she, on the trial, testified they became engaged in August, 1911, she said: ''In August, 1911, we
had gone to church at Walnut Grove and coming home
he was telling me, you should consider yourself engaged now, and not go with anyone else, and I promised him I would not go with anyone else if I could
avoid it. I never went with anyone else only when it
was necessary. So we were engaged the first Sunday
in August, 1911,'' and, she continued, ''so we went together all the time,'' and she follows this by testimony
that appellant began to make improper advances in
August, 1912, assuring her ''it was no harm'' and that
they ''would get married if anything happened.'' She
testifies she repulsed appellant, but the next day he
approached her again, and after that broached the matter every time she was with him. On being further
questioned for the State, she said appellant argued
there was no impropriety in what he asked, since they
were to be married, and said that ''if anything happened'' they would be married right-away, otherwise
they would put it off until they ''were better fixed.''
Upon November 24, 1912, she accompanied appellant
to a place near St. Joseph and for a time occupied a
room with him and submitted to his desires. She
testifies she protested vehemently against going to the
place and against the act itself, but also. testifies she
aided appellant in removing her clothing, corset and
shoes, preparatory to the illicit act. She testified at
the preliminary that she attended to these details herself, but says she was nervous then and was mistaken,
to the extent indicated. She says that appellant on this

occasion made the same arguments he had unsuccess-
fully employed before, as above set forth. Of the
visit to the same place on December 14, 1912, she says
appellant "made her go" despite her strong opposition; that she then told him she would never go to
town with him again, and that she never did so.

On the preliminary examination in August, 1913,
prosecutrix testified the engagement to marry was
entered into after wheat harvest and about threshing
time in 1912, but before November 24, 1912. On the
trial she attributed this discrepancy to the same cause
she assigned for that mentioned above.

On cross-examination she testified she told no one
of her engagement to marry appellant and knew of
no one appellant had told; that appellant did not ask
her parents for her hand, and that she did not tell them
of her engagement because she "was afraid to;" that
appellant gave her no engagement ring, but that he
offered to procure one, which offer she says she declined because she feared her parents, if they saw
the ring, would put an end to her association with appellant.

To bring out the relation between the two she was
asked how often appellant was at her home after she
became eighteen and prior to the date on which she
testified her ruin was accomplished, November 24,
1912. To this she replied: "Two or three times a
week and maybe more. He would come up and play
cards with us, and croquet, and sometimes he took
lunch with us, and whenever I had company I always
invited him.

"Q. How frequently were you together? A. I
saw him almost every day. Q. At those times what
would be the train of his conversation about your relations with each other? A. He would tell me how he
loved me. (Objection.) Q. State what passed between you and defendant at these meetings. A. He

would tell me how nice it would be when we got married and how much he thought of me and how much I thought of him.''

She admitted going out in company with other young men several times after August, 1911, and during October, November and December, 1912, and that she broke a social engagement with another young man in order to accompany appellant to St. Joseph on the occasion of the second visit to "Alex's," December 14, 1912.

The father of prosecutrix testified, in effect, that appellant's attentions to his daughter began in 1910 or 1911, but added that appellant had "always gone with" her since the two went to school together. He was permitted to state that appellant treated prosecutrix "like a sweetheart" and that "he seemed to think a lot of her." He testified he saw the two in each others' company "two or three times a week or more" at his home, adding: "If she had company from the city, or anywhere, she would invite him over." He said appellant would take prosecutrix out in his buggy or automobile "to different places and down to his sister's;" that prosecutrix "did not seem to care for any other company and wouldn't go with any one else;" that "she would turn everybody down for him. It didn't please me, but I seen she thought so much of him and thought I would have to let her have her own way about it."

One other witness, who lived in the vicinity of Saxton, testified she "believed . . . if she remembered right," that appellant escorted prosecutrix to a party at witness's home "one evening." When this occurred does not appear.

The mother, brother and grandfather of prosecutrix testified in the case, but none of them testified or attempted to testify to any circumstance tending to show that the relations between appellant and prosecutrix indicated an engagement to marry. The same thing is true of the numerous other witnesses from the neighborhood who testified in the case.

There is no pretense any date for a wedding was ever set or that any preparations, of any kind, were ever made by prosecutrix or her family, such as usually indicate an approaching wedding. There was no evidence of any gifts of any kind made by one to the other.

The State offered in evidence a card which prosecutrix testified she received through the mail. It is a postal card, mailed some time in 1909. On one side appears the then address of prosecutrix, in St. Joseph, where she was in school, and the initials "H. L. E." Prosecutrix testified the hand writing was that of appellant. The other side of the card bears a picture of a gentleman mailing a card or letter and, in one corner, the printed words, "To My Wife." This card was received by prosecutrix three years before the time the alleged seduction occurred and nearly two years prior to August, 1911, the date she became engaged to appellant, according to her testimony.

In this connection, however, prosecutrix was asked whether she and appellant were engaged when she received the card. An objection was made, and then she was asked to state "what understanding, if any," she had with defendant at the time she received the card. She answered: "When I was going to school he told me not to go with any one else and that we intended to be married, and that when I was eighteen we would be engaged. I was eighteen in 1910 (November 6th). We had always thought lots of one another and we always talked about when we got old enough to go together." On cross-examination prosecutrix testified she received the card in 1909, but was not engaged to appellant until August, 1911. Appellant denied addressing or mailing the card, and said it was done by a kinsman who placed his (appellant's) initials on it as a joke. No other card and no letters or other writings of any sort, sent or received by appellant, were offered or mentioned in evidence.

One Helsel testified he knew and lived near the principals, and that, after gossip had gotten well under way, about the 1st of August, 1913, he jestingly asked appellant "how his boy was;" that appellant said "all right," and asked witness "what would you do if you were in my place?" Witness said he replied: "I would have married the girl or got so far away nobody would ever see me." He says appellant then "said he did promise to marry her and would have, but R. T. [Moddrell] and Tadlock told him not to." Helsel testified appellant did not say when the promise alluded to was made.

Five witnesses testified prosecutrix bore a good reputation prior to the time she charges she was seduced.

She did not advise her parents of her condition until about July 1, 1913, six or seven weeks before the birth of her child. Her father testified he was sick when the information reached him and that he sent for appellant, but appellant did not come. On ruling on an objection to this statement, the trial court said it was competent for the State to show witness sent for appellant and that appellant *refused to go to see him.* There was no evidence how Jeffries' message was sent or what it was, and none that it ever reached appellant. Prosecutrix testified she told appellant of her condition on March 8, 1913. She also testified appellant, in May, 1913, solicited her to go again with him to "Alex's," but that she refused. On neither of these occasions does she claim she reminded appellant of a promise to marry her, nor does she testify she ever did so. The father was also asked concerning a conversation he had with some ladies whom he visited while looking up witnesses. He was asked about what they said about a specified matter affecting appellant, and he answered the question and then added: "From the way they talked about him they had no use for him," the reference being to appellant. The court, on objection being made to this that it was a conclusion, ruled it was competent, saying: "He is stating what she said, not what he said," and directed counsel for the State to "go ahead," which counsel did by asking witness whether that "was the substance of all the conversation that took place," to which the witness replied affirmatively.

Appellant testified in his own behalf. He denied there was ever any promise of marriage; stated that in October, 1912, he was told by R. T. Moddrell that he had had sexual intercourse with prosecutrix on the way home that night from a dance at the Adams' home near Saxton; that subsequently, he, appellant, broached this circumstance to prosecutrix, and that the ensuing conversation resulted in the trip to "Alex's," the place prosecutrix says appellant took her November 24, 1912; that he experienced no difficulty in securing the consent of prosecutrix to the sexual act; and that they visited the same place again December 14, 1912, as testified to by prosecutrix. He also testified prosecutrix never at any time asked him to marry her after she discovered her condition, and he denied telling Helsel he had ever promised to marry prosecutrix. He testified he had taken prosecutrix "to town and automobile riding" and to the homes of the best families in the country about Saxton, and had escorted her to parties and had visited in the Jeffries' home and "had meals there when they had company," and that prosecutrix visited his mother and sisters at their home, and that he and she and his mother and sisters attended gatherings together after December, 1912. In this he is corroborated by prosecutrix. He denied having said in August, 1912, that he had attempted to seduce prosecutrix, but had failed. He was contradicted as to this by one witness.

R. T. Moddrell and Winston Tadlock, young men living in the Saxton neighborhood, cousin and second cousin, respectively, of appellant, both testified they had been intimate with prosecutrix. Moddrell testified to one instance, and Tadlock to a number of them. As to their being in the company of prosecutrix on the occasions they named, Moddrell was corroborated by prosecutrix and other witnesses, and Tadlock was corroborated by prosecutrix as to some of the occasions and contradicted as to the rest. Prosecutrix strongly denied any improper relations with either of them or any other person except appellant. Moddrell testified he told appellant in October, 1912, of his experience with prosecutrix. There was testimony that both Moddrell and Tadlock had made statements out of court inconsistent with material portions of their testimony on the trial, and there were some inconsistencies in their testimony as given in the case. There was evidence tending to show Tadlock's reputation for truth, veracity and morality was bad, that as to the last mentioned quality being slight. There was as much testimony that his reputation was good. It appeared in evidence that Moddrell and Tadlock had taken considerable interest in appellant's behalf, and had each made an affidavit, for the use of the prosecuting attorney, stating their illicit relations with prosecutrix. There was evidence they had been led to believe this would result in a dismissal of the prosecution. Some inconsistencies between Tadlock's testimony and his affidavit were called to his attention, and he made explanations which had a tendency to harmonize them.

There was evidence tending to prove circumstances having a strong tendency to show that prosecutrix had been guilty of unchastity with one Opplinger in October, 1912. This individual was visiting in Saxton at the time, but lived in another State. As to the opportunity, the facts are indisputable. The testimony as to the circumstance which would practically convict prosecutrix outright was that of Moddrell.

George Thompson testified that in the summer or fall of 1912 he came upon prosecutrix, in the dusk of evening, in a compromising position near the roadside with a young man who was unknown to him. He was unable to describe the stranger, except as to size, and testified he had never seen him before and had not seen him since. He declared prosecutrix and her companion did not seem abashed but "grinned" at him. Prosecutrix denied all this.

There was some evidence that prosecutrix indulged in vulgar language and in unmaidenly conduct in the presence of men. This was chiefly supported by Tadlock's testimony.

Evidence tending to show prosecutrix, during the fall of 1912, went to various places with others than appellant was offered. Four or five young men figured on her social calendar, to some extent, during this time.

Appellant's mother testified that after the condition of prosecutrix was discovered by her parents and the talk began, she, the witness, was sent for by them and went to the Jeffries home and was there informed of the matter and, among other things, she asked prosecutrix in the presence of her parents, whether appellant promised to marry her, and that prosecutrix answered he had not; that then she asked prosecutrix "why she did it," and prosecutrix replied she "didn't know;" that the following morning prosecutrix and her mother came to the home of witness and in the conversation she asked the same questions and received the same answers. As to this second conversation she was corroborated by one of her daughters and by appellant, and was contradicted as to both occasions by prosecutrix and her mother, though not as to the fact that there were conversations at the times mentioned and not as to their presence. The father of prosecutrix also contradicted the witness as to the first conversation. There was no testimony, however, that prosecutrix claimed a promise of marriage on these occasions. Her mother testified prosecutrix wept, but said nothing at all.

In his opening statement counsel for the State, over appellant's objections, was permitted to say: "The young girl who was wronged by this young man has solicited him, and begged him and importuned him . . . (Objections) . . . has begged him to marry her . . . to give this bright little baby a father and a name. We will show that he has at all times and still refuses to become the husband of this little girl that he has wronged, and the father of this little baby that he has brought into the world."

During the argument to the jury by counsel for the State, appellant's counsel said: "I object to the statement that this girl begged the defendant to marry her; there is no testimony that she ever said anything except on the eighth day of March to him on the subject." The court said the jury was capable of determining which of counsel was correct, and then told the jury to decide the case from the testimony, not from the argument.

I. Appellant contends it was error to permit counsel for the State, in the opening statement and during the argument to the jury, to make the remarks which appear in the statement of the case. The learned Attorney-General insists that the matter objected to in the argument to the jury at the close of the case cannot be reviewed, for the reason that it was not properly preserved in the bill of exceptions, and that the attempt to preserve it in the affidavits is futile. In so far as the rule is applicable, this contention is correct. It does not cover the

Remarks of Counsel.

whole matter, however. During the argument of the
case by counsel for the State counsel for appellant
made this objection: "I object to the statement that
this girl begged the defendant to marry her; there is
no testimony that she ever said anything except on the
8th day of March to him on the subject." The court
said: "The jury heard the testimony and are capable
of deciding which statement is correct, Judge Strop's
or yours. Gentlemen of the jury you will decide the
case from the testimony as you remember it, and not
from the argument of counsel." Defendant excepted.
The reiteration in counsel's objection of the language
objected to, coupled with the ruling of the court, which,
by clear implication, concedes the correctness of the
recitation, in the objection, of the argument of counsel
for the State sufficiently preserves the argument in so
far as it is stated in the objection. This identical question was presented by the briefs in State v: Newcomb,
220 Mo. l. c. 57, and this court nevertheless ruled on the
objection to the argument, and rightly so. The record
shows the objectionable language was stated by appellant's counsel, as that used by counsel for the State,
that the trial court understood it so and ruled on the
matter on its merits. This portion of the argument
and the portion of the opening statement objected to,
as heretofore set out, are before us and will be considered together.

It is settled law that argument of counsel, when
objection is made, will be examined in the light of the
facts of the particular case.

In State v. Horton, 247 Mo. l. c. 666, BROWN, J.,
pointed out the reasons why those concerned in prosecutions, particularly of this kind, should perform their
duties "with scrupulous fairness;" and in State v.
Levy, 262 Mo. l. c. 193, it was said, in considering an
opening statement to which objection had been made:
"If the case was a very close one, and the conviction
rested upon testimony that was unsatisfactory, we-

might consider this point as worthy of serious consideration, for as we said" (in cited cases) "the misconduct of a public prosecutor will be weighed in connection with the facts of each case, and when the State's case is weak, it will require less misconduct on the part of the prosecutor to work a reversal than where . . . the evidence of defendant's guilt is very strong."

In State v. Helton, 255 Mo. l. c. 183, it was said: "Improper arguments are a class of errors unto themselves, and no hard-and-fast rule can be laid down by which their vicious effects shall be measured. When the evidence of guilt is overwhelming and the verdict is not unusually severe, it is difficult to say that the improper remarks produced any harmful effect . . . Quite a different rule arises in cases like the one at bar, where the evidence . . . is meager and unconvincing, and the prosecutor undertakes to secure a conviction by arousing prejudice in the minds of the jury through the use of epithets and other improper argument."

Under the statute (Sec. 4478, R. S. 1909) under which this prosecution was instituted, if appellant had married prosecutrix before the jury was sworn that would have barred his further prosecution; but no *offer* to marry prosecutrix would have aided him. Evidence of such an offer would not have been admissible even to mitigate the punishment. [State v. O'Keefe, 141 Mo. l. c. 273; State v. Brandenburg, 118 Mo. l. c. 185 et seq.] He could not show he had offered to marry prosecutrix and she had refused him. The fact, however, if it had been a fact, that she demanded of him the fulfillment of the promise under which she testifies her ruin was accomplished would, in view of her professed affection, have placed her before the jury in the light of acting according to the natural instincts of a woman wronged under a promise of marriage. The fact that she did not make any such demand, which appears clearly from this record, is one of the circumstances tending strongly to impeach her testimony that there was a promise of marriage.

In view of the rule announced by the cases cited, a recapitulation of some of the facts is warranted.

Prosecutrix testifies she told appellant of her condition March 8, 1913; that in May, 1913, he solicited her to revisit "Alex's;" that he visited her home, to play cards, after March 8, 1913; that she saw him and was with him, in the company of others, frequently after November 24, 1912, and prior to August, 1913; that she saw him at his home in about July 1, 1913; but she does not testify that on any occasion she ever referred to a promise of marriage in his presence. Her condition was the reason and theme of the conversation between her parents and appellant's mother in June, 1913, as it was of the conversation at appellant's home the following day, and on this last occasion she talked, or had an opportunity to talk with appellant, but she does not pretend she demanded, claimed or suggested reparation on the ground of any promise of marriage. Her mother's testimony is positive she did not do so. Even on the trial she does not testify to an unequivocal promise and a like acceptance by her, and on the preliminary examination her testimony was less satisfactory in this respect. On the trial she contradicted her testimony before the justice of the peace as to the time, place and circumstances of the origin of the engagement she asserted. The first appearance of her claim that a promise of marriage existed seems to have been at the time she commenced this prosecution.

In the light of all the circumstances, her failure to demand of appellant that he keep the promise she testifies he made, was a matter for the grave consideration of the jury. We do not mean to say that a demand of marriage by her was essential to the State's case, but simply that on a record showing the facts stated and indicating a claim of her continued affection and disclosing no obstacle to marriage which would explain her silence, the failure of prosecutrix to demand of appellant such reparation, as a fulfillment of his alleged promise would have given, is a fact of much importance upon the question of the truth of her testimony.

Whether or not it was the intent, the probable effect of the remarks objected to, was to break the force of this significant omission. The opening statement was inflammatory and argumentative. It was not a simple statement of expected proof to say the State would show prosecutrix "solicited, begged, importuned" appellant to marry her and that he had "refused at all times and still refuses" to marry the "little girl he had wronged" and give a name "to this litle baby he brought into the world." There is absolutely nothing in the evidence offered tending to warrant such a forecast, and it is hardly conceivable counsel for the State could have been ignorant that the testimony of the prosecutrix and her mother would furnish complete refutation of these statements. To follow such an opening statement with an argument to the jury in which the same unfounded declarations were repeated, indicates that, absent evidence on a vital point, counsel supplied the want with repeated and unchecked assertion.

We do not regard as important the fact that the name of one of counsel, as the offender, appears in the record in connection with the closing argument and that of another appears in the motion for new trial. The substance of the matter is that certain argument was objected to, and the objection to the same argument, so far as its substance, and even language, is concerned was preserved in the motion. The course pursued by counsel constituted reversible error.

II. It was error to permit the father of prosecutrix to state his conclusions and give his opinions as to the relations between appellant and prosecutrix. He had stated some facts concerning their association, and it is

Conclusions and Opinions.

suggested this made his opinions competent. Cases involving the issue of mental incapacity are cited. Such decisions are obviously inapplicable. Other dedecisions are placed before us. In Eyerman v. Sheehan, 52 Mo. l. c. 223, the question was the value of certain broken stone in place in a reservoir in the construction of which it had been used. It was shown that accurate measurement was impossible, and witnesses who had been employed in constructing the reservoir and had "ample data upon which to make their estimate" were•permitted to give an estimate of the average depth of the broken stone used. The court said: "The general rule is that witnesses must state facts, and not their individual opinions, but there are exceptions . . . When the subject of inquiry is so indefinite and general in its nature as not to be susceptible of direct proof, the opinions of witnesses are admissible. If the witness has had the means of personal observation, and the facts and circumstances upon which he bases this conclusion are incapable of being detailed so intelligently as to enable any one but the observer himself to form an intelligent conclusion from them, he may *add* his opinion. A witness who is such an expert may state facts and give his estimate of the work upon the facts detailed."

In State v. Ramsey, 82 Mo. l. c. 137, a murder case, it was held that a witness might be permitted to state that the slain man, just after the first interchange of blows, "looked scared" and "looked as if he wanted to get away." The court held the testimony admissible on the authority of Wharton on Crim. Ev., sec. 751, wherein it is said: "Evidence that defendant was confused, embarrassed, or under the influence of terror is receivable."

In State v. Buchler, 103 Mo. l. c. 206, 207, prosecution for felonious assault, it was held proper to admit testimony that the expression on defendant's countenance was "anger, ferocity, vulgar hate." The court said: "A person of ordinary understanding could not detail facts which would. give to a jury the remotest idea of the passions expressed on the countenance, though a child one year old would distinguish anger from love in its mother's face. Witnesses are allowed to testify to their impressions or opinions on such matters, for want of any other way to get the evidence before the jury; they admit of no more definite proof."

This rule is not applicable in this case. Jeffries' statement that appellant *treated* prosecutrix like a sweetheart discloses a mere conclusion from acts of defendant, and it does not appear these are unsusceptible of proof. That appellant "seemed to think a good deal of her" is clearly the inference drawn from observation of acts of appellant. The same is true as to what witness said prosecutrix "seemed to do."

These are conclusions, pure and simple. Manifestly, they do not fall within the rule of the cases from which we have quoted. The testimony was erroneously admitted.

III. Jeffries' conclusion, drawn from the conversation of some ladies to whom he talked before the trial, that "from the way they talked about him" (appellant) "they had no use for him," was not competent evidence. It was volunteered by the witness. No motion to strike out was made, and the usual rule is that, in such circumstances, such a motion is a prerequisite to a review of such matter. In this instance, however, the trial court, on the objection made, ruled on the point on its merits, despite the fact the approved method, by motion to strike out, had not been employed in raising the question. The justification of any method of procedure of this character is found in its results. The rule as to the employment of motions to strike out incompetent testimony volunteered, arises out of the fact such mo-

Opinions of Others.

tions present the point made sharply to the court and draw his attention and ruling to the very matter of which complaint is made. In this instance, the objection served the purpose, called the matter specifically to the court's attention, and elicited a ruling on the point on its merits. We think it preserved the question for review. The testimony was clearly inadmissible.

IV. The admission of the postal card is said to constitute error. Ordinarily, letters, cards and like

Prior Writings. missives, interchanged by the principals, are admissible for what they are worth. This card was received by prosecutrix about two years before August, 1911, the date she says she became engaged to appellant, and over three years prior to the date of her downfall. It contains a picture and three printed words. In no event could it be relied upon as corroborative of the promise of marriage, since there was, outside of the testimony of prosecutrix, no foundation laid for its introduction in evidence. [State v. McCaskey, 104 Mo. l. c. 647; State v. Davis, 141 Mo. l. c. 525.] Its worth as evidence of the relations between the parties is practically nothing, because (1) it was received two years before the engagement, and (2) it is inherently weak in character. The rule, ordinarily applied, is stated in State v. Walker, 232 Mo. l. c. 263, 264. However, in view of the circumstances, if this case is retried and the postal card is in evidence and the record made is like this one, the trial court should confine its evidentiary use to questions independent of corroboration of the marriage promise.

V. It cannot be disputed that, in the absence of some showing that the message reached and was under-

Remark of Court. stood by appellant, the remark of the trial judge in ruling on Jeffries' testimony that he sent for appellant was objectionable as assuming, before the jury, that appellant "refused to

go" to see Jeffries. However, no objection was made
to the remark or exception to it saved. The exception
saved, we think the record shows, was directed to the
ruling as applied to the question preceding the remark.
Further, the motion for new trial does not refer to the
matter or contain any ground broad enough to include
it.

VI. Helsel's testimony was concerning an admission made by appellant, eight months after the alleged
seduction, that "he did promise to
Admission
of Promise. marry" prosecutrix. Helsel stated appellant did not say when this promise
was made. Testimony showing a very similar admission was held sufficient corroboration in State v. Phillips, 185 Mo. l. c. 187, 188. In somewhat similar circumstances, a like rule was approved in State v. Sublett, 191 Mo. l. c. 170, 172, 173. This evidence was undoubtedly sufficient as an admission if it constituted an
admission of a promise made prior to the seduction;
otherwise, it amounted to nothing. The promise of
marriage must precede the seduction. [State v. Eisenhour, 132 Mo. 140.] On the authority of the cases first
cited, the testimony was admissible, and, in itself, sufficient corroboration of the marriage promise. Speaking for himself, the writer is of the opinion there is
nothing in the language used or in the evidence anywhere upon which a jury could reasonably determine
whether the promise said to have been admitted was
made before or after the seduction, and that the testimony was inadmissible, and the instruction which indicated corroboration might be found from admissions
alone, having in this particular no other support than
Helsel's testimony, was in this respect erroneous. In
a close case corroboration should be strong, and the
rule in State v. Teeter, 239 Mo. l. c. 488, ought to be applied here upon this phase of the case.

VII. For the reasons given in State v. Mintz, 245 Mo. l. c. 542 et seq., it was, in the writer's ópinion, error to give the instruction, commonly given the jury concerning the weight to be given a defendant's testimony, to take into consideration the fact he was the defendant. In the case cited a somewhat different question was presented, but most of the reasons given there are applicable here. The usual general instruction on the credibility of witnesses was given in this case. That applied to appellant with the rest. The other instruction referred to is such a palpable comment on the weight of the evidence and so clearly violative of the principle that the mere fact defendant is charged with crime is no evidence of his guilt, that it is too obviously erroneous to require discussion. When a few dollars, instead of a man's life or liberty, are involved, this court does not tolerate an instruction of the kind. [Stetzler v. Railroad, 210 Mo. l. c. 713, 714.]

Weight of Defendant's Testimony: Usual Instruction.

The decisions dealing specifically with the instruction given in this case, from the time of its first appearance here, State v. Maguire, 69 Mo. 197, until to-day, generally concede, expressly or by implication, that the instruction is not invulnerable, but hold, in a way, that it is harmless. That suggestion finds its complete answer in the reason given for holding erroneous, analogous instructions affecting the testimony of a party in a civil case. It is a plain and unquestionable comment on the weight of defendant's testimony. One reason advanced in support of the instruction is that the statute rendering defendants in criminal cases competent as witnesses (Sec. 5242, R. S. 1909) provides that when a defendant offers himself as a witness, the fact that he is the defendant "may be shown for the purpose of affecting the credibility of such witness." The writer is of the opinion that what is said of this particular suggestion in State v. Mintz, supra, l. c. 545, furnishes the answer to the argument mentioned. "In truth the statute, so far as now pertinent, merely lays down a rule of evidence and cannot be said to authorize giving a specific instruction as to the credence to be accorded any of those whom it renders competent as witnesses. It has no more of such efficacy than has any other rule admitting impeaching evidence, whether such rule emanates from a legislative or common-law source."

To hold the statute warrants this instruction is to hold that a mere legislative declaration of a rule as to the admission of an impeaching fact as evidence warrants a specific comment on that evidence by instruction to the jury. It is not possible to admit the correctness of this instruction without extending the practice to include all other legislative declarations of similar character, and there is no logical defense for discriminating, in this connection, between rules made by the Legislature and those of like kind which come from any other source. At any rate it could not be denied, if the argument based upon the clause quoted from section 5242, supra, is sound, that reason must require a like effect to be given to that provision in section 6354, Revised Statutes 1909, which renders competent parties to civil actions and expressly provides that the fact one is such a party "may be shown for the purpose of affecting his credibility." Neither does the legislative requirement that the court *shall* instruct the jury, etc., in criminal cases affect the matter. That mandate requires *instructions, on the law of the case, not comments on evidence.* Further, the duty of a court to instruct in a criminal case, "whether requested or not," is no greater than its duty to instruct in a civil case when *requested* to do so. If the argument based upon the command to instruct is sound and warrants the giving the instruction being considered, it must follow that a like instruction must be given as to parties testifying in civil cases when such an instruction is asked. Consequently, the command of the statute that the court shall instruct the jury in criminal cases in nowise creates any condition which warrants a distinction between the rule, so far as concerns the instruction under consideration, applicable in such cases and that applicable in civil cases.

Possibly there are cases in which no harm is done defendant by giving such an instruction as that being considered. The writer is unable to conceive such a case unless the accused pleads guilty. However, assume such a thing can be; in such a case the judgment ought not to be reversed on account of the instruction. This is so manifestly *not* a case of that kind that it needs no argument to show it.

In this case, therefore, it is the opinion of the writer that we should at least hold that in a case like this, in which the State's case is possessed of so much inherent weakness, the instruction is reversible error. Otherwise, we permit the State to supply its lack of convincing evidence by securing from the judge an adverse comment on defendant's testimony, which comment is based upon a practical assumption of the very guilt which is the subject of inquiry.

VIII. On the subject of corroboration, the rules of law are clearly established, and we need not go into

Corroboration.

a further discussion of the matter. There is no impropriety in saying, however, that the instructions should be drawn in such manner as to give the appellant full protection in this connection, and that the jury should be cautioned against a finding of corroboration from circumstances as easily referable to some other relationship of the parties as to an existing engagement to marry. [State v. Charles Spears, 183 S. W. 311.] Neither should the instruction leave any doubt the promise relied upon must have been an existing one and that a promise conditioned upon pregnancy resulting would not suffice.

The testimony of prosecutrix warrants an instruction upon this theory. Further, in the circumstances of this case, there should be given an explicit instruction upon the effect of previous illicit relations with other men. [State v. Patterson, 88 Mo. 88.] The correct rule may be reasoned out from the instructions given, but an express statement of it is fairer in a case disclosing the weaknesses apparent in this.

The judgment is reversed and the cause remanded. *Woodson, C. J.*, and *Graves, J.*, concur; *Bond, J.*, concurs in the result; *Faris, J.*, concurs in a separate opinion; *Revelle, J.*, dissents in opinion filed; *Walker, J.*, absent.

FARIS, J. (concurring except in paragraph seven)—I concur in the result of the able opinion of my learned brother BLAIR in this case, but I cannot consent to characterize the giving of the cautionary instruction as to the weight and credibility of the evidence of defendant as reversible error. So, I dissent to what is said on this question in paragraph 7 of Judge BLAIR's opinion. I do this because the unsettling of this question would cause much uncertainty and result in the reversal of many cases unnecessarily. Aside from the statute, infra, I concede the logic of his arguments, and admit the existence of a different rule in civil cases. But this question has been settled in this State for almost forty years (State v. Maguire, 69 Mo. l. c. 202, decided in 1878), and as the settlement thereof, as unanimously ruled by Division Two of this court and evidenced by dozens of rulings, *is well buttressed by a solemn statute* (Sec. 5242, R. S. 1909), it ought not to be disturbed. If this ruling is to be disturbed it is plainly the duty of the Legislature to create the disturbance by an amendment to said section 5242. For in view of the fact that such an instruction is comparatively innocuous, since it but tells the jury that they may do the identical thing which they would do without being told, no sufficient reason would seem to exist for our amending this section by judicial construction.

In the fairly recent case of State v. Shaffer, 253 Mo. l. c. 338, Division Two, discussing this identical question, unanimously said:

"It is also contended by defendant that the court erred in giving instructions numbered 3 and 4, which we have set out in the statement, and which deal with the weight and credibility of the testimony of the defendant and that of defendant's wife. Learned counsel cite us to a very late holding in a civil case, that of Benjamin v. Railroad, 245 Mo. 598, in which suit a similar comment upon the testimony of the plaintiff was held to be error. We have no fault to find with the holding of the court in that case. But learned counsel overlook the fact that the statute itself in conferring upon the defendant and defendant's spouse the right to testify, has seen fit to limit such right by permitting a showing of the fact that the witness is the defendant and on trial, and the fact of marriage to the spouse offered as a witness, for the purpose of affecting the credibility of either or both of them. [Sec. 5242, R. S. 1909.] We have no such statute touching the testimony of a plaintiff in a civil case, or of a defendant in such case; hence the difference between the two holdings. If the statute permits the showing of the fact of interest on account of the witness being a defendant or the spouse of a defendant, why may not the jury be likewise advised of the existence of the law applicable to such status by an appropriate instruction? We concede, however, that there is not much excuse for the giving of such instructions as these where the court instructs generally as to the credibility of witnesses and as to the fact that the interest of any witness or witnesses in the case may be considered by the jury for the purpose of affecting the credibility of such witness. But while these instructions have been

many times given, and while in the view of the writer
they ought not to be given, yet when we consider the
statute which we cite above, and when we have reference to the many holdings of this court that the giving
of instructions such as these do not constitute reversible error, we are not disposed to go farther than to say,
as has been many times said before by this court, that
in our view the giving of such instructions as these subserves no useful purpose, and would as well be omitted
and the labor of preparing the same saved. Similar
instructions have been before us in many cases. [State
v. Napper, 141 Mo. l. c. 407; State v. Fox, 148 Mo. 517;
State v. Dilts, 191 Mo. 673; State v. McDonough, 232
Mo. 219; State v. Lingle, 128 Mo. 528; State v. Newcomb, 220 Mo. l. c. 66.] And while the giving thereof
has often been criticized as unnecessary, we have not
been able to find a single case reversed on account of
these instructions.''

Brevity would seem to forbid the addition of anything to what was said on this point in the Shaffer case,
supra. But one further apposite thought, suggested by
inference but not fully enlarged on in the Shaffer case,
thrusts itself to the front here: This point is that trial
juries, unlike private citizens, are not governed by the
maxim, *ignorantia legis neminem excusat*. In no
case, barring slander and libel at least, is a jury presumed to know the law. Both by practice and a plain
statute (Sec. 5231, R. S. 1909), trial courts are required
in criminal cases to tell, i. e., *instruct*, the jury what the
law is. Section 5242 being the law by which the jury
must try the case, or to drop into metaphor, being the
section which furnishes the legal scales by which in trying the case, the jury are required to weigh the testimony of the defendant, or that of his or her spouse,
can there be any legal solecism in telling the jury
that such is the law? Is not the court *nisi* but performing a statutory duty in doing so? From what
other source are they permitted to know, or can they

know, that this is law? So, while adhering to all that Division Two of this court said in the Shaffer case as to the logical non-necessity of the instruction *in cases wherein a general instruction on the credibility of the witnesses is given,* I do not think that the occasion calls for the specific branding of this point as reversible error here or elsewhere. I think it should be left where Division Two has left it, that is, to be gradually worked out by the trial courts, in the light of the criticism directed toward it in the Shaffer case, which is after all but a type of many other similar rulings upon this point. [State v. Shaffer, supra; State v. Hyder, 258 Mo. 225; State v. Newcomb, 220 Mo. 1. c. 66; State v. McDonough, 232 Mo. 219; State v. Mintz, 245 Mo. 1. c. 547; State v. Dilts, 191 Mo. 673; State v. Fox, 148 Mo. 517; State v. Napper, 141 Mo. 1. c. 407; State v. Lingle, 128 Mo. 528; State v. Zorn, 71 Mo. 415; State v. McGinnis, 76 Mo. 326; State v. Cook, 84 Mo. 40; State v. Wisdom, 84 Mo. 1. c. 190; State v. Ihrig, 106 Mo. 1. c. 270.] Hence, I concur in the result and in the opinion, barring what is said in paragraph seven.

REVELLE, J. (dissenting)—I. In my opinion the only claim to judicial countenance that the cautionary instruction as to the testimony of a defendant can make, is its old age and gray hairs. It is supported by neither logic nor justice, and, like the proverbial wolf, first found its way into our midst in the guise of a harmless and mistaken thing. It frequently has been the subject of criticism but never of commendation, and I agree that it possesses all the frailties and infirmities that our learned brother BLAIR has so clearly pointed out. It is not only a palpable comment on the weight of defendant's testimony, but is predicated upon a principle inconsistent with the presumption of innocence, and car-

Weight of Defendant's Testimony: Usual Instruction.

ries with it that very inference. If the indictment is no evidence of guilt, and if the defendant is presumed to be innocent, what justification can there be for instructing that he is guilty to such a 'degree as to cast suspicion upon his credibility and require his evidence to be received with caution? I have always understood that the presumption of innocence attends an accused throughout the trial, and for all purposes, and this includes the time and manner of giving instructions. To justly attach the suspicion must we not presume his guilt, because there is no room for this poison in the case of the innocent, and it is contrary to human experience to say that the instruction does not have the effect of creating a suspicion whenever and wherever it is given, and suspicion once aroused is hard to down and likely to extend its fangs to all parts. After giving the general instruction on the credibility of witnesses, and the rule by which their testimony is to be weighed, then to single out the defendant, who presumably is equally innocent with the rest, and admonish the jury to *beware* of what he says, is giving entirely too much prominence to the isolated fact which it is said section 5242, Revised Statutes 1909, permits to be proved; and this is all contrary to the uniform holdings of this court. [State v. Heath, 221 Mo. 1. c. 592; State v. Edwards, 203 Mo. 1. c. 545; McFadin v. Catron, 120 Mo. 1. c. 274; Railroad v. Stockyards, 120 Mo. 1. c. 565; Jones v. Jones, 57 Mo. 1. c. 142; Barr v. Kansas City, 105 Mo. 550.]

In State v. Heath, supra, this court, in discussing a similar proposition, said: "In our opinion this instruction was properly refused. It was nothing more or less than selecting certain isolated facts and undertaking to comment upon them . . . This court has uniformly and repeatedly condemned instructions which undertook to treat of isolated facts which may be developed upon the trial."

In Barr v. Kansas City, supra, l. c. 559, it is said: "The vice of specially calling the attention of the jury to isolated facts or otherwise giving prominence to the facts of the case favorable to one side, while measurably retiring the view of the other side by ignoring it, or presenting it only in general terms, has been frequently condemned by this court. [Sawyer v. Railroad, 37 Mo. l. c. 263; Anderson v. Kincheloe, 30 Mo. l. c. 525; Fine v. Public Schools, 39 Mo. l. c. 67; Rose v. Spies, 44 Mo. l. c. 23; Jones v. Jones, 57 Mo. l. c. 142; Raysdon v. Trumbo, 52 Mo. l. c. 38; Chappell v. Allen, 38 Mo. 213.]" In the same case the court further says: "It is a vicious mode of instruction, trenches upon the province of the jury to weigh all the evidence, without bias or comment from the court."

Besides, the provisions of section 5242, supra, which is said to be responsible for the approval of this instruction, can hardly be said to have any real application to the *person on trial*. This section merely provides that no person shall be incompetent as a witness by reason of being the person on trial, or by reason of being the husband or wife of the accused, but "such fact may be shown for the purpose of affecting the credibility of the witness." In so far as it provides that such "fact may be shown for the purpose of affecting the credibility of witnesses," it can, in its very nature, be applicable only to the husband or wife, as the case may be, of the defendant, and not to the defendant himself, because, without any proof, we know the jury knows the identity of the accused, and when he testifies that he is the person on trial. This they know from the identity of name and things occurring during the proceedings.

The vice of this instruction is clearly apparent in at least certain cases which come before this court. For instance, in cases of rape, we have held that a conviction is warranted on the uncorroborated testimony of a prosecutrix, and while it may be conceded that a *guilty* person on trial has a strong incentive to testify falsely, and that his testimony should be received with caution, we also know that a prosecutrix, in such a case, frequently has an even greater inducement to commit perjury. In such a case where only the prosecutrix testifies to the facts of guilt, and such facts are denied by the defendant, this instruction is usually sufficient to break the scale balance and overcome the presumption of innocence. It casts suspicion upon the defendant and leaves the prosecutrix on a higher and more favorable plane, thus giving greater weight to her testimony.

Notwithstanding the frailties which this instruction possesses, and the somewhat stormy career through which it has passed, trial courts persist in giving it, and it has never yet been held sufficient in this State, to warrant a reversal. While I firmly believe that the instruction should *never* be given, I am of the opinion that there are numerous cases from whose records it appears that the same was not really prejudicial, and, therefore, insufficient to warrant a reversal, but I am further of the opinion that there are many cases where the evidence is so close, and the defendant's guilt so doubtful, or the nature of the trial and conditions such, that the giving of this instruction would change the result, and in such cases the error is of such magnitude that this court *should not hesitate* to hold it ground for reversal.

II. In the instant case I do not agree with the majority opinion as to the disclosures of the record. ___:___. As I have read it I have no such doubt **Non-Prejudicial.** of defendant's guilt or the orderly character of the trial as is indicated by the opinion, and am, therefore, unwilling to reverse the judgment because of this instruction.

III. Neither do I agree that the remarks of State's counsel in his opening statement are sufficient to work a reversal, nor do I think that the alleged closing argument is so preserved as to be open to review. It may be conceded that the opening statement was not warranted by either the law or facts, but, in my opinion, it was not prejudicial. It is but common knowledge and ordinary human experience that no juror will sit through the trial of a seduction case without the thought that the girl, whose shame and disgrace would be lessened by marriage, was anxious to and did what she could to bring about the marriage, and this statement of counsel could only have hastened the thought. Again, it was not prejudicial, because the jury knew the defendant had not married her, and her "importuning and begging" and his refusal to yield, if effective at all, would tend rather to corroborate his statement that he had not promised to marry her than to the contrary.

Remarks of Counsel.

IV. I am also of the opinion that it was not reversible error to permit the father of prosecutrix to make the general statements attributed to him, such as: Appellant treated prosecutrix "like a sweetheart;" "he seemed to think a lot of her." His knowledge and information upon which these alleged conclusions were predicated were completely brought out and developed in evidence, and the jury was in a position and fully capable of determining whether or not such conclusions were warranted. Cross-examination was a complete shield to this alleged vice.

Conclusions of Witness.

But there is another reason why this assignment is without force here. The record discloses that no exceptions were saved to the ruling of the court when this evidence was introduced.

V. Relative to the statement of Jeffries that "from the way they [meaning certain women] had talked about him [appellant] they had no use for him," the record discloses

that this came out in connection with his explanation of certain matters concerning which he had been interrogated on cross-examination. After the statement was made, defendant's counsel merely objected, and at no time requested that the answer be stricken out. We cannot justly anticipate what the trial court would have done had the proper motion been made, nor can we convict it of error in not acting when there was nothing calling for action. The court in ruling, simply directed that they "go ahead," and after this no further reference was made to this subject. I do not think the matter is open to review.

VI. The propositions discussed in paragraphs IV, V and VI are likewise, in my opinion, insufficient to warrant a reversal.

VII. Unless the facts in this case are sufficient to warrant an affirmance, we have judicially committed many grievous and unpardonable sins.

I, therefore, dissent from the majority opinion in this case, and am of the opinion that the judgment should be affirmed.

PARKER-WASHINGTON COMPANY et al., Appellants, v. JAMES R. DENNISON.

In Banc, March 1, 1916.

1. **LIMITATION: Written Promise to Pay.** In order to bring an "action upon any writing . . . for the payment of money or property" it must appear in the statement of the cause of

action that the money sued for is promised to be paid by the language of the writing. If such promise arises only upon proof of extrinsic facts it is barred by the five-year Statute of Limitations.

2. ———: ———: ———: **Bad Faith on Part of Promisor.** The plaintiff being the owner of asphalt used in paving streets in a certain city, and of a plant used in the preparation of asphalt for paving purposes, located in said city, entered into a written contract with defendant whereby defendant agreed to pay plaintiff (1) for the use of said plant, five cents per square yard for all asphalt paving laid under the contract to the extent of forty thousand square yards, and (2) for said asphalt, one-half the amount received for any pavement done by defendant, after deducting all expenses. The defendant was to make bids in good faith to obtain paving contracts from the city. The petition alleged that defendant made no effort in good faith to obtain any such paving contracts, and when he had obtained some such contracts did not perform them and never intended to perform, and never shipped any of the asphalt which had been tendered according to contract, and held the plant for a long time; and that the gain which would have accrued to plaintiff by the payment of said sum of five cents per square yard for all asphalt agreed to be laid by defendant was two thousand dollars, and one half the profits agreed to be paid and delivered to plaintiff was twenty thousand dollars, for which amounts judgment was asked. The suit was not brought within five years. *Held*, that the contract contained a promise to pay money only on condition that the pavement was laid, and the petition on its face alleges that no paving was laid, and therefore it does not state a promise to pay arising out of the words used in the written contract, but stated only a cause of action upon an implied promise arising in law out of the alleged torts of defendants: that such cause of action is not within the statute and was barred in five years.

Held, by WOODSON, C. J., dissenting, that all written contracts calling for things to be done in the future are conditional, and whether they have been performed or not must of necessity be shown by parol testimony; that the contract in suit contained a definite promise in writing to pay two separate sums of money upon its performance; that defendant did not relieve himself from his promise to pay those sums by fraudulently refusing to perform; and that the promise to pay is found in the contract itself, and no evidence *aliunde* is required to show a promise to pay, and hence the five-year Statute of Limitations does not apply.

Appeal from Jackson Circuit Court.—*Hon. Thomas J. Seehorn,* Judge.

AFFIRMED.

Ball & Ryland for appellants.

The action falls within Sec. 1888, R. S. 1909, providing what actions may be brought within ten years, and falls within the first paragraph thereof, "an action upon any writing, whether sealed or unsealed, for the payment of money or property." Miner & Frees v. Howard, 93 Mo. App. 569; Shinn v. Wooderson, 95 Mo. App. 6; Howe v. Mittelberg, 96 Mo. App. 490; Mathis v. Knapp, 45 Mo. 48; Bridges v. Stephens, 132 Mo. 549; Carr v. Thompson, 67 Mo. 476; Curtis v. Sexton, 201 Mo. 217; Ball v. Cotton Press Co., 141 Mo. 26; Knisely v. Leathe, 256 Mo. 341.

Scarritt, Scarritt, Jones & Miller for respondent.

(1) The sole question presented for determination upon this appeal is whether the five or ten-year Statute of Limitations applies to the pending action. The petition was demurred to on the ground that the action was barred within five years after it accrued and this appeal is from the order sustaining the demurrer. (2) If the action is one for the recovery of money or property which the writing pleaded and relied upon, shows upon its face to be due or transferable to the plaintiffs, either expressly or by implication arising from the face of the instrument sued on, although evidence *dehors* the writing sued on may be necessary to discover the amount of the debt, then that action may be commenced within ten years from the time it accrued; but if the cause of action sought to be enforced does not fall within that category, the five-year statute applies to it. Carr v. Thompson, 67 Mo. 472; Menefee v. Arnold, 51 Mo. 536. (3) The

nature of the action as well as the nature of the writing relied upon are both consequential in determining
whether the five-year or ten-year period of limitation
applies. The promise sued on, to pay money or transfer property, must be in writing if the ten-year and
not the five-year period is to be applied; and furthermore, the written promise sued on must be one to
pay money or to transfer property in order that the
ten-year period and not the five-year period shall
apply. Bridges v. Stephens, 132 Mo. 524; Kauz v.
Great Council, 13 Mo. App. 341; State ex rel. v. Brown,
208 Mo. 619. (4) Nowhere in the contract now at bar
did defendants' promise to pay plaintiffs any damages for non-performance of the contract, nor promise to pay them anything under the circumstances expressly shown to exist by the allegations of the petition itself; nor does the petition charge, or contract
show, that defendant promised in writing to pay plaintiffs any damages or any sum upon any contingency
that is alleged to have existed. This action therefore,
comes within section 1889. Gas Light Co. v. St. Louis,
11 Mo. App. 65, 84 Mo. 202; Brady v. St. Joseph, 84
Mo. App. 399; Ash v. Independence, 103 Mo. App.
299; Thomas v. Pacific Beach Co., 115 Cal. 136.

OPINION.

BOND, J.—This is an appeal by plaintiff from a
judgment of the trial court sustaining a demurrer to
defendants' third amended petition, on the ground
that the cause of action therein alleged had accrued
more than five years before the bringing of this suit.
Plaintiff declined to plead further. Its suit was dismissed, from which judgment its appeal was duly
taken to this court, since the amount in dispute ex-
ceeds the pecuniary limit of the jurisdiction of the
Kansas City Court of Appeals.

This case turn on the question, whether the action
is upon a writing for the payment of money or prop-

erty. [R. S. 1909, sec. 1888.] If that is the nature
of the action, then the demurrer interposed below
should have been overruled. The solution of this
question necessitates an interpretation of the petition
setting forth the plaintiffs' cause of action, and the
contract exhibited therewith. The substance of the
petition is, that plaintiffs and defendants entered into
a written contract, on the 9th day of May, 1898, wherein defendants agreed to, and did, purchase sufficient
Trinidad Lake asphalt to construct forty thousand
square yards of asphalt pavement. The price paid
being the cost to plaintiffs on the date of payment
when delivery of the asphalt should be made where it
was located and which was thereafter to be shipped
to Kansas City, where it was to be used by defendants
in laying pavements in said city, after proper preparation at an' asphalt plant owned by plaintiffs in
Kansas City, which it was agreed, should be put in
the possession and control of the defendants up to
September 15, 1898; and in case defendants had not
then obtained contracts for the laying of forty thousand square yards of pavement, then the said plant
was to remain in his possession for such time as necessary, up to November 15, 1898, or later, if such
paving contracts had been obtained, but not fully performed at that date. It was further provided that defendants should give their time to carrying out the
paving contracts and engage in no other business during the existence of said agreement, which should be
ended whenever forty thousand square yards of
asphalt pavement had been laid by defendants; that
they should bid on all such contracts when proposed
to be let, until they were awarded forty thousand
square yards of such paving. The contract between
the parties also restricted the plaintiffs from bidding
against defendants without their consent up to November 15, 1898, unless defendants had sooner gotten
contracts for forty thousand square yards of asphalt

paving. It further provided, that defendants should pay plaintiffs five cents per square yard for all asphalt paving *laid* pursuant to said contract, irrespective of any profit or loss in the matter, and that this payment should not be charged as an item of expense; that upon the completion of the work, the total price received (cash, bonds and special tax bills) should be divided equally, after deducting the actual cost and expense of the work, between plaintiffs and defendants; but in the event of loss, the whole burden thereof should be borne by defendants.

The petition then alleges that although plaintiffs were ready and offered to deliver said asphalt, defendants did not promptly accept and pay for the same, but only did so after the lapse of more than a year, and then failed to transport it to Kansas City and made no bids in good faith to obtain the laying of paving contracts and made no effort to get the confirmation of such contracts as were awarded to them by Kansas City, and never intended to perform any of the contracts which were awarded to them, or for which they submitted bids. The petition concludes, to-wit:

"Plaintiffs state that, while certain of public contracts for street paving were let to the defendants by Kansas City, Missouri, subsequent to the making of the aforesaid contract, said defendants never performed any of said contracts, and never intended or attempted to obtain and perform any contracts for the laying of asphalt pavements in said city; that defendants never shipped any of the asphalt, bought and delivered to them as aforesaid, to Kansas City; that defendants never laid a single yard of asphalt pavement in Kansas City under said contract.

"That had defendants shipped said asphalt to Kansas City as agreed, and had they endeavored to obtain contracts for paving as agreed, they could, and would have had awarded to them and confirmed during the time mentioned and stated in said contract sufficient paving contracts to have laid street pavement to the amount of 100,000 square yards with the asphalt purchased of the plaintiffs, and the failure of defendants so to keep and perform their contract, and to obtain awards and confirmations of contracts, as aforesaid, was solely due to their own neglect, bad faith and default as aforesaid.

"That defendants agreed to keep a complete set of books showing the cost of all material and labor used in and about the carrying out of said contract, but said defendants failed to keep any such account.

"Plaintiffs state that the defendants, under the contract aforesaid, held and controlled for more than a year the plant of the plaintiff, The Parker-Washington Company; that the defendants, as stated, never performed any part of said contract; that the plaintiffs at all times kept and performed their part of said agreement; that finally, and prior to the institution of this suit, the defendants repudiated said agreement and refused to do and perform the same.

"That the gain to plaintiffs, which would have accrued to them by the payment of said sum of five cents per square yard for all asphalt agreed to be laid by defendants under said contract was two thousand dollars, and the value of one-half of the profits in cash and tax bills, agreed to be paid and delivered to plaintiffs as aforesaid, was the sum of twenty thousand dollars.

"Wherefore, plaintiffs pray judgment against the defendants for said sum of twenty-two thousand dollars, with interest from the date of filing this suit at the rate of six per cent per annum."

II.   There are two causes of action alleged in the petition: The one for damages caused to plaintiffs by the alleged fraudulent failure of defendants to procure and perform contracts for street paving, and thereafter to pay to plaintiffs five cents per square yard for forty thousand square yards after that much street paving had been laid. Plaintiffs allege that these omissions prevented a "gain" to them of $2000. The other, for damages in the estimated sum of $20,000 as one-half of what would have been the earnings, if about one thousand tons of asphalt, sold to defendants by plaintiffs, had been properly prepared and laid in the form of street pavements under contracts let to defendants by Kansas City, which defendants fraudulently failed to obtain.

In order to bring an "action upon any writing . . . for the payment of money or property" (R. S. 1909, sec. 1888), it must appear in the statement of the cause of action, that the money or property sued for is *promised* to be paid or given by the language of the writing, and that such promise does not arise only upon proof of extrinsic facts. That nothing else meets the requirements of the statute, has been uniformly held whenever it has been under review. [Curtis v. Sexton, 201 Mo. l. c. 230; Menefee v. Arnold, 51 Mo. 536; Carr v. Thompson, 67 Mo. l. c. 476; Bridges v. Stephens, 132 Mo. l. c. 549 (separate opinion of BARCLAY, J.); Knisely v. Leathe, 256 Mo. l. c. 377.] Does the "promise sued on" in the present action, arise from the *words* of the written contract whose stipulations are recited in the petition? In support of that position, the learned counsel for appellant cites the following paragraphs from their contract with defendants:

"Said second parties shall pay said first parties five cents per square yard for all asphalt paving laid under this contract, said sum being in payment for the use of said plant, and shall be paid by second parties without regard to either profit or loss in the laying of any pavement, and in no event shall be charged as an item of expense.

"Upon the completion of any paving contract the

actual cost and expenses shall be ascertained by said parties, and such amount shall be deducted from the price received in cash, bonds or tax bills at their face, and the balance of such cash, bonds or tax bills shall be divided equally between the parties hereto, but in the event of loss upon any contract such loss shall be borne by said second parties.''

These clauses of the contract show on their face and by express terms, that the only promises to pay any money were: First, a promise to pay five cents per square yard for all asphalt paving *laid* under this contract; and second, a promise to pay one-half of the profits of the paving work after its *completion*. The petition states no asphalt was laid; no paving work was done and no price received for any such work in cash, bonds or tax bills, by defendants. It is clear, therefore, that neither of the conditional promises recited in the two above clauses, ever became absolute obligations on the part of the defendants, for no promise based upon a condition, can be enforced as such, until the contingency upon which it depends has happened. The fact that defendants tortiously prevented the happening of the contingency upon which their contractual obligations would have arisen, cannot be held to make a contract for them contrary to the terms in which their contract was expressed in the written agreement. Such wrongful conduct would constitute a legal basis for an implied assumpsit on their part to pay the damages caused thereby, but it could not alter the terms of the *conditional promise to pay,* as used in the written contract.

The petition alleges bad faith of the defendants in failing to procure lettings of paving contracts, thereby disabling them from performing the work, and thereby disabling plaintiff from enforcing the promise to pay five cents per square yard for forty thousands square yards of asphalt which had been laid in the construction of a pavement, and thereby preventing plaintiffs from enforcing the general promise to pay to them one-half of the net profits of the performance of all completed paving contracts. These allegations of the petition would entitle the plaintiffs to recover damages for the non-performance and breach by defendants of the terms of their written contract. Such a recovery is justified on elementary principles applicable to redress for breaches of contract. But they do not state a cause of action on a written contract to pay money upon certain conditions which never happened. Their whole legal intendment is to set forth a cause of action for damages for a tortious breach of a contract to do certain things, for the doing of which defendants promised to pay money or property to plaintiffs.

Under the contract referred to in the petition, if the defendants had *laid* the pavement, or if defendants had obtained the laying of paving work from Kansas City, and had performed such work and reaped a profit therefrom, and had failed to pay the specific or general sum agreed by them to be paid on said contingencies, then plaintiffs could have sued defendants on the promises to pay contained in their contract, and could have recovered in that action, whatever amount the evidence showed was due. For in that event, the promises to pay made by defendants, would have become consummate by the happening of the condition upon which they were made, and such promises could have been established by the intrinsic evidence of the language of the contract between parties, and would have been a proper foundation for a suit, and it would not have been necessary (as it was in this case), to go outside of the writings and show by evidence *aliunde*, certain tortious acts on the part of defendants as a legal basis of an implied assumpsit to pay the damages thereby caused to plaintiffs.

In the case at bar, the action of plaintiffs is not

based upon the promise to pay five cents per square yard on all the asphalt laid by defendants, nor one-half of the net profits of such work when completed. For if the action had been predicated upon the simple averment of such promises, coupled with the further averment that no asphalt pavement had ever been laid, and no paving business had ever been carried on, then the petition would have been subject to a general demurrer, for the reason, that it showed on its face two *conditional* promises, which had never ripened into legal obligations. To avoid that predicament, it was necessary for the pleader to allege some other ground of liability than the two conditional promises made in the written contract. And this was done in effect, when it was alleged in the petition that by reason of the torts, frauds and negligences of defendants, the contract made by them, and the promises to pay therein expressed, became unenforceable. For upon those allegations the law would imply a promise on the part of the tortfeasor to pay the damages caused by his wrongdoing. Hence, it is the implied assumpsit created by law upon the wrongful conduct of defendants in breaking the terms of their written agreement, which is the sole basis for the maintenance of the present action, which is therefore one limited by the Statute of Limitation of five years. [R. S. 1909, section 1889.]

This distinction between a suit for the enforcement of a conditional written promise to pay money or property, and a suit for damages caused by tortious failure to perform the conditions upon which such promises are made to depend by the terms of the instrument, necessarily arises from a consideration of the language employed in entering into a contract of the kind referred to in the petition. It is also fully recognized in the learned opinion of GRAVES, J., Knisely v. Leathe, supra, l. c. 368, in contrasting the positions taken by the parties to that case, one of which was that the suit then brought was not on the contract "but was one for damages of which the written contract might be purely evidential."

That is the distinction which justifies the action of the trial court in sustaining a demurrer to the petition in this case. It was not, and could not be, under the terms of the contract referred to, a suit upon a written promise to pay money or property, but was an action upon an implied promise imputed to defendants by the law to answer in damages for their tortious breach of the stipulations upon which the promises in the contract were conditioned.

The judgment of the lower court is correct, and is affirmed.

PER CURIAM.—The foregoing opinion of *Bond, J.,* in Division is adopted as the opinion of the Court in Banc. All concur except *Woodson, C. J.,* who dissents in opinion filed; *Revelle, J.,* concurs in separate opinion in which *Graves* and *Blair, JJ.,* concur.

REVELLE, J. (concurring).—I fully concur in the excellent opinion of our learned brother BOND, and my only reason for attempting to add anything thereto is the fact that the case of Knisely v. Leathe, 256 Mo. 341, is strongly urged as authority for a contrary view.

In the briefs and argument of appellant, as well as in the dissenting opinion of our learned Chief Justice WOODSON, this is used as "a deadly parallel." In my opinion there is such a difference between that and the instant case as to not only distinguish them, but to make the Knisely case, supra, if adhered to, an impassable barrier to plaintiff's recovery. In the Knisely case *a promise to pay* a specified sum became *absolute* when the plaintiff produced a purchaser that defendant would accept. The terms of the contract that such purchaser should be *able* to buy were purely preliminary and all complied with and terminated when the defendant actually *accepted* him as a *suitable* and *able* purchaser; and in that case it was shown that the defendant, in point of fact, did accept the purchaser and made a contract of sale; and when he did this he merged in that contract of sale an unconditional promise to pay plaintiff a designated amount. In that case, in order to make the *promise* absolute and unconditional, it was necessary to show *only* defendant's acceptance of the purchaser, and in law that required nothing more in the nature of parole evidence than is required when recovering upon a promissory note, namely: parole proof, when required, of the execution of the note. As is said in the Knisely case (l. c. 375-6): "When Leathe signed this contract with Wolcott [Wolcott was the purchaser with whom Leathe entered into the contract of sale] . . . his liability to Knisely, the procuring agent, became *fixed*, unless such liability was defeated by some express agreement to the contrary." To make the Knisely case authority for appellant's contention, it was necessary for it to allege and prove that paving contracts requiring the materials mentioned in the contract sued upon were actually made, and not merely that defendants might have made them had they, in good faith, complied with their agreement.

There is no doubt in my mind that defendant breached its contract, and that plaintiff was entitled to recover *damages* therefor had it pursued its timely and authorized remedy; and in that action the contract here would have been evidentiary of the damages, but we cannot change the law when the lawmaking authority has lawfully written it. The statements of the court in the Knisely case, as in all others, must be read in relation to the particular question to which they are being applied. Every declaration of the court in that case that has been seized upon as authority for appellant's contention here is found in a discussion of a purely incidental and subsequent matter. The contract in that case provided that the money which defendant had promised to pay plaintiff should be paid from the purchase price received from the sale of the property. The evidence discloses that the property was, in point of both law and fact, *sold,* but that, for some reason, the defendant refused to execute proper deeds to the purchaser, and, for this reason, the purchaser, of course, refused to pay the money out of which plaintiff's commission was to be paid. The court merely held that as the promise to pay had become unconditional, and as the liability of the defendant had become fixed, he could not, through his breaches and derelictions, unlawfully refuse to receive the fund from which the commission should be paid. As heretofore stated, the court's statements in that connection do not go to the character of the written instrument, but merely to the derelictions of one of the parties after the liability had become firmly fixed. The language of the Knisely case urged here, it should be noted, was used with reference to another contract, and not with reference to the contract sued upon in that case. The breach of that other contract was shown for the sole purpose of showing when the money sued for under the contract in suit was in fact due. When the Knisely case is read in view of the fact that two contracts (one in suit and one not in suit) were being discussed, it will be clearly seen that the Knisely case is not authority here.

Unless the action in this case sounds in tort, and is really one for a breach of contract, the distinction between an action for damages, because of a breach of contract, and an action on the contract itself, is clearly destroyed. The Legislature having made the distinction we can but observe it.

Graves and *Blair, JJ.,* concur.

WOODSON, C. J. (dissenting)—I dissent from
the majority opinion in this case for the reason that
in my judgment the suit is bottomed upon a written
promise to pay money, and not to recover damages
for a breach of contract or for fraud and deception.

The error counsel for defendant have fallen into,
as I view the record, is partially caused by not differ-
entiating between a suit brought by the obligee, payee
or vendee, based upon a written contract made by the
obligor, payor, vendor, whereby he promises to pay
to the former money or property, and a suit brought
by the former against the latter for damages for a
breach of a contract or for fraud or deception. The
distinction between the two is broad and deep, and
the rights and remedies of the respective parties
thereto are equally different, as will be pointed out
during the course of this opinion.

The petition contains but one count, and states
but one cause of action, not two, as the majority opinion holds. That cause of action is based upon the
written contract attached to the petition and made a
part thereof, which reads as follows:

"This Agreement, entered into this 9th day of
May, 1898, by and between The Parker-Washington
Company, a corporation, and David and
F. P. McCormick, parties of the first part,
and James R. McIlvried and James R. Dennison, par-
ties of the second part, all of Kansas City, Missouri.

"Witnesseth: That, whereas the parties of the
second part propose to engage in the building of
asphalt streets in Kansas City, Missouri, and desire to
purchase asphalt and other materials for such purpose, and also to secure the use of an asphalt plant
for the preparation of such material; and, whereas,
the parties of the first part own much more than a
sufficient amount of Trinidad Lake asphalt to lay
forty thousand square yards of asphalt surface, some
of which is in Kansas. City, Missouri, and some of

Contract.

which is located in the State of New York, and also
own a modern asphalt plant, located in Kansas City,
Missouri, with certain tools and appliances used in
and about the preparation of the material used in the
laying and construction of the asphalt portion of street
work.

"Now, therefore, in view of the promises, it is
hereby agreed by and between said parties as follows, that is to say:

"Said second parties hereby purchase from the
first parties, and the first parties hereby sell to the
second parties, a sufficient amount of Trinidad Lake
asphalt to lay forty thousand square yards of asphalt
paving, according to plans and specifications, in Kansas City, Missouri, and said second parties also agree
to purchase such other asphalt as may be legally used
in the laying of said 40,000 square yards of pavements
under this contract, provided that such asphalt other
than the Trinidal Lake asphalt shall be furnished for
cash at the market price, at such times as it shall be
called for by said second parties, provided no such
asphalt shall be used without consent of the board of
public works.

"Said second parties shall pay for the Trinidad
Lake asphalt the cost price to said parties, which
shall include freight, handling, insurance enroute, interest, etc., to date of payment, which payments shall
be made upon delivery of the asphalt where located,
and satisfactory evidence furnished of the genuine-
ness thereof, said first parties to give at least five
days' notice before making any delivery, and such
asphalt shall be shipped to Kansas City, Missouri, by
said second parties, upon such payments and delivery,
and no expense for the extra handling for the purpose ·
of storing said asphalt at Kansas City, Missouri, shall
be charged to the business.

"All asphalt sold to said second parties by first
parties in pursuance of this contract shall be used

by said second parties in the laying of pavements in said city, and not otherwise, and the preparation of all material for the asphalt portion of such paving shall be prepared at the asphalt plant of said first parties and for such purpose said second parties shall have the possession and control of said plant for the preparation of Trinidad Lake asphalt for Kansas City, Missouri, to September 15, 1898, and in case the contracts for the 40,000 square yards of paving have not been confirmed by the council by September 15, 1898, then said second parties shall have the possession and control of said plant for the preparation of said Trinidad Lake asphalt for such time as may be necessary, up to November 15, 1898, with the right of ingress and egress at all times, for the purposes of this contract. In case said contracts shall have been confirmed prior to November 15, 1898, but not fully executed, then said second parties shall have the necessary possession, control and use of said plant until such contracts shall have been fully executed. Said second parties to have the possession, control and use of said plant in its present condition, destruction by fire or otherwise excepted, with such employees as they may require in the preparation of the material to be used in the laying of such pavements and shall also have the use of the tools, and appliances of said first parties used in and about the laying of the asphalt portion of such pavements. The machinist and night watchmen of said first parties shall at all times be retained and shall be paid for their services, for the machinist not to exceed $3.50 per day, and for the night watchman not to exceed $1.50 per day, by said second parties, during the time said second parties shall have the use of said plant.

"Said second parties shall repair all damages to said plant, tools and appliances, sustained while in the use of said second parties, the usual wear and tear excepted, and damages by fire and the elements also excepted.

"Said second parties shall furnish such tools and appliances as are not furnished by said first parties, which may be necessary in and about said work, and charge the cost thereof to the expense account, and at the termination of this contract all such tools and appliances, including material on hand, except Trinidad Lake asphalt, shall be divided equally between said parties.

"Said second parties agree to give such time and efforts as may be necessary in promoting the business and carrying out contracts, and also agree not to engage in any other line of asphalt work or with other parties, either directly or indirectly other than those interested in this contract during the existence of this contract, and this contract shall be deemed to have been carried out and consummated upon the completion of the forty thousand square yards of asphalt paving by the second parties as herein indicated.

"The said second parties agree to bid on all Trinidad Lake asphalt paving contracts to be let hereafter by Kansas City, Missouri, up to forty thousand square yards, until they are awarded the forty thousand square yards, and said first parties will not bid, directly or indirectly, on any Trinidad Lake asphalt paving contracts in Kansas City, Missouri, before September 15, 1898, without consent of said second parties, unless said second parties have been awarded and have confirmed the contracts for forty thousand square yards before September 15, 1898. In case said amount has not been awarded and confirmed by September 15, 1898, then said first parties will not bid before November 15, 1898, unless said amount has been awarded and confirmed prior to November 15, 1898, except by agreement with said second parties.

"It is agreed that said second parties shall receive no compensation in the way of salary for any services which they or either of them render during the life of this contract, and no expense shall be incurred by said second parties in the procuring of contracts other than those approved by David and F. P. McCormick.

"It is agreed that David and F. P. McCormick shall have a voice as to the expense incurred in the purchasing of material and in the employment of all labor used in and about such work. It being understood that all material and labor shall be purchased and employed with the least expense consistent with good workmanship.

"Said David and F. P. McCormick will render, without compensation, any service that may be required by said second parties in and about the carrying out of the provisions of this contract, that does not interfere with the carrying on of the business of the Parker-Washington Company.

"That said second parties shall keep a complete set of books, showing the cost of all labor and material used in and about the carrying out of this contract, including vouchers for all moneys paid out, and showing for what purpose, and such books and vouchers shall be subject to the inspection of said David and F. P. McCormick, at all times, and upon the completion of each paving contract, a complete statement shall be rendered as to such work.

"Said second parties shall furnish all moneys necessary in and about the carrying out of their part of this contract, and no interest shall be charged upon such moneys as an item of expense.

"Said second parties shall pay said first parties five cents per square yard for all asphalt paving laid under this contract, said sum being in payment for the use of said plant and shall be paid by second parties without regard to either profit or loss in the laying

of any pavement and in no event shall be charged as
an item of expense.

"Upon the completion of any paving contract the
actual cost and expenses shall be ascertained by said
parties, and such amount shall be deducted from the
price received in cash, bonds or tax bills at their face,
and the balance of such cash, bonds or tax bills shall
be divided equally between the parties hereto, but in
the event of loss upon any contract such loss shall be
borne by said second parties. The one-half received
by said first parties is in consideration of said first
parties selling said asphalt, use of tools and appliances and the services of said David and F. P. McCormick as herein required. In pursuance of this agreement, said second parties shall counsel with David
and F. P. McCormick, and said second parties shall
not bid less than two dollars per square yard upon
any asphalt paving contract, without the concurrence
of said David and F. P. McCormick.

"The entering into this contract shall in no way
conflict with the business of The Parker-Washington
Company, except as such business is expressly limited by the terms of this contract, and said first parties agree in carrying on their business not to hinder
or delay said second parties in the conduct or carrying out of their business under the terms of this agreement and this agreement shall never be construed as
a partnership between said parties.

"It is further agreed by and between David and
F. P. McCormick and said second parties, that said
first parties will sell, if requested by said second parties, certain of the stock of said first parties, and will
cause to be issued to said second parties, unissued
stock of said first parties, to an amount, including such
stock as said second parties shall purchase, equal to
the stock held by other parties in said corporation.
Said second parties shall pay par value for all stock
issued by first parties, provided they elect to take

such stock, and shall pay for such' stock as they may purchase which has already been issued, such price as shall be agreed upon not to exceed one-twelfth of the amount of stock issued, to the end that said second parties shall hold one-half of the stock issued by said company at the time they become stockholders in said company.

"In case the said second parties take the stock in said company as herein indicated, then this contract shall be assumed by the Parker-Washington Company as of this date, and it shall bear all expenses and receive all profits arising out of this contract; and in case said second parties do not take the stock mentioned herein before the completion of this contract, then the net earnings of said first parties from the date hereof shall not be considered an asset of the Parker-Washington Company, but' shall inure to the benefit of the stockholders of said company.

"Said first parties do not intend that this offer for the sale of stock shall be an option, but in case first parties desire to make any other arrangement, it shall give said second parties fifteen days' notice of such intention, and said second parties shall have the fifteen days within which to take said stock under this agreement; and in case said second parties do not take said stock under this agreement within the fifteen days, then said first parties shall be free to make any arrangement they deem wise as to the sale of stock or the enlargement of their business, or the termination of this offer.

"The parties of the second part may desire to form a corporation in conjunction with at least one other person for the sole purpose of carrying out the requirements of this contract, and in case this is done, the second parties have the right to assign their interest in this contract to such corporation, and thereupon this contract shall bind the said corporation. The said corporation shall have all of the rights and be substituted to all of the liabilities of the second parties as fully and with the same effect as though the name of said corporation had been stated in this contract as the party of the second part, and such corporation, if organized, shall be dissolved upon the completion of this contract, but said second parties shall guarantee the payment for the asphalt sold them as herein set forth, and also the turning over to the first parties, the profits for all work as herein mentioned and the five cents per square yard for all pavements laid for use of plant.

"Witness the hands of said parties to duplicates hereof the day and year first above written."

(Then follow the signatures and attestation.)

The legal effect of this contract was pleaded paragraph by paragraph, nothing more nor nothing less, and wound up with a prayer for a judgment for the $2000, for rent due for the use of the shop and tools, etc., and $20,000, mentioned in the petition, for its estimated share of the profits it would have received, had the defendant performed his part of the contract, which he fraudulently refused to do.

To the petition, the defendant filed a demurrer which, with formal parts omitted, was as follows:

"1· That plaintiffs' alleged cause of action is not an action upon any writing for the payment of
Demurrer. money or property, and that the said action was not commenced within five years after said alleged cause of action accrued, and that plaintiffs' alleged cause of action became and was barred by the statute of this State within five years after the said alleged cause of action accrued, and was barred long prior to the institution of this suit.

"2. That it appears from the face of the said third amended petition that plaintiffs' alleged cause of action accrued on or about November 16, 1898, and that the period within which such an action may be commenced under the statutes of Missouri expired five years after the alleged cause of action accrued, to-wit, on or about November 16, 1903, and that this suit was not commenced until July 5, 1905.''

This demurrer was sustained; and the question is, was that proper in this case?

Before discussing the character of the written contract sued on and the liability of the defendant thereon, I wish to call attention, in passing, to the fact that my learned associate in writing the majority opinion, misconceives the character of this suit, for in Paragraph Two thereof, it is stated: ''There are two causes of action alleged in the petition: The one for damages caused to plaintiff by the alleged fraudulent failure of defendants to procure and perform contracts for street paving, and thereafter to pay to plaintiffs five cents per square yard for forty thousand yards after that much street paving had been laid. Plaintiffs allege that these omissions prevented 'a gain' to them of $2000. The other for damages in the estimated sum of $20,000, as one-half of what would have been the earnings, if about one thousand tons of asphalt, sold to defendants by plaintiffs, had been properly prepared and laid in the form of street pavements under contracts let to defendants by Kansas City, which defendants fraudulently failed to obtain.''

As previously stated, and as appears from the face of the petition, there is but one cause of action stated therein, and not two, as stated in the majority opinion; nor was the suit brought to recover damages from the defendant for a fraudulent breach of contract, as stated in that opinion. But the suit was brought, as appears from the petition and the contract sued on, for the *recovery of money conditionally* promised in writing, to be paid by the defendant to the plaintiff for the use of the shop and tools mentioned therein, and for one-half of the estimated prof-

Causes of Action.

its thereon promised to be paid, had the defendant
performed the terms and conditions of said contract,
as he agreed to do.

The fraud was not pleaded as the basis of the
suit, but for the purpose of showing the fraudulent

Fraud. breach of the promise, which would prevent
the defendant from shielding his liability behind the conditions of the contract, and which, if they
had not been performed by him, on account of inability, after exercising in good faith all proper efforts
on his part, would have excused his non-performance
thereof, and thereby have absolved him from all liability upon his conditional promise to pay money.
But, if upon the other hand, as the petition shows to
be true, the non-performance of the conditions was
the intentional design of the defendant, which had he
performed, would have made his promise absolute,
then the law will not permit him to rely upon his own
wrong, and say he was not liable to pay the money
promised, because the conditions stated in the contract had not been performed. [Knisely v. Leathe,
256 Mo. 341.]

I. Returning to the petition and contract sued
on: By reading the contract sued on in this case, it
will be seen that it either contains in its
Written Contracts. own terms or provides in express terms
that books and accounts shall be kept by the
defendant, showing each and every item of cost and
expense entering into the construction of the 40,000
yards of asphalt pavement mentioned therein; and
this court will take judicial notice of the fact that
under the Charter of Kansas City all such work must
be ordered by ordinance duly enacted, and that the
contracts, plans and specifications therefor, must be
in writing.

So, if we consider the terms of the contract, with
the records that it provided should be kept by the de-

fendant, in connection with the charter provisions of Kansas City and the ordinances and contracts mentioned, every element of the contract between the parties to its smallest detail, would have been in writing; and the default of the defendant in the non-performance of his part of the written contract sued on, prevented the entire transactions from being in writing, and that non-performance constitutes his whole defense in this case.

That being true, then, in my opinion, the well-known rule of law applies, which is to the effect that when the written contract refers to books, records, documents or other written instruments, and are made a part thereof, and when all of them are read together, they embrace the entire contract, then, in legal effect, it is the same for all purposes as though said books, records, etc., had been included in the contract proper. But it may be suggested that said ordinances, contracts, books and records, etc., were not in existence at the time the contract was executed, or at the date this suit was instituted, and, therefore, that rule is not applicable to this case. It is true they were not in existence at that time, and in the very nature of the case they could not have been in existence at the time of the execution of the contract sued on; they were matters that had to be performed after its execution, as a part of its performance. But there is a valid answer to that suggestion in my opinion.

In answer to that suggestion: That suggestion, in my opinion, is without merit, for the reason that the contract upon its face shows that they were to be made by the defendant and had he done so, then every element of the contract, including its performance, would have been in writing at the date of the institution of this suit; and had they been made by the defendant—showing the matters and things the contract provided they should contain—then I apprehend no lawyer of sound judgment would, for a moment, con-

tend that the entire contract was not in writing,
within the meaning of the ten-year Statute of Limitations. That must be true, for the reason that the acts
of performance of a contract, cannot, in the very
nature of the case, be included in the contract itself,
nor does the Statute of Limitations require such an
impossibility.

If that proposition is sound, and, in my opinion,
it is, then, the fact that said books and accounts were
not made and kept by the defendant, is unavailing to
him, for the reason that neither law nor equity will
permit him, or any other person, to take advantage
of his own wrong, positive fraud and deception, knowingly and deliberately perpetrated upon the plaintiff,
for the purpose of damaging and injuring it, if not to
destroy its business.

II. In the foregoing observations I have, for
argument's sake, assumed that all of the terms of
the contract sued on were not embraced
within the written contract between the
parties, which as I understand the majority opinion in effect holds; and, therefore, it was necessary to piece out the written contract in order to show the entire contract, which fact
brought the case within the five-year Statute of Limitations.

Performance
of Written
Contracts.

But as a matter of fact, I deny that such was the
case. What part of the contract sued on was not in
writing, as indicated by the writing sued on, and
where are the allegations in the petition so stating or
even intimating anything of that kind? The answer
is, where? They do not exist. If they do, neither
the court nor counsel have pointed a finger thereto,
nor have I been able to find any such provision in the
written contract or statement in the petition after
carefully reading them a number of times. But the
majority opinion does hold that it was necessary for

the plaintiff to resort to parol testimony in order to make out its case, and that said fact destroyed the written contract as one for payment of money or property, within the meaning of the ten-year Statute of Limitations, and brings it within the purview of the five-year statute. For that reason, as previously stated, the majority opinion must in effect hold that all of the terms of the contract made between the plaintiff and the defendant were not reduced to writing, and embraced in the written contract sued on; for otherwise, such parol testimony would have been wholly immaterial, irrelevant and incompetent—not tending to prove any issue whatever in the case.

I adhere to that time-honored rule of law which is to the effect that whenever a contract has been reduced to writing and signed by the parties, it cannot thereafter be varied, added to, subtracted from or altered by parol testimony, except where it appears from the face of the writing itself that all of the terms of the contract were not embraced therein; but where such fact does appear from the face of the writing, then the remainder of the contract may be shown by parol testimony, if properly pleaded, and provided, the contract is not one the Statute of Frauds requires to be in writing.

Clearly, as before stated, the writing sued on does not show upon its face that all of the terms of the contract actually entered into between the parties were not reduced to writing; and for that reason there were no parts of the contract resting in parol, which could have been pleaded or proven by parol testimony. In other words, if a written contract shows upon its face, as this one does, that all of the terms of the contract were reduced to writing, then there was no element of it resting in parol which could have been pleaded, and consequently could not have been proven by parol evidence.

An additional observation regarding the necessity of the contract providing for the acts of its performance: As previously stated, the contract may provide what acts shall be done in its performance, and by whom they must be performed; but whether they have been performed or not, must of necessity be shown by parol testimony, for the obvious reason the performance of a contract must be subsequent to its execution.

In the case at bar, had the defendant performed his part of the contract, except as to paying plaintiff its $2000, and one-half of the profits, the only facts which the plaintiff would have been required to prove by parol evidence in order to have been entitled to a recovery, would, at most, have been that it sold and delivered to the defendant the asphalt mentioned, that it was of the kind and standard specified in the contract; that it turned over to the defendant, the shops and tools also mentioned therein; and that the accounts of the cost of the labor and materials and other items of expense which entered into the street improvements were true or false, as the case may have been, and what balance, if any, there remained in favor of the contractors; one-half of which would have belonged to the plaintiff.

This is precisely what was done in the case of Knisely v. Leathe, 256 Mo. 341.   •

In that case the plaintiff had to show *by parol testimony,* that he had found a purchaser for the land, at the price stated, and that he was able, ready and willing to pay for the same in the manner stated in the contract. All of those matters pertained to the performance of the contract, and not to the promise to pay money or property.

The same is true in the case at bar. The matters mentioned in the majority opinion, which had to be proven by parol testimony, also pertained to the performance of the contract, and not to the promise of the defendant to pay the sums before mentioned. The promise in both cases was contained in other provisions of the contract.

The mere fact that the breach of the contract was brought about by fraud and deception on the part of the defendant is wholly immaterial in so far as the rights of the plaintiff to sue thereon are concerned. If the contract was, at the time of its execution, a promise to pay money, which clearly it was, then no subsequent act of the defendant, fraudulent or otherwise, could change the character of that promise, or have substituted one statute for another for its government.

Certainly the defendant stands in no better position for having broken his contract through means of fraud and deception, than he would have occupied had he stood idly by without exerting an effort to perform his part thereof; and had the defendant breached the contract in the manner last suggested, there could be no shadow of doubt in my opinion but that the suit thereon would have been for a breach of a contract for the payment of money; and in that case all that the plaintiff would have been required to prove in order to have entitled him to a recovery, was that the defendant made no effort to perform the contract; that the conditions therein stated could have been performed by him by the exercise of proper efforts; the contract price for laying the pavement and the cost and expenses for laying the same.

The apparent, not real, efforts of performance of the contract made by the defendant did not relieve him from his promise to pay the plaintiff the two sums of money mentioned in the contract; nor the fact that said promise was conditioned upon his ability to procure the contracts from the city for laying the pavement relieve him, when he made no effort to procure them or to have them confirmed when procured.

The conditions of the contract in this case are very much like those in the case of Knisely v. Leathe, supra. Here the conditions are that the defendant was to use his best efforts to secure contracts from the city to do the street paving mentioned in the contract; that he should construct the pavements according to the contracts, plans and specifications, and keep true and accurate accounts of the cost and expenses thereof, and pay, first, to plaintiff, $2000, for the use of shop and tools, regardless of the profit made or loss sustained in constructing the 40,000 yards of pavement mentioned in the contract, and, second, one-half of the net profits to be realized, if any, for constructing said pavements; while in the Knisely case the conditions of sale were that the real estate agent, Knisely, should find a purchaser for the land who was able, willing and ready to purchase the same upon the terms stated in the contract, and that the agent was to receive from Mr. Leathe, landowner, for his services, the sum of $107,500, payable in four installments, "the first one of $37,941.19, and each of the three additional payments of $23,186.27 each, at such time and place as the said Leathe should receive the principal payment on said real estate, as per the contract of sale entered into by him with Charles C. Wolcott of even date herewith."

In the former case the plaintiff was to be paid the $2000 for the use of the shop and tools, and the one-half of the net profits, if any, realized out of the contracts, as soon as the defendant constructed the pavements. In the latter case, Knisely was to be paid his commission for selling the real estate by Leathe, in said four installments, out of the four installments of the purchase price of the land, as they were paid by Wolcott to him.

Knisely performed his part of the contract, but Leathe refused to sell the land to Wolcott, and, therefore, contended that Knisely was not entitled to his commissions because they were only payable out of the installments of the purchase money as they were paid to him by Wolcott; and as the latter had never paid him any of the purchase money, Knisely was entitled to no commissions.

The court in that case said, "That is true; but it was your own wrong which prevented Wolcott from paying the purchase price, and you will not therefore be heard to say the purchase price was not earned by Knisely."

The same is true in the case at bar; it was the wrong of the defendant which prevented the plaintiff from receiving the $2000, for the use of the shop and tools and its portion of the estimated profits it would have been entitled to had the work under the paving contracts been done by the defendant.

The following parallel columns prepared by counsel for plaintiff, will show more clearly the analogy of the two cases and the applicability of rules of law laid down in that case, to the one at bar:

This Case.	*The Knisely Case.*
In this case the promises sued on are as follows:	In the Knisely case the promise sued on was as follows (supra, p. 376):
"Said second parties shall pay said first parties five cents per square yard for all asphalt paving laid under this contract, said sum being in payment for the use of said plant and shall be paid by second parties without regard to either profit or loss in the laying of any pavement and in no event shall be charged as an item of expense.	" 'I hereby promise and agree to pay to Charles H. Knisely, of St. Louis, Mo., trustee, or his order, the sum of one hundred and seven thousand five hundred dollars out of the purchase price of $850,000; the payment of said $107,500, to be made by me to said Charles H. Knisely, trustee, or his order, in four payments, the first one of $37,941.19,

"Upon the completion of any paving contract the actual cost and expenses shall be ascertained by said parties, and such amount shall be deducted from the price received in cash, bonds or tax bills at their face, and the balance of such cash, bonds or tax bills shall be divided equally between the parties hereto, but in the event of loss upon any contract such loss shall be borne by said second parties."

In this case it is said (Opinion, p. 180, *ante*):

"It (the contract) further provided that defendants should pay plaintiff five cents per square yard for all asphalt paving laid pursuant to said contract."

Again (p. 183, *ante*):

"These clauses of the contract show on their face and by express terms, that the only promises to pay any money were: First, a promise to pay five cents per square yard for all asphalt paving laid under this contract; and,

and each of the three additional payments of $23,-186.27 each, at such time and place as I receive the principal payment for said real estate as per contract of sale entered into by me with Charles C. Wolcott of even date herewith.' "

In the Knisely case (p. 368), it is said:

"It is clear that counsel for respondent were urging that plaintiff could not recover because there had been no money paid by Wolcott to Leathe [as it is here contended and held that plaintiffs cannot recover because there had been no asphalt laid]. So that, from all standpoints the character of this written instrument between Leathe and Knisely is a vital question here in view of the fact that this case must go back for trial below. Not only so, second, a promise to pay one-half of the profits of the paving work after its completion.''

Again (p. 183):
"It is clear, therefore, that neither of the conditional promises recited in the two above clauses ever became absolute obligations on the part of the defendant, for no promise based upon a condition can be enforced as such until the contingency upon which it depends has happened . . . Such wrongful conduct [of the defendant] would constitute a legal basis for an implied assumpsit on their part to pay the damages caused thereby, but it could not alter the terms of the conditional promise to pay as used in the written contract.

Again (p. 184):
"They do not state a cause of action on a written contract to pay money upon certain conditions which never happened. . . . Under the contract referred to in the petition, if the defendants

but the very character of the suit is challenged and the court below, having sustained the demurrer as a whole, we must take the view here that the trial court stood with respondent upon these contentions as to the character of the suit and the character of the contract. He could not have sustained the second ground of demurrer as he did without saying that the written contract was not one 'for the payment of money or property,' or without saying that the suit was not upon the written contract.",

Again (p. 372):
"The petition proceeds upon the theory, and rightfully so, that if Wolcott purchased the property and a completion of that purchase by exchange of deeds and trust deeds was prevented by

had laid the pavement or if defendants had obtained the laying of paving work from Kansas City and had performed such work and reaped a profit therefrom and had failed to pay the specific general sum agreed by them to be paid on said contingencies, these plaintiffs could have sued defendants on the promises to pay contained in their contract and could have recovered in that action whatever amount the evidence showed was due.''

the act of Leathe, then the money mentioned in the Leathe-Knisely contract at once became due, and this too without reference to the payment of any money by Wolcott. In other words, that Leathe could not wilfully refuse to enforce the Wolcott contract and thereby defeat the promise to pay made in the Knisely contract. It follows that counsel for respondent are in error when they insist that the action is one sounding in damages for a breach of contract. It also follows that the circuit court was in error if it followed this bent of counsel's mind. It is further true that the court was in error when in sustaining the second ground of the demurrer that the petition stated no cause of action without the allegation that the money had been paid by Wolcott.''

Again (p. 185):
"If the action had been predicated upon the simple averment of such promises, coupled with the further averment

Again (p. 376):
"This contract, at least when coupled with the allegation that Wolcott or his assigns stood ready and willing to perform

that no asphalt pavement had ever been laid and ho paving business had ever been carried on, then the petition would have been subject to a general demurrer, for the reason that it showed on its face two conditional promises which had never ripened into legal obligations."

and Leathe refused and failed to perform the Leathe-Wolcott contract, rendered Leathe liable at once for the full amount agreed to be paid in the Knisely contract, as and of the date of such refusal, this too, in a suit upon the contract."

Again (p. 377):

"The action is upon the contract, and at the very most it is only required to go outside of the contract to show that Wolcott was ready and willing to perform and Leathe refused to perform the Wolcott-Leathe contract."

The same principles of law announced in the Knisely case are controlling in this. There, in discussing what constituted a written promise to pay money or property, within the meaning of the ten-year Statute of Limitations, this court, on page 361, said:

"It makes no difference, however, whether the suit be in debt for the amount due upon a contract, or in covenant to recover unliquidated damages for its breach. Both are alike on the contract; and if the contract is 'for the payment of money or property' it fills the requirement of the provisions of the Statute of Limitations we have quoted. The following cases are more or less in point on the same question: Rey-

burn v. Casey, 29 Mo. 129; Moorman v. Sharp, 35 Mo.
283; Henoch v. Chaney, 61 Mo. 129, 133; Miner v.
Howard, 93 Mo. App. 569. We have no doubt that the
ten-year limitation would apply in a suit of this character brought on a similar contract in the lifetime of
the party.''

I have always understood the rule to be, that if
the contract contains an express agreement, or one by
necessary implication, to pay money or property,
then the ten-year Statute of Limitations and not the
five, governs the same. This is made clear by the
mere statement of the fact, that it is the *promise of
the obligor which must be in writing,* not the consideration .he received for entering into the same, nor
what acts he agreed therein to perform in carrying
the contract into execution.

Those matters have nothing whatever to *do with
the promise made, nor its character,* except of course,
in a proper case the promise might be shown to be
void for a want of consideration or a failure thereof.

The contract sued on contains the following provisions or promises made by the defendant, viz.:

''*Said second parties shall pay said first parties
five cents per square yard for all asphalt paving laid
under this contract, said sum being in payment for the
use of said plant, and shall be paid by second parties
without regard to either profit or loss in the laying of
any pavement, and in no event shall be charged as an
item of expense.*

''*Upon the completion of any paving contract the
actual cost and expenses shall be ascertained by said
parties, and such amount shall be deducted from the
price received in cash, bonds or tax bills at their face,
and the balance of such cash, bonds or tax bills shall
be divided equally between the parties hereto, but in
the event of loss upon any contract such loss shall be
borne by said second parties.*''

As well stated by counsel for plaintiff:

"The relief sought is:

"(1)   For the recovery of $2000, being five cents per square yard for 40,000 square yards of asphalt pavement, being the specific liquidated sum that at all events and in any event defendant, by the first of the foregoing provisions, agreed to pay; and,

"(2)   For the recovery of $20,000 for failure to pay, as promised in the second of the above provisions.

"If either or both of these express written promises to pay are promises to pay money or property, the action was well brought within the ten-year period, and the judgment of the circuit court must be reversed and plaintiffs awarded a trial."

Can there be any question but what the promise before quoted from the contract sued on, was for the payment of money—the $2000, and the one-half of the net profits of the street improvements, represented by the $20,000 mentioned? Clearly not, for the defendant never promised to pay anything else; but he did promise to pay the former sum, and one-half of the net profits to be derived from the street improvements to be constructed by him; which plaintiff estimates would have been $20,000, had the defendant complied with the other parts of the contract; and for that reason he sued for the $20,000.

In discussing a similar case the Court of Appeals in the case of Miner & Frees v. Howard, 93 Mo. App. 569, on page 572, said:

"By that instrument there arose a promise to pay for the labor and material; and it is therefore not true, as contended by defendants, that the claim for the material in controversy was barred, because more than five years allowed for actions on accounts had elapsed. . . . The fact that the sum to be paid was not ascertained when the bond was executed and therefore not named therein, does not prevent the application of the statute. [Carr v. Thompson, 67 Mo. 472; Reyburn v. Casey, 29 Mo. 129; Moorman v. Sharp, 35 Mo.

283.] Neither is it an objection to this view of the
statute that the bond in suit is a collateral or indirect
promise to pay money. [Martin v. Knapp, 45 Mo. 48;
Rowsey v. Lynch, 61 Mo. 560.] Though indirect, the
bond itself contains a promise and was a writing 'for
the payment of money,' which would sustain the action within ten years.''

In the case of Shinn v. Wooderson, 95 Mo. App.
6, the plaintiff made an agreement with the trustees
of the church to furnish moneys for the construction,
the trustees agreeing to reimburse him and to give
him a lien or mortgage on the church property for
such sum as they did not repay him when the improvements were completed. Shinn claimed a balance for
which he had not been paid and brought suit for it
after five years. The court says (p. 13):

''The rendition of the account by items will be
treated merely as evidence offered, upon the part of
the plaintiff, to show that in good faith he did pay out
the amount he agreed with the defendants to advance.
The petition sets out that he furnished that amount
to the trustees upon the understanding that if he was
not repaid he was to have his lien upon the lot. The
amount that he was to let the trustees have was agreed
upon and fixed at the sum stated. It follows, then,
that his is not a suit upon an account, but a suit upon
an agreement.''

The court held the ten-year statute applied.

In Howe v. Mittelberg, 96 Mo. App. 490, the court
says (p. 493):

''If we test the application of the Statute of Limitations, as appellant claims we should, by asking
whether the contract shows on its face a promise to
pay or requires evidence *aliunde* to show a promise
(Carr v. Thompson, 67 Mo. 472), the cause of action
falls within the ten-year limitation, because the contract carries on its face a promise to pay money.''

In the Martin v. Knapp case, 45 Mo. 48, the suit was on an administrator's bond, and the five-year statute was pleaded in bar. The court pointed out in the opinion that the Statute of Limitation of 1849 was amended in the revision of 1855 by omitting the word "direct" in describing actions on written instruments for the payment of money and that the Legislature did so with the object of including in the ten-year limitation all actions founded on such instruments, whether the promised payment was to be certain or contingent. That statute has never been amended since 1855.

In Bridges v. Stephens, 132 Mo. l. c. 552, the court said:

"The result of these decisions is that if the writing in question contains enough to raise the promise (to pay money or property) sued on, the ten-year limitation applies to an action for its breach. If the obligation is clearly apparent from the writing, a breach of it may be exhibited by facts outside the writing."

In Carr v. Thompson, 67 Mo. 472, referred to in Howe v. Mittelberg, supra, Thompson's written promise was that he " 'should pay the said Carr the amount for which he may be liable as security on the bond of one J. Henry Chiles as guardian of his daughter, Sally Chiles, as soon as the same is ascertained and known —say in twelve months from this date (September 11, 1866) by note and security, with interest from this date.' " The court, on page 476, said:

"The promise to pay was in writing and, though the sum to be paid was not expressed in the writing but was by the terms thereof to be thereafter ascertained, that fact would not take it from under the operation of the ten-year statute. Were the writing of such a character that evidence *aliunde* would be required in order to show a promise to pay, the limitation of five years would apply."

In Curtis v. Sexton, 201 Mo. 217, the court says (p. 230):

"Defendant also contends that the cause of action falls within the five-year Statute of Limitations and is therefore barred. The argument is that when evidence beyond the written document must be resorted to in order to make out the case it is not an action upon 'a writing . . . for the payment of money or property' within the meaning of section 4272, Revised Statutes 1899 (which is the ten-year limitation), and several cases are cited as supporting that argument, among them Menefee v. Arnold, 51 Mo. 536; Brady & Kerby v. St. Joseph, 84 Mo. App. 399, and others. But that is a misconception of those cases; they only mean to say that where the promise or agreement to pay on which the action is based is not found in express terms or by fair implication in the writing, but the cause of action arises out of facts collateral to the instrument, it does not fall within the provision of that section of the Statute of Limitations.

"'In the case at bar there is an express agreement to pay the amounts the plaintiff paid on account of his purchase and interest thereon, the only necessity for going beyond the paper writing to make out the case is to show the performance of the contract on the part of the plaintiff and the breach on the part of the defendant. The action is founded on the written contract and falls within the ten-year section of the Statute of Limitations."

To the same effect is the case of Ball v. Cotton Press Co., 141 Mo. App. 26. That was an action to recover a dividend on stock held in the defendant company and was bottomed on a minute record of the board of directors which recited that a certain sum should "'be paid pro rata according to the number of shares held by them [the stockholders].'" It was contended that the action was barred by the five-year Statute of Limitations. The court says (p. 42):

"In order for a writing to be a promise to pay money in the sense of the ten-year limitation section, the writing must contain words which either express a promise to pay or from which a promise may be implied. [Reyburn v. Casey, 29 Mo. 129; Carr v. Thompson, 67 Mo. 472; Howe v. Mittelberg, 96 Mo. App. 490.] What was written in the record of the meeting of the directors of the Peper Company imported a promise to pay plaintiff $1500 as his part of the dividend . . . The present action was instituted about nine years after the declaration of the dividend and is not barred.''

In the supplemental opinion of Judge GRAVES, in the case of Knisely v. Leathe, supra, the point is ably and thoroughly discussed. In that case the obligation to pay the plaintiff was to pay him out of moneys thereafter to be paid to the defendant under a contract which he had with one Wolcott. The court, on page 368, said:

"He [the trial judge] could not have sustained the second ground of demurrer as he did without saying that the written contract was not one 'for the payment of money or property' or without saying that the suit was not upon a written contract, but was one for damages of which the written contract might be purely evidentiary.''

Again (p. 372):

"The petition proceeds upon the theory, and rightfully so, that if Wolcott purchased the property and a completion of that purchase by exchange of deeds and trust deeds was prevented by the act of Leathe, then the money mentioned in the Leathe-Knisely contract at once became due, and this too, without reference to the payment of any money by Wolcott. In other words, that Leathe could not wilfully refuse to enforce the Wolcott contract, and thereby defeat the promise to pay made in the Knisely contract. It follows that counsel for respondent are

in error when they insist that the action is one sounding in damages for a breach of contract. It also follows that the circuit court was in error if it followed
this bent of counsel's mind. It is further true that
the court was in error, when in sustaining the second
ground of the demurrer, that the petition stated no
cause of action without the allegation that the money
had been paid by Wolcott. That one having an en-
forceable contract of sale with another person, induced and procured by an agent, cannot defeat the
agent's commission by refusing to enforce the contract, is well-settled law. His refusal to carry out the
contract, or, in the event he himself has signed the contract of sale with the purchaser, his refusal afterwards
to enforce such contract renders him liable for commission in the sum agreed upon.''

I state without fear of refutation, that the consensus of the authorities is to the effect just stated,
and that the contract sued on is a promise to pay
money, and, therefore, is governed by the ten-year
Statute of Limitation.

I will now carefully review the authorities cited
and relied upon by counsel for defendant in support
of their contention that the five-year statute controls
in this case.

The main cases cited by counsel for the defendant in support of his contention that this is not a suit
upon a written contract or promise for the payment
of money or property and therefore the action is
barred by the five-year Statute of Limitations, are:
Brady & Kerby v. St. Joseph, 84 Mo. App. 399; St.
Louis Gas Light Co. v. St. Louis, 11 Mo. App. 55, 84
Mo. 202; Ash & Gentry v. Independence, 103 Mo. App.
299; Thomas v. Pacific Beach Co., 115 Cal. 136.

The first case mentioned is that of Brady & Kerby
v. St. Joseph, 84 Mo. App. 399.

In that case defendant, a city of the second class,
in proper form and legal manner awarded to plain-

tiffs' assignor a contract to grade certain streets therein according to the plans and specifications then on file
in the office of the city engineer, showing among other
things the grade lines of the streets to which the grading had to conform, for and in consideration of
——————— dollars. The contract also provided that
after the grading should be completed according to
contract, the city would issue to the contractor special
tax bills against the abutting property in payment of
the contract price therefor; also that in conformity
to the provisions of the city charter, the city should
not be liable in any manner for the cost of grading
said streets, but that he should collect the cost thereof
through the means of said tax bills out of the abutting
property and not otherwise. That after the grading
had progressed to a certain stage the city, by ordinance, changed the grade lines of some of said streets,
which rendered it physically impossible for the contractor to complete the grading according to the contract and plans and specifications. Some eight or nine
years after the grade lines of the streets had been so
changed and the grading thereby having been prevented, that suit was brought, not on the *contract for
the payment of money or property* the city had promised to pay the plaintiff, because *no such promise was
contained in the contract,* but for damages sustained
by him because the city had wrongfully rendered it
impossible for the contractor to complete the grading
according to contract and plans and specifications,
which, under the law, was absolutely necessary for
him to do before he was entitled to the tax bills creating a lien upon the abutting property, out of which
alone he had to look to collect his money for doing the
work.

In all such cases the city acts more in the nature
of an agent for both parties, the property owners and
the contractors; ordering the improvements made for
the benefit of the property which must pay the cost

thereof and issuing the special tax bills to the contractor in payment.

From the foregoing it is clearly seen that the contract mentioned was not a promise made by the city for the payment of money or property to the contractor for doing the grading, but upon the contrary, it in specific terms provided that the city should *not be liable* for the cost of the improvements, and that the contractor should look alone to the abutting property for his pay. In other words, what did the city promise the contractor to do upon his completion of the grading according to contract? To pay him money or property? No; but to issue to him special tax bills creating a lien upon the abutting property in his favor, which alone the law provided, and he by the contract agreed to accept, as full compensation for doing the work. Did the contractor complete the grading? No. Did the city issue the tax bills? No. Why? Because the work was not completed according to contract, which alone would have benefited the abutting property and legally authorized the issuance of the tax bills. What effect did the change of the grades of the streets, by the city, have upon the contract of the plaintiff for doing the grading? It impaired the obligation of a valid contract, and therefore violated the contract clauses of the State and Federal Constitutions. Then what was the suit for in that case? To recover the special damages from the city the plaintiff had sustained by reason of the breach of said contract, and not on a written promise to pay money or property.

Moreover, suppose the city had not interfered with the grading, and the plaintiff had completed the same according to contract, but the city had wrongfully refused to issue the tax bills, would the city in that case have been liable under the law and the contract for the payment of money or property? Certainly not. The only agreement the city made was to issue the tax bills, and its failure to so do would not have metamorphosed that agreement into a contract to pay money or property and thereby have rendered it liable for the payment of money or property, instead of its duty to issue the tax bills.

In such a case, the city could have been compelled by mandamus to have issued and delivered the tax bills to the contractor. This court has so held in numerous cases.

That was an action against the city of St. Joseph, as the Court of Appeals stated in the opinion, to recover *special damages* because of its wrongful act in preventing the plaintiff from completing the grading according to the contract. Upon that performance depended the contractor's right to have the tax bills issued and delivered to him, through which alone he could have collected the contract price for the work. In other words, the abutting property to street improvements cannot be compelled to pay the cost thereof, without they have been constructed in conformity to the terms of the contract which alone adds the benefits to the property—for which it must respond. No excuse will or can be accepted for a non-compliance with the terms of the contract—not even the acts of God or man; but if the completion of the work is wrongfully prevented by the city, then it may be compelled to respond for the ensuing damages; but *the property* or property owner, never. For the reasons stated the Court of Appeals correctly held that that suit was not based upon a written promise to pay money and that the five and not the ten-year Statute of Limitations governed. Clearly that case has nothing in common with the case at bar, which was based upon a written promise to pay money; and it is equally clear that the five-year statute has no application to this case.

The second case cited by counsel is that of the St. Louis Gas. Co. v. City of St. Louis, 11 Mo. App. 55, affirmed in 84 Mo. 202. In that case the plaintiff in 1846 made a contract with the city of St. Louis, to sell to the city its gas plant in the year 1870, upon certain conditions named therein. For years subsequent to the last-named date, the company had furnished the city with gas for illuminating purposes, for, which the latter refused to pay. Thereupon the company sued the city for the sum of $545,670.48, the price of said gas so used. The city in its answer, by way of a counterclaim, set up the terms of the contract of 1846, whereby the company agreed to sell the plant to it in the year 1870, upon certain conditions named, and that it had performed those conditions, but nevertheless, the company had refused to sell and turn over the possession of the same to the city; and that in consequence of said refusal, the city had been damaged in the sum of $3,000,000, etc.

In that case it should be observed that there was no provision in the contract on the part of the company to pay to the city said $3,000,000, or any other sum. It simply agreed to sell to the city the gas plant; and the contract contained no promise to pay the city money or property in case it refused to sell and transfer the plant. But, as before stated, the company did agree to sell the plant to the city; and in the case of City of St. Louis v. St. Louis Gas Light Co., 70 Mo. 69, the former brought suit against the latter to specifically enforce the same contract which this court held was proper, but denied the city's right to the remedy prayed, because it had waived its right to insist upon the performance of the contract of sale. It is thus seen that the city in the case reported was not again suing for the enforcement of the contract of sale, but was suing for damages for its breach in not selling the plant to it. It is therefore perfectly clear the company never in writing or otherwise agreed to pay the city $3,000,000, or any other sum of money in case it refused to make the sale; and therefore said contract was not a written promise to pay to the city money or property. The suit was for damages, the law imposes for the breach of the contract. That is made clear by the case of City of St. Louis v. St. Louis Gas Light Co., supra, where the city brought suit to compel the company to sell and convey the gas plant to it. That suit was based upon the company's promise to sell and convey—the only promise it made to the city; and the city knowing that fact, brought that suit for its specific performance. But as before stated,. the Gas Company never agreed in writing or otherwise, to pay to the city $3,000,000, or any other sum, in case it should refuse to make the conveyance; and therefore the counterclaim of the city was not and could not have been based upon a promise of the company to pay it money. That counterclaim was based upon a breach of contract for the sale of the plant to the city, and nothing more. That case is totally foreign to the case at bar; and the principles of law announced therein regarding the Statute of Limitations have no application to this case.

The next case is that of Ash & Gentry v. Independence, 103 Mo. App. 299.

The facts of that case are very similar to those in the case of Brady & Kerby v. St. Joseph, supra, save in this one particular: In the former, the negligence and delay of the city of Independence prevented the contractor from completing his contract within the time prescribed therein; and in consequence thereof he was denied a recovery on the tax bills which were properly issued, but not in proper time; while in the latter case the change of grade prevented the contractor from completing the work. The legal proposition in both is identically the same; and the Brady case is cited and chiefly relied upon in support of the Ash-Independence case.

It is clear from this statement that the latter case was not a suit upon a contract for the payment of money or property nor a mandamus proceeding to compel the city to issue the tax bills—it had previously fulfilled that promise, the only one it had made to the contractor, but it was a suit predicated upon the negligence and delay of the city of Independence, which prevented the contractor from completing the work within the specified time. The court held, and properly so, that the five-year Statute of Limitations applied. That ruling was proper, but it has no application to the case at bar, where the suit is upon the written contract to pay money and not for the recovery of damages for its breach, as was true in all of the cases cited by counsel for defendant.

The last of said cases cited is that of Thomas v. Pacific Beach Co., 115 Cal. 136.

In that case the facts were substantially these: On December 12, 1887, the defendant entered into a written contract with the plaintiff to sell him certain lots of ground belonging to it, for the sum of $500, with interest, on deferred payments. The contract provided that the purchase price thereof should be paid in three equal installments, the first on the date of the contract, and the other two in one and two years thereafter, and that upon the payment of the deferred installments, the contract provided that the defendant should execute to the plaintiff a proper deed conveying the lots to him. That in due time the plaintiff paid the full purchase price of the lots to the defendant, and in September, 1891, he demanded from it a deed conveying the lots to him, which was by the defendant refused; and on October 7, 1893, that suit was instituted by the plaintiff to recover back from the defendant the purchase price paid by him to it for the lots. To that suit the defendant interposed the one-year Statute of Limitations of California, as a bar to the action, which is similar to our five-year statute. In opposition to that position the plaintiff contended that the suit was based upon a written contract for the payment of money, etc., and that the four-year statute of that State applied, which is similar to our ten-year statute. The court, in that case held, and properly so, in my opinion, that the one-year statute governed and that the demurrer was properly sustained.

In that case it should be borne in mind what was the real character of the contract sued on. In short, the defendant agreed to sell to the plaintiff certain lots for the sum of $500, and the plaintiff agreed to pay that sum to the defendant for the same; and nothing was said in the contract about the defendant repaying the purchase price of the lots to the plaintiff in case the former declined to execute the deed conveying the lots to him. Under that state of facts, what were the plaintiff's remedies? First: He could have brought suit on the contract for specific performance (which expressly promised to convey the lots to him). That suit could have been brought at any time within four years, for the reason that the promise was in writing and was governed by the four-year statute. And second: He could have waived his right to the specific performance of the contract and have sued for damages sustained, if any (which was not in writing) for defendant's refusal to convey the lots to him, which would not have been for the purchase price paid, with interest, but for damages sustained, which was the difference between the contract price and the value of the lots, if that exceeded the contract price, but if less than the contract price, then he could have recovered nothing, because, in that case, he would not have been damaged. In short, what was the promise the defendant made to the plaintiff in that case? To convey to him certain lots. Did the defendant promise or agree in the contract to repay to the plaintiff the $500 with interest in case the lots should not be conveyed to him according to the terms of the contract? No. It only promised to convey the lots—nothing was said regarding a repayment of the purchase price.

Upon that state of facts, the plaintiff could have, as he did, waived his right to sue for specific performance of the written contract, and have sued for damages for its breach, which could have been done in one year; or he could have sued for specific performance of the written contract, which could have been done in four years.

The four cases mentioned are the principal, if not the sole, cases relied upon to show that the five-year statute governs this case, which in my opinion, have no application to it whatever.

So it is seen that those cases have no bearing whatever upon a suit based upon a written contract, as this one is; and that the contention of counsel for defendant has no legal foundation upon which to rest.

Moreover, and independent of all that I have stated regarding the character of the contract and promises made by the defendant in this case, if the contract sued on is not a promise in writing made by the defendant to pay the plaintiff the $2000 for the use of the shop and tools mentioned and the $20,000, or so much of it as the evidence might show was due the plaintiff as the estimated share of its profits, then I feel perfectly confident in stating that it would be both a legal and physical impossibility to draw and execute such a contract as this, that is, one which promises to pay certain estimated profits upon conditions therein stated, to be performed by the promisor, and at the same time bring it within the ten-year Statute of Limitations. This must be true in the very nature of things. The performance of the terms and conditions of any and all contracts, must of necessity, as previously stated, be performed subsequent to the execution of the contract, and for that reason the acts of performance must also rest in parol, and be proven by that character of evidence. It would also be true, that such a contract could not be legally drawn and executed, whereby one person could promise to pay to another an unliquidated sum of money to be realized out of any business enterprise, and at the same time bring the contract within the ten-year statute. This seems to me to be a novel and startling proposition; and if that is true, then it must also be true that all of the terms of such a contract cannot be reduced to writing and embraced in the same contract, but part of it must rest in parol and be proven by that treacherous class of evidence.

There is much more that might be said regarding the law and facts of this case in confirmation of the position that this is a suit based upon a written promise to pay money, and, therefore, not barred by the five-year Statute of Limitations; but I believe I have sufficiently stated the law and facts of the case to show that the majority opinion is based upon a misconception of the facts, which renders the legal propositions therein stated (which, as abstract propositions of law, are correct) inapplicable to the real facts of the case.

For the reasons stated, I dissent from the majority opinion, and am of the opinion that the judgment of the circuit court should be reversed and the cause remanded for a new trial.

THE STATE v. RICHARD WADE, Appellant.

In Banc, March 1, 1916.

1. **INFORMATION: Sufficiency of Charge.** In criminal pleadings nothing material can be left to intendment or implication; and where a crime is created by statute the charge must be such as to specifically bring the accused within its material words.

2. ————: ————: **Aided By Proof.** The State cannot prove what it has not charged; it cannot by incompetent evidence supply an absent allegation. Even though the evidence establishes an offense forbidden by the statute, a conviction cannot stand if the allegations are insufficient to point out any crime denounced by it.

3. ——————: Ejusdem Generis: Gambling Device. When an enumeration of certain specified things in a statute is followed by general words or phrases, they are deemed to mean things of the same class and kind as those enumerated, and do not include things wholly different from those specifically mentioned. Section 4750, Revised Statutes 1909, condemning the setting up and keeping of certain enumerated gambling devices, or "any kind of gambling table or gambling device, adapted, devised, and designed for the purpose of playing any game of chance for money," is not broad enough to include all gambling devices regardless of their character, but does include all those of a kindred nature and similar kind to those enumerated.

4. ——————: ——————: ——————: Craps Table: Must Be Described. A table, duly marked and arranged for the purpose, on which the game of craps is played by means of dice for money or property, is within the purview of the statute; but it is not specifically enumerated therein, and therefore the rule of *ejusdem generis* applies, and the information must contain sufficient averments showing it to belong to the enumerated class. An information simply charging that the defendant set up and kept "a certain table and gambling device commonly called a crap table," with no allegation defining a crap table, or of what it consists, or how designed, or how and by what means the game of craps is played, is not sufficient to support a conviction, even though the evidence establishes the fact that the tables which were operated by defendant are of the class forbidden by the statute. Nor is the general allegation that the crap table was "a gambling device adapted, devised and designed for the purpose of playing games of chance for money and property" sufficiently descriptive of a crap table to supply an allegation necessary to show that such table is of a kindred nature and similar kind to one of those enumerated in the statute. [Overruling on this point State v. Rosenblatt, 185 Mo. 114; State v. Locket, 188 Mo. 415; State v. Holden, 203 Mo. 581; State v. Lee, 228 Mo. 480.]

5. GAMBLING DEVICE: Commonly Known: Proof: Variance. Where the information charges that the gambling table which defendant set up is one "commonly known as a crap table," the State must show that there is a table commonly so known, and that it was this particular kind of table that defendant set up and kept; and where all the witnesses testify that the tables which defendant maintained and operated were not of the kind which they commonly knew as crap tables, and that a crap table is of a radically different design and construction, a conviction cannot stand.

6. ——————: Location: Street Number: Variance. The information charged that defendant set up a craps table "at 118½ North Fifth street." The evidence tended to prove that de-

fendant set up gambling tables in the basement of premises
designated as 118 North Fifth street, the sole available entrance thereto being under a barber shop at said number, from
which initial point a tunnel, equipped with a series of automatic doors, led to the room where the tables were; that
the premises and entrance were commonly known as 118½
North Fifth street; that defendant's mail in accordance with
his direction, was addressed to 118½ North Fifth Street; and
that when arrested defendant gave that number as his address.

Held, by REVELLE, J., with whom FARIS and BLAIR, JJ.,
   concur, that there is no fatal variance between the allegation and proof; that it was unnecessary to allege the exact location, since it did not relate to a constitutive part
   of the offense, and if a variance at all it is cured by Sec.
   5114, R. S. 1909.

Held, by GRAVES, J., with whom WOODSON, C. J., concurs,
   that the variance is not cured by the statute, but is fatal
   to the judgment. WALKER and BOND, JJ., do not concur
   with either opinion.

Appeal   from   Buchanan   Criminal   Court.—*Hon.
Thomas F. Ryan,* Judge.

REVERSED AND REMANDED.

Kay G. Porter, Charles F. Strop and *Eugene Sil-
verman* for appellant.

(1)   It is the inflexible rule in criminal pleadings
that in all indictments or informations for felonies,
nothing can be left to intendment or implication, and
judged by this rule, the information in the present case
is insufficient.   The indictment nowhere alleges the
nature of the game which was played; it is not alleged
that the game of craps was played; it is not alleged
that a game of chance was played, and fails to allege
that any game was played for either money or property.   As sustaining the general principles which
should govern the present case, see State v. Keating,
202 Mo. 204, and many cases cited therein.   State v.
Evans, 128 Mo. 406; State v. Birks, 199 Mo. 271.   (2)
It is no answer to the above contention that the information follows the language of the statute.   The

rule that an information is sufficient when it follows the language of the statute has no application excepting in the cases where the statute so far individuates the offence that the offender has proper notice from the adoption of the statutory forms what the offence he is to be tried for really is. In no other case is it sufficient to follow the words of the statute. It is no more allowable under a statutory charge to put the defendant on trial without specification of the offence than if would be on a common-law charge. Wharton's Criminal Pleading and Practice, sec. 220; Sherwood's Commentaries on Crim. Law of Missouri, 638; State v. Hayward, 83 Mo. 299; Ex parte See, 241 Mo. 295; State v. Kruger, 134 Mo. 274; State v. Thierauf, 167 Mo. 442. (3) Not only was there no allegation that the game of craps was played, but there is no allegation as to what constitutes the game of craps. The information should have alleged that the game of craps was a game played with dice. This court has recently held that it would not take judicial notice that poker was a game played with cards and chips; it follows and for like reason, that this court will not take judicial knowledge that craps was played with dice. State v. Solon, 247 Mo. 672. (4) There was a fatal variance between the information and proof offered. The information charged the defendant with setting up a table commonly called a crap table. The proof was that the table set up was an ordinary pool table. The uncontradicted testimony was that a crap table, commonly called, which is the allegation, was a certain distinctive kind of table and established for a specific purpose, whereas, the table described in evidence was a different kind of table, and not such a table as is ordinarily used for gaming purposes. (5) The accepted doctrine is that where the place is stated not as venue, but as a matter of local description, a variance between the description in the indictment and the evidence will be fatal. Applying this rule to the present case, there was a fatal variance.

State v. Wade.

The uncontradicted testimony was that the device complained of was located in the basement of the building known as 424 Francis street, a separate and distinct number, and a separate and distinct building, State v. Kelley, 29 Atl. (N. H.) 843; Withers v. State, 17 S. W. (Tex.) 725; Bernero v. Commonwealth, 116 S. W. (Ky.) 312; Greenwood v. People, 83 Pac. 646; Bryant v. State, 62 Ark. 460; Moore v. State, 12 Ohio, 390; State v. O'Neal, 124 N. W. 69; State v. Crogan, 8 Iowa, 523; McAllister v. State, 116 S. W. (Tex.) 583; Ball v. State, 26 Ind. 155; Clark v. Commonwealth, 16 B. Mon. (Ky.) 216; People v. Slater, 5 Hill, 401; Levy v. State, 42 So. (Miss.) 875; Johnson v. State, 58 S. E. 265; State v. Kelly, 132 N. W. (N. D.) 223. (6) If it be conceded, which we do not, that there was any evidence tending to show that the basement of the premises ordinarily known as 118 North Fifth street was known as 118½ North Fifth street, yet the great weight of the testimony and all of the credible testimony was to the effect that 118½ North Fifth referred to the second story, and undoubtedly the jury upon the testimony in the case, had room to find that 118½ was the second story, in which event there should have been an instruction to the jury to have further assisted the jury, to the effect that unless the offence was committed at 118½ North Fifth street, the defendant should be acquitted. State v. Conway, 241 Mo. 271; R. S. 1909, sec. 5231; State v. Nicholas, 222 Mo. 434; State v. Taylor, 118 Mo. 153; State v. Banks, 73 Mo. 592; State v. Palmer, 88 Mo. 568.

John T. Barker, Attorney-General, and *Lee B. Ewing*, Assistant Attorney-General, for respondent.

(1) The information herein is good. Sec. 4756, R. S. 1909; State v. Lee, 228 Mo. 480; State v. Holden, 203 Mo. 582; State v. Rosenblatt, 185 Mo. 120. (2) The instructions are in approved form and fully cover all the law of the case. State v. Lee, 228 Mo. 480;

State v. Mathis, 206 Mo. 604; State v. Holden, 203 Mo. 584.

REVELLE, J.—On the 2nd day of March, 1914, the prosecuting attorney of Buchanan County filed in the criminal court of that county an information, which, omitting formal parts, is as follows:

"That at said county Richard Wade at 118½ North Fifth Street, in the city of St. Joseph . . . did then and there wilfully, unlawfully and feloniously set up and keep a certain table and gambling device commonly called a crap table, which said crap table was then and there and on said other days and times a gambling device adapted, devised and designed for the purpose of playing games of chance for money and property; and did then and there . . . unlawfully and feloniously induce, entice and permit certain persons, to-wit . . . to bet and play at and upon a game played on and by means of such gambling device."

On this information defendant was tried and convicted, and his punishment assessed at four years' imprisonment in the penitentiary. The judgment was affirmed by Division Two, but, owing to the dissent of FARIS, J., and upon defendant's application, the cause was transferred to Court In Banc.

The evidence adduced by the State tends to prove that defendant, as tenant, occupied and had under his exclusive control, the basement of the premises designated 118 North Fifth Street, in the city of St. Joseph. The particular basement room in which the alleged gambling device was set up and kept was under a restaurant fronting on Francis street, the sole available entrance thereto being under a barber shop at 118 North Fifth Street. From this initial point of entrance a tunnel or underground passageway led to the room in question. The tunnel was equipped with a series of doors, which closed automatically through the operation of certain convenient and ready devices. A system of electric signals had been duly installed in order to warn of the approach of undesirable persons. In the room, besides some other furniture and fixtures, were two pool tables, on each of which was chalked off what is referred to in the evidence as a "crap game lay-out." The evidence also discloses that in this room was a full equipment for pool tables, such as racks, balls and cues. The "crap game lay-out" is described as certain chalk marks with numbers thereon at different points.

On the 7th of February, 1914, when this room was raided by the officers, thirty or forty persons were found in the room, some of whom were engaged at the time in playing what is called the "game of craps," which is described as a game played with dice. At that time there was about $300 in money found on the tables. One table was in charge of and being operated by Frank Dorsal, and the other by William Garnett, both of whom were in the employ of defendant. Defendant was at the cigar counter in another part of the room.

A deputy sheriff, who had been a police officer for fourteen years, and two of defendant's employees, testified that the premises and the entrance thereto were commonly known as 118½ North Fifth Street. The evidence also discloses that defendant's mail, and that of his employees, in accordance with his directions, was addressed to 118½ North Fifth Street, and, when arrested, defendant gave this number as his address.

The State's witnesses testified to their knowledge and familiarity with what is commonly known as a "crap table," and stated that the pool tables with the "crap lay-out" thereon were not such tables. All witnesses for the State testified, however, that the game of craps was, in point of fact, played on such tables.

The defendant offered some evidence tending to show that there was no such number as 118½ North

Fifth Street in the city of St. Joseph, and that if there were such a number it referred to the second story of the building at 118 North Fifth Street, and not to the basement in which defendant was conducting his business.

Defendant also offered a picture of a table which had been identified by the State's witnesses as a correct representation of the table commonly known as a "crap table," and this discloses no similarity between such a table and the one which the witnesses described as being kept by defendant.

I. The record discloses several assignments of error, the most important being the challenge to the sufficiency of the information. In the absence of a valid and sufficient charge a judgment cannot stand, and, under such circumstances, the question of a defendant's guilt or innocence is not food for the judicial mind. The organic law entitles every person charged with crime to be informed of the nature and cause of the accusation against him, and, in keeping with the spirit of this salutary and fundamental principle of justice, courts have evolved an inflexible rule that in criminal pleading nothing material can be left to intendment or implication. Where a crime is created by statute, the charge must be such as to specifically bring the accused within the material words thereof. One is not required to wait until the State's evidence is in to know whether he is *charged* with a crime. This much at least must appear from the allegations of the indictment or information—indeed, the State cannot prove what it has not properly alleged, and particularly can it not supply by incompetent evidence an absent allegation in the charge. We do not allow this even in civil pleading and practice, although, in such cases, we have not the same constitutional inhibition as we have in criminal cases.

The information in this cause is bottomed on section 4750, Revised Statutes 1909, which is as follows:

"Every person who shall set up or keep any table or gaming device commonly called A B C, faro bank, E O, roulette, equality, keno, slot machine, stand or device of whatever pattern, kind or make, or however worked, operated or manipulated, or any kind of gambling table or gambling device, adapted, devised and designed for the purpose of playing any game of chance for money or property and shall induce, entice or permit any person to bet or play at or upon any such gaming table or gambling device, or at or upon any game played or by means of such table or gambling device or on the side or against the keeper thereof, shall, on conviction," etc.

It will be observed that the Legislature first specifically names and denounces certain tables and gambling devices, thus giving them a legal signification, and then proceeds, in general terms, to level its pronouncement against "any kind of gambling table or gambling device adapted, devised and designed for the purpose of playing any game of chance for money or property and shall induce, entice or permit any person to bet or play at or upon any such gaming table or gambling device," etc.

In construing statutes we have so frequently applied the familiar rule of *ejusdem generis*, that we would not now be warranted in departing therefrom. We have said this doctrine meant that when an enumeration of certain specified things in a statute is followed by general words or phrases, such words or phrases of general description shall be deemed to mean things of the same class and kind, and not include things wholly different from those specifically mentioned, or otherwise expressed; that when general words follow particular words they must be construed as applicable only to the things of the same general

class as the particular words by which they are preceded.

Although, as said by Judge Faris in State v. Solon,
247 Mo. 672, when discussing the present section (1. c.
683), "Clearly this section has been by construction
strained almost to the breaking point," nevertheless,
this court has, at all times, declared, in determining
the devices to which it is applicable, that it recognized
the *ejusdem generis* rule.

In State v. Rosenblatt, 185 Mo. 114, Judge Gantt
said: " 'Craps' are not named and therefore do not
have a legal signification within the meaning of the
statute, but if prohibited at all must come within the
general prohibition of the section. Conceding that all
other gambling tables and devices not specifically
named must, under the doctrine *ejusdem generis*, be of
the same general class with those devices specifically
named, we think there can be no doubt that . . . a
crap table is of that class."

In State v. Locket, 188 Mo. 1. c. 422, Judge Fox, in
passing upon the same question approvingly quotes
this language from Judge Gantt.

In State v. Gilmore, 98 Mo. 206, this court held that
a pack of playing cards, although used for playing
games for money or property, was not a gambling device within the meaning of this section, the court
tersely stating that any other construction is condemned by the rule of *ejusdem generis*.

In State v. Lemon, 46 Mo. 375, the statute was declared inapplicable to a horse race; and in State v. Bryant, 90 Mo. 534, it was held that a gun and a target
were not of a kindred nature and similar kind to those
enumerated, and were, therefore, not within the purview of the act.

In the recent case of State v. Solon, 247 Mo.
672, it was held that the court will not take judicial
notice that poker is a game of chance, and that where
there is no evidence that the game of poker alleged to

have been played on the table was played with cards
and that chips or other gambling paraphernalia were
used, a demurrer to the evidence should be sustained,
since it is not sufficient to show that a game of poker
was played upon an ordinary hotel dining table, and
that defendant acted as "banker" therein and actually
took a "rake-off" therefrom.

In State v. Patton, 255 Mo. l. c. 261, the court said:
"In the case of State v. Solon, supra, we labored to
show the elements which distinguish the felony of setting up a gambling device, from those which go to
make up the ordinary misdemeanor of gaming. We
often find a dangerous twilight zone where the facts
so imperceptibly shade into a felony on the one side and
into a misdemeanor on the other, that it is almost impossible to distinguish the line of demarcation. The
Legislature has the right to say that a pack of cards
carried by a traveler; a writing table, or a washstand
in a guest room of an inn; an idle hour, an idle friend
or two and a game of five-cent ante, make a crime meet
for the taint of felony and two years in the penitentiary. But they have not so written it; neither
will we."

From these cases it is clear that this statute is
not broad enough to, and does not, include the setting
up or keeping of every and all kinds of gambling devices, regardless of their character, but is leveled
against only those of a certain class.

We yield to the holding in the case of State v. Rosenblatt, 185 Mo. 114; State v. Lee, 228 Mo. 480; State
v. Holden, 203 Mo. 581; and State v. Locket, 188 Mo.
415, that a table, duly marked and arranged for the
purpose, on which the game of craps is played by
means of dice for money or property, is within the purview of the section.

We further find from the evidence in this case
that the tables operated by defendant are of the class
forbidden by this section, but it is by virtue of the evi-

dence alone, and not the information, that we are able
to so. determine. The State proved more than it alleged. In these days of reform this might be sufficient
to warrant an affirmance of the judgment were it not
for what seems an insurmountable obstacle, namely:
the constitutional provision prohibiting a conviction
except upon a valid and sufficient charge. As heretofore stated, the tables which the evidence shows defendant maintained are not among those enumerated by
the statute, but fall within the general terms thereof.
Where the offense charged is the setting up and keeping of the gaming tables enumerated no more need be
averred, for the statute, in specific terms, denounces
that as a penal offense. In such cases it is a familiar
rule that it is sufficient to charge the offense in the
words of the statute, but where the device charged is
not among those enumerated, must there not be, recognizing the rule of *ejusdem generis,* sufficient averments showing it to be one belonging to the enumerated
class, and, therefore, within the general inhibition?
Absent this, can the defendant be said to be constitu-
tionally charged with a crime? Must not the indictment show on its face, and from its allegations, that
the thing for which an accused is placed upon trial
comes within the definition of the statute? Only
games of a certain distinctive character are denounced
by this section, and this is of the very essence of the offense. The correct rule is stated in 20 Cyc. 906, as follows: "The general rule is that an indictment for
keeping, setting up, or exhibiting a gaming-table or
other gambling device is sufficient if it follows the
language of the statute. But where the indictment alleges the keeping of other implements or gambling devices than those *named* in the act, they should be sufficiently described to show them to be gambling tables
or devices within the purview of the statute." This
doctrine was clearly recognized in the case of State v.
Etchman, 184 Mo. 193, the opinion in that case being

State v. Wade.

written by Judge Fox, who also wrote the opinion in State v. Locket, 188 Mo. 415, which will be noticed later.

The present information charges that defendant set up and kept "a certain table and gambling device commonly called a crap table." There is no allegation defining a crap table or of what it consists, or how designed, or how and by what means the game of craps is played—in short, there is no allegation bringing it within the class of the enumerated devices, unless (first) we take judicial notice of what constitutes a crap table, and how the game of craps is played; or (second) unless the general allegation that it was "a gambling device adapted, devised and designed for the purpose of playing games of chance for money or property" is sufficiently descriptive thereof to supply the missing information.

As to the first proposition, we have abundant authority that we do not so judicially know (State v. Solon, 247 Mo. 672; State v. Etchman, 184 Mo. 193), and this soft impeachment we also on other and purely personal grounds deny.

As to the second proposition, it is sufficient to say that the allegatioin is more in the nature of a conclusion than a statement of fact. [State ex rel. v. Railroad, 240 Mo. l. c. 50.] It can, with fitness, be applied to and be said to be equally descriptive of a pack of playing cards (State v. Gilmore, supra), a poker table without other paraphernalia (State v. Solon, supra), gun and target (State v. Bryant, supra), a horse race (State v. Lemon, supra); or, in fact, any of the "gaming tables and devices" included and prohibited by the misdemeanor section, to-wit: Section 4753, Revised Statutes 1909. In truth, substantially the same language is used and necessary when charging an offense under the misdemeanor section (State v. Howell, 83 Mo. App. 198); so the use of that phrase alone cannot possibly bring the alleged offense within the definition of the felony statute. Something more evidently is required. In State v. Miller, 132 Mo. 297, this court said: " 'The statutory indictment must specify on its face "the criminal nature and degree of the offense . . . and also the particular facts and circumstances which render the defendant guilty of that offense.'' ' [1 Bishop, Crim. Proc. (3 Ed.), sec. 625.]" See also State v. Terry, 109 Mo. 601.

In discussing a statute in substance like ours, and an indictment similar to the one at hand, it is said in Huff v. Commonwealth, 14 Gratt. 648: "Where the offense charged is for keeping and exhibiting a game not enumerated, there must be some averment showing it to be one of the unequal games belonging to the same class with the enumerated games. . . . The charge that the game is unlawful does not cure the defect. The offense must be so charged as to appear to be unlawful; otherwise, the allegation that an act was unlawful, would dispense with all averments showing it was unlawful."

While the employment of the general words heretofore quoted are, under another rule of construction, essential to a valid charge, they cannot supply other material allegations of fact.

In the case of State v. Solon, supra, suppose the indictment had not alleged the element of which the court found there was no evidence, namely: the means by which poker is played, and which caused the reversal thereof, should defendant have been put upon trial? And yet without so alleging the indictment would have been just as good as the one in the instant case. Must we impute to a defendant a knowledge of what constitutes a poker table or a crap table and how they are operated when we judicially disclaim such knowledge? Is he not entitled to be advised of this by the indictment?

Our conclusion is that the information in this case is wholly insufficient, and in this we are sustained by both logic and the weight of authority. It has been so held in Tummins v. State, 18 Tex. App. 13; Huff v. Commonwealth, 14 Gratt. 648, and numerous other cases.

It is true that the present information has heretofore been held sufficient by this court, and this alone is responsible for our hesitancy to hold to the contrary, but we have frequently said that a question of law is not settled until it has been correctly decided.

In the first case (State v. Rosenblatt, 185 Mo. 114) there is a brief discussion of the indictment, but an analysis thereof discloses that the conclusion that the indictment is sufficient is predicated upon the statement that the statute under discussion is broad enough to and does, include the setting up and keeping of *all* devices which may be used for playing games of chance. With this in mind, the court held that the statute individuated the offense, and that it was unnecessary to allege more than the words of the statute. Further consideration of this case indicates a glaring inconsistency. In discussing and determining the character of games and devices to which the statute is applicable the court, as heretofore stated, recognized the rule of *ejusdem generis,* but when it came to determining the sufficiency of the charge, the court expressed the opposite view and held it applicable to all devices. This error on the part of the court is again apparent from what it says at page 123, when attempting to distinguish our statute and the indictment then under discussion from the case of Huff v. Commonwealth, 14 Gratt. 648. The court in this connection said: ''It was not necessary to allege that chuck-a-luck or craps or both were of a *like kind* of gambling device as A B C, faro bank, E O, roulette, keno or equality. The decision in Huff v. Commonwealth, 14 Gratt. 648, was predicated on a statute which, after designating certain gambling devices, proceeded to say, '*or a table of like kind.'* No such words appear in section 2194, Revised Statutes 1899.''

In the case of Huff v. Commonwealth, supra, the court held that an indictment in the form of the instant one was insufficient for the reasons heretofore pointed out. It is clear that the statute in that case, by the use of the words ''or a table of like kind,'' added nothing whatever thereto, and did not change the construction which the courts would have placed thereon even in their absence. In that case the Legislature merely expressed in the statute that which we attach in such cases by construction, and the distinction which this court attempted to make in the Rosenblatt case only emphasizes the incorrectness of the decision.

The cases of State v. Locket, State v. Holden and State v. Lee, supra, were decided upon the strength of the Rosenblatt case, and the opinions therein contain nothing throwing light on this question. These opinions were written by Judges GANTT and Fox, and it is not amiss to note that in the case of State v. Etchman, 184 Mo. 193, Judge Fox wrote the opinion, and in it Judge GANTT concurred. In that case the indictment charged the setting up of a roulette *wheel*, where the statute denounces, among other devices, a roulette *table*. In that case the indictment was held insufficient, the court saying: ''It may be said that those who are familiar with the game know that 'roulette wheel' has reference to 'roulette table.' That does not meet the difficulty.'' (So might it be said by those familiar with a crap table that it is of the same class of devices as those named in the statute, but ''that does not meet the difficulty.'') The opinion in this case was rendered at the same term as was the opinion in the Rosenblatt case, and is clearly inconsistent therewith. Neither in the Rosenblatt, Locket, Holden or Lee cases is there any satisfactory authority cited sustaining the conclusion that the indictments therein are sufficient, but, in our opinion, such authorities as are cited, when analyzed, tend to the contrary. To the extent that these cases hold an information or indictment in the form of the one in this case sufficient they should be and are overruled.

II. This record also presents another question requiring consideration. In prosecuting alleged offenders the State must not take inconsistent positions. If, as the State contends, the information in this case is rendered sufficient by the description that the table is one *commonly known* as a crap table, was

Commonly Known: Proof. it not incumbent upon the State to show that there is a table *so commonly known,* and that it was this particular kind of a table that defendant set up and kept? Each witness for the State who testified relative to this subject stated that the tables which defendant maintained and operated were not of the kind which they commonly knew as a crap table. To the contrary, the tables are of radically different design and construction, as is evidenced by the uncontradicted exhibit offered by defendant, and positively identified by the State's witnesses. If there is such a table as has, through common and popular usage, become generally known as a crap table, and defendant's exhibit truly and correctly represents the same, this defendant could not plead as a bar to a subsequent prosecution his conviction of having set up and kept the tables which the evidence here shows he did. This only emphasizes the importance and necessity of fairly describing the character of the device intended to be charged. Under this information the most that could be said is, that defendant was called upon to answer the charge of keeping a table which had become generally known as a crap table. It did not require him to answer to the charge of maintaining tables of an entirely different design and construction.

State v. Wade.

It follows that if the information in this case were held sufficient we would necessarily have to hold that the proof disclosed a fatal variance and that the judgment could not stand. We have gone to a considerable extent in holding that section 5114, Revised Statutes 1909, cured questions of variance, but in none of our former holdings have we gone so far as to hold that a variance of this character was thereby cured.

Not only was there no evidence upon which a jury could find that the tables kept by defendant were of the kind commonly known as a crap table, but the court instructed, in effect, that this was immaterial.

III. It is further urged that there is a fatal variance between the charge and proof as to the location of the room in which the alleged games were played. Relative to this, it is sufficient to say that several witnesses for the State testified positively that this place was generally known and recognized by the number and description which the information alleges, and was so designated by defendant himself, and from this the jury was warranted in finding that the room was located as alleged. While it is unnecessary for the purposes of this case to go further, nevertheless, it is my opinion that if such a variance were disclosed it is one of that type that is cured by section 5114, Revised Statutes 1909. We have repeatedly and uniformly so held. [State v. Carragin, 210 Mo. l. c. 371; State v. Barker, 64 Mo. l. c. 285; State v. Smith, 80 Mo. l. c. 520; State v. Harl, 137 Mo. l. c. 256; State v. Sharp, 106 Mo. l. c. 109; State v. Waters, 144 Mo. l. c. 347; State v. Wammack, 70 Mo. l. c. 411; State v. Sharp, 71 Mo. l. c. 221; State v. Ward, 74 Mo. l. c. 255; State v. Nelson, 101 Mo. l. c. 482; State v. Dale, 141 Mo. l. c. 287; State v. Sharpless, 212 Mo. l. c. 202.] The allegation of the exact location of the place where the game was conducted

Location of Tables.

was unnecessary and did not relate to any constituent part of the offense. Unless the above statute was held to apply to instances of this character it would, in effect, be meaningless.

IV. The record discloses several other assignments of error, but, since they relate to matters which the State can easily guard against on a retrial, we deem it unnecessary to discuss or decide them.

For the reasons heretofore assigned the judgment is reversed, and, in order to enable the State, if it sees fit, to further proceed on a valid and sufficient charge, the cause is remanded. *Faris* and *Blair, JJ.*, concur; *Woodson, C. J.*, and *Graves, J.*, concur in separate opinion by *Graves, J.; Bond* and *Walker, JJ.*, dissent.

GRAVES, J. (concurring)—I concur in all of my brother's opinion except paragraph three. In that I neither concur in the law announced nor the facts stated. I think the facts shown as to where

Variance. these tables were found are at variance with the charge in the information, and therefore fatal to the judgment here. Nor do I agree that such a variance is cured by the statute named. I therefore not only agree that the judgment should be reversed for the reasons stated by the majority opinion, but for the additional reason suggested above. *Woodson, C. J.*, concurs in these views.

IN RE MINGO DRAINAGE DISTRICT. In the
Matter of the Articles of Association and Petition
of GEORGE S. DEAN et al. for the Incorporation
of MINGO DRAINAGE DISTRICT v. B. F. WIL-
SON et al., Appellants.

In Banc, March 1, 1916.

1. **DRAINAGE DISTRICT: Construction of Statutes.** Drainage
and reclamation statutes are to be liberally construed.

2. ————: **Objections.** Objections to the organization of the
proposed drainage district, timely filed by any person other
than the signers of the proposed articles, inure to the benefit of all non-signing owners of property liable to taxation in
the proposed district.

3. ————: **Ownership of Land: How Shown.** The matter of
title of lands within the proposed drainage district is only
incidental, and only a prima-facie showing of ownership is required, where no attempt is made to show that the signers of
the articles are not owners. The law does not require proof
of ownership to be made by deraignment from the Government
down to the present owners, by offering muniments of title or
certified copies thereof; secondary evidence of any kind that
establishes a prima-facie ownership is sufficient for the purposes of incorporation to constitute the signer of the articles
an owner, in the absence of proof to the contrary.

4. ————: ————: **Specific Objection: Should Be Pleaded.** If
certain persons who are not owners of land sign the articles of
incorporation for some fraudulent or ulterior motive, the objectors should deny by name that they are owners and upon
the hearing break down by evidence their prima-facie showing
of ownership; or, at least, deny generally that divers persons
who signed the petition were competent signers or owners of
land, and destroy the prima-facie case by proof.

5. ————: **Inclusion of Hills.** The inclusion of hills and other
high lands which do not overflow within the drainage district
does not necessarily render the incorporation invalid. If
such lands are not benefited and only by their inclusion a competent number of petitioners is obtained, that would have the
effect to oust jurisdiction; but it may well be that that drainage of wet, low or swamp lands lying around and about will
so far benefit hills and other high land in matters of sanitation
and easier egress and ingress as to render it entirely equitable
that they should bear a modicum of the cost of draining the
low land.

6. ————: **Petitioner: President of Corporation.** An objection, made only by other landowners, that the president of a corporation owning land in the proposed district had no authority, in the name of the company, to sign the articles of incorporation without being specifically authorized to do so by the board of directors or by a vote of its stockholders, is not allowed.

7. ————: ————: **Attorney In Fact.** Likewise, an objection by other landowners only, that a certain person who held a power of attorney to act generally for a corporation which owned certain lands in the proposed district had no authority to sign the articles, is disallowed.

8. ————: ————: **Holder of Deed in Escrow.** And an objection by the owners of other land only that a certain person who had contracted to buy the land for which he signed the name of the then apparent owner, was not authorized to sign the articles, is disallowed, the fact being that the deed to him was then actually executed and lying in escrow and before the hearing was taken down by him and recorded.

9. ————: **Title of Case.** Prior to a final judgment incorporating a drainage district the title of the case on appeal should run thus: "In re Petition for Incorporation of Mingo Drainage District; George S. Dean et al., Petitioners, Respondents, v. B. F. Wilson et al., Appellants."

10. ————: ————: **Right to Sue.** After the decree incorporating a drainage district has been made final it can sue and be sued in its own corporate name.

Appeal from Stoddard Circuit Court.—*Hon. W. S. C. Walker*, Judge.

AFFIRMED.

Brown, Pradt & Genrich and *V. V. Ing* for appellants.

No persons but those who are owners of swamp, wet or overflowed lands or lands subject to overflow are qualified signers and petitioners in a proceeding to organize and incorporate a drainage district. Laws 1913, p. 233, sec. 2. The acreage majority must be swamp, wet or overflowed lands or lands subject to overflow, and such land must lie in a contiguous body.

Laws 1913, p. 233, sec. 2. Owners of real estate in
the sense in which the term "owners" is used in the
act under which this proceeding is prosecuted, are
the owners of the freehold estate as appears by the
deed record. Laws 1913, p. 253, sec. 39. A freehold
estate in lands is an estate vested and cannot be
established by oral statements of witnesses. Turner
v. Williams, 76 Mo. 617. The deed record is the
best evidence of the ownership of the lands in the
drainage district. Laws 1913, sec. 39, p. 253. Where
the best evidence is available it must be used. Secs.
2818, 2819, R. S. 1909. The second best evidence
(a copy of the conveyance or a copy of the record)
is not admissible unless such copy is under the oath
of some person knowing the requisite facts, or the
certificate of the recorder under his official seal.
Sec. 2819, R. S. 1909. All of the testimony of witnesses
as to what they say they found relative to the ownership of the lands in the drainage district, and their
opinions relative thereto, by examination of the abstract books of Weber Abstract, Land & Loan Company concerning lands in Stoddard County, was improperly admitted, because the abstract books themselves could not have been admitted in evidence (if
they had been offered, which was not done) because
there was no evidence whatever as to the correctness
of the abstract books by persons who knew. Einstein
v. Land & Lumber Co., 118 Mo. App. 184. In the second
place, it was improper for the court to admit as evidence of ownership the oral testimony of witnesses
as to what they understood the deed records and in-
dexes of deed records to show, concerning the question
as to who were the owners of the lands in the drainage
district. The question of ownership is a question of
law, for the court to pass on, and not to be decided by
the testimony of witnesses. Brown v. Railway Co., 101
Mo. 484; Land Co. v. Thompson, 157 Mo. 647; Whittle-
sey v. Kellogg, 28 Mo. 404; Milan v. Pemberton, 12 Mo.

598. The custodian of the record, in this case, the recorder of deeds, is the only person who may testify as
to what the records in his office show or do not show,
and this rule applies in all cases where the ownership
of real estate is involved. Sec. 2819, R. S. 1909. Even
records other than the records of the conveyances
of real estate are subject to the rule that no person
except the custodian thereof may give oral testimony
of its contents. Blodgett v. Schaffer, 94 Mo. 652; Martin v. Brand, 182 Mo. 116. The best evidence available to the party offering evidence must be offered.
Montgomery v. Dormer, 181 Mo. 5. The deed records of
Stoddard County were all in the office of the recorder
of that county at the time of the trial, and no offer of
any of these records as evidence in this case was made.

Wammack & Welborn and *J. F. Meador* for respondents.

The court might very well require some showing
by the petitioners as to the ownership of the land—a
sufficient showing to induce the court to see that it
is not being imposed upon, but in the absence of any
showing whatever on behalf of the objectors (and there
is no such showing in this case) the objectors would
have no right to demand anything more than the showing made by the articles themselves and would not be
in a position to question the character of evidence by
which such showing was made. Birmingham Drainage District v. Railroad, 178 S. W. 897; Little River
Drainage District v. Railroad, 236 Mo. 94.

FARIS, J.—This is an appeal from a proceeding
in the circuit court of Stoddard County for the incorporation of a drainage district under the provisions of
the Act of March 24, 1913. [Laws 1913, p. 232 et seq.]
Upon a hearing on the question of entering a *pro forma*
decree of incorporation and from a judgment decreeing incorporation, appellants here, who are some of
the objectors below, have appealed.

The questions which are involved turn upon the objections filed by appellants and others who were not signers of the proposed articles of incorporation. Except for the alleged errors in the admission of evidence upon the hearing of the case and which are specifically set forth in the opinion, a full understanding of the points of contention may be had from the objections filed by appellants. These objections, caption, merely formal parts and the names of the objectors other than these appellants, omitted, are as follows, so far as they are pertinent:

"Now come B. F. Wilson, C. S. Gilbert, L. A. Pradt, Neal Brown [and eighteen other named persons] and state that they are the owners of the lands and real estate which it is alleged that they own in the articles of association, made and executed by George S. Dean, Robert H. Bailey, Timothy T. Beach and others asking and praying that the lands and other property therein described be organized and incorporated as a drainage district. to be named Mingo Drainage District, and filed in the office of the clerk of this court in vacation of the court.

"These objectors, B. F. Wilson, C. S. Gilbert, L. A. Pradt, Neal Brown [and eighteen other named persons] further state that they did not sign the articles of association herein.

"The said B. F. Wilson, C. S. Gilbert, L. A. Pradt, Neal Brown [and eighteen other named persons] come now into court here for the purpose of objecting, most respectfully to the incorporation of the said proposed Mingo Drainage District under the said articles of association filed in this court, and do object most earnestly and sincerely to the organization and incorporation of said Mingo Drainage District for the following reasons, to-wit:

"1st. For the reason that the drainage and reclamation of the lands and other property in said proposed district from the effects of water, which is

contemplated if said Mingo Drainage District be organized and incorporated, is not practical or feasible, even
if the same be possible.

"2nd. For the reason that the effects of the water
upon the lands and other property within the said proposed district are not so injurious as to justify imposing the burdens and costs and expenses upon the
owners of the lands and property in the district for
the purpose of draining the said lands.

"3rd. For the reason that the drainage of the
said lands is impracticable for want or lack of sufficient fall or slope in the land to carry off the water
that accumulates thereon by rainfall and natural
flowage.

"4th. For the reason that there is not sufficient
outlet or channel or other body of water into which
the water may be drained off the lands in the proposed
district, nor any way of draining it off without throwing it onto other lands of great value, thereby entailing
great damage to such other lands and placing heavy
burdens of taxation on the lands in the said district
to pay the same.

"5th. For the reason that there are many acres
of lands in said proposed district that would not in
any way be benefited by the drainage of the swamp
and overflowed lands therein.

"6th. For the reason that there are many acres
of lands in said proposed district that are not swamp,
nor overflowed land, nor subject to overflow by water.

"7th. For the reason that the burden of taxation
upon the lands in the proposed district would, necessarily, be so great that the making of the improvements contemplated, and draining the lands in the
district would be out of reason and proportion to the
benefits that would result therefrom to the property
in said drainage district.

"8th. For the reason that there are now in process
of drainage and reclamation about 5,000,000 [sic] acres

of swamp, wet and overflowed lands and lands subject to overflow in the Little River Drainage District
immediately north and east of the proposed Mingo
Drainage District, which project, if practicable and
consummated, will reclaim and throw upon the market, no doubt, many thousands of acres of land and
open up to use many thousands of acres of land, if the
project of drainage is practicable and feasible, which ·
will render the present drainage and reclamation of
the lands in the proposed Mingo Drainage District
impracticable, for the reason that there will be no demand nor necessity for the reclamation of said lands
at the present time and for several years; and, if said
lands in said Little River Drainage District be not
reclaimed and made useful for agricultural purposes
and other purposes, then that fact will demonstrate
the impracticability of the reclamation of the swamp,
wet and overflowed lands in the proposed Mingo
Drainage District, hence it is best and most judicious
to await the result of the efforts at the reclamation of
the lands in the Little River Drainage District before
proceeding to the organization and incorporation of
the proposed Mingo Drainage District, which, if organized and incorporated, will entail large and burdensome expenses and costs on the owners of the property
in said district, even if it should be demonstrated
later that the project is impracticable.

"9th. For the reason that there is no demand
or necessity for the drainage of the lands in the proposed Mingo Drainage District at the present time
that justifies the organization and incorporation of
the district. . . .

"11th. For the reason that the owners of a majority of the acreage of the lands in said proposed Mingo
Drainage District have not signed said articles of association.

"12th. For the reason that the owners of a majority of the acreage of the swamp, wet and overflowed

lands and lands subject to overflow by water have not signed said articles of association.

"13th. For the reason that the owners of a majority of the acreage of the swamp, wet and overflowed lands and lands subject to overflow by water in a contiguous body have not signed the said articles of association.

"14th. For the reason that the lands and other property in said proposed drainage district owned by each person who owns land and property therein are not described as belonging to the respective owners thereof and the name and post-office addresses of each owner given in said articles of association.

"15th. For the reason that the names of the individual owners of lands and other property in said proposed Mingo Drainage District is not given and the lands and other property owned by each is not described in the said articles of association.

"16th. For the reason that there are swamp, wet and overflowed lands and lands subject to overflow by water in the said proposed Mingo Drainage District which are not described in said articles of association.

"17th. For the reason that much of the lands described in said articles of association filed herein are not swamp, wet or overflowed lands, nor lands subject to overflow.

"18th. For the reason that there are persons who own lands in said proposed drainage district whose names are known by the persons who signed said articles of association, or by some of such signers, and whose names are not stated in said articles of association. . . .

"23rd. For the reason that many of the persons whose names appear as signers to the articles of association did not, in fact, sign said articles of association and did not authorize their respective names to be signed thereto.

"24th. For the reason that many of the persons whose names appear as signers to said articles of association do not own any lands or other property within said Mingo Drainage District.

"25th. For the reason that said articles of association contain no description of any property other than lands, and there is no allegation that there are any other kinds of property in said drainage district other than real estate and lands, and no allegation that the owner or owners of any kind of property in said district than lands, have or has signed said articles of association, and no allegation that there are no .other kinds of property in said district other than lands.

"26th. For the reason that the lands belonging to these objectors within said proposed drainage district would not be benefited by the drainage and alleged improvements contemplated by the petitioners as disclosed by said articles of incorporation, but on the contrary, would thereby be greatly injured and damaged.

"These objectors to the organization and incorporation of the said Mingo Drainage District earnestly object to the organization and incorporation of said Drainage District for the above and foregoing reasons, and they respectfully ask the court to find and to adjudge and decree that the lands described in said articles of association be not organized and incorporated as a drainage district, and to render its order, judgment and decree dismissing said articles of association and said drainage proceedings, and to adjudge the costs of this proceeding against the said signers of said articles of association according to law, and that these objectors recover of and from the said signers to said articles of association their costs and expenses in this behalf expended, and that they have execution therefor, and that they be permitted to go hence without day."

OPINION.

I. Objectors raised *nisi* twenty-six alleged reasons why the Mingo Drainage District should not be incorporated. Many of these were premature and could not have been considered by the court *nisi* at this incorporating stage of this proceeding. For many, if not the majority of the twenty-six points mooted, will save themselves till the report of the viewers and engineers comes in, should that stage ever be reached. Such of the points as were timely, but not prematurely raised, are here for review as questions of fact or as alleged errors of the court below, in admitting evidence. Some of these timely mooted points have apparently been waived, since no steps to review them are taken here. So, three points only confront us: (a) That the court *nisi* allowed, over appellant's objections, the ownership of the lands in the proposed district to be proved by secondary evidence, instead of requiring such proof of ownership to be made by deraignment from the Government down to the present owners, by offering in proof the best evidence, to-wit, original muniments of title, or certified copies thereof, upon a proper foundation laid; (b) that there are unlawfully included within the limits of the proposed district certain lands which are not swamp, but high and hilly; and (c) that certain persons, to-wit, Collins, Shantz and Keaton, had no legal authority to sign the proposed articles of incorporation for certain owners of lands within the proposed district.

We must bear in mind *that not one scintilla of evidence was offered by the appellants,* or by any other objector. These objectors merely stood by and contented themselves with objecting to the form of proof offered by the petitioners for the district to show ownership of the lands therein.

Generalizing, we but state a well-settled truism when we say that since drainage and reclamation statutes are manifestations of one of the very highest phases of the police power, that, to-wit, having an intimate relation to the betterment of health through sanitation and the destruction of breeding-places for germ-bearing insects, courts in this, as in practically every other jurisdiction, have held that such statutes are to be liberally construed. [State ex rel. v. Bugg, 224 Mo. l. c. 554; State ex rel. v. Bates, 235 Mo. l. c. 293; Osborn v. Maxinkuckee Lake Ice Co., 154 Ind. 101.] Indeed, our statute in express terms declares its own remedial character, and requires at our hands a liberal construction. [Sec. 62, Laws 1913, p. 267.]

Coming specifically to the provisions of our statute, we note that there are provided time and place for both general and specific objections and exceptions. By section 4 of the Act of March 24, 1913, Laws 1913, p. 235, any person, barring those who are signers of the proposed articles of incorporation, may appear and file objections "why such drainage district should not be organized and incorporated." Such objections, it is obvious, inure to the benefit of all non-signing owners of property liable to taxation in the proposed district. After the district is, in a way of speaking, "conditionally organized and incorporated" (Carder v. Fabius River Drainage District, 262 Mo. l. c. 554), any individual owning such property therein (whether he signed the articles or not), or even the district itself, may file individual exceptions, covering apparently any and every possible phase of accruing damage to the property or interests of the exceptor. [Sec. 16, Laws 1913, p. 241.]

The general objection first above mentioned is that which is said to be in controversy here. Touching it our statute provides that "any owner of real estate or other property in said proposed district, who

may not have signed said articles of association,
objecting to the organization and incorpo-
Proof of Ownership of Land. ration of said drainage district, shall, on or
before the first day of the term of court at
which the cause is to be heard, file his objection or objections why such drainage district should not be organized and incorporated. Such objection or objections
shall be limited to a denial of the statements in the
articles of association, and shall be heard by the court
in a summary manner, without unnecessary delay."
[Laws 1913, p. 235, sec. 4.]

It will be noted that *objections may be filed on
the day set for hearing* in the circuit court, and that
when so filed they are to be heard *"in a summary
manner,"* and *"without unnecessary delay."* It is
not so clear that we are aided, for that in the determination of the troubling point, the Legislature may
have had in mind a trial according to the rule governing summary proceedings, that is, a trial which is not
regulated, or bound by the rules of the common law
or by the statutes of pleading and procedure which
govern practice and procedure in ordinary civil cases.
For such proceedings yet follow the common-law rules
of evidence, absent a statute otherwise providing.
[Comm. v. Borden, 61 Pa. St. 272.] However, it is fairly deducible that the Legislature held in mind the utter
impossibility in practice in the ordinary case of requiring ownership of lands in a proposed drainage district to be shown by a formal deraignment from the
Government through original muniments of title, or
by certified copies upon a proper foundation laid. In
the case at bar more than thirty thousand acres of land
are included in the proposed district. There are more
than three hundred separate tracts described. These
said tracts have as owners, or incumbrancers whose
titles or claims are evidently evidenced by paper conveyances, many more than three hundred persons or

corporations. If there were but one conveyance to each
tract much expense and labor would be involved in
making strict proof to meet the contentions of appellants here. If there were an average of ten conveyances
to each tract, the matter of proof of title in the way
urged on us would instantly become impracticable to
a point approaching the impossible. And if it were
ever desired to be made a matter of review here by
appeal, such appeal would likewise be impossible on
account of the labor and expense of printing a record
of the three thousand or more conveyances offered in
evidence below. Being permitted by law to be no more
ignorant than the ordinary citizen, of matters of con-
temporary progress, public moment and history, we
know (in fact such acreage *is writ at large in the instant record*) that the Little River Drainage District
contains much more than half a million acres of land.
The strict rule here contended for would have forbidden for all time the organization of that district. Yet
it seems that in the organization of that district the
court *nisi* permitted, and this court sanctioned, the use
of evidence which did not prove ownership (as deraignment by muniments of title from the source would
have done, as inevitably as the demonstration of a
problem in Euclid), but merely "evidence tending to
prove the *ownership* as alleged in the articles of association." [Little River Drainage District v. Railroad,
236 Mo. l. c. 112.]

It is manifest that the circuit court could not pause
in the organization of a drainage district under a statute worded as ours is, to try out and determine between
all possible contenders each and every title to each
of the three hundred parcels of land in the district at
bar. Such a view is so restricted and narrow as to
trench upon the ridiculous. So, while conceding that
where the question of title is directly in issue the best
evidence thereof is required as appellants contend,
that is not the case before us. Here the matter of title

is only incidental, and all that is required is a prima-
facie showing of ownership. The ownership shown, it
would seem, may be that only which arises from a recorded deed, or a deed not recorded if there be in fact
ownership, or no deed at all where there is sufficient
possession. The *pseudo* owner may not have
an indefeasible title; his title may be so flimsy as
to fall at the first attack by the true owner, but if
it be of record and be of the stature connoted by the
phrase prima-facie, it is sufficient to constitute the
claimant an owner so that he may petition for the
incorporation of a drainage district. Being only
incidentally involved therefore, title, or ownership,
may be shown prima-facie by secondary evidence.
[Railroad v. Gilbert, 3 C. C. A. 264; Joy v. State,
41 Tex. Crim. App. 46; Sleep v. Heymann, 57 Wis.
495; Babcock v. Beaver Creek Township, 65 Mich.
479; Grevenberg v. Borel, 25 La. Ann. 530.] The
reason for the distinction is not far to see. For whenever an action is brought wherein the question of title
to land is the sole issue to be determined the case
and wherein the judgment will become final and conclusive proof of such title, the best evidence of which
the conditions permit should be adduced. But where
as here it is merely collateral, and the producing of
the best evidence would involve so great a labor and
so huge a volume of record evidence as to render the
making of proof impossible from the view point of
practicability, we are permitted to hold in consonance
with the authorities that the rule as to the best evidence does not apply. Besides, the fact that any other
view would render this statute so cumbersome and
onerous in the making of proof of ownership, as to
forbid the organization of any but small districts, when
the converse must have been intended, inclines us to the
opinion that the Legislature intended to relax the harsh
rules of evidence in the making of this proof. That

such a view was in the legislative mind is to be gathered from the statutory requirement that such objections as those now at bar shall be heard in a "summary manner, without unnecessary delay."

We hold that the showing made by oral testimony of persons who are shown to be competent abstractors, familiar with land titles, and who had examined the abstracts of title to the lands in the proposed district, and the records of the recorder's office touching same, as also the tax books, was sufficient, as prima-facie proof of such ownership for the purposes of incorporating this drainage district.

We could have reached this conclusion by another road: For while both the appellants and the respondents treat this point of ownership as well raised by the objections filed, we do not think that it is so raised. But because both sides so agree, and because it has, it seems, been raised before and never ruled (Little River Drainage District v. Railroad, supra; Birmingham Dr. Dist. v. Railroad, 266 Mo. 60), we have thought best to notice it. Yet one will read in vain through the exceptions to find *specifically* this objection mooted. It is objected, to-wit:

"13th. For the reason that the owners of a majority of the acreage of the swamp, wet and overflowed lands and lands subject to overflow by water in a contiguous body have not signed the said articles of association," and,

"24th. For the reason that many of the persons whose names appear as signers to said articles of association do not own any lands or other property within said Mingo Drainage District."

But nowhere is it said specifically who of the signers do not own lands in the proposed district, or that the ostensible owners of a majority of the acreage who signed the petition do not in fact own the lands they therein claim to own. Rather do the two allegations seem to hint, while most adroitly avoiding, a di-

rect charge of a signing by others than the owners of
the lands. Taking the two charges together they may
seem to make this direct charge; considering them separately they do not so charge. The thirteenth allegation may mean that, granting good faith and truth in
the averment of ownership, there are yet, upon a bare
inspection and mathematical addition, not enough
owners of acreage signing to amount to a majority.
The twenty-fourth allegation may mean that there are
enough signers to confer jurisdiction, but yet by accident or inadvertence, names of unnecessary persons
have gotten upon the lists.

Conceding that it might be possible for a fraud
to be perpetrated upon the court to which a petition
for the incorporation of a drainage district is presented, and that in such case there should be at hand
a plain way to circumvent such fraud, yet it is apparent
that such protection both to the court and to non-
signing and opposing owners of property liable to taxation, is plainly afforded without raising for such chim-
erical situation an insuperable barrier to the organization of these districts at all. For if A, who is not
an owner of any land of the mentioned sort in the
proposed district yet signs the petition for some fraudulent and ulterior motive, nothing is easier than to so
charge specifically in the objections filed, by denying
that A is such owner, and upon the hearing to break
down the prima-facie case made by proof of A's lack
of competency as a signer. Or, even to deny generally that divers persons who signed the petition were
competent signers or owners of the lands they claim
to own, and therefore that their signing was designed
to work a fraud upon the court and impose an illegal
tax and hardship upon the property owners. But as
forecast, in such case some proof of the allegation
ought to be made to destroy the prima-facie case made
by proof from persons who had examined the records,
abstracts and tax books. We mention this lest it be

urged that no protection against fraud is afforded
by the ruling we have found it necessary to make in
compliance with the statutory demand of a liberal
construction of this law at our hands.

II. It is contended that there are some high, hilly
lands embraced in the proposed district; and that such
fact renders the incorporation illegal. We do not think
it necessarily follows that because certain high lands
which neither floods nor water cover, are included,
such fact conclusively shows a lack of benefit to such
lands making the inclusion of them *ipso facto* error.
This would seem to be true here for at least three
reasons: (a) Appellants here do not own any of these
hill lands so here included; (b) it is not shown that
the petitioners who signed would cease to be a majority,
if the signing owners of the hill lands were excluded,
and (c) it may well be that the drainage of low, wet and
swamp land lying about, around or near high hill land
will so far benefit the latter in matters of sanitation
and ease of egress and ingress as to render it entirely equitable that the hill land should bear a modicum
of the cost of draining the low land. Besides, it was
said in oral argument and not denied, that such inclusion of hill land does not change the status of the
case as to the forum, or jurisdiction, or as to the requisite number of signing owners, and that such inclusion
was largely for the purpose of convenience in description. Moreover, it appears by the record that the
petitioners sought to amend the proposed articles by
striking out these hill lands, but their motion to this
end was overruled. If this was error, it was not one for
which petitioners should suffer. [In re Big Lake Drainage District v. Rolwing, 265 Mo. 450.]

The owners of this hill land, if so it be that they
are not benefited, have provided for them in the statute under discussion a place and time to moot this
question. [Sec. 16, Laws 1913, p. 241.] That such a
question might be raised successfully at this juncture,

we may concede without deciding, contenting us with holding that it has not been so raised upon the facts here. In such latter case, however, the inclusion of the hill land should have the effect to oust jurisdiction by destroying the competency of a jurisdictional number of petitioners; absent, perhaps, even in such case, proof of contingent benefit from betterment of health or access.

III. The proof shows that one Shantz, who was president of a corporation owning certain of the lands sought to be included, signed the articles of incorporation without being in that behalf specifically authorized by the board of directors or by a vote of the stockholders. Likewise the proof showed that one Collins, having a power of attorney to act generally for the Connecticut Mutual Life Insurance Company touching certain lands which said company owned in the proposed district, signed for said company without specific authorization. It is urged that these persons were not upon these facts competent to sign for their respective principals.

We held in the case of Sibbett v. Steele, 240 Mo. 1. c. 94, in substance that a petition for the incorporation of a drainage district was in effect the first pleading in the case; that such pleading might be signed by the attorneys who appeared in court and therein represented the petitioners, and that so assuming to represent them, such attorney would be held to possess the power of binding the petitioners by the judgment rendered, no objection from the latter appearing showing lack of power so to bind them. These petitioners are not here objecting for themselves. They do not question the authority of their agents. Appellants are seeking to question it for them. We think the holding in the Sibbett case disposes of this contention, either directly or by the very strongest analogy. Also that case disposes of the contention that Keaton had

no authority to sign for Sloan and Mrs. Clayton; the
facts being that Keaton had contracted to buy the land
for which he signed the names of Sloan and Mrs. Clayton, and the conveyance to him therefor was actually
executed and lying in escrow. Before the case came
on for hearing Keaton had taken down the deed and
had it recorded. Neither Keaton, the present owner,
nor the Shantz Company, nor the Insurance Company
was objecting; the others may not. We disallow these
several contentions.

No point is made touching the style of this case.
Consequently, we style it here cumbersomely, as it
came up to us. We think, however that prior to a final
judgment decreeing incorporation, the better style
would be: "In re.Petition for Incorporation of Mingo
Drainage District; George S. Dean et al., Petitioners,
Respondents, v. B. F. Wilson et al., Appellants."
[Little River Drainage District v. Railroad, 236 Mo.
94.] After the decree of incorporation has been made
final, the district may of course sue and be sued in its
own corporate name. [Carder v. Fabius River Drainage District No. 3, 262 Mo. 542.] We but mention this
in passing, lest by silence, we should seem to approve
the style herein adopted, and for the sake of uniformity, of which virtue there has been so little, as a glance
at the Missouri drainage cases indicates.

It follows that the judgment incorporating this
district should be affirmed. Let this be done. All concur, except *Walker, J.,* absent.

J. C. SIMPSON, Appellant, v. O. L. VAN LANING-
HAM.

In Banc, March 1, 1916.

1. **NEGOTIABLE NOTE: Notice of Infirmities.** Notes made
    payable to the maker and indorsed in blank by him become
    payable to bearer and negotiable by delivery; and a transferee

before maturity with actual knowledge of a concurrent dependent agreement, and a transferee after maturity without actual knowledge, take the notes with notice of the agreement and that it makes them non-payable.

2. ———: **Concurrent Dependent Agreement.** A negotiable promissory note and a concurrent collateral agreement, connected by direct reference or necessary implication, the stipulations of which are mutual and dependent, are to be construed together as one entire contract; and a transferee of the note after maturity, without actual knowledge of the agreement, cannot recover, if the agreement, when so construed, bars a re recovery.

3. ———: ———: **Option to Surrender Stock for Notes.** The maker of negotiable notes received a concurrent written agreement, signed by a corporation and its president, reciting that the maker had purchased one hundred shares of the capital stock of the company, for which he had given his two notes in settlement, due in six months, and guaranteeing that the maker, at their maturity might, at his option, surrender the stock, whereupon the notes would be cancelled and returned to him. The certificates of stock, indorsed in blank, were attached to the notes, and the notes were transferred to a bank, whose cashier had full actual knowledge of the agreement. Shortly afterwards the bank went into the hands of a receiver, who, after the maturity of the notes, sold them to plaintiff. *Held*, that the notes and agreement did not constitute independent contracts, but they are dependent, and the agreement constitutes a defense to an action on the notes; and since the payee of the notes, when the agreement was delivered, was the holder, and the holder signed the agreement, the rule is not changed by the fact that another also signed it.

4. **GUARANTEE.** The fact that the makers of an agreement "guarantee" certain things does not of itself constitute the agreement a guaranty. The word may be used simply to give emphasis and not to change the plain character of the agreement.

5. **NEGOTIABLE NOTES: Conditioned on Return of Stock: Failure to Return as Part of Defense.** Where negotiable notes, given for the purchase of certificates of stock of a corporation, indorsed in blank, attached to the notes and delivered with them to the payee, were accompanied by a concurrent dependent agreement that upon the maturity of the notes the certificates could be surrendered and the notes cancelled, and that agreement is set up as a defense to an action on the notes, the instructions may authorize a finding for defendant without requiring a finding that he returned the stock or relinquished his right to it, since the certificates were already in possession of the holder of the notes, and it was

Simpson v. Van Laningham.

impossible for defendant to tender the physical return of the stock.

6. ———: ———: **Evidence of Demand for Return of Notes.** And, under such circumstances, evidence that the maker demanded from the signers of the concurrent dependent agreement (the corporation and its president) the return of the notes, in accordance with the agreement, and being told they were in possession of a bank as transferee had his attorney to demand them from the bank, was competent to show an effort on defendant's part to comply with the agreement, as far as he could.

7. ———: ———: **Evidence of Election.** And evidence that, when defendant was approached by the attorney of the corporation on the theory that he was a stockholder, he announced that he had elected to surrender the stock and cancel the notes in accordance with the agreement, could not have prejudiced the rights of a holder of the notes with notice of the agreement.

8. **EVIDENCE: Hearsay.** A general objection that all the testimony on a particular subject contained in two depositions was hearsay should not be allowed if part of it is clearly not hearsay.

Appeal from Jackson Circuit Court.—*Hon. W. A. Powell,* Judge.

Affirmed.

Robinson & Goodrich for appellant.

(1) The existence of the guaranty, even if the cashier had knowledge thereof at the time the bank purchased the note, constituted no defense to this action. Jennings v. Todd, 118 Mo. 305; Miller v. Altsway, 81 Mich. 196; Adams v. Smith, 35 Me. 324; Dow v. Tuttle, 4 Mass. 414; Davis v. McCurdy, 17 N. Y. 230; R. S. 1909, secs. 10022, 10024, 10025. (2) The court committed error in admitting in evidence defendant's testimony as to conversations he had had with, and statements made to, other persons, not parties to this suit, in regard to the guaranty given him by the Refrigerating Company and J. E. Brady, and in

regard to the bank cashier's knowledge of said guaranty. (a) They were simply self-serving declarations of the defendant, not made in the presence of his adversary. Milliken v. Green, 5 Mo. 489; Gordon v. Klapp, 38 Ala. 357; Nicholson v. Tarply, 70 Cal. 608; Williams v. English, 64 Ga. 546; Adams Express Co. v. Boskowitz, 107 Ill. 660; Handley v. Cal., 30 Me. 9; Neisbaum v. Thompson, 11 Md. 557; Kehrig v. Peters, 41 Mich. 475; Cain v. Cain, 140 Pa. St. 144. A party's own statements, not made in the presence of his adversary, are not admissible in his own favor. McLean v. Rutherford, 8 Mo. 109; Teller v. Patten, 61 U. S. 125; Alexander v. Handley, 96 Ala. 220; Rogers v. Schulenberg, 111 Cal. 281; Alston v. Grantham, 26 Ga. 374; Cotton v. Holliday, 59 Ill. 176; Corbel v. Beard, 92 Iowa, 360; Talbott v. Talbott, 25 Ky. 3; Boston v. Worcester, 67 Mass. 83; Griffin v. Bristle, 39 Minn. 456; Howard v. Hunt, 57 N. H. 467; Moody v. Gardner, 42 Tex. 411; McKesson v. Sherman, 51 Wis. 303. (b) Said conversation were hearsay evidence, and therefore not admissible. Chouteau v. Searcy, 8 Mo. 733; Atkisson v. Castle Garden, 28 Mo. 124; Coble v. McDaniel, 33 Mo. 363; O'Neil v. Crain, 67 Mo. 250; Fougue v. Burgess, 71 Mo. 389; St. Louis v. Arnett, 94 Mo. 275; State v. Sibley, 131 Mo. 530; Gordon v. Burris, 141 Mo. 611; Allen v. Transit Co., 183 Mo. 437; Bevis v. Railroad, 26 Mo. App. 19; Love v. Love, 98 Mo. App. 509; 16 Cyc. 1200; 11 Am. & Eng. Ency. Law, p. 520. (c) Moreover, said conversations and statements were wholly irrelevant to any issue in the case, and for that reason inadmissible. Irrelevant testimony is never admissible. 1 Greenleaf on Ev., secs. 50, 52 and 448; Eddy v. Baldwin, 32 Mo. 369; Ferguson v. Thatcher, 79 Mo. 511; Frederick v. Allgaier, 88 Mo. 598; State v. Blunt, 91 Mo. 503; Mathias v. O'Neill, 94 Mo. 520; Carlin v. Bank, 86 Mo. App. 592; Bank v. Bank, 64 Mo. App. 253; Thompson v. Bowie, 4 Wall. 463; Whitelaw v. Whitelaw, 96 Va. 712. (3) Defendant's instruction authorized the jury to return a verdict for defendant without finding a performance on his part of the conditions necessary to entitle him to the benefit of the guaranty given him by J. E. Brady and the Refrigerating Company.

William Thomson and *D. C. Payne* for respondent.

Plaintiff cannot recover in this action. (a) Plaintiff is not a holder in due course. R. S. 1909, secs. 10022, 10024, 10025, 10026. (b) A trustee cannot delegate his power. Cassady v. Wallace, 102 Mo. 575; Garesche v. Inv. Co., 146 Mo. 436; Bailes v. Perry, 51 Mo. 449; Graham v. King, 50 Mo. 22. (c) One buying commercial paper after maturity takes it subject to equities. (d) Equities between maker and payee brought to actual knowledge of indorsee of negotiable note before his purchase of same before maturity, defeats recovery. Johnson v. Machinery Co., 144 Mo. App. 436; Bank v. Brisch, 154 Mo. App. 631; Bank v. Salmon, 117 Mo. App. 506; Bank v. Reeper, 121 Mo. App. 688; Bank v. Ornsdorff, 126 Mo. App. 654; 7 Cyc. 947-949-956. (e) When a collateral and contemporaneous agreement, forming a whole or a part of the consideration on the part of the payee of a negotiable instrument, has been breached by the payee and actual knowledge of such breach has been given to an indorsee who takes before maturity, such knowledge will defeat recovery in the hands of such indorsee. Bank v. Ornsdorff, 126 Mo. App. 654; Hunter v. Johnson, 119 Mo. App. 487; Jennings v. Todd, 118 Mo. 296; Studebaker Mfg. Co. v. Dickson, 70 Mo. 272; Davis v. McCready, 17 N. Y. 230; R. S. 1909, secs. 10022-10024, 10025, 10026, 10028. (f) Where one of the parties to a contract, either before the time for performance or in the course of performance, makes performance or further performance by him impossible, the other party is discharged and may sue at once for the breach. Wolf v. Marsh, 54 Cal.

228; Miller v. Ward, 2 Conn. 494; Dare v. Spencer, 5 Blackf. 491; Crabtree v. Messersmith, 19 Iowa, 179; Jones v. Walker, 13 B. Mon. 163, 56 Am. Dec. 557; Bassett v. Bassett, 55 Me. 127; Tel. Co. v. Semmes, 73 Md. 9; Grice v. Noble, 59 Mich. 515; Bolles v. Sachs, 37 Minn. 315; Hammer v. Breidenbach, 31 Mo. 29; Crump v. Mead, 3 Mo. 233; Clendennen v. Paulsel, 3 Mo. 230; Gibson v. Whip Pub. Co., 28 Mo. App. 450; True v. Bryant, 32 N. H. 241; Wollner v. Hill, 93 N. Y. 576; Nav. Co. v. Wilcox, 52 N. C. 481; Camp v. Barker, 21 Vt. 469; Hinckley v. Steel Co., 121 U. S. 264. (g) Courts incline strongly against the construction of promises as independent, and if possible they will be held to be concurrent or dependent so that a breach by one party will discharge the other. Larimore v. Tyler, 88 Mo. 661; Turner v. Mellier, 59 Mo. 526; Caldwell v. Dickson, 26 Mo. 60; Denny v. Kile, 16 Mo. 450; Randolph v. Frick, 57 Mo. App. 400; Billups v. Daggs, 38 Mo. App. 367; Kirkland v. Oates, 25 Ala. 465; Haney v. Caldwell, 43 Ark. 184; Peasley v. Hart, 65 Cal. 522; Smith v. Lewis, 24 Conn. 624, 63 Am. Dec. 180; Houston v. Spruance, 4 Harr. 117 (Del.); Clark v. Weis, 87 Ill. 438, 29 Am. Rep. 60; Harshman v. Heavilon, 95 Ind. 147; White v. Day, 56 Iowa, 248; Water Co. v. Winfield, 51 Kan. 104; Foster v. Watson, 16 B. Mon. 377; Golding v. Petit, 20 La. Ann. 505; Williams v. Hagar, 50 Me. 9; Coates v. Sangston, 5 Md. 121; Gates v. Ryan, 115 Mass. 596; Fultz v. House, 6 Sm. & M. (Miss.) 404; Railroad v. Cochran, 42 Neb. 531; Elliott v. Heath, 14 N. H. 131; Shinn v. Roberts, 20 N. J. L. 435, 43 Am. Dec. 636; Duffield v. Johnston, 96 N. Y. 369; Ducker v. Cochrane, 92 N. C. 597; Mehurin v. Stone, 37 Ohio St. 49; Becker's Estate, 166 Pa. St. 313; Hood v. Raines, 19 Tex. 400; Faulkner v. Hebard, 26 Vt. 452; Lowber v. Bangs, 2 Wall. 728, 17 L. Ed. 442. (h) No one claiming by virtue of the title which was obtained in said notes by the National Bank of Commerce can recover.

Jacobs v. Mitchell, 46 Ohio St. 601; Lancaster v. Callins, 7 Fed. 338; Rogers v. Smith, 47 N. Y. 324.

BLAIR, J.—From a judgment in the Jackson Circuit Court in a suit on two notes for $5000, plaintiff appeals.

Plaintiff sues merely as an assignee for collection purposes. The notes sued on were negotiable in form, dated September 17, 1907, and payable at the National Bank of Commerce of Kansas City, six months after date. Each was signed by defendant and was payable to himself or order.

There was evidence that these notes were executed in consideration of the purchase or proposed purchase by defendant of one hundred shares of the stock of the Merchants' Refrigerator Company, of which J. E. Brady was president. The stock of this last-named company had been increased, and Brady desired to dispose of some of this increase to defendant. There was evidence defendant was a reluctant buyer, but was persuaded by Brady and the cashier of the National Bank of Commerce to yield, and the result was defendant executed the notes in suit, payable to himself, indorsed them in blank and delivered them to Brady for his company, attaching to each note as collateral, fifty shares of the stock of the company contemporaneously issued to him, having indorsed the certificate of stock in blank. As a part of the same transaction the Refrigerator Company and Brady executed and, simultaneously with the delivery of the notes, delivered to defendant a contract in writing as follows:

The Great Western Life Insurance Co.

Office of President.   Kansas City, Mo. 9-16-1907
Mr. O. L. Van Laningham,
        City.

Dear Sir:
    You have this day purchased of the Merchants' Refrigerator Company 100 shares of the capital stock represented by

certificates Nos. 134 and 135 for 50 shares each for which you have given two notes of $5000 each in settlement due in six months.

This statement is for the purpose of guaranteeing to you that at the maturity of said notes you may, at your option, surrender the stock and if you do surrender said stock, we jointly and severally agree to cancel and return to you your two notes of $5000 each upon the delivery to us of said stock.

MERCHANTS REFRIGERATOR CO.
BY J. E. BRADY, PRES.
J. E. BRADY.

The answer to each count set up this agreement and averred it was part of the consideration of the notes sued on.

A few days after the notes were executed and delivered and the contract delivered to defendant, Brady and the Refrigerator Company transferred the notes by delivery only and for value to the National Bank of Commerce. There is evidence the bank had full notice of the contract or agreement delivered to defendant and, in fact, that the bank's cashier assisted in formulating the agreement set out and participated in the negotiations out of which it and the notes grew.

The bank subsequently went into the hands of a receiver, who sold the notes in suit, after maturity, with a multitude of others, to the Terrace City Realty Company and Dr. Woods, who jointly authorized plaintiff to collect them by this suit.

Plaintiff contends the agreement constitutes no defense, without regard to the question of notice to the bank, and complains of certain testimony admitted and instructions given and of rulings on objections to argument of defendant's counsel. The evidence, instructions and argument complained of need not now be set out, but will be adverted to in the course of the opinion.

I. The notes being payable to the maker and indorsed in blank by him thereupon became

Negotiable Note: Dependent Collateral Agreement. payable to bearer and negotiable by delivery and were so negotiated by defendant and then negotiated to the bank by his transferee. It appears from the evidence that the bank became a holder for value before maturity.

Plaintiff contends the agreement accompanying the note was collateral and independent and constitutes no defense to this action even though it be conceded that the bank took with notice and that plaintiff, a transferee after maturity, is affected with all equities attaching to the note in the bank's hands.

Practically this identical question was decided in American Gas & V. M. Co. v. Wood, 90 Me. 516. In that case the action was upon a note. In defense there was offered a written agreement to the effect that if the maker did not wish to pay the note at its maturity, he should "receive it back on the surrender by him" to the payee "of one hundred shares of stock" which constituted the consideration of the note.

The court in that case discusses at some length the authorities holding that independent collateral agreements constitute no defense to promissory notes but afford separate actions for their breach, but holds that the note and agreement there considered are "connected by direct reference or necessary implication" and are to "be construed together as an entire contract, the stipulations of which are mutual and dependent, rather than independent and collateral." The basis of this rule was stated to be that "two contemporaneous writings between the same parties, upon the same subject-matter, may be read and construed as one paper; and this rule applies notwithstanding one of the writings is a promissory note, when the action is between the parties to it or their representatives." It is indisputable that the same rule applies to a transferee with notice or after maturity. [Hill v. Huntress, 43 N. H. 480.]

The agreement in the case at the bar is in writing, and the cases dealing with the admissibility of parol agreements are not in point. Neither, for obvious reasons, are the cases applicable in which attempts were made to defend on the ground that the consideration of the note sued on was an executory contract which had been breached but of which breach the transferee had no notice before he brought the note. The same thing is true of cases in which the defense was that the note was for property accompanied by a warranty, and the transferee of the note had notice of the warranty, but not of its breach. In such cases the note and executory contract or the note and warranty are consistently construed to be independent agreements and the maker is remitted to his action upon his contract or warranty. To this class belong the cases cited by plaintiff in this case. In Jennings v. Todd, 118 Mo. l. c. 301, it is expressly stated that at the time Bush purchased Jennings's note "neither the fraud nor breach of contract had developed." In that case the note was payable at a fixed time. The fulfillment of the contract to furnish the maker certain books for a stated price depended upon the maker himself and was to be fulfilled "from time to time in such quantities" as the maker desired. The note was to become void upon the payee's violation of its contract to furnish the maker the books described. When what is said in the opinion is confined, as it should be, to the facts in the case, it accords with the general current of authority upon the subject and in no way is in conflict with the conclusion reached in American Gas & V. M. Co. v. Wood, supra.

Other cases cited are Adams v. Smith, 35 Me. 324; Miller v. Ottaway, 81 Mich. 196; Dow v. Tuttle, 4 Mass. 414; Davis v. McCready, 17 N. Y. 230.

In Miller v. Ottaway, the note was for the purchase price of two mares, the seller warranting that they were in foal. The note was negotiated before maturity, and the indorsee had knowledge of the warranty, but none of any breach of it. The court states the rule to be that it is not a "defense against a bonafide holder for value that he was informed that the note was made in consideration of an executory con-

tract, unless he was also informed of its breach,"
though the defense might be interposed if he knew of
the breach. The court cites 1 Parsons on Bills &
Notes, 261, wherein the other cases cited by plaintiff
on this point are cited and relied upon, with others.

It is clear the case at bar does not fall within this
principle. The condition upon which the **agreement** in
this case provides that the note is to be returned is
quite different in character from that contemplated by
the rule announced in Miller v. Ottaway. In that case
the stipulations were clearly independent and independently actionable. The intent of the parties is the principal thing, and the question is usually to be resolved
upon the inquiry, as has been said, whether that intent
was that performance should be mutual, dependent
and simultaneous. [Turner v. Mellier, 59 Mo. l. c. 535,
536.] It is also true that in case of doubt, covenants
are ordinarily held to be dependent. These principles
distinguish the cases cited by plaintiff and confirm
the soundness of the conclusion in American Gas & V.
M. Co. v. Wood, which we think correct, and which, applied here, negatives plaintiff's contention that the
agreement in evidence did not affect the right to sue on
the notes. If the bank took with knowledge of the
agreement, it took subject to it and, further, can even
be said to have taken with knowledge of a breach, since
it took with the notes the stock attached to them and
dealt with in the agreement. Plaintiff's principals
bought from the bank after maturity and stand in the
bank's shoes, so far as the agreement is concerned.

It is suggested the agreement is not between the
parties to the note and that it cannot, therefore, be construed with the note. The evidence makes it clear
enough that the note was transferred by delivery to
the maker of the agreement. It was payable to bearer,
being indorsed in blank by the payee who executed it to
himself. It was this note, so transferred, with which
the agreement had to do. The payee, when the agree-

ment was delivered, was the holder, and the holder signed the agreement. That another also signed does not change the rule.

It is also contended that the agreement was a mere guaranty and intended merely to afford an action in case of non-compliance with its terms. This argument is based upon the use of the word "guarantee" in the agreement. The term "guarantee" was doubtless used with the intent to give emphasis and not to change the plain character of the agreement.

II. It is urged that the instructions given for defendant authorized a finding for him without requiring a finding that he complied with the conditions of the agreement by returning the stock or relinquishing his rights to it. Plaintiff offered in evidence the notes and, attached thereto, the certificates of stock, *indorsed in blank*. From their date, the holders of the notes had the stock, so indorsed, in their possession. Defendant was wholly disabled to tender physically the stock in return for the notes, and that because plaintiff's assignor had possession of the stock when the notes matured. Having proved that the bank, in whose shoes he stands, had the stock in its possession and that it was indorsed in such manner that the bank could avail itself of it at will, and that he now has the same stock in the same condition, it does not lie in his mouth to complain because the jury was not required to find that defendant tendered to the bank the stock which the bank already had, under its full control, so far as this question is concerned.

III. Defendant, in his deposition, on cross-examination, testified that after the bank went into the hands of a receiver he was called into a meeting of the officers and directors of the National Bank of Commerce and reorganization committee. The receiver, also, was present. Dr. Woods, one of the plain-

Return of Stock.

Hearsay.

tiff's present principals (one of the present owners of
the note) and Mr. Rule, cashier of the bank, were there.
Defendant said he was questioned as to the notes, and
said he "went into the case fully and stated Mr. Rule's
connection with the matter and also stated he did not
care to purchase the stock, but that he exercised his
right to cancel" in accordance with the contract, and
demanded his notes. He said he offered to produce
the contract, but the chairman said it was not necessary, stating that if the notes were in the hands of innocent parties they would have to be paid. Defendant
testified he replied they were not in the hands of innocent parties, but of the Bank of Commerce, which had
notice of the whole transaction. This testimony appears, piecemeal, in two depositions.

The objections made in this connection were that
the above was hearsay. One fault with the objection
now relied upon is that it included in the scope of the
matter objected to defendant's offer to produce the contract and other things clearly not hearsay. It was too
broad. Further, it was competent to show that Dr.
Woods had notice of the bank's knowledge of the agreement before he purchased the notes in suit, particularly
since these notes were purchased by him and another,
in connection with other paper of the face value of
$432,000 for the sum of $30,000.

IV. Objection is also made to testimony of defendant that he demanded from Brady and the Merchants' Refrigerator Company the return of his notes,
in accordance with his agreement; that he was told the
bank had the notes, and he then caused his attorney to
demand the notes from the bank. In this he is supported by Brady and his attorney. This testimony was
competent to show an effort to comply with the agreement, so far as defendant could. The principle relied
upon by plaintiff in connection with this complaint concerning the instructions would have required of defendant an effort to surrender the stock and a demand that

the notes be canceled under the agreement had the stock not been in the possession of the holder of the note. The testimony could not have injured plaintiff in any way. The same is true of defendant's testimony that when approached by the attorney of the Refrigerator Company on the theory that he was a stockholder thereof he announced that he had elected to surrender the stock and cancel the notes. This evidence could not have prejudiced plaintiff, since it is conceded the written agreement authorized defendant to make such election as against the Refrigerator Company, and plaintiff stands simply upon the ground that the bank had no notice of the contract and that, even if it had, the notes in its hands would not have been affected by it. Practically all of the testimony objected to was elicited by plaintiff's counsel on cross-examination but read to the jury by defendant's counsel.

V. Several objections were made during the argument of defendant's counsel. In all instances except one, the court ruled with plaintiff and admonished counsel for defendant. No requests for stronger rebukes were made. At one point counsel for defendant said: "The Terrace Company was formed for the very purpose of manipulating this stuff, nearly all the assets of that bank." Counsel for plaintiff objected on the ground that "the instruction of the court is, that does not constitute a defense." Counsel for defendant rejoined that the instruction did not state it was "a circumstance the jury cannot consider." The court merely remarked "Go on." The objection now made, that the statement would prejudice the jury, was not made in the trial court. Further, there was evidence tending to show the statement had truth in it. At the most there is nothing indicating that the trial court, who had heard all the argument in the case, abused its discretion in ruling as it did. The judgment is affirmed. All concur, except *Woodson, C. J.,* and *Graves* and *Bond, JJ.,* who dissent.

THE STATE ex rel. WABASH RAILWAY COMPANY v. CORNELIUS ROACH, Secretary of State.

In Banc, March 24, 1916.

1. **CORPORATION: Franchises: Sale.** The franchises of a railway company are divisible into two classes: first, the mere right of being a body corporate; and, second, all other powers or privileges granted by the sovereign power. The first is not subject to barter and sale; the second are.

2. **———: ———: What Passes by Mortgage Sale.** Both by the laws and Constitution of Missouri and by the general law, all the franchise rights of a railway company except the mere right to be a corporation, including the right to do business within this State, pass to the purchaser at a foreclosure mortgage sale, where the franchise rights have been conveyed by the mortgage.

3. **———: Wabash Railroad: Right of Purchaser to do Business.** On December 26, 1906, the Wabash Railroad Company, then possessed of the right, privilege and franchise to do a railroad business in this State, mortgaged all those rights, and they passed by foreclosure sale in 1915 to the Wabash Railway Company, a new corporation, organized under the laws of Indiana. Ever since the building of the North Missouri Railroad under the Act of 1851, there has been a State grant of a right to do intrastate business over that railroad and its after-acquired and after-constructed portions, which has successively passed, by statutory authority, to divers successors of the old railroad company, and is now vested, by reason of said foreclosure sale and purchase, in the said Wabash Railway Company.

4. **———: ———: Police Power.** The grant of a right to construct and own a railroad and to do a railroad business within the State is not a right that falls within the police power. The control of common carriers, such as, for instance, the fixing of maximum passenger or freight rates, is an exercise of police power, but that is a totally different question from the right to do business at all.

5. **———: ———: ———: Violation of Charter Rights.** The Legislature cannot, in the exercise of assumed police powers, violate charter contracts and overthrow vested rights. The Wabash Railway Company, being the owner of a franchise right

to own and operate a railroad and do a railroad business in this State, granted by the State to the North Missouri Railroad Company prior to the adoption of the Constitution of 1875, and passed by successive mortgages and foreclosure sales to said present company, cannot by a legislative act be deprived thereof, for such right does not pertain to police powers, but is a contract right.

6. ——: ——: **Permission to Do Business: Retroactive Statute.** The Act of 1913, Laws 1913, p. 179, declaring that no railroad corporation, except one incorporated under the laws of this State, shall be permitted to do an intrastate business in this State, does not have a retroactive operation, and does not apply to a foreign corporation which has succeeded to the rights of another railroad company which long prior to the enactment of said statute had been granted by the State the right to own and operate a railroad in this State and to carry on an intrastate railroad business, and the Secretary of State cannot lawfully withhold from said corporation a permit or license to do business in Missouri. That act cannot contravene existing rights lawfully granted by the State. It applies to railroads built subsequently to its enactment, and does not affect those then operating in the State.

Held, by WOODSON, C. J., dissenting, that the Act of 1913 applies simply to intrastate business and railroads, and the Constitution (Art. 12, sec. 18) retained jurisdiction over so much of a consolidated railroad as is in this State.

7. ——: ——: ——: **Due Process: Impairment of Contract.** To hold that a foreign corporation which by purchase has acquired the railroad of another company and its franchise right to do business in this State, acquired prior to the enactment of the Act of 1913, Laws 1913, p. 179, cannot do a railroad business in this State, would be to take valuable property rights without due process of law, and to impair the obligation of contracts, not only of said company, but of all other foreign corporations now owning and operating railroads under franchises granted prior to its enactment.

Mandamus.

WRIT ISSUED.

James L. Minnis and *Nagel & Kirby* for relator.

(1) Relator owns the portion of the Wabash Railroad situated in Missouri and is not only authorized by

section 13, article 12, of the Constitution to carry persons and property as a common carrier "between any points within this State," but is required to do so by section 14 of the same article, which declares relator "a common carrier" and its railroad "a public highway." Sec. 3078, R. S. 1909; Brown v. Railroad, 137 Mo. 537; Dietrich v. Murdock, 42 Mo. 284; Branch v. Jessup, 106 U. S. 483; Gamble v. Q. C. W. Co., 123 N. Y. 91. (2) The Act of 1913 is void because, if given effect, it would impair the obligations of contracts and deprive relator of its property without due process of law, in violation of the Constitution of the United States. Sec. 1, art. 14, of Amendments to U. S. Constitution; Daniels v. Railroad, 62 Mo. 43; Railroad v. Delamore, 114 U. S. 501; Julian v. Trust Co., 193 U. S. 93; Railroad v. Commissioners, 112 U. S. 609; Vicksburg v. Waterworks Co., 202 U. S. 453; Lawrence v. Hennessey, 165 Mo. 659; State ex rel. v. Lesueur, 145 Mo. 322; Railroad v. Missouri, 152 U. S. 301; Pullman Car Co. v. Railroad, 115 U. S. 587; Muller v. Dows, 94 U. S. 444; Dodd v. Railroad, 108 Mo. 581· (3) Relator purchased at the foreclosure sale, with the railroad, the right to conduct thereon in the State of Missouri, the business of a common carrier, and as such to transport passengers and freight locally between points in Missouri, subject only to filing the statement and affidavit and paying the tax and fees required of foreign corporations as a condition precedent to their right to do business in this State. Julian v. Trust Co., 193 U. S. 93; New Orleans v. Delamore, 114 U. S. 501; Railroad v. Commissioners, 112 U. S. 609; Christian Union v. Yount, 101 U. S. 352; Railroad v. Allison, 190 U. S. 326; Burgess v. Seligman, 107 U. S. 20. (4) The Act of 1913, in prohibiting foreign railroad companies from entering this State with instrumentalities of interstate commerce and operating the same in local business, is void because violative of the "commerce" and "due process" clauses of the Constitution of the United States. Sec. 8, art. 1, U. S. Constitution; Sec. 1, art. 14, Amendments to U. S. Constitution; Crutcher v. Kentucky, 141 U. S. 47; Telegraph Co. v. Kansas, 216 U. S. 1; Pullman Car Co. v. Kansas, 216 U. S. 56; Ludwig v. Tel. Co., 216 U. S. 146; Harrison v. Railroad, 232 U. S. 318; Railroad v. Arkansas, 235 U. S. 350. (5) The laws of Missouri authorize the incorporation of a company similar to relator. Secs. 2990, 2991, 2992, 3048, 3049, 3065, 3067, 3077, 3078, R. S. 1909; State ex rel. v. Cook, 171 Mo. 362.

John T. Barker, Attorney-General, and *Shrader P. Howell*, Assistant Attorney-General, for respondent.

(1) A foreign corporation can do business in a State other than that of its creation only upon complying with the terms and conditions prescribed by the Legislature thereof. Beale on Foreign Corporations, p. 156; Elliott on Railroads, sec. 30; Daggs v. Ins. Co., 136 Mo. 393; State ex inf. v. Oil Co., 194 Mo. 149; State ex rel. v. Vandiver, 222 Mo. 206; Koenig v. Railroad, 27 Neb. 703; Oil Co. v. Texas, 177 U. S. 28; Ins. Co. v. Daggs, 172 U. S. 566; Cable v. Ins. Co., 191 U. S. 307; Ins. Co. v. Prewett, 202 U. S. 246; Maine v. Railroad, 142 U. S. 227. (2) The application of the terms of the Act of 1913 to the relator will not operate as an impairment of the obligation of contract within the meaning of section 10, article 1, of the Federal Constitution. Roeder v. Robertson, 202 Mo. 535; Ins. Co. v Daggs, 172 U. S. 566; Packing Co. v. Arkansas, 212 U. S. 344. The right to complain on the ground of impairment of a contract is limited to the contractual party or the person injured by such alleged impairment. Hooker v. Burr, 194 U. S. 419; Williams v. Eggleston, 170 U. S. 304. When a transfer of a fran-

chise is made a new corporation is created, and the
grantee takes subject to the laws then existing, and the
right to complain must be based on the impairment of
a contract executed prior to the passage of the law
questioned. Owen v. Railroad, 83 Mo. 460; Denny v.
Bennett, 128 U. S. 489; State ex rel. v. Lesueur, 145
Mo. 328; Rockwell v. Railroad, 51 Conn. 401; Railroad v. Commissioners, 112 U. S. 621; Pullman Car Co.
v. Railroad, 115 U. S. 594; Lehigh Co. v. Easton, 121
U. S. 391; Baldwin's Am. R. R. Law, sec. 12, p. 39.
But even if relator were operating under a franchise
acquired at the foreclosure sale, still the State would
not be deprived of its right to enact legislation under
its police powers to regulate the exercise of such franchise rights. State ex inf. v. Oil Co., 218 Mo. 377;
State ex rel. v. Vandiver, 222 Mo. 223; Ins. Co. v.
Prewett, 202 U. S. 246; Packing Co. v. Arkansas, 212
U. S. 345; Baldwin's Am. R. R. Law, p. 213; Railroad v. Ohio, 173 U. S. 296; Railroad v. Emmons, 149
U. S. 367; Railroad v. Bristol, 155 U. S. 571. (3) The
Act of 1913 does not in any manner take away, abridge
or interfere with the right of relator to carry on interstate commerce and therefore does not impinge upon
the provisions of section 8, article 1, of the Federal
Constitution. State ex inf. v. Oil Co., 218 Mo. 376;
State v. Railroad, 239 Mo. 296; Pac. Exp. Co. v. Seibert, 142 U. S. 349; Railroad v. Arkansas, 235 U. S.
350; 2 Elliott on Railroads, sec. 690; Express Co. v.
Minnesota, 223 U. S. 335. Although State legislation
may incidentally affect interstate commerce, yet that
fact alone does not render such legislation invalid.
People v. Railroad, 104 Ill. 476; Quachita v. Packet
Co., 121 U. S. 44; Mobile Co. v. Kimball, 102 U. S. 691;
Railroad v. Illinois, 118 U. S. 564; Glue Co. v. Glue Co.,
187 U. S. 616. (4) The act in question does not violate
the fourteenth amendment to the Federal Constitution,
which prohibits the taking of property without due

process of law. Roeder v. Robertson, 202 Mo. 535; 8 Cyc. 1116; Ins. Co. v. New York, 119 U. S. 119; Railroad v. Bristol, 151 U. S. 571.

GRAVES, J.—Original action in mandamus. against the Secretary of State. The relator, Wabash Railway Company, is a new corporation, organized under the laws of Indiana, in October, 1915, and more particularly under the Act of March 3, 1865, of that State. The petition has been treated as and for the alternative writ, and a demurrer has been filed thereto, which reads:

"Now at this date comes the respondent, Cornelius Roach, Secretary of State of the State of Missouri, and after entering his appearance and waiving the issuance of an alternative writ in this case, demurs to the petition of relator for the following reasons:

"1st. Because said petition does not state facts. sufficient to constitute a cause of action.

"2nd. Because it appears upon the face of relator's petition that relator is not entitled to the relief asked.

"3rd. Because under the law of Missouri, as enacted by the Legislature of said State and approved April 16, 1913, relator cannot operate a railroad in the State of Missouri and transport passengers or freight from one point in the State to another point in the State unless relator is incorporated under the laws of the State of Missouri, and upon the face of relator's petition it appears that it is not thus incorporated.

"4th. Because under the laws of the State of Missouri relator is not entitled to a certificate to do business in the State of Missouri.

"5th. Because the laws of the State of Missouri do not authorize the formation of a corporation of a character similar to that of the relator.

"Wherefore, respondent prays the court to quash the alternative writ and to deny relator the relief asked and for such further orders as to the court shall seem just and proper."

The petition is one of great length, but counsel for relator has fairly summarized its pertinent features thus:

"The relator is a railroad corporation organized under the laws of the State of Indiana, and particularly under an act approved March 3, 1865, by which it was provided in substance and in part:

"(1) That a railroad situated in Indiana and other States, may be sold as an entirety under foreclosure of a mortgage, at one time and place.

"(2) That the purchasers at such a sale, by filing a certificate as therein provided, may form a new corporation and become a body corporate, 'with power to sue and be sued, contract and be contracted with, and maintain and operate the railroad in the said certificate named, and transact all business connected with the same.'

"(3) That 'such corporation shall possess all the powers, rights, privileges, immunities and franchises in respect to said railroad, or the part thereof purchased as aforesaid, and all of the real and personal property appertaining to the same, which were possessed or enjoyed by the corporation that owned or held the said railroad, previous to such sale, by virtue of its charter and amendments thereto and other laws of this State, or of any State in which any part of said railroad is situated, not inconsistent with the laws of this State.'

"(4) That 'said corporation shall have capacity to hold, enjoy and exercise, within other States, the aforesaid faculties, powers, rights, franchises and immunities, and such others as may be conferred upon it by any law of this State, or of any other State in which any portion of its railroad may be situated, or in which it may transact any part of its business.'

"Relator was incorporated for the purpose of acquiring, owning, maintaining and operating the Wabash Railroad, and acquiring owning and exercising the franchises pertaining to it.

"With a view to laying a foundation for our contentions, we will indicate briefly the facts stated in the petition.

"By the Acts of 1851 (Laws 1851, page 483), as amended by the Act of 1853 (Laws 1853, page 323) and the amendatory Act of 1865 (Laws 1865, pages 89, 90), the State of Missouri created the North Missouri Railroad Company, and granted to it, its successors and assigns, the franchises, rights and privileges to locate, construct, own, maintain and operate a railroad as a common carrier for hire, and it accordingly thereafter constructed or acquired, maintained and operated as a common carrier for hire substantially the lines of the Wabash Railroad, now existing in Missouri.

"On October 1, 1868, pursuant to express power conferred by said acts, the North Missouri Railroad Company mortgaged its railroad, franchises, rights and privileges, which were sold, pursuant to said mortgage, to one Jessup, acting for himself and his associates, who, on January 2, 1872, conveyed said railroad, franchises, rights and privileges to the St. Louis, Kansas City & Northern Railway Company (hereinafter called the Northern Company), a Missouri railroad corporation organized for the purpose of acquiring, owning, maintaining and operating said railroad as a common carrier for hire.

"On August 14, 1879, the Northern Company, pursuant to the provisions of what are now sections 3077-8, Revised Statutes 1909, entered into a contract of consolidation with the Wabash Railway Company, a consolidated corporation organized under the laws of the

States of Illinois, Indiana and Ohio, which owned substantially the lines of the Wabash Railroad east of the Mississippi River as they now exist, and the franchises, rights and privileges to maintain and operate the same as a common carrier for hire.

"By virtue of this consolidation the Wabash lines east and west of the river were consolidated or unified, so that the two railroads became a single, continuous railroad, and the rights, privileges and franchises granted by the above States to the constituent companies were unified so that they pertained to each and every part of the continuous railroad, and the contract vested this road and the rights, privileges and franchises pertaining thereto, in the consolidated corporation, the Wabash, St. Louis & Pacific Railway Company.

"On June 1, 1880, the Wabash, St. Louis & Pacific Railway Company, pursuant to express power, mortgaged its railroad, rights, privileges and franchises, which were thereafter, pursuant to said mortgage, sold to a purchasing committee. The purchasing committee caused a railroad corporation to be organized under the laws of each of the States of Missouri, Illinois, Indiana, Michigan and Ohio, and conveyed to each of said corporations the railroad, rights, privileges and franchises local to the State in which it was organized.

"In May, 1889, these several corporations entered into a contract of consolidation pursuant to what are now sections 3077-8, Revised Statutes 1909, and the laws of said other States, and thereby formed The Wabash Railroad Company and vested in it the consolidated or continuous railroad and the unified rights, privileges and franchises to own, maintain and operate the same as a common carrier for hire.

"On December 26, 1906, The Wabash Railroad Company, pursuant to express power conferred by all of said States, mortgaged its railroad, rights, privileges and franchises, and thereafter made default, and appropriate proceedings were instituted in the Federal court at St. Louis, Missouri, to foreclose the mortgage. A decree was entered on January 30, 1914, wherein it was adjudged that the mortgaged railroad, rights, privileges and franchises 'were indivisible, of such a nature, and so situated' that they should be sold as an entirety, and they were, pursuant to said decree, sold as an entirety to a purchasing committee, who organized relator corporation pursuant to the Indiana act hereinbefore set out. The purchasers assigned to relator their bid, and pursuant to the decree of foreclosure a special master conveyed to relator the Wabash Railroad and the rights, privileges and franchises pertaining thereto.

"Thereafter, on October 23, 1915, on the coming in of the special master's report that the purchasing committee had assigned its bid to relator, and that he had, accordingly, conveyed the Wabash Railroad and franchises to relator, an order was entered, approving and confirming the master's report and adjudging relator to be the assignee of the purchasing committee.

"On November 1, 1915, relator entered into the possession, use and enjoyment of the Wabash Railroad and the rights, privileges and franchises pertaining thereto, and shortly thereafter tendered to the Secretary of State, for filing in his office, a copy of its charter or certificate of incorporation duly authenticated by the Secretary of State of Indiana, together with a sworn statement under its corporate seal, setting forth the business in which it was engaged in Missouri, viz., that it owned the Wabash Railroad and the franchises pertaining thereto, was operating same as a common carrier for hire, and was exercising or would exercise all the rights and privileges vested in it by virtue of said special master's deed and by the law under which

it was incorporated; and also a statement of the proportion of the capital stock represented by its property
and business transacted in Missouri, and other statements required by law, and also tendered to the Secretary of State $19,671.50, being the corporation tax and
fees due from relator to the State of Missouri, and demanded that he issue to relator a permit or license to do
business in Missouri. No point is made on the form of
the statement, and it is agreed that the amount of
money tendered is correct.

"The Secretary of State refused to file the papers
and accept the money for reasons heretofore stated.

"It is also conceded that relator has kept its said
tender to the Secretary of State good by insisting continuously on the filing of said documents and the acceptance of said money."

The facts well pleaded stand confessed by the
demurrer as a matter of law. Among others, the following pertinent propositions are suggested: (1) Does
the Act of 1913 apply to this relator, and (2) if it does,
is it violative of constitutional provisions?

I. The real foundation of respondent's objection
to granting a license to relator is evidently our Act of
1913 (Laws 1913, p. 179), which reads:

"That no railroad corporation, whether steam,
street, electric, transfer or terminal, except one incorporated and chartered in and under the laws of the
State of Missouri, shall be authorized or permitted to
carry passengers or freight of any kind from one point
in this State to another point in this State."

The foregoing is section 1 of the act. Sections 2
and 3 of the act are penal in character, and provide
penalties and fines as to violators of the act.

It stands admitted by the pleadings that the
predecessors in title to the railway lines involved here

Mortgage and Sale of Franchise Rights. had the right or franchise (given them by this State) to do an intrastate business. The franchises of a railway company are divisible into two classes: (1) The mere right of being a body corporate and (2) all other grants of power or privileges by the sovereign power. The first is not subject to barter and sale, but those rights and privileges falling within the second division, supra, are subject to barter and sale. In this case among those rights or franchises, was the right to carry passengers and freight from point to point in Missouri; in other words, was the right to do an intrastate business as a railroad. This franchise or right was subject to sale or mortgage along with the physical property. This right or franchise was first granted to the "North Missouri Railroad Company, its successor or assigns," by the State. Under a mortgage sale this right passed to Jesup and associates, who in turn assigned it to the St. Louis, Kansas City & Northern Railway Company. By law this corporation, a Missouri product, was authorized to consolidate with other corporations of like character, and in 1879, did consolidate with railroad corporations east of the Mississippi River, having a line running to such river opposite the Missouri side of such river. This consolidation was under the name of Wabash, St. Louis and Pacific Railway Company. The franchise right to do intrastate business passed to this consolidated company, both by virtue of our laws and our Constitution. By foreclosure sales these rights passed from the Wabash, St. Louis and Pacific Railway Company to "The Wabash Railroad Company," where they remained until in 1915, when by virtue of a mortgage foreclosure sale they passed to the relator herein.

That the franchise rights of the old North Missouri Railroad Company, passed through Jesup to the St. Louis, Kansas City & Northern Railway Company, has been twice held in this State. [Daniels v. St. Louis, Kansas City & Northern Railroad Co., 62 Mo. 43; State ex rel. v. St. Louis, Kansas City & Northern Railway Co., 3 Mo. App. l. c. 193.] It should be noted that this was a sale under a mortgage at which Jesup acquired the rights which he afterward conveyed.

Besides these express authorities in this State, it seems to be the general rule that at a foreclosure sale, where the franchise rights have been conveyed by the mortgage, all such franchise rights will pass to the purchaser, save and except the mere right to be a corporation. [Daniels v. Railroad, 62 Mo. 43; State ex rel. v. Railroad, 3 Mo. App. l. c. 193; Railroad v. Delamore, 114 U. S. l. c. 510; Julian v. Central Trust Co., 193 U. S. l. c. 106.]

On December 26, 1906, The Wabash Railroad Company, then being possessed of the right, privileges and franchise to do an intrastate railroad business in the State of Missouri, mortgaged such rights, privileges and franchises, and these passed by the sale in 1915 to the relator.

In other words, since the building of the North Missouri railroad under the Act of 1851, there has been a State grant to a right to do intrastate business over that particular railroad, and its after-acquired and constructed portions. This was a substantial property right, and has passed successively to the divers successors of the old railroad company, and is now vested in the present relator. Every step taken, by which the right or franchise has passed from one to the other corporation, has been taken by statutory authority. The corporations were all along authorized to mortgage their roadbeds and other property rights, including franchise rights. The Missouri corporation had both constitutional and statutory authority for consolidation. So that if the right to do an intrastate business is one not violative of the police power of the

State, the relator here acquired a valuable existing and vested right. But more of this in another connection.

II. Whatever else may be said of the legislative grant of rights to the predecessor in title to the relator here, it is clear that by these acts the State granted the original corporation the right to do an intrastate business upon the railroad it was given authority

Police Power. to build and construct. Not only so, but the original act (Laws 1850-1, p. 483) further contemplated that the road to be built by the corporation then chartered by the Legislature would also do an interstate business, because in section 7 of the act, after providing for the construction of the road from St. Charles, Missouri, to the northern boundary line of the State, it is added: "With a view that the same may be hereafter continued northwardly into the State of Iowa, in the direction of Fort Des Moines, in that State."

This valuable right of doing an intrastate railroad business was a grant which the State could make. In other words, it was a proper subject-matter of a contract between the State and corporation. The charter of a corporation is its contract with the State. GANTT, J., in Mathews v. Railroad, 121 Mo. l. c. 310, said:

"It is wholly unnecessary to review the decisions which sustain the view adopted in the Dartmouth College case (4 Wheat. 518), that defendant's charter is a contract between it and the State. It has been uniformly followed by this court."

As to grants made prior to 1875, the Constitution of that year expressly recognized the validity thereof. Section 1 of article 12 reads:

"All existing charters, or grants of special or exclusive privileges, under which a bona-fide organization shall not have taken place, and business been commenced in good faith, at the adoption of this Constitution, shall thereafter have no validity."

The converse would be the case where the corporation was organized and the contemplated charter
powers exercised.

It must of course be conceded that the State cannot by grant disrobe itself of its police powers, but the
grant of a right to construct and build a railroad within her borders, and the further grant of the right to
use such railroad in the transportation of passengers
and freight, for hire, between points and places within
this State, is not the exercise of the police power of the
State. It has been said that such a power is an inde-
scribable one, but we find no case where the grant to
construct and use (within this State) a railroad, has
ever been held to be an exercise of the police power of
the State. If the State by such grant, and in addition
thereto undertook to divest itself of the power to regulate such corporation in the use of the railroad, to the
detriment of the health, safety and general welfare of
the public, then such attempted release of the power
might be invalid. For our Constitution, article 12, section 5, says:

"The exercise of the police power of the State
shall never be abridged, or so construed as to permit
corporations to conduct their business in such manner
as to infringe the equal rights of individuals, or the
general well-being of the State."

But this is not the case here. A grant of the right
to do an intrastate railroad business does not of itself
contravene this section of the Constitution. [Sloan v.
Railroad, 61 Mo. 24; State ex rel. Haeussler v. Greer,
78 Mo. 188; Scotland County v. Railroad, 65 Mo. l. c.
135; State ex rel. v. Laclede Gaslight Co., 102 Mo. l. c.
486.]

The control of common carriers under and by virtue of the police power is a totally different question.
The general terms of the rule pertaining to control un-

der the police power is well expressed in 8 Cyc. 874, thus:

"Common carriers have from the earliest time been controlled by police power; accordingly, railroad companies being allowed to charge only reasonable rates, the Legislature may make a valid enactment that certain maximum rates shall not be exceeded; likewise railroad companies may be compelled to make connections with other railroads suitable to the convenience and safety of the public, and to obey many other kindred regulations."

But these matters of regulation under a proper exercise of the police power do not cover the right of the State to grant the privileges to construct and operate a railroad in this State and to do intrastate business. This Act of 1913 (Laws 1913, p. 179) should be given a construction which would, if possible, save it from constitutional darts. In other words, it should be given a prospective rather than a retroactive construction. It should be construed and read as to railroads thereafter built, rather than as affecting railroads already operating in the State. It should not be so construed as to make it contravene existing rights. We have adopted this method of construction even as to constitutional provisions. [State ex rel. Haeussler v. Greer, 78 Mo. 188, supra.] We have no doubt if a foreign corporation, without a railroad in this State, and without any previous grant of rights by this State, should apply for admission to do business in this State, and ask to construct and operate a railroad in this State, that, under this law, it might be kept out of the State. But that is not this case.

In the Greer case, supra, Haeussler, the relator therein, was a stockholder in the German Savings Institution, and he and some other friendly stockholders tendered their votes for Haeussler, as director of such corporation, under the cumulative plan of voting provided for by section 6 of article 12 of the Constitution. The corporation was one created by legislative charter prior to the Constitution of 1875. Under this legislative charter the other system of voting was provided for, and the respondent Greer was elected over Haeussler. The action was by *quo warranto* to test Greer's right to hold the office. This court, through HENRY, J., said that whilst the language of the Constitution was broad enough to apply to all corporations, yet it should not be so construed as to give it retroactive action, when such would strike down existing contract or charter rights. So in the case at bar. This law should not be given an application or a construction which would strike down contract or charter rights. The relator in this case is the legal owner of certain charter rights granted by the State, i. e., the rights to own and operate a railroad in Missouri, and to do an intrastate business thereon. These rights are such as could be properly granted by the State, and do not pertain to the police powers of the State. [State ex rel. v. Laclede Gaslight Co., supra, and other cases cited.] The State cannot in the exercise of mere *assumed police powers* pass a law violative of charter rights. In the Laclede Gaslight Co. case (102 Mo. l. c. 486), BLACK, J., said:

"It is not to be doubted that there is a limit to the power of the Legislature to tie the hands of subsequent Legislatures in respect to the exercise of what is termed the 'police power.' Thus it is said: 'No Legislature can bargain away the public health or the public morals.' [Stone v. Mississippi, 101 U. S. 814.]

"But certainly there is a limit in this regard over which legislatures and municipalities cannot pass; they cannot, in the exercise of assumed police powers, violate charter contracts and overthrow vested rights. On this subject Judge COOLEY aptly says: 'The limit to the exercise of the police power in these cases must be this:

The regulations must have reference to the comfort, safety or welfare of society; they must not be in conflict with any of the provisions of the charter; and they must not, under pretense of regulation, take from the corporation any of the essential rights and privileges which the charter confers. In short, they must be police regulations in fact, and not amendments of the charter in curtailment of the corporate franchise.' [Cooley, Const. Lim. (5 Ed.), 712]."

This and the other cases cited announce the proper general rules, but they may not accord fully with the present line of demarcation between the police and other powers of the State. Some of these cases discuss rates allowed by State grant. The modern rule as to grants of this character, is that they fall within the category of regulatory measures in the interest of the general public welfare, and therefore are within the police power of the State. But we repeat, the grant of the right to construct and own a railroad in Missouri and to do an intrastate business thereon is not such a right as falls within the police power of the State.

We hold therefore that the Act of 1913 should not be given a construction which would make it strike down the vested rights of relator or other corporations similarly situated. We hold that it has no application to a corporation which in due course has acquired the right to own and operate a railroad in this State for the doing of intrastate business, which right to so own and operate such road has been previously granted by this State.

III. If this Act of 1913 is to be construed as contended for by the State officials it would be violative of several constitutional provisions. It would be the taking of valuable property rights without due process of law. It would be the striking down of contract

Due Process of Law. rights in violation of both the State and Federal Constitutions. This relator, as to these contract rights, stands in no different situation than do the other foreign corporations now owning and operating railroads in this State. The other foreign corporations now operating railroads in this State in intrastate business, are doing so by virtue of grants heretofore made. The only difference is (and in law that is no difference) the relator has but recently acquired these rights, whilst the others have possessed them for some years.

It is a fundamental rule that a statute should be so construed, if possible, as to make it valid under all constitutional provisions. As previously said, if a foreign corporation, possessed of no contract or charter rights from this State, should apply for license to do business in this State, and to construct and operate a railroad therein, the Act of 1913 would apply and prevent such a corporation from coming into the State. The State, save where it has previously granted the right, can stop any foreign corporation at the State line. The law, whether wise or otherwise, seems to have that effect, but it should not be construed to apply to corporations owning or legally acquiring railroads already in the State, where, in the acquisition of them, they also acquire the franchise right to do an intrastate as well as other business in the State. We so construe this act. To otherwise construe it, would make it violative of more than one constitutional provision, both of State and Federal Constitution.

It follows that the alternative writ of mandamus should be made peremptory, and the respondent herein required to accept and receive the license fees tendered, and issue to relator a license to continue the business of its railroad in this State. It is so ordered. All concur except *Walker, J.,* absent, and *Woodson, C. J.,* who dissents in opinion filed.

WOODSON, C. J. (dissenting)—That portion of the plaintiff's railway lying in this State was constructed and owned by a Missouri corporation, and was so owned at the date of the adoption of the Constitution of this State in 1875; and that being so, the plaintiff and those through whom it claims took that part of the road located in this State with all the rights, powers, duties, burdens and limitations granted and imposed upon it by the Constitution and laws of this State.

At the date of the consolidation of the roads mentioned in the majority opinion, under the name of the Wabash Railway Company, section 18 of article 12 of the Constitution of 1875 was in full force and effect. It reads as follows:

"Sec. 18. *Consolidation with foreign companies.*—If any railroad company organized under the laws of this State shall consolidate, by sale or otherwise, with any railroad company organized under the laws of any other State, or of the United States, the same shall not thereby become a foreign corporation; but the courts of this State shall retain jurisdiction in all matters which may arise, as if said consolidation had not taken place. In no case shall any consolidation take place, except upon public notice of at least sixty days to all stockholders, in such manner as may be provided by law."

According to the plain letter and spirit of this constitutional provision, the company which owned that part of the road lying within this State at the date of said consolidation remained and still remains a domestic corporation, and its property, rights and duties, in so far as intrastate transportation is concerned, remain subject to and are governed by the laws of this State to the same extent as if the consolidation had never taken place.

The consolidations mentioned become new companies, so is this reorganized company. [State ex rel. v. Keokuk & W. Ry. Co., 99 Mo. 30; State ex rel. v. Chicago, Burlington & K. C. Ry. Co., 89 Mo. 523.]

But that is not true regarding interstate commerce, for under both the State and Federal Constitutions, as well as under the statutes of this State authorizing the consolidation of the railroads of this State with those of other States, those parts of the consolidated road situate in Missouri are authorized and required to carry interstate commerce; and consequently the Act of 1913 (Laws 1913, p. 179) does not and could not apply to that character of commerce. [State ex inf. v. Standard Oil Co., 218 Mo. 1, l. c. 376.]

In other words, in my opinion, in construing said Act of 1913 we must view that part of plaintiff's road located in this State from two aspects, viz.: First. That as a matter of law the Missouri company still owns the physical property and possesses all the rights, powers and privileges it possessed, and owes all the duties to the public imposed upon it prior to the date of its consolidation with the plaintiff, in so far as intrastate shipments are concerned. Second. That said company, property, rights, powers and privileges are subjected by said statutes and constitutional provisions to the paramount duty of carrying interstate commerce, but not totally destroyed, as I understand the majority opinion in effect holds.

If I am correct in the foregoing observations, then the Act of 1913 is only applicable to intrastate commerce and is valid in that regard.

I am, therefore, of the opinion that the alternative writ of mandamus should be quashed.

THE STATE ex rel. W. G. LOGAN v. JAMES ELLISON et al.

In Banc, March 30, 1916.

1. **JUDGMENT: Finality: Setting Aside at Subsequent Term.** After a final judgment has been rendered at one term, the court, in the absence of a statute to the contrary and of a pending motion or other proper step to carry the case over to the next term, has no jurisdiction, at such next term, to modify or annul that judgment.

2. ————: ————: **After Motion for Rehearing Overruled.** Where the Court of Appeals affirmed the judgment of the trial court, and a motion for rehearing having been timely filed was overruled on the last day of the term and an order was made on said day giving all parties ten days in which "to file motions in cases ruled on this day," the judgment was a finality, and the Court of Appeals had no power at the next term to sustain a motion filed at said next term to set aside the order overruling the motion for a rehearing, nor did it have any power on the last day of the term to make the order extending the time to the next term in which to file a motion to set aside said order, but all its orders and judgments made at such subsequent term were null and void.

3. ————: ————: **Court of Appeals: Certification of Cause to Supreme Court.** The Court of Appeals has no power to certify a cause to the Supreme Court at a subsequent term after its judgment therein has become a finality. The Constitution requires such transfer to be made at "the same term" at which the judgment is rendered "and not afterwards."

Mandamus.

WRIT ISSUED.

John I. Williamson for relator.

(1) When a court has rendered final judgment in a cause and overruled a motion for a rehearing and the term has ended with no motions pending, the jurisdiction of the court over the judgment is at an end. This

rule applies to appellate courts. Padgett v. Smith, 205
Mo. 122; Gratiot v. Railroad, 116 Mo. 470; Danforth
v. Lowe, 53 Mo. 218; Hill v. St. Louis, 20 Mo. 587;
1 Black on Judgments (1 Ed.), sec. 306, p. 383; 1 Freeman on Judgments (4 Ed.), sec. 96, p. 132; 3 Cyc. 474,
sub-sec. b; 17 Am. & Eng. Ency. Law (2 Ed.), 816,
sec. 7; Sibbald v. United States, 12 Pet. 491; Bank v.
Moss, 6 How. 39; Bronson v. Schulten, 104 U. S. 410;
Hawkins v. Railroad, 99 Fed. 322; Brown v. Aspden's
Admr., 14 How. 24. (2) If, under the circumstances in
this case, respondents should have issued the mandate
of their court upon the judgment of affirmance in the
original case, the fact that they have attempted to
transfer the case to this court is no defense to the
alternative writ. State ex rel. v. Homer, 249 Mo. 58;
Smith v. Mo. Pac. Ry. Co., 143 Mo. 33; State ex rel. v.
Philips, 96 Mo. 573. (3) The filing of a supplemental
motion to transfer and of a motion to set aside the
order overruling the motion for a rehearing, after the
expiration of the time allowed by order of court, was
ineffective for any purpose. Rule 20 of Kansas City
Court of Appeals; State ex rel. v. Smith, 172 Mo. 446;
St. Louis v. Dorr, 145 Mo. 485.

Morrison, Nugent & Wylder for respondents.

(1) The order of February 28, 1914, allowing parties ten days within which to file motions retained jurisdiction in the Kansas City Court of Appeals to the
ensuing March, 1914, term, and all orders and judgments thereafter entered by said court in said cause are
valid and subsisting orders of said court. State ex rel.
v. Philips, 96 Mo. 570; Childs v. Railroad, 117 Mo.
428; Gratiot v. Railroad, 116 Mo. 450; State v. Guer-
inger, 178 S. W. 65. (2) The motion to transfer to the
Supreme Court was a proper and legal motion. Rule
35, Supreme Court; Sec. 6, Amend. 1884 to Mo.

Constitution. (3) The supplementary motion and motion to set aside the order denying a rehearing was properly before the court. (4) Relator expressly and impliedly consented to the jurisdiction of the court at the March, 1914, term. Philadelphia v. Coulston, 118 Pa. St. 541; Cooney v. Bonfield, 172 Ill. App. 657; Hair v. Moody, 9 Ala. 399; Gage v. Chicago, 141 Ill. 642; Hewetson v. Chicago, 172 Ill. 112; Kidd v. McMillan, 21 Ala. 325; Cowles v. Curry, 96 N. C. 331; Harrison v. Osborn, 114 Pac. (Okla.) 331; 23 Cyc. 905; 17 Am. & Eng. Ency. Law (2 Ed.), 838. (5) The principal case is already in this court for consideration on the merits; hence a peremptory writ of mandamus cannot issue. State ex rel. v. Hickman, 150 Mo. 629; Johnson v. Fecht, 185 Mo. 339; Clark v. Railroad, 179 Mo. 56; Sutton v. Cole, 155 Mo. 206.

WOODSON, C. J.—This is an original proceeding by mandamus brought in this court to compel the respondents, the Judges of the Kansas City Court of Appeals, to set aside an order and judgment of reversal by them rendered, at the October term, 1914, thereof, on the 5th day of said month, in a cause then pending in said court, wherein the Kansas City Coal & Material Company was appellant and W. G. Logan, the relator herein, was the respondent, to reinstate a former judgment of affirmance rendered therein by said court at the October term, 1913, thereof, and on the 5th day of January, 1914, and to issue the mandate of said court upon the last-mentioned judgment.

In response to the alternative writ, the respondents made their return, which in substance discloses these facts:

That on January 5, 1914, during the October term, 1913, of said court, a judgment of affirmance was by said court rendered in said cause; that on January 15, 1914, during the same term of said court, the appellant filed in said cause a motion for a rehearing; that on February 28, 1914, during the same term of court, said motion was overruled. On the last-named date, that being the last day of the October term, 1913, of said court, the court made a general order to the effect "that all parties be given ten days to file motions in cases ruled on this day," and then finally adjourned the October term, 1913, to court in course.

At the March term, 1914, of said court, and on the 2nd day of said month, the appellant in the original cause filed a motion to have the cause certified to the Supreme Court, and on the 11th of the same month the appellants filed in said cause a supplemental motion to have the same certified to this court, and also a motion to set aside the order overruling the motion for a rehearing; that on April 15, 1914, during the same term, the motions to certify the cause to this court were overruled, and an order for a rehearing was granted.

On June 1, 1914, during the same term, the cause was argued and submitted, and on July 6, 1914, said term of court was adjourned to court in course.

On October 15, 1914, at the October term of said court, a judgment was rendered by said court reversing the judgment of the circuit court and remanding the cause, and at the same time it made an order certifying the cause to this court, of its own motion.

The order of February 28, 1914, made by the court, continuing all motions and other matters pending in said court until the March term, was as follows:

"Now, the court doth order that all motions and other matters pending be continued until the next March term of this court, and the court doth further order that all parties be given ten days to file motions in cases ruled on at this date."

The respondents base their right to set aside the judgment of affirmance in the original case, and to reverse, remand and certify said cause to this court, upon the ground stated in their return, viz.:

"That in and by the order aforesaid, entered in said court on the 28th day of February, 1914, and in and by the filing of said motion by the said company to transfer said cause to the Supreme Court, filed on the 2nd day of March, 1914, and in and by the said supplemental motion and motion to set aside the order overruling the motion for rehearing filed in said cause on the 11th day of March, 1914, and by each of said orders and said motions the jurisdiction of the said Kansas City Court of Appeals, and the judges thereof, was retained in said cause in and to the said March, 1914, term of the said Kansas City Court of Appeals."

As a further defense, respondents also make the following statement in their amended return:

"Respondents further say that they, as judges of the Kansas City Court of Appeals, and the said Kansas City Court of Appeals have no jurisdiction in this cause, because it has been certified to the Supreme Court of the State of Missouri, under the provisions of section 6 of the Amendment of 1884 to article 6 of the Constitution of the State of Missouri, as will appear from the record entry of judgment of the said Kansas City Court of Appeals, entered on the said 5th day of October, 1914, and as will appear from the copy of the opinion of this court hereto attached and made a part hereof."

To this return counsel for relators filed a demurrer.

I. There are but two legal propositions presented by this record for determination, and the first is, did the Court of Appeals, under the order of February 28, 1914, before mentioned, have jurisdiction

Finality of Judgment. at the October term, 1914, thereof, to set aside the judgment of affirmance rendered by it at the October term, 1913, when no motion of any kind was pending in said cause?

Counsel for the relator contends that the Court of Appeals had no such jurisdiction, while the respondents insist that it had.

There is an irreconcilable conflict between authorities in this State upon this question.

The cases of State ex rel. v. Philips, 96 Mo. 570, and Childs v. Railroad, 117 Mo. 414, l. c. 428, squarely hold that the filing of a motion for a rehearing in an appellate court after the adjournment of the term, under an order allowing the motion to be filed in vacation, continues the cause so that the opinion filed does not become the opinion of the court until the motion is disposed of at the next term.

There is this distinction between those cases and the case at bar: In those cases no motion for a rehearing had been filed at the time the order was made extending the time to the next term for parties to file such motions, while in the case at bar the motion for a rehearing had been filed and overruled at the time the order of extension was made.

Under Rule 21 of this court, regarding motions for a rehearing, that fact alone would. be a finality of the case, unless the court of its own motion, during the same term, should for some good cause resting in the breast of the court set the judgment aside; but Rule 20 of the Kansas City Court of Appeals governing motions for a rehearing is not so definite and clear as is said rule of this court.

But from the view we take of this case it is not necessary for us to construe or give effect to said Rule 20; it is more becoming to leave that duty with the Court of Appeals, except perhaps in a case where it might become absolutely necessary for this court to do so, in order to properly decide the case.

The rule invoked by counsel for relator is firmly established in this State, as well as many others; and the two cases before cited seem to be the only cases in conflict with it. In fact, it is elementary that after a final judgment has been rendered in a cause, at one term of the court, in the absence of a statute to the contrary, with no motion or other proper step having been taken therein, to carry the cause over to the next term of court, the court possesses no jurisdiction to set aside, modify or annul that judgment at such succeeding or any subsequent term of the court. [Jeude v. Sims, 258 Mo. 26.]

In discussing this question this court, in the Jeude-Sims case, on page 39, used this language:

"In all cases, except those provided for by these statutes, a court has no authority to disturb its judgment after the lapse of the term. This has been so universally ruled, that citations would be to become superfluous.

"The defendants, therefore, are in no position to lay hold of either of these two statutes, and the original judgment was wrongfully set aside after the lapse of the term, unless such action can be upheld upon one of the other two theories remaining to be discussed."

The same question was under consideration in the case of State ex rel. v. Reynolds, 209 Mo. 161, and in disposing of it this court, on page 176, used this language:

"If the circuit court of St. Louis County had made in express terms an order at a subsequent term setting aside the final decree granting the injunction and ordering the receiver appointed, it would have been absolutely void and of no effect, because that court had no authority to make such order after the expiration of the term at which the decree was made. And there is nothing in the Hirzel case (State ex rel. v. Hirzel, 137 Mo. 435), which indicated anything to the contrary.

[State ex rel. v. Walls, 113 Mo. 42; Appo v. People, 20 N. Y. 531.]

"In the former case the judge of the court which tried the case, after overruling the motion for a new trial, died, but before signing the bill of exceptions. His successor in office attempted at a subsequent term of the court to set aside the judgment and grant a new trial. In that case this court held that prohibition would lie to prevent the successor in office from setting aside the judgment previously entered, for want of jurisdiction in the court to make the order. The decision was not based upon the ground that the matter involved had been adjudicated and could not on that account be again litigated, but was based squarely upon the ground that the court had no jurisdiction to make the order.

"The same proposition was involved in the Appo case, supra, and it was there contended that when the inferior court or tribunal has jurisdiction of the action or of the subject-matter, before it, any error in the exercise of that jurisdiction can neither be corrected nor prevented by a writ of prohibition. In the discussion of that proposition the Court of Appeals of New York said: 'It is true that the most frequent occasions for the use of the writ are where a subordinate tribunal assumes to entertain some cause or proceeding over which it has no control. But the necessity for the writ is the same where, in a matter of which such tribunal has jurisdiction, it goes beyond its legitimate powers; and the authorities show that the writ is equally applicable to such a case. . . . These cases prove that the writ lies to prevent the exercise of any unauthorized power, in a cause or proceeding of which the subordinate tribunal has jurisdiction, no less than when the entire cause is without its jurisdiction. The broad remedial nature of this writ is shown by the brief statement of a case by Fitzherbert. In stating the various cases in which the writ will lie, he says: ''And if a man be sued in the spiritual court, and the judges there will not grant unto the defendant the copy of the libel, then he shall have a prohibition, directed unto them for a surcease,'' etc., until they have delivered the copy of the libel, according to the statute made Anno 2 H., 5 [F. N. B., title Prohibition.] This shows that the writ was never governed by any narrow technical rules, but was resorted to as a convenient mode of exercising a wholesome control over inferior tribunals. The scope of this remedy ought not, I think, to be abridged, as it is far better to prevent the exercise of an unauthorized power than to be driven to the necessity of correcting the error after it is committed. I have no hesitation, therefore, in holding that this was a proper case for the use of the writ.' [Appo v. People, 20 N. Y. l. c. 541-2.]

''And the same conclusions have been reached by this court in the following cases: Morris v. Lenox, 8 Mo. 252; Railroad v. Wear, 135 Mo. l. c. 256; State ex rel. v. Scarritt, 128 Mo. l. c. 338-9; High on Ex. Legal Rem., sec. 789; Spelling on Ex. Legal Rem., sec. 1741.''

The following authorities are also directly in point: Padgett v. Smith, 205 Mo. 122; Gratiot v. Mo. Pac. Ry. Co., 116 Mo. l. c. 470 (concurring opinion of BARCLAY and BRACE, JJ.); Danforth v. Lowe, 53 Mo. l. c. 218; Hill v. St. Louis, 20 Mo. l. c. 587; 1 Black on Judgments (1 Ed.), sec. 306, p. 383; 1 Freeman un Judgments (4 Ed.), sec. 96, pp. 132-3; 3 Cyc. 474, subsec. b.; 17 Am. & Eng. Ency. Law (2 Ed.), 816; Sibbald v. United States, 12 Pet. 491; Bank v. Moss, 6 How. 39; Bronson v. Schulten, 104 U. S. 410; Hawkins v. C. C. C. & St. L. Ry. Co., 99 Fed. 322; Brown v. Aspden's Admrs., 14 How. 25; Priddy v. Hayes, 204 Mo. 358; Wilson v. Darrow, 223 Mo. 520.

We have been cited to no statute or rule of common law or chancery which authorized the Court of

Appeals to make the order of February 28, 1914, extending the time to the next term of court in which to file motions in the causes mentioned therein. That authority existed, if at all, upon the rule announced in the cases of State ex rel. v. Philips, supra, and Childs v. Railroad, supra.

Those cases were not well considered, nor was any authority cited in support of the rule there announced. They stand alone in this State, and have no foreign support that I know of; they are against the consensus of authority in this State and elsewhere, and should, in my opinion, be overruled, which is accordingly done.

It therefore follows that the order of the Court of Appeals made on February 28, 1914, extending the time to the next term of the court for appellants in the original case in which to file the motion mentioned was and is null and void, and all orders and judgments of the court made therein at said succeeding term are likewise null and void, and of no force or effect whatever.

II. It is next insisted by counsel for respondents that notwithstanding the fact that the order of February 28, 1914, may have been unauthorized by law, and, therefore, null and void, yet the Court of Appeals, under section 6 of the Amendment of 1884 of article 6 of the Constitution, had the authority to certify the original cause to this court for any of the reasons stated therein, and the cause having been certified here by it, the peremptory writ of mandamus should be denied, and the cause decided by this court upon its merits.

While that section of the Constitution authorizes the various courts of appeals of the State to certify cases to this court for any of the grounds stated therein, yet in express terms it further provides that said Court of Appeals must, of its own motion, make such transfers to this court at "the same term" at which the judgment is rendered "and not afterward."

The return discloses the fact that the certification of the original cause to this court was made at the second or third term of the court subsequent to the one at which the original judgment was rendered.

Upon that state of facts, under the plain mandate of said constitutional provision, the order of the court certifying the original cause to this court was not authorized, and is therefore *coram non judice.*

It is true this court may in the exercise of its constitutional control of all other courts of the State, require the Court of Appeals to certify a cause to this court after the expiration of the term at which the judgment therein was rendered, but that fact does not signify that said court may so do of its own motion. [State ex rel. v. Philips, 96 Mo. l. c. 575; State ex rel. v. Patterson, 207 Mo. 129.]

For the reasons stated we are of the opinion that the peremptory writ of mandamus should issue; and it is so ordered.

Revelle, J., concurs; *Faris, J.,* concurs in a separate opinion in which *Graves, Walker* and *Blair, JJ.,* concur; *Bond, J.,* dissents.

FARIS, J. (concurring).—I concur in the result of the opinion of the learned Chief Justice, but I do not think that any necessity exists in this case to overrule the cases of State ex rel. v. Philips, 96 Mo. 570, and Childs v. Railroad, 117 Mo. 414.

I am of opinion that sufficient differences are apparent between the facts of those cases and the facts of the case at bar, to clearly distinguish those cases from the instant one. It may be that both of the cases marked for overruling in the Chief Justice's opinion were incorrectly decided—touching that I do not think we need here to give an opinion—therefore I do not think we need here trouble ourselves with their correctness or incorrectness. In the case on which the one at bar is bottomed a motion for rehearing *had been filed and overruled*, and appellant therein had come absolutely to the end of all legal steps for a review. In the Philips case no motion for rehearing *had ever been filed;* in the Childs case the ruling appears merely *arguendo*. In fairness, since time to file a motion for a rehearing in the Philips case—absent the order—was lacking, the Kansas City Court of Appeals gave by its general order time in the next term to file such motion for a rehearing, and upon mandamus brought here we approved their action fully. Since the matter strikes me largely as one of practice, touching which we possess inherent power to make rules, and since we have a rule—as also has the Kansas City Court of Appeals —allowing ten days after judgment to file a motion for rehearing, and since no statute expressly forbids, it would be to curtail both our convenience and the expediting of business and to run the risk of doing great injustice, if we thus cut off our right to retain by express order jurisdiction in a case so that time (otherwise lacking) might be had to file therein a motion for rehearing. In short, our convenience and the hurry of events might necessitate our deciding a case on the last day of any given term. If we have no right to make an order to the end that the losing party may have the same opportunity to file a motion for rehearing as we give by our rules' to others, it may be questionable whether the loser in such case has been accorded due process of law. [State v. Guerringer, 265 Mo. 408.] Certainly this is so, if the privilege given by a rule of an appellate court to file a motion for a rehearing and have it considered is a right *given* by law at all.

Under the facts at bar as they are so lucidly set out by the learned Chief Justice, so patent a difference appears to me that I vote not to overrule the cases mentioned, but to distinguish them upon their facts from this one; and so voting I concur fully otherwise. *Graves, Walker* and *Blair, JJ.,* concur in these views.

R. G. RAMSEY v. PETER H. HUCK, Judge of Circuit Court, and GEORGE W. COVINGTON.

In Banc, March 30, 1916.

1. **PROHIBITION: Circuit Courts.** The Supreme Court is given authority by the Constitution to prohibit, by its writ of prohibition, circuit courts and other inferior tribunals from exercising jurisdiction which they do not legally have.

2. ———: **Justice of Peace: Title to Office.** The Constitution gives the Supreme Court exclusive jurisdiction in cases involving title to any office under this State, and the office of a justice of the peace is such an office.

3. ———: **Jurisdiction of Appeal.** Jurisdiction to hear and determine upon appeal the original case out of which the application for a writ of prohibition arose, is not a prerequisite to the right of the Supreme Court to issue the writ.

4. **JUSTICE OF PEACE: Election Contest: Jurisdiction.** The county court, except in cities of three hundred thousand inhabitants, has jurisdiction to hear and determine a contested election for the office of justice of the peace; but such court is an inferior tribunal, and the grounds of its jurisdiction must appear affirmatively upon the face of the record.

5. ———: **Notice of Election Contest.** The service of notice of contest for the office of justice of the peace, fifteen days before the term of the county court at which the election is to be contested, is, by the statute, made essential to the validity of the proceeding; and where only twelve days' notice is given to contestee the court has no jurisdiction, and the proceeding must be dismissed.

6. ———: ———: **Amendment.** Notice of contest of less than fifteen days cannot be made sufficient by an amendment fixing the time of hearing at fifteen days from the date of service. It is only where jurisdiction has been obtained by proper notice, in the manner pointed out by the statute, that an amendment may be made to a notice of contest.

7. ———: ———: **Appeal.** If the county court had no jurisdiction over the contest for the office of justice of the peace, because notice of contest was not timely served, the circuit court acquired none by reason of an appeal.

Prohibition.

WRIT ISSUED.

Edward A. Rozier, B. H. Boyer and Clyde Morsey for relator.

Benjamin H. Marbury for respondents.

· WALKER, J.—Prohibition. Relator invokes this writ to prevent the circuit court of St. Francois County from entertaining jurisdiction in a proceeding to contest the right to the office of justice of the peace.

At the general election held in November, 1914, Ramsey, the relator, and Covington, one of the respondents, were opposing candidates for the office of justice of the peace in one of the townships of said county. Ramsey at said election received the greater number of votes, a commission was delivered to him and he was inducted into office.

On November 25, 1914, Covington notified Ramsey, by delivering to him a copy of the petition in the proceeding, that "at the next term of the county court of St. Francois County, to-wit, on Monday, December 7, 1914, he would contest Ramsey's right to said office." On said day Ramsey, appearing to plead to the jurisdiction of the court, filed a motion therein which alleged, among other things, that the return of the sheriff of the service of notice of contest showed upon its face that it was served on the 25th day of November, 1914, and that he was in fact served on said day, or only twelve days before the next term of said county court, whereas section 5924, Revised Statutes 1909, provides that in all such matters a notice shall be served upon the contestee fifteen days before the term of court at which such election is to be contested and hence said county court was without authority to hear said cause.

Covington thereupon asked leave to amend the notice which constituted the petition by striking out these words: "On Monday, December 7, 1914," and by inserting in lieu thereof the following: "And on the first day of said term which shall be held fifteen days or more after November 25, 1914, or the day of the service of this notice of contest." The court refused to permit this amendment to be made and sustained Ramsey's plea to the jurisdiction and dismissed the proceeding. Covington thereupon applied for and was granted an appeal to the circuit court. Upon the perfecting of this appeal Ramsey appeared therein and challenged the jurisdiction of the circuit court to hear said cause on the ground that the county court had no authority to hear same and that the circuit court had acquired none by reason of the appeal. This motion was by the circuit court overruled, whereupon Ramsey applied for the writ herein.

It has been questioned whether this is the proper forum in which to invoke this writ in a case of this character. The Constitution (Sec. 8, art. 6, Amdt. 1884) gives express power to this court to issue the writ to regulate the actions of the courts of appeals, but such power is not expressly given in regard to other inferior tribunals, the provision in regard thereto being as follows: "The Supreme Court shall have a general superintending control over all inferior courts. It shall have power to issue writs of *habeas corpus,* mandamus, *quo warranto, certiorari* and other original remedial writs, and to hear and determine the same." [Sec. 3, art. 6, Constitution.] However, the general words "and other original remedial writs" were held in Thomas v. Mead, 36 Mo. 232, to authorize the issuance of the writ of prohibition against a circuit court in a case involving title to the office of clerk of the Supreme Court. This ruling has been followed in a number of subsequent cases in which the court has supervised circuit courts and other inferior tribunals, the

(Marginal note: Prohibition to Circuit Court.)

last expression on the subject being found in State ex
rel. v. Williams, 221 Mo. l. c. 256.

Whatever individual opinion may, therefore, be
entertained as to the correctness of the construction of
the rule in regard to general words following particular words, as announced in Thomas v. Mead, supra,
must be subordinated to the conclusion reached in that
case and subsequent cases, and discussion in regard
thereto is foreclosed and the right of the court to issue
the writ in the exercise of its supervisory control over
any inferior tribunal is completely established.

The proceeding sought to be prohibited involves
title to the office of justice of the peace. The Constitution provides that the Supreme Court
shall have exclusive jurisdiction ''in cases
involving . . . title to any office under this State.'' [Sec. 12, art. 6, Constitution; Sec. 5, art. 6, Amdt. 1884.] This provision
means any office held under the authority of the laws
of this State, and has been held to apply to give this
court jurisdiction in contests involving title to the following offices: ˙clerk of the circuit court (State ex rel.
Blakemore v. Rombauer, 101 Mo. l. c. 501); members of a school board (State ex rel. Macklin v. Rombauer, 104 Mo. 619; State ex rel. Rogers v. Rombauer,
105 Mo. 103; State ex rel. Walker v. Bus, 135 Mo.
325); school directors (State ex inf. Sutton v. Fasse,
189 Mo. 532; State ex rel. Frisby v. Stone, 152 Mo. l.
c. 204; State ex rel. Frisby v. Hill, 152 Mo. 234); and
county collector (Sanders v. Lacks, 142 Mo. 255); and
certain township officers (Macrae v. Coles, 183 S. W.
578).

Under these rulings the conclusion is authorized
that the office of justice of the peace is one held under
the authority of the laws of this State, and hence this
court has jurisdiction.

Jurisdiction:
Title to
Office.

The court's power in the premises, as defined in the cases cited, is based primarily upon its jurisdiction to hear and determine upon appeal the original cases out of which the application for the writs arose; such appellate jurisdiction, however, is not a prerequisite to the right of this court to issue the writ herein. [State ex rel. v. Eby, 170 Mo. l. c. 516.]

We come now to a consideration of the jurisdiction of the county court to hear and determine the contest proceedings upon which the application for the writ herein is based. The Constitution provides in this regard that "the General Assembly shall, by general law, designate the court or judge by whom the several classes of election contests shall be tried," etc. [Sec. 9, art. 8, Constitution.] Under this provision section 5294, Revised Statutes 1909, was enacted, giving county courts, except in cities now or hereafter attaining three hundred thousand inhabitants, jurisdiction in contests of township offices; and section 7372, Revised Statutes 1909, which provides that in contested elections for justice of the peace the county courts shall decide same. Under these sections county courts are given power to hear and determine contested elections for the office of justice of the peace. [Taaffe v. Ryan, 25 Mo. App. 563.]

Election Contest: Notice.

Such courts being, therefore, clothed with general power herein, it remains to be determined whether the statute prescribing the procedure relative hereto has been complied with—because to the statute alone, upon which contests of elections are solely based, we must look to determine the regularity of the court's proceeding. [State ex rel. v. Hough, 193 Mo. l. c. 645.] Furthermore, the fact must be borne in mind that county courts are inferior tribunals, not proceeding according to the course of the common law, but confined to the authority given them by statute, and that the grounds of their jurisdiction must appear affirmatively on the face of their records. [Ex Parte O'Brien, 127 Mo. 477; Strouse v. Drennan, 41 Mo. 289; State ex rel. Sanks v. Johnson, 138 Mo. App. 306.]

It is contended here that the notice of the contest of election was insufficient. The statute requires, among other things, that "the notice shall be served fifteen days before the term of court at which the election shall be contested," etc. The object of the statute in requiring the notice has two distinct purposes. One is to bring the party into court and the other to set forth and advise the court of the grounds of the contest. The notice, therefore, stands in lieu of and performs the functions of a writ and a petition in an ordinary suit. [State ex rel. Wells v. Hough, 193 Mo. l. c. 642; Hale v. Stimson, 198 Mo. l. c. 145.] Possessed of this importance, the service of the notice as required by law becomes jurisdictional and is absolutely essential to the validity of the proceeding. [State ex rel. Sale v. McElhinney, 199 Mo. l. c. 78.] The rule is well established and uniform in its operation that where the jurisdiction of a court is made to depend upon the time either of the giving of notice or of taking an appeal, the requirement is peremptory. In Castello v. Court, 28 Mo. 259, we held that the notice required in a contested election case must be given within the time pescribed by the statute, and in Wilson v. Lucas, 43 Mo. 290, which was a contest of an election to the office of circuit judge, the statute required a certain number of days' notice of the contest and the petition was dismissed because the requirement was not observed. In Bowen v. Hixon, 45 Mo. 340, involving a contest for the office of county clerk, the notice of the contest required by the statute was not complied with and the proceedings were held to be invalid. In Adcock v. Lecompt, 66 Mo. 40, a contest for the office of county collector, the proceeding was dismissed on account of a defective notice. In State ex rel. v. Ross, 245 Mo. l. c. 46, it was held that notice of the contest within the time designated in the statute was one of the rights of the contestee and a failure to give same forfeited the right to the contest.

In the instant case the notice of contest was served on the contestee on the 25th day of November, 1914, in which he was notified that at the next term of the county court of St. Francois County, to be begun on Monday, the 7th day of December, 1914, a proceeding would be begun and prosecuted in said court by contestant to determine the contestee's right to the office of justice of the peace. From these facts it is evident that the contestee was only given twelve days notice of said contest, which was not sufficient under the statute, and it was so held by the county court. It is contended, however, that this defect was cured by the amendment proposed to be made after the filing of the contestee's plea to the jurisdiction, which attempted to fix the time of hearing of the proceeding at fifteen days from the date of the service of the notice on the contestee. This proposed amendment was not permitted by the county court. It is only where jurisdiction has been obtained by proper notice in the manner pointed out by the statute that an amendment may be made to a notice of contest. It was so held in Nash v. Craig, 134 Mo. 347, which ruling was approved in State ex rel. v. Hough, 193 Mo. l. c. 650. The correctness of this ruling is evident from the nature of the proceeding. The notice constitutes the petition in the case. Jurisdiction is acquired by properly serving it upon the contestee. Unless it has been so served the court is without authority to make any order in the premises except to dismiss the proceeding and upon a proper application to grant the contestant an appeal. The county court being without jurisdiction, the circuit court acquired none by reason of the appeal (Tie & Timber Co. v. Drainage Co., 226 Mo. 1. c. 444; Sidwell v. Jett, 213 Mo. 601), and it should have so ruled by sustaining the contestee's motion to dismiss.

It is therefore ordered that the preliminary writ of prohibition issued be made absolute and that the circuit court refrain from further exercise of jurisdiction herein. All concur.

JOHN McMENAMY INVESTMENT & REAL ESTATE COMPANY v. STILLWELL CATERING COMPANY, Appellant.

Division One, March 30, 1916.

JURISDICTION: Non-Resident Corporation: Service. For the reasons stated in the minority opinion of the St. Louis Court of Appeals, 175 Mo. App. 1. c. 679 et seq., in this case, the judgment is reversed, and the cause remanded, in order to give plaintiff opportunity to obtain valid service on defendant corporation.

Appeal from St. Louis City Circuit Court.—*Hon. J. Hugo Grimm,* Judge.

REVERSED.

George W. Lubke and *George W. Lubke, Jr.,* for appellant.

F. A. & L. A. Wind and *F. X. Geraghty* for respondent.

GRAVES, P. J.—This cause reached this court by a certification, under the Constitution, made by the St. Louis Court of Appeals. Two opinions were filed in that court. The majority opinion affirmed the judgment of the circuit court. The minority opinion held that the judgment should be reversed, and the writer

of the minority opinion asked for the certification of
the cause here on the ground that the majority opinion
conflicted with Priest v. Capitain, 236 Mo. 446, and
other cases in this court. The case is fully reported
in 175 Mo. App. 668. All sides of the question involved
are thoroughly threshed out in these two opinions.

The question of the jurisdiction of the circuit
court, and that is the vital question, is discussed from
all angles in these two opinions. The dissenting opinion in my judgment follows the views of this court
upon the question involved. The record facts are so
thoroughly stated, and the case law so thoroughly discussed by Judge ALLEN in his dissenting opinion, that
we feel that it would be a useless expenditure of vital
force to try to add to them. For the reasons expressed
by Judge ALLEN in his dissenting opinion (Real Estate
Co. v. Catering Co., 175 Mo. App. l. c. 679 et seq.), the
judgment of the circuit court is reversed. All concur.

ON MOTION TO MODIFY JUDGMENT.

GRAVES, P. J.—We are asked to so modify our
judgment in this case that the cause may be remanded. It is suggested that perhaps proper service
of process can be obtained. Our judgment was a
simple reversal of the judgment *nisi*. Under the views
we have expressed as to the law, we do not know
whether plaintiff can get a valid service of process or
not, but we see no objection to a remanding of the cause
to give the plaintiff such an opportunity. So, whilst
adhering to all the views of the opinion, we will sustain the motion to modify our judgment, so that such
judgment shall be to the effect that the judgment *nisi* is
reversed and the cause remanded to the circuit court
to be proceeded with in accordance with the law as declared in our opinion. Motion to modify judgment
sustained and judgment modified as herein indicated.
All concur.

MABEL L. SMITH v. RESERVE LOAN LIFE IN-SURANCE COMPANY et al., Appellants.

Division One, March 30, 1916.

1. **TENDER: Draft or Order.** A tender of bank notes, checks or drafts or orders for the payment of money, if not objected to for failure to produce legal tender money, is a legal tender in payment of a private debt.

2. ———: ———: **Implied Waiver.** The creditor, if he objects to a payment in bank notes or such things as represent money in the marts of trade and commerce, should put his refusal on that ground, and if he suppresses his objection at the time the offer is made, he is estopped from subsequently making the objection, if his later insistence thereon would inflict a loss or damage upon his debtor who in reliance upon his implied waiver failed to produce the kind of money made legal tender by law.

3. ———: ———: ———: **Submitting Issue to Jury.** The facts stated in the opinion authorized the trial court to submit to the jury the issue of implied waiver of a tender of actual money.

4. ———: **Evidence: Telegraph Order: Bankable Paper.** Testimony that a telegraph money order, tendered by the company's agent to an insurance company in payment of a premium note, is bankable paper in the sense that the banks of the town would put it to the credit of the holder and permit him to check out the amount thereof, is competent evidence, where the sufficiency of the tender of such order is the issue in the case.

5. ———: **Telegraph Money Order.** A telegraph money order drawn by the cashier of the sendee office of the Postal Telegraph-Cable Company upon its treasurer in New York is equally as satisfactory and trustworthy in the payment of debts as bank drafts or individual checks.

Appeal from Jackson Circuit Court.—*Hon. James H. Slover*, Judge.

AFFIRMED.

Guilford A. Deitch, Ed. E. Yates and *Perry S. Rader* for appellants.

(1) The Postal Telegraph-Cable Company "was bound to deliver to appellant the money," not its check, nor a draft, nor an order on itself. Robinson v. Tel. Co., 24 Ky. L. Rep. 456; Tel. Co. v. Gougar, 84 Ind. 178. (2) The order drawn by "C. Fred Knight, Money Transfer Agent," at Indianapolis, directing the "Treasurer of Money Transfer Department Postal Telegraph-Cable Co." at New York to "pay to the order of Reserve Loan Life Insurance Company $595.40," was not negotiable, was not a check or a bankable draft, and it is very doubtful if it had any bankable or negotiable quality unless and until accepted by the treasurer in New York, either in his own name or in such way as to bind the telegraph company.. (a) It was not negotiable because it was expressly made payable out of a particular fund; "and charge same to account of Money Transfers." School Township v. Andress, 56 Ind. 163; McGee v. Larramore, 50 Mo. 427; 1 Daniel on Negotiable Instruments (6 Ed.), sec. 50; Richardson v. Carpenter, 46 N. Y. 664; Hoagland v. Erck, 11 Neb. 580; Hannay v. Trust Co., 187 Fed. 686. (b) It was not a bank draft because it was not drawn by one bank upon another bank. (c) It was not a check because not drawn on a bank. 2 Daniel on

Negotiable Instruments (6 Ed.), secs. 1566, 1568; Bank
v. Bank, 10 Wall. (77 U. S.) 647; Hawley v. Jette, 10
Ore. 34. (d) It was not a bill of exchange: Because
it was not drawn on the general funds of the Postal
Telegraph-Cable Company, but against the money in
"Money Transfer Department." Espy v. Bank, 18
Wall. (85 U. S.) 152; Wood's Byles on Bills & Notes,
sec. 1; Daniel on Negotiable Instruments (6 Ed.), secs.
27, 29. It was not a bill of exchange of the Postal Telegraph-Cable Company because it was not signed by
such company or by any person in its name, and does
not purport to be drawn by it or for it. It could not
have been enforced against said company, if accepted
by defendant, and resisted by said company. 7 Cyc.
549 (e); Wood's Byles on Bills & Notes, sec. 1; Daniel
on Negotiable Instruments (6 Ed.), secs. 27, 29; Bank
v. Hooper, 71 Mass. 567; Crum v. Boyd, 9 Ind. 289;
Snow v. Goodrich, 14 Me. 235; Stackpole v. Arnold, 11
Mass. 27, 29; Banking Co. v. Van Antwerp, 51 N. Y.
Supp. 812; Pentz v. Stanton, 10 Wend. (N. Y.) 271; 1
Am. & Eng. Ency. Law (2 Ed.), 1047 (5); Bank v. Anderson, 32 Pac. (Cal.) 168; Freman's Note, 48 Am. St.
919; McClellan v. Robe, 93 Ind. 298; Bank v. Steel
Co., 155 Ind. 581. The order unless accepted by the
Postal Telegraph-Cable Company, or by its treasurer
in New York, or at least by "the Treasurer Money
Transfer Department Postal Telegraph-Cable Com-
pany, 253 Broadway, New York," could not have been
enforced as a legal demand against said telegraph company. The liability of the drawee on a bill begins with
its acceptance. Reilly v. Daly, 159 Pa. St. 611;
McGinn v. Bank, 131 Pa. St. 364; Bank v. Bank, 69
Ind. 480; Marriner v. Lumber Co., 113 N. C. 52. (3)
"A bill of exchange is not money in any sense, and is
not made a legal tender by any statutory enactment."

Ins. Co. v. Clark, 41 Ind. App. 351; Goss v. Bowen, 104
Ind. 209; Boyd v. Olvey, 82 Ind. 298. (4) Even if the
transfer order had been received by defendant it would
not have been a payment of the note unless at the time
it was accepted there was a positive agreement that it
was being accepted as full payment and satisfaction of
the debt. Appleton v. Kennon, 19 Mo. 637; Howard v.
Jones, 33 Mo. 583; Wiles v. Robinson, 80 Mo. 47; Com-
misky v. McPike, 20 Mo. App. 66; Holland v. Rongey,
168 Mo. 16; Way v. Caddell, 82 Mo. App. 144. And the
same is true even though the telegraph money order be
considered a check or draft. Johnson-Brinkman Coms.
Co. v. Bank, 116 Mo. 570; Hall & Robinson v. Railroad,
50 Mo. App. 183; Prewitt v. Brown, 101 Mo. App. 259.
A payment other than in money necessarily rests upon
an independent agreement. Moore v. Renick, 95 Mo.
App. 643; Rider v. Culp, 68 Mo. App. 531; Ulsch v.
Muller, 143 Mass. 379. The giving and accepting of
an order for prior indebtedness will not be regarded as
payment thereof unless there be an express agreement
between the parties to that effect. Farwell & Co. v.
Salpaugh, 32 Iowa, 583; Railroad v. Burns, 61 Neb.
794; Estey v. Birnbaum, 9 S. D. 175; Cliver v. Heil,
95 Wis. 365. (5) If the order signed by "C· Fred
Knight, Money Transfer Agent," is considered the obligation of the Postal Telegraph Company, the drawer
and drawee were one and the same person, or a bill
drawn by the drawer upon himself (if the "Treasurer
of Money Transfer Department" can be considered the
company); and such an order is in effect the promissory note of the drawer or telegraph company or of
Knight, and defendant was entitled to consider it as a
promissory note and nothing more. Railroad v. Davis,
20 Ind. 8; Road Co. v. Branegan, 40 Ind. 362; Board

of Commissioners v. Day, 19 Ind. 452; Railroad v.
Dillon, 7 Ind. 405; Fairchild v. Railroad, 15 N. Y. 340;
Haney v. Beet Sugar Co., 1 Dougl. (Mich.) 197; 1 Daniel on Negotiable Instruments (6 Ed.), sec. 424; 1 Parsons on Bills & Notes, p. 63; Randolph v. Parish, 9
Port. (Ala.) 76; Poydras v. Delmare, 13 La. 98. If
defendant was entitled to treat said order as a promissory note, then it was no tender. It was not money,
or "that which by common consent is considered and
treated as money." One promissory note is not a legal
tender in payment of another, unless expressly agreed
to be accepted as such. Holland v. Rongey, 168 Mo.
16; Keyser v. Hinkle, 127 Mo. App. 75; Bradway v.
Groendyke, 153 Ind. 508; Ins. Co. v. Chappelow, 83
Ind. 429.

*Edward L. Scarritt, Constantine J. Smyth, Ed. P.
Smith* and *W. A. Schall* for respondent.

(1) There was no error in admission of testimony.
Supreme Tent v. Fisher, 90 N. E. (Ind.) 1044; Berth-
old v. Reyburn, 37 Mo. 587; Land Co. v. Moody, 198
Fed. 7; Breed v. Hurd, 23 Mass. 356. (2) The burden
of proof was on the defendants. Harris v. Insurance
Co., 248 Mo. 317; Crenshaw v. Insurance Co., 71 Mo.
App. 52; 25 Cyc. 925-927; Life Assurance Society v.
Cannon, 201 Ill. 250. (3) The facts show that the in-
sured made a good tender of the amount due upon the
premium note with interest, within the time provided
in the note. (4) The tender made was sufficient in law.
Willcotts v. Ins. Co., 81 Ind. 300; Mathews v. Modern
Woodman, 236 Mo. 344; Halsey v. Insurance Co., 258
Mo. 662; Graham v. Ins. Co., 62 Atl. (N. J.) 681; Beatty
v. Miller, 94 N. E. (Ind.) 897; Gradle v. Warner, 140
Ill. 123; Kitchell v. Schneider, 103 N. E. (Ind.) 647;
Gunby v. Ingram, 36 L. R. A. (N. S.) 232; Edmonds
E. C. Company v. Kilpatrick, 166 Mo. 262; Potter v.

Schafer, 209 Mo. 586; Schaeffer v. Coldron, 85 Atl.
98; Bristol v. Mente, 80 N. Y. S. 52; McGrath v. Gag-
ner, 77 Md. 331; Bonding Co. v. Bruce, 13 Ind. App.
550; Cox v. Hayes, 18 Ind. App. 220; Mahon v. Waters, 60 Mo. 170; McMahn v. Insurance Co., 128 Fed.
388.

OPINION.

I.

BOND, J.—This is a suit on an insurance policy
taken out by Frank H. Smith on November 11, 1909,
in favor of his wife, Mabel L. Smith, the respondent
herein, in the sum of $10,000 in the Reserve Loan Life
Insurance Company, upon payment of the first annual
premium thereon of $732.

On the 11th day of November, 1910, when the second annual premium became due, the said Frank L.
Smith was unable to pay the same and applied to the
defendant company for an extension of time; to-wit,
to the 11th of February, 1911, which extension was
granted by said defendant company, in consideration
of which the said Frank L. Smith paid to the defendant company the sum of $108.93 in cash and sent the
defendant company one of the coupons mentioned in
said policy for $36.60, and executed an extension pre-
mium note for $595.40 payable on February 11, 1911,
providing that if said note be not paid upon maturity
the policy shall be without notice null and void.

On Thursday, February 9, 1911, one Arthur A.
Remillard, the brother-in-law of Mrs. Smith, acting for
Mr. Smith, tried to pay the premium at the local office
of the said company in Philadelphia. Finding the local agent was not authorized to receive money he went
to the office of the Postal Telegraph Company and
turned over to them $595.40 plus $9 to pay the transfer

charges and requested them to transmit the money to
the defendant company. At the same time Remillard
telegraphed the defendant; to-wit,

"Philadelphia, Pa., Feb. 9, 1911.

The Reserve Loan Life Insurance Co.,
900 Odd Fellows Bldg.

I this day telegraph you five hundred and ninety-
five dollars and forty cents in payment of note given by
Frank H. Smith, for premium on policy No. 25684, is-
sued to Frank H. Smith, and due Feb. 11th, this year.
Return note and send receipt for premium to Frank H.
Smith, Aldan, Delaware Co., Pa.

"ARTHUR A. REMILLARD."

And after sending the telegram, and within the
hour, he wrote and took to the post office, stamped and
registered the following letter:

"Postal Telegraph-Cable Company,
"Night Lettergram.
"Philadelphia, Pa. Feb. 9-11.
"Reserve Loan Life Insurance Company,
900 Odd Fellows Bldg.,
Indianapolis, Ind.,
"Gentlemen:—

"I sent you today by the Postal Telegraph Co.
five hundred and ninety-five dollars and 40 cents
($595.40) in payment of note given by Frank H. Smith
for premium on policy No. 25684 said note maturing
Feb. 11, 1911. I exacted a report from the Postal Company of delivery of the message I sent notifying you I
forwarded the money and for what purpose.

"Kindly answer at once and return note and also
send receipt for premium to Frank H. Smith, Aldan,
Delaware Co., Pa., formerly 1532 Arch St.

"Hoping for a prompt reply, I am respy,
"ARTHUR A. REMILLARD,
"Aldan, Delaware Co. Pa."

The money sent by Remillard had an order of waiver of identification, in which case the Telegraph Company testified they would pay in money if so requested.

The testimony shows that on the 9th and 10th of February, 1911, the Telegraph Company notified the defendant company of the arrival of the money to pay the premium, which might be obtained by calling at the office of the Telegraph Company.

Upon the defendant failing to call at the office of said Telegraph Company, after being so notified, Mr. Knight, the cashier of said Telegraph Company, on the 11th of February, 1911, called personally at the office of the defendant and displayed a draft of the Postal Telegraph Company drawn upon its treasurer in New York for the amount of the extension note, $595.40. Knight presented this draft at the cashier's window. The space behind the window was occupied by Miss Dickson, who was authorized to receive collections. The conflicting testimony as to what was said and done on this occasion will be stated later.

On the following Monday, February 13, 1911, Knight again went to the office of the defendant company where he saw Mr. Zulick, its vice-president, and delivered the draft or order to him in the presence of Mr. Deitch and Mr. West (the appellant claims Miss Dickson was also present), Mr. Zulick refused to accept the postal order and testified that he demanded money. Knight testified that the draft or order was returned to him but no demand was made for money.

Mr. Zulick testified that on Saturday at eleven-thirty-nine o'clock he wired Frank H. Smith that he could not send the premium receipt unless the premium note be paid in cash before due, sending the wire over the Western Union.

Mr. Smith was sick at the time the second annual premium fell due, of which the company was informed.

Evidence was introduced by the defendant of the Indiana law governing legal holidays (February 12, 1911, was Lincoln's birthday) and claimed that under such law the note would not mature until Tuesday, February 14, 1911.

The case was tried at the May term, 1915, of the Jackson Circuit Court at Kansas City. A verdict was found in favor of the plaintiff for $9874.83, upon which judgment was rendered. The defendant duly appealed.

II.

The controlling question on this appeal is whether there was a sufficient tender of payment of the note for a part of the second premium payable on the policy in suit?

Prior to the legal tender acts of 1862 making United States treasury notes a legal tender for all debts public or private not payable in a particular kind of coin or commodity, only gold or silver coin of the realm was a legal tender of payment of private debts. [30 Cyc. 1212.] But before and after these Congressional enactments a tender of bank notes, checks or drafts or orders for the payment of money (if not objected to for failure to produce legal tender money) would not be invalid because not falling within the description of money made legal tender by the Constitution of the United States and the Federal Statutes. [Williams v. Rorer, 7 Mo. 556; Shipp v. Stacker, 8 Mo. 145; Berthold v. Reyburn, 37 Mo. l. c. 595; Beckham v. Puckett, 88 Mo. App. l. c. 639; Thompson v. St. Charles County, 227 Mo. l. c. 234.]

Legal Tender.

The reasoning of these cases is that the creditor when offered such representatives of legal tender money if he is not willing to accept them as such, should put his refusal on that ground so that the debtor may have the opportunity to secure the specific money which the law prescribes shall be accepted in payment of any debts express to be payable in dollars. Hence, it is deemed only just that the holder of such an obligation upon tender of the payment thereof in bank notes or such things as represent money in the marts of trade and commerce, shall state expressly the ground of his rejection in order that the debtor may comply with the technical law requiring a tender of a particular kind of money. The non-observance of this duty necessarily misleads the debtor and may inflict a loss which would be avoided if the creditor had stated that he objected to the form and character of the tender. He should therefore be estopped from subsequently urging an objection which he suppressed at the time of the offer if his later insistence thereon would inflict a loss or damage upon a creditor who in reliance on his implied waiver failed to produce the kind of money made a legal tender by law. This thought has been accurately and pithily stated by LAMM, J., viz., "Who does not speak when he should may not when he would." [Thompson v. St. Charles County, supra.]

In the case at bar defendant had actual knowledge two days before the note given to it for part of the second premium on the policy matured; that the money for the full payment thereof had been telegraphed to Indianapolis where its home office was located, for the satisfaction of the note and was requested by wire and letter sent from Philadelphia coincidentally with the transmission of the money to apply the same on said note and return receipt thereof. The defendant was also notified by the forwarder of the money (the Postal Telegraph Company) two days before the maturity of the note that it held the money order for the amount which would be due on the maturity of the note and was requested in said notice to apply for the same. Getting no reply to this written request the forwarding company phoned the office of the defendant stating it held such order for it and received a phone answer indicating that the matter would be taken up or information given about it. Failing to receive such information the forwarder sent its cashier on the morning of the 11th day of February to the office of the defendant with a draft or order drawn upon the treasurer of the forwarding company for the full amount due on the note. This was displayed to the person at the cashier's window who did not receive it, excusing herself on the ground that the cashier was not in and that she would refer the matter to a Mr. Woodbury. Her account of the matter is, to-wit, "I was only passing. I just referred him at once to Mr. Woodbury and went back to my desk. Mr. Woodbury came forward and I went to the next counter and back to my desk."

The account of this transaction by C. F. Knight, the cashier of the transmitter of the money, was in substance that after unavailing efforts for two days to get definite instructions from defendant as to the money held for it and after repeated notices given, he called in person with a draft in the usual form payable to defendant, upon the New York treasurer and presented the same to the lady occupying the cashier's window, adding, to-wit, "I told her I was from the Postal Telegraph Company with a money order for the Reserve Loan Life Insurance Company for $595.41 from Arthur A. Remillard, Philadelphia." That she walked away and then came back. "When she came back she said that the cashier was not in and that he would take it up and let us know," whereupon he (Knight) returned to his office.

It was shown that this lady had full authority to accept payment of premiums and give receipt therefor. This being the last day upon which the note could be paid according to its terms, Knight, however, appeared with the same draft on the Monday following and handed it to the vice-president of the defendant company. As to what took place at that interview there is a sharp conflict of testimony. The testimony of the cashier of the Postal Telegraph Company is to the effect that the draft or order which he delivered to the vice-president was handed back to him without any objection to the form of the tender and without any request that money should be produced instead. The testimony of the vice-president, corroborated by others whom he called to witness the interview and a hotation upon a memorandum, was to the effect that the vice-president refused to accept the order and demanded the production of money. The evidence was undisputed that the vice-president had received notice from the sender of the money two days before the maturity of the note by letter and wire and that he delayed his reply until the lapse of two days, when, only a few minutes before the maturity of the note, he wired the assured that the note must be paid in cash before he would send a receipt or return it. This belated reply was sent over the wire of another company than that which transmitted the money.

These and other facts adduced on the trial presented issues of fact which were submitted to the jury under appropriate instructions. Upon this conflicting evidence their verdict was in favor of the testimony relied upon by the plaintiff to show an implied waiver on the part of the defendant of the production of the money at the times when the draft or order was presented for payment of the note.

The testimony for the plaintiff leads to the conclusion that the verdict of the jury was supported by evidence affording a legitimate basis for the inference that the defendant intended at all times, after it was informed two days in advance of the maturity of the note that the money to pay it had been transmitted by telegraph, to baffle the efforts which might be made to extinguish that obligation and thereby forfeit the policy and thus avoid its liability for the death of the insured whose ill health and impecunious condition the record discloses had been brought to the attention of the defendant.

The anxiety to pay this note is manifest from what was done by Mr. Remillard to that end. He appeared at the office in Philadelphia with the money in his possession and was told that it could not be received there but would have to be sent to the home office in Indianapolis. Without risking the delay of the mail and uncertainty of his individual check or draft reaching defendant in time, he at once deposited with the Postal Telegraph Company the entire amount which would be due on the note two days thereafter, with directions to wire it, waiving identification, to the order of defendant at Indianapolis and paid $9 for that method of sending the money. This was immediately done, the defendant was promptly notified both by the telegraph company and by the sender, as has been shown and with the result as has been shown.

In view of this testimony there was substantial evidence to support the verdict of the jury; for upon the theory of the evidence relied upon by plaintiff the transaction was one to which the doctrine of implied waiver of the production of money under the authorities hereinbefore cited is strictly applicable.

We conclude, therefore, that there was no error on the part of the trial court in submitting the issue as to the validity of the tender of payment to the jury.

III.

Error is claimed as to the instructions. A careful examination of these shows that they were submitted in accordance with the rules of law governing the validity of payment where there is an implied waiver of the production of the money itself.

Some complaint is made as to the evidence adduced tending to show that the draft or order pre-

sented by the Postal Company of Indianapolis to the
defendant was bankable in the sense that the banks of
Evidence.   Indianapolis would put it to the credit of a
holder and permit him to check out the
amount thereof. Plaintiff was entitled to make this
proof in order to show the commercial value of the paper tendered on her behalf as the representative of
money, and she was further entitled to show that the
drawer of the order, the Postal Telegraph Company,
kept sufficient funds deposited in a bank in Indianapolis to pay this draft or order.

It seems to us to be a matter of common knowledge
that the transmission of money by telegraph through
such companies as the Postal Telegraph and the Western Union Telegraph Company has become well established in modern business in the States of this Union
and amongst most civilized nations having dealings
with the people of this country; and that such a draft
or order, considering its use in certain emergencies
requiring the rapid transfer of cash, and the immense
resources of the two companies who are engaged in
affording that business facility to their customers,
would be equally as satisfactory and trustworthy as
the cashier's checks of banks or the checks of individuals, and that persons willing to accept these for money
would not hesitate to receive the former which has now
become a recognized medium of quick exchange of money of such pecuniary value and security that it is accepted by banks on the same basis upon which they
receive drafts or cashier's checks of other banks.

The judgment in this case is free from any reversible error and is affirmed. All concur.

BOARD OF EDUCATION OF CITY OF ST. LOUIS
v. CITY OF ST. LOUIS et al., Appellants.

Division One, March 30, 1916.

1. **POLICE REGULATION: Water-closets: Conflicting Authority of City and School Board.** The Board of Education of the city of St. Louis is not subject to the ordinances and regulations of the city in respect to the manner of construction of water-closets and vents therefrom in a public school building. Under the statute the Board of Education is specifically "charged with the care of the public school buildings of said city, and with the responsibility for the ventilation and sanitary condition thereof," and under the Constitution that statute makes their authority exclusive.

2. ———: ———: ———: **Presumption of Application to Sovereign: Repeal by Implication.** Where the sovereignty itself has dealt with the subject of the construction and management of property which is held and used by its agents for the highest governmental purposes, no presumption that laws of the character of the charter of the city of St. Louis and ordinances passed in pursuance thereof are applicable to the sovereign, can prevail, for then the power does not rest upon presumption, but upon express legislative declarations.

3. ———: ———: ———: **Paramount Authority of Statute.** The general charter of the city of St. Louis must yield to the provisions of a law having special application to particular matters and things within the field of its operation; and where there is such a general law, the question of whether the charter and ordinances are impliedly repealed without being mentioned in the general law, is not in the case.

Appeal from St. Louis City Circuit Court.—*Hon. J. Hugo Grimm*, Judge.

AFFIRMED.

William E. Baird for appellants.

(1) The Board of Education is a public corporation formed for a special and limited purpose; its charter is found in the statutes, which must be construed by

the same rules as are applied to other statutes. Heller v. Stremmel, 52 Mo. 311; State v. Lockett, 54 Mo. App. 202; Peers v. Board, 72 Ill. 508; Smith v. Proctor, 130 N. Y. 319; McQuillin, Mun. Corp., sec. 114. (2) The property controlled by the board is not owned by the State or used for governmental purposes; the presumption that the sovereign or the State is not bound by local regulations cannot be indulged. Kansas City v. Fee, 174 Mo. App. 510; School Dist. v. Pasadena, 166 Cal. 7; Public Schools v. St. Louis, 26 Mo. 468; Bank v. State, 69 Iowa, 30; Sioux City v. School Dist., 55 Iowa, 150; City, Trustee, v. Chicago, 207 Ill. 37; Board v. People, 219 Ill. 87. (3) The city of St. Louis, by its charter, had and still has plenary power over sewers, drains, sanitation and other local subjects of regulation. Ex parte Smith, 231 Mo. 111; Gunning Co. v. St. Louis, 235 Mo. 99. (4) No such power has been given the Board of Education; a modification of the city charter will not be implied in the law creating the board. R. S. 1909, secs. 11030-11062; Dillon, Mun. Corp. (5 Ed.), sec. 235; State ex rel. v. Severance, 55 Mo. 386; Wills v. Railroad, 133 Mo. App. 625; E. St. Louis v. Maxwell, 99 Ill. 443; Wood v. Comrs., 58 Cal. 563; State v. Williams, 80 Tenn. 251.

Robert Burkham for respondent.

(1) Education is a governmental function. Article 11, Missouri Constitution; Lehew v. Brummell, 103 Mo. 550; Heller v. Stremmel, 52 Mo. 309; State ex rel. v. St. Louis School Board, 112 Mo. 213. The members of the Board of Education of the city of St. Louis are officers under the State and exercise functions of government. State ex rel. v. Rombauer, 104 Mo. 619; State ex rel. v. Gordon, 231 Mo. 547; Secs. 11030–11062, R. S. 1909. The Board of Education is a public corporation separate and distinct from and entirely independent of the municipality of St. Louis.

Waterworks Co. v. School Districts, 23 Mo. App. 241; State ex rel. v. Tracy, 94 Mo. 221; School District No. 7 v. School District of St. Joseph, 184 Mo. 156. (2) School buildings being maintained by the State in the exercise of a governmental function, the presumption arises, at least so far as their internal construction is concerned, that they are not subject to municipal regulation or control. (a) The general principle: Bank v. United States, 86 U. S. 227; 26 Am. & Eng. Ency. of Law, p. 644; 36 Cyc. 1171. (b) The application of the principle to local governmental subdivisions: Cole v. White Co., 32 Ark. 43; Whitehead v. Board of Education, 139 Mich. 490; Cincinnati v. Volk, 72 Ohio St. 469. (c) The application of the principle to local building regulations. Institution v. Louisville, 123 Ky. 767; Milwaukee v. McGregor, 140 Wis. 35. (3) Regardless of any presumption of independence from municipal control arising from the fact that school buildings are maintained by the State and controlled by State officers, existing legislation clearly indicates that the Board of Education of the city of St. Louis is intrusted with the power to determine what kind of interior plumbing in school buildings is best adapted for its purposes. Charter of the Board of Education of City of St. Louis, Secs. 11030 to 11062, R. S. 1909.

BROWN, C.—This suit was instituted April 11, 1912, against the defendant city and Stephen H. Gilmore, its supervisor of plumbing, to obtain an injunction restraining them from interfering with work in course of construction under contract for a new school building in said city to be known as the Horace Mann School. The contract provided for a system of vents from the water-closets known as "a continuous venting system, doing away with all local vents to the fixtures," while a regulation of the Board of Public Improvements of the city of St. Louis provided for a different system, requiring "sewer, soil, waste, and ventilation pipes to be arranged and constructed to admit of a free circulation of air from the fresh air inlet to each fixture trap and through the roof." The petition charged that the defendants threatened to apply the ordinances and rules of the city, which are fully set out, to this work, and cause the arrest of any and all of plaintiff's agents, servants, or employees who may go upon the premises under plaintiff's direction to prosecute said plumbing work, on the charge of violating said ordinances, rules and regulations. There is no question raised as to reasonableness of the ordinances of the city or regulations of its Board of Public Improvements, nor as to whether either system of venting is superior to the other, but the case is presented and discussed upon the broad proposition as to whether or not the Board of Education, in this particular, is subject to the ordinances and regulations of the city in this respect. A general demurrer to the petition was overruled, and defendants declining to further plead, final judgment was rendered granting the injunction and the case is here upon the defendants' appeal.

Section 26 of article 3 of the charter then in force provided, among other things, that the mayor and assembly shall have power, within the city, by ordinance *not inconsistent with the Constitution* or any law of this State or of this charter, to do the following things: In clause two, to construct and keep in repair all bridges, streets, sewers and drains, and to regulate the use thereof; in clause twelve, to provide for the safe construction, inspection and repairs of all private and public buildings within the city; and in clause fourteen, to pass all ordinances not inconsistent with the provisions of the charter or the laws of the State as may be expedient in regard to the peace, good government, health and welfare of the city.

It also provides (Sec. 3, art. 4) for a board of public improvements to consist of an elective president and five commissioners with certain prescribed powers, and adds the following provision: Section 42: "The municipal assembly shall provide by ordinance such additional duties of and requirements from the board of public improvements and its several members, as it may deem necessary, and for the appointment by them of such assistants and employees as the demands of the several departments may require."

It was under these powers and ordinances passed in pursuance of them that the defendant superintendent of plumbing was appointed and the rule relating to the ventilation of water-closets, which the city is now attempting to apply to the Horace Mann School, was made.

When the framers of the present Constitution conferred upon the freeholders of the city the power to make their present charter they provided, with the most careful foresight (Sec. 23, art. 9) that "such charter and amendments shall always be in harmony with and subject to the Constitution and laws of Missouri, except only that provision may be made for the graduation of the rate of taxation for city purposes in the portions of the city which are added thereto by the proposed enlargement of its boundaries."

In the same Constitution, and in pursuance of the uniform policy of the State from the beginning, it was provided (Sec. 1, art. 11) that "a general diffusion of knowledge and intelligence being essential to the preservation of the rights and liberties of the people, the General Assembly" (not the freeholders of the city of St. Louis) "shall establish and maintain free public schools for the gratuitous instruction of all persons in this State between the ages of six and twenty years." It was in obedience to this constitutional mandate that the Act of 1897 (as amended by the Act of

May 28, 1909) under which the public schools of the city of St. Louis have ever since been operated was enacted. It provided that "every city in this State now having or which may hereafter have five hundred thousand inhabitants or over, together with the territory now within its limits, or which may in the future be included by any change thereof, shall be and constitute a single school district, shall be a body corporate, and the supervision and government of public schools and public school property therein shall be vested in a board of twelve members, to be called and known as the 'Board of Education of . . .'" [R. S. 1909, sec. 11030.]

The powers and duties of this board were highly specialized in the act, and included the general and supervising control, governing and management of the public schools, and public school property in such city; the power to appoint such officers, agents and employees as it may deem necessary and proper; to make, amend and repeal rules and by-laws for the government, regulation and management of the public schools and school property in such city and exercise generally all powers in the administration of the public school system therein; and have all the powers of other school districts under the laws of the State except as herein provided. Particularizing further, it provides for the appointment by the Board of Education of a commissioner of school buildings who "shall be charged with the care of the public school buildings of such city, and with the responsibility for the ventilation, warming, sanitary condition and proper repair thereof," and "shall prepare, or cause to be prepared, all specifications and drawings required, and shall superintend all the construction and repair of all of such buildings." [R. S. 1909, sec. 11036.] In the performance of these duties he was required to appoint such assistants as should be authorized by the Board of Education, one of whom "shall be a trained and educated engineer, qualified to design and construct the heating, lighting, ventilating and sanitary machinery and apparatus connected with the public school buildings." [R. S. 1909, sec. 11037.]

It will be noted that this act not only gives the Board of Education plenary power with reference to the construction, maintenance and care of the public school buildings of the city, but descends into matters connected with the health and comfort of the pupils including the designing as well as the construction and maintenance of the very appliances which are the subject of this litigation, ventilating and sanitary machinery and apparatus to be installed and maintained for the removal from the building of foul and noxious air necessarily generated in the use of the water-closets.

We have been favored by counsel on both sides with exhaustive and highly interesting briefs and arguments relating to the presumptions which should prevail in determining whether laws of the character of the charter of St. Louis and ordinances passed in pursuance of its terms are applicable to the sovereign, and whether they are repealed by general laws which do not in terms mention them. We cannot appreciate the application of either of these questions to this case. The first does not rest upon presumption, for the sovereignty itself has dealt with the subject of the construction and management of the property which is held and used by its agents for the highest governmental purposes, and we have to look no further than its legislative declarations to determine in whom the authority claimed by each of the parties to this proceeding is vested; and as to the second question so ably argued, we have only to look to the converse of the proposition stated by counsel for appellant. The question is not whether a law of general application in the city of St. Louis impliedly repeals any of the provisions of a special act or charter for the government of that community, but it is whether the general charter yields to the provisions of a law having special application to particular matters and things within the field of its operation. The statement of this question includes its answer.

It cannot even be claimed that there is a question in this case relating to the intention of the Legislature to apply the Act of 1897 from which we have quoted, to the schools of the city of St. Louis. By its terms it describes the city of St. Louis as the only community in the State in which it can apply. That it gives to the Board of Education through its lawfully constituted officers the power to design, construct and maintain the very apparatus now in question is not and cannot be denied by any English-speaking person, and the constitutional power of the Legislature to enact it is unquestioned and unquestionable.

We have carefully examined the authorities cited by the appellant and find but one, Pasadena School District v. Pasadena, 166 Cal. 7, which seems to question the view we have taken with reference to the effect we give to the statute giving authority to the Board of Education to supervise and govern public school property within the city, and charging it through its officers possessing special qualifications for that purpose with the responsibility for the ventilating, warming and sanitary condition of such building, and the designing as well as the construction of the machinery and appliances for that purpose. In the California case the city by ordinances established an elaborate building code providing that only certain classes of buildings should be erected in certain fire districts and for the inspection of plumbing construction and electrical wiring and equipment of buildings, the use of permits and the collection of fees therefor, and making it unlawful to commence the erection of any building within the city other

than those erected by the United States unless plans
and specifications are submitted to the building in-
spect and a permit for the erection thereof first obtained and the fee paid. The school district denied that
it was subject to these regulations and an agreed case
was submitted to the court to determine it. The court
stated, in substance, that the Constitution of the State
had invested the city with the powers to make these
regulations and that the sole contention of the school
district was that it was an independent governmental
agency of the State created under a general law which
invested its trustees with the *control and management*
of all school property within its limits, and hence insisted that its authority in that respect was not subject
to be controlled by the police regulations of a municipality in which a part of the territory of the school district was embraced. The trustees of the school districts
were required by statute before building school houses
to submit the plans to the superintendent of schools.
The court stated that it was not claimed that these code
provisions *expressly gave any power to the trustees or
enjoined upon them the duty of adopting sanitary* building regulations, or regulations in the nature of provisions for the public health and comfort and safety in
the construction of such buildings, and held that in the
general powers mentioned no such power was conferred, and that their power was not different from that
possessed by private corporations and other owners of
land to control it and plan and erect buildings thereon
and sustained the city in its contention that a permit
was required. It will be seen that the issue in that case
was entirely different from the issue in this.

Here the right to erect a building within the limits
of the city is not involved, but only the question as to
which of these two contending municipalities is clothed
by statute with the right to determine interior sanitary
arrangements for the ventilation of its water-closets,

so as to promote the health and comfort of the pupils and teachers who should be its inmates. We think it is peculiarly appropriate that those charged with the custody and control of the pupils while in the building should also be charged with the protection of their health while engaged in their studies. The Legislature seems to have taken this view of the matter, and has, in our opinion, in unmistakable terms, placed that responsibility upon the board. We therefore affirm the judgment of the circuit court. *Railey, C.,* concurs.

PER CURIAM.—The foregoing opinion of BROWN, C., is adopted as the opinion of the court. All of the judges concur.

AUGUSTA E. HASSLER, Appellant, v. MERCANTILE BANK OF LOUISIANA.

Division One, March 30, 1916.

1. **DEED OF TRUST: Validity of Foreclosure Sale: Failure to Name Grantor in Notice.** The omission from the notice of sale under a deed of trust of the name of one of two grantors, all other requirements being met, the grantor whose name was omitted having previously parted with his equity, the representative of the owner of the entire equity being present at the sale, a fair price being obtained for the property, and the balance of the secured note afterwards being paid, so that the grantor whose name was omitted from the notice is no longer liable directly or indirectly for any sum by reason of his signature on the note secured, does not render the sale void, in spite of the statute (Sec. 2843, R. S. 1909) which requires that "such notice shall set forth . . . the grantors."

2. ——: ——: **Proof of Time of Publication.** Where the recitals in the trustee's deed show a compliance with the statutory requirements and are not contradicted, further proof of the time during which the notice of sale was published is not necessary.

Appeal from Louisiana Court of Common Pleas.—
Hon. B. H. Dyer, Judge.

AFFIRMED.

John W. Matson for appellant.

(1) The deed of trust, and the note that it secured
was given by M. J. Hassler and S. C. Hassler, and
under the laws the interest of either of them could
have been sold, or, either could have been sued without
joining the other one. The failure of the trustee in
his notice of sale and his trustee's deed to mention the
name of S. C. Hassler shows failure to foreclose and
convey that interest. Secs. 2842, 2843, R. S. 1909;
Chamberlain v. Trammell, 131 S. W. 227; Fisher v.
Simon, 95 Tex. 234; 28 Am. & Eng. Ency. Law (2
Ed.), p. 789; Youker v. Treadwell, 4 N. Y. Supp. 674;
Reside v. Peter, 33 Md. 120; 9 Ency. Pl. & Prac., p.
166; Thomas v. Loan Co., 79 N. Y. 54; Morgan v. Joy,
121 Mo. 677; Freeman v. Moffitt, 119 Mo. 280. (2) A
sale upon foreclosure by advertisement has been held
a nullity as to the owner of the premises not notified.
St. John v. Bumpsted, 17 Barb. (N. Y.) 100; Watson
v. Spence, 20 Wend. (N. Y.) 260; Van Slyke v. Shel-
den, 9 Barb. (N. Y.) 278. In the equity court the title
of the purchaser will not be recognized as valid unless
the terms of the power and statutes have been strictly
followed. 28 Am. & Eng. Ency. Law, p. 786, and notes.

David A. Ball and *Robert A. May* for respondent.

(1) Is not the plaintiff estopped from setting up
any interest, title or claim to this property? She joined
in the deed of trust to Tinsley, trustee for the bank.
She knew that S. C. Hassler had signed that deed of
trust. She knew that S. C. and M. J. Hassler and herself had conveyed all their equity in this property to
the Diamond Flour Manufacturing Company; and she

knew that the name of S. C. Hassler had been omitted
from the notice of sale of this property under said
deed of trust, and she attended the sale by and through
her husband and agent, and stood by and said not a
word. Can she now be heard to question the sale under said deed of trust? Tyler v. Hall, 106 Mo. 313;
Brown v. Appleman, 83 Mo. App. 70; Pentz v. Knester,
41 Mo. 447; Barnett v. Smart, 158 Mo. 167. (2) S. C.
Hassler not only executed the deed of trust, but afterwards conveyed all his equity in said property to the
Diamond Flour Manufacturing Co. So that he had
parted with all of his interest and nothing remained for
him to convey. So his deed to plaintiff passed no title
or interest in the property to plaintiff. (3) The principal object in publishing notice of sale, is not so much
to notify the grantor or mortgagor, as it is to inform
the public generally, so that bidders may be present at
the sale and a fair price obtained. 28 Am. & Eng. Ency.
Law, 790; De Jarnette v. De Giverville, 56 Mo. 440.
Accordingly, the notice should contain such facts as
are reasonably sufficient to apprise the public of the
nature of the property to be sold, and of the time, place
and terms of sale. 28 Am. & Eng. Ency. Law, 791;
Powers v. Vienckhoff, 41 Mo. 425; Stephenson v. January, 49 Mo. 465. (4) The notice of sale should, ordinarily, contain the name of the grantor but the omission
may perhaps be cured by reference to the book and
page where the instrument is recorded. 28 Am. & Eng.
Ency. 792; Baker v. Cunningham, 162 Mo. 134; Morgan v. Joy, 121 Mo. 677. (5) Even if the trustee's notice of sale were defective, it would be of no avail to
plaintiff, unless by petition she had offered to redeem
by paying the amount due on the note secured by the
deed of trust. Schoenwerk v. Hoberecht, 117 Mo. 22;
Kennedy v. Siemers, 120 Mo. 73; Springfield v. Donovan, 120 Mo. 423. (6) The grantor, S. C. Hassler, in
the deed of trust, was not injured by the sale, because

he had parted with all interest he had left to the Diamond Flour Manufacturing Co. Appellant knew this and she knew that all the stock, books, etc., had been turned over to the bank, so she is not hurt nor was she in the least deceived or defrauded by the sale. Ohnsorg v. Turner, 13 Mo. App. 541. The trustee in a deed of trust given upon land to secure a debt takes the title. McNutt v. Life Ins. Co., 181 Mo. 94. A purchaser at a void foreclosure sale will, nevertheless, hold under color of title and may, in suit in ejectment brought against him, set up the forfeited mortgage to protect his possession against all except the mortgagee and those claiming under him on a regular foreclosure sale. Jackson v. Magruder, 51 Mo. 55; Russell v. Whitely, 59 Mo. 196; Johnson v. Houston, 47 Mo. 227; Wheeler v. Drake, 129 Mo. App. 547. (7) It follows that the deed by the acting trustee, although the sale was not advertised according to law, passed the title to plaintiff. Springfield v. Donovan, 120 Mo. 423; Kennedy v. Siemers, 120 Mo. 73; Fowler v. Carr, 63 Mo. App. 486; Biffle v. Pullman, 125 Mo. 108.

BLAIR, J.—This is an appeal from a judgment for defendant in an action in ejectment, instituted in the Louisiana Court of Common Pleas. In the view we take of the case it is unnecessary to state all the facts in detail, since plaintiff's case depends upon the question whether a sale under a trust deed was valid or invalid.

Plaintiff's husband, M. J. Hassler, and his brother, S. C. Hassler, formerly owned the land in suit and executed a deed of trust thereon to secure a $5,000 note they gave to defendant. In this trust deed plaintiff joined with her husband. Subsequently the equity in the property was conveyed to a corporation whose capital stock was almost all owned by plaintiff. A few shares were in her husband's name and he was presi-

dent of the concern and plaintiff was its secretary. Default in the payment of the $5000 note was followed
by the advertisement and sale of the property in suit
under the trust deed,. and at this sale one McCune
bought and later conveyed the property to defendant.
Plaintiff's husband and agent, M. J. Hassler, president
of the corporation owning the equity, attended the sale.
S. C. Hassler, one of the signatories of the trust deed
but who had conveyed his interest in the equity to the
corporation mentioned, is not shown to have been present at the sale. The amount bid by McCune was the
full and fair value of the property sold, and this sum
was credited on the note secured, leaving an unpaid
balance of several hundred dollars. By a subsequent
transfer of other property and all the stock of the corporation mentioned, its books and papers, and certain
personal property, this unpaid balance was extinguished and the note fully paid. Subsequently certain
sales of the property in suit were made under judgments against the corporation obtained in actions begun about the time of the transfer of the corporate
stock to defendant, service being had upon M. J. Hassler as president of the corporation. One of these
judgments was upon a claim by plaintiff for an alleged
dividend declared some years previously. M. J.
Hassler furnished the data for the institution of this
suit and then was served as president of the defendant corporation. The other judgment is also subject
to some suspicion. The title acquired under these sales
is of no value unless the trustee's sale is void.

Plaintiff contends the trustee's sale was and is a
nullity because the name of S. C. Hassler, one of the
grantors in the deed of trust, was omitted from the notice. Section 2843, Revised Statutes 1909, requires
that: "Such notice shall set forth the date and book
and page of the record of such mortgage or deed of

trust, *the grantors*, the time, terms and place of sale, and a description of the property to be sold, and shall be given by advertisement, inserted . . .".etc.

The question is whether under the section the omission from the notice of sale of the name of one of two grantors renders void the sale, all other requirements being met, the person whose name has been omitted having parted with his equity and the representative of the owner of the entire equity being present at the sale, a full and fair price being obtained for the property, and the balance of the secured note afterward being paid so that the person whose name was omitted from the notice is no longer liable directly or indirectly for any sum by reason of his signature on the note secured.

We have no hesitancy in saying the omission of S. C. Hassler's name from the notice in the circumstances in no way affects the validity of the trustee's sale and the full title passed thereby to McCune and by his deed now resides in defendant.

The principle necessitating this conclusion was substantially approved in Trust Co. v. Ellis, 258 Mo. l. c. 708 et seq. In that case the trustee's notice of sale omitted to give the book and page of the record of the trust deed, and this court held the facts of the case failed to show loss or injury on account of the omission and declared the sale valid.

In this case the owner of the equity, the corporation, was represented at the sale by its president; the public was advised sufficiently, since the book and page of the record was given and a reference thereto disclosed the deed of trust; full value was bid and paid for the property. S. C. Hassler no longer owned the equity and was in no wise injured by the sale, since he had no equity to protect, and since also the subsequent payment of the balance due on the notes entirely extinguished his obligation. In accordance with the ruling in the case cited, we hold the sale valid. We are aware there are decisions in other States rigidly holding trustees to exact compliance with statutes as to notice, but this court has long adhered to the rule announced in the Ellis case and sees no good reason for departing from it.

The trustee's deed is criticised somewhat, but an examination of it discloses it contains language apt to convey the entire title. Neither is there any substance in the suggestion that there should have been further evidence of the time during which the notice was published. The recitals in the trustee's deed showed compliance with the statute and were not contradicted. This was sufficient. [Sec. 2858, R. S. 1909.]

The judgment is affirmed. All concur.

THE STATE ex inf. JAMES S. SIMRALL, Prosecuting Attorney, ex rel. BENJAMIN M. CLEMENTS et al., Appellant, v. GEORGE CLARDY et al.

Division One, March 30, 1916.

1. **CONSOLIDATED SCHOOL DISTRICT: Area: Pleading.** No consolidated school district can be formed unless it contains an area of at least twelve square miles, or has an enumeration of at least two hundred children of school age; and when its directors are called upon collectively, and directly by the State in a suit in the nature of *quo warranto*, to show a right to exist, their answer unless it states one or the other of these necessary statutory requirements, is insufficient.

2. ——: ——: ——: **Assumed at Trial.** But if no point was made, either at the trial or in the appellate court, that the answer of the directors, sued by the State in *quo warranto* to determine the validity of the organization of an alleged consolidated school district, does not contain an allegation that the district contains an area of at least twelve square miles, and if both plaintiff and defendants proved, conclusively, without objection, that the area of said district is more than twelve square miles, the court will assume on appeal that the answer was amended so as to include such necessary allegation.

3. ——————: Filing Papers: Indorsement by Depositary. The
petition, notice, plat, proceedings of meeting, etc., required by
section 3 of the Consolidated School District Act (Laws 1913,
p. 721) need not be indorsed "filed" in order to be filed with
the county clerk and county superintendent. Indorsement on
the paper of the fact of filing is not a necessary element of
filing, unless the statute specifically so says.

4. ——————: Validity of Organization: Recital in Minutes:
Manner of Voting. If the minutes of the special meeting to
organize a consolidated school district state that the vote was
taken by ballot and that a certain number of votes were cast,
of which a certain number were for consolidation and a less
number against it, the organization will not be held invalid on
the sole ground that the minutes do not recite that each voter
advanced to the front of the chairman and deposited his ballot
in a box provided for that purpose, nor because they do not
recite that the tellers announced each ballot aloud. The statute
(Sec. 10865, R. S. 1909) does not require the minutes to recite
the details of each act constituting the statutory requirements
of the meeting.

Appeal from Clay Circuit Court.—*Hon. Frank P.
Divelbiss*, Judge.

AFFIRMED.

Kenneth McC. DeWeese for appellant.

(1) The fact that a city, town or other community
has become incorporated by performing the conditions
and complying with the statutory requirements prescribed by a general law must be proved. 1 Jones on
Evidence, sec. 115, p. 550; Hamilton v. Carthage, 24
Ill. 22-23. Upon a direct proceeding by *quo warranto*
or otherwise to test the validity of the organization of
a municipal incorporation, it is necessary to show the
manner of the organization under the charter, or that
all of its requirements have been complied with. State
v. Frost, 103 Tenn. 685; State v. Bilby, 60 Kan. 130;
People v. Linden, 107 Cal. 94; Kane & Co. v. School
District, 48 Mo. App. 408. (2) If a statute creating a
corporation and providing for its proceedings shall re-

quire such proceedings to be preserved in a record kept for that purpose, then such record is the only proper evidence of such proceedings and the proceedings of a board of school directors must be shown by their record. Kane & Co. v. School District, 48 Mo. App. 408; State v. Lawrence, 178 Mo. 374. (3) The answer of the defendants did not state facts sufficient to show or constitute any lawful warrant of authority to the defendants, to use or exercise the functions of a board of directors of said consolidated school district.

Ralph Hughes and *Martin E. Lawson* for respondents.

There seems to be no question about the fact of compliance with the law, but appellant questions the proof of those facts. The errors claimed are based upon the proposition that parol evidence cannot be adduced to show facts which actually transpired at the meeting for the purpose of organizing said district which the clerk did not record in the minutes. It will be observed that the minutes of the meeting of organization are very brief, being in fact but a synopsis of what really transpired at the meeting. It is practically the uniform rule that in such instances parol evidence is permissible to explain the record and supply omissions therein. Trustees v. Wimberly, 2 Tex. Civ. App. 404; Morgan v. Wilfley, 71 Iowa, 212; Township v. Codding, 42 Kan. 649; Gilmer v. School District, 136 Pac. 1086; Tucker v. McKay, 131 Mo. App. 728; Nehrling v. Herold Co., 112 Wis. 558; Railroad v. Douglas County, 103 Wis. 75; Watts v. Levee District, 164 Mo. App. 263.

RAILEY, C.—This is an information in the nature of *quo warranto*, exhibited by the prosecuting attorney of Clay County, Missouri, at the relation of Benjamin M. Clements, John Filger and Philip Klamm as the

board of directors of School District Number Four in
Clay County, against George Clardy, Ernest Capps,
John Filger, John M. Blevins, James Allen and Lee
Williams, assuming to act as the board of trustees of
an alleged consolidated school district styled "Consolidated School District Number One of Clay county, Missouri." Its purpose is to test the validity of the organization of the district under the act of the Legislature approved March 14, 1913, entitled, "An Act to provide for the organization of consolidated schools and
rural high schools, and to provide State aid for such
schools, with an emergency clause."

The answer denies the usurpation charged and proceeds as follows:

"Further answering, these defendants say that
heretofore a petition signed by more than twenty-five
qualified voters of the community hereinafter described, was filed with the county superintendent of
public schools of Clay County, Missouri, showing that
they desired to form said community into a consolidated
school district under the provisions of an act of the
Legislature of the 47th General Assembly of Missouri,
entitled, 'An Act to provide for the organization of consolidated schools and rural high schools, and to provide State aid for such schools, with an emergency
clause,' approved March 14, 1913; that on receipt of
said petition, the county superintendent of schools visited said community and investigated the needs of the
community and determined the exact boundaries of the
proposed consolidated district, locating the boundary
lines as in his judgment would form the best possible
consolidated district, having due regard also to the welfare of adjoining districts; that said county superintendent of schools called a special meeting of all the
qualified voters of the proposed consolidated district
for considering the question of consolidation, by posting within the proposed district ten notices in ten pub-

lic places, stating the place, time and purpose of said
meeting, at least fifteen days prior to the date set for
said meeting, and also posted within said district fifteen days prior to the date of said special meeting at
least five plats of the proposed consolidated district,
which plats and notices were posted within thirty days
after the filing of said petition; that said special meeting was called to meet at the hall in Linden, Missouri,
on April, 20, 1914, at two o'clock P. M., as stated in
said notices.

"These defendants further state that the said county superintendent of schools filed a copy of the petition
and of the plat aforesaid with the county clerk of Clay
County, Missouri, and that he sent and took one of said
plats to the said special meeting, which he attended in
person, and on the date and at the hour aforesaid, said
county superintendent of schools called said meeting
to order in person; that at said meeting, John M.
Blevins was elected chairman and Ernest Capps was
elected secretary of said meeting; that thereupon, the
meeting proceeded to vote by ballot upon the proposition to organize the said consolidated district, those
voting for such organization having upon their ballot
the words 'For Organization,' and those voting against
the organization having on their ballots 'Against Organization,' and each person desiring to vote advanced to
the front of the chairman and deposited his ballot in
the box used for that purpose. When all present had
voted, the chairman appointed two tellers who called
each ballot aloud and the secretary kept a tally and reported to the chairman who announced the result of
the vote, and a majority of the votes being cast for organization, the chairman so declared, and declared the
Consolidated District No. 1 organized, and called for
the next order of business, which was the election of six
directors, two of whom were to be elected for three years,
two for two years, and two for one year, each director

being elected separately and the result announced in the manner prescribed for organization, and these defendants were, in said manner and in accordance with law, duly elected directors of said Consolidated School District No. 1, they duly qualified and have since then been, and are now, acting as such board of directors; that the chairman and secretary of said special meeting kept a record of the proceedings thereof, which they certified to the county clerk of Clay County, Missouri, in which said entire consolidated school district is located, and the county school superintendent of Clay County, Missouri, filed a copy of the petition and of the plat of said proposed county school district with the county clerk of said Clay County, Missouri.''

The appellants, not challenging the sufficiency of the answer, replied with a general denial. On the trial the appellant assumed the burden of showing the validity of the organization of the defendant district, and introduced: (1) A copy of a petition for the consolidated district, addressed to James A. Robeson, the superintendent of schools of the county, purporting to be signed by forty-one qualified voters of school districts number 50 and 63 and adjoining districts, notifying him of their purpose to organize a consolidated school district in accordance with said act, and asking him to visit the community to investigate its needs, and to make and post plats and notices of a special school meeting to vote on the organization of such consolidated district. This petition and notice purported to be filed in the office of the superintendent March 17, 1914. (2) A notice of such special meeting to be held at a place therein named, on April 20, 1914, at two o'clock, P. M., to consider the organization of such district and elect six directors therefor. This was signed by the county superintendent of public schools, and dated April 4, 1914. This was by the superintendent, taken to and laid before the special meeting, as was also

the original plat made by him, a copy of which he filed
in the office of the county clerk. (3) A plat of the proposed Consolidated School District No. 1, of Clay
County, in townships 51 and 52, ranges 32 and 33 in
said county. This plat was endorsed: "Filed in my
office this 4th day of April, 1914. T. C. Stean, Clerk."
Evidence was introduced showing that copies of the
petition and notice were deposited with the clerk in
his office at the time of the filing of the plat, and had
been kept there ever since. (4) Another plat, substantially like the foregoing from the office of the
county clerk, who testified that he made it for his own
use. (5) "Minutes of Special Meeting of Patrons of
Proposed Consolidated District," held at the time and
place named in the notice. This was marked: "Filed
in my office the 23rd day of April, 1914. T. C. Stean,
County Clerk." It recited, among other things, the
adoption of the proposed consolidation by a vote sixty-
two to forty-nine, and the election by ballot of these respondents as directors. (6) A copy of the foregoing
minutes with the addition that the meeting was held at
two o'clock, P. M. This was certified to be a true copy
of the minutes of the meeting by John M. Blevins,
chairman, and Ernest L. Capps, secretary, of the same,
and verified by their affidavit made May 18, 1914, before the clerk of the county court, and filed in his office on the following day. (7) A copy of the same similarly certified and verified and filed in the office of the
superintendent of public schools on the same day. (8)
A copy of the petition above mentioned, marked: "Filed
in my office this 17th day of March, 1914, James A.
Robeson, County Superintendent." (9) A copy of the
above mentioned notice endorsed: "Filed in my office this 23rd day of April, 1914. James Robeson,
County Superintendent of Public schools." (10) Copies of plats from the records in the office of the clerk
of the county court indicating that all of school district

number 50, and parts of 51, 62, 63, 64 and 65, were included in the new consolidated district. All except two of the forty-one signers of the petition were shown to reside within the limits of the consolidated district, and to be qualified voters at the places of their residences. Mr. Robeson, county superintendent of schools at the time, testified that he posted the ten notices of the special election and five plats of the proposed district in public places within the territory included, on April 4, 1914. The plat is drawn on a sectional plat of the United States survey of the four townships 51 and 52 of ranges 32 and 33 in which the consolidated district is situated, and shows that it contains an area at least equal to twenty-seven sections.

With reference to the enumeration of the children of the territory included, the following is the only reference we find in the record.

"By the Court: What about the enumeration? It says none should be formed unless they have two hundred children, unless that is admitted.

"By Mr. DeWeese: No."

Mr. Stean was then recalled and testified:

"Q. Can you get the enumeration showing the number of school children within this consolidated school district?

"By Mr. Hughes: The last enumeration made before the proceedings to form the consolidated district.

"A. It's made in five first and then one.

"Q. I wish you would get those records, the five that were made just before and the one before."

There were two small towns in the district, Linden and Gashland, neither of which was incorporated. The directors of the consolidated district met after the election and on the same day, and organized by the election of John M. Blevins, president, George T. Clardy, vice president, and Ernest Capps, secretary, took the oath of office, and proceeded to the transaction of their business. The record of this meeting was written on loose sheets of paper and afterward copied in a book procured for such purpose, and the sheets were lost or destroyed.

Objections were properly made and exceptions saved by the plaintiff with reference to all the questions we shall consider.

The appellant's assignment of errors is as follows:

"1.   The answer of defendants did not state facts sufficient to constitute a legal response to the several matters and things set forth in the information and inquired for, or to constitute any lawful warrant of authority to use or exercise the functions of a board of directors of said consolidated school district.

"2.   The court erred in the admission of parol evidence to supply the deficiency of the record.

"3.   No sufficient petition was filed with the county superintendent of schools, as required by section 3 of the Act of March 14, 1913.

"4.   No sufficient notice of a special meeting was given by the county superintendent of schools.

"5.   No sufficient plats of the proposed consolidated district were posted as required by law.

"6.   The proceedings of the special meeting, certified by the chairman and secretary to the county clerk and to the county superintendent of schools, as required by said act, were insufficient.

"7.   The copy of the petition and plat filed in the office of the county clerk were insufficient in law.

"8.   The record did not show that the proposed consolidated school district contained an area of at least twelve square miles. This was undertaken to be supplied by parol evidence.

"9.   The evidence did not show that the proposed consolidated school district had an enumeration of at least two hundred children of school age. This was undertaken to be supplied by parol evidence.''

I. The appellant's counsel have furnished us with an excellent brief of points and authorities which he evidently believes to be applicable to this case, and considerately, and not without hazard, has entrusted to us the work of finding the facts which fit them in a somewhat obscure record. The public interests involved are such that it has been advanced upon our docket for argument and disposition, and we have given careful consideration to the record to ascertain the real questions upon which the parties differ. At the outset we are met with the unexplained assertion that the answer is not sufficient to show the right of the respondents, which depends entirely upon the question whether or not the organization of Consolidated School District No. 1, in Clay County, Missouri, of which they assume to exercise the office of directors and, collectively, to act as a board of directors, is valid; in other words, whether there is such a school district by virtue of the proceedings here called in question. This depends entirely upon the provisions of the act of the General Assembly entitled, ''An Act to provide for the organization of consolidated schools and rural high schools, and to provide State aid for such schools, with an emergency clause,'' approved March 14, 1913. [Laws 1913, p. 721.]

II. The statute referred to provides: ''No consolidated district shall be formed under the provisions of this act unless it contains an area of at least twelve square miles, or has an enumeration of Consolidated at least two hundred children of school School District: age.'' [Laws 1913, p. 722, sec. 2.] Validity of Organization. These conditions are evidently jurisdictional. They are not mere requirements relating to the proceedings by which the organ-

ization is to be accomplished, but are expressed in
terms of prohibition, and relate to the nature and constitution of the thing which may be incorporated, so
that if they are not met the incorporation would necessarily be a nullity. In this proceeding the respondents
are called upon directly by the State to show their
right to exercise, collectively, the duties of the governing body of a quasi-municipal corporation for school
purposes. That right depends upon the existence of
the office and the existence of the office depends on the
existence of the municipality to which it pertains.
They must show its existence in return to the challenge
of the State, and in doing so must plead the existence
of the facts necessary to its creation. They have failed
in their answer to plead the conditions prescribed by
the statutory requirements we have stated with respect to area and number of children which it must contain, and their pleading is therefore insufficient. But
as appellant assumed the burden of showing that the
proposed consolidated district had not been legally established; and as both plaintiff and defendant proved
conclusively, without objection, that the area of said
proposed consolidated district contains more than
twelve miles square; and as no point was made, either
in the trial court, or in this court, respecting this matter; and as the answer could have been amended at the
trial in accordance with the proof aforesaid, we will
consider the answer as having been amended so as to
set out the area of the proposed consolidated district
aforesaid, and dispose of the case as though said
amendment had been made. [Darrier v. Darrier, 58
Mo. l. c. 233; Baker v. Railroad, 122 Mo. l. c. 547-8;
State ex rel. v. McQuillin, 246 Mo. l. c. 594.]

III. Section three of the act provides that "when
the resident citizens of any community desire to form
a consolidated district, a petition signed by at least
twenty-five qualified voters of said community shall be

filed with the county superintendent of public schools.''
It becomes his duty on receipt of this to visit the community, investigate its needs and deter-
mine the exact boundaries of the proposed
district, and make plats thereof. He shall
then call a special meeting, giving at least
fifteen and not more than thirty days' notice thereof,
by posting ten notices stating the place, time and purpose of such meeting and five plats in public places
within the proposed district. The meeting shall commence at two o'clock P. M. It also provides that he
shall file a copy of the petition and of the plat with the
county clerk and shall take one plat to the special meeting, which ''shall be called to order by the county superintendent of schools or some one deputized by him
to call said meeting to order.'' It shall then choose a
chairman and secretary and proceed in accordance
with section 10865, Revised Statutes 1909. It further
provides that ''the proceedings of this meeting shall
be certified by the chairman and the secretary to the
county clerk or clerks and also to the county superintendent or superintendents of schools of all the counties affected.'' The superintendent is also required to
file a copy of the petition and plat with the county clerk.
The proof was unquestioned that all the papers so required to be filed with the superintendent and clerk of
the county court were, in due time, deposited in their
several offices and were kept there; but the course of
the counsel in introducing and resisting the introduction of the evidence upon the trial indicates the theory
of the plaintiff to have been that the fact of filing included an indorsement to that effect upon all the several papers, to constitute a record which would be the
sole evidence of the fact; while the proof was made
in some instances by the production of the papers by
the proper custodian and parol evidence that they were
deposited and kept among the papers of his office.

*Filing:
Necessity of
Indorsement.*

This is an erroneous view of the question, which is an old one and has long been settled by adjudication, and the *dicta* of many courts and writers. Even the word "file" is a form of the Latin word which signifies a thread, and is suggestive of the manner in which those papers and documents not considered of sufficient importance to justify spreading upon the record, were strung for preservation. A distinguished author defines the word "file" as follows: "To file, and filing, mean the act either of the party in bringing the paper and depositing it with the officer, for keeping, or the act of the officer in folding, indorsing and putting up the paper." [Abbot's Law Dictionary.] Another distinguished legal lexicographer, Bouvier, under the same title, defines it as follows: "In the sense of a statute requiring the filing of a paper or document it is filed when delivered to and received by the proper officer to be kept on file." That the statement of the officer upon the document does not constitute a filing is illustrated in Sternberger v. McSween, 14 S. C. 35, 42, where it was held that a paper which was taken to the officer to be filed, and was marked "filed" by the officer, who handed it back, and it was taken away, had not been filed.

All these papers had been deposited with the clerk and superintendent, as the case might be, to be kept among the papers of the office, and it was competent to prove that fact by parol. If the paper was in existence it could be produced by the officer; if not, its loss or destruction while it constituted a record of the proper office, could be proven in the same manner.

IV. One other point which we have been able to glean from the record, consists in a general complaint as to the sufficiency of the minutes of the special meet-

ing filed in the respective offices of the clerk of the
county court and county superintendent of
public schools. It is founded upon the requirement of section 10865, Revised Statutes 1909, which governs the proceedings of the special
meeting. This requires that the vote on the organization of town and city school districts shall be taken by
ballot, ''and each person desiring to vote shall advance
to the front of the chairman and deposit his ballot in a
box to be used for that purpose. When all present shall
have voted, the chairman shall appoint two tellers,
who shall call each ballot aloud, and the secretary shall
keep a tally and report to the chairman, who shall announce the result.'' The minutes in this case speak as
follows:

Recitals in Minutes.

"After stating business of meeting, Chairman
called for vote by ballot on matter of proposed consolidation. Ballots to contain words, 'For Consolidation,' or 'Against Consolidation.'

"Remarks on question before the house called for
and made by Prof. Robeson along lines of general information.

"Balloting resulted as follows: For Consolidation, 62, against Consolidation, 49. Majority for Consolidation, 13. Total vote, 111. Proposition carried."

The statute does not undertake to say in what form
the minutes of the meeting shall be kept or how mi-
nutely, if at all, they shall go into the details constituting each act of the meeting. It is evident that the
highest degree of verbal skill cannot be expected from
the secretaries of such meetings. We think that the
statement that the vote was taken by the chairman by
ballot and the result ascertained and declared necessarily includes the details which constitute the taking
of the vote under the statute. To be sure, the minutes
do not say that each person voting advanced to the
front of the chairman or that a box was provided for

the ballots or that the chairman appointed two tellers to read the votes aloud to the secretary, who kept a tally and reported the result to the chairman. It is unnecessary to decide that these things are not of such vital consequence that if one or all had been omitted the proceeding would have been void, because they are necessarily included in the general statement contained in the minutes.

Finding no error in the record, we affirm the judgment.

Brown, C., dissents as to result only on the ground that he thinks the Act of March 14, 1913, requires an enumeration of 200 as a condition of organization under it.

PER CURIAM.—The foregoing opinion of RAILEY, C., is adopted as the opinion of the court. All of the judges concur.

IRWIN H. PIPES v. MISSOURI PACIFIC RAILWAY COMPANY, Appellant.

Division One, March 30, 1916.

1. **PLEADING: Personal Injuries: Action Given by Statute.** It is not necessary that the statute of this State or of Congress which gives to plaintiff his cause of action be pleaded; all that is required is that the facts which bring the case within them be stated in the petition. The laws of Congress are not foreign laws that must be pleaded or proven in this State.

2. **INTERSTATE COMMERCE: Personal Injuries: Jurisdiction of State Court.** If the petition states the facts which, under the statute of this State and the statute of Congress, constitute a cause of action for personal injuries due to defendant's negligence, the court should refuse an instruction directing the jury that if the car which the crew was attempting to couple at the time plaintiff was injured was employed in interstate commerce, their verdict must be for defendant; for, the State courts have jurisdiction to enforce the liability created by those statutes for such injuries so inflicted.

267 Mo 25

3. **EVIDENCE: Cause of Stopping Cars.** Where plaintiff fell from the running board of a car and was injured, when the drag of sixteen cars, which the crew were attempting to couple with other loose cars, suddenly stopped, it is error to permit plaintiff to testify what caused them to stop and deny that right to defendant—where the cause of the sudden stop is the vital issue in the case.

Appeal from Jackson Circuit Court.—*Hon. Clarence A. Burney,* Judge.

REVERSED AND REMANDED.

White, Hackney & Lyons for appellant.

(1) The court erred in permitting plaintiff to testify that in his opinion undoubtedly the brakes were set on the engine thereby causing the drag to stop suddenly. Permitting him to answer this question and give his conclusion of the most vital fact in issue in the case was glaringly prejudicial to the defendant. Landers v. Railroad, 134 Mo. App. 87; Taylor v. Railroad, 185 Mo. 255; Castanie v. Railroad, 249 Mo. 192; Glasgow v. Railroad, 191 Mo. 364; Roscoe v. Met. St. Ry., 202 Mo. 595; Gutridge v. Railroad, 94 Mo. 472; Nash v. Dowling, 93 Mo. App. 164; Wesner v. Railroad, 177 Mo. App. 122; 6 Thompson on Negligence, p. 684. (2) But in any event, and on any theory, the court, after having permitted the plaintiff to give his opinion as to what stopped the drag, when the plaintiff was not in a position to see what actually occurred, should have permitted Hogan, of like experience with the plaintiff and who had occupied a position enabling him to tell what stopped the drag, to give an opinion on the same matter on which the plaintiff had given his opinion. If Hogan's testimony was inadmissible then plaintiff's testimony was also inadmissible. (3) The plaintiff did not bring his action for damages under the Federal Employers' Liability Act, but sued under the State law and was not entitled to recover. When it appeared

from the evidence that the plaintiff and the defendant were, at the time of the accident, engaged in interstate commerce, the State law was not applicable to the transaction and the rights, duties and liabilities of the parties, but the Federal Employers' Liability Act having superseded the State law in such a case was alone applicable, and this completely barred the plaintiff's right to recover under the State law. The case pleaded by the plaintiff, to-wit, one under the State law was, therefore, disproved, and the case proved, to-wit, one under the Federal Employers' Liability Act, was not pleaded, hence there could be no recovery for the plaintiff, and the jury should have been so instructed. Moliter v. Railroad, 180 Mo. App. 84; Railroad v. Seale, 229 U. S. 156; Railroad v. Slavin, 236 U. S. 454.

Percy C. Field and *Clarence S. Palmer* for respondent.

(1) The testimony of the plaintiff as to the cause of the sudden stopping of the train was proper. He was stating a fact made known to him by his trained senses. Railroad v. Johnson, 38 Ga. 409; Wigmore on Evidence, sec. 659; Hunter v. Halsley, 98 Mo. App. 621; Smith v. Railroad, 34 Nova Scotia, 22; Bryce v. Railroad, 129 Iowa, 342. (2) There was no error in the ruling of the trial court on the admissibility of the testimony of the witness Hogan. He testified to all the facts about which he was asked. (3) The rights of the parties to this action were exactly the same under the facts, whether the case was controlled by the State or Federal law. By no possibility were the rights of the appellant materially affected by the rulings of the trial court on this question, and there should therefore be no reversal. Railroad v. Wulf, 226 U. S. 570; Railroad v. Slavin, 236 U. S. 306; Sec. 2082, R. S. 1909; Railroad v. Yurkonis, 220 Fed. 429; Railroad v. Hayes, 234 U. S. 86; Hogarty v. Railroad, 245 Pa. St. 443;

Railroad v. Nelson, 212 Fed. 69; McIntosh v. Railroad, 182 Mo. App. 288.

BROWN, C.—This is an action for personal injury suffered by the plaintiff in the course of his employment as a switchman in defendant's yard at Kansas City. Verdict and judgment for $8000, from which the defendant has taken this appeal.

The petition states, in substance, that the plaintiff was a member of a switching crew employed by defendant in said yard. On June 12, 1914, he, with the crew, which consisted of a foreman, an engineer and fireman who operated the engine, and himself and another switchman, was engaged in handling cars in said yard; that in doing this work the engine was attached to the east end of a drag consisting of sixteen freight cars, for the purpose of shoving it west on one of the tracks to couple it to three freight cars standing on said track, and shoving the drag so made up to a gravity lead at the west end of the yard; that in executing the movement it was his duty to get on the top of the cars and pass along the running boards to the head of the drag, or farthest car from the engine; that in pursuance of this duty he mounted one of the cars, climbed to the top, and walked west along the footboard; that while he was doing this the last car had been apparently coupled to the three that were standing on the track so that there were nineteen cars in the drag; that while plaintiff was still walking along the footboard on the top of the sixteenth car toward the head of the drag, and was at the west end of the sixteenth car, the fireman, who was driving said engine, without any signal to stop, applied the brakes to the engine and caused it to stop suddenly and with a jerk, so that the three front cars which had not been securely coupled to the one on which he was walking separated from it and plaintiff was thrown from the top of the car to the track below and injured.

It specifies particularly that the "defendant was negligent, in that, the said fireman carelessly and negligently caused said engine and drag to stop with a jerk, when no signal had been given to stop, when the defendant, by and through its agents and servants, in charge of said engine and drag, knew, or by the exercise of ordinary care, could have known that plaintiff was walking upon the running board of said cars of said drag and would be jerked off of said drag and injured by the stopping of said engine and drag with a jerk when no signal to stop had been given;" and that the agents and servants of defendant in charge of said engine and drag carelessly and negligently pushed it along without the three head cars being securely coupled, so that they would separate from the drag being stopped with a jerk, when they knew or by the exercise of ordinary care could have known of the dangerous position of plaintiff and that he was relying on the car being securely coupled.

The answer consisted of a general denial and the ordinary general plea of contributory negligence.

There was no suggestion in any of the pleadings that the employment of the defendant at the time of the injury related in any way to commerce between the States.

There was evidence tending to prove that these three cars had been delivered at the yard that day by the Chicago, Milwaukee & St. Paul Railway Company, which had brought them from Laredo, Missouri, and that one of them had been delivered at Laredo that morning from Ottumwa, Iowa.

There was also evidence tending to prove the allegations of the petition, unless there was a failure with respect to setting the brakes. On this subject the plaintiff testified as follows: "I was standing there looking

back over my shoulder and just at the time I was looking back the stop came, and the stop was so sudden
that undoubtedly the stop was made by the application of the brakes, or else.—'' At this point he was
interrupted by an objection from defendant's attorney, who immediately moved to strike out the statement of the cause of the stopping, on the ground that
it was mere speculation. This was overruled by the
court and the witness continued, stating that the jerk
came with such an abrupt stop that in his estimation or
knowledge the brakes were undoubtedly set or the engine reversed—that it was made by the stopping of the
engine. The defendant moved to strike out this portion
of the answer as being a mere opinion. The objection
was overruled by the court and to this action in admitting this evidence and refusing to strike it out the defendant excepted.

The defendant introduced Mr. Hogan, the other
switchman of the crew, who testified that at the time
Mr. Pipes fell from the top of the car he (Hogan) was
standing at about the middle of the original drag of
sixteen cars, transmitting to the engines such signals
as were given by the foreman, who was at the place
where the coupling was to be done. During his examination by Mr. Hackney for defendant (Mr. Field representing the plaintiff), the following took place:

"Q. Could you tell what if anything caused the
sixteen cars to stop?

"Mr. Field: Objected to as calling for a conclusion of the witness.

"Q. Could you see what caused it?

"Mr. Field: I suppose that is a conclusion. Let
him state what he did see.

"The objection was by the court sustained. To
which ruling of the court the defendant then and there
duly excepted.

"Mr. Hackney: I offer to show by this witness that the cars stopped in consequence of striking the three cars and not from the application of the brake on the engine.

"Mr. Palmer: Objected to for the reason that it would be a mere conclusion of the witness unless the witness could see what was being done by the engineer on the engine, which he testifies was eight cars away.

"The objection was by the court sustained. To which ruling of the court the defendant then and there duly excepted."

The defendant, at the close of plaintiff's evidence and again at the close of all the evidence, asked the court to instruct the jury to find a verdict in its favor, which it refused, and defendant duly excepted. It also asked the court to instruct that if the plaintiff was negligent, and his negligence contributed in any way to his injury, they should find for the defendant. This was also refused and exception taken. It also asked the court to instruct that if the jury should find from the evidence that the east car of the three to which the crew were trying to couple the drag "was U R T car No. 3832; that said car was loaded, and had been transported in such loaded condition by the Chicago, Milwaukee & St. Paul Railway Company from Ottumwa, Iowa, to Kansas City, Missouri, and there delivered to the Missouri Pacific Railway Company for further transportation or delivery, then regardless of the other defenses in this case, the plaintiff is not entitled to recover and your verdict must be for the defendant." This was refused, to which defendant excepted. The cause was then submitted to the jury upon the sole theory, affirmatively expressed in substance in plaintiff's instructions and negatively in those given for defendant, that the liability of defendant depended upon the fact that after the drag of sixteen cars struck the east car of the three to which they were attempting to couple it, and while the engine was pushing the nineteen cars westward, the engineer or fireman operating it, without any signal to do so, suddenly stopped "with a jerk," letting the three cars, which had failed to couple, pass on, and throwing the defendant from the west end of the sixteenth car on which he was walking.

The appellant assigns for error the action of the court in refusing its instruction intended to direct the jury that if the car to which the crew was attempting to couple was, at the time, employed in interstate commerce, their verdict must be for the defendant. The instruction is without foundation. This is a common-law action excepting in so far as it is modified by the terms of section 5434 of the Revised Statutes of 1909 of Missouri, and by section one of the Act of April 22, 1908 (35 U. S. Statutes at Large, p. 65). The former is as follows: "Every railroad corporation owning or operating a railroad in this State shall be liable for all damages sustained by any agent or servant thereof while engaged in the work of operating such railroad by reason of the negligence of any other agent or servant thereof: Provided, that it may be shown in defense that the person injured was guilty of negligence contributing as a proximate cause to produce the injury." The latter provides that "every common carrier by railroad while engaged in commerce between any of the several States . . . shall be liable in damages to any person suffering injury while he is employed by such carrier in such commerce . . . for such injury . . . resulting in whole or in part from the negligence of any of the officers, agents or employees of such carrier."

These statutes constitute the law of the State with reference to the liability of railroad companies to their servants for injuries inflicted upon them by fellow-servants in the course of the common employment, and

Jurisdiction: Interstate Commerce.

the State courts of general jurisdiction have cognizance
of suits to enforce the liability created by them. This
jurisdiction must be exercised in accordance with the
procedure prescribed by the statutes of the State. The
procedure provides (Sec. 1794, R. S. 1909) that the
petition shall contain a plain and concise statement of
the facts constituting the cause of action and the relief
to which the plaintiff may suppose himself entitled.
Its sufficiency is judged by the answer to the question,
do these facts entitle the plaintiff to relief under the
laws in force in this State, and in considering it, the
general laws, whether State or Federal, must be considered. It is not necessary that these laws be mentioned or in any way identified in the pleading. It is
only required to state the facts which bring the case
within them. [Emerson v. Railway Co., 111 Mo. 161,
165; Lore v. Manufacturing Co., 160 Mo. 608, 621;
McKenzie v. United Railways Co., 216 Mo. 1, 17; Railway Co. v. Wulf, 226 U. S. 570, 576; Railway Co. v.
Gray, 237 U. S. 399, 401.] The laws of Congress are
not foreign laws that must be pleaded and proven in
the courts of this State. Had the answer in this case
pleaded that the injury was suffered while the defendant and its switching crew were engaged in commerce
between the States, it would have been no defense, but
merely the statement of an immaterial fact attending
the creation of the liability, and to have proven it without pleading could have no greater effect.

Since the trial of this case, the Supreme Court of
the United States, which is the paramount authority
upon the construction of the Federal laws, has decided
this question in Railway v. Gray, supra. In doing so
it said: "There are differences and similarities between the Wisconsin and Federal statutes, but we do
not perceive that there is any difference that made the
railway company's position worse if tried on the hypothesis that the State law governed." In this case

there is no suggestion of any such difference in the application of these statutes. [See, also, C. R. I. & P. Ry. Co. v. Wright, advance sheets U. S. Sup. Ct. Reports, Feb. 15, 1916, p. 185.]

The only case to which our attention has been directed which tends to support the theory of defendant is Moliter v. Railroad, 180 Mo. App. 84. In that case the Kansas City Court of Appeals held that actions upon the liability created by the State and Federal statutes were so essentially different in their nature that they cannot be substituted for each other by amendment to the petition. This was probably a mere inadvertence, and ought not to be followed.

II. The next question presented will be simplified by bearing in mind the facts upon which the plaintiff depends for his recovery. He was thrown from the top of a freight car over the front end, falling upon the track. The car from which he fell was the last or front car of a drag of sixteen which had been shoved westward to be coupled to the east one of three cars standing upon the same track. The moving car, upon the top of which he was walking forward for the purpose of stepping upon the running board of the other car as soon as the coupling should be made, struck it, but the automatic couplers failed to work, so they were not locked together. Up to this point there is no difference between the plaintiff and defendant. Here, however, their theories diverge. The plaintiff says that the sixteenth car upon which he stood continued westward, shoving the three before it when the engineer, without any signal therefor, either by the application of the brakes, or by reversing the movement of the engine, suddenly stopped it with a jerk, and the three cars passed on, leaving a space in which the plaintiff fell to the track. On the other hand, the defendant claims that the sixteen cars stopped by reason of their impact against the three, which, not

Evidence.

having coupled, moved away from them by the force of the impact, leaving the space into which plaintiff was thrown by the sudden stop.

The jury were instructed that if they should believe the former theory they must find for the plaintiff; if the latter, they were to find for the defendant. During the occurrences that resulted in the accident Mr. Lonergan, the foreman of the crew, stood at the east end of the three cars, where the coupling was to take place, directing the movement of the engine by signalling with his hands. Mr. Hogan, a switchman, stood about half way between Mr. Lonergan and the engine, for the purpose of transmitting the signals from the former to the latter by repeating them.

Upon the trial it was admitted that Mr. Lonergan was not available as a witness to either party. The plaintiff testified: "I was standing there looking back over my shoulder and just at the time I was looking back the stop came, and the stop was so sudden that undoubtedly the stop was made by the application of the brakes." At this point he was interrupted by defendant's attorney, who objected, and moved to strike out the statement on the ground that it was mere speculation. It was overruled by the court and the witness was permitted to continue, repeating this statement in substance: stating that the jerk came with such an abrupt stop that in his estimation or knowledge the brakes were undoubtedly set or the engine reversed—that it was made by the stop of the engine. The defendant moved to strike out this additional statement as being a mere opinion. The court refused and defendant excepted. These matters are assigned for error.

The defendant introduced Mr. Hogan and asked him if he could tell what, if anything, caused the cars to stop—if he could see what caused it? The plaintiff objected on the ground that the question called for the conclusion of the witness. This objection was sustained and defendant excepted. The defendant's counsel then said: "I offer to show by this witness that the cars stopped in consequence of striking the three cars and not from the application of the brakes on the engine." To this the plaintiff objected for the reason that it would be a mere conclusion of the witness, unless he could see what was being done on the engine, eight cars away. The objection was sustained and defendant excepted. These matters are also assigned as error. It will be seen that the question raised upon the admission and exclusion of this testimony was of the most vital importance. It seems to us, that the same reasons upon which the admissibility of the testimony of plaintiff must rest would apply with equal force in favor of the testimony offered through Mr. Hogan. Both were experienced railroad men, and as such, must be assumed to have been equally competent to draw inferences from the facts which surrounded them relating to the operation in which they were engaged. The plaintiff was sixteen cars away from the engine when it stopped, and it is not suggested that he was able to see anything that was taking place in the cab. In fact he places his knowledge upon the nature of the stop alone.

Of course he could hear the rattle of drawbars and couplers as the eight or ten feet of slack of which he testifies were taken up or payed out, and felt the final jerk attending the change from movement to absolute rest. If this was not sufficient to indicate to his trained senses the cause of the stop the admission of his testimony was vital error. If he was qualified to speak in that respect so that the testimony was admissible, Mr. Hogan, a man of equal experience and intelligence, must have been equally qualified. He stood half way between plaintiff and the engine, his duty requiring him to watch Mr. Lonergan, who stood at the place where the impact must occur, and in communication, by sight, with the man controlling the engine, to whom he must be prepared to signal with his hands, and who must be in plain sight of him to receive such signals. His instincts and perceptions were trained like those of the plaintiff. It seems impossible under these circumstances that he should not have been as well prepared as the plaintiff to speak of the cause of the stop and as to whether it originated from force applied at the engine or at the front end of the drag. We think it was error to refuse to permit him to say whether or not he could, under the circumstances, tell what caused these sixteen cars to stop and whether or not he could see what caused it. If he could, he was perfectly competent to state, as the plaintiff stated, the cause, and could be asked what it was, for the purpose of proving that it was from the impact against the three cars ahead of it, and not from the application of the brakes. We think that the court committed prejudicial error in refusing to permit him to be so examined. It follows that the judgment of the Jackson Circuit Court must be reversed and the cause remanded. *Railey, C.,* concurs.

PER CURIAM.—The foregoing opinion of BROWN, C., is adopted as the opinion of the court. All the judges concur.

FRANK HOWARD et ux. v. SCARRITT ESTATE
COMPANY, Appellant.

Division Two, March 31, 1916.

1. **NEGLIGENCE: Injury to Child: Care of Parents: Instruction.**
In an action by parents for the negligent killing of their child
of tender years while riding in the passenger elevator of defendant's office building, an instruction which told the jury
that if the failure of either of the child's parents to guard and
look after him "contributed in the least degree" to the happening of the "accident" to the child, the finding should be for defendant, was erroneous. Contributory negligence sufficient to
prevent recovery must be negligence that entered into and
formed the direct, producing and efficient cause of the casualty.
Besides, the instruction should not place the burden of guarding the child upon both parents at the same instant.

2. ——————: **Customary Method of Operating Elevator: Instruction.** Where the effect of closing the sliding doors of a passenger elevator with one hand while the operator threw the
speed lever with the other was that the accelerated car was
six or eight feet above the floor before the doors became
closely shut, and plaintiff's child, a passenger thereon, fell
through and was killed, an instruction which tells the jury that
if they believe from the evidence that the elevator doors were at
the time operated "in the usual and customary way that this and
other similar elevators and doors in this and other buildings
were operated" the defendant was not negligent in the operation thereof, was erroneous. The apparatus is not so intricate
as to require expert exposition, or an instruction based thereon.

Appeal from Jackson Circuit Court.—*Hon. T. J. Seehorn,* Judge.

AFFIRMED AND REMANDED.

Boyle & Howell, Joseph S. Brooks and *George L.
Boyle* for appellant.

(1) Instructions 7 to 13, inclusive, given on behalf
of the defendant, and Instruction 5 for plaintiff, as
modified, properly declared the law applicable to the
case and it was error on the part of the court to grant

a new trial on account of error in the instructions. Minnier v. Railroad, 167 Mo. 120; Spencer v. Bruner, 126 Mo. App. 102; Brunke v. Tel. Co., 115 Mo. App. 39. (2) Under the law and evidence in the case the verdict of the jury was properly returned for the defendant and the verdict of the jury should not have been set aside.

Ellis, Cook & Barnett for respondents.

(1) The court erred in giving defendant's instruction 10, making failure to use the least degree of care contributory negligence precluding recovery. Oates v. Met. St. Ry. Co., 168 Mo. 535; Moore v. Railroad, 126 Mo. 265; Whalen v. Railroad, 60 Mo. 323; Kennayde v. Railroad, 45 Mo. 255; Klockenbrink v. Railroad, 172 Mo. 688; Hof v. Transit Co., 213 Mo. 468. (2) The court erred in giving defendant's instruction 9, justifying gross carelessness by custom. Hughes v. Railroad, 127 Mo. 447; Peterson v. Met. St. Ry. Co., 211 Mo. 498; Penney v. Stock Yards Co., 212 Mo. 309; Lee v. Knapp, 55 Mo. App. 390; Reichla v. Gruensfelder, 52 Mo. App. 43.

FARIS, P. J.—Plaintiffs, who are husband and wife, sued the defendant, a corporation, engaged in Kansas City in operating an office building, for the alleged negligent killing of their infant son in a passenger elevator in said building. Upon trial the jury found for defendant, whereupon the court granted plaintiffs a new trial, and defendant appealed. The amount sued for being $10,000 and within our jurisdiction, the case is here.

This is the second appeal in this case. Heretofore it was tried and plaintiffs had judgment for $5000. Thereon an appeal was taken to the Kansas City Court of Appeals; wherein for errors, the case was reversed and remanded. [Howard v. Scarritt Estate Co., 161 Mo. App. 552.]

The facts upon the instant appeal, so far as they are pertinent, do not so greatly differ from those shown upon the first trial and set out in the report of this case in Howard v. Scarritt Estate Co., supra, as to make it necessary to again use space in reciting them. They have been published once and the curious may read them in the book cited above.

Upon the instant trial the testimony tended to show that the operator of the elevator in question had given the two sliding doors (which closed the entrance to the elevator shaft) a shove with one hand while he threw the starting lever over with the other. The starting apparatus was equipped with five electrical contact points, the office of which was to start the car with different degrees of rapidity, increasing till the last point of contact was reached, which gave a very rapid movement to the car. The effect of such contemporaneous closing of the sliding doors and throwing on of the speeds, so rapidly accelerated the car as that it was always some six or eight feet above the floor before the doors had time to become closely shut. There was some testimony offered by plaintiffs from the operator of the elevator in question, as well as from other witnesses engaged in operating elevators in the same building and in similar buildings, that the method thus pursued in closing the doors in question in the instant case and in contemporaneously starting the elevator cage, was the usual and customary way of so operating these appliances.

Upon the trial an instruction was offered by defendant and given by the court upon this phase of the case. This instruction will be found set out at length in the opinion herein in connection with the discussion of its alleged incorrectness. The court also upon the trial of the case gave an instruction upon the theory of the alleged contributory negligence of plaintiffs herein in failing to properly guard the child while he

was riding in the elevator and just before he fell
through and was killed. This instruction will also be
found in the opinion, and so we need not set it forth
here.

I. The new trial herein was granted "on account
of error in instructions." Of this error, or errors, no
further and more definite specifications are furnished
us. Counsel for appellant broadly urge

Contributory Negligence of Parents. that instructions seven to thirteen inclusive, given for defendant, are each the law, citing us as proof of the faith which
is in them to the case of Minnier v. Railroad, 167 Mo.
l. c. 120; and to two cases in the Courts of Appeals,
Spencer v. Bruner, 126 Mo. App. l. c. 102, and Brunke
v. Telephone Co., 115 Mo. App. l. c. 39.

These cases are not in our view authority sufficient
to sustain all seven of the instructions complained of;
some one or more of which must have been held in mind
by the court below.

Among others the court *nisi* gave for the defendant this instruction, numbered ten in the record, to-wit:

"The court instructs the jury that inasmuch as the
son of plaintiffs was a child of tender years, it was
their duty at all times to guard and look after him, and
that it was the duty of the parents to take care for their
child in proportion to the dangers of his surroundings,
and if you believe from the evidence that plaintiffs or
either of them failed to watch and care for their child
in manner and form as defined by these instructions, in
the elevator in question, and that such failure on the
part of the parents, or either of them, contributed in
the least degree to cause the accident to their child,
then plaintiffs cannot recover in this suit and it is your
duty to return a verdict for defendant."

We think it is evident from a mere casual reading
that the above instruction is erroneous and that the

267 Mo. 26

giving of it alone was a sufficient warrant for the action of the learned court in setting aside the verdict for defendant. For it will be seen that the jury are advised by this instruction that if the failure of either of the parents of the dead child to guard him and look after him "contributed in the least degree" to the happening of the "accident" to the child, then the finding should be for defendant.

It is not the law that *the least negligence of him who is hurt* will excuse an otherwise guilty tortfeasor for his negligent act. [Moore v. Railroad, 126 Mo. l. c. 277; Oates v. Railroad, 168 Mo. l. c. 548.] It is plain (and it has so been ruled) that to hold otherwise would be to hold that there exists in this State the doctrine of comparative negligence; a doctrine which has been, when sought to be invoked, always expressly repudiated. [Hurt v. Railroad, 94 Mo. l. c. 264; Oates v. Railroad, supra.] The rule as to the quantum of contributory negligence which is sufficient to prevent recovery is that it must be such as to enter into and form the direct, producing and efficient cause of the casualty, and absent which the casualty would not have happened.

The unfortunate facts of this casualty present a peculiarly difficult case in which to apply the doctrine of contributory negligence. The circumscribed area in which the child and his parents were confined and the closeness of the child to the door opening, were such that a mere step may have caused his fall and death. We think, however, that defendant was entitled to have this issue presented to the jury by a proper instruction; we are convinced that the instruction given was improper.

In addition to the error above pointed out this instruction put upon plaintiffs too great a burden of care. It might well be proper to leave to the jury the question of the care of one parent, but to say to the

jury, as this instruction in effect does, that unless both
parents were guarding the child no recovery could be
had, was in a practical sense to instruct the jury to find
for defendant. If *both parents* were negligent in performing the duty of guarding the child then no recovery should be had; but one parent at a time ought to
be all the guard a four-year-old child needs in order to
ride safely in a passenger elevator.

II. While it necessarily results that this case must
for the error noted above be affirmed and remanded
for the new trial properly granted by the learned trial
court, it may be well to say that in our opinion instruction nine was likewise erroneous. This instruction
reads thus:

"The court instructs the jury that if you believe
from the evidence the elevator doors to the elevator
shaft were operated at the time in question in the usual
and customary way that this and other similar elevators and doors in this and other buildings
are operated, then you should not find that
defendant was negligent at the time in question in the operation thereof, and your verdict should be in favor of defendant."

Customary
Method of
Operating
Elevator.

If the matter of time and manner of closing a door
to an elevator shaft were a peculiarly intricate one,
which, by reason of its abstruseness, the populace, lacking scientific knowledge, are unable to grasp and know
and understand, then evidence of experts as to the safe-
ness or unsafeness of a given method of operation
might be permissible, and an instruction based on such
testimony be allowable. But no such case is presented.
Rather is this a case analogous in all substantial respects as to this feature to that of Hughes v. Railroad,
127 Mo. 447, wherein it was said at page 454:

"The giving of the instruction would amount to
the assertion that a custom, however dangerous to human life it might be, had it been pursued for a period

of eight months by defendant without injury to any
one up to the date of the injury complained of, might
be interposed as a defense, by the party exercising it,
from the consequences of its dangerous continuance.
The duty enjoined upon defendant to exercise care,
caution and vigilance is not dependent upon the fact
that on some former occasion a like injury had happened at this exact place and under similar circumstances and conditions. The act itself was dangerous.
The consequences of it could have been reasonably
foreseen, and injuries from it reasonably been avoided
only by the exercise of the greatest care on part of
defendant to warn all persons on its platform to be on
the lookout.''

Conceding that a rule similar to that stated in the
above instruction exists in matters demanding expert
exposition, and likewise as to the duty of the master
to furnish only customarily used appliances, and not
the very best and newest and most improved appliances
to an employee, we yet do not think it can apply in a
case like this. [Reichla v. Gruensfelder, 52 Mo. App.
43; Peterson v. Railroad, 211 Mo. 498; Penney v.
Stock Yards Co., 212 Mo. 309.]

The question of the degree of duty, if any, which
defendant owed to plaintiffs upon the facts, is not raised
here by appellant, and while respondent tacitly calls
it to our attention, we are not for that called on to discuss it. But pass it, saying simply that it is not before
us upon the record. If it was ever in the case it has
been waived in this review.

It results from what is said that the action of the
learned trial court in granting a new trial was correct
and that the case should be affirmed and remanded for
the new trial properly ordered by the court *nisi.* Let
this be done. All concur.

I. J. WOLF v. HENRY HARRIS, Appellant.

Division Two, March 31, 1916.

1. **ABSTRACT: Transfer from Court of Appeals.** When a case reaches the Supreme Court by transfer from a court of appeals, on the ground that a constitutional question is involved, the rule is not to scrutinize too closely the abstract of the record, lest appellant be caught unwittingly between the rules of that court and of this and thereby be pinched out of any appeal at all.

2. **PETITION: Cause of Action.** The point that the petition does not state a cause of action may be raised for the first time in the appellate court.

3. **INJUNCTION: Publication of Libel.** Injunction, when that is the only relief prayed for, will not lie to restrain the threatened publication of either a libel or slander.

4. **————: ————: Remedy.** The issue of libel or no libel is an issue of law and a matter for the jury; and before plaintiff can have an injunction to restrain a further publication of libelous statements, there must be a verdict of the jury finding the statements to be false and libelous. If he goes to a jury with the alleged libel and obtains a judgment, which owing to defendant's insolvency he is unable to collect, further publication of a libel of like or similar import may be enjoined in a separate suit; or he may couple a count for injunction in his petition with a count at law for damages, and having sustained before a jury his law count, the court, upon allegation and proof of defendant's insolvency and threatened continuance of the libelous publication, or to avoid a multiplicity of suits, can enjoin a continued publication thereof.

Appeal from Jackson Circuit Court.—*Hon. W. A. Powell*, Judge.

REVERSED.

T. A. Frank Jones for appellant.

(1) Under the Constitution defendant had the right to make the publications complained of, being responsible for all abuse of that liberty. Mo. Constitu-

tion, art. 2, sec. 14.   (2) Under the allegations of the
petition plaintiff had no right to an injunction against
the defendant. Life Assn. v. Boogher, 3 Mo. App. 173;
Flint v. Smoke Burner Co., 110 Mo. 492.

Kimbrell & White for respondent.

FARIS, P. J.—Respondent herein, who was plaintiff below, brought this action in equity in the circuit
court of Jackson County to perpetually restrain and
enjoin defendant from publishing certain alleged false,
defamatory and libelous statements concerning respondent. From a judgment for plaintiff enjoining defendant as prayed, the latter appealed.

The case turns on the application to plaintiff's
petition of section 14 of article 2 of the Constitution
of Missouri, which section is pleaded by defendant in
his answer. This petition is lengthy and we do not
deem it necessary to set it out *in haec verba,* but will
content ourselves with stating the substance of it. It
may help toward an understanding of the case to say
that the petition sounds in equity only and contains
but one count.

The plaintiff, after averring that he is a practicing
physician and surgeon in Kansas City, Missouri, and
that he has been such for nearly a quarter of a century,
and reciting the extent of his studies, practice and
experience, avers that he was called to treat a young
daughter of defendant, and though exercising in that
behalf the utmost care and skill, the patient without
fault of plaintiff, died; that thereafter defendant demanded of plaintiff in divers ways, and at divers times
and places the sum of $10,000 because of the death of
said patient, and threatened that unless said sum was
paid, defendant by circulating charges of criminal negligence of plaintiff in connection with the death of the
patient aforesaid, would destroy the reputation, business and professional standing and income of plain-

tiff, which plaintiff avers to be lucrative and large, and that in pursuance of said threats defendant circulated and published more than a thousand copies of a certain false and libelous writing concerning plaintiff. This writing is set out in the petition, and is if untrue manifestly libelous.

It is further alleged that thereafter defendant with the same malicious intent and design, published and circulated among plaintiff's patients, friends and acquaintances, more than five thousand copies of a certain pamphlet, in which were repeated the same, or similar, false, defamatory and libelous statements, and that subsequently defendant procured the printing of a large placard, likewise containing false and libelous statements concerning the plaintiff, and that all this was done for the purpose of wrongfully extorting from plaintiff the said sum of $10,000.

Plaintiff further alleged that all charges so made by defendant touching the wrong doing and alleged malpractice of plaintiff were false and were known by defendant to be false, and that they were made and circulated solely to gratify the spite and ill will of defendant against plaintiff and for the purpose of extorting money from plaintiff.

It is further alleged that defendant threatens to continue and until and unless restrained and enjoined will continue, to print, publish and circulate the same, or similar libelous statements touching plaintiff; that if plaintiff has any property the same is so wholly encumbered and covered up and so insufficient in quantity and value that plaintiff would be unable to collect any judgment which might be rendered in his favor as damages in any action at law that plaintiff might bring on account of the publication of said libelous statements; that if he were to sue defendant on each successive libelous publication he would be compelled to bring a multiplicity of actions at law, at great cost, inconvenience and expense and that said actions would be so numerous and would for that so encumber the dockets of the courts of Jackson County as to obstruct the administration of justice therein, and so by reason of the premises plaintiff avers that he has no adequate remedy at law and is compelled to resort to his action in equity.

The prayer for relief is substantially followed in the decree as first above stated; that is to say, that defendant be perpetually restrained and enjoined from printing or publishing or attempting so to do, the false, defamatory and libelous statements aforesaid, or any others of like or similar import.

As stated, defendant in his answer invoked the provisions of section 14 of article 2 of the Constitution of Missouri, and denied that when measured thereby, plaintiff's petition stated any cause of action; denied that defendant is insolvent, but averred his solvency, and being solvent averred that plaintiff had an adequate remedy by an action at law for damages; further answering defendant pleaded the truth of the statements made by him; that is to say, in substance admitting publication, but averring justification.

The case went first to the Kansas City Court of Appeals, but on account of the invocation of the Constitution by defendant in his answer, the latter court, upon motion, sent the case up to us. ...

Such further facts as will suffice to make the points clear will be found in the opinion.

OPINION.

As a foreword we may say that the abstract and the brief in this case upon appellant's part (we have not been favored with a brief from respondent) are

Abstract.   exceedingly meagre and are not such as our rules require. But since the case comes here on transfer by order of a Court of Appeals, on aocount of a constitutional question, the rule in such case is not to scrutinize too closely the abstract of the record, lest an appellant caught unwittingly between their rules and ours should be pinched out of any appeal at all.

There are set forth in the abstract the petition in full and the answer of the defendant invoking section 14 of article 2 of our Constitution. One point in his brief keeps alive this contention that an absolute defense is afforded him by the Constitution; another point urges that "under the allegations of the petition plaintiff had no right to an injunction against the defendant." We will treat these points thus coupled together, as we have the right to do under authority, as an attack upon the sufficiency of the petition. For where a petition states no facts upon which a judgment may be bottomed, in short, where it states no cause of action, that point may be raised here for the first time. [Sexton v. Metropolitan Street Railway Co., 245 Mo. 254; Monmouth College v. Dockery, 241 Mo. 522.]

Coming then to a consideration of this contention, we are constrained to hold that the point is well taken; that the petition states no cause of action, because injunction (when as here, that is the sole relief prayed for) will not lie to restrain the threatened publication of either a libel or a slander. Any other view overlooks the spirit if not the letter of the Constitution (Sec. 14, art. 2, Constitution 1875), which substantially guarantees to the citizen the privilege of saying, writing and publishing whatever he desires on any matter, subject only to liability (either civil or criminal, or both), for any abuse of that privilege. So far, it could not be said with any certainty from the bare language set forth, that an abuse of the liberty so guaranteed, when such abuse is so flagrantly present as is conceded by the appellant's brief to be the fact here, could not be remedied by injunction. If the Constitution had stopped with this we might well say that such a remedy lies. But this section continues: "In all suits and prosecutions for libel the truth thereof may be given in evidence and the jury under the direction of the court shall determine the law and the fact." It follows that if the statements made are true the appellant is permitted to publish them when and where and as often as he will, and that he is entitled to a jury of his country to determine whether these statements are true or false. That the statements on which this action is bottomed seem upon their face to be malicious and obviously untrue, does not change the case. It has been so often ruled that in a plain case of slander of the person or slander of title, injunction will not lie, that reiteration should be unnecessary. [Flint v. Hutchinson Smoke Burner Co., 110 Mo. l. c. 500; Life Association v. Boogher, 3 Mo. App. 173; Thummel v. Holden, 149 Mo. l. c. 685; Clothing Co. v. Watson, 168 Mo. l. c. 148; Sec. 14, art. 2, Constitution of 1875; American Malting Co. v. Keitel, 209 Fed. 356.] In the case of Flint v. Hutchinson Co., supra, at page 500, BLACK, J., speaking for this court, said:

"We live under a written Constitution which declares that the right of a trial by jury shall remain inviolate; and the question of libel or no libel, slander or no slander, is one for a jury to determine. Such was certainly the settled law when the various constitutions of this State were adopted, and it is all-important that the right thus guarded should not be disturbed. It goes hand in hand with the liberty of the press and free speech. For unbridled use of the tongue or pen the law furnishes a remedy. In view of these considerations a court of equity has no power to restrain a slander or libel; and it can make no difference whether the words are spoken of a person or his title to property.

"In either case it is for a jury to first determine the question of slander or libel in an action at law. This, we conclude, is the result of the better cases in this country and in England."

The facts before us lacking the element of conspiracy obviously distinguish the instant case from the case of Lohse Patent Door Co. v. Fuelle, 215 Mo. 421, and from the case of Shoemaker v. South Bend Spark Arrester Co., 135 Ind. 471. For the former case was bottomed upon the theory of conspiracy, while the latter case dealt not only with a false publication amounting to slander of title, but with threats toward divers and sundry others, and toward all who might buy, or use the alleged patent-infringed article. Besides, *the ultimate fact had been already ruled in a proper action,* to-wit, that there was no infringement and therefore the *alleged* slanders of title which the court enjoined had beforehand (but in the same action) been found and declared to be false and therefore as to title, slanderous.

It is stated in the Flint case, supra, that after an action at law in which there is a verdict finding the statements published to be false, plaintiff on an otherwise proper showing could have injunction restraining any further publication of that which the jury has found to be actionable libel or slander, and of slanders or libel of a like or similar import. So say we in this case. If plaintiff had gone to a jury with this alleged libel and obtained a judgment, which owing to the insolvency of defendant he was unable to collect, further publication of a libel of like or similar import ought to be enjoined. Or, even if plaintiff had joined a count at law for damages for libel with a count for injunction on the theory of a threatened continuance of the false publication, and had alleged and proved, either the inadequacy of remedy by reason of the libeller's insolvency, or, the legal necessity of the remedy sought in order to avoid a multiplicity of suits, the court *nisi* upon a finding by the jury of the libel, and by the court of the said necessary facts on the equity side, could have enjoined continued publication thereof. Since, however, there is in the instant case neither conspiracy, nor threats to others, nor a verdict of a jury upon the fact of libel, we are constrained to say that this judgment cannot stand. Let it be reversed. All concur.

THE STATE ex rel. FRANK N. ABERCROMBIE v. CHARLES W. HOLTCAMP, Judge of Probate Court, Appellant.

Division Two, March 31. 1916.

1. ADMINISTRATION: Removal Causes: Ascertainment Before Appointment. Section 50, Revised Statutes 1909, announcing the causes for which letters testamentary or of administration may be revoked, is not to be read into and made a part of section 14, which designates persons who cannot qualify as executor or administrator. The probate court cannot refuse to appoint an executor named in the will on the ground that such person if appointed could be removed for the causes mentioned in section 50.

2. ————: Executor: Renunciation. The person named as executor in a will may renounce his right to be appointed, either by an express renunciation, or by acts and conduct *in pais*.

3. ————: ————: ————: Determination a Judicial Matter. The probate court must determine from the facts whether the person nominated executor in the will has renounced his right to be appointed, and in doing so exercises a judicial function; his act must not be arbitrary, or an abuse of power, or wholly unsupported by facts showing a renunciation; but if such facts are present, the appointment of another cannot be annulled by mandamus brought by the named executor to compel his appointment.

4. ———: **Title to Estate: Domiciliary and Ancillary Executor.**
The executor who has duly qualified in the domiciliary jurisdiction succeeds to the title of all testator's estate, wherever
situated, and continues to hold such title until an ancillary
administrator is appointed, whereupon the title to the estate
in the ancillary jurisdiction vests in the latter.

5. ———: **Executor: Acts of Renunciation: Recall.** Testator
died in Ohio, leaving a will which named relator and two
women as executors. All qualified in Ohio, but within a few
days relator filed his resignation, which was accepted. He did
not qualify in the Missouri city in which he lived and where
the most of testator's property was situate. He also immediately resigned as director of the corporation in which testator's
Missouri assets were principally invested, and avowedly severed
all relations with the management and preservation of the
estate, and did other things which tended to establish a renunciation *in pais.* *Held,* that the probate court did not act
arbitrarily, in holding relator had renounced his rights under
the will and in appointing another administrator with the will
annexed; and the renunciation being complete, it could not
be recalled, but was lost to relator forever.

6. **WILL: Intention as to Executors.** The rule that the expressed
intention of the testator must be the guide in construing a will,
applies to every part of it—to the expressed desire that a nominated executor should administer the whole estate, the assets
in the State where testator died and those in other States, as
well as to other parts of it.

7. **ADMINISTRA TION: Executor: Renunciation of Domiciliary
Right: Is Renunciation of Ancillary Right.** A resignation
in the domiciliary jurisdiction by an executor named in the will
who is qualified under the laws of the various jurisdictions in
which the estate is located, is a renunciation of his right to
administer so much of the estate as is situate in the ancillary
jurisdiction in which he resides. So that where relator, a resident of this State, who was named executor in the will of a
testator who died in Ohio, qualified in that State and soon
afterwards resigned, his resignation, there accepted, operated
automatically as a renunciation of his right to administer so
much of the estate as was located in this State.

Appeal from St. Louis City Circuit Court.— *Hon.
George H. Shields,* Judge.

REVERSED (*with directions*).

Jones, Hocker, Hawes & Angert and *George B. Webster* for appellant.

(1) The circuit court was without jurisdiction to entertain mandamus because the action of the probate court was the exercise by it of a judicial function. 4 Words and Phrases, p. 3850; State ex rel. v. County Court, 227 Mo. 460; State ex rel. v. Guinotte, 113 Mo. App. 319; 1 Bouvier, 884. (2) An executor appointed under a will need not accept such appointment, but may renounce or resign his appointment at any time prior to intermeddling with the affairs of the estate or doing any act which amounts to an acceptance of the trust. Woerner's Administration, sec. 234. (a) This renunciation may result from acts *in pais*. Thornton v. Winston, 4 Leigh. 152; Solomon v. Wixon, 27 Conn. 520; Ayers v. Weed, 16 Conn. 291; Wood v. Sparks, 1 Dev. & Bat. 395. (3) Abercrombie was competent to act as executor under the will both in Ohio as regards the primary administration and in Missouri as regards the ancillary administration. Woerner's Administration, sec. 230. (4) Abercrombie had the option to accept the office of executor or to resign and renounce the same. He had not the option to accept in part and renounce in part. Having resigned or renounced his office as executor under the will, that resignation being filed in and accepted by the court administering primary administration, operated as a resignation of his office *in toto*, and not in part only. Ross v. Barclay, 18 Pa. St. 179. (5) A renunciation once made and accepted cannot be recalled. State ex rel. v. Romyne, 136 Mo. App. 658; Thornton v. Winston, 4 Leigh. 164; Wood v. Sparks, 1 Dev. & Bat. 296; Stockdale v. Conaway, 14 Md. 99; Lutz v. Mahan, 80 Md. 237; Estate of Kirtlan, 16 Cal. 161; Triplett v. Wells, Littell's Cases (Ky.), 49; Carpenter v. Jones, 44 Md. 625.

Jeptha D. Howe for respondent; *Marshall & Henderson* of counsel.

(1) Mandamus is the proper remedy. There is no merit in the appellant's contention that the judge of the probate court exercised judicial discretion in appointing Steininger administrator with the will annexed. The will appointed relator as executor and the probate court had no power to refuse to permit him to qualify, it being conceded that he was a resident of the State of Missouri. Flick v. Schenk, 212 Mo. 275; State ex rel. v. Guinotte, 113 Mo. App. 339; State ex rel. v. Fowler, 108 Mo. 465; State ex rel. v. Reynolds, 121 Mo. App. 699. (2) The resignation of relator as executor applied only to the administration in Ohio and did not apply, and was not intended to apply, to the right of relator to qualify as executor in Missouri. (3) Even if the resignation of relator, directed to the probate court in Ohio, should be held to apply also to Missouri, nevertheless relator had the right to retract his renunciation as to the administration in Missouri at any time before an administrator, with the will annexed, was appointed in Missouri, and this relator did, and the probate court in St. Louis had no power or jurisdiction to refuse to allow him to qualify as such executor in Missouri and no power or jurisdiction to appoint Steininger administrator with the will annexed. 1 Woerner's Am. Law of Adm., pp. 229, 230, 513; Casey v. Gardiner, 4 Bradf. 13; Robertson v. McGeoch, 11 Paige's Chan. 640; Taylor v. Tibbatts, 13 B. Mon. (Ky.) 177; Davis v. Inscoe, 84 N. C. 396; Wood v. Sparks, 1 Dev. & Bat. 389; Staunton v. Parker, 55 Hun, 60; McDonnell v. Prendergast, 3 Haag. Ecc. 216; In re Benton, 2 Hayw. & H. (U. S.) 315; 30 Fed. Cas. 18234; Thompson v. Dixon, 3 Haag. Ecc. 212; Dempsey's Estate, Tuck. (N. Y.) 51; In re True, 120 Cal. 352; Judson v. Gibbons, 5 Wend. 224;

Codding v. Newman, 3 Thomp. & C. 364; Percy v. De-Wolf, 2 R. I. 103.

REVELLE, J.—This is an appeal from a judgment of the circuit court of the city of St. Louis granting a peremptory writ of mandamus, commanding the probate judge of that city to permit relator to qualify as executor under the will of Martin Stanford Robison, deceased, and to revoke the appointment theretofore made of Edward A. Steininger as administrator with will annexed.

The material facts are as follows:

On March 24, 1911, Martin Stanford Robison, a citizen of the city of Cleveland, Ohio, died, leaving a will, in which Mrs. Sarah C. H. Robison, Mrs. Helene H. R. Britton and relator were named executors. Mrs. Robison and Mrs. Britton were at the time of the death of testator residents of the State of Ohio, while relator was then, and yet is, a resident of the State of Missouri. Immediately upon the death of the testator relator proceeded to the city of Cleveland to attend the funeral, and while there, to-wit, on March 28, 1911, the will was admitted to probate in the county of testator's residence, and relator, Mrs. Robison and Mrs. Britton duly qualified as executors. On April 6, 1911, relator filed his resignation as executor of the will, and on April 7th the probate court accepted same. Three days after the death of testator, to-wit, on March 27th, letters of administration were granted to Edward A. Steininger by the probate court of the city of St. Louis, upon the written request of the legatees named in the will, these letters going only to the ancillary administration.

It appears that the greater portion of testator's estate consisted of property located in Missouri, he being the dominant owner of the stock of a Missouri corporation owning the baseball club known as "The

Cardinals.'' On June 19, 1911, the public administrator of the city of St. Louis filed in the probate court
of that city an authenticated copy of the will, and at
the same time filed his notice that he had taken charge
of the estate. On the same day Edward S. Steininger,
who had theretofore been granted letters of administration, also filed in the probate court of the city of St.
Louis another copy of the will, whereupon a *dedimus*
was issued to take the testimony of the subscribing witnesses who lived at Cleveland, Ohio. On the 29th of
June relator applied to the probate court for leave to
qualify as executor under the will. On July 8th Steininger filed a certified copy of the resignation of relator, which had been filed with the probate court of Ohio,
said copy having been procured on April 12th. On
June 20th the public administrator filed a motion in
the probate court to quash the *dedimus* theretofore issued to take the testimony of the subscribing witnesses
to the will; and on June 30th filed a motion to require
Steininger to settle with him as administrator with
will annexed. The hearing on these various applications and motions began in the probate court on July
10th, and, upon completion thereof, the probate court
found, from the facts adduced in evidence, that relator had no absolute right to qualify as an executor,
because he had theretofore renounced and waived such
right. After so disposing of relator's claims, it appointed Steininger administrator with the will annexed.

The evidence discloses that at about the same time
that relator tendered his resignation to the probate
court of Ohio, he also resigned as a director in the
Missouri corporation in which the testator's assets
were chiefly invested. It also appears that three days
after the death of testator, and before relator resigned
in Ohio, he had arranged for his bond as ancillary ex-

ecutor, but after he resigned in Ohio he made no effort whatever to qualify in Missouri until the time and after the occurrences heretofore recited.

At the hearing before the probate court relator testified that some differences had arisen between him and one of the principal legatees, and that he did not desire to be in a position where it would embarrass this party, and that he therefore resigned as executor under the will and as a director of the Missouri corporation, and had entirely severed his connection with the estate. On April 10th, following his resignation on April 6th, he wrote a letter to Mrs. Robison clearly indicating his intention to have nothing further to do with the management or administration of any part of the estate.

I. At the inception we are confronted with appellant's insistence that mandamus is not a proper and available remedy, for that the action of the probate court, which the writ seeks to control, involved the exercise of both a judicial discretion and function. On the other hand, it is contended that, since the will nominated and appointed relator as executor, the duty of the court was purely ministerial, and after the probate of the will it had no authority to do other than grant letters testamentary to relator.

Executor:
Renunciation
of Appointment:
Recall: Mandamus.

A determination of this question makes necessary an examination of the statutory provisions relating to wills.

Section 19, Revised Statutes 1909, provides: "After probate of any will, letters testamentary *shall* be granted to the persons *therein appointed executors* . . . If all such persons *refuse to act,* or be *disqualified,* letters of administration shall be granted to the person to whom administration would have been granted if there had been no will."

Section 14 provides that "no judge or clerk of any probate court, in his own county, or his deputy, and no male person under twenty-one years of age, or female person under eighteen years of age, or of unsound mind, shall be executor or administrator. No married woman shall be executrix or administratrix, nor shall the executor of an executor, in consequence thereof, be executor of the first testator."

Section 17 provides: "Letters testamentary and of administration may at any time be granted to any person deemed suitable *if* the person or persons *entitled to preference* filed their renunciation thereof, in writing, with the clerk of the court, or if proof be made that no such persons reside in this State."

Section 50 provides: "If any executor or administrator become of unsound mind, or be convicted of any felony or other infamous crime, or has absented himself from the State for a space of four months, or become an habitual drunkard, or in anywise incapable or unsuitable to execute the trust reposed in him, or fail to discharge his official duties, or waste or mismanage the estate, or act so as to endanger any co-executor or co-administrator, or failed to answer any citation and attachment to make settlement, the court" (upon written complaint and after notice and hearing) "shall revoke the letters granted."

It is insisted on the part of appellant that the causes announced in section 50 for which letters may be *revoked* must be incorporated and read in connection with section 14 which designates the persons who cannot be *appointed* and who cannot *qualify* as executor or administrator, and that when the probate court is called upon to grant letters testamentary it is not only its privilege but duty to judicially ascertain and determine whether any of the removal causes exist.

With this we do not agree, as it is clear that section 50 relates only to persons who have already qual-

ified, while section 14 prescribes the class of persons
who can neither be appointed nor qualified. We further find from the administration laws that an appeal
is allowed from orders and judgments *revoking* letters
for the causes mentioned in section 50, but no such
right is given in cases where letters testamentary or
of administration are denied to persons lawfully thereto entitled. [Flick v. Schenk, 212 Mo. 275; Marshall
v. Estate, 164 Mo. App. 429.] That relator possessed
the qualifications required, and was not disqualified by
reason of any of the disabilities mentioned in section
14, is conceded, and we have abundant authority in this
State for giving relief by mandamus when, under such
circumstances, the probate court fails to perform its
plain legal duty. [State ex rel. v. Guinotte, 113 Mo.
App. 399; State ex rel. v. Fowler, 108 Mo. 465; State
ex rel. v. Reynolds, 121 Mo. App. 699; Flick v. Schenk,
212 Mo. 275; State ex rel. Knisely v. Holtcamp, 266
Mo. 347; State ex rel. v. Homer, 249 Mo. 58.]

We, therefore, conclude that, unless other facts appear which preclude relator from asserting his original
rights to letters testamentary, such rights were absolute, and mandamus is a proper remedy to compel the
probate court to grant to him such letters. [Cases
supra.]

This, however, does not dispose of the subject, in
so far as this case involves it, as the pleadings and evidence disclose that the refusal of the probate court to
grant letters to relator was predicated upon its findings of fact, that relator had, prior to making his demand for letters, duly and completely *renounced* and
waived his rights thereto.

The law is well-settled that, although an executor,
if not disqualified by statute, has the absolute right to
letters testamentary upon the probate of the will, he is
not required to exercise this right or accept this position of trust and responsibility. He is free, if he so

desires, to renounce his rights thereunder, and this he can do by an express renunciation, or by acts and conduct *in pais*. [Thornton v. Winston, 4 Leigh, 152; Solomon v. Wixon, 27 Conn. 520; Ayres v. Weed, 16 Conn. 291; Wood v. Sparks, 1 Dev. & Bat. l. c. 395.]

In case of such renunciation it becomes the duty of the probate court to appoint another, and it is clear that in performing its duty, that is, appointing the person entitled thereto, that court must determine, from the facts, whether there has been a renunciation. It may be conceded that in such a case the court can-not act arbitrarily, or abuse its power, or make a finding which is wholly unsupported; but, absent these, it cannot be gainsaid that the court, when determining this question, exercises a discretion and performs a judicial function. In the instant case we find no such arbitrary abuse of power as to warrant outside interference or the use of the extraordinary writ. The relator had duly qualified in the domiciliary jurisdiction as executor of the will, and as such, was in charge of the principal and primary administration. The law is that such an executor succeeds to the title of all of testator's estate, *wherever* situated, and continues to hold such title until an ancillary administrator is appointed, when the title to the estate in the ancillary jurisdiction vests in the latter. [13 Am. & Eng. Ency. Law, 931.]

When relator voluntarily resigned he did not state in his resignation that he was attempting to resign only in Ohio, but made it general. He followed this up by immediately resigning as a director in the corporation in which the Missouri assets were principally invested, and avowedly severed all relations with the management and preservation of the Missouri estate. He wrote a letter to Mrs. Robison clearly indicating an intention to have nothing further to do with the estate, or any part thereof. For a period of about three months, although a resident of the city where the prop-

erty was located, and well knowing that the estate was
in the process of administration by another, he took no
interest therein, and made no effort to file the will or
qualify thereunder, and when the will was finally presented it was not by him, but by another. He had
made arrangements for his bond as executor in Missouri in March, but, after resigning in Ohio, he abandoned these. He testified at the hearing, in explaining
some of his actions, that his relations with the interested parties had become unfriendly and unpleasant,
and that he had no desire to embarrass them by continuing his relations with the business.

In view of these facts, it cannot be reasonably said
that the probate court, in determining the question as
to whether relator had renounced his right, acted arbitrarily and without sufficient facts; and for this reason, if no other, the writ should be denied, unless relator is correct in his insistence that, notwithstanding he
had renounced, he, nevertheless, had the right to change
his mind and accept the trust at any time after the will
was filed and before another person was appointed with
the will annexed.

In State ex rel. v. Romjue, 136 Mo. App. 650, the
Kansas City Court of Appeals held that where a person entitled to administer renounced his right thereto,
it was forever lost and could not be recalled, and this
notwithstanding that there was coupled with the renunciation an express condition that certain other persons should be appointed to administer. In that case
the court held that this right was purely a personal
privilege, and that if the members of the privileged
class renounce their right, or lose it by failing to exercise it, then the duty devolves upon the probate court of
selecting another. The court in that connection said
(1. c. 658-9):

"We regard the renunciations filed by relators as
unconditional, and pass to the question of whether rela-

tors could retract them at any time before the appointment of an administrator. In our opinion, the better doctrine is that when the privilege once is renounced or waived, it is lost forever and cannot be recalled. Two very potent reasons may be given in support of this doctrine. First, as a general rule, the estates of deceased persons demand speedy attention and injury would result from delays that might be caused if resident heirs could renounce and recall their privilege at will, and, second, the right of revocation, if it existed, might be used as was attempted in the present case, not in good faith for the purpose of enjoying the privilege, but as a club to hold over the probate court to compel it to appoint, not the persons whom the court in the exercise of its judgment found were best qualified to administer, but those whom the resident heirs favored. The doctrine just announced is abundantly, though not unanimously, sustained by the authorities. We refer to the briefs of counsel where the authorities for and against it are collated. We conclude that respondent acted within the scope of his right and duty in refusing to acknowledge the right of relators to recall their renunciations and, as the appointment made by him appears to have been the result of the exercise of sound judgment and not of an arbitrary abuse of power, we find no occasion to interfere.''

And we might add, that when the choice of the testator refuses to act, the duty of preserving the estate and the selection of another person to act becomes important and immediately necessary, and this incurs expense and trouble, a part of which would be made useless and wasteful if the vacillating person who first refused to serve, and then changed his mind, were permitted to play thus fast and loose. [Stocksdale v. Conaway, 14 Md. 99; Estate of Kirtlan, 16 Cal. 161.]

Again, in cases like the present, where a full administration had been in progress (although not under

the will) for three months, the right to revive should
not exist. During that period relator stood idly by,
watching others handle the laboring oar, and failing
and refusing to perform the very duties which gave
life to his right. To permit him to then claim his volun-
tarily-waived right would be to pervert the very object
of his appointment and reward his dereliction. It
would mean that he could accept a part of the trust, and
reject the remainder, even in the same jurisdiction.

We are, therefore, of the opinion that the probate
court was not only called upon to determine the legal
effect of the resignation filed in Ohio, but also the question of fact as to what relator's intentions were, and
how far he had renounced *in pais;* and, in this connection, it had a perfect right to weigh and consider all
of relator's acts and conduct. This required the exercise of judicial discretion, and it is too well settled
to even warrant the citation of authorities that such
discretion cannot be controlled by mandamus.

II. In the preceding paragraph we have not directly dealt with one question which the record presents, namely: whether, under the law of administration, an executor who is qualified under the laws of the
various jurisdictions in which the estate is located, can,
as a matter of absolute right, accept a
part of the trust and reject that which
he deems undesirable; or can refuse to
act in the principal jurisdiction and yet
retain his absolute rights in the ancillary jurisdiction. The absolute rights
of an executor to letters testamentary
are derived solely from the act of the
testator in naming him as such. [18
Cyc. 74, and cases cited.] The dominant object of a
testator in naming a person as executor is not to be-
stow favor, but to impose duties—the duty of manag-

Executor:
Renunciation
of Domiciliary
Right a
Renunciation
of Ancillary
Right.

ing, directing and administering upon his estate and carrying out his expressed wishes, and we give effect to his nomination, not because of inherent rights in the person nominated, but because of the expressed desire and intention of the testator. A testator may have good reasons for confiding his whole estate to one person, and for wanting the same person to administer upon it in its entirety, and thus have pursued one general and harmonious policy in relation thereto. In many cases the property and estate are of such a character that such a policy is absolutely essential to a profitable preservation and distribution thereof. Is it not reasonable to assume that all testators desire this uniformity of action and administration when they name persons as executors for all purposes, and refrain from naming some for one jurisdiction and others for other jurisdictions? A testator, if capable of making a will, knows the location of his property, its particular character, as well as the laws of the States where located, and how he desires it handled. He selects his representative with all this in mind and with reference thereto.

In this case testator knew that a resident of this State was legally qualified to become the legal representative of both the principal and ancillary administration. He named relator executor of his whole will, not a part thereof, as he might have done had such been his desire and intention. [Hunter v. Bryson, 25 Am. Dec. 313; Despard v. Churchill, 53 N. Y. 192; Mordecai v. Boylan, 59 N. C. 365; Gibbons v. Riley, 7 Gill, 81.] In construing wills we have always said that the expressed intention of the testator must guide and govern us, and this applies to every part of the will. It was the expressed desire and intention of testator that relator act as one of the legal representatives of both the principal and ancillary administration, and we are unwilling to hold that this intention can not only be defeated, but may be used for the purely personal advantage of the person defeating it. He should not be permitted to select from the trust thus imposed the things which he deems pleasurable and profitable, and reject those which may seem burdensome and unprofitable. He should accept or renounce the whole, thus giving full effect to the intention of the one who created his right. In 18 Cyc. 80, it is said: "A person nominated as an executor cannot be compelled to act as such, but the office may be accepted or refused at discretion, although one should refuse entirely or not at all."

It has been held in some jurisdictions that the right of renouncement is available only in the tribunal of the testator's domicile, and that after a person has qualified as executor in that tribunal his resignation in an ancillary jurisdiction is absolutely void. [Ross v. Barclay, 18 Pa. St. 179. See, also, Slaughter v. Garland, 40 Miss. 172; Wilson v. Cox, 49 Miss. l. c. 542; Lindsley v. Patterson, 177 S. W. l. c. 833.] This, as well as the proposition that when there is a resignation in the domiciliary jurisdiction it applies to ancillary rights, seems entirely sound. The principal administration of an estate must take place in the jurisdiction of the deceased's domicile, and to this all ancillary administration is subordinate and subservient. [18 Cyc. 67; In re Estate of Gable, 79 Iowa, 178; Spraddling & Keeton v. Pipkin, 15 Mo. l. c. 134.] The tribunal there has the exclusive power to admit the will to probate, and the right to issue letters testamentary or to receive resignations and renouncements is an incident to that jurisdiction; and when there made should operate automatically as a renouncement in all ancillary jurisdictions. We so hold.

For the reasons heretofore assigned the judgment is reversed with directions to quash the peremptory writ of mandamus. *Faris, P. J.,* and *Walker, J.,* concur.

LOUIS BERNERO, An Infant, by His Curatrix, LO-
RAINE T. BERNERO, Appellant, v. THERESA
L. GOODWIN et al.

Division Two, March 31, 1916.

1. **ADOPTED CHILD: Right of Heirs to Inherit.** If an adopted
   child dies during the life of its adopting parent, leaving children, such children inherit as grandchildren upon the death of
   such adopting parent intestate.

2. ———: ———: **Statute.** Section 1671, Revised Statutes
   1909, providing that a person may, by deed, "adopt any child
   or children as his or her heir," by the use of the word "heir,"
   and section 332, providing that the estate of an intestate shall
   descend "to his children, *or their descendants*," mean that the
   child of an adopted child who dies during the lifetime of the
   adopting parent, inherits from such adopting parent dying intestate. An adopted child is a child within the meaning of the
   descent laws, and the words in section 332 mean the same as
   if they had read that the estate shall descend "to his children
   (either natural-born or adopted), or their descendants."

3. ———: ———: **How Determined.** The rights of the natural child of the adopted child to claim a distributive share in
   the estate of the adopting parent is not limited solely to the
   adoption statutes and the deed of adoption, to the exclusion
   of all rights given by the statutes of descents, but those statutes lay down the general rules of inheritance, and the deed
   of adoption created the status of the adopted child, or gave to
   him the status of an heir.

Appeal from St. Louis City Circuit Court.—*Hon. Hugo
Muench*, Judge.

Reversed and remanded.

*Thomas D. Cannon, Moses N. Sale, D. Goldsmith,
E. P. McCarthy* and *John A. Burke* for appellant.

(1) The legal status of the child of an adopted
child is that of grandchild to the adoptive parent. R.
S. 1909, secs. 332, 1671, 1672, 1673; Healey v. Simpson,
113 Mo. 340; Gray v. Holmes, 57 Kan. 217; Power v.

Hafley, 85 Ky. 671; Pace v. Klink, 51 Ga. 220; In re
Estate of Walworth, 85 Vt. 322; In re Winchester's Estate, 140 Cal. 468; Harle v. Harle, 166 S. W. (Tex.)
676; Fiske v. Lawton, 124 Minn. 85; Vidal v. Com-
magere, 13 La. Ann. 516; Note to 118 Am. St. 688;
Humphries v. Davis, 100 Ind. 274; Gilliam v. Trust Co.,
186 N. Y. 127; 1 Corpus Juris, 1367, p. 1401; 1 R. C.
L. 613.   (2) The legal status in this State of an
adopted child is the same as that of a child born in
lawful wedlock with respect to the statute of descent
and distribution. R. S. 1909, secs. 332, 1671, 1672, 1673;
Fosburg v. Rogers, 114 Mo. 122; Moran v. Stewart,
122 Mo. 299; In re Estate of Moran, 151 Mo. 557;
Thomas v. Maloney, 142 Mo. App. 198; Horton v. Troll,
183 Mo. App. 693.   (3) The law places no limit upon
the age of the child adopted. The child adopted may be
over the age of twenty-one years. In re Estate of
Moran, 151 Mo. 557.

McShane & Goodwin and *Stewart, Bryan & Williams* for respondents; *John M. Goodwin* and *George
H. Williams* on brief.

(1) Where one inherits a share in an estate which
his deceased parent would have inherited, he inherits
not from the latter, but directly from the intestate.
Barnum v. Barnum, 119 Mo. 67; Records v. Fields, 155
Mo. 325; Heady v. Crouse, 203 Mo. 119; Wattenbarger
v. Payne, 162 Mo. App. 436; Hockaday v. Lynn, 200
Mo. 470.   (2) Sec. 332, R. S. 1909, does the same thing
for the grandchildren of an intestate that section 546
does for the grandchildren of a testate; the latter
makes the child of a deceased parent an original legatee of the grandfather, and the former makes him an
heir, taking in his own right directly from the intestate
by virtue of their propinquity of blood. Wattenbarger
v. Payne, 162 Mo. App. 434; Hockaday v. Lynn, 200
Mo. 470.   (3) The right of inheritance is purely statu-

tory, and he who claims a share in the inheritance must point to the law which transmits it to him. Goldstein v. Hammell, 236 Pa. St. 309; Wattenbarger v. Payne, 162 Mo. App. 440. (4) The statutes of adoption being in derogation of the common law are strictly construed as against the adopted child. Hockaday v. Lynn, 200 Mo. 464; Reinders v. Koppelmann, 68 Mo. 482; Clarkson v. Hatton, 143 Mo. 58; Sarazin v. Railroad, 153 Mo. 485; Beach v. Bryan, 155 Mo. App. 50; Furguson v. Jones, 17 Ore. 204; Baker v. Clowser, 43 L. R. A. (N. S.) 1056; Thomas v. Maloney, 142 Mo. App. 197; Van Der Lyn v. Mack, 137 Mich. 146; Phillips v. McConica, 59 Ohio St. 9. (5) Consanguinity is so fundamental in statutes of descent and distribution that it should only be ignored by construction when courts are forced so to do either by terms of express statute or by inexorable implication. (6) The general statutes of inheritance are modified and set aside by statutes regulating the effect of adoption, only so far as there is some specific provision in the statutes of adoption inconsistent with the application in such cases of the general inheritance statutes. Like an invading force upon a hostile domain, the adoption law prevails only so far as its lines extend. Beyond those limits all remains under the original control. Baker v. Clowser, 43 L. R. A. (N. S.) 1056; In re Jobson, 164 Cal. 312, 43 L. R. A. (N. S.) 1065; Reinders v. Koppelmann, 68 Mo. 482; Clarkson v. Hatton, 143 Mo. 47. (7) The Missouri statute of adoption is silent as to the children of adopted children. Laws 1856-7, p. 59, secs. 1-4; G. S. 1865, p. 478, secs. 1-4; R. S. 1879, secs. 599-602; R. S. 1889; secs. 968-971; R. S. 1899, secs. 5246-5249; R. S. 1909, secs. 1671-1674; Reinders v. Koppelmann, 68 Mo. 496; Beach v. Bryan, 155 Mo. App. 53. (8) Where the statute is silent, since nothing can be supplied except by inexorable implication, the right of inheritance must be determined by the statutes of descent and distribution

and against the children of the deceased adopted child.
Phillip's Estate, 17 Pa. Sup. Ct. 103; Goldstein v.
Hammell, 236 Pa. St. 305; Reinders v. Koppelmann,
68 Mo. 482; Hockaday v. Lynn, 200 Mo. 456; Clarkson v. Hatton, 143 Mo. 47; Van Der Lyn v. Mack, 137
Mich. 146; Phillips v. McConica, 59 Ohio St. 9.   (9)
The adopted child is let into inheritance only for the
purpose of preserving in full its right of inheritance
from its adopting parent; and the door to inheritance
is shut and its bolt shot at that precise point. Hockaday v. Lynn, 200 Mo. 468; Phillip's Estate, 17 Pa.
Super. Ct. 103.   (10) There is no shooting of bolts as
to "kindred" or "relatives by blood" under the statutes of descent and distribution; under those statutes
all property of an intestate "shall descend and be distributed to his kindred without end." R. S. 1909, sec.
332.   (11) By the act of adoption the child is entitled
to inherit from his adoptive parent as his heir in the
degree of a child. Hockaday v. Lynn, 200 Mo. 465.
(12) The act of adoption creates a contractual relation
between the adopter and adoptive. Reinders v. Koppelmann, 94 Mo. 344; Clarkson v. Hatton, 143 Mo. 58;
Hockaday v. Lynn, 200 Mo. 473.   (13) And this contractual relation is purely personal to the foster-parent
and the child. Helms v. Elliott, 89 Tenn. 446; Merritt
v. Morton, 136 S. W. (Ky.) 429; Kettel v. Baxter, 100
N. Y. Supp. 529; Lawson on Contracts, sec. 115.   (14)
The laws of Missouri recognize two classes of persons
to whom rights of inheritance go: (1) Those who are
designated as heirs by our statutes of descent and distribution called "heirs at law," "heirs by law" or
"right heirs;" (2) those who take as an heir by contract of adoption called "heirs by contract." Both
classes are separate and distinct, and heirs by contract
of adoption do not partake of any of the rights or at-
tributes of heirs at law, unless the statute authorizing
such contracts and the contract itself gives such right.

Reinders v. Koppelmann, 68 Mo. 482, 94 Mo. 338; Clarkson v. Hatton, 143 Mo. 47; Hockaday v. Lynn, 200 Mo. 456. (15) The adopted child, by the event of the adoption, has itself *ex contractu* the right of inheritance from its adoptive parent, and nothing more. Hockaday v. Lynn, 200 Mo. 473; Thomas v. Maloney, 142 Mo. App. 198.

WILLIAMS, C.—This is a suit to contest the validity of what purports to be the last will and testament of Theresa Bernero, deceased, on the ground of undue influence and unsoundness of mind. The proceeding was instituted in the circuit court of the city of St. Louis. Some of the defendants filed a pleading in the nature of a plea in abatement, which alleged that plaintiff would have no interest in the estate of deceased in the event there had been no will and, therefore, he did not have such an interest as to entitle him to bring the suit. Trial was had by the court which resulted in a judgment finding that plaintiff did not have such an interest in the estate as would entitle him to maintain the action to contest the will. The plaintiff thereupon duly perfected an appeal to this court.

The facts are undisputed and may be stated, substantially, as follows:

Louis Bernero, Sr., and Theresa Bernero (the alleged testatrix) were husband and wife. The husband died in August, 1904. On April 10, 1905, said Theresa Bernero, by deed of adoption, executed and acknowledged as provided by the statutes, adopted Emanuel C. Bernero as her child and heir. The deed of adoption recites that said Theresa and her husband, in 1880, while in Italy, agreed with the parents of said Emanuel to adopt him and brought him home with them to the city of St. Louis, where he lived with them as their child and as a member of the family, but no deed of adoption was ever recorded as required by the statutes. The deed of adoption further recites that it was made so as to comply with said statutes.

At the time of the deed of adoption, Emanuel Bernero, the adopted child, was twenty-eight years of age. On November 30, 1904, said Emanuel Bernero, the adopted son, married Loraine Thompson, now Loraine T. Bernero, appearing as the curatrix of the plaintiff infant in this suit. There was born of this marriage, on October 14, 1905, Louis Bernero, plaintiff in this case. Emanuel Bernero, the natural father of plaintiff, died in April, 1910, leaving surviving him his widow and his son Louis Bernero, the plaintiff. On July 15, 1911, said Theresa Bernero (alleged testatrix) died in the city of St. Louis. It does not appear that she left any natural children or their descendants surviving her, but that she left surviving her two sisters. After her death, her alleged will, dated June 25, 1910, was admitted to probate by the probate court of the city of St. Louis. The present plaintiff was made beneficiary under the will in the sum of ten thousand dollars. The remainder of her property was left to several different legatees and devisees.

The condensed facts, therefore, appearing from the record, necessary to a determination of the question here raised, are that an adopted child died during the life of his adopting parent and left surviving him a natural child (the plaintiff herein), and, thereafter, the adopting parent died, leaving a will. Plaintiff brings this suit to contest the validity of the will. Defendants raise the issue that plaintiff could not inherit from the adopting parent in the event she died intestate, and that, therefore, plaintiff had not such an interest as would permit him to contest the will. Plaintiff contends that he inherits from the adopting parent of his natural father the same as if his father had been the natural child of the adopting parent.

The question now presented for our review is whether or not the natural child of an **Rights of Heir of Adopted Child.** adopted child shall share in the distribution of the estate of the adopting parent dying intestate, the adopted child having predeceased the adopting parent.

This identical question has never been before the court for determination.

After a careful consideration of the question, we have reached the conclusion that the question should be answered in the affirmative.

The rule, here applicable, and supported by the great weight of authority, is stated in 1 R. C. L. 614, as follows:

"If an adopted child dies during the life of its adopting parent, leaving children, such children are for most, if not for all, purposes regarded as natural grandchildren of the adopting parent, and are entitled to represent their parent and to receive from the estate of his adopting parent what he would have been entitled to receive had he lived until after such parent's death."

To the same effect and directly in point are the following authorities: Gray v. Holmes, 57 Kan. 217; Power v. Hafley, 85 Ky. 671; Pace v. Klink, 51 Ga. 220; In re George Walworth's Estate, 85 Vt. 322; In re Estate of Winchester, 140 Cal. 468; In re Webb's Estate, 95 Atl. 419 (Pennsylvania Supreme Court, not yet officially reported); 1 Corpus Juris, 1402, sec. 137.

It appears that in the majority of the foregoing authorities, the principal argument or reason given in favor of the holdings is that since adoption was a creature of the civil law and unknown to the common law, the courts would look to the civil law for aid in construing the respective statutes; that under the civil law the children of an adopted child stood in the position of grandchildren of the adopting parent.

In the case of In re Webb's Estate, supra, the reason given in support of the holding was that the word "heir" used in the adoption statute of Pennsylvania, *"ex vi termini,* implies representation" and that, therefore, upon the death of an adopted child her children succeeded to her rights as heir of the adopting parent. Respondent attacks the correctness of the reasoning given as a justification for the holdings in some of the above entitled cases.

Without here undertaking to determine whether the respective reasons given in the authorities cited would be sufficient to sustain a like result in the present case, we will state that we think a sufficient reason can be given in justification of the conclusion reached in the present case without calling to our aid the precepts of the civil law or without relying upon the implication of representation springing from the word "heir" as discussed in the Pennsylvania case.

We have reached the conclusion that, in this State, the natural child of an adopted child (the adopted child having predeceased the adopting parent), inherits from the adopting parent for the following reasons:

Section 1671, Revised Statutes 1909, provides that a person may, by deed, "adopt any child or children as his or her *heir,"* etc. The deed of adoption in the present case was in compliance with that statute. Section 332, Revised Statutes 1909, being one of the statutes of descent of the estate of an intestate, provides, among other things, that the estate "shall descend and be distributed in parcenary to his kindred, male and female, subject to the payment of his debts and the widow's dower, in the following course: First, to his children, *or their descendants,* in equal parts."

It has been held by this court that an adopted child was a child within the meaning of the above quoted statute on descents. [Fosburgh v. Rogers, 114 Mo. 122, l. c. 133.] And also that an adopted child is a child within the meaning of other sections of the descent laws. [Moran v. Stewart, 122 Mo. 295, l. c. 299.] The above mentioned portion of the statutes on descent as construed, therefore, means the same as if it read: "First, to his children (either natural-born or adopted) or their descendants in equal parts."

Since Emanuel C. Bernero (the adopted child) was the inheriting child of Theresa Bernero (the adopting parent) within the meaning of the foregoing statute of descent, and since Louis Bernero, appellant here, was the blood child and, therefore, unquestionably the descendant of said Emanuel, deceased, we think it inevitably follows that, *under the statute of descent,* Louis is entitled to the said distributive share in said estate in the event said Theresa died intestate.

As we have gathered it, from the briefs and oral argument, respondent's main contention is that the appellant, the blood child of the adopted child, must receive its rights to a distributive share, if any, solely under the deed of adoption executed by his natural father and the adopting parent, and that since the adoption statute makes no provision for the descendants of the adopted child, and since the rights created by the deed of adoption are personal between the contracting parties and not such as extend to other parties, the appellant can receive no share in the estate of the adopting parent. The error of the above position, as it appears to us, is in assuming that the rights of appellant to claim a distributive share in the estate is limited solely to the adoption laws and deed of adoption, to the exclusion of all rights given by the statute on descents.

It was pointed out in the case of Fosburgh v. Rogers, supra, that the statute of descents merely laid down the general rules of inheritance, but did not undertake to accurately define "how the status is to be created which gives the capacity to inherit" (Id. l. c. 133), and that this status might be created elsewhere, as for example, by compliance with the adoption law or the law providing a way for making illegitimate children legitimate. In the present case, appellant, the natural child of the adopted child, does not, in a proper sense, take under the deed of adoption. The deed of adoption created the status of an inheriting child in appellant's father, and the right of appellant to represent his father is given him by the statute of descents, by use of the words, "or their descendants."

So, as in the first instance, it is not necessary to refer to the civil law to ascertain whether an adopted child, in Missouri, is thereby given the right to be an heir—this because the Missouri adoption statute expressly says he is an heir, neither is it necessary, in the second instance, to look to the implication of representation arising from the use of the word "heir" in the adoption statute—this because the statute of descent takes hold of the matter when once the status of an inheriting child is given the adopted child and provides for representation or succession by use of the words "or their descendants."

The fact that the courts of other States have reached the same conclusion as herein reached, but by a different process of reasoning, but strengthens the soundness of the result herein reached. An examination of the adoption laws of the different States cited above, where the question has been discussed, discloses that the rights of an adopted child to inherit from the adopting parent in those States, so far as they affect the point now discussed, are the same, in effect, as the rights of inheritance given the adopted child in Missouri. In none of those States, as well as in Missouri, does either the adoption statutes or the descent statutes expressly say that the natural child of an adopted child inherits from the adopting parent, but in each case cited the same result has been reached as we have reached in the present case.

We do not consider that anything herein decided conflicts in any manner with the ruling in Hockaday v. Lynn, 200 Mo. 456, which held that the adopted child does not inherit from the collateral kindred of the adopting parent.

The judgment is reversed and the cause remanded. *Roy, C.,* concurs.

PER CURIAM.—The foregoing opinion by WIL-LIAMS, C., is adopted as the opinion of the court. All the judges concur.

THE STATE v. CHARLES E. McWILLIAMS.

Division Two, March 31, 1916.

1. **INFORMATION: Sufficiency: Embezzlement.** Where the statute sets out the specific facts constituting the crime, as does Sec. 4550, R. S. 1909, concerning embezzlement, an information based thereon which is definitively descriptive of the offense as defined therein, is sufficient.

2. ——: ——: ——: **Intent.** Where the embezzlement consists of doing the act itself, that is, where it consists of the fraudulent conversion of money by one to whom it has been intrusted, the information need not allege the intent with which the act was done, since the criminal intent will be inferred from the fraudulent conversion.

3. ——: **Former Jeopardy: Based on Assumption.** A defendant cannot be put in peril by being placed upon his trial under an invalid amended information upon the assumption that a valid information was then pending undisposed of. To constitute former jeopardy there must have been a valid information or indictment charging the same offense, and in a proceeding under that valid information or indictment a jury must have been impaneled and sworn for defendant's trial.

4. ———: ———: **Amended Information: Quashed: Former Restored.** An information, in one count, charging defendant with embezzlement, was filed in one county, and after the case was transferred to another county the prosecuting attorney of the first filed an amended information in two counts, the first charging embezzlement of money, and the second embezzlement of a check, and a jury was impaneled and sworn and the trial proceeded, but before a verdict was rendered the court, of its own motion, quashed the amended information and ordered defendant to be held for trial under the original information. *Held*, that by being put upon his trial on the amended information defendant was not, because of its invalidity, put in jeopardy under the original valid information.

5. **CONTINUANCE: Contradictory and Insincere Application.** An application for a continuance, which is inconsistent, contradictory, does not import the truth as to defendant's knowledge of what the absent witness would testify and does not show reasonable diligence, should be denied.

6. ———: **Diligence: Deposition.** Where the application states that the defendant had sent to the absent witness money with which to pay her traveling expenses from another State to the place of trial and that she had agreed to attend, the trial court would be justified in granting a continuance, if the allegation therein of defendant's recent knowledge of what her testimony would be bears the impress of truth; but if the facts reveal that he did know what her testimony would be, then proper diligence required him to take her deposition, and having failed to do that the trial court did not abuse its discretion in denying the application.

7. **EMBEZZLEMENT: Agency of Loan Agent.** Where the borrower called at defendant's office to employ him to secure a loan of $3400, and gave him a note for $127.50 for his services in that behalf, and in addition signed an order directed to the loan company in which he requested that the proceeds of the loan be paid to defendant and in which he said he thereby appointed defendant his agent to settle with the company for said loan, and the loan company, after deducting its own commission, sent a check payable to defendant for the balance, the defendant was the agent of the borrower, in all that was necessary to establish the relation of agency, in a prosecution for having embezzled the proceeds of the check.

8. ———: ———: **Circumstances.** Circumstances arising out of a transaction, even in establishing the fact that defendant, charged with embezzlement, was the borrower's agent, are sometimes as strong in probative force as sworn testimony.

9. ———: **Ownership of Check.** Where the loan company contracted to loan $3400 to a farmer, to be evidenced by his note,

which was to be secured by a deed of trust on his land, and upon the receipt of the note and deed of trust executed by him caused the deed of trust to be recorded, and forwarded a check for the amount of the note less commission, payable to defendant, the agent who had negotiated the loan, the company parted with the title to the check, and the nominal ownership passed to defendant; and it thereafter became his duty to either indorse it to the farmer, or convert it into cash and pay the proceeds to him, or apply it to the discharge of a prior lien for which the money had been borrowed; but as it was indorsed and placed to defendant's credit in the bank, his act became embezzlement of the money when he drew it out and without the farmer's consent converted it to his own use.

10. ———: **Felonious Intent: Concealment.** A defendant's felonious intent, in a charge of embezzling his principal's money, is to be measured by his acts; and it may be shown by his evasion of his principal, a concealment from him of the fact that he has received the money, and a neglect or refusal to account for it.

11. ———: ———: **Use of Money.** Where defendant is charged with embezzling money, in that he as the agent of a farmer undertook to borrow for him a sum of money to be used in paying off a farm mortgage, and when the check for the loan was sent to him it was deposited to his own credit in a bank and drawn out for his own personal uses, it is not error to permit an officer of the loan company to testify that defendant had not used the money in paying off the prior lien on the land, nor returned it to the company.

12. ———: ———: **Depositing Check.** Nor under such circumstances is it error to permit the State to show that the check payable to defendant's order and received by him was indorsed and deposited to his credit in a bank, and later checked out by him.

13. ———: ———: **Other Loans.** Where the defendant was the agent of the borrower in a particular case and was authorized to receive the proceeds of the loan from a certain company, whatever relationship he may have sustained to that company in previous or subsequent like transactions can have no bearing upon the issue of whether he embezzled the money received by him in that case.

Appeal from Daviess Circuit Court.—*Hon. Fred Lamb,* Judge.

AFFIRMED.

W. S. Herndon, R. H. Musser, John Leopard and *Paul D. Kitt* for appellant.

(1) The court erred in overruling defendant's motion to quash the information. The information did not contain an essential element 'of the offense, viz., the intent. This information is based on the first subdivision of Sec. 4550, R. S. 1909. State v. Lentz, 184 Mo. 234; 15 Cyc. 491. When the intent with which an act is done is a necessary ingredient of the offense it must be alleged in the information. Kelley's Criminal Law & Practice (3 Ed.), sec. 199; State v. Haney, 130 Mo. App. 95; State v. Dowd, 95 Mo. 163; State v. McCollum, 44 Mo. 345; State v. Burke, 151 Mo. 136; 22 Cyc. 329; 15 Cyc. 513. (2) The court erred in overruling the demurrer to the evidence offered by defendant at the close of the State's evidence, and in overruling the demurrer offered by defendant at the close of all the evidence, and in refusing to give instruction number 1 requested by defendant, because: (a) In order to constitute embezzlement, as agent, as charged in the information, the accused must occupy the designated fiduciary relation and the money or property must belong to his principal, the one designated and named in the information, and come to the possession of the defendant by virtue of that relation. State v. Brown, 171 Mo. 480; Griffen v. State, 4 Tex. App. 390; State v. Myers, 68 Mo. 266; State v. Dodson, 72 Mo. 283; State v. Moreaux, 254 Mo. 406; Ex Parte Hedley, 31 Cal. 108. Appellant was not the agent, clerk, collector and servant of Gregor and did not receive this check or money as agent, etc., of Gregor; nor did the check or money come to him by virtue of his relation, if any, to Gregor, nor in the course of his employment, if any, by Gregor; it came to defendant by virtue of defendant's relation to Bartlett Brothers Land & Loan Company and as that company's agent or bailee. Day v.

Dages, 46 N. E. 589; Jensen v. Investment Co., 53 N.
W. 179; Figley v. Bradshaw, 53 N. W. 148; McLean v.
Ficke, 62 N. W. 753; Ins. Co. v. Jones, 27 Pac. 807;
Gibson v. Davenport, 29 Ohio St. 309; Stockton v. Watson, 101 Fed. 490; Bowman v. Lickey, 86 Mo. App. 47;
Savings Fund Society v. Bank, 36 Pa. St. 498, 78 Am.
Dec. 390; Insurance Company v. Ives, 56 Ill. 402. The
check or money in question did not belong to Gregor
but belonged to Bartlett Brothers Land & Loan Company, or someone whom they represented; it had not
been turned over unconditionally as Gregor's money;
the title to the check and money still remained in Bartlett Brothers Land & Loan Company. State v. Cooper,
71 N. W. 197; Bowman v. Lickey, 86 Mo. App. 47; Guthrie v. Waite, 129 Mo. App. 587; Plow Co. v. Porter,
82 Mo. 23. (b) The check or money was not received
by defendant as agent, clerk, collector or servant of
Gregor, but it was received by him, as agent of Bartlett
Brothers Land & Loan Company, or a bailee or trustee
for a certain purpose, viz.: to apply as payment on the
mortgage on Gregor's farm. State v. Castleton, 255
Mo. 201; State v. Myers, 68 Mo. 266; State v. Betz,
207 Mo. 589; 3 Ruling Case Law, sec. 2, p. 72; Sec. 4552,
R. S. 1909. A bailment is defined to be a delivery of a
thing in trust for some special object or purpose, and
upon a contract, express or implied, to conform to the
object or purpose of the trust. Watson v. State, 70
Ala. 13, 45 Am. Rep. 70; Story on Bailments (9 Ed.),
sec. 2; 5 Cyc. 161-170; Railroad v. Railroad, 61 N. J.
L. 287; 3 Am. & Eng. Ency. Law, 733; Knapp v.
Knapp, 118 Mo. App. 685; Guthrie v. Waite, 129 Mo.
App. 587. (c) If defendant was guilty of the offense
of embezzlement it was not of money, but of the check
sent him by Bartlett Brothers Land & Loan Company;
if guilty of embezzlement at all he was guilty of wrongful conversion the moment he cashed the check and
placed the money to his credit; this was contrary to

his instructions. State v. Castleton, 255 Mo. 210; State v. Schilb, 159 Mo. 142; State v. Mispagle, 207 Mo. 574; Sansberry v. State, 59 So. 340; State v. Crosswhite, 130 Mo. 355; State v. Salmon, 216 Mo. 522; Spaulding v. People, 172 Ill. 55; 2 Bishop's New Criminal Law, secs. 372-373-379. (3) The court erred in refusing to sustain the defendant's plea in bar and of former jeopardy. The State having admitted the facts stated in the plea in bar, to be true, it then became a question of law, on the facts stated, and was equivalent to a demurrer to the plea. State v. Anderson, 186 Mo. 25; State v. Wiseback, 139 Mo. 214. The facts set forth in the plea in bar, show that the defendant was in jeopardy, and that the plea should have been sustained. Article 5, Amendments Constitution United States; Cooley Const. Lim. (6 Ed.), 399; Secs. 22, 23, 28 and 30, article 2, Constitution Missouri; State v. Snyder, 98 Mo. 555; State v. Hays, 78 Mo. 605; State v. Webster, 206 Mo. 558; State v. Keating, 223 Mo. 86; State v. Wiseback, 139 Mo. 214. The act of the court in discharging the jury must be treated as an acquittal of the defendant. 12 Cyc. 261-270, and cases cited in Notes 85-86 and 87, p. 270; Kelley's Criminal Law and Practice (3 Ed.), sec. 229; State v. Webster, 206 Mo. 558; Cooley on Constitutional Limitations (7 Ed.), 467; State v. Webster, 206 Mo. 558. The court erred in overruling defendant's application for a continuance.

John T. Barker, Attorney-General, and *Shrader P. Howell*, Assistant Attorney-General, for the State.

(1) The information in this case is in an approved form and is sufficient in all respects. Sec. 4550, R. S. 1909; Kelley's Crim. L. & Pr., sec. 675; State v. Adams, 108 Mo. 211; State v. Mohr, 68 Mo. 303; State v. Lipscomb, 160 Mo. 131; State v. Shour, 196 Mo. 205. In charging the completed offense of embezzlement it is

unnecessary to further allege that such act was committed with the intent to deprive the owner of the property so converted. State v. Larew, 191 Mo. 199; State v. Cunningham, 154 Mo. 179; State v. Lentz, 184 Mo. 237; State v. Silva, 130 Mo. 463; State v. Martin, 230 Mo. 690; State v. Adams, 108 Mo. 214. (2) The plea of twice in jeopardy will not avail where the former trial was based upon an invalid information. State v. Keating, 223 Mo. 94; State v. Manning, 168 Mo. 429; State v. Owen, 78 Mo. 374; State v. Wilson, 39 Mo. App. 187; State v. Buente, 256 Mo. 241; Kelley's Crim. L. & Pr., sec. 229. In this case the trial had on the amended information was a nullity for the reason that the prosecuting attorney of Livingston County was without authority to file an amended information in the circuit court of Daviess County. State v. Bartlett, 170 Mo. 672; State v. Vinso, 171 Mo. 585; State v. Billings, 140 Mo. 204; State v. Blunt, 110 Mo. 337. Upon the quashing of the amended information the valid original information resumed its full force and effect. Sec. 5102, R. S. 1909; State v. Mayer, 209 Mo. 396; State v. Melvin, 166 Mo. 572; State v. Anderson, 96 Mo. 245; State v. Williams, 191 Mo. 212; State v. Vincent, 91 Mo. 665. (3) This court will not interfere with the finding of the trial court where the record on appeal shows substantial evidence to support the verdict returned. State v. Concelia, 250 Mo. 424. Under the facts of this case it is manifest that the defendant was constituted and recognized by all parties concerned as the agent of the borrower as charged in the information. May v. Ins. Co., 72 Mo. App. 290; Robinson v. Jarvis, 25 Mo. App. 427; County v. Goggin, 105 Mo. 191; Robinson v. Kreisel, 187 Mo. App. 55; Mortgage Co. v. People, 102 Ala. 245; Mortgage Co. v. King, 105 Ala. 392; Cooper v. Headley, 12 N. J. Eq. 48; Johnson v. Shattuck, 67 Ark. 159; Thomas v. Demsey, 57 Iowa, 58; Engleman v. Reuse, 61 Mich. 395.

The testimony submitted on the trial was amply sufficient to show that the defendant converted and embezzled the money as charged. State v. Wissing, 187 Mo. 106; State v. Laughlin, 180 Mo. 361; State v. Martin, 230 Mo. 697.

WALKER, J.—In November, 1913, appellant was charged in an information filed in the circuit court of Livingston County with embezzlement, under section 4550, Revised Statutes 1909. Upon a trial in the circuit court of Daviess County, to which the case had been transferred by change of venue, appellant was convicted and sentenced to four years' imprisonment in the penitentiary. The original information was in one count. Appellant moved to quash same on the general ground that it did not state facts sufficient to constitute a cause of action. This motion was by the court overruled. After the case had been transferred to the circuit court of Daviess County, in June, 1914, the prosecuting attorney of Livingston County filed in the circuit court of Daviess County an amended information charging the appellant with the same offense as in the original, but in two counts, one for the embezzlement of money and the other for the embezzlement of a check. On the day said amended information was filed, the appellant announcing ready for trial, a jury was sworn and impaneled and the trial proceeded, but before a verdict was rendered the court, on its own motion, stopped the proceedings and quashed the amended information and ordered that the appellant be held for trial on the original information. Thereafter, on December 10, 1914, appellant filed a plea in bar on the ground that having been put upon his trial on the amended information and a jury having been impaneled and sworn to try him, he had been put in jeopardy and hence should not again be required to answer for the same offense. This plea was overruled. Appellant then filed an application for a continuance on the ground of the absence from the State of a stenographer who had formerly been in his employ, alleging that said witness, if present would testify that Greger had told appellant to use the money he had obtained from Bartlett Bros. until the second loan was obtained and pay him (Greger) interest on same. This motion was overruled, and appellant waived formal arraignment, entered a plea of not guilty and a jury was impaneled and sworn to try the cause. The trial progressed and on December 12, 1914, the jury returned a verdict finding the appellant guilty as stated, and from this judgment he appeals.

In the spring of 1913 Charles E. Greger owned a farm in Livingston County burdened with two deeds of trust, one for $3000 and the other for $1600. Both were held by Frank B. Caesar. The notes secured by these deeds of trust becoming due, the owner desired their payment. The appellant at the time was in the real estate and loan business in Chillicothe, and Greger approached him for the purpose of securing a loan to enable him to take up these notes and release his farm from the deeds of trust. The first conversation in regard thereto between appellant and Greger was in the latter part of March, 1913, and as a result of same Greger filled out, at appellant's direction, an application to Bartlett Bros. of St. Joseph for a loan of $3600. After some correspondence between Bartlett Bros. and the appellant, the former agreed to make the loan to the amount of $3400 on the Greger land, and on April 14, 1913, a note and deed of trust were executed by Greger to Bartlett Bros. for that amount and same were delivered to appellant to be forwarded to Bartlett Bros.; at the same time another note and deed of trust were executed for the sum of $1400, which sum of money was to be obtained from a source other than Bartlett Bros. When it had been ascertained that the money could be obtained from Bartlett Bros., Greger made and delivered to the appellant, at the latter's request and direction, the following paper: "Utica, Mo., April 1, 1913. Bartlett Bros. Land and Loan Company, St. Joseph, Mo. Gentlemen: Please pay to Charles E. McWilliams or order the proceeds of my loan of $3400 negotiated by you for me. I hereby appoint said Charles E. McWilliams my agent to settle with you in full for said loan. Charles E. Greger."

On the completion of the abstract of title of the Greger land and its examination and approval by Bartlett Bros., on June 14, 1913, they forwarded to appellant their check, payable to him, for $3298, being the proceeds of the $3400 which they had agreed to loan Greger, less the commission. A few days prior to the forwarding of this check appellant had written Bartlett Bros. that he had completed the arrangements for the second loan, but it is further shown by the evidence that this had not been done, and that the second deed of trust was never recorded, nor was the note representing it ever negotiated. The check for $3298 sent by Bartlett Bros. to appellant was indorsed by a stenographer in his office and placed to his credit in the Peoples Savings Bank of Chillicothe. None of this money was ever paid to Greger, but all of it was checked out, either by the appellant or persons in his office authorized to check on his account, and in November preceding the trial the entire amount had been thus withdrawn from the bank, leaving only a balance of ninety-four cents. Nor was any of the proceeds of this check ever paid to Caesar, the owner of the two deeds of trust. Appellant never at any time disclosed to Greger that he had received the $3298 or any other amount of money from Bartlett Bros. by reason of the execution of the note for $3400 and deed of trust by Greger to said Bartlett Bros. to secure same. Upon the consummation of this loan by the delivery made by appellant to Bartlett Bros. of the note and deed of

trust for $3400 they at once placed the deed of trust
upon record. Greger made frequent visits to appellant's office in Chillicothe after he had delivered the
note and deed of trust to him, in an effort to ascertain,
whether he had received the money, but could not find
him, although these visits were repeated at intervals
from July, 1914, to the day of the trial, December 10,
1914. He says that during this time he was in California for his health. Appellant, on the witness stand,
testified that a few days after the receipt of the money
from Bartlett Bros. he told Greger the money had been
received, but that he had not yet been able to negotiate
the second loan for $1400. At that time appellant says
Greger suggested that he would see the owner of the
notes secured by deed of trust and endeavor to induce
him to take the second loan. In the meantime appellant says he talked to Caesar and tried to get him to
take the $3298 which had been received from Bartlett
Bros. and apply it on the two notes aggregating $4600,
but that Caesar had refused so to do. Appellant could
not remember that Greger had ever given him a note
in payment for his services in securing the loan.
Shown a letter that he had addressed to Bartlett Bros.
on June 13, 1914, in which he said, "We have been
ready for a long time for our part of the deal and have
the papers for the second loan on record and are awaiting your money," he admitted that the statement therein made was not true, but said when he wrote the letter
he had the promise of the money to cover the second
loan for $1400, and had given directions to some one
in his office to have the deed of trust recorded and
thought it had been done. He further admitted that
the check received from Bartlett Bros. in the sum of
$3298 had been deposited to his credit in the Peoples
Savings Bank in Chillicothe and had been checked out,
either by himself or some one in his office. When asked
if it had been spent for his private benefit he answered

evasively but admitted that he had never paid the
money to Greger, his excuse being that no demand had
ever been made for it, that he had been gone several
months and had not seen Greger during that time, that
he had never paid the money to Bartlett Bros., and had
never given Greger a slip of paper or anything else
showing he had used it, and that this was his customary
way of transacting business of this character. Caesar,
who owned the first and second deeds of trust, denied
that appellant had ever offered to pay him the $3298
which had been received by, appellant from Bartlett
Bros. or any other sum, or that appellant had offered to
give him any additional security as an inducement for
him to take a second mortgage.

The charging part of the original information is as
follows:

"That Charles E. McWilliams on or about the 14th
day of June, A. D. 1913, at said county of Livingston
and State of Missouri, being then and there the agent
of a certain private person, to-wit—of one Charles E.
Greger, and the said Charles E. McWilliams, being
then and there, not a person under the age of sixteen
years, did then and there by virtue of his said employment as agent of the said Charles E. Greger, have,
receive and take into his possession and under his care
certain money to a large amount, to-wit, to the amount
of thirty-four hundred dollars, lawful money of the
United States and of the value of thirty-four hundred
dollars, of the property and moneys belonging to the
said Charles E. Greger, and the said Charles E. Mc-
Williams the same money then and there feloniously
did embezzle and fraudulently convert to his own use,
without the assent of his employer, the said Charles E.
Greger, the owner of said money; and the said Charles
E. McWilliams, the said money, in manner and form
aforesaid, feloniously did steal, take and carry away;
against the peace and dignity of the State."

I. The information charges a statutory embezzlement under section 4550, Revised Statutes 1909. Its sufficiency is assailed generally. The well-established rule in regard to charging an offense based on a statute is that where the statute sets out the **Information.** specific facts constituting the crime, an information or indictment based thereon which is definitely descriptive of the offense, as defined by the statute, will be held sufficient. [State v. Perrigin, 258 Mo. l. c. 236.] The necessary constituent elements of the offense are set forth in the statute in the instant case and hence the information which embodies its language is not subject to valid objection. [State v. Moreaux, 254 Mo. l. c. 405; State v. Blakemore, 226 Mo. l. c. 574.]

In addition to the general objection urged by appellant to the information, it is contended that it does not allege a criminal intent.

The statute upon which this charge is based creates two offenses: one consisting of the doing of the act itself, and the other of doing certain things in regard to the subject-matter with the intent to do the prohibited act. The information here is based upon the first offense denounced by the statute and charges the commission of the act itself and not the doing of something else with the intent to commit the act.

Embezzlement is the fraudulent conversion of another's property by one to whom it has been intrusted or into whose hands it has lawfully come; and when it has been embezzled or converted, within the meaning of the statute, it is not an improper inference that the act was intended by the perpetrator of same. While it is true that no one can be convicted of a felony in the absence of a criminal intent, such an intent in a case of embezzlement may be inferred from a felonious or fraudulent conversion and need not be alleged in the information or indictment. This ruling as to the sufficiency of a charge under the first class of offenses defined by the statute received the careful consideration of this court in State v. Lentz, 184 Mo. 223, in which it was held that it was not necessary to allege the intent with which the act charged was committed. This ruling was approved in State v. Larew, 191 Mo. l. c. 199.

II. Appellant interposes the plea of former jeopardy. This is not based upon the proceeding against him on the amended information, which he admits to have been a mere nullity, no other alternative remaining under our ruling in State v. Bartlett, 170 Mo. l. c. 672. But he contends that while put upon his trial in the first instance on the amended information he was, in law, by reason of its invalidity, put in jeopardy under the original information, it being the only valid charge against him.

Jeopardy.

The fallacy of this contention becomes apparent upon an analysis of same. It bases the plea of jeopardy upon an assumption and not upon a fact. A defendant cannot thus be put in peril within the meaning of the Constitution. [Art. 2, sec. 23, Constitution.] It will not suffice to assume that because appellant could not be injured by the invalid proceeding that he must perforce have cause of complaint because there was pending against him in the same case a valid charge which he was not then required to answer. If the appellant was only required at the time the amended information was preferred against him to answer the charge therein—and no further demand could the State then make—under what rule of reason or law can it be said that he was answerable under the original information? It is true that it formed the foundation for the prosecution and gave the circuit court of Daviess County derivative jurisdiction of the case upon the perfecting of the change of venue, but this did not give it power while simply lying in the files and undisposed of to operate as a charge against appellant because of the invalidity of the proceeding he was then being required to answer.

If the fallacy of appellant's contention be not sufficiently shown by the foregoing concrete reasons, let us see what light is thrown on the question by the authorities.

A rule well established here and elsewhere requires that before a plea of former jeopardy can be sustained these facts must be made to appear; that a valid charge either by indictment or information has theretofore been preferred against the accused in a court of competent jurisdiction charging him with the same offense of which he is on trial, and that in the former proceeding a legal jury was impaneled and sworn. [State v. Buente, 256 Mo. l. c. 239, and cases; State v. Keating, 223 Mo. l. c. 94; 12 Cyc. 261.] There are exceptions to this rule well stated in the Buente case, supra, p. 241, but not necessary to be considered here. Appellant was at no time before his arraignment and the trial which resulted in his conviction, required to answer, on a trial, a valid charge preferred against him. This is one of the essentials necessary under the rule stated. The amended information, as he admits, lacked the requisite of validity, for the reasons set forth in State v. Bartlett, supra. He was not arraigned upon or required to answer the original information when the proceeding of which he complains was pending against him, nor was a jury impaneled and sworn to try him on this charge. To hold, therefore, that it operated to his injury in the absence of these essentials would be in violation of precedent and contrary to reason.

No provision of our Bill of Rights was violated in the trial of appellant, nor was he entitled to be heard on the plea that the proceeding against him contravened the Fifth Amendment to the national Constitution; this, as has been repeatedly held, is applicable only to crimes against and trials under Federal laws. [Capital City Dairy Company v. Ohio, 183 U. S. 238; Thorington v. Montgomery, 147 U. S. 490; State v. Buente, supra; 12 Cyc. 259.] There is no merit in the plea in bar.

III. Appellant complains of the action of the trial court in refusing to grant him a continuance. The ap-

Continuance.
plication was properly refused. It is inconsistent, if not contradictory, in alleging that the appellant had conferred with the witness by correspondence, knew what her testimony would be and sent her money to enable her to attend the trial, while at the same time alleging that he had only learned what her testimony would be during the last few days preceding the making of the application. Further than this, the allegation as to appellant's recent knowledge of the witness's testimony does not savor of sincerity. If true it is contrary to all human experience. He was charged with a felony. She was his employee when he received the check from Bartlett Bros., the cash proceeds of which he subsequently embezzled. She, as his evidently trusted employee, deposited this check to his credit in the bank. On account of her relation to his business requiring her daily attention thereto and his alleged frequent conversations with Greger, he must have known of her presence when he had these conversations concerning which it is stated she will testify. This testimony if true was vital to his defense and she was his most important witness. Yet, according to his statement, he did not know what she would testify until a few days prior to the making of the application. In addition, therefore, to the application in this respect lacking the import of truth, it does not show such diligence as must reasonably be expected will be exercised by a man of ordinary

intelligence under like circumstances. [State v. Pagels, 92 Mo. l. c. 308.]

No intendments are to be taken in favor of applications of this character (State v. Good, 132 Mo. l. c. 129); from its express allegations the conclusion is reasonable that appellant knew not only what the testimony of this witness would be but her whereabouts in ample time between the date of the filing of the information and the trial to have enabled him to take her deposition.

If the allegation as to appellant's then recent knowledge of the witness's testimony bore the impress of truth, which it does not, then the trial court would have been justified in granting the application, in view of the statement that he had sent her money to defray her traveling expenses to the place of trial and that she had agreed to attend; but under the facts as we view them a proper exercise of diligence required him to take her deposition. This being true, the overruling of the application, which was addressed to the sound discretion of the trial court, was not unwisely or oppressively exercised and we refuse to interfere with same. [State v. Cain, 247 Mo. l. c. 705; State v. Crane, 202 Mo. l. c. 74; State v. Clark, 170 Mo. 207.]

IV. The uncontroverted facts show that appellant was the agent of the borrower (Greger) in securing this loan. Greger testified that on the day he called at appellant's office to employ him to secure the loan he gave appellant a note, payable to the latter, for $127.50 for his services in that behalf. Further than this, the order given by Greger to appellant on Bartlett Bros. (set forth in full in the statement of facts), which was to be delivered to the latter in the event the loan was secured, expressly declared appellant to be Greger's agent. Appellant does not deny either the execution of this note or the delivery to him of the order, but contents him-

Agency of Appellant.

self with a resort to a lack of memory in regard to the first and silence as to the second. Forgetfulness and evasion have never been regarded as indicative of truth.

If it be conceded that appellant was the agent of the loan company at the beginning of the transaction this does not militate against the conclusion, supported by the facts stated, that he was the agent of the borrower to negotiate the loan and apply the proceeds thereof as had been directed; but the credibility of appellant's testimony as to his agency for the loan company, at any time, is shaken by the testimony of Peterson, a representative of the company, that up to the time the appellant made the application for Greger he was a stranger to the company and that even the formal blank used in this application was not procured by the appellant from the company's office. Subsequently this witness stated that appellant during the year 1913 negotiated four or five loans through the company, but this does not tend to show appellant's agency in the matter at bar or in the cases of which the witness testified.

Circumstances naturally arising out of a transaction are sometimes as strong in probative force as sworn testimony. This case affords an illustration of this fact. Appellant was not compensated for his services in securing this loan by the company, as he would naturally have been had he been its agent, but by Greger. When the note and deed of trust had been executed and delivered to the loan company it forwarded to appellant for Greger, not $3400, but a check for $3298, or $102 less than the face of the note, which latter sum it deducted and retained for its services in making the loan. While it is stated in one of the letters from the company to appellant that "it will, when the loan has been completed, pay him his part of the commission," so far as the evidence discloses none of the sum thus deducted or retained was ever claimed by or paid to him, nor did the company ever compensate him in any other manner. The reasonable conclusion from this fact is that he was not employed by the company to negotiate the loan, but by Greger to obtain it, and by the latter he had been fully paid. It is clear, however, whether he was paid by the company or not, that in all that is necessary to constitute the relation, he was the agent of the borrower.

The cases cited in respondent's brief under this head, by reason of the similarity of their facts to those in the instant case, sustain the conclusion we have reached in regard to appellant's agency.

V. Appellant contends that the title to the check forwarded by the Bartlett Bros. Loan Company to appellant, the cash proceeds of which were to be paid to Greger or applied in part satisfaction of certain prior liens on his land, never left the company and at all times belonged to it. This contention is mystified by many words, principally copied from the formal application made by appellant to the company for Greger and the correspondence between appellant and the company prior to the making of the loan. The relevant facts from which ownership must be determined are that the company contracted to loan $3400 to Greger to be evidenced by his note, which was to be secured by a deed of trust on his land, and upon the receipt of such note and deed of trust caused the latter to be recorded and forwarded a check payable to appellant for the amount of the loan less the company's commission. Upon the acceptance by the company of the note and the recording of the deed of trust, the contract for the loan was consummated, whereby the obligation of the company to pay the amount called for in the note became fixed. Upon the transmittal, therefore, of the check to appellant by the company it parted with the title to same and the nominal ownership therein passed to the appellant who became burdened, upon the receipt of same, with the obligation to either indorse it to Greger, convert it into cash and pay the proceeds to him, or apply it to the discharge of the prior lien on Greger's land. He did neither, but indorsed same to a bank and had the amount called for therein placed to his credit. This created a technical appropriation, as the money realized from the check belonged to Greger, but until appellant indicated a purpose to do with this money as the thief does with the property of another in a case of larceny, such a felonious conversion did not occur as to create the crime of embezzlement. But when it did occur the crime was complete. Nor is it material as to the manner in which the money was drawn out if converted to appellant's own use. [State v. Woodward, 171 Mo. 593; State v. Moyer, 58 W. Va. 146, 6 Am. & Eng. Ann. Cas. 344.]

VI. Appellant's felonious intent is to be measured by his acts. According to the testimony, to which the jury gave credence, the sufficiency of which is ample to sustain the verdict, it is shown that appellant, when the loan had been secured, evaded Greger. He concealed the fact from him that the loan had been consummated and that he had received the check. He placed the same to his own credit in a bank and admits that he drew the money out for his own use and has not accounted for same.

Felonious Intent.

These facts sufficiently show a felonious intent on the part of the appellant, and his relation to Greger as an agent having been established, his act is clearly within the purview of that general rule that if one who has the possession of the property of another, instead of delivering it to the owner as his duty requires, neglects or refuses to account for it or otherwise diverts it so as to exercise dominion over it to the exclusion of the owner and to make it his own, he is guilty of embezzlement. [State v. Lentz, 184 Mo. l. c. 239.]

VII. Appellant complains because the trial court permitted the State to show by the witness Peterson that the appellant had neither used the money received

Rulings on Testimony. from Bartlett Bros. in paying off the prior liens nor had he returned the money to the loan company. The question at issue was whether or not the money so received by him had been applied as directed by Greger, and it was therefore pertinent for the State to show that the appellant had violated his directions as to the manner in which the loan should be applied.

Further objection is made that the court erred in permitting the State to show that the check received by appellant from the loan company had been indorsed and deposited to his credit in a bank and had later been checked out by him. The check was made payable to appellant, and necessarily under the authority given him by Greger he could not commit the crime of embezzlement until after it had been indorsed and converted into money. If in the latter form he used it as directed, he was guiltless; on the other hand if he used the money for purposes other than to pay it to Greger or to discharge the prior liens, he was guilty as charged. It is manifest, therefore, that the court's ruling in this respect was not erroneous. Moreover, appellant admitted on the witness stand that the check had been received and deposited and the money drawn out of the bank by himself or others authorized to do so and that he had used the same for personal purposes. Therefore, whether the action of the trial court in permitting a witness to state the condition of the bank was erroneous is immaterial, as the evidence given by such witness was in accord with that given by the appellant himself. Harmless error will not work a reversal.

Appellant also urged that the court erred in refusing to permit the witness Peterson to state the number of applications appellant had submitted to the loan company during the year 1913. This witness did state that appellant had forwarded to his company possibly half a dozen applications for loans during that time. Presumably, from the witness's former testimony, these were made subsequent to procuring the loan for Greger. But even if the court had refused to permit the witness to answer the question it would not have been error. The matter at issue was whether the appellant had embezzled the money represented by the check which had been forwarded to him, and his relationship to other borrowers and the loan company prior or subsequent to this transaction was not material. The evidence shows that he was authorized to receive the proceeds of this loan and was made the agent of the borrower in this particular case. Therefore, whatever relationship he may have sustained to the loan company in previous or subsequent like transactions could have no bearing upon the issue to be determined by the jury in the instant case.

VIII. The instructions given by the court advised the jury as to the elements constituting the offense charged and the punishment prescribed therefor; that the charge is sustained if it was shown that the money was embezzled in one sum or in less amounts at different times; that want of assent to the appropriation of the money by the appellant may be shown either by direct and positive evidence or from all the facts and circumstances in the case; what facts must appear from the evidence to constitute the appellant the agent of the prosecuting witness; that the crime may be established either by direct c: circumstantial evidence; that the criminal intent to deprive the owner of his property may be inferred when conversion is established. Other formal

Instructions.

instructions were given as follows: as to the presumption of innocence and reasonable doubt; the weight to be attached to appellant's testimony; that the jury is the judge of the credibility of witnesses; that if the prosecuting witness gave his consent for appellant to make personal use of the money in question a verdict of acquittal must be returned; that if it appears from the evidence that the appellant was the agent of the loan company and received the money conditionally, he must be acquitted; and that the mere failure to pay over the money to his principal does not constitute the crime charged. These instructions fully advised the jury as to all the principles of law arising under the evidence in this case and are in substantial compliance with similar ones which have heretofore met with the approval of this court. See cases cited in respondent's brief approving instructions similar in all their material particulars to those given in this case. These instructions rendered the giving of those asked by appellant and refused unnecessary.

There was ample evidence to sustain the verdict. Appellant was awarded a fair trial and has no just cause of complaint. We find no error authorizing a reversal and the judgment of the trial court is affirmed. All concur.

HERMAN SCHROEDER et al. v. GEORGE L. EDWARDS et al., Appellants.

HERMAN SCHROEDER et al; JOHN D. GERLACH, Administrator of Estate of HARVEY NEVILLE, Appellant, v. GEORGE L. EDWARDS et al.

Division Two, March 31, 1916.

1. **SUFFICIENCY OF EVIDENCE: Judgment of Foreign Court: Raised By Motion for New Trial.** An assignment in the mo-

tion for a new trial that "the verdict and judgment is unsupported by any substantial evidence" raises the question of the sufficiency of the evidence, and that proposition necessarily embraces a contention that the judgments against a corporation rendered by a court of another State, which are made the basis of plaintiff's suit against its stockholders for the amount of the unpaid stock issued to them, and introduced in evidence, were insufficient in law to support a finding for plaintiff.

2. ———: ———: Presumption: Cognovit. Where the plaintiff's cause of action is bottomed on the judgment of a circuit court of another State, proof of a judgment entered by the clerk of that court in vacation, is not sufficient, unless there are also introduced in evidence the statutes of that State establishing the jurisdiction and the authority to do that which was done by the clerk in vacation. In such case the presumption that the judgment so entered was regular and valid cannot be indulged, because such a judgment, being unknown to the common law, must depend for its validity upon the statutes authorizing it.

3. STATUTES OF ANOTHER STATE: Proof. In Missouri the statutory law of another State must be proven the same as any other fact in the case.

4. CORPORATION: Payment for Stock: Services Rendered By Financial Agent. Where nothing was paid in money by its stockholders at the time the Illinois corporation was organized, but the plan of its incorporators was to issue the company's bonds to the full amount of its capitalization and use the money derived from their sale in the construction of the electric light plant, it cannot be held that one of them, who, as the company's financial agent, indorsed its notes upon which money was obtained for the first work of construction, which notes when the bonds were sold were paid out of the proceeds, thereby, as against general creditors of the company, paid for the stock issued to him in services rendered the company.

5. MOTION TO STRIKE OUT: Waiver. Any error of the trial court in overruling defendant's motion to strike the amended petition from the files, on the ground that it constituted a departure, is waived by filing an answer to the merits and going to trial.

6. APPEAL: Insufficient Assignment: Striking Out Answer. An assignment under "Points" that "the portions of defendants' answer stricken out by the court on the motion of the plaintiffs were material to the defense of these defendants, and error was, therefore, committed by the court in such action," with nothing more except the citation of authorities, does not

comply with Rule 15, and does not designate any facts from which the court may comprehend what the point is.

7. **CORPORATION: Unpaid Stock: Creditor Participating in Wrong.** A stockholder who participated in the transaction whereby the services of a financial agent were received and accepted by the corporation in full payment of stock issued to such agent, cannot be heard to say that the stock is not full paid, even though he has loaned money to the company, and cannot hold said agent as a stockholder as for unpaid subscriptions on his stock, to satisfy a judgment against the company in the amount of the money loaned. [Following Meyer v. Min. & Mill. Co., 192 Mo. 162, and distinguishing Gillett v. Chicago Title & Trust Co., 230 Ill. 373.]

8. **REMANDING CAUSE: Confining Issue.** Where all issues in an equity case except one have on appeal been settled, the court, instead of remanding the cause generally, may remand it with directions that upon a retrial the case be confined to the one issue upon which the evidence at the first trial was insufficient to support a decree for plaintiff.

Appeal from St. Louis City Circuit Court.—*Hon. George C. Hitchcock,* Judge.

REVERSED AND REMANDED (*with directions*).

Eliot, Chaplin, Blayney & Bedal for plaintiffs.

(1) A shareholder's liability to creditors of a corporation is determined by the statutes of the State in which the corporation was incorporated, and the construction of its statutes by the court of last resort of that State is followed in all jurisdictions. Meyer v. Mining Co., 192 Mo. 162; Hodgson v. Cheever, 8 Mo. App. 318; Bagley v. Tyler, 43 Mo. App. 195; Guerney v. Moore, 131 Mo. 650; Leucke v. Tredway, 45 Mo. App. 507; Kimball v. Davis, 52 Mo. App. 194; McClure v. Iron Co., 90 Mo. App. 567; Pfaff v. Gruen, 92 Mo. App. 560; 4 Thompson on Corporations (2 Ed.), sec. 5050, p. 1440; 10 Cyc. 670. This liability will be enforced in all other jurisdictions unless the statute creating the right gives an exclusive remedy for its enforcement. Hodgson v. Cheever, 8 Mo. App.

318; Bagley v. Tyler, 43 Mo. App. 195; Guerney v.
Moore, 131 Mo. 650; Leucke v. Tredway, 45 Mo. App.
507; Schickle v. Watts, 94 Mo. 411; Van Cleve v.
Berkey, 143 Mo. 109; Meyer v. Milling Co., 192 Mo.
162; Euston v. Edgar, 207 Mo. 287. (2) The services
of Mr. Edwards in raising $19,500 for the company
under the circumstances disclosed in evidence were not
such services as could be given or received in payment
of capital stock. 1 Cook on Corporations (7 Ed.), pars.
17 and 18; Thompson on Corporations (1 Ed.), sec.
1605; 4 Thompson on Corporations (2 Ed.), secs. 3962-
3964; Clark and Marshall on Corporations, sec. 384;
Sand Co. v. Crematory Co., 205 Ill. 42; Liebke v.
Knapp, 79 Mo. 22; 10 Cyc. 472. (3) Under the law of
Illinois, shares of stock must be paid for in money or
money's worth. Where an agreement is made to that
effect, shares may be paid for in property, but to constitute payment the property must have been bona
fide sold to and received by the corporation at its market or cash value. Coleman v. Howe, 154 Ill. 458;
Van Cleve v. Berkey, 143 Mo. 109; Sprague v. Bank,
172 Ill. 149; Sand Co. v. Crematory Co., 205 Ill. 42;
Gillett v. Title & Trust Co., 230 Ill. 373. (4) In the
absence of an express agreement on the part of a corporation, an officer is not entitled to payment for services rendered as such officer. Gridley v. Railroad, 71
Ill. 200; Fritze v. Bldg. & Loan Soc., 186 Ill. 183;
Macaroni Co. v. Boggiana, 202 Ill. 312. (5) Payment
for the capital stock of a corporation in property must
be made under an agreement with the corporation.
An agreement between the promoters to this effect is
not sufficient. 1 Cook on Corporations (7 Ed.), sec.
18; Jewell v. Paper Co., 101 Ill. 57. (6) The appellants having failed to make the point below that respondents must introduce the Illinois statutes showing the authority of the clerk to enter a judgment in
vacation cannot make the point on appeal. The judgments cannot be collaterally attacked for defects in

procedure; being judgments of a court of general
jurisdiction of a sister state authenticated under the
act of Congress they are entitled to full faith and
credit, and it will be presumed that the court had jurisdiction unless it is affirmatively shown to the contrary. 2 Black on Judgments (2 Ed.), secs. 889 and
896; Dodge v. Coffin, 15 Kan. 277; 23 Cyc. 1090, 1095;
Lackland v. Pritchett, 12 Mo. 485; Assurance Co. v.
Walden, 238 Mo. 49; Hurd's R. S. Ill., ch. 110, sec.
88; Conkling v. Ridgely, 112 Ill. 36; (7) The law of
Illinois, as determined by its court of last resort, al-
lows a corporate creditor to recover against shareholders for the unpaid portion of their stock even
though the creditor at the time of extending credit
knew the shares were unpaid. Gillett v. Title & Trust
Co., 230 Ill. 373; Sprague v. Bank, 172 Ill. 149; 4
Thompson on Corporations (2 Ed.), sec. 5028, p. 1423.

Jeffries & Corum for defendants.

(1) The consideration for shares of stock of a corporation may be paid in services rendered or to be
rendered. Cook on Corporations (7 Ed.), sec. 20;
Shannon v. Stevenson, 173 Pa. St. 419; Beach v. Smith,
30 N. Y. 116; Liebke v. Knapp, 79 Mo. 22; Vogeler v.
Punch, 205 Mo. 574. (2) A loan of credit is such a
service as a corporation may accept in payment for
its stock. Saunders v. Marble Co., 25 Wash. 475;
Cook on Corporations (7 Ed.), sec. 20; Bank v. Slater,
117 Fed. 1002. (3) In determining the question as to
whether or not the property or services are of adequate value in the payment for shares of stock, the
courts of Illinois and elsewhere have adopted what is
known as the "good faith" rule, which provides that
in the absence of express fraud the adequacy of the
consideration cannot be questioned by creditors of the
corporation. Kunz v. Valve Co., 29 Ohio Cir. Ct. 519;
Coleman v. Howe, 154 Ill. 458; Car Seat Co. v. Rankin,

45 Ill. App. 226; Bank v. Northrup, 82 Kan. 638; Farwell v. Tel. Co., 161 Ill. 52; McBride v. Farrington, 131 Fed. 797; Coit v. Amalgamating Co., 119 U. S. 343; Fogg v. Blair, 139 U. S. 118; Cook on Corporations (7 Ed.), sec. 46; Trust Co. v. McMillan, 188 Mo. 547; Hall v. Henderson, 134 Ala. 455, 63 L. R. A. 673; McClure v. Iron Co., 90 Mo. App. 567; Carp v. Chipley, 73 Mo. App. 22; Vogeler v. Punch, 205 Mo. 558; Peck v. Coal Co., 11 Ill. App. 88; Chemical Works v. Glass Co., 34 Ill. App. 404; Young v. Iron Co., 65 Mich. 411; Netherly v. Baker, 35 N. J. Eq. 301; Beckley v. Schlog, 46 N. J. Eq. 533. (4) No statute of the State of Illinois being introduced in evidence prohibiting the payment of stock in services, the common-law rule in regard thereto will be applied. Horton v. Lbr. Co., 147 Ky. 227; McClure v. Iron Co., 90 Mo. App. 567; 10 Cyc. 649; Coffin v. Ransdell, 110 Ind. 424. (5) Where a judgment of confession in vacation by the clerk is authorized by a statute of a foreign State, such statute must be introduced in order to prove a valid judgment. Otherwise the common-law rule that a judgment is a judicial act and must be entered in open court applies. Roundy v. Hunt, 24 Ill. 598; Trimble v. Stamper, 179 Mo. App. 300; Secs. 6281, 6282, R. S. 1909. (6) Where a creditor participated in the scheme whereby the capital stock of a corporation has not been fully paid and therefore knew at the time he extended credit to it that it was not fully paid, he cannot thereafter enforce his claim by suing the stockholders for the unpaid portion of their stock. This is conceded by appellant to be the well-settled law of Missouri. He asks this court to apply to this case the law of Illinois as declared by the courts of that State, wherein he claims all question of knowledge of, or participation in, the scheme by which the stock is issued for less than its expressed par value, is eliminated from the right of a creditor of the corporation to recover from the stockholders. If this be the set-

tled law of Illinois as declared by the courts of that
State, and is relied upon by appellants to control this
case, it should have been pleaded and proved in the
lower court. Morton v. Supreme Council, 100 Mo.
App. 88; Garrett v. Conklin, 52 Mo. App. 654; Gin-
nochio v. Railroad, 155 Mo. App. 163; Thompson v.
Railroad, 243 Mo. 336; Tennent v. Ins. Co., 133 Mo.
App. 345. (7) The common law of Illinois applicable
to this case is the same as the general common-law
rule. When the evidence shows that the capital stock
of a corporation was to be paid for in property or services under an agreement between the corporation and
the stockholders, and said agreement to render services in payment for the stock has been made and carried
out in good faith, in the absence of fraud, creditors
are foreclosed from a recovery against such stockholders on the ground that the stock has not been paid for.
McClure v. Iron Co., 90 Mo. App. 460; Carp v. Chip-
·ley, 73 Mo. App. 22; Vogeler v. Punch, 205 Mo. 558;
Kunz v. Valve Co., 29 Ohio Cir. Ct. 519; Coleman v.
Home, 154 Ill. 458; Car Seat Co. v. Rankin, 45 Ill. App.
226; McBride v. Farrington, 131 Fed. 797; Meyer v.
Milling Co., 192 Mo. 162; Berry v. Rood, 168 Mo. 333;
Woolfolk v. January, 131 Mo. 620; Trust Co. v. Mc-
Millan, 188 Mo. 1; Shield v. Hobart, 172 Mo. 491;
Biggs v. Westen, 248 Mo. 333; Bonet Const. Co. v.
Westen & Kline, 153 Mo. App. 185; Millinery Co. v.
Trust Co., 251 Mo. 553.

WILLIAMS, C.—This is a proceeding in equity by
judgment claimants of the Chester Light, Water & Ice
Company, a corporation organized under the laws of
the State of Illinois, to recover from the defendants,
residents of St. Louis, Missouri, as stockholders of
said corporation, an amount alleged to be unpaid on
the stock held by them in said corporation, and to have
said amount, due on said stock, applied to the payment

of the plaintiffs' respective claims. Trial was had, in the circuit court of the city of St. Louis, resulting in a judgment and decree in favor of all of the plaintiffs, except plaintiff Neville, and judgment was rendered against defendant George L. Edwards for the sum of $10,226.26 and against defendant Grant for the sum of $343.16, making a total judgment of $10,569.42, which was the total amount of judgments and claims held by the respective plaintiffs, less the claim of plaintiff Neville. Cross appeals were duly taken to this court, one appeal by plaintiff Neville and another appeal by the defendants Edwards and Grant.

The third amended petition, upon which the case was tried, alleged the incorporation of the Chester Light, Water & Ice Company, under the laws of the State of Illinois, with an authorized capital of $35,000, divided into three hundred and fifty shares of the par value of $100 each, and that defendant George L. Edwards and one J. D. Gerlach were the original incorporators and promoters of said corporation and that all but five shares of said capital stock were originally subscribed for by A. D. Grant as a "straw man" and that said Grant paid no consideration to said corporation for said stock.

That immediately after said corporation was organized said Grant transferred 340 shares of said stock to defendant Edwards; that said Edwards, afterwards, transferred all but 147 shares of said stock to other parties, among them J. D. Gerlach, 146 shares; that an understanding existed between Edwards and Gerlach whereby each was to receive approximately one-half of the capital stock of said corporation; that said defendant Edwards became the owner of and holder of one hundred and forty-eight shares of stock in said corporation, and now owns and holds the same on the books of the corporation and that no consideration has ever been paid to the corporation, nor has the corporation ever received any value for the one hundred and forty-eight shares of stock so held by defendant Edwards.

The defendant Edwards, in 1901, indorsed and delivered to said J. D. Gerlach a certificate for said one hundred and forty-eight shares of stock held by said Edwards, but that said transfer has never been recorded upon the books of the corporation, and that, at the time of the transfer, the corporation was insolvent and said Gerlach was insolvent and said transfer was made by said Edwards to avoid liability on said stock; that under the common law of Illinois, the transferrer of stock remains liable thereon until the transfer is recorded on the books of the corporation and that such liability has not been removed by statute in said State; that there is now due and unpaid on said 148 shares of stock held by said Edwards the sum of $14,800, for which said defendant is liable to these plaintiffs; that said defendant Grant owns five shares of the capital stock of said company, upon which there has been nothing paid, and that there is due on such shares the sum of five hundred dollars; that said defendants Grant and Edwards are the only solvent stockholders, holding unpaid stock, within the jurisdiction of said circuit court.

The petition further alleges that section 8, chapter 32, of the Revised Statutes of Illinois, provides as follows:

"Every assignment or transfer of stocks on which there remains any portion unpaid shall be recorded in the office of the recorder of deeds of the county within which the principal office is located, and each stockholder shall be liable for the debts of the corporation to the extent of the amount that may be unpaid upon the stock held by him to be collected in the manner herein provided. No assignor of stock shall be released from any such indebtedness by reason of any assignment of his stock, but shall remain liable therefor jointly with the assignee until said stock be fully paid. Whenever any action is brought to recover any indebtedness against the corporation, it shall be competent to proceed against any one or more stockholders at the same time to the extent of the balance unpaid by such stockholders upon the stock owned by them respectively, whether called in or not, as in cases of garnishment. Every assignee or transferee of stock shall be liable to the company for the amount unpaid thereon, to the extent and in the same manner as if he had been the original subscriber.''

The petition further alleges that plaintiff Herman Schroeder, on December 14, 1904, recovered judgment in the circuit court of Randolph County, in the State of Illinois, against said Chester Light, Water & Ice Company, in the sum of $56.70, together with costs amounting to $4.85. That execution was duly issued upon said judgment, addressed to the sheriff of said Randolph County, and was, by said sheriff, duly returned *nulla bona*. That said judgment still remains due and unpaid, and under the laws of the State of Illinois bears interest at the rate of five per cent per annum.

The judgments of the other respective plaintiffs are set forth in the same manner as the judgment of plaintiff Schroeder.

The prayer of the petition asks that the court enter a decree against said defendants, in proportion to the amount of their respective stock liability, an amount sufficient to satisfy the total claims and judgments of the respective plaintiffs.

Defendants filed a motion to strike out the third amended petition on the ground that it was a departure from the original cause of action pleaded. This motion was overruled and defendant saved an exception.

Defendants' answer to said third amended petition alleged:

1st. That the court had no jurisdiction of the subject-matter.

2nd. That the plaintiffs, or some of them, have no legal capacity to sue.

3rd. They admit that defendant Edwards, in 1901, sold and transferred all of his stock in said company to said J. D. Gerlach for a consideration of five dollars per share and executed to said Gerlach a power of attorney to cause said shares of stock to be transferred on the books of the company to said Gerlach, and that, by reason thereof, the defendant Edwards ceased to be a shareholder in the company, and that if the company is indebted to the plaintiffs, as alleged in their amended petition, said indebtedness accrued long subsequent to the time when defendant Edwards ceased to be a shareholder, as aforesaid.

4th. That when the company was organized, it was mutually agreed between the incorporators thereof and all the subscribers to the capital stock that its capital stock should be paid, wholly, in services, contract and franchise rights to be rendered to and transferred to the company, or for its use and benefit, either before or after the incorporation of the company, and that all of the services and contract and franchise rights agreed to be rendered to and transferred to the company, in payment of the capital stock of the company, were rendered to and transferred to the company, as agreed, and its capital stock fully paid as agreed, all of which was known to the plaintiffs and each of them, and particularly to the plaintiff Harvey Neville, who was an incorporator of the company, shareholder, director and treasurer thereof, from its organization to its final dissolution, and that neither of the plaintiffs gave or extended credit to the company on the faith that its capital stock had been paid in money or its equivalent in property value, but well knew that the capital stock of the company was not intended to be paid in money or in its equivalent in property.

5th. That the liability of shareholders in a corporation, organized under the laws of Illinois, to said corporation or its creditors, is a contractual liability, and that, under and by virtue of the laws of the State of Illinois, which form a part of the said contract, the shareholders of a corporation, organized under the laws of said State, can only be sued upon their stockholders' liability in the courts of that State, and such liability could not be enforced by suit or otherwise except by such suit or proceeding prescribed for that purpose by the laws of the State of Illinois, and in the courts of said State. That under and by virtue of section 8 and section 25, chapter 32, of the Revised Statutes of Illinois, it is provided as follows:

(Section 8 is the same section as is copied in plaintiffs' petition.)

''Section 25. If any corporation or its authorized agents shall do, or refrain from doing, any act which shall subject it to a forfeiture of its charter or corporate powers, or shall allow any execution or decree of any court of record, for a payment of money, after demand made by the officer, to be returned 'No property found,' or to remain unsatisfied for not less than ten days after such demand, or shall dissolve or cease doing business, leaving debts unpaid, suits in equity may be brought against all persons who were stockholders at the time, or liable in any way, for the debts of the corporation, by joining the corporation in such suit; and each stockholder may be required to pay his pro rata share of such debts or liabilities to the extent of the unpaid portion of his stock, after exhausting the assets of such corporation. And if any stockholder should not have property enough to satisfy his portion of such debts or liabilities, then the amount shall be divided equally among all the remaining solvent stockholders. And courts of equity shall have full power, on good cause shown, to dissolve or close up the business of any corporation, to appoint a receiver therefor who shall have authority, by the name of the receiver of such corporation (giving the name), to sue

in all courts and do all things necessary to closing up
its affairs, as commanded by the decree of such court.
Said receiver shall be, in all casès, a resident of the
State of Illinois, and shall be required to enter into
bonds, payable to the People of the State of Illinois,
for the use of the parties interested, in such penalty
and with such securities as the court may, in the decree or order, appointing the same, require.   In all
cases of suits for or against such receiver, or the corporation of which he may be receiver, writs may issue
in favor of such receiver or corporation, or against him
or it, from the county where the cause of action accrued to the sheriff of any county in this State for
service.''

That the plaintiffs have not commenced any suit
as provided by.the laws of the State of Illinois to determine the liabilities and assets of the company and
have not applied to the payment of the creditors of the
company all the assets of the company and have not
determined, in such a suit, the pro rata liability of all
the shareholders of the company and, by reason thereof, are not entitled to maintain this suit.

6th. That on the ―― day of ――――, in a certain
cause, entitled ―――――― ·v. The Chester Light, Water and Ice Company, pending in the United States
Circuit Court for the ―――――――― District of Illinois,
――――――――was appointed receiver to take charge of
and administer the property and effects of the company, and he, if any one, is the proper party to collect
any dues or liabilities which may be owing to the company or its creditors from the shareholders or others.

7th. That under the laws of the State of Illinois a
shareholder is not liable to the creditors of a corporation upon their unpaid stock, unless the overvaluation
of the property turned in for said stock was fraudulently and knowingly made, with the intent of evading
the statutes of Illinois.

8th. That plaintiffs' claims are barred by the Statutes of Limitation of the State of Illinois.

9th. A general denial.

Upon plaintiffs' motion, the court struck out of defendants' said answer the following portions thereof:

1st. The allegation that plaintiffs did not have legal capacity to sue.

2nd. The allegation that defendant Edwards executed and delivered to Gerlach proper power of attorney to transfer upon the books of the company the stock sold to him in 1901.

3rd. The allegation that, after said sale of stock in 1901, the defendant Edwards ceased to be a shareholder in the company and that if the company was indebted to the plaintiffs, said indebtedness accrued long subsequent to the time when said defendant Edwards had ceased to be a stockholder in the company.

4th. The entire portion of paragraph five of said answer.

Defendants excepted to the action of the court in sustaining said motion. Plaintiffs thereafter filed an amended reply to the remaining portions of said answer. The reply contained a general denial and an allegation that the matters pleaded in the fourth paragraph of said answer constituted no defense to the plaintiffs' cause of action under the laws of the State of Illinois as decided by the highest court of said State in the case of Gillett v. Chicago Title & Trust Co., 230 Ill. 373.

The record in this case is very large, but the facts shown by the evidence are not complex and may be stated substantially as follows: In 1892, one Gerlach, a resident of Chester, Illinois, having procured certain electric light and water franchises from the city of Chester, was desirous of promoting a corporation to take over said franchises and erect an electric light plant and a water plant in said city. In furtherance of this plan, Gerlach called upon defendant Edwards in

St. Louis and laid the plan before him. Gerlach was, at that time, cashier of a bank at Chester, but was not a man of any great financial resources. Mr. Edwards was engaged in the brokerage business in the city of St. Louis and was a man of means. It was agreed between Edwards and Gerlach that they would organize a corporation, under the laws of Illinois, with a capital stock of $35,000, each to receive, approximately, one-half of the stock. Gerlach was to superintend the construction of the plants and Edwards was to act as financial agent. The plan was to bond the company for $35,000 and, by the sale of the bonds, raise funds with which to construct the plants for the corporation. Gerlach's stock was to be paid for by his transferring to the company the franchises which he held in the city of Chester. Edwards's stock was to be paid for by services to be rendered by him as the financial agent of the corporation. The company was organized, J. D. Gerlach, A. D. Gordon, George L. Edwards, William H. Bryan and Harvey Neville each subscribing for one share and A. D. Grant (who acted as "straw man") subscribing for three hundred and forty-five shares. After the corporation was organized, all of the stock subscribed for by Grant, with the exception of five shares, which he retained, was transferred on the books of the company, so that, finally, defendant Edwards held one hundred and forty-eight shares of the capital stock, Gerlach one hundred and forty-seven shares and the remaining stock divided in small amounts among other stockholders. Plaintiff Neville held two shares of the capital stock. After the corporation was organized, Gerlach transferred his franchises to the corporation and the corporation began the construction of an electric light plant at Chester. The company had no funds with which to construct the plant but the money was raised by the corporation giving its notes, with Edwards as indorser. In this manner, five thousand dollars was first raised; then six thousand dollars was raised, out of which the first five thousand dollars of indebtedness was paid, and, at another time, thirteen .thousand five hundred dollars was raised. The obligations upon which defendant Edwards became endorser were retired later with the money obtained from the sale of the mortgage bonds of the corporation. At the time that defendant Edwards was lending his name to the credit of the company, he was also the president of the company. Plaintiff Neville was treasurer of the company and also a director; and was the father-in-law of Gerlach. Gerlach was elected general manager.

At a meeting of the directors, on January 30, 1894, a resolution was passed allowing Gerlach the sum of $14,700 in payment for his franchises and, *on motion of H. Neville, George L. Edwards, defendant, was allowed the sum of $14,900 for "services as financial agent and other services."* It appears that the stock of Gerlach and Edwards was paid for in this manner and that neither Edwards, Grant nor Gerlach paid any money to the corporation for their stock and did not render any further consideration to the corporation than that above mentioned.

There was evidence tending to show that the company was insolvent in 1901, but the failure of the company did not occur until about 1903, at which time the bond-holders filed a petition to foreclose the mortgage and a sale of the company property was had in such foreclosure.

Some of the witnesses testified that the services of defendant Edwards, as financial agent, were worth $15,000; one of the witnesses stated that he did not mean to say that they were worth that much in cash. There was evidence tending to show that the company would not have been able to build its plants if it had not been for defendant Edwards indorsing the company's paper to raise temporary funds. It also appears, from the evidence, that defendant Edwards sold his stock to Gerlach, in November, 1901, Gerlach paying Edwards five dollars per share for the stock; but no transfer of the stock was ever made on the books of the company.

A number of opinions by the Supreme Court of the State of Illinois were offered in evidence; also the statutes referred to in the pleadings.

Defendants offered in evidence an order made by the circuit court of the United States, at the city of Springfield, Illinois, on the twentieth day of November, 1903, appointing a receiver for the company. The order appointed Don E. Detrich receiver, and ordered him to take and hold the property of the company, described in the bill, until further order of the court, and enjoined the defendant corporation, and all other persons, from interfering with any of said property and from prosecuting against said defendant corporation any suits or actions at law or equity.

The petition, applying for the receiver, is not set forth in the record, neither are any of the subsequent proceedings in said foreclosure proceeding set forth in this record, but it appears, in the evidence, that the corporate property sold for much less that the mortgage indebtedness.

All of the plaintiffs, except one, made proof of their claims by duly authenticated, certified copies of the record of the circuit court of Randolph County, Illinois, showing judgment for the respective amounts claimed by each plaintiff to have been rendered by the clerk, in vacation. The following is a copy of the record as to one of said judgments. All the judgments were similar as to form.

"Herman Schroeder v.
The Chester Light, Water & | Cognovit.
Ice Company.

"Now, on this 14th day of December, A. D. 1904, it being in vacation after September Term, A. D. 1904, of this court, comes the plaintiff, Herman Schroeder, by A. E. Crisler, his attorney, and files his declaration in a plea of trespass on the case on promises, and files also the instrument in writing on which this suit is brought, to-wit: One promissory note, the execution of which is duly proven by the affidavit of Wm. H. Miller, on file in this cause.

"And now comes also the said defendant, by Don E. Detrich, attorney, and files herein his warrant of attorney, duly executed by the said defendant, authorizing him to appear in any court of record in behalf of said defendant and waive service of process, and confess judgment in favor of said plaintiff, and against said defendant, for the amount found to be due upon said certain promissory note annexed to said warrant of attorney, besides the costs of suit, the execution of said warrant of attorney being duly proved by the affidavit of Wm. H. Miller on file herein; and said defendant's attorney also files his cognovit, by which he waives service of process upon the said defendant and confesses the said action of the plaintiff, and that said plaintiff, by reason of the non-performance of the promises in the plaintiff's declaration mentioned, has sustained damages in the sum of fifty-six dollars and seventy cents, it being the amount due on said note, over and above his costs by him in this behalf expended; and the said defendant, by its said attorney, consents and agrees that judgment may be entered in this behalf in favor of the said plaintiff and against said defendant for the amount of damages aforesaid, to-wit, for the sum of fifty-six dollars and seventy cents and for costs of suit; and release all errors in entering up this judgment, or in issuing execution thereon, and consents to the issuing of immediate execution on the same.

"By virtue whereof and in pursuance of the statute in such case, made and provided, it is considered that said plaintiff have and recover of and from the

said defendant the said sum of fifty-six dollars and
seventy cents, being the amount of damages so confessed as áforesaid, together with his costs and charges
by him about this suit in this behalf expended and that
he have execution therefor.

"Attest: W. Geo. Beever.
                                          Clerk."

Evidence was also introduced showing that ex-
ecutions were issued on these judgments and returned
not satisfied.

It appears, from the evidence, that Gerlach, prior
to the institution of this suit, had received his discharge as a bankrupt.

It further appears, from the evidence, that plaintiff Neville, who was a stockholder and a director of the
company, held two shares of the company's stock and
was elected treasurer of the company; that he was the
father-in-law of Gerlach and was made a stockholder
and director of the company so as to help supply a
sufficient number of directors for the company and that
all of his acts, in connection with the company, were
done at the suggestion of Gerlach. Mr. Neville was engaged in steamboating and paid very little attention to
the affairs of the corporation in question. However,
we think that there is sufficient evidence to show that
he knew that defendant Edwards's stock was attempted to be paid up by the financial services rendered to
the company by Edwards and, in fact, Neville made the
motion, at a directors' meeting, to allow Edwards
$14,900 for his services as financial agent of the corpor-
ation. This resolution was passed by the board of
directors. Mr. Neville had nothing to do with the
books of the company and knew nothing about the company's affairs, except information given to him by
Gerlach and information obtained by him at directors'
meetings. Neville loaned the company money, from
time to time, and, at the time the company failed, it
owed him for borrowed money the sum of $5,065.74.

Since the trial was had in the circuit court, Neville died, and the suit, as to him, has been revived in the name of John D. Gerlach, his administrator.

We will first consider the appeal of the defendants below:

I. Appellants contend that the judgments introduced in evidence were insufficient in law to support the finding for plaintiffs. In this regard, it is contended Judgment that, in the petition, it is alleged that the as Proof. plaintiffs' respective claims are based upon judgments "in the circuit court of Randolph County in the State of Illinois against said Chester Light, Water & Ice Company" etc., whereas the proof offered show only judgments entered by the clerk of said court in vacation and that, since no proof of statutory provisions of Illinois authorizing a procedure of this character was offered in evidence, no presumption as to their validity can be allowed. Respondents attempt to meet this contention by saying (1st) that the point was not raised below and hence cannot be reviewed here, and (2nd) although it had been properly raised below, yet the judgments were of a court of general jurisdiction and that it will be presumed that the court had jurisdiction to enter the judgment unless it is affirmatively shown to the contrary.

Was the point sufficiently raised below? One of the grounds of the motion for a new trial was the following: "Because the verdict and judgment is unsupported by any substantial evidence." We think this ground in the motion for a new trial raises the question as to the sufficiency of the evidence, which proposition, necessarily, embraces the point now urged by appellants.

This brings us to the discussion of the question upon its merits, to-wit, Was there a failure of proof which rendered the evidence insufficient to support the decree? The petition pleads the judgments as judgments of the circuit court. The proof shows judgments entered by the clerk of the court in vacation. Is the proof sufficient to establish the validity of the judgments offered in evidence? The only possible way that this proof could be established would be either (1st) by presumption arising from the record offered, or (2nd) by introducing in evidence the statutes of Illinois establishing the jurisdiction and authority to do that which it appears was done by the clerk in vacation. Since there was no attempt to make proof by introducing the statutes of Illinois, it leaves us to a determination of the sole question, to-wit, Will it be presumed that the judgments introduced in evidence were regular and valid? We are of the opinion that the situation cannot be aided by presumption. This because the proceeding upon its face appears to be one unknown to the common law, and must, therefore, derive its validity from some statutory provision, and it also appears upon the face of the judgments that the judgments were not rendered by a court of general jurisdiction, but rather by one of the ministerial officers of the court, the clerk, in vacation.

Discussing the subject of the presumption to be indulged concerning judgments of a sister state, Black on Judgments, vol. 2, sec. 875, states the correct rule, here applicable, as follows:

"And it is further to be observed that if the court rendering the judgment was one of limited, inferior, or *statutory jurisdiction, or if the proceedings were in derogation of the common law,* jurisdiction will not be presumed, but must be affirmatively shown by the face of the record or fully and distinctly pleaded and proved." (Italics ours).

It would appear that the manner of pleading such judgments in this State is regulated by section 1836, Revised Statutes 1909. The foregoing rule, stated in Black on Judgments, supra, was, by this court in Banc, quoted with approval in the case of State ex rel. v.

Grimm, 239 Mo. 340, l. c. 356, and should, therefore, be considered as controlling here.

In discussing the matter of the presumptions attending judgments of a sister state, Division One of this court, in the case of Norman v. Insurance Company, 237 Mo. 576, l. c. 584, said:

"Further, no matter whether the court of common pleas [of Philadelphia] is or is not a court of general jurisdiction, its jurisdiction in attachment and garnishment proceedings, they being special and statutory, is not supported by the presumptions which usually attend the acts of courts of general jurisdiction."

Applying said rule to the situation here, it, necessarily, follows that the evidence is insufficient to support the decree, because of a failure to prove any statutory authority for the rendition of such judgments.

Respondents, in support of their contention, rely upon the case of Dodge v. Coffin, 15 Kan. 277, which appears to be in point. It appears, however, that the court's ruling in that case was influenced, largely, by the fact that it took judicial notice of the statutory law of the State of Illinois. That is not the rule in this State. In Missouri, the statutory law of another State must be proven the same as any other fact in the case. [Gibson v. Railroad, 225 Mo. 473, l. c. 483; Norman v. Insurance Co., 237 Mo. 576, l. c. 582.]

II. It is contended that the court erred in failing to find that the services rendered the corporation by appellant Edwards were such services as could be given in payment of capital stock and that they were reasonably worth the sum of $14,900, the par value of the stock received by Edwards.

Payment for Corporate Stock in Services.

It appears that Edwards, the president of the company, and one of its active promoters, claims to have paid for his stock by services rendered the company as financial agent. His said services consisted in aiding the corporation to procure temporary loans, Edwards lending his credit to the company as indorser on the paper. It does not appear that Edwards had to pay any of these notes upon which he was indorser, but that the same were paid by money derived from the sale of bonds of the corporation. It further appears that the scheme of organization was that the company should be organized for $35,000 and that the stockholders intended to build the company's plant, not from money paid upon the stock, but by bonding the company for an amount equal to the capital stock and then selling the bonds. In carrying out this plan, it was perhaps necessary that the work be started before the bonds could find a suitable market, and to this end Edwards aided, as above stated, in temporarily financing the proposition until the money could be realized on the bonds. Edwards paid no other consideration for his stock, and it would appear that even the services which he rendered were made necessary because of the fact that he had not paid anything on his stock. It appears that the plan was that the corporation should acquire its working capital from the proceeds of a liability (bonds) rather than from assets derived from stock subscriptions. And the said services of Edwards were expended in thus promoting and financing the company. If services of this kind can be given by an officer of a company, in payment of his stock subscription, then the whole purpose of the law requiring stock to be paid in ''money or money's worth'' can easily be defeated.

We think that the chancellor did not err in finding that, as against the claims of the general creditors, the services of Edwards, as financial agent, could not be given in payment of his stock. We have been unable to find a discussion of this exact point in any of the authorities, but it occurs to us that a bare statement of the matter is sufficient to justify the action of the learned trial court in the ruling made.

III.   Appellants cannot now avail themselves of the point that the court erred in overruling their motion to strike the third amended petition from the files

Waiver.   on the ground that it constituted a departure, this because error, if any, occurring thereby, was waived by appellants filing answer to the merits and going to trial. [Castleman v. Castleman, 184 Mo. 432, l. c. 440.]

The same also may be said with reference to the point that the court erred in overruling appellants' motion requesting an election. [White v. Railroad, 202 Mo. 539, l. c. 561-562; Hanson v. Neal, 215 Mo. 256, l. c. 270-271.]

IV.   Appellants contend that the court erred in striking out the several portions of their answer. Under the head of ''Points and Authorities,'' in their

Assignment of Point.   brief, appellants, concerning this proposition, state, as follows: ''The portions of defendants' answers stricken out by the court on the motion of the plaintiffs, were material to the defense of these defendants, and error was, therefore, committed by the court in such action,'' citing thereunder ''31 Cyc. 639, and Hoffman v. Wight, 137 N. Y. 621.''

There were many portions of the answer stricken out by the court and, with the aid only of the foregoing, it is difficult to ascertain what the point is, upon which appellants rely. The above statement under ''Points and Authorities'' is, in fact, nothing more than a mere assignment of error. Rule 15 of this court provides that ''all briefs shall be printed and shall contain, separate and apart from the argument or discussion of authorities, a statement in numerical order, of the points relied on, together with a citation of authorities appropriate under each point. And any brief failing to comply with this rule may be disregarded by the court.''

In the recent case of Harrison v. Cleino, 256 Mo. 607, l. c. 608, in discussing this rule, WOODSON, P. J., said:

''Clearly the meaning of the rule is, that the statement of the points shall be clearly and fully stated, in order that the court may comprehend therefrom the facts upon which the legal propositions presented for determination are predicated.''

For the foregoing reasons, therefore, we will not attempt a discussion of this assignment of error.

V. We will now consider the appeal of the plaintiff, John D. Gerlach, administrator of the estate of Harvey Neville, deceased.

The points involved in this appeal do not differ, materially, from those discussed in the foregoing appeal, except in one important particular.

The trial court found against the claim of plaintiff Neville on the theory that since Neville had participated in the organization scheme whereby the

Stockholders. financial services of Edwards were agreed upon and allowed to be given in payment of his stock, he could not now be heard to question that the stock was fully paid. The trial court based its ruling upon the authority of Meyer v. Mining & Milling Company, 192 Mo. 162, l. c. 191 et seq.

Appellants contend that the court erred in so holding and that the decree should have been in favor of plaintiff Neville's claim, in accordance with the rule of law announced in Gillett v. Chicago Title & Trust Co., 230 Ill. 373, which rule of law was pleaded by plaintiff in the reply. Respondents contend that the case of Gillett v. Chicago Title & Trust Co., supra, is not in point.

In the Meyer case, supra, l. c. 192, it was held that "a party to the transaction whereby property was turned over to the company as payment in full for the stock issued, cannot be heard to say that the stock is not full paid stock, even though he has loaned money to the company, and cannot hold his fellow stockholders as for unpaid subscriptions on their stock, to satisfy a judgment in his favor for money actually loaned to the corporation." In that case, the case of Sprague v. Bank, 172 Ill. l. c. 168-9, was relied upon by the losing party as controlling. In the Sprague case, it was held that the stockholder's liability upon unpaid stock "is not dependent, in any degree, upon the knowledge possessed by the creditor that such subscription was or was not paid in full. If unpaid to the corporation, it must be paid to the creditor." [Sprague v. Bank, 172 Ill. l. c. 168-9.] In the Meyer case, after stating that the facts, of that case, were unlike those in the Sprague case, in that the creditor in the Meyer case was one of the original parties agreeing to the method by which the stock should be paid, while the creditor in the Sprague case did not stand in such a position, the court reached the conclusion that the Sprague case should not be considered as controlling, and used the following language (l. c. 194):

"If the facts in judgment in the Sprague case were like the facts in judgment here, this court might feel bound to enforce the interpretation placed upon the Illinois statutes by the court of last resort of that State, but the decision in the Sprague case imposes no such obligation on this court; and as such a result as is here sought is directly contrary to the rules that obtain in this State, this court will adhere to the rule heretofore announced by it in cases like this, until a similar case has been brought before the Supreme Court of Illinois and that court has otherwise declared the law in that State upon similar facts."

The basic facts involved in the case at bar are the same, in effect, as those held in judgment in the Meyer case and, under the above ruling, the Meyer case should be followed in the case at bar unless it appears that the Supreme Court of Illinois has held otherwise on similar facts.

Appellants contend that the above mentioned case of Gillett v. Chicago Title & Trust Co., is such a case, and that, since the facts involved in the Gillett case are similar, in effect, to those held in judgment in the Meyer case, the Gillett case should control. If the principal facts underlying the Gillett case were the same as those discussed in the Meyer case, the position of appellants would be sound. But, after a careful consideration of the Gillett case, we are unable to discover that the facts discussed were similar. The discussion of this point in the Gillett case appears to be confined merely to the effect that the creditor's knowledge of the unpaid stock has upon his rights to recover against the stockholder. [Gillett v. Chicago Title & Trust Co., supra, l. c. 414-415.] The opinion, in no manner, undertakes to discuss the legal proposition passed upon in the Meyer case and now presented in the case at bar. In the Gillett case, it does not appear that either of the original incorporators who agreed that the capital stock should be paid up by certain prospective patents, etc., were creditors, as is the case of creditor Neville in the case at bar.

It, therefore, follows that the trial court was correct in following the Meyer case and in finding against plaintiff Neville.

VI. By reason of the conclusions reached in the foregoing discussion concerning the respective appeals, it follows that that portion of the judgment disallowing the claim of plaintiff Neville should be affirmed, and that the portion of the judgment finding in favor of the claims of the remaining plaintiffs and

against the defendants should be reversed and the
cause remanded.

It is so ordered. *Roy, C.,* concurs.

PER CURIAM.—The foregoing opinion by WIL-
LIAMS, C., is adopted as the opinion of the court. *Faris,
P. J.,* and *Walker, J.,* concur; *Revelle, J.,* not sitting.

ON MOTION TO MODIFY.

PER CURIAM.—Herman Schroeder et al., respondents in the above entitled cause, have duly filed
a motion to modify the foregoing opinion so the retrial of the cause, when remanded, shall be confined to
the single issue as to whether or not there was statutory authority in Illinois authorizing the entry and
rendition by the clerk of the circuit court, in vacation,
of the various judgments relied upon by the respective
plaintiffs (respondents herein), as a basis of their
respective claims.

It appears that all other issues in the cause were
properly tried and determined before and that the
motion to modify should be sustained. [McLure v.
Bank of Commerce, 252 Mo. 510, l. c. 524.]

It is therefore ordered that the foregoing opinion
be modified so that instead of remanding the cause
generally for a new trial, the cause be remanded with
directions that the new trial shall be confined to the
single issue as to whether or not there was statutory
authority in Illinois authorizing the clerk of said circuit court to enter or render the respective judgments
upon which said respondents base their respective
claims. Either party may, if they so desire, so amend
the pleadings as to more clearly draw the issue upon
this question.

After a determination of this single issue, the
circuit court will thereupon enter its judgment or decree, in accordance with the facts heretofore found and
the facts then found upon this issue.

WARREN M. MILLER et al., Appellants, v.
GEORGE BOULWARE et al.; WILLIAM T.
COX, Intervenor.

Division Two, March 31, 1916.

1. **PARTIES TO ACTON: Suit to Quiet Title: Right of Person in
   Interest to Intervene.** Section 2541, Revised Statutes 1909,
   is a part of the Act of 1873, Laws 1873, p. 49, relating to the
   right of persons whose deeds or other evidences of title are
   lost or destroyed, to have the title adjudged to them and the
   record title restored to them, and does not apply to proceedings
   under section 2535, and does not authorize one who claims title
   by adverse possession to intervene and file an answer in a suit
   to quiet title.

2. ——: ——: ——: **Section 1733.** One who is not
   united in interest with any other party to the suit to quiet
   title is not authorized by section 1733, Revised Statutes 1909,
   to intervene, nor to be joined either as plaintiff or defendant.

3. ——: ——: ——: **Section 1732: Adversary Interests.**
   Section 1732, Revised Statutes 1909, does not authorize one in
   possession of land and claiming by adverse possession to in-
   terevene and to be made a party defendant to a suit to quiet title brought against the record title owner by one who bases
   his title upon the Statute of Limitations by actual possession
   and does not ask for possession. Such an intervenor does not
   (1) have or claim an interest in the controversy adverse to
   the plaintiff, nor (2) is he a necessary party to a complete determination or settlement of the question involved, nor (3)
   is such a suit one for possession of the real estate.

Appeal from Osage Circuit Court.—*Hon. R. A. Breuer,*
Judge.

REVERSED AND REMANDED (*with directions*).

Vosholl & Monroe for appellants.

(1) The court committed error when it allowed
Cox to become a party to this suit, thereby amending
in effect the proceedings, not only against appellant,
but all defendants. This suit was originally commenc-

ed by appellant against George Boulware, if alive, or if dead, his unknown heirs or devisees, and service of process upon them was by publication. An amendment of the proceedings was made by making Cox a party, which could not be done after service by publication. Smith v. Kiene, 231 Mo. 232. (2) No judgment that could have been rendered in the original suit could in any way affect the rights Cox could have had. Whatever claims he could have had could be determined in a separate action between himself and Miller. No right or title could be determined save that asserted by plaintiff or defendants in original action. Graton v. Land Co., 189 Mo. 332; Chaput v. Bock, 224 Mo. 81. (3) There was no issue between plaintiff and Cox and the judgment rendered does not bind them as against each other. Bank v. Bartte, 114 Mo. 276; Boogher v. Frazier, 99 Mo. 325; McMahon v. Geiger, 73 Mo. 145; O'Rourk v. Railroad, 142 Mo. 342.

Gove & Davidson for respondents.

(1) The application and motion of Cox to be made a party defendant was properly sustained. Greene v. Conrad, 114 Mo. 651; Railroad v. Hattod, 102 Mo. 45; Valle v. Cerre's Admr., 36 Mo. 584; Secs. 1732, 1733, 2541, R. S. 1909. (2) This is a suit under our statute to quiet title which though not technically a suit in equity is designed to determine all the questions whether of law or equity relating to the respective title of the parties and to put at rest the controversy. Wheeler v. Land Co., 193 Mo. 287. The pleading makes it a suit at law and the issues could have been tried by jury, which was waived by the parties. Lee v. Conrad, 213 Mo. 404; Minor v. Burton, 228 Mo. 583. (3) Plaintiff has not been injured by the action of the court in allowing Cox to become a party defendant, and the error if any was committed, does not affect the merits of the case, and the Supreme Court will disregard such

error as produces no injury. Sec. 2082, R. S. 1909; Logan v. Field, 192 Mo. 70. (4) There is no error materially affecting the merits of the action. Freeland v. Williamson, 220 Mo. 229; Stumpe v. Kopp, 201 Mo. 412; Manse v. Boerr, 222 Mo. 115; Berry v. Railroad, 214 Mo. 293.

ROY, C.—This is a proceeding to quiet title under section 2535, Revised Statutes 1909. The petition among other things contains the following:

"For cause of action plaintiff says that he is the absolute owner of the south one-half of the northwest quarter, section 35, township 43, range 7, all situate in Osage County in the State of Missouri, he and those under whom he claims having acquired title to said realty by actual, peaceable, open and continuous and adverse possession thereof for more than thirty years next preceding the filing of this suit and under claim and color of title thereto.

"That the above named George Boulware is the apparent owner of record to said land by deed duly entered of record in Osage County, Missouri, deed records, by purchase from one George Mann, who entered said land in the year 1835 as shown by the Osage County records. That whatever title said Boulware ever had has long since passed away by reason of long possession under claim of title as aforesaid."

It prays for a determination of the rights of the parties, but does not ask for the possession of the land.

Respondent Cox, on his own motion, over plaintiff's objection, was made a party defendant and filed an answer in which he alleged title in himself to a part of the land (describing that part) by adverse possession. Plaintiff moved to strike out that answer but the motion was overruled. There was judgment in favor of respondent as to the part claimed by him and judgment in favor of the plaintiff as to the residue. The plaintiff has appealed.

Defendant Cox, respondent here, was improperly made a party to this suit. He claims the right to be made such party under sections 1732, 1733 and 2541, Revised Statutes 1909.

The writer was at first of the opinion that the latter section authorized Cox to be made a defendant, but his attention has been called to the fact that such section was originally enacted in 1873 (Laws 1873, p. 49, sec. 3) as a part of an act entitled "An act to establish evidence of title to real property and to restore the records of the same, and to provide for the recording of deeds." Section 1 of that act provided that persons whose deeds or other evidence of title are lost or destroyed may have their title to the land adjudged to them. Section 3, the original of our present section 2541, provides that any person claiming an interest or estate in the lands adverse to that alleged in the petition may be made a party defendant, and that the decree rendered in such cause shall be conclusive against the parties to the suit, and shall be prima-facie evidence against all other persons.

Parties to Suit to Quiet Title: Intervenor.

In the connection in which section 2541 appears in our Revised Statutes it seems to apply to proceedings under section 2535 to quiet title. Section 8086, Revised Statutes 1909, provides that "the provisions of the Revised Statutes, so far as they are the same as those of prior laws, shall be construed as a continuation of such laws and not as new enactments."

Section 2541 had no application to section 2535 prior to the revision, and, for that reason, can have none now.

Section 1733, Revised Statutes 1909, provides that persons who are united in interest must join as plaintiffs, and that, in case of a failure of one of such persons to consent to be plaintiff, he may be made a defendant. That section does not justify making Cox a defendant herein. He is not united in interest with any other party to the suit.

Section 1732 does not authorize making the respondent a party defendant herein. There are three classes of persons provided for in that section:

1. Those having or claiming an interest *in the controversy* adverse to the plaintiff.

2. Those who are necessary parties to a complete determination or settlement of the question involved therein.

3. The landlord and tenant and "any person claiming title or a right of possession to real estate" may be made defendants in a suit *for the possession* of such real estate.

We will consider those classes of persons in the order named.

I. This respondent is not of the first class.

In Cape Girardeau S. W. Ry. Co. v. Hatton, 102 Mo. 45, the county judges had executed a deed purporting to convey a large tract of land from the county to the railroad company. That deed was placed in escrow in the hands of one of the judges. The railroad company sued the judges of the county court to determine its rights to the deed. It did not make the county a defendant. It was held that the county was properly made a defendant on its own motion, because, as there stated, it was "the real party in interest." It should be kept in mind that the deed purported to be executed by the county and to convey the land of the county, consequently its delivery to the grantee therein was a matter in which the county was deeply interested. If that deed had been made between the parties other than the county, though it purported to convey the county land, the county would not have been interested in the controversy as to such deed. The fact that the county owned the land did not of itself make it a proper party defendant, but that fact coupled with the additional one that it was a party to the deed, gave it an interest *in the controversy.*

In this cause Cox claimed and actually owned a part of the land by adverse possession. He had no paper title from anybody, and had no interest in any controversy between other parties as to such paper title. If he had remained out of the suit a decree therein would have had no effect whatever on his rights. He neither claimed nor possessed any interest *in the controversy.*

II. The respondent was not a necessary party to a determination or settlement of the question involved. In Carr v. Waldron, 44 Mo. 393, one of several mortgagees of real and personal property sued another of the mortgagees to recover plaintiff's share of the money realized by the sale of the property. It was there said:

"In the present case the parties were all mortgagees, and had an interest in the mortgaged property. There had been no ascertainment or adjustment of the respective amounts to which each was entitled; and, where such is the case, all should be brought in, in order that there may be a final determination binding all the parties."

That case illustrates the meaning of the statute, but furnishes no ground for respondent's contention here.

III. The third class includes only those who are interested in a suit *for the possession* of real estate, and for that reason cannot include the respondent here. This is not a suit for the possession of real estate. The petition alleges possession in the plaintiff, and that he has title by adverse possession.

The plaintiff had the right to choose his opponent, to frame his petition in such a way as not to affect the respondent, and to have his controversy settled without being interfered with by the respondent.

The judgment is reversed and the cause remanded with directions to strike out respondent's answer and overrule his motion to be made a party defendant herein, and to enter judgment in favor of the plaintiff and against the original defendants in the cause. *Williams, C.,* concurs.

PER CURIAM.—The foregoing opinion of Roy, C., is adopted as the opinion of the court. All of the judges concur.

THE STATE ex rel. JOHN T. BARKER, Attorney-General, Appellant, v. D. H. SAGE, Doing Business Under Name of SAGE BANKING COMPANY.

In Banc, April 10, 1916.

1. **PRIVATE BANKS: Assets and Rights of Creditors: Power of State Court to Construe Own Laws.** This court has the constitutional power to construe all constitutional provisions and legislative acts of this State applicable to private banks and bankers organized and existing under its laws, and to decide to whom the assets of an insolvent bank belong, and the priority of the rights of creditors thereto.

2. **NATURAL PERSON: Right to Engage in Business.** There is no constitutional inhibition against any natural person engaging in any business he may choose which is not *malum in se.*

3. ———: ———: **Private Banking.** Nor is there any constitutional provision limiting the power of the General Assembly to enact general laws providing for the organization of private banks, authorizing them to engage in a banking business, declaring their legal status, and prescribing the terms and conditions upon which they may carry on that business within this State. .

4. **PRIVATE BANKS: Corporations Sole.** Since a private bank, though owned by a single individual, is by statute granted powers and privileges not possessed by natural persons or partnerships, and possesses only such powers and privileges as are

State ex rel. v. Sage.

granted by statute, and cannot exist until it has complied with these statutes, and since the statutes completely segregate the bank's assets and business from its owner's private assets and business, it is a legal entity, a corporation sole, under the provisions of the Constitution (Art. 12, sec. 11) declaring that the term corporation "shall be construed to include all joint stock companies or associations having any powers or privileges not possessed by individuals or partnerships." If owned by more than one person, it is still a separate entity or *quasi*-corporation. [Disapproving Gupton v. Carr, 147 Mo. App. 105.]

5. ———: ———: **Notwithstanding Words of Statute.** The words of the statute (Sec. 1116, R. S. 1909) declaring that the owner or owners of a private bank may carry on a banking business "without being incorporated," were used to distinguish private banks from banks incorporated under the general banking laws; they were not intended to declare that a private bank, organized under the statutes and conducted according to their requirements, it not a separate legal entity, or a *quasi*-corporation, or a corporation sole.

6. ———: ———: **Application of Assets.** The assets of a private bank, belonging to a single individual, belong to the bank, and upon its insolvency should be used to pay its creditors, and if any surplus remains after they are paid, it should be used in paying the owner's individual creditors, if he too, is insolvent or has been adjudged a bankrupt in the Federal court.

7. ———: **Insolvency: Priority of Jurisdiction of State and Federal Court.** The taking possession of a private bank by the Bank Commissioner is the first step in the bringing of a suit for the appointment of a receiver, and that step gives the circuit court jurisdiction of the cause, and a subsequent application for a receiver and the appointment of one cannot be said to be *coram non judice* because of the fact that, before the receiver is appointed, a petition asking that the bank's owner be adjudged a bankrupt is filed in the Federal court.

8. ———: ———: ———: **Bankrupt Proceedings Against Owner.** Besides, the filing of a petition in the Federal court, asking that the owner of a private bank be individually adjudged a bankrupt, does not place the assets of his said bank *in custodia legis*—certainly not to the extent of depriving the State court of its jurisdiction to decide whether or not the creditors of the bank are entitled to be paid out of its assets before they can be used to satisfy its owner's individual creditors.

Appeal from Clark Circuit Court.—*Hon. N. M. Pettingill*, Judge.

REVERSED AND REMANDED.

John T. Barker, Attorney-General, and *W. T. Rutherford,* Assistant Attorney-General, for the State, plaintiff and appellant; *T. L. Montgomery* for McDermott Turner, Receiver, intervener and appellant and *W. M. Fitch* and *James P. Gilmore* for Erwin Fox, George W. Cannon and James Fulton, interveners and appellants.

(1) The Sage Banking Company was and is, under the laws of Missouri, a corporation, or corporate or artificial entity, separate and apart from D. H. Sage, individually, its organizer, and its assets, therefore, are not, and cannot be, affected by, nor subjected to, any proceeding in bankruptcy in and by any Federal courts. Sec. 11, art. 12, Mo. Constitution; Sec. 2963, R. S. 1909; Section 1, Clause 6, Bankruptcy Act, Collier on Bankruptcy, p. 2; Secs. 1117-1119, 1095, 1081, 1088, R. S. 1909; Clark & Marshall on Private Corporations, sec. 18; Dwight on Law of Persons and Personal Property, p. 580; State v. Turley, 142 Mo. 410; Jones v. Williams, 139 Mo. 25; State ex rel. v. Payne, 129 Mo. 477; Matthews v. Skinker, 62 Mo. 329; Sec. 2990, R. S. 1909; Fargo v. Railroad, 6 Fed. 767; Insurance Co. v. Oliver, 10 Wall. 507; Society v. Brown, 213 U. S. 43. (2) In any view of the case, an individual or private banker or bank, created by and organized under the statutes of Missouri, is not a natural person within the meaning of the bankruptcy acts of Congress, and the assets of the Sage Banking Company, therefore, are not, and cannot be, affected by, nor subjected to, any proceedings in or by any Federal court. Articles 1 and 2, Chap. 12, R. S. 1909; In re Guaranty & Trust Co., 121 Fed. 74; Perkins v. Smith, 116 N. Y. 441; People v. Young, 207 N. Y. 529; Ratcliffe v. People, 22 Colo. 78; Bassmet v. Jackson, 19 Fla. 667; Shadwell v. Phillips, 72 Minn. 521; Helena v. Rogan,

27 Mont. 138; United States v. Bashaw, 50 Fed. 753; Sener v. Ephrate, 176 Pa. St. 87; Nudgett v. Leibes, 14 Wash. 485; Ashland W. Co. v. Ashland Co., 87 Wis. 485; Lucas Co. v. Railroad, 67 Iowa, 211. (3) The Sage Banking Company, or D. H. Sage doing business under that name, if the court should hold the company not to be a corporate entity, is not a "natural person" within the meaning of the bankruptcy laws of the United States, but is, in any event, a separate entity from D. H. Sage, or David H. Sage, individually, and the assets of the Sage Banking Company, therefore, cannot be affected by, nor subjected to, any bankruptcy proceeding solely against David H. Sage. People v. Doty, 80 N. Y. 251; In re Kehler, 153 Fed. 237; In re Funk, 101 Fed. 244; In re Funk, 117 Fed. 786; Curtis v. Hollingshead, 14 N. J. L. 409; Lumber Co. v. Covert, 35 Mich. 260; Bank v. Burt, 93 N. Y. 245; Forsyth v. Woods, 11 Wall. 486; Walker v. Wait, 50 Vt. 675; Cooley v. Corsett, 39 Mich. 784; Cross v. Bank, 17 Kan. 340; In re Bertenshaw, 157 Fed. 363; Fidelity Trust Co. v. Gaskell, 195 Fed. 865; In re Junk & Balthazard, 169 Fed. 482. (4) No title passed to the trustee in bankruptcy in the proceedings in the Federal court of Iowa, for the reason that, prior to the filing of the petition in bankruptcy therein, said David H. Sage could not have by any means transferred the assets of the Sage Banking Company, and the same could not have been levied upon and sold under any judicial process against him, and, by reason thereof, the State court was without power to transfer said assets to said trustee. Maynard v. Bond, 67 Mo. 315; Casey v. Cavaroc, 96 U. S. 467; Kennedy v. Gibson, 8 Wall. 506; Casey v. Sociate, 2 Woods 77, 5 Fed. Cases 265; 3 Am. & Eng. Ency. Law, 98; Fish v. Olin, 76 Vt. 120; Relf v. Rundle, 103 U. S. 225; Parson v. Ins. Co., 31 Fed. 305; Gilman v. Ketchum, 84 Wis. 69; Ford v. Gilbert, 44 Ore. 262; Barnes v. Newcomb, 80 N. Y. 113; Walling v. Miller, 108 N. Y. 173; Thomp-

son v. McCleary, 159 Pa. St. 183; Edwards v. Norton, 55 Tex. 410; In re Tyler, 149 U. S. 164; Ells v. Water Co., 86 Tex. 109; Campau v. Club, 130 Mich. 417; Groscup v. Society, 162 Fed. 947; Martin v. Davis, 21 Iowa, 535. (5) The money, assets and property of the Sage Banking Company were *in custodia legis* long prior to the filing of the petition in bankruptcy, or were so situated as not to be affected thereby, and the circuit court of the State having first acquired jurisdiction thereover, has the right, and should be required, to retain jurisdiction and administer the estate and wind up the affairs of the Banking Company, under the statutes of Missouri. Collier on Bankruptcy, par. b, p. 992; Casey v. Cavaroc, 96 U. S. 488; Metcalf v. Barker, 187 U. S. 175; Jaquith v. Rowley, 188 U. S. 625; In re Rathman, 183 Fed. 924; Harris v. Bank, 216 U. S. 382; In re McMahon, 77 C. C. A. 668; Frank v. Volkmmoer, 205 U. S. 521; Hiscock v. Bank, 206 U. S. 41; Skilton v. Coddington, 185 N. Y. 80.

Boyd & McKinley for respondent.

(1) Where an adjudication of bankruptcy has been made by a court of bankruptcy the jurisdiction of that court to administer the property of a bankrupt is exclusive. Fidelity & Guaranty Co. v. Bray, 225 U. S. 205; Harvester Co. v. Lumber Co., 222 U. S. 300; In re Watts, 190 U. S. 1; Bank v. Gudger, 212 Fed. 49; In re McLoughlin v. Knop, 214 Fed. 260; In re Naval Stores Co., 214 Fed. 563; Morehouse v. Powder Co., 206 Fed. 204; Dry Goods Co. v. Crating Co., 206 Fed. 817; In re Telegraph Co., 196 Fed. 153; Lea v. West Co., 91 Fed. 237; In re Wagon Co., 110 Fed. 927; In re Fuller's Earth Co., 186 Fed. 578; In re Zeigler Co., 189 Fed. 259; In re Knight, 125 Fed. 35; Hooks v. Aldridge, 145 Fed. 865; In re Electric Supply Co., 175 Fed. 612. (2) The title to all the property of the bank-

rupt vests in the trustee in bankruptcy as of the date of filing the petition asking for the adjudication of bankruptcy. In re Sage, 224 Fed. 525; County Commissioners v. Hurley, 169 Fed. 94; Pugh v. Loisel, 219 Fed. 417; Toof v. Bank, 206 Fed. 250; In re Contracting Co., 212 Fed. 691; Bryan v. Bernheimer, 181 U. S. 188; Mueller v. Nugent, 184 U. S. 1; Everett v. Judson, 228 U. S. 474; Remington on Bankruptcy (2 Ed. 1915), secs. 117, 1112; Sec. 70, U. S. Bankruptcy Act, 30 Stat. L. 565; Sec. 47, U. S. Bankruptcy Act, 36 Stat. L. 840; Lazarus v. Prentice, 234 U. S. 263. (3) The title to the property of D. H. Sage, doing business under the firm name and style of Sage Banking Company, passed to the trustee in bankruptcy on the adjudication of bankruptcy in accordance with the provisions of the Bankrupt Act. Sec. 4-B, U. S. Bankruptcy Act, 36 Stat. L. 839; Sec. 1-A6, Bankruptcy Act, 30 Stat. L. 544; Sec. 1116-1118, R. S. 1909; In re Salmon & Salmon, 143 Fed. 395; In re Purl's Estate, 147 Mo. App. 105; 1 Remington on Bankruptcy (2 Ed. 1915), sec. 79; Burkhart v. Bank, 137 Fed. 958; In re Surety Trust Co., 121 Fed. 73; Couts v. Townsend, 126 Fed. 249; In re Kersten, 110 Fed. 929; In re Sage, 224 Fed. 525. (4) The special agent of the Missouri Banking Department and the receiver, McDermott Turner, were not and are not adverse claimants having a beneficial title to or claim upon the property of D. H. Sage, doing business under the firm name and style of Sage Banking Company. Bryan v. Bernheimer, 181 U. S. 188; Mueller v. Nugent, 184 U. S. 1; Harvester Co. v. Lumber Co., 222 U. S. 300; Shawnee County v. Hurley, 169 Fed. 94; Lazarus v. Prentice, 234 U. S. 266; Bank v. Cox, 143 Fed. 91; In re Sage, 224 Fed. 525. (5) State insolvency laws are superseded by or give way to Federal insolvency laws. In re Salmon & Salmon, 143 Fed. 395; In re Sage, 224 Fed. 525; In re Watts & Sachs, 190 U. S. 1. (6) The State court cannot incumber the assets of the bankrupt estate with

any liens or make any order appropriating or dis-
tributing any of the assets of the bankrupt estate after
the bankruptcy proceedings attach. In re Sage, 224
Fed. 540; Black on Bankruptcy, sec. 27; Remington
on Bankruptcy (2 Ed. 1915), sec. 1620; In re Hecox,
164 Fed. 875; In re Stave Co., 199 Fed. 952; In re
Fuller's Earth Co., 186 Fed. 578; In re Rogers, 116
Fed. 435. (7) The Supreme Court of Missouri has no
jurisdiction to determine this controversy as the act
of the State court in appointing the receiver was *coram
non judice.* In re Stave Co., 199 Fed. 952; In re Sage,
224 Fed. 540; Hickman v. Parlin-Orendorff Co., 88
Ark. 519; Harvester Co. v. Lumber Co., 222 U. S. 300;
Pugh v. Loisel, 219 Fed. 417; County Commissioners
v. Hurley, 169 Fed. 94. (8) The receiver appointed by
the State court, McDermott Turner, has complied with
the order of the lower court and paid or satisfied the
judgment, and therefore this appeal should be dismissed. Noah v. Insurance Co., 78 Mo. App. 370;
King v. Campbell, 107 Mo. App. 496; Cassell v. Fagin,
11 Mo. 207; Aull v. Trust Co., 149 Mo. 15; 3 Corpus
Juris, 360, 368, 665, 675.

WOODSON, C. J.—This suit was instituted in the
circuit court of Clark County, under the banking laws
of this State, to determine the priority of the rights of
the depositors and other creditors of the Sage Banking
Company, of Alexandria, Missouri, a private bank,
duly organized under the laws of this State, to the assets thereof, to the rights of the general creditors of
D. H. Sage, the owner of the bank, who is a bankrupt.

The facts, in so far as this case is concerned, are
briefly as follows:

On December 31, 1910, D. H. Sage subscribed and
swore to, and acknowledged, the regular application or
form for establishing or creating a private bank, under
the provisions of articles 1 and 2, chapter 12, Revised
Statutes 1909, and particularly sections 1116 and 1117

thereof, naming the person interested therein as D. H. Sage, residence, Alexandria, Missouri, the amount of capital as ten thousand dollars, the name in which the business was to be conducted as Sage Banking Company, and the business to be conducted at Alexandria, Missouri. This application was regularly filed in the office of the Recorder of Deeds for Clark County, Missouri, on the 3rd day of January, 1911, and a certificate to that effect made by the Recorder. Afterwards, the recorded document was filed with the Bank Commissioner of Missouri, and on the 9th of January, 1911, he duly issued his certificate to that effect, establishing the Sage Banking Company, at Alexandria, Missouri, with a capital of ten thousand dollars.

The Sage Banking Company, as thus organized and created, continued in the general banking business, receiving deposits, paying checks, etc., until October 17, 1914, when, under the provisions of section 1081, it posted on its door the following notice: "This Bank Is In The Hands Of The Bank Commissioner." Thereupon, the Bank Commissioner appointed McDermott Turner, special agent, under the provision of that section, who took charge of the bank and the assets thereof. He held the custody and charge of the bank and its assets until November 21, 1914, when the State, upon proper notice to the Attorney-General, by the Bank Commissioner, instituted the suit of "The State of Missouri, at the Relation of John T. Barker, Attorney-General, Plaintiff, v. D. H. Sage, doing business under the Style and Firm Name of Sage Banking Company, of Alexandria, Missouri, Defendant," in the circuit court of Clark County, Missouri, this suit, and, upon proper application and petition, the judge of that court, under the provisions of section 1081, appointed said McDermott Turner, theretofore special agent, the receiver of said Sage Banking Company, who immediately qualified and took charge of the bank and its assets as receiver of the Sage Banking Company.

On November 19, 1914, there was filed in the United States District Court for the Eastern Division of the Southern District of Iowa, a petition in bankruptcy, by creditors of David H. Sage, individually, praying that he be adjudged an involuntary bankrupt.

On November 25, 1914, an answer was filed for Sage, alleging that he had been domiciled at Keokuk, Iowa, for more than six months past, but that his actual residence during all of that time and prior thereto was at Alexandria, Missouri. Sage also admitted therein his willingness to be adjudged a bankrupt.

On November 27, 1914, David H. Sage, individually, was adjudged a bankrupt by the Referee in Bankruptcy of the Federal Court, reference having been made to him on November 25, 1914, by the clerk of that court.

On December 28, 1914, the attorney for Sage filed a schedule of his assets for him in the bankruptcy proceedings. The schedule is sworn to by the attorney, who, in affidavit, alleges the absence of Sage from Keokuk at that time. The schedule also alleges that the bankrupt was not sufficiently advised to know whether or not he should schedule the assets and liabilities of the Sage Banking Company, but undertook to attach a list of them.

David H. Sage, at the time of the filing of the petition in bankruptcy, was engaged in business at Keokuk, Iowa, operating a retail grocery store, under the name and style of Sage Bros. He was also engaged in the general mercantile business at Alexandria, Missouri, in his own proper name, David H. Sage, and also engaged in the general mercantile business, at Wayland, Missouri, under the name and style of Sage Mercantile Company.

On January 7, 1915, at a meeting of the creditors of David H. Sage, they elected and appointed Johnson B. Angle, Trustee in Bankruptcy, which action was approved by the referee.

On March 8, 1915, Johnson B. Angle filed his interplea in this case in the circuit court of Clark County, setting forth the filing of the petition in bankruptcy, the adjudication of David H. Sage as a bankrupt, the appointment and qualification of Johnson B. Angle, as trustee, and praying for an order vacating the appointment of the receiver, Turner, and to have the receiver turn over to the trustee in bankruptcy the property of the Sage Banking Company.

On April 5, 1915, the plaintiff, the State of Missouri filed its verified plea or answer to the trustee's interplea or application, and on the same day McDermott Turner, the receiver of Sage Banking Company, by leave of court, and Erwin Fox, George W. Cannon and James Fulton, depositors and creditors of Sage Banking Company, for themselves, and all others similarly situated, filed their separate verified pleas or answers to said interplea or application, denying the trustee's right to the assets of said bank, and claiming them for the use of the creditors of the bank.

Thereafter a hearing was had in the circuit court, evidence introduced, and the cause decided by the court in favor of the trustee in bankruptcy. ·

It was shown that at the hearing, the receiver, with the amount that had been turned over by the special agent, had collected and had on hand $30,068.32, and there were notes not yet collected in the sum of $43,-236.34, making the amount involved, at least, $70,000. It was also shown that the claims of the depositors against the bank amounted to $59,517.16, and that there were 205 depositors.

In due time the State filed motions for a new trial, and in arrest of judgment, which were by the court overruled, and it duly appealed the cause to this court.

Thereupon, the trustee in bankruptcy presented an application in the United States District Court of Missouri for an order on Turner to turn over the assets of the bank to him, and on June 20, 1915, the application was sustained.

From that order and decision the appellants in this court have taken an appeal to the United States Circuit Court of Appeals, but without giving a supersedeas bond, and the appellant, McDermott Turner, has complied with the order and turned over all of the assets in his possession belonging to "D. H. Sage, doing business in the name of Sage Banking Company," to the trustee in bankruptcy, as shown by exhibits to the motion to dismiss, the originals of which are filed with the clerk of this court.

The trustee in bankruptcy contended that the property and assets of the Sage Banking Company passed to him, and that he was vested with the right of possession thereto and the administration thereof. The State, the receiver, and the depositors and creditors contended that no title or right of possession ever passed to the trustee; that the Sage Banking Company was really a corporate entity, by virtue of the statutes of Missouri, or, in any event, an artificial being or entity, separate and apart from Sage individually; that the character of bank or banker involved was not within the meaning of the Bankruptcy Act; that the depositors and creditors of the bank were the beneficial owners thereof; that the capital, surplus and assets of the bank were separate and apart from the property and assets of Sage individually; that they were pledged and dedicated solely to the banking business, when the bank was established, and that, in any event, the depositors and creditors had a lien on or preferential, primary and exclusive claim thereto, which must be satisfied and discharged, prior to any rights of the other creditors of Sage attaching to any interest of his therein; that the property and assets of the Sage Banking Company were *in custodia legis* prior to any time involved that would give the Iowa court any right to take the same, and that the State court first became possessed of them, and that its jurisdiction could not be in any way affected by the proceedings in the Federal court.

I. Counsel for the interpleader, the respondent, contends that there is but one legal proposition presented here for determination, and they state it in this language:

"The sole and only question for consideration is the right to the control of the assets of the Sage Banking Company. It is not a question of priority among creditors or preferred liens, as those

Administration of Assets of Insolvent Private Bank.

questions are not an issue in this controversy and cannot be injected into the same through any straw men put up by appellants. Preferences and priority would have to come up on a proper issue in either the circuit court of Clark County, Missouri or in the United States Bankruptcy Court. The sole question in this litigation is to determine who shall administer the assets of the bankrupt."

This contention is most vigorously denied by counsel for the appellants; and upon the contrary, they insist that the primary and controlling questions are: first, that the Sage Banking Company is in the nature of a corporation sole, or is such a distinct entity that it and its business are entirely separated from D. H. Sage individually and his general business, and consequently that his bankruptcy in no manner affects the banking company; and, second, that because of said corporate character or distinct entity of said banking company, the acts of Congress regarding bankruptcy matters have no application thereto.

In my opinion the contention of counsel for the respondent is not sound; and I am also of the opinion that the contentions of counsel for the appellants correctly state the law of this State regarding the character of the Sage Banking Company, and that said acts of Congress were never designed to apply to or embrace such an institution, any more than they would apply to an ordinary banking corporation, where one of its stockholders has been adjudged a bankrupt. In each case, the surplus of his interest in the bank, if any, remaining, after paying the corporate creditors, would be available under proper proceeding, for the payment of the bankrupt's general creditors.

Before proceeding to the discussion of the laws of this State, which in our opinion sustain the contentions of counsel for appellants, as before stated, we will dispose of a preliminary question regarding the authority of this court to decide the questions of law involved in this case, as presented by the record thereof.

Counsel for appellants insist that this court possessed that authority, while counsel for respondent deny that insistence.

There can be no question but that this court has the constitutional power to construe all constitutional provisions and legislative enactments of this State applicable to private banks and bankers organized and existing under the laws thereof, and to decide to whom the assets thereof belong, as well as their priority of rights thereto; but we do not deem it wise or proper to decide the incidental question thereto, as to whether or not the circuit court of Clark County has the legal right to administer the assets of the bank, for the reason the Federal court has the actual custody of the same; whether rightfully or wrongfully, we express no opinion, and we presume that court will finally dispose of the assets according to law.

II. This brings us to the discussion of the questions, what is a "private bank" and "a private banker," within the meaning of the laws of this State, and to whom do the deposits and assets thereto belong?

It should be borne in mind that there is no constitutional prohibition against a person engaging in any business he may choose, which is not *malum in se,*

A Private
Bank is a
Corporate
Entity.

nor is there such a provision limiting the power of the Legislature to enact general laws providing for the organization of private banks to engage in and carry on a banking business. That being true, and the Legislature being thus unrestrained in that regard, possessed the constitutional authority to enact the statutes of this State providing for the incorporation of general banking companies, and for the organization of private banks and bankers, and to declare their status before the law, and·to prescribe the terms and conditions upon which they may do business in this State. Conceding that much to be true, which must be done, the constitutionality of said statutes must also be conceded, which only leaves the two questions for this court to decide, viz.: (1) What is a private bank or banker? and (2) To whom do the assets thereof belong, within the meaning of said statutes?

I will undertake to answer those questions in the order stated: First: This statement of the case necessarily calls for a careful consideration of the statutes providing for the organization of "private banks" or "private bankers" (the two terms being used interchangeably by the Legislature), their status before the law, as well as those conferring their power, imposing their duties and those which prescribe the terms and conditions upon which they may transact business in this State.

In order to correctly interpret those statutes, it should be remembered that prior to the Act of 1877 (Laws 1877, p. 34, secs. 22 to 29) there was no statutory law specially applicable to private banks.

Prior to the enactment of those statutes all such institutions were practically, if not literally, established by the person or persons desiring to enter into such business, who conducted the same according to his or their own ideas, as a part and parcel of his or their general business, the precise thing counsel for respondent is here contending for, with the exception as to the organization of the bank and its supervision by the State—similar to the State's supervision of public warehouses.

Under those conditions counsel for respondent contend that when the owner of the bank failed in business the bank constituting an integral part of it, the deposits or assets of the same constituted a part and parcel of the general assets of his estate and should be administered accordingly in the payments of all of his creditors; and that the bank depositors have no preference over other creditors.

That condition of things, in many cases, would lead to great injustice and many hardships, in that the depositors parted with their money without receiving anything in return therefor, usually deposited it only for safe-keeping, while other creditors would become such for value received.

That act has been amended from time to time, with the design to protect the depositors from the injustice and hardships before mentioned; and as amended it has been carried into the various revisions of 1879, 1889, 1899 and 1909, and now constitutes a part and parcel of articles 1 and 2 of chapter 12 of the last named revision.

We will now set forth such of those statutes and parts thereof as are material to the legal propositions presented.

Section 1116, Revised Statutes 1909, declares what private bankers or private banks are, in the following language:

"Sec. 1116. *Private bankers defined.*—Private bankers are declared to be those who carry on the business of banking by receiving money on deposit, with or without interest, by buying and selling bills of exchange, promissory notes, gold or silver coin, bullion, uncurrent money, bonds or stocks, or other securities, and of loaning money, without being incorporated.''

Section 1117 prescribes the terms and conditions upon which private bankers may conduct business in this State, which reads as follows:

''Sec. 1117. *Requirements for private banker— change of ownership.*—No person or company of persons shall engage in the business of banking as private bankers without a paid-up capital of not less than ten thousand dollars, and if said banking business is to be carried on in a city having a population of one hundred and fifty thousand inhabitants or more, then without a paid-up capital of not less than one hundred thousand dollars, nor until he or they shall have made a statement, subscribed and sworn to as correct and true before a notary public by each person connected with such business as owner or partner, setting forth: First, the names and places of residence of all persons interested in the business, all of whom shall be residents of this State, and the amount of capital invested; and second, the name in which the business is to be conducted and the place at which it is to be carried on; which statement shall be acknowledged, recorded in the office of the recorder of deeds of the county in which the bank is to be located, and a certified copy of such recorded instrument shall be filed in the office of the Bank Commissioner: Provided, however, that in order to accomplish a change in the ownership of a private bank, it shall be necessary for all the partners of the new bank to make, record and file in the office of the Bank Commissioner a statement in form and manner required by this section for establishing a new bank.''

And section 1118 confers upon a private banker the same powers and rights, and imposes upon him the same duties and obligations that are imposed upon duly incorporated banking companies; and in so far as is here material is as follows:

ᵀoᐧprivate banker, who receives general deposits ᴜne manner of banks of deposit and discount, ᴊl employ any part of his capital, or any funds de- ₚosited with or borrowed by him, in dealing or trad- ing in, buying or selling lands, goods, chattels, wares or merchandise, but he may sell and dispose of all kinds of property which may necessarily come into his pos- session in the collection of his loans or discounts. Nor shall any such banker use or employ his capital or funds deposited with or borrowed by him in any other manner than banks of deposit and discount are by this article permitted, or loan a greater amount to any person or loan any sum whatever, except upon like se- curity as is required to be taken by banks of deposit and discount. Neither shall the profits of such private bank be distributed to the owners thereof without first setting apart to surplus account at least twenty per cent of the net profits of each year until the surplus equals twenty per cent of the capital, and said surplus shall not be diminished except for the payment of any losses which may occur: Provided, if there are un- divided profits, these shall first be used in payment of such losses.''

Section 1119 provides that: ''All the provisions of this article shall, so far as the same are applicable, apply to all private bankers doing business in this State.''

Section 1095, Revised Statutes 1909, provides that, when any banking corporation, individual banker or trust company shall have filed the requisite certificate, paid incorporation fees and other fees, before such banking corporation or individual banker shall be au- thorized to do business, the Bank Commissioner shall ascertain whether or not the capital of the same has been paid in cash. It further provides as follows:

''In case the Bank Commissioner shall find that all the provisions of the law have been complied with by the institutions herein named, which desire to be authorized to do business, he shall grant them a certificate to that effect. Such certificate, or certified copies thereof, shall be taken in all the courts of this State as evidence of such incorporation."

Section 1087 provides that:

"No private bank or banker in this State shall make any loan or discount on account of the personal security or obligation of the proprietor, owner or partner in such private bank in excess of ten per cent of the paid-up capital and surplus of such private bank or banker. For any violation of the provisions of this section, the Bank Commissioner shall have authority, in his discretion, to make application for the appointment of a receiver for such private bank or banker, as now provided by law in case of insolvent banks and trust companies."

Section 1081, Revised Statutes 1909, places individual or private banks under the same regulations as those incorporated under the first sections of article 2 of chapter 12. It reads:

"If, from an examination made by the bank commissioner, or by one of his examiners, it shall be discovered that any bank, private banker, savings and safe deposit company or trust company is insolvent, or that its continuance in business will seriously jeopardize the safety of its depositors or other indebtedness, and if the action is taken from an examination by an examiner, and such examiner shall recommend the closing of the bank, then it shall be the duty of the Bank Commissioner, if he approve such recommendation, by himself or one of his examiners, immediately to close said bank, private bank, savings and safe deposit company or trust company, and to take charge of all the property and effects thereof. Upon taking charge of any bank, private bank, savings and safe deposit company or trust company, the Bank Commissioner shall, as soon as practicable, ascertain, by a thorough examination into its affairs, its actual financial condition, and whenever he shall become satisfied that any such bank, private banker, savings and safe deposit company or trust company cannot resume business or liquidate its indebtedness to the satisfaction of all its creditors, he shall report the fact of its insolvency to the Attorney-General, who shall immediately, upon the receipt of such notice, institute proper proceedings in the proper court for the purpose of having a receiver appointed to take charge of such bank, private bank, savings and safe deposit company or trust company, and to wind up its affairs and business thereof, for the benefit of its depositors, creditors and stockholders; and it is made the duty of the court, or the judge thereof in vacation, summarily to appoint said receiver to take possession of the property and assets of said bank, private banker, savings and safe deposit company or trust company, for the purpose of winding up the business thereof; any complaints or opposition of the bank, private banker, savings and safe deposit company or trust company or its officers subsequently to be heard in open court. The Bank Commissioner may appoint a special agent to take charge of the affairs of an insolvent bank, private banker, savings and safe deposit company or trust company temporarily, until a receiver is appointed; such agent to qualify, give bond and receive compensation the same as a regularly appointed examiner of the department of banking; such compensation to be paid by such bank, private banker, savings and safe deposit company or trust company, or allowed by the court, as costs in case of the appointment of a receiver: Provided, that in no case shall any bank, private banker, savings and safe deposit company or trust company continue in charge of such special agent for a longer period than sixty days. Any bank, private banker, savings and safe deposit company or trust company receiving deposits and doing business in this State under the laws cited in this chapter, may place its affairs and assets under the control of the Bank Commissioner by posting a notice on its front door as follows: 'This bank (or trust company) is in the hands of the Bank Commissioner.' The posting of this notice or of a notice by the Bank Commissioner that he has taken possession of any bank, private bank, savings and safe deposit company or trust company, shall be sufficient to place all of its assets and property, of whatever nature, in the possession of the Bank Commissioner and shall operate as a bar to any attachment proceedings whatever.''

This section uses the words ''individual'' bank or banker and ''private'' banks or bankers as synonymous terms.

Section 1088 makes it the duty, among other things, of every bank, private bank or banker, savings and safe deposit company or trust company, receiving deposits, to cause to be made, not less than once each year, by a committee of at least three of its shareholders, an examination of the condition of its affairs, assets and liabilities, and the books and other documents thereof, and file their written report, one copy thereof with the institution, and a duplicate thereof with the Bank Commissioner: ''Provided, however, that should any such corporation or private bank or banker not have any owners or directors, other than the officers thereof, that then and in such event, said examination and report may be made by such officers, and it is hereby made their duty so to do, under the same penalties as above provided.''

By a careful reading of statutes before set out, it will be seen that section 1116 defines a private bank or banker to be one or more persons ''who carry on the business of banking by receiving money on deposit, with or without interest, by buying and selling bills of exchange, promissory notes, gold or silver coin, bullion, uncurrent money, bonds or stocks or other securities, and of loaning money, *without being incorporated.*'' (Italics are ours.)

Private bankers have no other rights and powers than those just stated, for the reason that "*expressio unius est exclusio alterius;*" and section 1117 provides for the creation of an individual or private bank, and forbids any other person or company from engaging in the business of private bankers unless they comply with the provisions thereof, which have been hereinbefore copied.

From the foregoing observations it will be seen that no person or persons can engage in the private banking business, except upon compliance with the terms of said section 1117; and not until then are they private bankers, nor until then do they possess the rights and powers of private bankers, which are stated in said section 1116; but when they have complied with the provisions of that section, then they become and are private bankers; and consequently possess the powers and privileges not possessed by other individuals or partnerships. That being true, then under the plain and unambiguous language of section 11 of article 12 of the Constitution of 1875, all such bankers constitute a corporation.

That section reads as follows:

"The term corporation, as used in this article, shall be construed to include all joint stock companies or associations *having any powers or privileges not possessed by individuals* or partnerships."

A foreword before proceeding:

The Sage Banking Company was originally organized by D. H. Sage and his brother; the latter having retired from business, the former reorganized the bank individually, as provided for by said section 1117.

It has been suggested that the last three words, "without being incorporated," of section 1116, declaring what is a private bank, are inconsistent with the idea that private banks are corporations. That would be true if read alone; but when read in connection with all the other statutes applicable to such banks and those governing banks incorporated and to be incorporated under the general bank laws, it will be seen that those words were used to distinguish private banks from banks incorporated under the general banking laws of the State.

It has been suggested that because of the facts that a private bank may, under the statute, be organized by a single individual or more, that no charter is issued to it; that no provision is made for the issuance of stock to the incorporators, or for the election of officers and a board of directors, etc., it cannot be logically maintained that it was the design of the Legislature that private banks should be incorporated.

It is true private banks are not incorporated under the statutes as other banks are, yet under a general statute, the Bank Commissioner is empowered to issue to such person or persons, as may desire to engage in the private banking business, a certificate authorizing him or them to so do, upon complying with the provisions of section 1117, which, at least, constitutes such an institution a separate legal entity, or a quasi-corporation, completely separating its business from the general business of the proprietors thereof.

This idea will be enlarged upon during the course of the opinion.

I fully appreciate the force of that argument; but if we consider the unlimited power of the Legislature in that regard, as I have previously pointed out, with no design expressed on its part to abolish private banks which were numerous at the time of the adoption of the Constitution and at the time the statutes mentioned were enacted, I am of the opinion that the Legislature intended to remedy the evils previously mentioned and not to abolish the private banking business, and that in order to do so, it was necessary to completely segregate the private banking business of the State from the solidarity of the owner's general busi-

ness and make each rest upon its own bottom, and
thereby make a private bank a separate and distinct
entity from the general business of the owner and subject the assets thereof, first, to the payment of the
bank's creditors, and, second, if thereafter any remains, they might go under the general laws to the payment of the general creditors; and yet not to disturb
the ownership of the bank or its management or control by the owners, as provided by law.

Such an entity, as before suggested, might more
properly be designated as a *quasi*-corporation when
owned by more than one person, and a *quasi*-corpora-
tion sole, when owned by but one person, with their
rights, powers, duties and obligations conferred and
defined by statute.

This is the clear common sense reading of the statutes, and they fully remedy the evils which led to
their enactments.

Sections 1118 and 1119 before quoted place the business of a private bank in the same situation as that of
an ordinary incorporated bank under the laws of this
State, and provide that "all the provisions of this article (2) shall so far as the same are applicable, apply
to all private bankers doing business in this State."

Further clarity will be added to the conclusions
before stated when we consider those sections of the
statute governing general banks and general banking
business in connection with those that are specially applicable to private banks.

The following provision found in section 1087
strongly indicates a complete separation of the private
bank and its business from all other business of the
organizers and owners thereof, viz.:

"No private bank or banker in this State shall
make any loan or discount on account of the personal
security or obligation of the proprietor, owner or partner in such private bank in excess of ten per cent of
the paid-up capital and surplus of such private bank or

banker. For any violation of the provisions of this
section, the Bank Commissioner shall have authority,
in his discretion, to make application for the appointment of a receiver for such private bank or banker,"
etc.

This language of the statute clearly indicates that
the Legislature understood that it had segregated the
private bank from the general business of the owner
thereof, had formed it into a separate entity or a *quasi-*
body corporate, and had thereby prevented the assets
thereof from being commingled with and owned by the
organizers of the bank in his individual capacity; and
at the same time had subjected those assets to the payment of its creditors in preference to the other creditors of the owner of the bank as previously stated. If
that was not the intention of the Legislature, then why
did it provide in said section that a *private bank* shall
not lend more than ten per cent of its paid-up capital
stock and surplus to the owner of the bank, etc.? If
the money deposited in the bank, and its assets belong
individually to the proprietor or owner thereof, as contended for by counsel for respondent, and that, therefore, the bank is only a coffer or a vault in which they
are placed by him for safe keeping, then why did the
Legislature make it unlawful for that coffer or that
vault to lend to the owner of the same more than ten
per cent of his own money, which he had placed therein
for safe keeping, and could lawfully use any or all of
it as he saw proper to do? I am unable to understand
how a strong box or an arched structure with strong
doors can act in any manner whatever, much less to
count out and lend money, and to distinguish its owner
from other persons. Nor can I understand, if counsel
for respondent is correct, why a receiver should be appointed for said coffer or vault, or how it could be dissolved by an order of court, and its business affairs
wound up and its assets distributed among its creditors, as is provided for by section 1081, when it never

had any being (except a physical one), assets or creditors. In that case the bank or coffer and its contents
oelong to the organizer of the bank, and all may be
seized and taken to pay the owner's general creditors.
In other words, according to the contention of counsel
for respondent, a private bank, under the laws of this
State, has no legal existence, nor capacity to transact
business upon its own account; but at most, it is only
a depository for the safe-keeping of the money deposited therein, which belonged to the owner of the bank,
and it may be taken for the payment of his individual
debts in general.

If that is true, then there is but one theory under
the sun, known to man, by which it can be lawfully
done, and that is upon the theory that when a person
deposits money in a private bank he is simply lending
the same to the owner of the bank, through it as his
agent; and therefore it may be taken for the payment
of his general indebtedness. No such design can be
gathered from the legislation of this State upon that
subject; and I am sure that such is not the understanding of the depositors of such institutions. Moreover, if
such banks are not separate entities, then the law of
the State has clothed the wolf in sheep's clothing, and
thereby induced the people of this State to lend their
money to individuals under the belief and understanding that they were depositing them in such institutions
for safe keeping, safeguarded by stringent penal laws
against being used and speculated with by the proprietors thereof. All of those matters point to the fact
that such banks are separate entities—transacting
business upon their own account, just the same as all
other classes of banks do, and their assets must be first
used for the payment of their liabilities.

Again: By sections 1080 and 1085, all private
banks of this State are required to be examined so
often by the Bank Commissioner, and a penalty is prescribed for any such bank refusing to submit to such

examination. Is that consistent with the idea that the
bank and all of its assets are the individual property
of the owner of the bank? I think not; for the very
object of such examinations is to ascertain the solvency
or insolvency of the bank, for the protection of the
depositors and other creditors of the institution, as
well as the community at large. That being true, what
good purpose would be served by such examinations if
the bank is not a corporate body and does not transact business on its own account, but is, as contended
for by counsel for respondent, only an instrumentality
with which the owner of the bank transacts a part of
his individual business; and that the assets thereof belong to him in the same sense that he owns a farm with
the stock thereon, a store with the merchandise therein
or any other business enterprise? I submit no good
whatever would be realized therefrom, for the obvious reason that if the bank is not a separate entity, but
is an integral part of the general assets of its owner,
then his solvency or insolvency would determine the
solvency or insolvency of the so-called bank; and the
financial condition of the latter could not be ascertained
by an examination made by the Bank Commissioner
without he should also investigate the financial condition of the owner of the bank. The owner of the bank
might be indebted, for instance, in the sum of $250,000,
and have only $50,000 worth of individual assets out-
side of those deposited in the bank, and $100,000 de-
posited therein. In that case his indebtedness would
exceed his combined assets, those in and out of the
bank, by the sum of $100,000, yet that fact would not
and could not appear from an examination of the financial condition of the bank only; and consequently the
examination of the bank would not be worth a penny
to any one.

Again: Suppose the contention of counsel for respondent is right, and that a private bank is absolutely
solvent, that is, it has more money and other valuable

assets on hand than are necessary to pay every dollar of its indebtedness; and at the same time the owner of the bank is hopelessly insolvent, that is, his assets in and out of the bank are wholly insufficient to pay his indebtedness, which of course, according to the contention of said counsel, includes the indebtedness of the bank; and suppose further that under those conditions the owner of the private bank should receive deposits for the bank when he knew of said insolvency, would the owner in that case be guilty, under the statutes of this State, of the crime of receiving deposits for the bank after he knew of *his insolvency?* In my opinion, that question should be answered in the negative, for the reasons that the statute refers to the insolvency of the bank itself, and not to the insolvency of the individual owner thereof; and there is no statute of that character applicable to a person who receives deposits of money from others in his individual capacity.

Moreover, section 1089 provides that if the Bank Commissioner shall report that any such bank is insolvent when it is solvent, or solvent when it is insolvent, he shall be liable on his official bond for all damage done thereby.

Now, if the contention of counsel for respondent is correct, then how could the Commissioner ascertain whether the bank is solvent or insolvent if it is not a separate entity, and he has no authority to investigate the financial condition of the owner of the bank? Under that assumption he could by no possible means ascertain the financial condition of any private bank in the State, and would thereby render himself liable on his bond in every case where the owner of the bank should happen to be insolvent at the time the examination is made, notwithstanding the fact that the bank itself was perfectly solvent.

Not only that, section 1091 provides that whenever the Bank Commissioner shall neglect or violate any of the duties of his office regarding such banks, etc., he shall be deemed guilty of a felony, etc.

This clearly shows that such a bank is a separate institution from all other business of its owner, for otherwise the Commissioner would have no authority to examine such banks or discharge his numerous other duties regarding them.

There are other provisions of the statutes lending strength to the views herein expressed; but in my opinion those considered clearly establish the fact that *all private banks* in this State are *separate entities* from all other business enterprises of the owners or proprietors thereof; and therefore no good would flow from a further consideration of those statutes.

The St. Louis Court of Appeals, in the case of Gupton v. Carr, 147 Mo. App. 105, held contrary to the views here expressed; but we are clearly of the opinion that our learned brothers of that court misconceived the very object and purpose the Legislature intended to accomplish by the enactment of the statutes under consideration, and, therefore, drew erroneous conclusions as to the meaning of said legislation. We are, therefore, of the opinion that said case should be overruled, and it is accordingly done.

I am therefore clearly of the opinion that the assets of the Sage Banking Company belong to that institution, and for that reason its creditors have a priority of right to them over the rights of the creditors of D. H. Sage, and that they should be first applied in payment of their claims, and second, if any remains thereafter, then in payment of his individual creditors as provided by law.

III. The respondent has filed a motion in this court to dismiss the appeal for the reason that the act of the circuit court of Clark County appointing Turner

receiver of the Sage Banking Company,
Priority of was *coram non judice*—the application
Jurisdiction.
for said appointment having been made
subsequent to the filing of the petition asking that said
Sage be adjudged an involuntary bankrupt.

There are other grounds also assigned, but they
are all germane to.the one stated; and the disposition
of that will dispose of all.

There is no merit in the motion, for two reasons:
first, because the bank was in the hands of the Bank
Commissioner, through his agent, Turner, before the
petition in bankruptcy had been filed against D. H.
Sage. The taking possession of the bank under section
1081 is the first step taken in bringing suit under sections 1082 and 1083, for the appointment of a receiver
thereof, and to wind up the affairs of the bank; and
that possession of the property by the Commissioner
was sufficient custody thereof to give the circuit court
jurisdiction of the cause. And, second, the filing of the
petition in bankruptcy against D. H. Sage, individually, did not place the assets of the Sage Banking Company *in custodia legis;* evidently not to the extent of
depriving the circuit court of its jurisdiction to pass
upon the questions here presented.

For the reasons stated, the motion to dismiss the
appeal is overruled.

For the reasons stated the judgment of the circuit
court is reversed and the cause remanded. *Graves,
Blair* and *Revelle, JJ.,* concur; *Bond, J.,* dissents;
Walker and *Faris, JJ.,* absent.

ON MOTION TO MODIFY.

GRAVES, J.—The motion to modify the opinion
should be sustained *in toto.* All except the first ground
of the motion refer to mere clerical oversights, and
should be granted without argument, and as I understand, the opinion will be corrected in these details.

The first ground of the motion requests us to strike out the following clause from the opinion:

"But we do not deem it wise or proper to decide the incidental question thereto, as to whether or not the circuit court of Clark County has the legal right to administer the assets of the bank, for the reason the Federal court has the actual custody of the same; whether rightfully or wrongfully, we express no opinion, and we presume that court will finally dispose of the assets according to law."

This clause should be stricken out because it conflicts with the real holding in this case. The opinion elsewhere decides just what this clause says we will decline to decide. To get the connection we will state the facts. The opinion holds, and rightfully holds, that this court can decide the question as to whom these assets belong. The opinion then discusses our State laws, and very rightfully concludes that the circuit court of Clark County rightfully became possessed of these assets by and through a receiver appointed by it. The opinion, in the last paragraph thereof, after correction by inserting the word "not," rightfully holds, that "the filing of the petition in bankruptcy against D. H. Sage, individually, did *not* place the assets of the Sage Banking Company *in custodia legis*."

Further the appeal in this case was taken from the order of the circuit court directing its receiver to turn over these assets to the trustee in bankruptcy of the Federal court, appointed on an application which we say did not place the assets *in custodia legis*. This judgment of the circuit court of Clark County our opinion reverses. In other words, we say the judgment directing the receiver in the circuit court to transfer the assets to the trustee in bankruptcy was wrong, and that the circuit court should have held that the trustee in bankruptcy had no title or interest in the assets, and was not entitled to the possession.

These holdings in the opinion are in direct conflict with the clause asked to be stricken out by this motion. That clause says we will not decide whether or not the circuit court has the legal right to administer the assets of the bank, which directly contravenes all else that is said in the opinion. When we reverse the judgment of the circuit court, as we do, it is tantamount to saying that the administration of the estate was properly in that court. This for the reason that the judgment we reverse is one by which the circuit court of Clark County divested itself of the administration of the estate. Not only this, but when we said that the petition in bankruptcy did not place the assets involved here *in custodia legis,* we in effect said that the bankruptcy court could not administer these assets. And yet further, when we say, as we do in the opinion, that the Sage Banking Company is, under our law, such a legal entity as not to bring it within the terms of the bankruptcy act, we necessarily say that the administration of these assets is in the State court.

The clause mentioned in appellant's motion to modify our opinion should be stricken from the opinion. It escaped my attention at the time I concurred in the opinion.

We should do in this case, just as this court did in State ex rel. v. Woodson, Judge, 164 Mo. 440. In that case, as in this, the court of the State had divested its receivers of the right to administer the estate and directed them to turn over the assets to the receivers of the Federal court. In that case, as it is claimed in this case, the receivers in the State court had turned over to the receivers in the Federal court.

The appeal in that case, just as in this case, was from the order of the State court divesting itself and its receivers of the administration of the estate. This court held that the administration was properly in the State court, and quashed the order which took such administration from the State court to the Federal court. In other words we decided which court had jurisdiction of the estate, as we have done in this case, save and except what is said in the clause mentioned.

The motion to modify the opinion should be and is sustained and opinion modified as herein indicated. *Faris, Blair* and *Revelle, JJ.,* concur; *Woodson, C. J.,* dissents to this opinion; and *Bond, J.,* dissents as to both opinions.

THE GOLD ISSUE MINING & MILLING COMPANY v. PENNSYLVANIA FIRE INSURANCE COMPANY OF PHILADELPHIA, Appellant.

In Banc, April 10, 1916.

1. **JURISDICTION: Foreign Insurance Company As Defendant: Foreign Plaintiff: Right to Sue In This State.** An Arizona corporation, not licensed to do business in either Colorado or Missouri, can bring and maintain a suit in the circuit court of any county in Missouri, against an insurance company organized under the laws of Pennsylvania and licensed to do insurance business in this State, upon an insurance policy issued and delivered in Colorado, insuring property in that State against loss by fire, by having the summons served by the sheriff of Cole County upon the Superintendent of Insurance as the statutory agent of said insurance company, in accordance with the provisions of section 7042, Revised Statutes 1909. [GRAVES, BOND and WALKER, JJ., dissenting.]

2. ————: ————: ————: ————: **Limitation to Contracts Made In this State.** The statute (Sec. 7042, R. S. 1909) does not limit the right of holders of policies issued by an insurance company licensed to do business in this State to sue in the courts of this State upon contracts made in this State, but gives them the right to sue such a company in the courts of this State upon policies wherever made.

> *Held*, by GRAVES, J., dissenting, with whom BOND and WALKER, JJ., concur, that the substituted method of service of process provided by the statute is limited to actions arising on contracts made or acts done in this State.

3. ———: ———: ———: ———: **So Long as Policies Are
Outstanding.** The language of the statute declaring that the
authority of the Superintendent of Insurance to accept service
of process for an insurance company licensed to do business in
this State shall continue "so long as it shall have any policies
or liabilities outstanding in this State," is not a limitation upon
the authority of the Superintendent to act for such company,
and not a limitation upon the character of the actions that may
be brought and maintained in the courts of this State, and
does not distinguish between contracts made in this State and
contracts made elsewhere, but is a mere limitation of the time
within which suits may be brought.

Held, by GRAVES, J., dissenting, with whom BOND and
WALKER, JJ., concur, that the language of the statute declaring that service of process upon the Superintendent of
Insurance shall be valid and binding upon said company
"so long as it shall have any policies or liabilities outstanding in this State," does characterize the kind of litigation to which foreign insurance companies can be required to respond in the courts of this State, and fixes a
limitation upon the causes over which they can assume
jurisdiction; and when read in connection with the preceding clause, which mentions policies issued when the
company was in the State, it is apparent that the substituted method of service of process is limited to suits on
contracts made within the State, and does not apply to contracts made outside the State.

4. **STATUTORY CONSTRUCTION: In the Light of Prior Condition.** There are few guides to the construction of a statute more
useful than that which directs attention to the prior condition
of the law as an aid in determining the meaning of any change
therein.

5. **JURISDICTION: Foreign Insurance Company: Licensed to
Do Business in State: Process: Application of Statutes.**
Neither section 7042 nor section 7044, Revised Statutes 1909,
authorizes service of process in suits brought in the courts of
this State against a foreign insurance company doing business
herein without a license, based upon a policy of insurance issued by it in another state or country. Section 7042 does not
apply to suits based on contracts of insurance written in this
State by a foreign company having no license to do business
herein, but section 7044 applies to such a situation. Section
7042 limits the service of process therein provided to foreign
insurance companies doing business in this State under authority from the State duly granted to them; and by section 7044 the process therein mentioned is limited to suits upon
policies issued in this State by companies which do not have
authority from the State to do business here.

6. ———: ———: ———: ———: Constitutionality of Statute. Section 7042, Revised Statutes 1909, designed to authorize service of process against foreign insurance companies doing business in this State in pursuance to a license properly granted, based upon insurance contracts made in another state, by service of summons upon the Superintendent of Insurance appointed as its agent for the purpose of process, is not unconstitutional, either as denying to said companies due process of law, or on the theory that the Legislature has no power to authorize suits to be brought in the courts of this State for a breach of an insurance contract made in another state.

7. ———: ———: ———: ———: ———: Transitory Action. In pursuance to broad and specific provisions of the State and Federal Constitution, the Legislature of this State has made ample provision by which a suit on a transitory cause of action—that is, a personal action founded on a violation of rights which, in contemplation of law, have no locality, but follow the person—may be brought in the courts of this State by a citizen of any other State or country, with the same freedom as is accorded to a citizen of this State. The Legislature has enacted, and had constitutional authority to enact, laws conferring jurisdiction upon the courts of this State to try and determine actions brought by a citizen of another state or country against a foreign insurance company licensed to do business in this State, upon contracts of fire insurance made in another state or country, whether the property destroyed was located in this State or elsewhere. [GRAVES, BOND and WALKER, JJ., dissenting.]

8. INSURANCE POLICY: Forfeiture Clauses: Estoppel: Evidence. Where the general agents of an insurance company, at the time or subsequent to the issuance of a policy of fire insurance, are informed of the existence of any fact regarding the property which is violative of conditions expressed in the policy (such as vacancy or failure to operate a manufacturing plant for more than thirty days), then the company is estopped to interpose a violation of such conditions of forfeiture as a defense to a suit based on the policy to recover damages sustained; and testimony that the company's agents were informed at the time the policies were issued and subsequently that such conditions were not being kept and the reasons therefor and waived objection thereto, is competent evidence.

9. ———: ———: ———: Waiver. The general agent of the insurance company who on its behalf issues a policy is the company's *alter ego*; and his knowledge that a forfeiture condition of the policy is being violated and his assurance of "all right" is a waiver of the condition; and a waiver may be inferred from the conduct and acts of the agent, and need not be proved by express agreement; his failure to express dissent

when informed of a breach of the condition, is such evidence of waiver as to carry the question to the jury.

10. ———: ———: ———: ———: **Acceptance of Premium.** Acceptance by the general agent who issued the policy of payment of an unpaid premium after the fire has occurred, with knowledge, is a waiver of the conditions of forfeiture.

11. ———: **Conspiracy of Agent and Insured: Telling Truth.** Telling the true facts by the agents as to knowledge and waiver of policy conditions is no evidence of a conspiracy or collusion between them and the insured.

12. **CORPORATION: Authority to Do Business: Payment of Fees.** Where the smelting company organized under the laws of Arizona, at the time insurance policies were issued to it on its plant in Colorado, had not taken out a license to do business, but had purchased the property insured, and prior to the fire had obtained a license from Colorado, the fact that it had not obtained such license prior to the issuance of the policy is, under the laws of Colorado and Missouri, immaterial in a suit on the policies for damages by fire.

13. **JURISDICTION: Raised by Answer.** Jurisdiction over the person is a proper subject-matter of a plea in the answer, when the lack of jurisdiction does not appear on the face of the petition, but when such lack so appears it should be raised by demurrer. [Per GRAVES, J.].

14. ———: ———: **Waiver By Appearance.** A motion to quash the service of process, which is in effect a demurrer to the jurisdiction of the court over the person of defendant and limited to that purpose, is not an appearance, such as amounts to a waiver of jurisdiction. [Per GRAVES, J.].

Appeal from Audrain Circuit Court.—*Hon. J. D. Barnett*, Judge.

AFFIRMED.

David H. Robertson, Lewis & Grant and *Fred Herrington* for appellant.

(1) The court erred in permitting the witness Doepke to testify, over defendant's objections, to conversations between witness and defendant's agent had prior to and at the time of the issuance of the policy with reference to the effect and binding force of the

terms and conditions thereof. All such prior conversations were merged in the subsequently issued policy under the familiar rule of evidence, that parol contemporaneous evidence is inadmissible to contradict or vary the terms of a valid written instrument. Ijams v. Providence Ins. Soc., 185 Mo. 466; Graham v. Merc. Ins. Co., 110 Mo. App. 95; Gillum v. Fire Assn., 106 Mo. App. 673; Riley v. Ins. Co., 117 Mo. App. 229; Dircks v. Ins. Co., 34 Mo. App. 43. (2) The court erred in permitting the witness Doepke to testify, over defendant's objections, to conversations between witness and the agent of insurer had after the policy was issued and while the property was occupied and in operation, as to shutting down operations and vacating the property at some time in the future, for a longer period than permitted under the terms of the policy, for the purpose of showing a waiver of the requirements of the policy in that respect. Such conversations, before the vacancy occurred, were inadmissible for the reason that such conversations or any agreement then made could have no effect, because there could be no waiver of a forfeiture until after the ground of forfeiture had occurred. That "a waiver is a voluntary relinquishment of a known right" is familiar law. Rogers v. Ins. Co., 155 Mo. App. 276; Patterson v. Ins. Co., 174 Mo. App. 37; Patterson v. Ins. Co., 164 Mo. App. 157. (3) The court erred in refusing to instruct a verdict for the defendant at the close of the evidence for the plaintiff, and at the close of all the evidence, and the verdict is contrary to the law and the evidence. Because it is undisputed that no actual notice of the facts sought to be charged to the principal was ever given to the latter and the notice to and knowledge of the agent cannot be, in law, imputed to the principal. Bank v. Nichols, 223 Ill. 41; Cowen v. Curran, 216 Ill. 598; Booker v. Booker, 208 Ill. 529. (a) The agent, to the knowledge of the insured, had an interest adverse to his principal. Bank v. Nichols, 223 Ill. 41;

Cowen v. Curran, 216 Ill. 598; Booker v. Booker, 208 Ill. 529; Safé Dep. Co. v. Lord, 67 N. J. Eq. 489; Bank v. Bridges, 39 Okla. 359; Bank v. Miller, 229 U. S. 517. (b) The agent was acting in collusion with and in the interest of the insured and against the interest of his principal. Scripture v. Ins. Co., 20 Tex. Civ. App. 153; Ins. Co. v. Minch, 53 N. Y. 150; Pennoyer v. Willis, 26 Ore. 1; Terry v. Cotton Co., 138 Ga. 656. (c) The agent was attempting to act as the agent of both parties without the knowledge or consent of his principal. Fiske v. Royal Exch. Assn. Co., 100 Mo. App. 545; Ins. Co. v. Ins. Co., 138 N. Y. 446; Ramspeck v. Patillo, 104 Ga. 772; Rockford Ins. Co. v. Winfield, 57 Kan. 576. (4) The court erred in instructing the jury in effect that if they found from the evidence that, prior to the institution of this suit, plaintiff paid all necessary corporation fees to the State of Colorado and obtained from the Secretary of State of Colorado a certificate of authority to do business in the said State, the fact that plaintiff had not paid said fees and obtained said certificate of authority prior to its alleged acquisition of title to the property in question, or prior to the issuance of the policy in suit, or prior to the fire, was immaterial. Respondent did not have title to the ground on which the insured buildings stood at the time of the issuance of the policy and, hence the policy is void. Overton v. Ins. Co., 79 Mo. App. 1; Roberts v. Ins. Co., 26 Mo. App. 92; Holloway v. Ins. Co., 48 Mo. App. 1; Brenner v. Ins. Co., 99 Mo. App. 718; Appendix, 3 Mo. App. 603; Ins. Co. v. Manning, 160 Fed. 382; Lane v. Parsons, Rich & Co., 97 Minn. 98. (5) The court erred in overruling defendant's motion to quash the writ and in refusing to sustain the defense, set forth in the first paragraph of defendant's answer, which defense was based upon the grounds that the Superintendent of the Insurance Department of the State of Missouri, upon whom service was at-

tempted to be made, was not authorized by the laws
of Missouri to acknowledge or receive service of process for the defendant in this action and that Sec. 7042,
R. S. 1909, is unconstitutional and void, because it
denies to the defendant due process of law as guaranteed to it by the Constitution of Missouri and by section 1, article 14, Constitution of United States. Simon
v. Southern Ry. Co., 236 U. S. 115; Old Wayne Life
Assn. v. McDonough, 204 U. S. 22; Harkness v. Hyde,
98 U. S. 476; Southern Pac. Co. v. Denton, 146 U. S.
202; Goldey v. Morning News, 156 U. S. 518; Mechan-
ical Appliance Co. v. Castleman, 215 U. S. 437; Cain
v. Pub. Co., 232 U. S. 124.

Percy Werner and *Sutton & Huston, amici curiae.*

Fauntleroy, Cullen & Hay, Fry & Rodgers and
Fred D. Shaw for respondent.

(1) The insurance company is estopped to claim a
forfeiture of the policy for the reason the mill was
shut down at the time of the fire and waived the necessity for permission for the shutting down of the mill
to be in writing endorsed upon the policy. Hyman v.
Ins. Co., 42 Colo. 156; Nixon v. Ins. Co., 2 Colo. App.
265; Thompson v. Ins. Co., 169 Mo. 12; Rissler v. Ins.
Co., 150 Mo. 366; Huestess v. Ins. Co., 70 S. E. 406;
Millis v. Ins. Co., 95 Mo. App. 211; Rudd v. Ins.
Co., 120 Mo. App. 1. (2) Colorado has a like rule.
There, as here, if the agent who wrote the policy
knows of any fact existing which will cause a forfeiture of the policy and causes the assured to rely
upon the fact that the policy will not be avoided, the
insurance company is estopped to claim a forfeiture.
Wich v. Ins. Co., 2 Colo. App. 488; Nixon v. Ins. Co.,
2 Colo. App. 265; Hyman v. Ins. Co., 42 Colo. 162;
Allis v. Ins. Co., 11 Colo. App. 264; Smith v. Ins. Co.,
3 Colo. 422; Taylor v. Ins. Co., 14 Colo. 499; Strauss v.

Ins. Co., 42 Pac. 822; Donlon v. Ins. Co., 16 Colo. App. 416; Kittenring v. Assn., 22 Colo. 257; Strauss v. Ins. Co., 9 Colo. App. 386. (3) Kilpatrick & Hanley were the *alter ego* of the insurance company, and their knowledge of the fact that the factory was shut down and their assurances to Doepke that it was "all right"' is a waiver. Thompson v. Ins. Co., 169 Mo. 25; Rissler v. Ins. Co., 150 Mo. 368; Shutts v. Ins. Co., 159 Mo. App. 441; Prentice v. Ins. Co., 77 N. Y. 487 Wooldridge v. Ins. Co., 69 Mo. App. 413; Hyman v. Ins. Co., 42 Colo. 156; Crouse v. Ins. Co., 79 Mich. 249; Andrus v. Ins. Co., 91 Minn. 358; Hart v. Ins. Co., 9 Wash. 620; Haight v. Ins. Co., 92 U. S. 51; Burnham v. Ins. Co., 63 Mo. App. 85; Montgomery v. Ins. Co., 80 Mo. App. 500; Ross Langford v. Ins. Co., 97 Mo. App. 79. (4) Policy is not void by reason of the plant being shut down, but only voidable, and the insurance company must cancel and return unearned premium. Not having done so, policy continues in force. Patterson v. Ins. Co., 176 Mo. App. 37; Flannigan v. Ins. Co., 46 N. Y. Supp. 687; Springfield Co. v. Ins. Co., 151 Mo. 98; Miller v. Ins. Co., 106 Mo. App. 211; Anthony v. Ins. Co., 48 Mo. App. 73; Brix v. Ins. Co., 171 Mo. App. 518; Smith v. Ins. Co., 3 Colo. 422. (5) Accepting premium after fire is a waiver of any violation of policy after the agent of the insurance company knew of it. Flannigan v. Ins. Co., 46 N. Y. Supp. 687; Raddin v. Ins. Co., 120 U. S. 195; Baker v. Ins. Co., 77 Fed. 550; Ins. Co. v. Wolff, 95 U. S. 326; Freeman v. Ins. Co., 47 S. W. 1025. (6) This mortgage did not render the policy void, only voidable at the election of the insurance company. It only suspended the policy while the mortgage was upon the property. As soon as the mortgage was paid the policy revived and was in full force and effect at the time of the fire. Brix v. Ins. Co., 171 Mo. App. 518; Obermeyer v. Ins. Co., 43 Mo. 579; Born v. Ins. Co., 110 Iowa, 379; Viele v. Ins. Co., 26 Iowa, 9. (7) The fact that the record did not show a satisfaction of the mortgage is immaterial. If the mortgage was paid off, it ceased to be an encumbrance. Hawkes v. Ins. Co., 11 Wis. 188; Schreck v. Ins. Co., 27 Neb. 527; Vanlue v. Ins. Co., 26 N. E. 119; Born v. Ins. Co., 110 Iowa, 379. (8) Kilpatrick, the company's agent, who wrote the policy, knew that the mortgage was filed of record. Under such circumstances the insurance company waived its right to claim that the policy was void by reason of such mortgage. Hyman v. Ins. Co., 42 Colo. 156; Weinberger v. Ins. Co., 170 Mo. App. 270; Rissler v. Ins. Co., 150 Mo. 368; Laundry Co. v. Ins. Co., 151 Mo. 98; Thompson v. Ins. Co., 169 Mo. 28. (9) Notice to Kilpatrick, the company's agent, before the fire, that Peters held the $25,000 mortgage on the property was notice to the company. Where one agent represents several companies, what he knows is imputed to all. Hyman v. Ins. Co., 42 Colo. 156; Mesterman v. Ins. Co., 5 Wash. 524; Hamilton v. Ins. Co., 94 Mo. 355; Russell v. Ins. Co., 55 Mo. 585; Howitz v. Ins. Co., 40 Mo. 557. (10) Another defense which the insurance company urges is based upon its claim and assertion that Doepke, the president of the respondent, knew that Kilpatrick, the agent of the insurance company, was betraying his principal by withholding the information of the existence of the aforesaid mortgages, and of the fact that the plant was shut down and was idle. That therefore Doepke was "in collusion" with Kilpatrick to cheat and defraud the insurance company, and therefore Kilpatrick did not waive the forfeiture of the policy, which appellant claims existed, and for this reason a verdict should have been directed for the defendant. (a) Fraud is an affirmative defense which the insurance company should have set up in its answer by a statement of the facts which constitute fraud. There is no suggestion of any such defense in defendant's answer. Such defense must be specially pleaded. Hill v. Ins. Co., 127 S. W. 283; Harris v. Ins. Co., 248

Mo. 315; Cheevers v. Ins. Co., 83 N. Y. Supp. 728; Cade v. Ins. Co., 67 Pac. 603. (b) Any such doctrine, *ipso facto,* wipes out the whole principle of waiver or estoppel. Hyman v. Ins. Co., 42 Colo. 156; Spieser· v. Ins. Co., 97 N. W. 209; Allis v. Ins. Co., 11 Colo. App. 264; Huestess v. Ins. Co., 70 S. E. 405. (c) If Doepke entertained no fraudulent intent in regard to these matters, the policy was not void. Cohen v. Ins. Co., 78 Atl. 911; Reynolds v. Ins. Co., 46 N. W. 659; Hill v. Ins. Co., 127 S. W. 290; Prentiss v. Ins. Co., 77 N. Y. 487; Rissler v. Ins. Co., 150 Mo. 366. (11) Upon the return day of the writ of summons, the insurance company duly appeared in this case, and filed its written motion to "dismiss the cause," and set out numerous reasons therefor. This motion having been overruled by the trial court, appellant herein thereupon applied to the Supreme Court of Missouri for a writ of prohibition against respondent. An alternative writ of prohibition having been issued, the whole matter came up for decision in the case of State ex rel. v. Barnett, 239 Mo. 193. This court held the service good and that the circuit court of Audrain County had jurisdiction. Therefore the whole question of proper service and jurisdiction of the Audrain Circuit Court has been settled by the decision in that case and is *res adjudi-cata.* State ex rel. v. Barnett, 239 Mo. 193; Chapman v. Railroad, 146 Mo. 494; Bridge Co. v. Stone, 194 Mo. 184; Bank v. Taylor, 62 Mo. 338; Bank v. Donnell, 195 Mo. 591. Defendant, at a subsequent term of the court, by "leave of court had and obtained," filed its answer herein to the merits. This was a general appearance, and waived all questions of jurisdiction. Outside of appellant appearing, generally when it filed its motion to quash the writ and "dismiss the cause," it had lost its right, as a matter of right, to file any answer at the subsequent term, and could only then file its answer, as it did, as a matter of grace. Asking the court for and obtaining "leave" to file its

answer, when its motion to "dismiss" had been overruled, appellant voluntarily submitted itself to the
jurisdiction of the court, when it asked and obtained
"leave" to file its answer to the merits. Pry v. Railroad, 73 Mo. 124; 3 Cyc. 507; Tennison v. Perryman,
49 Mo. 110; Cement Co. v. Gas Co., 255 Mo. 3; Forgey
v. Co., 140 Mo. App. 605; Bank v. Railroad, 119 Mo.
App. 10; Baisley v. Baisley, 113 Mo. 544.

WOODSON, C. J.—This is a suit instituted June
6, 1911, in the circuit court of Audrain County, Missouri, by the plaintiff against the defendant, to recover
the sum of $2,500, alleged to be due the former under
the terms of a policy of insurance dated October 5,
1909, insuring certain property in the State of Colorado against damage and loss by fire.

A trial was had which resulted in a judgment for
the plaintiff, and the defendant, in proper time and
in due form, appealed the cause to this court.

We will briefly state the pleadings.

The petition was in due form, charging that the
plaintiff was a corporation duly organized under the
laws of Arizona; that at all the times therein stated
the defendant was a foreign insurance company, organized under the laws of Pennsylvania, and was duly
licensed under the laws of this State to carry on a
general fire insurance business herein, and was at all
of said times carrying on said business herein.

That the plaintiff on October 5, 1909, was the
absolute owner of the property insured, situated in
the State of Colorado; and that upon that date the defendant issued the policy mentioned, insuring the same
against loss or damage by fire for a period of one
year, for a consideration of————————dollars.

That on August 13, 1910, said property was struck
by lightning and destroyed and damaged to the amount of $134,000; and that proofs of loss were duly
given.

The policy was a regular standard policy, containing the usual terms and conditions.

At the September term, 1911, of said court the defendant filed in the cause a motion to quash the summons and the return of service thereof made by the sheriff of Cole County on the Superintendent of Insurance of this State, which was by the court overruled.

Thereupon the cause was passed to await the decision of this court in the case of State ex rel. v. Barnett, 239 Mo. 193.

After that case had been decided, the defendant, after leave of court had been obtained, filed an answer, which is substantially as follows:

The answer alleges the service was had upon the Superintendent of Insurance; that the court acquired no jurisdiction over defendant, because neither party was a resident of Missouri and the action accrued in Colorado, and therefore section 7042, Revised Statutes 1909, did not apply; that said section is unconstitutional and void, because in violation of section 30, article 2, of the Missouri Constitution, and section 1, article 14, of the Federal Constitution; also that section 7042 was enacted in 1885, Laws of Missouri 1885, page 183, in violation of section 28 and of section 34, of article 4, of the Missouri Constitution, and therefore void, so that the service of process gave no jurisdiction over the defendant.

That in violation of the terms of the policy the property had been permitted to remain idle more than thirty days without the written permission of the defendant; also that in violation thereof, said property had been encumbered by the execution of a mortgage thereon, to secure the sum of $25,000, without defendant's knowledge or consent.

Further, that the item "gold in process" mentioned in the policy was not destroyed; that contrary to the terms of the policy, the property insured was not in operation at the time of the fire, nor for more than six months prior thereto; that the property was mortgaged at the time of the issuance of the policy and at the time of the fire without the consent of the defendant; and that the plaintiff was guilty of fraud and false swearing in claiming in its proofs of loss that "gold in process" to the value of $9,000 was destroyed; that the plaintiff was not the sole and unconditional owner of the property insured, nor did it own the property in fee simple, because it had not been licensed to do business in Colorado under the provisions of section 904 and section 910, Revised Statutes of Colorado 1908, and therefore it did not have title to the property, pleading decisions of Colorado to this effect; and that the defendant had tendered to the plaintiff all the premium with interest thereon.

The reply denied the unconstitutionality of section 7042; admitted that the building was not in operation as charged by defendant, but pleaded waiver of such condition of the policy; that the mortgage on the property was paid off before the insurance was taken out; denied making false statements regarding "gold in process;" denied any information sufficient to form a belief as to whether section 910, Revised Statutes of Colorado 1908, and cases cited by defendant, were ever in force or rendered by the court; alleged that it paid taxes upon the property prior to the fire; pleaded that the courts of Colorado had decided that after a foreign corporation has paid a license fee, it may sue in the courts of Colorado; and pleaded that the doctrine of waiver was the law of Colorado.

The policy in suit was dated and delivered along with the other policies, amounting to about $50,000, to a Mr. Doepke, president of the respondent company, on or about October 5, 1909, and covers the insured property for one year thereafter. The insured property was destroyed by fire on August 13, 1910, and this action was instituted in the circuit court of Audrain County on June 6, 1911; summons being served upon Frank Blake, Superintendent of the Insurance Department of the State of Missouri, on June 7, 1911.

We will first state the undisputed facts of the case; and then briefly state what the evidence tended to show regarding those that were disputed, viz.:

The plaintiff herein is a corporation duly organized under the laws of the State of Arizona. The defendant is a fire insurance corporation duly organized under the laws of the State of Pennsylvania, and at all times mentioned in this suit and at the time this suit was commenced was, and ever since had been, duly licensed as a foreign insurance company to do business in the State of Missouri.

On October 5, 1909, the defendant duly made and delivered its policy and contract of insurance to plaintiff herein at Cripple Creek, Colorado, where it had a general insurance agency, which was represented by. Kilpatrick & Hanley. In that section of Colorado the insurance company had no other representative, and Kilpatrick & Hanley had authority to make contracts of insurance. At the time the insurance was effected plaintiff owned certain valuable mining property and was engaged in the building of a large smelter for the purpose of smelting gold from its mines, which were located two or three miles out of Cripple Creek, Teller County, Colorado. On October 5, 1909, for and in consideration of a premium of $74.12, defendant, through Kilpatrick & Hanley, its general agents at Cripple Creek, did issue its policy and contract of insurance to plaintiff, whereby it was insured against all loss or damage by fire for a period of one year from October 5, 1909, to October 5, 1910, to the smelter, buildings, machinery, etc., which went to make up the smelter, which are described in the policy and which were owned by plaintiff, and which was finished and ready for use the day it was destroyed by lightning. Lightning struck the buildings August 13, 1910, and they were all destroyed by fire resulting therefrom.

The evidence shows that the insured buildings and property, which were totally destroyed by fire, were worth $134,000, and that the loss and damage occasioned thereby was about that sum. There was a large amount of other insurance upon the property besides that which was issued by appellant herein, amounting to about $50,000. The insurance premiums were not paid in cash when the policies were delivered, but a credit was given to plaintiff therefor by Kilpatrick & Hanley, and prior to the fire plaintiff paid $500 to Kilpatrick & Hanley on the premiums, which amounted to between $1,500 and $1,600.

August 15, 1910, two days after the fire, Kilpatrick and Hanley sent a telegram from Cripple Creek, Colorado, to J. F. W. Doepke, the president of respondent, and one who was in sole charge of respondent's business, and the only one with whom Kilpatrick & Hanley ever had any business, requesting that respondent send the balance of the premiums, which amounted to $1,124. The telegram is as follows:

Cripple Creek, Aug. 15, 1910.

J. F. W. Doepke,
    Mercantile Building, St. Louis, Missouri.
    Mail draft for your protection eleven hundred and twenty-four dollars,

KILPATRICK & HANLEY.

Immediately upon receipt of that telegram Deopke sent a draft to Kilpatrick & Hanley for said sum of $1,124, which made payment in full of all the premiums upon all the policies, including the policy of defendant herein, which Kilpatrick & Hanley had issued upon the property in question.

At the time the insurance was effected and at the time the fire occurred the plaintiff had not received a license to do business in the State of Colorado from that State, although it had for a long time past owned the mining property in question and had been engaged in the erection of the smelter and buildings which were insured and destroyed by fire and had been regularly paying taxes to the State of Colorado upon the property in question.

After the fire the plaintiff gave due notice of the fire to defendant and made due proofs of loss through the Kilpatrick & Hanley agency, the agents of the defendant.

The policy provided that the property should not be idle for more than thirty days without the written permission of defendant. The evidence for plaintiff tended to show that at the time the policy was issued and delivered to plaintiff, its president informed the agents of defendant that because of the scarcity of fuel and the difficulty in delivering it at the plant, a tramway might have to be constructed, and on account of those matters the smelter might be idle at times for periods of more than thirty days at a time, and asked them what he should do in the premises. That in reply thereto said agents stated to him that that would be all right; and thereupon he accepted the policies and paid the premium as previously stated. That thereafter, and before the fire occurred, the same inquiry had been addressed a number of times to said agents, to which they made substantially the same answer, as that before stated. This was corroborated by Kilpatrick, one of defendant's agents and witnesses.

That when it was found out that the business would have to shut down, Doepke, the president of the plaintiff company, went to defendant's agents and informed them that he was unable to procure the necessary fuel with which to operate the smelter and would have to close down on that account, and asked them what was necessary for him to do in regard to the insurance, as he did not want any question raised as to its validity. This was on January 10, 1910; and Kilpatrick said to him, "All right; go ahead."

That each and every month thereafter said agents were notified of the fact that the mill was idle, and inquiry made of them as to what should be done. That at no time did they make ".any objections to it." Kilpatrick, one of defendant's agents says that was true, and that he made no objection, "because I expected he (Doepke) would start up in a short time, and I didn't want to lose the business and premiums."

The policy prohibited encumbrances upon the property; and at the time of the issuance of the policy or shortly thereafter, the company executed to one Peters a mortgage on the property to secure the sum of $25,000.

The undisputed evidence shows that in "June, 1910," Doepke informed Kilpatrick & Hanley about "this mortgage" and the agents made no objection "whatever" to it. They did not, upon being informed of the existence of this mortgage, cancel the policy or offer to return any of the premiums. Under date of July 11 and 21, respectively, 1910, Kilpatrick & Hanley wrote to plaintiff and cancelled certain other policies which they had issued to it upon this property for the reason that the Peters mortgage of $25,000 was upon the property, and in the place of the canceled policies wrote other policies to take the place of the cancelled ones. On July 10, 1910, more than a month before the fire, the Peters mortgage was paid off and satisfied in full. A second mortgage on the property is mentioned in the evidence, but not set out, and the amount it was given to secure is not made clear, but whatever was the amount, it was fully paid and satisfied June 11, 1908, more that two years before the fire. The note had been "surrendered up and canceled." The testimony in regard to both of these mortgages having been fully paid and released before the fire is proven by the uncontradicted testimony in this case.

It is conceded that the plaintiff company had not complied with the laws of Colorado, and secured a license to do business thereín, at the time the policy in question was issued.

Such additional facts as may be necessary for a proper disposition of the case will be stated in the opinion.

I. Counsel for the appellant (defendant) assign many grounds for a reversal of the judgment of the circuit court; a number of them are constitutional questions.

We will dispose of the latter first, because if appellant's position is sound in that regard, then there will be no necessity for a determination of the former.

Counsel for appellant state their position in the following language:

"The court erred in overruling defendant's motion to quash the writ and in refusing to sustain the defense, set forth in the first paragraph of defendant's answer, which defense was based upon the grounds that the Superintendent of the Insurance Department of the State of Missouri, upon whom service was attempted to be made, was not authorized by the laws of the State of Missouri to acknowledge or receive service of process for the defendant in this action and that section 7042, Revised Statutes 1909, is unconstitutional and void because it denies to the defendant due process of law as guaranteed to it by the Constitution of Missouri and by section 1, article 14, of the Constitution of the United States."

Constitutional Right.

While counsel state their general proposition in the language just quoted, yet when they come to brief and argue the same they subdivide it, at least by necessary implication, into five propositions, which, if I correctly understand them, are as follows:

First: That said section 7042, Revised Statutes 1909, was only designed to provide for service of pro-

cess issued in suits against foreign insurance companies doing business in this State founded upon contracts
of insurance made in this State, and not elsewhere.

Second: That, if said section 7042 was designed
to authorize service of process issued in suits against
foreign insurance companies doing business in this
State under authority of the statute properly granted,
growing out of contracts of insurance made in another
state or country, then it is unconstitutional, null and
void under both the State and Federal Constitutions,
as stated by counsel in their general proposition before
quoted.

Third: That the Legislature has no constitutional power to enact laws conferring jurisdiction upon the
courts of this State to try suits against foreign insurance companies based upon contracts of insurance executed in another State or country.

Fourth: That said section 7042 was not designed
to provide for service of process issued in suits against
foreign insurance companies doing business in this
State unlawfully, that is, without permission of the
State, founded upon contracts of insurance made in
this State; but if that was the design then the section
is unconstitutional for the reasons before stated.

Fifth: That, if said section 7042 was designed to
authorize service of process in suits against foreign
insurance companies doing business in this State based
upon a contract of insurance made in another State
with or without a license from that State, then it is
unconstitutional, null and void, for the reasons before
stated.

Regarding the first: While this question is embraced within the general proposition before mentioned,
yet in fact, it presents no constitutional question whatever, but simply involves the meaning of section 7042.

A foreword: Because of the misapprehension, in
my opinion, of counsel for appellant, and some of my

learned associates regarding the meaning of section 7042, Revised Statutes 1909, and its

Jurisdiction: Venue: Foreign Corporation: Contracts Made in Other States. constitutionality under the ruling of the Supreme Court of the United States in the cases of Old Wayne Mutual Life Assn. v. McDonough, 204 U. S. 8, 1. c. 22, and Simon v. Southern Railway Company, 236 U. S. 115, and because of the far-reaching, detrimental and injurious effect such a rule would have upon the jurisprudence of this and the other States of the Union and upon the speedy and orderly administration of justice, I feel justified in devoting more time and space to the case than would otherwise be necessary. This may, and doubtless will, lead to more or less repetition, and some illustrations to show the application of the principles of law to the facts; and consequently a prolongation of the opinion.

Returning to that statute: Every phase of this statute save its constitutionality was carefully considered and determined by this court in the case of State ex rel. v. Grimm, 239 Mo. 135, l. c. 159. Since, however, its meaning has again been questioned and its constitutionality assailed I will add some additional views as to its meaning and then carefully consider its constitutionality.

In order to grasp the real meaning of this statute we should have it before us. It reads as follows:

"Sec. 7042. Any insurance company not incorporated by or organized under the laws of this State, desiring to transact any business by any agent or agents in this State, shall first file with the Superintendent of the Insurance Department a written instrument or power of attorney, duly signed and sealed, appointing and authorizing said superintendent to acknowledge or receive service of process issued from any court of record, justice of the peace, or other inferior court, and upon whom such process may be served for and in behalf of such company, in all proceedings that may

be instituted against such company, in any court of
this State or in any court of the United States in this
State, and consenting that service of process upon said
superintendent shall be taken and held to be as valid
as if served upon the company, according to the laws of
this or any other State.   Service of process as aforesaid, issued by any such court, as aforesaid, upon the
superintendent, shall be valid and binding and be
deemed personal service upon such company, so long
as it shall have any policies or liabilities outstanding
in this State. . . . Every such instrument of appointment executed by such company shall be attested
by the seal of such company, and shall recite the whole
of this section, and shall be accompanied by a copy of
a resolution of the board of directors or trustees of
such company similarly attested, showing that the
president and secretary, or other chief officers of such
company, are authorized to execute such instrument in
behalf of the company; and if any such company shall
fail, neglect or refuse to appoint and maintain, within
the State, an attorney or agent, in the manner hereinbefore described, it shall forfeit the right to do or
continue business in this State."

This section should be read with sections 7040 and
7041, Revised Statutes 1909, for the former prohibits
all foreign insurance companies from doing business
in this State without first taking out a license, etc.,
and the second prescribes the mode of procuring such
license, etc.

This statute was first enacted in 1845, and was carried into the Revised Statutes of 1845 as section 3, on
page 610.

This statute was amended in 1885 (Laws 1885, p.
183, sec. 1) so as to read as we now have it in said
section 7042, and it was first carried into the Revised
Statutes of 1889, as section 5912.

On May 11, 1899, the appellant filed with the Superintendent of Insurance an instrument in the nature of a consent and appointment in compliance with the requirements of the Revised Statutes 1889, stating the desire of the appellant to transact business in the State of Missouri pursuant to the laws thereof, setting forth fully said section 5912.

And thereupon and under that authority the appellant has continued to the present time to transact its said business in this State under said license.

This places before us clearly the law under which the appellant came into the State to transact an insurance business, and its status before the law of the State, including its agreement for service of legal process upon it through the Superintendent of Insurance of this State.

It is one of the elementary rules of statutory construction that in trying to ascertain the meaning of a statute or an amendment thereto, we should first look at the status of the subject-matter of the contemplated legislation as well as the law or lack of law governing the same. If there is no law upon the subject, and some evil exists in connection therewith, which the Legislature desires to remedy, then a new statute must be enacted in order to remedy the evil; but if there is an existing law governing the matter, statutory or common law, which is defective or insufficient to properly govern the same and in consequence thereof evil lurks in or about the same, which should be abolished, then that end is generally accomplished by an enactment supplementing the deficient statute or the insufficiency of the common law, as the case may be. [Dowdy v. Wamble, 110 Mo. l. c. 283; Mooney v. Buford & George Mfg. Co., 72 Fed. l. c. 36.]

Prior to 1845 the insurance business transacted in this State, both life and fire, was comparatively small,

and principally done by foreign companies. For that
reason there had been but little legislation needed or
enacted upon the subject; no means were provided by
which service of process could be had against such a
company issuing policies in this State. This led to
great injustice and hardship in many cases, because
when a loss occurred the insured was compelled to settle with the company upon its own terms or go to the
State of its incorporation and sue it for the sum due on
the policy. This led to much loss of time, trouble and
expense on the part of the policy-holders in going to
and from the place of trial, to say nothing of the cost
and expense of the litigation.

This injustice appealed to the Legislature, and
in 1845, for the first time in so far as I have been able
to ascertain, it undertook by legislation to remedy that
injustice in so far as concerned contracts of insurance
made in this State, and thereby authorized suit to be
brought on such policies in the courts of this State,
and provided for service of process against any such
company in the manner stated therein, which will presently be copied.

As previously stated, the first legislation in this
State which took any definite form looking to a remedy
of the injustice and hardships mentioned, was enacted
in 1845, which is chapter 87, Revised Statutes 1845.

While this entire chapter should be considered in
connection herewith, as throwing light upon the general design the Legislature had in mind, yet space compels me to confine my observations to section 3, page
610, Revised Statutes 1845, thereof. It reads as follows:

"The agent or agents of any such company aforesaid, shall also be required before commencing business, or, in case he or they have already commenced
business, then, on or before the first day of July, eighteen hundred and forty-five, to furnish to the clerk of

the county court, to be placed on the records of said
court, a resolution of the board of directors of the company for which he or they may propose to act, or are
already acting, duly authenticated, authorizing any
citizen or person residing in the State of Missouri, or
elsewhere, having a claim against any such company
aforesaid, growing out of a contract of insurance, made
with the agent or agents of any such company aforesaid, doing business in this State, to sue for the same
in any court in said State having competent jurisdiction; and further authorizing service of process on
said agent or agents to be sufficiently binding on said
company to abide the issue of said suit, and that such
service shall authorize judgments in the same manner
that judgments are taken against private individuals;
and it is hereby enacted, that the service of process on
the said agent or agents, in any action commenced
against such company, shall be deemed a service upon
the company, and shall authorize the same proceedings
as in case of other actions at law; the process shall be
served and returned in the same manner, as if the action were against the agent or agents personally.''

In addition to what was held by this court in the
case of State ex rel. v. Grimm, 239 Mo. 135, l. c. 159 to
171, as to the meaning of section 7042, I have this to
say: That section 3 of the Act of 1845 required all
foreign insurance companies desiring to do business
in this State to first place on record a resolution of
the board of directors, ''authorizing any citizen or person residing in the State of Missouri or elsewhere, having a claim against any such company aforesaid *growing out of a contract of insurance, made with the agent
or agents of any such company aforesaid doing business in this State to sue for the same in any court in
said State.''*

The italics are ours, and are made for the purpose
of accentuating the fact that this original statute did,
as contended for by counsel for the petitioner, provide

and was designed to limit the service of process in suits against such. companies growing out of contracts of insurance *made by them in this State.*

This statute was amended by an Act of 1855 (R. S. 1855, p. 885, sec. 1) which also required a resolution of the board of directors of such foreign insurance company "authorizing any person having a claim against such company *growing out of a contract of insurance made in this State* with the agent or agents thereof doing business in this State *to sue such company* for the same in any court of this State."

This amendment also limited the service of process in suits against such company to actions upon contracts of insurance made in this State.

This statute appears as section 3, page 402, General Statutes 1865, and concludes as follows: "And the service of process on such agent or agents as aforesaid shall be deemed a service upon the company sued, and shall authorize the same proceedings in suit as in the case of other suits in such court," etc.

And the following amendment was added (Laws 1869, page 38, section 31, amended) by section 6013, Revised Statutes 1879:

"Service of process as aforesaid issued by any such court, as aforesaid, upon any such attorney appointed by the company or by the superintendent, as aforesaid, shall be valid and binding and be deemed personal service upon such company so long as it shall have any policies or liabilities outstanding in this State," etc.

The latter amendment was designed to limit the time of service of process upon the company *"to such time as it has policies or liabilities outstanding in this State,"* etc.

As time passed the insurance business grew by leaps and bounds, in proportion to the general business of the country, and policies of insurance were issued by the thousands in and out of this State by for-

eign corporations on property located herein and elsewhere, and in order to meet the new order of things,
additional legislation was necessary.

Under this new order of things there was no provision contained in the Act of 1845 or in any of the
amendments thereof prior to 1885, by which a resident
or a non-resident of this State could sue a foreign insurance company doing business herein, upon a policy
of insurance issued by it out of this State, insuring
property located in this State or elsewhere, and in order to meet that condition section 3 of the Act of 1845,
as amended, as previously stated, was further amended
by the Act of 1885. [Laws 1885, p. 183.]

After the various amendments mentioned had been
enacted, this statute, as before stated, passed into the
revision of 1889, and is section 5912, and into the revision of 1909, and is now section 7042.

Section 7042 was in full force and effect when appellant applied for a license to do business in this
State, and on the 11th day of May, 1899, it fully complied with the requirements of that statute, and among
other things filed with the Superintendent of Insurance
of the State the instrument mentioned in said section,
appointing him its agent to accept service of such process as therein provided for as might be issued against
it by any court of proper authority in this State, and
consented that service had upon him as such should be
legal and personally binding upon it in the same manner as other proceedings had in said court.

By the amendment of 1885, which is now section
7042, the Legislature broadened and extended the scope
and operation of the Act of 1845, and the various
amendments thereto, by striking out the words which
limited it to suits brought on contracts of insurance
made in this State, and by inserting in lieu thereof, the
provision requiring all such companies to appoint the
Superintendent of Insurance of this State as their
agent to accept service of process for them and to ac-

knowledge receipt of the same when "issued from any court of record, justice of the peace or other inferior court, and upon whom such process may be served for and in behalf of such company *in all proceedings that may be instituted against such company in any court of this State* or in any court of the United States in this State, and consenting that service of process upon said superintendent shall be taken and held to be as valid as if served upon the company, according to the laws of this or any other State," and that service of process as aforesaid issued by any such court as aforesaid upon the Superintendent of Insurance "shall be valid and binding and be deemed personal service upon such company so long as it shall have any policies or liabilities outstanding," etc.

The omission from this statute of the limitation of the process of the courts of this State to causes of action arising out of contracts of insurance made in this State, as originally enacted, and enlarging or extending the process of the courts to *"all proceedings that might be instituted against such company in any court of this State,"* clearly authorized the Superintendent of Insurance to acknowledge the receipt and service of process for any such company in any and all transitory causes of action that might be brought by anyone against it in the courts of this State, except those mentioned in section 7044, Revised Statutes 1909, regardless of place where the contract of insurance was entered into; and the language of this amendment is sufficiently comprehensive to embrace residents and non-residents of the State at the time of the issuance of the policy and at the time of the institution of the suit thereon. This it seems to me is too plain for argument, and to attempt to do so would but confuse the plain meaning of the language of the amendment of 1885, and the steadfast purpose the Legislature had in mind when the amendment was enacted. Nor does the amendment of 1869, which in substance provides

that the authority of the Superintendent of Insurance
to acknowledge and accept service for such company
shall continue "so long as it shall have any policies or
liabilities outstanding in this State," militate in the
least against the construction heretofore placed upon
this section of the statutes, for the obvious reason that
said amendment is a limitation upon the duration of
the authority of the Superintendent of Insurance to
act for such company, and not a limitation upon the
character of suits that may be brought and prosecuted
in the courts of this State under such a service of process.

This court in the case of Dowdy v. Wamble, 110
Mo. l. c. 283, in discussing this rule, said:

"There are few guides to construction more useful
than that which directs attention to the prior condition of the law to aid in determining the full legislative
meaning of any statutory change thereof."

In discussing the same question the United States
Court of Appeals for the Seventh Circuit, in the case
of Mooney v. Buford & George Mfg. Co., 72 Fed. l. c.
36, said:

"The earlier provisions quoted from the Indiana
Code and statutes expressly limit the right to process
against foreign corporations to suits arising out of
transactions had in this State, and, from the mere omission of that limitation in the latter enactments, there
would arise a just inference that an enlargement of
jurisdiction in this particular was intended; but the
broad terms employed in the Act of 1883, 'process in
any suit against such company may be served,' etc.,
need not to be helped out by inference. . . . There
is no reason to be found in the context or in the course
of previous legislation in the State or in considerations
of policy for believing that in the enactment before us
the word was intended to be used in a more restricted
sense."

I am therefore clearly of the opinion that said section 7042 embraces the policy mentioned in this case and authorized the holders thereof to sue thereon in the circuit court of Audrain County.

II. This brings us to the consideration of the constitutional questions presented.

We will try to discuss these questions in the order stated, but they are so closely related and interdependent that what is said of one may necessarily apply to others; and for the purpose of preventing confusions in discussing the constitutionality of said section 7042, it should be borne in mind that it does not apply to suits arising out of contracts of insurance written in this State, by a foreign insurance company, without a license from it to do business herein; all such suits are governed by section 7044. *Nor do either of those sections authorize service of process* in suits brought in the courts of this State against foreign insurance companies doing business herein *without a license from the State to so do,* based *upon a policy of insurance issued thereby in another state or country.* That question will be considered in Paragraph Five of this opinion.

Due Process and Equal Protection.

In discussing sections 7042 and 7044, even though our language may be general, yet what is said of the one is not intended to apply to the suits mentioned in the other.

Regarding the first constitutional question presented, which is the second subdivision of appellant's general contention, before quoted: In brief, counsel for appellant contend that section 7042 is violative of section 30 of article 2 of the Constitution of Missouri and section 1 of the Fourteenth Amendment of the Constitution of the United States, because: first, it does not afford appellant due process of law; and, second, because the Legislature of this State has no power to authorize suits to be brought in the courts of this State for a breach of a contract of insurance not made in this State.

These two propositions are so closely and inseparably connected that we will discuss them together.

Does said section 7042 provide for due process of law, and was the appellant served with due process of law?

The respondent answers this question in the affirmative, while the appellant answers it in the negative.

The latter bases its answer upon the authority of the dissenting opinion filed in the Grimm case, supra, and the opinion of the Supreme Court of the United States in the case of Simon v. Southern Ry. Co., 236 U. S. 115.

By reading the dissenting opinion in the Grimm case it will be seen that it was predicated upon the idea that said section 7042 only applied to service of process in cases involving controversies growing out of insurance contracts *made in this State* with a foreign insurance company doing business herein under a license duly issued to it; and therefore service of process upon such a company, under that section of the statutes conferred no jurisdiction upon the courts of this State to try a case arising out of such a contract made in some other state or country.

This contention of the petitioner, in my opinion, is a clear misconception of the meaning of said section 7042, and of the class of cases to which it applies.

In addition to what was said upon this question in the Grimm case I wish to say that in the light of the history of this statute, as shown by the various amendments made thereto from time to time and the evils the Legislature intended thereby to remedy, there is no longer left a shadow of doubt but what it was the design of the Legislature, by enacting section 7042, to provide for process in suits involving controversies arising out of all lawful contracts of insurance issued

by such companies outside of this State as well as
those made in it, except those mentioned in section
7044 and the classes of cases mentioned in the case of
Old Wayne Life Association v. McDonough, 204 U. S.
l. c. 22, which will be carefully considered later. That
being unquestionably true, then if that section is constitutional, clearly the petitioner here was served with
due process of law within the meaning of the due process clauses of the State and Federal constitutions.

The Grimm case, therefore, has no bearing whatever upon the constitutional questions presented.

While there is some language used in the opinion
of the court in the case of Simon v. Southern Ry. Co.,
supra, which seems to lend support to the contention
of counsel for the petitioner, yet when read in the light
of the facts of that case and the statute the court had
under consideration, both of which are totally different
from those presented by this record, it does not, in my
opinion, bear the construction placed upon it by counsel for the petitioner, nor is it *applicable or controlling*
in the case at bar. In order to get a clear comprehen-
sion of that case I will briefly state the principal facts
thereof, as they appear in the statement of them, as
made by that court.

In that case the petition charged that the plaintiff
was a resident of Louisiana and the defendant was a
Virginia railroad corporation doing business in the former State; that the plaintiff purchased a ticket from
defendant, from Salem, Alabama, to Meridian, Mississippi, and that while traveling over the lines of the defendant in Alabama, through its negligence, a collision
occurred in which the plaintiff was injured. The suit
was brought in the district court for the Parish of
Orleans in the State of Louisiana, and the petition
alleged several items of damages, aggregating something over $13,000.

At all the times mentioned there was in force in
the State of Louisiana, an act of the Legislature known

as Act 54 (Louisiana Acts 1904, p. 133), two sections
of which are as follows:

Section 1: "That it shall be the duty of every foreign corporation doing any business in this State to
file in the office of the Secretary of State a written declaration setting forth and containing the place or locality of its domicile, the place or places in the State
where it is doing business and the name of its agent or
agents or other officers in this State upon whom process may be served."

Section 2: "Whenever any such corporation shall
do any business of any nature whatever in this State
without having complied with the requirements of section one of this act, it may be sued for any legal cause
of action in any parish of the State where it may do
business, and service of process in such suit may be
made upon the Secretary of State the same and with
the same validity as if such corporation had been personally served."

Having availed himself of these statutes the plaintiff had a summons issued for the defendant, directed
to "the Southern Railway Company, through Hon.
John T. Michel, Secretary of State of Louisiana, New
Orleans," and required the defendant to answer in
ten days.

The deputy sheriff on December 3, 1904, served the
citation and petition "on the within named Southern
Railway Co. in the Parish of East Baton Rouge, State
of Louisiana, by personal service on E. J. McGivney,
Asst. Secy. of State, Jno. T. Michel, Secy. of State,
being absent at the time of service." The Assistant
Secretary of State filed the citation and petition in
his office.

No notice, however, was given to the defendant by
the Secretary of State of the service of the citation
upon him or of the fact that suit had been brought
against it. It therefore made no appearance in the
suit, and on January 10, 1905, a judgment by default

was entered against the defendant; and thereafter on
January 20th, upon evidence introduced by the plaintiff, the court rendered a judgment for him for the
full amount sued for.

On February 6, 1905, the defendant, having heard
of the rendition of the judgment against it, filed a bill
in the circuit court of the United States for the District of Louisiana, asking that Simon be perpetually
enjoined from enforcing said judgment. The bill of
the railway company asking for the injunction charged
fraud on the part of Simon in procuring the judgment.

Proceeding, that court says:

"The bill further alleged that the Southern Railway was not doing business in the State of Louisiana;
that the service upon the Secretary or Assistant Secretary of State was not a citation upon the railway
company and was null and void for the purpose of
bringing it under the jurisdiction of the Civil District
Court; that any judgment rendered upon such attempted 'citation would be, if rendered without appearance of the defendant, a judgment without due process of law, and consequently, in violation of the Constitution;' that the railway company had never received the citation issued in the suit, nor was it advised,
nor had it any knowledge of the pendency of said proceedings until after the rendition of the judgment;
that the verdict of the jury having been rendered upon
false testimony and without notice, it would be against
good conscience to allow the judgment thereon to be enforced against the railway company, which has no remedy at law in the premises and has a complete meritorious defense to the claim on which the judgment is
based; that by fraud and accident, unmixed with its
own negligence, the railway company has been prevented from making such defense."

The cause was by the circuit court referred to a
master to hear the evidence and to report his conclusions of law and facts. He found that the railway was

not doing business in Louisiana in the sense of the statute; that the judgment was not fraudulent, but was void because service upon the Assistant Secretary of State was not the "service upon the Secretary of State" required by the statute.

The circuit court found that the railway company was doing business in New Orleans; but ruled that Act 54 did not provide for service on the Assistant Secretary of State, and hence that the judgment by default in the State court was void for want of jurisdiction of the person of the defendant.

The circuit court did not consider the question of fraud, but, as before stated, held that the State judgment was void because the Louisiana statute providing for service on foreign corporations was unconstitutional; and it entered a permanent injunction against said Simon, as prayed for in the bill. From that judgment Simon appealed the case to the Supreme Court of the United States.

Before taking up the Simon-Railway case, it should be borne in mind that section 1 of the Louisiana statute before quoted was not before the Supreme Court of the United States for consideration, because the service of summons in that case was had, if at all, upon the railway company, under the authority of section 2 of that act, and was served upon the Assistant Secretary of State instead of the Secretary, as the act required. This is made clear and set at rest by the following language quoted from page 129 of opinion of Mr. Justice LAMAR, who delivered the opinion in that case:

"The broader the ground of the decision here, the more likelihood there will be of affecting judgments held by persons not before the court. We therefore purposely refrain from passing upon either of the propositions decided in the courts below, and without discussing the right to sue on a transitory cause of action and serve the same on an *agent voluntarily appointed*

by the foreign corporation, we put the decision here on
the special fact, relied on in the court below, that in this
case the cause of action arose within the State of Alabama, and the suit therefor, in the Louisiana court,
was served on an agent designated by a Louisiana
statute.

"Subject to exceptions, not material here, *every
State has the undoubted right to provide for service
of process upon any foreign corporations doing business therein; to require such companies to name agents
upon whom service may be made; and also to provide that in case of the company's failure to appoint
such agent, service, in proper cases may be made upon
an officer designated by law.* [Mutual Reserve Assn.
v. Phelps, 190 U. S. 147; Mutual Life Ins. Co. v. Spratley, 172 U. S. 602.]"

After thus stating the facts of the Simon-Railway
case, copying the statute under which service of process in that case was attempted to be had, and what the
court in that case *did not consider or decide,* we will
now review what it *did decide therein.*

Following immediately the quotation last made
from that opinion, the Supreme Court of the United
States held that the second section of the Statute of
Louisiana, the one under which the pretended service
was had, was unconstitutional, in the following language:

"But this power to designate by statute the officer
upon whom service in suits against foreign corporations may be made relates to business and transactions
within the jurisdiction of the State enacting the law.
Otherwise, claims on contracts wherever made and suits
for torts wherever committed might by virtue of such
compulsory statute be drawn to the jurisdiction of any
State in which the foreign corporation might at any
time be carrying on business. The manifest inconvenience and hardship arising from such extra-terri-
torial extension of jurisdiction, by virtue of the power

to make such compulsory appointments, could not defeat the power if in law it could be rightfully exerted. But these possible inconveniences serve to emphasize the importance of the principle laid down in Old Wayne Life Association v. McDonough, 204 U. S. 22, that the statutory consent of a foreign corporation to be sued does not extend to causes of action arising in other States.

"In that case the Pennsylvania statute, as a condition of their doing business in the State, required foreign corporations to file a written stipulation agreeing 'that any legal process affecting the company served on the Insurance Commissioner . . . shall have the same effect as if served personally on the company within this State.' The Old Wayne Life Association having executed and delivered, in Indiana, a policy of insurance on the life of a citizen of Pennsylvania was sued thereon in Pennsylvania. The declaration averred that the company 'has been doing business in the State of Pennsylvania, issuing policies of life insurance to numerous and divers residents of said county and State,' and service was made on the Commissioner of Insurance. The association made no appearance and a judgment by default was entered against it. Thereafter suit on the judgment was brought in Indiana. The plaintiff there introduced the record of the Pennsylvania proceedings and claimed that, under the full-faith-and-credit clause of the Constitution, he was entitled to recover thereon in the Indiana court. There was no proof as to the company having done any business in the State of Pennsylvania, except the legal presumption arising from the statements in the declaration as to soliciting insurance in that State. This court said:

"'But even if it be assumed that the company was engaged in some business in Pennsylvania at the time the contract in question was made, it cannot be held that the company agreed that service of process upon the Insurance Commissioner of that Commonwealth would alone be sufficient to bring it into court in respect of all business transacted by it, no matter where, with or for the benefit of citizens of Pennsylvania . . . Conceding, then, that by going into Pennsylvania, without first complying with its statute, the defendant association may be held to have consented to the service upon the Insurance Commissioner of process in a suit brought against it there in respect of business transacted by it in that Commonwealth, such assent cannot properly be implied where it affirmatively appears, as it does here, that the business was not transacted in Pennsylvania. . . . As the suit in the Pennsylvania court was upon a contract executed in Indiana; as the personal judgment in that court against the Indiana corporation was only upon notice to the Insurance Commissioner, without any legal notice to the defendant association and without its having appeared in person or by attorney or by agent in the suit; and as the act of the Pennsylvania court in rendering the judgment must be deemed that of the State within the meaning of the Fourteenth Amendment, we hold that the judgment in Pennsylvania was not entitled to the faith and credit which, by the Constitution, is required to be given to the . . . judicial proceedings of the several States, and was void as wanting in due process of law.' "

As before stated, it should be *remembered* that in that case Simon *purchased his ticket at and from Salem, Alabama, to Meridian, Mississippi,* and that while riding on that ticket *he was injured in Alabama;* also that *service of the summons* in that case *was not had under the authority of the first section* of the Louisiana act mentioned, which authorizes service of process in such cases upon *one of the company's own agents* or officers in the State; but said service was had under the *second section* of said act which only applies whenever any such company transacts any business in that

State *without having complied with the requirements of section 1* of said act, and then and only then, could service of process be had upon the Secretary of State. That is, service under the second section could never be had where the railway company had complied with the requirements of the first section of the act, for in that case the service would have to be had under it, and not the second section; and there was not a *scintilla* of evidence introduced in that case which tended to show said company had not complied with the requirements of that section which of itself was sufficient to render inoperative the second section, for the obvious reason that it expressly provides whenever any such company transacts any business in that State without complying with the requirements of the first section, then service may be had under the authority of the second section. But concede that the railway company had complied with the requirements of the first section, then of course, in the express language of the second section it could not apply or become operative in that case, for the company had complied with the requirements of the first section.

And it should also be noted in this connection that two concurring facts had to affirmatively appear before the second section could, under its express provisions, apply to that case: first, that the railway company had not complied with the requirements of section one; and, second, that the company was doing business in that State without authority from the State to do so. There was no showing of non-compliance with the former, and therefore all business shown to have been transacted in that State by the railway company must be presumed to have been lawful, and not unlawful, under the laws of that State, as well as that of other States. In other words, the second section was designed to provide for service upon all such corporations which were poachers or interlopers, transacting business illegally in that State. In other words, by reading, the second section of the Louisiana act, it will be seen that it *only applies* to suits brought against a foreign corporation doing business *in that State without authority therefrom,* and therefore it could not apply to the Simon-Railway case, because that suit was based upon a tort committed, not in Louisiana, but in the State of Alabama. The mere fact, if it was a fact, of which there was no evidence either way, that the railway company may have been doing business illegally in Louisiana, that is, without authority from the State, could not expand the provisions of that section so as to embrace suits based upon torts committed or contracts executed in another State. Nor was the railway company in that case guilty of any conduct from which the law could or would presume that it had by implication consented to service upon the Secretary of State or the Assistant Secretary. Such implication can only arise from the fact that the transaction out of which the suit grew was transacted in the State without authority.

The second section, therefore, in the very nature of the case, was only applicable to suits growing out of said illegal transactions. That must be true, for the reason that said section by express terms limits its operation to suits brought in that State growing out of such illegal operations. Let me make this point clear, for it is the differentiation between this and the Simon case, and the one upon which the members of this court differ. The second section of the Louisiana act was designed to afford redress in the courts of that State, to only such persons who had been induced to make contracts therein with a foreign corporation which had not complied with the requirements of the first section thereof; and consequently the process authorized to be issued and served by the second section was of necessity limited to suits growing out of said poaching contracts so made in that State; and it could not possibly apply to any contract made in any other State or country.

This is the principle upon which the cases of Mutual Reserve Association v. Phelps, 190 U. S. 147, and Mutual Life Insurance Co. v. Spratley, 172 U. S. 602, are based; and that is the reason and the sole reason upon which the learned judge who wrote the opinion in the Simon-Railway Case used this language:

"But this power [the power to serve the Secretary of State without the consent of the company] to designate by statute the officer upon whom service in suits against foreign corporations may be made relates to business and transactions within the jurisdiction of the State enacting the law."

This is clearly the meaning of the second section; and I am unable to see what other meaning that court or any other court could give to it.

Moreover, if under the second section, because of the fact that a foreign corporation illegally transacted business in Louisiana—perchance just one transaction (and the record discloses in that case it was not extensive)—it may be sued in the courts thereof upon all lawful business transactions conducted in another State, as well as upon the illegal transactions conducted in that State, then why was the first section, which is general in its provisions, enacted? I respectfully submit, none whatever; and to answer the question otherwise would permit the second section (which is an exception to, or more accurately speaking, is an assisting adjunct to the first, designed to cover the poaching transactions not embraced in the first) not only to control the first, the principal part of the act, but would practically repeal it and wipe it from the statutes of Louisiana; and that, too, would be brought about by the illegal act of a wrongdoer.

This was the identical question that was involved in the case of Old Wayne Life Association v. McDonough, 204 U. S. 22; and the ruling of the court in that case was just as it was on the Simon-Railway case. This is made clear from the following language quoted from the former:

" 'But even if it be assumed that the company was engaged in some business in Pennsylvania [which was without authority] at the time the contract in question was made, it cannot be held that the company agreed that service of process upon the Insurance Commissioner of that Commonwealth would alone be sufficient to bring it into court in respect of all business transacted by it, no matter where, with or for the benefit of citizens of Pennsylvania . . . Conceding, then, that by going into Pennsylvania, without first complying with its statute, the defendant association may be held to have consented to the service upon the Insurance Commissioner of process in a suit brought against it there in respect of business transacted by it in that Commonwealth, such assent cannot properly be implied where it affirmatively appears, as it does here, that the business was not transacted in Pennsylvania. . . . As the suit in the Pennsylvania court was upon a contract executed in Indiana; as the personal judgment in that court against the Indiana corporation was only upon notice to the Insurance Commissioner, without any legal notice to the defendant association and without its having appeared in person or by attorney or by agent in the suit; and as the act of the Pennsylvania court in rendering the judgment must be deemed that of the State within the meaning of the Fourteenth Amendment, we hold that the judgment in Pennsylvania was not entitled to the faith and credit which, by the Constitution, is required to be given to the . . . judicial proceedings of the several States, and was void as wanting in due process of law.' "

By the use of the words, "Conceding, then, that by going into Pennsylvania, without first complying with its statute [which made its contract illegal], the

defendant association may be held to have consented
[by implication] to the service upon the Insurance
Commissioner of process in a suit brought against it
there in respect of business transacted by it in that
Commonwealth [which was without permission of the
State, and therefore illegal], such assent cannot properly be implied where it affirmatively appears, as it
does here, that the business was not transacted in
Pennsylvania,'' the court meant to say, and did in
effect say, that the fact that the Old Wayne Company
had previous to the time it executed and delivered the
policy there in suit to the insured in the State of Indiana it had been transacting business in Pennsylvania
without authority, constituted no ground, within the
meaning of the Pennsylvania statute, from which the
court could presume that the company had consented
by implication that the Insurance Commissioner of
Pennsylvania might accept service of process in a suit
based upon the policy so executed and delivered in the
State of Indiana, notwithstanding the fact that such
a presumption would have been indulged in against
the company, had that suit been based upon one of the
policies mentioned, executed and delivered by it in
Pennsylvania, without authority given by that State.

In that case, as in the Simon case, there was no
express agreement that service might be *had upon any
one,* yet the court stated that it might have implied
consent of service in that case, had the company illegally entered said State, and there have transacted the
business out of which that litigation arose, in violation
of its laws; but in that case it refused to indulge in such
presumptions because the uncontradicted evidence
showed that the transaction out of which that litigation arose was not conducted in the State in which the
suit was brought and process served; and therefore
held that in the very nature of the case it could not be
presumed that the company by implication consented
to service in the State of Pennsylvania, from the mere

fact that it had illegally transacted other business
therein than that out of which that litigation arose,
without first complying with the laws of that State,
when it affirmatively appeared that the illegal transaction sued on, and upon which the implied consent was
predicated, was not conducted in Pennsylvania; but
was transacted in the State of Indiana; and in the
Simon case, in the State of Alabama; but neither of
those suits was brought in the State where the policy
was executed.

It was for this reason that the Supreme Court of
the United States held in the Old Wayne and the Simon
cases that such a statute, as the second section of the
Louisiana act, was unconstitutional and void, if its. design was to authorize service of process upon any such
company in a suit based upon other than illegal transactions conducted in the State where the suit was
brought; and that was correct because that section
only applies to suits based upon policies illegally issued
in that State.

Suppose the service in the Simon case had been
under the first section of the Louisiana act, which provides for service upon the statutory agent of the company (I use the words, statutory agent, in the sense
that those mentioned in the first section are statutory
agents as well as actual agents, in so far as service of
process is concerned) then could it be seriously contended that the service in that case would not have
been valid; that is, if it was doing a legitimate business there at the time? I think not. Otherwise, no suit
could be brought in the courts of this, that or any other
State against any foreign corporation doing business
here, by *anyone, resident or non-resident, upon any
cause of action accruing outside of the State.* That is
not the law, nor ever will be, as long as the immaculate
flower of justice continues to bloom in the human heart.

The service in this case was had under the authority of section 7042, Revised Statutes 1909, which cor-

responds to the first section of the Louisiana act, and
not under section 7044, Revised Statutes 1909, which
is substantially the same and designed to serve the
same purpose as did the second section of the Louisiana act. Section 7044 reads:

"Sec. 7044. Service of summons in any action
against an insurance company, not incorporated under
and by virtue of the laws of this State, and not authorized to do business in this State by the Superintendent
of Insurance, shall, in addition to the mode prescribed
in section 7042, be valid and legal and of the same force
and effect as personal service on a private individual,
if made by delivering a copy of the summons and complaint to any person within this State who shall solicit
insurance on behalf of any such insurance corporation,
or make any contract of insurance, or collect or receive
any premium for insurance, or who adjusts or settles
a loss or pays the same for such insurance corporation, or in any manner aids or assists in doing either."

Had this suit been brought under section 7044 instead of section 7042, then the case would have been
on all-fours with the Old Wayne and Simon cases, for
the reason the former section only applies where the
policy sued on is issued in this State by such a company without first complying with sections 7040, 7041
and 7042, Revised Statutes 1909.

This is based upon the express authority of Mutual Reserve Assn. v. Phelps, 190 U. S. 147; Mutual
Life Ins. Co. v. Spratley, 172 U. S. 602, and New
England Mutual Life Ins. Co. v. Woodworth, 111 U. S.
138, and the same process of reasoning is used by the
Supreme Court of the United States in the Old Wayne
and the Simon cases, that is, that the said statute only
applies to poachers or interlopers who have issued policies in a State without first complying with her laws;
consequently had the policy sued on been illegally issued in this State, then as the court said in the Old
Wayne and Simon cases, there would have been an

implied consent that service of process in a suit brought thereon in the courts of this State might have been had upon the persons specified in said section 7044.

Since, however, it affirmatively appears that the appellant had fully complied with the requirements of said section 7042 and the policy having been issued in the State of Colorado, the case is not embraced within the provision of said section 7044, but falls squarely within the letter and spirit of section 7042, and therefore removes it from the operation of the rule announced in the Old Wayne and Simon cases, and brings it completely within the principles of law laid down in the case of State ex rel. v. Grimm, 239 Mo. 135, l. c. 159 to 171.

The case of the New England Mutual Life Ins. Co. v. Woodworth, 111 U. S. 138, is directly in point here. It was an action upon a life insurance policy issued upon the life of Ann E. Woodworth, who was domiciled at the time the policy was taken out in the State of Michigan, and who died at Seneca Falls, New York. She had never been domiciled in the State of Illinois and had no assets in the State of Illinois, unless the policy of insurance constituted assets. The probate court of Champaign County, Illinois, appointed the husband, S. E. Woodworth, administrator of the estate of Ann E. Woodworth, and he brought suit in the court of the State of Illinois against the New England Mutual Life Insurance Company, a corporation of the State of Massachusetts. Stephen E. Woodworth, appointed administrator, was the husband of Ann E. Woodworth and the said Stephen E. Woodworth, since the death of his wife, had been a resident of the county of Champaign, and State of Illinois, and had possession of the policy at the time the suit was instituted. On this state of facts, the defendant requested the presiding judges to rule that the plaintiff, as administrator appointed in Illinois, could not maintain this action. The request was overruled and the case carried to the

Supreme Court of the United States and that court sustained the proceeding, though the service was upon the defendant by virtue of a statute requiring the defendant to appoint a person upon whom lawful process could be served. In deciding the case, the Supreme Court of the United States said:

"In view of this legislation and the policy embodied in it, when this corporation, not organized under the laws of Illinois, has, by virtue of those laws, a place of business in Illinois, and a general agent there, and a resident attorney there for the service of process, and can be compelled to pay its debts there by judicial process, and has issued a policy payable, on death, to an administrator, the corporation must be regarded as having a domicil there, in the sense of the rule that the debt on the policy is assets at its domicil, so as to uphold the grant of letters of administration there. The corporation will be presumed to have been doing business in Illinois by virtue of its laws at the time the intestate died, in view of the fact that it was so doing business there when this suit was brought (as the bill of exceptions alleges), in the absence of any statement in the record that it was not so doing business there when the intestate died. In view of the statement in the letters, if the only personal property the intestate had was the policy, as the bill of exceptions states, it was for the corporation to show affirmatively that it was not doing business in Illinois when she died, in order to overthrow the validity of the letters, by thus showing that the policy was not assets in Illinois when she died.

"The general rule is that simple contract debts, such as a policy of insurance not under seal, are, for the purpose of founding administration, assets where the debtor resides, without regard to the place where the policy is found, as this court has recently affirmed in Wyman v. Halstead, 109 U. S. 654. But the reason why the State which charters a corporation is its dom-

icil in reference to debts which it owes, is because there
only can it be sued or found for the service of process.
This is now changed in cases like the present; and in
the courts of the United States it is held, that a corporation of one State doing business in another, is suable
in the courts of the United States established in the
latter State, if the laws of that State so provide, and
in the manner provided by those laws. [Lafayette
Insurance Company v. French, 18 How. 404; Railroad
Company v. Harris, 12 Wall. 65; Ex parte Schollen-
berger, 96 U. S. 369; Railroad Company v. Koontz,
104 U. S. 5, 10.]''

This cause had been cited and approved in the
following cases: Southern Pacific Co. v. Denton, 146
U. S. 202, l. c. 207; Shaw v. Quincy Mining Co., 145
U. S. 444, l. c. 452; Fitzgerald Const. Co. v. Fitzgerald,
137 U. S. 98, l c. 106; In re Louisville Underwriters,
134 U. S. 488, l. c. 493; In re Magid-Hope Mfg. Co.,
110 Fed. l. c. 353; Burger v. Grand Rapids & I. R. Co.,
22 Fed. l. c. 563; Kibbler v. St. Louis & S. F. R. Co.,
147 Fed. l. c. 881; Elk Garden Co. v. T. W. Thayer Co.,
179 Fed. l. c. 558; Mich. Aluminum F. Co. v. Aluminum
Castings Co., 190 Fed. l. c. 883; Mooney v. Buford &
George Mfg. Co., 72 Fed. l. c. 40; Hazeltine v. Mississippi Val. Fire Ins. Co., 55 Fed. l. c. 745; Overman
Wheel Co. v. Pope Mfg. Co., 46 Fed. l. c. 579; Riddle
v. New York, L. E. & W. R. Co., 39 Fed. l. c. 291; Zam-
brino v. Galveston, H. & S. A. Ry. Co., 38 Fed. l. c. 452.

Since the opinion in the Simon-Railway case was
handed down a case similar to the one at bar came before the United States District Court of New York, and
it was there said:

"In Simon v. Southern Railway, 236 U. S. 115,
the Supreme Court decided that a court of Louisiana
had not acquired jurisdiction under the following facts:
The defendant was a railroad company organized in
another State, having none of its railroad in Louisiana; but doing some business there. The statutes of

Louisiana directed all foreign corporations doing business in the State to appoint an agent on whom process should be served, and provided that if the corporation failed to make an appointment, service might be made upon the Secretary of State. The defendant not having appointed any such agent, Simon served his process on the Assistant Secretary of State in an action arising upon the tort of the defendant committed within the State of Alabama. The ground of the decision was that the implied consent of the corporation arising from its doing business in Louisiana must be limited to actions arising out of the business done within the State. The same rule was laid down in Old Wayne Life Association v. McDonough, 204 U. S. 8; the action there being in Pennsylvania upon a life insurance contract executed in Indiana by an Indiana corporation.

"In Simon v. Southern Railway, supra, the court especially reserved from the decision a case such as those at bar, where a foreign corporation has complied with the State statute and appointed an agent upon which process may be served. Such a case at first blush presents an apparent contradiction. Since 1839 (Bank of Augusta v. Earle, 13 Pet. 519), it has been the doctrine of the Supreme Court that a foreign corporation was a fictitious entity which had no existence outside of the territory of the sovereign which created it. All its acts elsewhere must be viewed as those of an absent principal, acting through an authorized agent. It resulted that personal jurisdiction could arise only when some agent had been appointed who was expressly authorized to appear or to accept service for the absent principal. [St. Clair v. Cox, 106 U. S. 350.] Otherwise the foreign State must proceed *in rem* against the property of the corporation, or *in personam* against agents within its borders. In 1855 (Lafayette Ins. Co. v. French, 18 How. 404), the court modified the extreme application of this doctrine by holding that, when a corporation did business within a foreign State which required as a prerequisite the appointment of an agent, consent to such an appointment must be assumed from the doing of the business, and that jurisdiction *in personam* would be acquired just as if there had been in fact an appointment. [St. Clair v. Cox, supra.]

"The defendant here argues that the terms of such an implied consent cannot be supposed to be other than those which the State statute attempts to exact, and that if the implied consent is to be limited, as has now been indubitably done, the express consent must be limited in exactly the same way. Were this not true, the defendant urges, an outlaw who refused to obey the laws of the State would be in better position than a corporation which chooses to conform. The theory of implied consent dialectically requires the same limitations to be imposed upon express consents, at least in the absence of some explicit language to the contrary in the State statute.

"The plaintiffs, on the other hand, urge that the express consent of a foreign corporation to the service of process upon its agent (Section 16, General Corporation Law; Section 432, Code of Civil Procedure) must be interpreted in the light of the statutes of the State giving jurisdiction to its own courts, and that in the cases at bar, residents of New York, may, under the New York Code, section 1780, sue foreign corporations upon any cause of action whatever. While, of course, the jurisdiction of this court over the subject-matter of suits depends altogether upon Federal statutes, the question now is of personal jurisdiction, and that depends upon the interpretation of the consent actually given, an interpretation determined altogether by the intent of the State statutes. That intent being determined, there is no constitutional objection to a State's exacting a consent from foreign corporations to any jurisdiction which it may please, as a condition of doing business. Intent and power uniting in the sections in question, how is it possible to confine the provision to actions arising from business done within' the State? [See State ex rel. v. Vandiver, 222 Mo. 1. c. 220, where the opinions of the Supreme Court of the United States are reviewed.]

"These two arguments treated as mere bits of dialectic, lead to opposite results, each by unquestionable deduction, so far as I can see. One must be vicious, and the vice arises I think from confounding a legal fiction with a statement of fact. When it is said that a foreign corporation will be taken to have consented to the appointment of an agent to accept service, the court does not mean that as a fact it has consented at all, because the corporation does not in fact consent; but the court, for purposes of justice, treats it as if it had. It is true that the consequences so imputed to it lie within its own control, since it need not do business within the State, but that is not equivalent to a consent; actually it might have refused to appoint, yet its refusal would make no difference. The court, in the interests of justice, imputes results to the voluntary act of doing business within the foreign State quite independently of any intent.

"The limits of that consent are as independent of any actual intent as the consent itself. Being a mere creature of justice it will have such consent only as justice requires; hence it may be limited, as it has been limited in Simon v. Southern Railway, supra, and Old Wayne Insurance Co. v. McDonough, supra. The actual consent in the cases at bar has no such latitudinarian possibilities; it must be measured by the proper meaning to be attributed to the words used, and where that meaning calls for wide application, such must be given. There is no reason that I can see for imposing any limitation upon the effect of section 1780 of the New York Code, and as a result I find that the consents covered such actions as these. This does not,

of course, touch the question of the jurisdiction of this
court over the subject-matter in either case.

"Motions denied." [Smolik v. Philadelphia &
Reading Coal & Iron Co., 222 Fed. 148.]

Of course I know that the district court has no
power to overrule the United States Circuit Court of
Appeals or the Supreme Court, yet the opinions of
that court, when founded upon reason and authority
and not in conflict with those superior tribunals, are
worthy of careful consideration in trying to ascertain
the meaning of the opinions of either of those great
courts upon any question left in doubt by them, and
for that reason I have quoted quite extensively from
the case last cited.

There is another marked distinction between this
case and the Old Wayne and Simon cases, and that is
the statute there under consideration was only applicable to exceptional cases, as previously stated, while
in the case at bar, section 7042 constitutes an important part of article 7 of chapter 61, Revised Statutes
1909, which contains the *General Provisions* applicable
to all kinds of insurance transacted in this State, including life, fire and accident, whether by a domestic
or a foreign company. That article places all of said
foreign companies upon an equality before the law with
domestic companies, including the rights to open offices, appoint agents, issue policies in every portion
of the State, and to sue and be sued.

Any such foreign company which has complied
with sections 7040, 7041 and 7042, Revised Statutes
1909, for all practical purposes becomes a citizen of
this State in the same sense as do domestic companies
of the same character; and are considered citizens of
this State and possess all of the rights, privileges and
immunities that are possessed by the latter. Of course
the foreign company must renew its license to do business within the State every year; but so long as that
license remains in force there is no distinction between

the rights, powers, duties and obligations of the foreign and domestic corporation; and such a "corporation must be regarded as having a domicile" in this State. [New England Life Insurance Co. v. Woodor , supra.]

And "within the contemplation of the statute relating to service of summons upon foreign insurance companies, such companies are regarded as residing in each county of the State." [State ex rel. v. Grimm, 239 Mo. 1. c. 166; Meyer v. Ins. Co., 184 Mo. 1. c. 486.]

And "it must be conceded that the only mode by which a foreign insurance company can be served with process in this State is by the method provided for in said section 7042." [State ex rel. v. Grimm, 239 Mo. 1. c. 160; Baile v. Equitable Fire Ins. Co., 68 Mo. 617; Middough v. Railroad, 51 Mo. 520.]

But how about section 7044, Revised Statutes 1909, the statute of this State corresponding to the second section of the Louisiana act, under which the service of summons in the Simon case was had? This section was not dealing with the general rights, powers, duties and obligations of foreign insurance companies duly licensed to do business in this State, as section 7042 does, but was designed for a single purpose, viz.: to procure service upon *poaching companies issuing policies of insurance in this State* without permission from her to so do.

The service provided for by this section is, therefore, *confined to suits brought in the courts of this State, upon policies unlawfully issued herein;* and as previously stated, *does not and cannot, in the very nature of the case, apply to suits brought in the courts of this State upon policies issued in another state or country, nor to policies lawfully issued in this State, provided of course, such a company is domiciled here, that is, has authority to transact business herein.*

If this was not the law, then the courts of this State could never acquire jurisdiction over the person or subject-matter of any suit brought in the courts hereof against any insurance, railroad, telegraph, telephone or other foreign corporation, either lawfully or unlawfully doing business in this State, *upon any cause of action growing out of any transactions not negotiated in this State, notwithstanding the fact that the plaintiff might be a resident of Missouri and the transaction may have been negotiated in California or New York.* In such a case the party having the cause of action would have to go to one of those States, the one in which his cause of action arose, and sue there, notwithstanding such company was lawfully domiciled in this State, with equal powers and rights of the domestic companies of like character. But in principle it is wholly immaterial whether the plaintiff is a resident or non-resident in such case, if the position of counsel for the appellant is correct. But if that of counsel for the respondent is sound, and the cause of action is transitory in character, then a person owning the same may sue any such company thereon in the courts of this State and have due process of law, regardless of the place, state or nation where the cause of action arose. Of course service in such cases would have to be had under section 7042, and not 7044; only under the latter when the cause of action arose in this State under a poaching transaction. [New England Life Association v. Woodworth, supra; The King of Prussia v. Kuepper, 22 Mo. 550; Mutual Reserve Assn. v. Phelps, 190 U. S. 147; Mutual Life Ins. Co. v. Spratley, 172 U. S. 602.]

I am, therefore, clearly of the opinion that section 7042 is not unconstitutional, for the reason assigned by counsel for appellant in the second subdivision previously stated; and their contention in that regard is ruled against them.

III. This brings us to the third subdivision of appellant's contentions.

In effect counsel for appellant contend therein that the Legislature of this State has no constitutional power to enact laws conferring jurisdiction upon the courts of this State to try and determine suits against foreign insurance companies duly licensed and doing business in this State, based upon contracts of insurance executed in another state or country, whether the property is located in this State or not.

Rights of Non-Resident to Sue in Missouri Courts.

The contention is that such legislation would do violence to section 30 of article 2 of the Constitution of Missouri, and section 1 of the Fourteenth Amendment of the Constitution of the United States, known as the equal rights and due process clauses of those beneficent instruments.

If this contention is true, such a ruling would be no less novel than astounding. In the light of the constitutional provisions just referred to and others to be presently mentioned, and those of similar import contained in the constitutions of the various States of the Union, also in the light of the numerous other statutes of this and those States enacted in pursuance thereof, giving force and effect to them, as well as the common law governing transitory actions, coupled with innumerable decisions of the courts of last resort of the various States and those of the Supreme Court of the United States, it seems to me that the mind which discovered the pregnable point here contended for, hidden behind such a barricade of constitutional provisions, legislative enactments, common law rules and judicial decisions, possessed a keener perception for the discovery of the vulnerable points in our jurisprudence than any of the great military geniuses of the world has ever possessed for the discovery of the weak positions in the enemy's position, and was more daring and self-reliant in his

attack than any of the bold knights mentioned in the
Legends of the Rhine.

But before taking up the question of the power of
the Legislature to enact laws conferring jurisdiction
upon the courts of this State to try such cases, I will
briefly consider what is a transitory action, and where
it may be brought, both at common law and under the
Constitution and laws of this State and of the United
States.

It is elementary that all transitory, or what are
known as personal actions, may be brought by anyone
capable of suing in any county, State or Nation where
the defendant may be found, subject, of course, to any
express constitutional or valid statutory restrictions
that may exist.

After treating of local actions, Mr. Boote, in his
Historical Treatise of an Action or Suit at Law (4 Ed.),
on page 96, in considering transitory actions, says:

"With respect to the Venue, it is said, that on the
settling of *Nisi Prius*, they obliged the plaintiff to try
his action where it accrued because the jury was to
come from where the fact was committed. But while
the Process was by Attachment and Distress, which
could be only where the defendant's goods were, it
begat a distinction between Actions; the one being
called Transitory, which related to goods and chattels, and was to follow the defendant wherever he
could be found; the other was called Local, because it
related to lands, and the process was to be on the
lands. These were to be laid in the County where the
lands lay; but in Transitory Actions the plaintiff had
liberty to choose his venue, being supposed to lay it
where the action accrued; and in case the defendant
fled from that place, the plaintiff had liberty to try
his Action in the County wherein the defendant was
summoned. But this came at length to be much abused,
for the plaintiff would lay his Action far from the
place where the Action arose, which put the defendant

under a necessity of carrying his Witnesses into a County far from the place. In order to prevent this, the 6 R. 2 was made, which enacts that Writs of Account, Debts, etc., should be commenced in the County where the contracts were made; for if the contracts were made in another County than contained in the Original, the Writ should abate. But this Statute (it is said) was never put in use, for it was thought the plaintiff could not then follow the defendant into another county, and it was foreseen that many other mischiefs would arise."

Blackstone announces the same rule. In volume 3, page 294 (4 Ed.—Lewis), he states the law thusly:

"*In transitory actions*, for injuries that might have happened anywhere, as debt, detinue, slander and the like, the plaintiff may declare in what county he pleases, and then the trial must be had in that county in which the declaration is laid."

Mr. Gould in his work on Pleading (5 Ed.), page 103, section 104, lays down this rule:

"In the application of this ancient rule, however, a distinction, suggested by general convenience, was soon established between things local and transitory; and consequently between local and transitory actions. . . . But in actions transitory, the ancient rule as to the locality of actions and trials, is now, and has long been, entirely disregarded, or rather *evaded*, to every purpose except the mere *form of laying some venue*, and the power of the court, under special circumstances, to change it, i. e. to change the county, on motion. In transitory actions, therefore, the plaintiff is at liberty to lay the venue in what county he pleases." [Citing: Bac. Abr. Actions Local, etc., B.; Com. Digest Pleadings, S. 9; Cowp. 177; 1 Saund. 74 (n. 2.); Gilb. H. C. page 89-90.]

Mr. Gould, also on page 108, section 112, says:

"But personal actions, that is to say, actions which seek nothing more than the recovery of money, or personal chattels of any kind, are in most cases transitory, whether they sound in tort or in contract: Because actions of this class are, in most instances, founded on the violation of rights which, in contemplation of law, have no locality. And it will be found true, as a general position, that actions *ex delicto*, in which mere personalty is alone recoverable, are, by the common law, transitory—except when they are founded upon, or arise out of some local subject. Thus actions for injuries to the person, or to personal chattels,—as for assault and battery, false imprisonment, slanderous words, libel and malicious prosecution—trespass for taking away or injuring personal chattels, trover, trespass on the case for escapes, false returns, deceit in the sale of goods, etc., are in general transitory; and may consequently be laid in any county, even though the cause of action arose within a foreign jurisdiction." [Citing: Com. Digest, Actions, N. 12; Coke's Littleton, 282; Cowp. 161; 1 T. R. 571; 2 Black. Rep. 1058; 2 Chitty on Pleading, 242 (n. p.); 2 Salk. 670; 12 Mod. 408; Sayer, 54; 1 Wils. 336; 1 East. 114; Cro. Car. 444; 9 Johns. R. 67, and 4 East. 162-3.] See also Browne on Actions at Law, pages 228 and 229.

The common law definitions of local and transitory actions were in full force and effect when the Constitution of the United States was adopted, and consequently, section 2 of article 4 thereof, has an important bearing upon all the common law adopted and statutes enacted by this State since that time (as will be presently shown), which provides: "*The citizens of each* State shall be entitled to all privileges and immunities of *citizens in the several States.*" (Italics ours.)

And in connection with said section two of the Constitution must be read section 1 of the Fourteenth Amendment thereof, for the reason it relates to the same subject-matter, and greatly enlarges the provisions of said second section. This amendment reads:

"All persons born or naturalized in the United States and subject to the jurisdiction thereof are citizens of the United States and of the State wherein they reside. No State shall make or enforce any law which shall abridge the privileges or immunities of citizens of the United States, nor shall any State deprive any person of life, liberty or property without due process of law, nor deny to any person within its jurisdiction the equal protection of the laws."

Section 30 of the Missouri Bill of Rights is along the same line, and reads: "That no person shall be deprived of life, liberty or property without due process of law."

So also will section 10 of article 2 of the Constitution of Missouri shed much light upon this question, especially when read in the light of article 6 of the Constitution of Missouri. Said section 10 reads as follows:

"*Courts of justice must be open.*—The courts of justice shall be open to every person, and certain remedy afforded for every injury to person, property or character, and that right and justice should be administered without sale, denial or delay."

Upon the ancient common law character of personal or transitory actions, and their venue, or places where to be brought and tried, Judge BLISS in his excellent work on Code Pleading, page 414, section 284, says:

"I am not speaking of the obsolete venue. At common law the pleader must allege a place in reference to every traversable fact, and that place, wherever the fact occurred, is charged as being within the county where the cause is to be tried. The code obligation to state the facts of itself forbids a fictitious venue, and, unless the place is material, it does not become one of the facts which constitute the cause of action. But actions are still divided into local and transitory, and as to the former, the issues

must be tried in the county where the cause of action
has arisen.

"The several States have designated the classes of
actions which require such trial, and they are usually
made to conform to local actions at common law."

So I feel safe in saying that if not predicated upon
and enacted in pursuance to that common law doctrine,
the Legislature of this State largely followed and
fashioned the Code of Civil Procedure of this State
closely after it, especially sections 1751, Revised Statutes 1909, the general statute providing *where suits*
instituted by summons shall be brought except as
otherwise provided for therein. That section of the
statute reads:

"Sec. 1751. Suits instituted by summons shall, except as otherwise provided by law, be brought: First,
when the defendant is a resident of the State, either
in the county within which the defendant resides, or
in the county within which the plaintiff resides and the
defendant may be found; second, when there are several defendants, and they reside in different counties,
the suit may be brought in any such county; third,
when there are several defendants, some residents
and others non-residents of the State, suit may be
brought in any county in this State in which any defendant resides; fourth, when all the defendants are
non-residents of the State, suit may be brought in any
county in this State; fifth, any action, local or transitory, in which any county shall be plaintiff, may be
commenced and prosecuted to final judgment in the
county in which the defendant or defendants reside, or
in the county suing and where the defendants, or one
of them, may be found."

This statute, in substantially the same form in
which we now find it, has been upon the statute books
of this State almost from its organization.

This section of the statute, with all kindred sections which were enacted at the same time or subse-

quently thereto, were designed to open the doors of
the courts of this State to all persons who have valid
claims against any and all persons within the jurisdiction of this State; and it was never the intention of
the framers of the Constitution, State or Federal, or
the Legislature, to close them against justice and to
shield wrong.

These and all kindred laws are designed to make
effective the old maxim, *Ubi jus, ibi remedium.* In
fact, that is one of the chief corner stones of all government. This appears in section 4 of the Bill of Rights,
which among other things provides: "That all persons have a natural right to life, liberty and the enjoyment of the gains of their own industry; that to
give security to these things is the principal office of
government, and that when government does not confer this security, it fails of its chief design."

With these objects and those designs in view,
whenever the lawmakers of the State discovered that
for any deficiency in the law, exact and even justice
could not be done and measured out to each and all,
whether plaintiff or defendant, they have steadfastly
endeavored, by enacting new laws or amending old
ones, to remedy that injustice, and at the same time deprive no one of life, liberty or property without due
process of law, as provided for in the State and Federal Constitutions.

Among the numerous laws so enacted by the Legislature of this State for the purposes mentioned, are
those providing where foreign railroad companies, telegraph companies, telephone companies, insurance companies, including life, fire and accident, doing business
in this State, may be sued in the courts hereof, and
how they may be served with process.

Moreover, there are many private corporations
organized under the laws of other States doing business herein, and we have statutes providing where they
may be sued and how served.

And in addition to the constitutional provisions and statutory enactments before mentioned governing the questions in hand, the Legislature of this State, by an amendment in the year 1905, of sections 547 and 548, Revised Statutes 1899, provided *generally* that whenever any cause of action has accrued under or by virtue of any of the laws of any other State or Territory, such cause may be brought in the courts of this State by the person entitled to the proceeds of such cause of action. Those statutes are now sections 1736 and 1737, Revised Statutes 1909, and read as follows:

"Sec. 1736. Whenever a cause of action has accrued under or by virtue of the laws of any other State or territory, such cause of action may be brought in any of the courts of this State, by the person or persons entitled to the proceeds of such cause of action: Provided, such person or persons shall be authorized to bring such action by the laws of the State or territory where the cause of action accrued.

"Sec. 1737. Whenever any cause of action has accrued under or by virtue of the laws of any other State or territory, and the person or persons entitled to the benefit of such cause of action are not authorized by the laws of such State or territory to prosecute such action in his, her, or their own names, then, in every such case, such cause of action may be brought and prosecuted in any court of this State by the person or persons authorized under the laws of such State or territory to sue in such cases. Such suits may be brought and maintained by the executor, administrator, guardian, guardian *ad litem*, or any other person empowered by the laws of such State or territory to sue in a representative capacity."

From this reading of these two sections it will be noticed that they place no limitation whatever upon the persons who may bring such a suit, save, of course, that it must be brought by the party who under the law of said state or territory is entitled to the proceeds of said cause of action, and of course that might be either an individual or a corporation.

The clear purpose of all of our statutes when taken together was to give full force and effect to said section 10 of article 2 of the Missouri Constitution, which provides that, "The courts of justice shall be open to *every person*." Not a part of them. Not to the citizens or residents of Missouri only, nor to the citizens of the United States only, but to all persons of the world who demand justice at the hands of our courts against any one who may be found within the jurisdiction of this State, whether resident or nonresident, individual or corporation. This is perfectly clear from the reading of that section of the Constitution which says *every person* may sue. Not only that, but the same section further provides that "certain remedy [shall be] afforded for *every injury to person, property or character, etc.*" This provision is not limited to *some of the injuries* that have or may be done to the person, property and character of those mentioned in the preceding clauses, but by clear and unambiguous words, includes *every one of the character mentioned*.

The case of the King of Prussia v. Kuepper's Admr., 22 Mo. 550, while not discussing all of the questions suggested regarding this section of the Constitution, yet in fact it recognizes and gives full force and effect to most, if not all of them; and by the express terms of section 1 of the Fourteenth Amendment all the constitutional and statutory provisions of this State regarding these questions, which apply to the citizens of Missouri, are extended to all other citizens of the United States, even though said section 10 of our Constitution did not include them. But in a sense, that is a moot question, for the reasons as previously shown, said section 10 embraces not only the citizens of

Missouri, but those of the United States also, as well as all persons of the world.

This is not a theory, but cold, stern law; and our reports and those of the Supreme Court of the United States are full of cases recognizing and enforcing those laws.

Such of these legal propositions as are material to this case will be considered at the proper place in connection with the facts they govern.

Of course, all constitutional and statutory provisions, State and Federal, are limited in their scope and operation, to those cases of which the court acquires jurisdiction by summons duly served; and if perchance, through the imperfection of the law, there should be a cause of action for which no provision is made for due process of law, then the person interested would have a loss without a remedy, an exception to the maxim, "No right without a remedy."

It was for the purpose of embracing these exceptional cases that the various amendments of the Act of 1845 were enacted, and the various new statutes mentioned were passed by the Legislature; all of which, in my opinion, amply provide for due service in all cases they were designed to embrace.

I have given this brief summary of the origin, growth and history of transitory actions in England, and their importation, adoption and expansion by means of legislative enactments, which are along the lines of the State and Federal constitutional provisions before mentioned, providing a remedy for every wrong and guaranteeing equal protection to all, and preventing anyone from being deprived of life, liberty or property without due process of law, whether residents or non-residents, corporations or individuals.

I will now address myself to the question. has the Legislature of this State the constitutional authority to enact a statute conferring jurisdiction upon the courts of this State to try a case against a foreign

insurance company duly licensed and doing business
in this State, upon a policy issued in another State or
country? The answer must be in the affirmative if not
restricted by State or Federal Constitution.

Counsel for appellant answer that question in the
negative, but assign no reason therefor, except the
contention that the Supreme Court of the United States
has so held in the Old Wayne and Simon cases, previously mentioned.

If our conclusions announced in Paragraph Two
of this opinion, as to the holding of those cases, are
correct, then counsel for appellant have no solid basis
upon which to predicate that answer. This is for the
reason that if those cases do not support their contention, then the case at bar must be determined according
to the rules of law governing ordinary transitory actions. That this suit is transitory in character cannot
be questioned, and, therefore, according to the authorities cited, a suit on the policy might have been brought
in any State where the defendant might have been
found.

This is not denied by counsel for appellant, but
they contend that the appellant was not a resident of
this State at the time this suit was instituted, except as
to the business transacted herein, and that in regard
to all other matters it was a non-resident.

This contention was decided against the appellant
in Paragraph Two of this opinion, and correctly so,
we think. But concede for the sake of the argument,
that the defendant was not a resident of this State in
the strict sense of that term, at the time this suit was
brought, yet it voluntarily came here and was by permission of this State authorized to transact all kinds
of business that a domestic company of like character
could have transacted, and could sue and be sued
in the courts of this State. The mere fact that the
appellant was not, technically speaking, a resident of
this State, makes no difference in my opinion, since it

was found within the jurisdiction of Missouri, whose laws provide that it might be sued in the courts hereof, and prescribed ample means for service of due process of law upon it, in all transitory actions brought against it. That is all the State and Federal Constitutions require.

As previously stated, all such companies doing business in this State under authority of our laws stand precisely upon the same footing and equality with domestic companies of like character, yea, even with individuals, whether residents or non-residents, if found within the jurisdiction of this State.

In such a case, what possible difference does it make where such a contract was made? I submit, none whatever. To illustrate, suppose an individual, a resident of New York, should execute a note in California, promising to pay another a certain sum of money, and should then come to this State and remain until the note matures: could it be seriously contended that the maker of the note could not be sued thereon in the courts of this State, simply because the note was not made in this State and that the maker was not a resident of the State of Missouri? I apprehend not. The test in transitory actions, as laid down by all of the authorities, is, does the law of the State where the defendant is found provide: first, that suit may be brought upon such a cause against any and all persons found within the jurisdiction of the State, whether residents or non-residents thereof; and, second, does the law amply provide for due process of law upon the defendant in such a case? If so, then it is wholly immaterial where the cause of action arose, and what is the residence of the defendant.

Not only that, if the contention of counsel for the appellant is sound, then our general statutes, articles 3 and 4 of chapter 21, Revised Statutes 1909, prescribing the place where transitory actions must be brought in the courts of this State, against residents and non-residents found in the jurisdiction of Missouri and how service of process may be had upon them, in so far as *non-residents are concerned,* and in so far as it *relates to all causes of action not originating in this State,* are void also. This would be true inevitably; and not only as to this State, but to every other State in the Union, because said section 1 of the Fourteenth Amendment applies equally to all of the States. Yea, even the attachment laws of this and other States authorizing the property of non-residents to be attached would be unconstitutional in all cases where the cause of action is based upon a transaction which was made in some other state or country. This would be true, because, as said by counsel for appellant, the Legislature of this State has no constitutional power to draw to its jurisdiction a cause of action arising elsewhere. The fallacy of this position is this: the Legislature of this State has never attempted to draw to its jurisdiction any cause of action that it did not possess at common law. Said section 7042, in that regard, is declaratory of the common law, only changing it as to the country where suit may be brought, and prescribing the mode of service of process, which is ample, as is shown by the record in this case; the appellant was duly served and given ample time and opportunity to make its defense. Not only that, but section 1 of the Fourteenth Amendment of the Constitution of the United States prohibits just what counsel for appellant is contending for, namely: that no resident or non-resident of this State can sue a foreign insurance company in the courts of this State, although it is authorized to, and is doing business here, upon a contract of insurance executed in another State or country; yet, they admit, which is true, that such a suit may be brought against such a company on a contract executed elsewhere, in the courts of this State. If that is not true, then according to appellant's contention, it could not be sued at all, anywhere.

What difference is there in legal effect, between the two? None; both companies are of the same character; they issue the same class of contracts within and without this State; they possess the same rights and powers, and the same duties and obligations are imposed upon them; the contracts of each are transitory in character; both may sue and be sued in the same courts of this State; when plaintiffs they have the same character of process issued in their behalf and served alike for them upon the defendants; and when defendants, the same kind of summons is issued in their behalf, and served upon their respective agents, appointed by the respective companies, differing only in that in the case of the domestic company the statute providing for service of process is upon certain persons who have been chosen by the company as its agents or officers to represent it in other capacities, that is, persons who are in the employ of the company, to perform its ordinary business, while in the case of the foreign company, the service is had upon a person also chosen by the company, but not in the employ of the company, but who is an officer of this State, the Superintendent of Insurance.

Again, if not conceded, it is true nevertheless, that if an individual non-resident of this State should execute a note outside of this State it could not be sued thereon in the courts hereof, when it becomes due. Why not? Each had the right to execute the note mentioned; both were made outside of this State; both are transitory causes of action, the laws of the State provide the same courts in which such suits thereon may be brought, and provide for the same kind of process and upon whom service may be had. In the case of the individual it must be served upon him personally or upon some member of his family, if not found, etc., while in the case of the company, domestic or foreign, because of its artificial character, the service *must be had upon its duly constituted agent* (whether sued at home or abroad), the Superintendent of Insurance.

Upon this state of facts, there can be no question, in my opinion, but what said Fourteenth Amendment equally applies to foreign insurance companies doing business in this State under license duly issued to it, as it does to domestic companies engaged in like business, and to transactions of like character transacted by individuals; otherwise, they would not enjoy the equal protection of the laws, either in suing or being sued.

If that is not the law, then a person residing or stopping in this State, or a corporation organized under the laws hereof, might execute a note for $1000 in the State of Illinois to a foreign insurance company doing business in this State, yet it could not sue and recover the money due thereon from the individual nor from the domestic company, for the reason that the note was not executed in this State, and for the further reason, as contended for by counsel for appellant, that this "State has no *constitutional power to draw to its jurisdiction a cause of action arising elsewhere.*" Nor in such a case could suit be brought in the Federal court; because the amount of the note would not bring the case within its jurisdiction. I think that is indisputable (International Textbook Co. v. Pigg, 217 U. S. 91, and cases cited), yet if the same note had been executed by the same party or company, at the same place, to an *individual* instead of a foreign corporation, he could, under a long unbroken line of decisions of this court and of the Supreme Court of the United States, have maintained the suit.

This question has been decided by the Supreme Court of the United States in the case of the International Textbook Co. v. Pigg, supra. That court in that case cited the case of Chambers v. Baltimore & Ohio Ry. Co., 207 U. S. 142, l. c. 148, and quoted with approval therefrom the following language:

"This court held in Chambers v. Baltimore & Ohio
R. R. Co., 207 U. S. 142, 148, that a State may, subject to the restrictions of the Federal Constitution,
'determine the limits of the jurisdiction of its courts,
and the character of the controversies which shall be
heard in them.' But it also said in the same case: 'The
right to sue and defend in the courts is the alternative
of force. In an organized society it is the right con-
servative of all other rights, and lies at the foundation
of orderly government. It is one of the *highest and
most essential privileges of citizenship, and must be
allowed by each State to the citizens of all other States
to the precise extent that it is allowed to its own citizens. Equality of treatment in this respect is not left
to depend upon comity between the States, but is granted and protected by the Federal Constitution.'* "

While it is true the former case involved a question of interstate commerce, yet that question was but
one of the two questions presented and decided; and
it had but little or no bearing upon the question of the
validity of the State statute, barring State courts to
non-residents while they were left open to those within
the jurisdiction of the State. This is clear, for the obvious reason that the interstate commerce clause of
the Constitution of the United States in no "manner,
shape or form" attempted to confer or define the jurisdiction of State courts; nor was any such authority
necessary to be lodged in that clause of the Constitution in order to give Congress full and complete power
to regulate that subject.

The remedy for the violation of the laws of the
United States, including those governing interstate
commerce, rests primarily with the Federal courts, and
secondarily with the State courts, which are and have
ever been opened to all persons, natural and artificial,
residents and nonresidents, by section 2 of article 4
and section 1 of the Fourteenth Amendment of the Constitution of the United States. In other words, the

commerce clause of the Constitution confers upon Congress the power to regulate interstate commerce, but the remedy for the violation thereof must primarily be in the .courts created by article 3 of the Constitution of the United States, and supplemented by section 1 of the Fourteenth Amendment thereof, which guarantees to every citizen of the United States the same right and privilege to sue in the courts of this State upon all transitory causes of action on which a citizen of this State might sue, under the laws hereof. Or in other words, if, under the laws of this State, a citizen hereof may maintain a suit on a given cause of action, then under said constitutional provision, any citizen of any other State of the Union may do likewise.

This court in the case of International Textbook Co. v. Gillespie, 229 Mo. 397, followed the rule announced by the Supreme Court of the United States in the case of International Textbook Co. v. Pigg, supra. See also: Cement Co. v. Gas Co., 255 Mo. 1; Roeder v. Robertson, 202 Mo. 522; United Shoe Machinery Co. v. Ramlose, 231 Mo. 508; State ex rel. v. Grimm, 239 Mo. 135, l. c. 179.

All of those cases decided by this court were instituted under section 1751 of our Practice Act, before quoted; and those decided by the Supreme Court of the United States were brought under similar statutes of other States where the suits were instituted; but that makes no difference in principle, in so far as this question is concerned, for the reason that it does not involve the question as to who may sue or be sued, or upon whom service of process may be had in such cases, for those questions were decided in Paragraph Two of this opinion, but the question in hand is, *where may suits on contracts, torts and other transitory actions be brought?*

Of course it cannot be said, nor do any of the cases cited hold, that non-residents can sue *all persons within*

the jurisdiction of this State, under the section of the
Practice Act before mentioned, but they do hold that if
a resident of this State can sue any or all persons
within the jurisdiction of this State in the courts hereof
on any transitory cause of action, under that or any
other statute of this State, or under the rules of the
common law, then, under said section 1 of the Fourteenth Amendment, any citizen of the United States,
though residing elsewhere, whether an individual or
a corporation, is guaranteed the same right to sue
upon a similar cause of action in the courts of this
State. In other words, the effect of that section of the
Constitution is to extend to all citizens of the United
States, who are residents of other States or countries,
the same right to sue persons found within the jurisdiction of this State, upon the same causes of action,
that is enjoyed by our citizens under the Constitution
and laws of this State; or, to express the same idea in
different language, the Constitution and laws of this
State, in the regard mentioned, were designed principally for the citizens of Missouri, and secondarily
for all persons of the world, as previously stated; but
be that as it may, the first section of the Fourteenth
Amendment extends all such constitutional provisions
and statutory enactments of this State, of the character
mentioned, to all citizens of the United States residing
elsewhere.

That is the plain meaning and effect of the ruling
of the Supreme Court of the United States in the cases
before cited upon this question; and also of the rulings
of this court in the cases cited in connection therewith.

Therefore, if we are correct in the conclusions
reached in Paragraph Two of this opinion regarding
that clause of section 7042, providing for process
against foreign insurance companies doing business in
this State and upon whom process may, or rather, must
be served, and also in our conclusions just stated regarding the legal rights of citizens of the United States

residing elsewhere, to sue in the courts of this State upon the same causes of action that our own citizens enjoy, then it necessarily follows that the respondent, a citizen of Arizona, had the legal right to sue appellant in the courts of this State upon the policy mentioned in the petition and evidence. '

IV. This brings us to the consideration of the fourth ground assigned by counsel for appellant in support of their general contention that section 7042 is unconstitutional.

In substance, that contention is, that said section, in so far as it authorizes service of process in a suit based upon a policy of insurance issued in **Domestic Contract by Foreign Citizen.** this State by a foreign insurance company doing business herein *without authority of law*, is unconstitutional, null and void under both the State and Federal Constitutions.

This contention can easily and briefly be disposed of. It is purely a moot question in this case. The policy sued on was not issued in this State, but in the State of Colorado. Therefore it was not unlawfully issued in this State, and this contention of counsel has no foundation whatever upon which to stand.

If, however, the policy had been issued in this State *without authority of the State first had and obtained,* then clearly the service of process could not have been had under said section 7042, for the reason that its express terms exclude service of process thereunder in suits founded upon all such policies; but service in all such cases could be had under section 7044, which was enacted for the express purpose of providing for service in suits on a policy of insurance issued in this State against a foreign company doing business herein *without authority of law.*

This was expressly decided by the Supreme Court of the United States in the cases of Mutual Reserve Assn. v. Phelps, 190 U. S. 147; Mutual Life Ins. Co. v. Spratley, 172 U. S. 602; and Commercial Mutual

Accident Co. v. Davis, 213 U. S. 245; and that ruling is expressly approved by the same court in the case of Simon v. Southern Ry. Co., 236 U. S. 115, l. c. 130.

The same result was correctly reached by the Court of Civil Appeals of Texas in the case of El Paso & South Western Ry. Co. v. Chisholm, 180 S. W. 156; but on page 159, that court undertook to state what the Supreme Court of the United States held in the Simon case, which shows that that court, like counsel for appellant here, misconceived and did not understand the ruling in the Simon case. The latter case has no application whatever to this case, as I think I have clearly shown.

My attention has just been called to the case of Fry v. Denver & R. G. Ry. Co., 226 Fed. 893. In that case the opinion does not disclose the statute under which process therein was served, and for that reason sheds but little light upon the question here presented; but the language used indicates that the manner of service was wholly immaterial. The opinion seems to proceed upon the theory that a suit cannot be maintained in a State without the transaction out of which it arose occurred in the State where the suit was brought. The Old Wayne and Simon cases are cited in support thereof, regardless of the statute under which process was had. If I correctly understand the opinion, then I have no hesitancy in saying that the court does not understand those cases. Instead of those cases supporting the views there expressed, they hold directly to the contrary.

But in the case at bar it must be remembered that the service was had under section 7042 and not under section 7044; but had the service in this case, under the facts thereof, been had under the latter section, then clearly the appellant would not have been served with due process of law, as was held and properly so, by the Supreme Court in the Simon-Railway case, supra. But the court in that case did not decide the moot question here presented, but expressly declined to express an opinion upon it because not properly before the court. In that case, as in this, the cause of action did not accrue in the State where the suit was brought, and therefore in neither case could the second section of the statute apply.

What is here said about section 7044 is clearly *obiter*, but is said to dispel some of the confusion it seems to me counsel are laboring under regarding the Simon-Railway case.

V. The fifth and last ground assigned by counsel for appellant in support of their general contention that said section 7042 is unconstitutional, is substantially as follows:

That said section 7042 is unconstitutional, because it authorizes services of process in suits brought in the courts of this State against foreign insurance companies doing business herein *unlawfully, that is, without authority first had and obtained* from the State, based ·upon a policy of insurance issued in another State. In support of this contention we are cited to the cases of Old Wayne Life Assn. v. McDonough, 204 U. S. l. c. 22, and Simon v. Railway Co., 236 U. S. 115.

This contention may also be briefly and easily disposed of. In the first place, it may be stated generally, that neither section 7042 nor 7044 applies to the state of facts upon which counsel's contention is predicated, nor to the facts of this case. Section 7042 in express terms limits the service of the process therein mentioned to foreign insurance companies doing business in this State *under authority from the State* duly granted to them; and there is no language contained in that section which remotely indicates that it applies to any such company doing business in this State *without such authority.* Therefore, this contention of counsel is not well founded; and the cases cited in support thereof have no application whatever to this case.

Those cases, however, will be further considered presently.

Nor does section 7044 authorize service of process in suits brought in the courts of this State against a foreign insurance company, based upon a policy *issued in another State.* By its express terms the process mentioned therein is limited to *suits brought upon policies of insurance issued in this State* by such companies *without authority* from the State first had and obtained.

Not only that, but there is no other statute or law of this State that I am familiar with, which authorizes service of process in a suit brought in the courts of this Commonwealth against a foreign insurance company *not authorized to do business* herein, based upon a *policy issued* by it in *another State or country;* but if there are any such, then they would *clearly be unconstitutional* under both the State and Federal constitutional provisions previously mentioned. This is precisely what was held by the Supreme Court of the United States in the Old Wayne and Simon cases.

In the Old Wayne case, the policy was issued in the State of Indiana, to a person residing in Pennsylvania, and the suit based thereon was brought in the State of Pennsylvania, where the company had *no authority to transact business,* but had (at least presumably, as that court stated) issued *some other policies* in that State *without authority.* Upon that state of facts, the plaintiff sued the company in Pennsylvania, and had service under a statute similar in all respects to section 7042, Revised Statutes 1909, of this State. In that case the court, in effect, held that said section of the Pennsylvania statute did not apply to policies issued in another State, unless the company was lawfully doing business in Pennsylvania; and because it was not lawfully doing business in that State, and because the policy was not issued therein, the court held that the service had under that statute was void. That ruling was clearly correct, because that statute, like said section 7042 of this State, in express terms *limited the service therein mentioned* to suits on policies *issued in that State under permission therefrom,* and did not embrace policies issued in another State.

In the Simon case the injury occurred in the State of Alabama, and the suit was brought in the State of Louisiana, and service was had under the second section of the Louisiana act, which is similar to section 7044 of our statutes. In that case the court ruled, and correctly so, that the service mentioned in that section was by its express terms limited to suits based upon torts committed in that State by a foreign corporation *not authorized to do business therein;* and therefore the service had upon the defendant was void because the injury did not occur in Louisiana.

The court went further in both of those cases and held that if the Pennsylvania statute mentioned authorized the service had in that case, then it would have been unconstitutional.

But suppose in the Old Wayne case the company had been doing a lawful business in Pennsylvania in pursuance to its authority, and service of process had been had upon the company under the same statute, then could it be said that said statute was not applicable and did not authorize the service? Certainly not; for any other answer would be in direct conflict with the plain language of the statute, and would violate section 1 of the Fourteenth Amendment of the Constitution of the United States.

The same would have been true in the Simon case, had the Railway Company been doing business in Louisiana under permission of the State and the service had been had under the first section of the act, instead of the second.

Likewise, the same rule applies to the case at bar, because the appellant was *doing business in this State, under its authority,* and service was had upon it *under section 7042*, which in express terms authorized service of process in suits brought in the courts of this State against all such companies so doing business in this State, regardless of the place where the policies are issued, as before shown.

In this class of cases there would not exist that inconvenience and hardship mentioned by the court in the Simon case, for the reason that all such companies lawfully doing business in this State are domiciled here and have their offices, agents and attorneys, just as they have in the States of their creation. Any such company can try any such case in the courts of this State with as little expense and inconvenience as they could be tried in the State of its organization or in the State where the policy was issued; but be that as it may, it has nothing whatever to do with the question of jurisdiction of the courts of this State in such cases, and the hardship and inconvenience mentioned would not be one-tenth as great upon the company as it would be upon the various policyholders, should they be compelled to go to the various States where the various companies were incorporated, or to those where the policies were issued, in order to enforce their claims.

Certainly the inconvenience and hardship which might be imposed upon such a company lawfully doing business here, when required to defend suits in the courts of this State based upon a policy issued in another State, where it has its offices, agents and attorneys, would not be greater than they would be in a suit brought here against such a company based upon a policy issued by it in this State unlawfully, where it would have no office, agent or attorney; yet the Supreme Court of the United States in the cases of Mutual Reserve Assn. v. Phelps, supra, Mutual Life Ins. Co. v. Spratley, and Simon v. Southern Ry. Co., supra, hold that the latter class of suits may be maintained in the courts of this State.

If according to those cases, such a company may be sued under section 7044 in the courts of this State on a policy unlawfully issued here, then why may it not be sued under section 7042 on a policy lawfully issued elsewhere? But as stated by the Supreme Court of the United States in the Simon case, as to inconvenience, etc., this is foreign to the question of jurisdiction.

Again: If such a company can by implication consent to the trial of such cases in the courts of this State, and agree to the impositions of such hardship and inconveniences as are incident to the necessary defense of the case, then why may not such a company consent thereto by express agreement, as the appellant has done in this case?

I am, therefore, clearly of the opinion that said section 7042 is constitutional, and that it provides for ample service of process in all cases which it was designed to embrace, one of which is the case at bar; I am also of the opinion that appellant was duly served according to the provisions of that statute, and was properly in court.

We are, therefore, of the opinion that the general contention of counsel for appellant, as well as the five subdivisions thereof, are without merit, and should be disallowed, which is accordingly done.

VI. Counsel for appellant assign as error the action of the trial court in permitting the witness Doepke to testify to certain conversations had between him and Kilpatrick & Hanley, the general agents **Estoppel and Waiver.** of the company at Cripple Creek, prior to and at the time the policy was issued, regarding the binding force of its terms and conditions respecting incumbrances upon and the vacancy of the property; also that the court erred in permitting said Doepke to testify as to conversations had between himself and said agents after the policy had been issued, regarding the vacancy of the property, and cite scores of cases in support thereof.

We will consider these two assignments together, as the same principle of law underlies each.

While there is some conflict of authority on these questions in other States, but in so far as Colorado, Missouri and many other States are concerned, it is well settled that where the general agents of an insurance company, at the time of or subsequent to the issuance of the policy, are informed of the existence of any fact regarding the property which is violative of any of the terms or conditions thereof, and which would work a forfeiture, and assent thereto, then the company is estopped from interposing such conditions of forfeiture as a defense to a suit brought upon the policy to recover the damages sustained.

It is undisputed, in this case, that the respondent, at the time the policy was issued, informed the general agents of the company that the scarcity of fuel and the difficulty in getting it to the smelter until a tramway could be built, would in all probability necessitate the shutting down of the smelter for periods of more than thirty days at a time, and asked said agents what effect such idleness would have upon the policy. In reply, the agents, in substance, said, that is "all right, go on." Not only that, the same matters were discussed between the same parties each and every month, from the time the policy was issued until the date of the fire, and upon each occasion the insured asked said agents what effect would the vacancy of the smelter have upon the policy; and each time they answered, that is "all right, go ahead."

Upon these undisputed facts there can be no doubt but what the appellant is estopped from interposing these forfeiture clauses as a defense in this case; a long line of authorities so hold. [Ins. Co. v. Hyman, 42 Colo. 156; Ins. Co. v. Nixon, 2 Colo. App. 265; Thompson v. Ins. Co., 169 Mo. 12; Rissler v. Ins. Co., 150

Mo. 366; Ins. Co. v. Allis Co., 11 Colo. App. 264; Huestess v. Ins. Co., 70 S. E. 403; Millis v. Ins. Co., 95 Mo.
App. 211; Rudd v. Ins. Co., 120 Mo. App. 1; Wein-
berger v. Ins. Co., 170 Mo. App. 266; Combs v. Sav-
ings & Ins. Co., 43 Mo. 148; McCullough v. Ins. Co.,
113 Mo. 606; Loeb v. Ins. Co., 99 Mo. l. c. 55; Prentice
v. Ins. Co., 77 N. Y. 483; Hartley v. Ins. Co., 33 Ins.
L. J. 329, 91 Minn. 382; Ins. Co. v. May, 43 S. W. 73;
Trustees St. Clara Academy v. Ins. Co., 98 Wis. 257;
Ins. Co. v. Mahone, 21 Wall. 152; McCollum v. Ins.
Co., 67 Mo. App. l. c. 80; Harness v. Ins. Co., 76 Mo.
App. 410; Gandy v. Ins. Co., 29 S. E. 655; Ins. Co. v.
Hart, 149 Ill. 513; Trust Co. v. Ins. Co., 79 Mo. App.
362; Benefit Assn. v. Tucker, 157 Ill. 194; Gibson v.
Ins. Co., 53 Ark. 494; Ins. Co. v. Dowdall, 159 Ill. 179;
Pechner v. Ins. Co., 65 N. Y. 195; Frye v. Equitable
Society, 89 Atl. 57; Wilson v. Ins. Co., 91 Atl. 913;
Ins. Co. v. Stanley, 82 S. E. 826; Clay v. Ins. Co., 25
S. E. 417; Blass v. Ins. Co., 46 N. Y. Supp. 392; Pren-
dergast v. Ins. Co., 67 Mo. App. 426; Wich v. Ins.
Co., 2 Colo. App. 484; Ins. Co. v. Smith, 3 Colo. 422;
Ins. Co. v. Taylor, 14 Colo. 499; Ins. Co. v. Donlon,
16 Colo. App. 416; U. S. Accident Assn. v. Kittenring,
22 Colo. 257; Strauss v. Ins. Co., 9 Colo. App. 386.]

Also under the facts of this case, the authorities
hold that Kilpatrick & Hanley were the *alter ego* of
the insurance company, and their knowledge of the fact
that the smelter was shut down and their assurances
to Doepke that it was "all right" is a waiver. [Thomp-
son v. Ins. Co., 169 Mo. l. c. 25, and cases there cited;
Rissler v. Ins. Co., 150 Mo. 366; Shutts v. Ins. Co.,
159 Mo. App. l. c. 441; Prentice v. Ins. Co., 77 N. Y.
l. c. 487; Wooldridge v. Ins. Co., 69 Mo. App. 413;
Ins. Co. v. Hyman, 42 Colo. 156; Crouse v. Ins. Co.,
79 Mich. 249; Andrus v. Casualty Co., 91 Minn. 358;
Hart v. Ins. Co., 9 Wash. 620; Haight v. Ins. Co., 92
N. Y. 51; Burnham v. Ins. Co., 63 Mo. App. 85; Mont-

gomery v. Ins. Co., 80 Mo. App. 500; Ross-Langford
v. Ins. Co., 97 Mo. App. 79.]

A waiver may be inferred from the acts and conduct of the agents of the insurance company and need
not be proved by express agreement. When Doepke
informed Kilpatrick, the agent of the insurance company who wrote this policy, that the mill was shut
down, even though Kilpatrick had not assured him that
everything was "all right," yet if he expressed no dissent, such conduct on his part would be a waiver. At
least, it would be such conduct as would send the question of waiver to the jury. [Ins. Co. v. Dowdall, 159
Ill. 179; Bowen v. Ins. Co., 69 Mo. App. 272; Millis
v. Ins. Co., 95 Mo. App. l. c. 217; Appel v. Surety Co.,
132 N. Y. Supp. 200; Hatcher v. Ins. Co., 127 Pac. 588;
Ins. Co. v. Fahrenkrug, 68 Ill. 463; Ins. Co. v. Johnston, 42 Ill. App. l. c. 73; Draper v. Ins. Co., 190 N. Y.
12; Loeb v. Ins. Co., 99 Mo. l. c. 58; Coppoletti v. Ins.
Co., 143 N. W. 787; Bank v. Ins. Co., 109 Mo. App.
l. c. 660; St. John v. Ins. Co., 107 Mo. App. 700; Ins.
Co. v. Lewis, 187 U. S. l. c. 353; Ins. Co. v. Norton, 96
U. S. 234.]

A policy of insurance is not void by reason of the
plant being shut down, but only voidable, and the insurance company must cancel and return unearned premium. Not having done so, the policy continues in
force. [Patterson v. Ins. Co., 174 Mo. App. 37; Flannigan v. Ins. Co., 46 N. Y. Supp. 687; Laundry Co. v.
Ins. Co., 151 Mo. l. c. 98; Miller v. Ins. Co., 106 Mo.
App. l. c. 211; Anthony v. Ins. Co., 48 Mo. App. l. c.
73; Brix v. Fidelity Co., 171 Mo. App. 518; Ins. Co.
v. Ashby, 102 N. E. (Ind.) 45; Ins. Co. v. Smith, 3
Colo. 422; Prentice v. Ins. Co., 77 N. Y. l. c. 488; Ins.
Co. v. Koehler, 168 Ill. 293; Ins. Co. v. Catlin, 163 Ill.
256; Ins. Co. v. Johnston, 42 Ill. App. 76; Born v. Ins.
Co., 110 Iowa, 379; Cassimus Bros. v. Ins. Co., 135
Ala. 256; Viele v. Ins. Co., 26 Iowa, 9; Ins. Co. v.
Knutson, 67 Kan. 71; Schreiber v. Ins. Co., 43 Minn.

367; McCollum v. Ins. Co., 61 Mo. App. l. c. 354; Saville v. Ins. Co., 8 Mont. 419; New v. Ins. Co., 31 N. E. 475; Ins. Co. v. Jones, 92 N. E. 879; Weinberger v. Ins. Co., 170 Mo. App. 266; McIntyre v. Ins. Co., 131 Mo. App. l. c. 93; Ins. Co. v. Johnston, 143 Ill. 106; Ins. Co. v. Richmond Mica Co., 102 Va. 429; Rissler v. Ins. Co., 150 Mo. 366.]

After the fire occurred the agents of the company demanded the balance of the unpaid premiums from the assured, which it paid; and the law is that the acceptance of the premium after fire is a waiver of any violation of policy after the agent of the insurance company knew of it. [Flannigan v. Ins. Co., 46 N. Y. Supp. 687; Ins. Co. v. Raddin, 120 U. S. l. c. 195; Baker v. Ins. Co., 77 Fed. 550; Ins. Co. v. Wolff, 95 U. S. 326; Ins. Co. v. Freeman, 47 S. W. 1025.]

We are, therefore, of the opinion that under the great weight of authority, under the facts of this case, the appellant has waived the forfeiting conditions of the policy, and is estopped from interposing them as a defense to this case.

VII. What is said regarding the vacancy clause of the policy is applicable to and controlling as to the incumbrance clause of the policy.

The agents of the appellant not only knew of the mortgages being upon the property, but canceled two other policies they had issued on it because of those incumbrances, and issued two others in their stead.

This company should not be permitted to thus blow hot and cold. If it wished to rely upon these forfeiting clauses of the policy, it should have returned the unearned premiums and declared the policy void before the fire occurred; but having failed to do either, it will not, at this late date, be heard to say that the policy was void because of the violations of said forfeiting clauses.

VIII. It is next insisted by counsel for appellant that its agents, Kilpatrick & Hanley, were acting in collusion with the respondent and against the interest of the appellant.

Counsel do not make it clear as to when or how this conspiracy was formed, or the purpose they intended to accomplish by it. Certainly they did not

Collusion.   enter into a conspiracy to burn the smelter by a stroke of lightning from heaven; nor did the vacancy of the smelter or the incumbrances thereon contribute or operate as conductors of the lightning from the clouds to the smelter, nor were they inducing causes of the lightning striking the same.

Moreover, the undisputed evidence is that the mortgages were paid and satisfied long before the fire occurred. So I am unable to see in what possible way the vacancy of the smelter and the satisfied incumbrances thereon had to do with the fire, or how the alleged conspirators could have co-operated with the lightning in destroying the smelter. Such a thing is preposterous.

The agents of the company did nothing but tell the true facts of the case as disclosed by the physical facts and the undisputed evidence in the case. If an agent may not do that, even though it may be detrimental to the interest of his principal, then the time has come when such agencies should be abolished.

There is not a scintilla of evidence in this case that tends to show that Kilpatrick & Hanley were acting collusively against the appellant.

IX. Counsel for appellant complain of the action of the trial court in refusing to give their instructions numbered three, four and five, as asked, and in modifying them and giving them in the modified form.

Counsel say that, "By its modification of these instructions, the court told the jury that they could not find for the defendant on the question of waiver unless they believed from the evidence that 'Doepke for the plaintiff company agreed and consented that said agents Kilpatrick and Hanley should conceal from the defendant company' the facts constituting the breaches of the conditions of the policy.''

These instructions should not have been given at all, either as asked by counsel or as modified by the court, for the reason that there was no evidence upon which to base them.

We disposed of this question in Paragraphs Six and Seven of this opinion, and no good purpose would be served by discussing it further at this place.

X. It is finally insistèd by counsel for appellant that:

''The court erred in giving plaintiff's instruction numbered 6 and thereby instructing the jury in effect that if they found from the evidence that, prior to the institution of this suit, plaintiff paid all necessary corporation fees to the State of Colorado and obtained from the Secretary of State of Colorado a certificate of authority to do business in the said State, the fact that plaintiff had not paid said fees and obtained said certificate of authority prior to its alleged acquisition of title to the property in question, or prior to the issuance of the policy in suit, or prior to the fire, was immaterial.''

Authority to do Business.

The evidence discloses the fact that at the time the policy in suit was issued, the respondent had not taken out a license to do business in the State of Colorado; and had not done so at the time it purchased the property upon which the buildings insured stood, for which it paid about $175,000, and received a general warranty deed thereto; but subsequently thereto, it took out a license to do business in the State, and paid all fees and taxes due on the property, long before the fire occurred.

That instruction correctly declared the law.

This question has been passed upon by the Supreme Court of Colorado and by the Supreme Court of the United States in a case which went up from Colorado.

In the case of Ins. Co. v. Allis Co., 11 Colo. App. 264, l. c. 269, the court said:

"There is no provision that the contracts of a corporation which has failed in compliance with the law shall be avoided; on the contrary, their validity is recognized and they are enforcible not only against it, but against its officers, agents and stockholders; nor does the statute assume to deprive it of any remedy which it would otherwise have upon its contracts or for the protection of its property rights. No consequence is attached to the failure except the subjecting of its officers, agents and stockholders to a personal liability on its contracts; and the courts cannot very well go further than the Legislature has gone. We feel entirely safe in saying that there is nothing in the statute by which the plaintiff's capacity to sue, or its right to maintain its action to enforce its demand, is in any way affected." The following cases are cited: Utley v. Mining Co., 4 Colo. 369; Tabor v. Mfg. Co., 11 Colo. 419; Kindel v. Lithographing Co., 19 Colo. 310.

In the case of Kindel v. Lithographing Co., 19 Colo. 310, the Supreme Court of Colorado expressly holds that failure of a foreign corporation doing business in Colorado to file a certificate, as required by the Constitution, article 15, section 10, subjects its officers, agents and stockholders to certain personal liabilities, but does not affect its right of action against a resident of the State for goods sold and delivered.

This same question came before the Supreme Court of the United States in the case of Fritts v. Palmer, 132 U. S. 282. This case arose under the laws of Colorado. In that case, the court said (Syl.): "The

Constitution of Colorado provided that no foreign corporation should do business in the State without having a known place of business in the State and an agent upon whom process might be served. . . . Said act further provided that no corporation, foreign or domestic, should purchase or hold real estate except as provided in the act. The act did not indicate a mode by which a foreign corporation might acquire real estate in Colorado." A foreign noncomplying corporation took a deed to property and its title was attacked on the ground "that the company violated the laws of the State [Colorado] when it purchased the property without having previously designated its place of business and an agent." The United States Supreme Court held that the grantee held a good title to the property, inasmuch "as the Constitution and laws of Colorado did not prohibit foreign corporations from purchasing and holding real estate within its limits," and that no one could question the title but the sovereignty.

In Seymour v. Mines, 153 U. S. 523, syl., it is held: "The State only can challenge the right of a foreign corporation to hold real estate within its limits."

In Smith v. Sheeley, 12 Wall. 358, syl. 2, it is held: "A conveyance of land cannot be treated as a nullity by the grantor who has received the consideration for the grant, there being no judgment of ouster against the corporation at the instance of the Government."

In Summet v. Realty Co., 208 Mo. l. c. 512, this court said:

"This court is next asked to reverse the judgment in this cause because the record discloses that the insurance company held the land in question for a period of more than six years, which is in violation of section 7 of article 12 of the Constitution of 1875.

This question can be raised by the State alone. It is a matter which does not concern the individual, as held in the following cases." [See cases there cited.]

In Bank v. Matthews, 98 U. S. l. c. 629, the court said: "A private person cannot, directly or indirectly, usurp this function of the Government" and question such title. [Bank v. Whitney, 103 U. S. l. c. 101; Ins. Co. v. Hyman, 42 Colo. 156.]

It is expressly held by the Supreme Court of Colorado: "Where a foreign corporation actually complies with the Act of April 6, 1901 (Laws 1901, p. 116, c. 52), prescribing the terms on which a foreign corporation may do business within the State, and prohibiting the exercise of corporate powers or the prosecution or the defense of actions until the required fee shall have been paid and the prescribed certificate obtained, subsequent to the commencement of an action on a contract made with a domestic corporation, it may maintain the action and enforce the contract; the prohibition being only provisional, subject to removal at any time." [Trust Co. v. Rope Co., 41 Colo. 299, 92 Pac. 727, syl. 5.]

The statute in question, and the contract of purchase of the land mentioned, being products of the State of Colorado, and her courts holding that under that statute said contract was valid, it would be presumption on the part of this court to hold otherwise, especially when this court has repeatedly ruled the same way in cases arising under similar statutes of this State.

There are some other minor points discussed, but they in no manner affect the merits of the case, and I will therefore pass them by.

Finding no error in the record, the judgment is affirmed. *Faris, J.,* concurs in the result; *Blair* and *Revelle, JJ.,* concur; *Graves, Bond* and *Walker, JJ.,* dissent in a separate opinion by *Graves, J.*

GRAVES, J. (dissenting).—I cannot concur in the majority opinion. The facts of the case and the questions raised are as follows:

Plaintiff is alleged to be an Arizona corporation, and defendant is alleged to be a Pennsylvania corporation, doing a general fire insurance business. The petition is an ordinary petition upon a fire insurance policy, issued by defendant to plaintiff in the State of Colorado. The property is alleged to have been destroyed by fire during the life of the policy.

This suit was brought in Audrain County, Missouri, and there tried, resulting in a judgment for the plaintiff in the sum of $2689.57, the amount of the policy for $2500 and interest thereon. Service of summons in the case was had by the sheriff of Cole County, Missouri, delivering a copy of the petition and summons to Frank Blake, the then Superintendent of the Insurance Department of Missouri.

Preserved in the bill of exceptions by the plaintiff, we have the motion to quash the service in this cause, which motion reads:

"Now comes the defendant herein and appearing for the purposes of this motion and for the purposes of this motion only, moves to quash the writ herein issued and the return thereon by the sheriff of Cole County and dismiss the cause for the following reasons, to-wit:

"1. The circuit court of Audrain County and no other court of the State of Missouri has jurisdiction over the person of the defendant herein nor over the subject-matter of said action.

"The plaintiff is a corporation existing under the laws of the Territory of Arizona, but attempting to engage in business in the State of Colorado and also attempting, according to the allegations of the petition herein filed, to exercise its corporate powers in the State of Colorado; and according to the alle-

gations of plaintiff's petition, was the owner of the
property in said petition described in the State of
Colorado; and the defendant is a foreign corporation
of the State of Pennsylvania doing business as an insurance company in the State of Missouri and also
in the State of Colorado;

"That the alleged contract sued upon by plaintiff
was made in the State of Colorado, and the insurance
against fire by said alleged policy was against loss
of property located in the State of Colorado; and
said fire by which said property is alleged to have
been destroyed took place in the State of Colorado.
Hence, the alleged contract sued upon and the alleged
cause of action in plaintiff's petition, if any, is a contract under the laws of Colorado and the cause of
action arose in the State of Colorado and is located
in the State of Colorado;

"That the defendant corporation is an insurance
company of the State of Pennsylvania, and hence is
a resident and a citizen of the State of Pennsylvania;

"That the said contract and said cause of action
is located in the State of Colorado and is not a contract nor a cause of action in the State of Missouri;

"That under and by virtue of section 7042, Revised Statutes 1909, a foreign insurance company is required upon condition of doing business in the State of
Missouri to make the Superintendent of the Insurance
Department of the State of Missouri its agent upon
whom service of process issuing out of the courts
of the State of Missouri might be had; but said Superintendent of Insurance is and can be an agent for
the purpose of service of process only for the benefit
of the State of Missouri and a cause of action arising in the State of Missouri out of contracts made
in the State of Missouri; and said section is solely
for the benefit of actions located in the courts of the
State of Missouri; and said Superintendent of Insur-

ance is not an agent for the purpose of having process served upon him for a cause of action arising outside of the State of Missouri and in behalf of nonresidents of the State of Missouri; and the said Frank Blake, the said Superintendent of the Insurance Department of the State of Missouri, upon whom service was had in said action, is not an agent for this defendant upon whom process could be served in the alleged cause of action set forth in plaintiff's petition.

"Wherefore, this defendant says that this court has not jurisdiction over the subject of this action nor over the person of this defendant.

"2. The bringing of this action in the State of Missouri and outside of the State of Colorado is an attempt on the part of the plaintiff to make use of the courts of the State of Missouri to deprive the defendant of judicial process by which it may procure the attendance of witnesses on its behalf in a defense of the merits of said cause of action; that this defendant is entitled to a defense on the merits of said cause of action and has a defense thereto consisting as follows: First, said policy is void; second, said policy became void by reason of acts of the defendant after the issue of said policy; third, it is void in fact and in law; fourth, the defendant was not the sole and unconditional owner of said property described in said petition at the time of the issuing of said policy, neither was it the sole and unconditional owner thereof at the time of the alleged fire; and further the plaintiff has avoided said policy and caused the same to become null and void by its violation of the terms of said policy, and said plaintiff did not have destroyed by fire a portion of the property as alleged in its said petition.

"That said petition presents many issues which the defendant acting on its own behalf will be com-

pelled to defend against, and there is a large amount
of testimony in the way of witnesses and in the way
of documentary evidence, all located in the State of
Colorado, which this defendant cannot produce in
any court of the State of Missouri by judicial process, and for that reason this court should not take
jurisdiction of said cause and cannot have jurisdiction of said cause; and to be allowed to maintain
said action in the State of Missouri would be to deprive the defendant of that due process of law which
the Constitution of the State of Missouri guarantees
to every foreign insurance company entering the State
for the purpose of doing business therein; and to
allow said action to be prosecuted in the State of
Missouri is to deny to the defendant the equal protection of the laws, and is, therefore, in disobedience
of section 1 of article 14 of the Constitution of the
United States, which provides that no State shall deprive any person of life, liberty or property without
due process of law, nor deny to any person within
its jurisdiction the equal protection of the laws."

This motion the court nisi overruled, and the defendant answered. In this answer the jurisdiction is
thus challenged:

"The defendant herein admits that at all dates
herein the plaintiff was and now is a corporation duly
organized and existing under and pursuant to the
laws of Arizona, and that at all of said times such
defendant was and now is a foreign corporation duly
existing under the laws of the State of Pennsylvania,
and at all of said times said defendant as such company and corporation has been and now is engaged
in a general fire insurance business in the State of
Colorado, and also in the State of Missouri, and was
and now is licensed and authorized to do business in
both of said States. Defendant says that the policy
or contract of insurance issued was made and exe-

cuted in the State of Colorado upon property located in the State of Colorado and further says that therefore said contract of insurance is a contract under the laws of the State of Colorado and not a contract under the laws of the State of Missouri.

"That the said Frank Blake, Superintendent of the Insurance Department of the State of Missouri, upon whom service was had in said cause, was not authorized by the laws of the State of Missouri to acknowledge or receive service of process issued from any court of record in the State of Missouri for this defendant in said cause of action, hence this court has no jurisdiction over this defendant, nor the subject-matter of this action, and section 7042, Revised Statutes 1909, does not apply to this action, for the reason that said contract of insurance is a contract of the State of Colorado and not of the State of Missouri and the cause of action can only be maintained in the State of Colorado, and said section 7042 is unconstitutional and void because it denies to this defendant due process of law and is an effort to take the property of this defendant without due process of law, and is therefore in conflict with section 30 of article 2, of the Constitution of the State of Missouri, which provides that no person shall be deprived of property without due process of law, and is in conflict with section 1, article 14, of the Constitution of the United States, which provides that no state shall make or enforce any law which shall deprive any person of property without due process of law, nor deny to any person within its jurisdiction the equal protection of the law.

"Defendant further says that said section 7042 was enacted by the General Assembly of the State of Missouri in the year 1885, as shown by Laws 1885, page 183, and that the title to said act is as follows:

" 'An act to amend section 6013, article 4, of the Revised Statutes of Missouri of 1879, entitled, "General Provisions" relating to insurance and service of legal process therein.'

"Whereas in truth and in fact, said act of the Legislature did not amend said section 6013, but repealed said section and enacted a new section in lieu thereof, and is therefore in conflict with section 28, article 4, of the Constitution of Missouri, which provides that no bill shall contain more than one subject, which shall be clearly expressed in said title, is contrary to the body of said act, and the subject of the body of the act is not expressed in the title, either clearly or otherwise.

"And defendant further says that said act is contrary to the terms of section 34 of article 4 of the Constitution of Missouri which provides that: 'No act shall be amended by providing that designated words thereof be stricken out, or that designated words be inserted, or that designated words be stricken out and others inserted in lieu thereof; but the words to be stricken out, or the words to be inserted, or the words to be stricken out and those inserted in lieu thereof, together with the act or section amended, shall be set forth in full as amended.'

"Wherefore, defendant says that said section 7042, Revised Statutes 1909, is unconstitutional and void and that the service herein is void and this court has no jurisdiction over the defendant or over the subject-matter of this action, and to entertain further jurisdiction in this cause would be to deprive the defendant of its property without due process of law."

Further parts of the answer set out various defenses to the suit upon the policy, which matters can be best stated, if necessary, with the points made. Reply placed in issue matters in the answer.

I. In this dissent I am not unmindful of the ruling of this court in State ex rel. v. Grimm, 239 Mo.

Jurisdiction: Contracts Made Outside of State.
135, and cases following it. I take it that the United States Supreme Court has fully sustained the dissent in the Grimm case, and no specious argument can change the force and effect of the very recent holding of that court. This, however, we discuss later.

It is clear in this case that the defendant did nothing more to give the circuit court of Audrain County jurisdiction over its person than the filing of the two documents we have set out in the statement. One is called a motion to quash the service, and the other is the answer. It is clear that jurisdiction over the person was challenged from start to finish. Jurisdiction over the person is the proper subject-matter of a plea in the answer. Section 1804, Revised Statutes 1909, reads:

"When any of the matters enumerated in section 1800 do not appear upon the face of the petition, the objection may be taken by answer. If no such objection be taken, either by demurrer or answer, the defendant shall be deemed to have waived the same, excepting only the objection to the jurisdiction of the court over the subject-matter of the action, and excepting the objection that the petition does not state facts sufficient to constitute a cause of action."

Section 1800, Revised Statutes 1909, referred to in section 1804, supra, reads:

"The defendant may demur to the petition, when it shall appear upon the face thereof, either: First, that the court has no jurisdiction of the person of the defendant, or the subject of the action; or, second, that the plaintiff has not legal capacity to sue; or, third, that there is another action pending between the same parties, for the same cause, in this State;

or fourth, that there is a defect of parties plaintiff or
defendant; or, fifth, that several causes of action have
been improperly united; or sixth, that the petition
does not state facts sufficient to constitute a cause
of action; or seventh, that a party plaintiff or defendant is not a necessary party to a complete determination of the action.''

From this it appears that jurisdiction over the
person is a subject-matter of demurrer, if it appears
from the face of the petition, but if it does not so
appear, then it is a subject-matter of answer, and is
only waived in the event it is not challenged by one
or the other methods. The challenge in this case was
not only timely, but continuous. Jurisdiction over
the person can only be acquired by service of the
person had according to law, or by consent, expressed
or implied. Implied consent consists in doing such
things as would indicate a willingness for the court
to try the case—i. e. as filing answer or doing some
similar thing, without questioning the jurisdiction of
the court. Implied consent is more frequently denom-
inated waiver of jurisdiction. In the case at bar the
defendant has waived nothing as to jurisdiction.
Dragged into court by the ears, as it were, it has
persistently protested want of jurisdiction. It has
lodged the plea where the statutes of this State say
it may be lodged, i. e., in its answer. The reply of
the plaintiff filed herein admits all the facts necessary
to show want of jurisdiction, if our views of the law
are correct. In other words, the reply admits that
plaintiff is an Arizona corporation, and the defendant
is a Pennsylvania corporation, and that ''the contract of insurance was made and executed in Colorado, upon property in Colorado.'' This admission
shows that it was not the result of business done in
Missouri. The full effect of this omission is not in
the petition, and therefore demurrer was not necessarily the pleading for defendant. Under the plea

to the jurisdiction found in the answer, and the admission found in the reply, the circuit court of Audrain County should have found for defendant upon the issue of jurisdiction.

Our statute, section 7042, Revised Statutes 1909, requires a foreign insurance company to designate the Superintendent of Insurance as its agent to receive service of process in suits filed against such foreign insurance company in the courts of this State. This designation is a pre-requisite to a license to do business in this State. A close reading of our statute, however, will disclose no legislative intent to make service of process in this manner effective in any case except one arising through contracts made and acts done in this State, whilst the corporation was licensed to transact business therein. In the Grimm case, supra, 239 Mo. 1. c. 187, I then took occasion to say:

"Neither do I believe section 7042, Revised Statutes 1909, charges our courts with the duty of hearing a case such as is now pending in the court of the respondent Grimm in the city of St. Louis. That section compels foreign insurance companies doing business in this State to make our State Superintendent of Insurance an agent to accept service of process. I believe that this section only confers jurisdiction upon our courts to hear and determine controversies growing out of insurance contracts made in this State, whilst a foreign insurance company is doing business in this State under a license from the State. It is said in the opinion by my learned brother that there is no limitation in this statute, and hence cases from other jurisdictions where there is a limitation in the statute are not in point. I think the statute, when considered as a whole, has a limitation. I think from its language there can be gathered a clear legislative intent to limit the jurisdiction of courts to actions upon contracts made in this State.

Note the language: 'Service of process as aforesaid, issued by any such court, as aforesaid, upon the Superintendent, shall be valid and binding and be deemed personal service upon such company, so long as it shall have any policies or liabilities outstanding in this State.' This follows the language emphasized by my brother, and to my mind characterizes the kind of litigation to which foreign insurance companies can be called upon to respond in our courts. In other words, it fixes a limitation of the kind of causes over which our courts can assume jurisdiction. The statute specifically refers to policies 'outstanding in this State.' It is true that this clause refers to a time when such company has withdrawn from the State or is no longer doing business in the State, but it also refers to contracts made when in the State. The policies above mentioned in the statute are policies issued when the company was in the State. The question then arises, why preserve this method of service after the company has left the State and limit it to cases upon policies outstanding in this State only, if the previous portion of the statute referred to all kinds of actions, whether upon contract in this State or contracts made out of this State?

"To my mind the substituted method of service provided for in this statute only applies to actions arising upon contracts made in this State, and not to actions upon contracts made out of this State. In other words, the statute limits the class of cases in which this kind of service can be effectively had, and the case pending in respondent's court is not one of the class, if the averments in the complex motion are true. How the relator may now avail itself of the situation, with jurisdiction over its person having been decided by the majority, may be a question, but not one for discussion at this time. To do so would be but to suggest to counsel how to try their cases.

"For these reasons, somewhat hurriedly drawn, I dissent in this case, as well as in those which follow it upon the questions discussed. *Valliant, C. J.,* concurs in these views."

The exact question, since the writer expressed the foregoing views, has come up in the U. S. Supreme Court in construing a similar statute in the State of Louisiana. By section 1 of the Louisiana act a foreign corporation was required to file a written declaration setting forth the places in the State where it was doing business and the name of its "agents . . . in this State upon whom process may be served." Section 2 of the act reads:

"Whenever any such corporation shall do any business of any nature whatever in this State without having complied with the requirements of section 1 of this act, it may be sued for any legal cause of action in any parish of the State where it may do business, and service of process in such suit may be made upon the Secretary of State the same and with the same validity as if such corporation had been personally served."

In Simon v. Southern Ry. Co., 236 U. S. 115, l. c. 130, Mr. Justice LAMAR, in discussing these statutes, says:

"Subject to exceptions, not material here, every State has the undoubted right to provide for service of process upon any foreign corporations doing business therein; to require such companies to name agents upon whom service may be made; and also to provide that in case of the company's failure to appoint such agent, service, in proper cases, may be made upon an officer designated by law. [Mutual Reserve Assn. v. Phelps, 190 U. S. 147; Connecticut Mut. L. Ins. Co. v. Spratley, 172 U. S. 602.] *But this power to designate by statute the officer upon whom service in suits against foreign corporations may be made relates to business and transactions within the*

jurisdiction of the State enacting the law. Otherwise, claims on contracts, wherever made, and suits
for torts, wherever committed, might, by virtue of
such compulsory statute, be drawn to the jurisdiction
of any State in which the foreign corporation might
at any time be carrying on business. The manifest
inconvenience and hardship arising from such extra-
territorial extension of jurisdiction by virtue of the
power to make such compulsory appointments could
not defeat the power if in law it could be rightfully
exerted. *But these possible inconveniences serve to
emphasize the importance of the principle laid down
in Old Wayne Mut. Life Assn. v. McDonough, 204 U.
S. 22, that the statutory consent of a foreign corporation to be sued does not extend to causes of action
arising in other States.*

"In that case the Pennsylvania statute, as a condition of their doing business in the State, required
foreign corporations to file a written stipulation
agreeing, ' "that any legal process affecting the company, served on the Insurance Commissioner . . .
shall have the same effect as if served personally on
the company within this State." ' The Old Wayne
Life Association having executed and delivered, in
Indiana, a policy of insurance on the life of a citizen
of Pennsylvania, was sued thereon in Pennsylvania.
The declaration averred that the company 'has been
doing business in the State of Pennsylvania, issuing
policies of life insurance to numerous and divers residents of said county and State,' and service was made
on the Commissioner of Insurance. The association
made no appearance, and a judgment by default was
entered against it. Thereafter suit on the judgment
was brought in Indiana. The plaintiff there introduced the record of the Pennsylvania proceedings and
claimed that, under the full faith and credit clause of
the Constitution, he was entitled to recover thereon
in the Indiana court. There was no proof as to the

company having done any business in the State of
Pennsylvania, except the legal presumption arising
from the statements in the declaration as to soliciting insurance in that State. This court said:

"'But even if it be assumed that the company
was engaged in some business in Pennsylvania at the
time the contract in question was made, it cannot be
held that the company agreed that service of process
upon the Insurance Commissioner of that Commonwealth would alone be sufficient to bring it into court
in respect of all business transacted by it, no matter
where, with or for the benefit of citizens of Pennsylvania. . . . Conceding, then, that by going into
Pennsylvania, without first complying with its statute, the defendant association may be held to have
consented to the service upon the insurance commissioner of process in a suit brought against it there
in respect of business transacted by it in that Commonwealth, such assent cannot properly be implied
where it affirmatively appears, as it does here, that
the business was not transacted in Pennsylvania.
. . . As the suit in the Pennsylvania court was
upon a contract executed in Indiana; as the personal
judgment in that court against the Indiana corporation was only upon notice to the Insurance Commissioner, without any legal notice to the defendant association, and without its having appeared in person
or by attorney or by agent in the suit; and as the
act of the Pennsylvania court in rendering the judgment must be deemed that of the State within the
meaning of the Fourteenth Amendment, we hold that
the judgment in Pennsylvania was not entitled to the
faith and credit which, by the Constitution, is required to be given to the . . . judicial proceedings of the several States, and was void as wanting
in due process of law.'

"*From the principle announced in that case it
follows that service under the Louisiana statute*

would not be effective to give the district court of Orleans jurisdiction over defendant as to a cause of action arising in the State of Alabama. The service on the Southern Railway, even if in compliance with the requirements of Act 54, was not that kind of process which could give the court jurisdiction over the person of the defendant for a cause of action arising in Alabama." (The italics are ours).

To my mind this ruling of our highest tribunal will stand the test of reason. There is no doubt that a State can require a foreign corporation to come into the State upon terms. Among those terms may be the designation of an agent to receive service of process in suits brought in the courts of the State, but the reasonable construction of all such statutes is, that they refer to suits arising out of business done in the State, and not elsewhere. The laws of a State are presumably for the benefit of its own citizens, and not for outsiders.

The State when it imposes conditions upon foreign corporations is imposing conditions with reference to the business which the corporations expect to do in the State when they apply for licenses. These conditions are imposed for the purpose of protecting the State and its citizens. So that we maintain that this condition imposed by section 7042, supra, should be read in that light. This State has no special interest in making its courts the rendezvous of all alleged causes of action arising in other States, whose laws and procedure may render difficult the procurement of a judgment in such States. Section 7042 was never passed with the legislative intent to authorize such process to be served in cases arising in other jurisdictions. It should be construed (as we think it clearly reads) to have reference only to causes of action growing out of the contracts made and the acts done within this State. When thus construed, the trial court was without jurisdiction in the case, and it should have so adjudged under the pleadings and admissions made in the pleadings.

II. It was said in the Grimm case that the form of the motion to quash the execution was such as to make a general appearance. To this I did not then agree and do not now. In the case at

Appearance.   bar a similar contention is made. The suggestion in the Grimm case is that there are matters which go to the merits. In this case when the motion is read, whilst it is voluminous, it must in fairness be said that all that is said therein goes to the question of want of jurisdiction, and reasons why jurisdiction should not be assumed. The first paragraph of this motion in a rather lengthy way challenges the jurisdiction. It goes to nothing else. The second paragraph, at most, simply sets up reasons why the court should not assume jurisdiction over the person. Taken as a whole it is but a challenge to the jurisdiction and the appearance was special and not general.

It is further suggested that because the first line or so of the answer uses the words:

"Now comes the defendant herein and after leave of court had and obtained, for its answer herein, says:"

The record proper shows no application for leave to answer. The whole record proper so far as relates to the matter here involved, reads:

"During the regular September term, 1911, on September 4, 1911, the defendant filed a motion to quash writ and return.

"Further during said September term, 1911, on September 6, 1911, the court overruled defendant's motion to quash writ and return.

"Further during said September term, 1911, on September 14, 1911, awaiting the action of the Supreme Court and its decision, this cause was ordered passed without action by this court.

"In Vacation, on December 16, 1911, this cause was by the court continued, awaiting the action of the Supreme Court.

"During the regular March term, 1912, on March 4, 1912, the defendant filed its answer, and deposited with the clerk of this court the sum of $80.05 as tender of premiums and interest paid by the plaintiff to the defendant on said policy; which answer, omitting caption and signatures, is as follows:"

It will be noted that after the ruling upon the motion to quash the service every other act was done by the court itself, until this answer was filed. Nothing in this record shows that defendant ever waived the matter of jurisdiction prior to filing its answer. If so, then by the very terms of section 1804, Revised Statutes 1909, the defendant did not waive the question, when it made such a question a part of its answer. It had the right to plead want of jurisdiction over its person along with other matters of defense. So that under the statutes of the State, sections 1800 and 1804, Revised Statutes 1909, this question of jurisdiction (although it be jurisdiction of the person) is well preserved and is here for our review.

Under the law there can be no question that by filing an answer which only goes to the merits of the case, jurisdiction of the person is waived. It may also be waived by a general appearance for any other purpose in the case, and it is useless to review the cases cited by counsel. Those cases are not this case. Here, like Houston v. Publishing Co., 249 Mo. 332, we have a case where the question of jurisdiction over the person has been kept a live issue from start to finish. Under the law the trial court should have found for defendant upon this plea in the answer. Other questions in the record need not be discussed. Nor should our previous ruling in the Grimm, and the school of cases here with the Grimm case, be taken as *stare decisis* and preclude a further review of the question.   In my humble judgment the question is of such grave concern that it should never be considered settled until it is settled right.   [Mangold v. Bacon, 237 Mo. 496, and cases cited therein.]

The judgment appealed from should be reversed and I so vote. *Bond* and *Walker, JJ.* concur in these views.

CASES DETERMINED

BY THE

SUPREME COURT

OF THE

STATE OF MISSOURI

AT THE

APRIL TERM, 1916.

SAMUEL SPERRY v. JAMES HURD et al., Plaintiffs in Error.

Division Two, April 10, 1916.

1. **PETITION: Motion to Make Definite and Certain: Waiver.** Defendant by answering over and going to trial on the merits waives any error to the action of the court in overruling his motion to require plaintiff to make his petition more definite and certain, and cannot urge any error in that ruling on appeal.

2. **ARGUMENT TO JURY: No Exception.** A failure of defendant to save an exception to the court's ruling on his objection that plaintiff's remarks to the jury are prejudicial precludes any consideration of the remarks on appeal.

3. **TRESPASS: Destruction of Fence: Loss of Pasture: Speculative Damages.** Plaintiff is entitled to the loss of grass in his pasture caused by the repeated destruction of his fence, whereby his cattle passed out of the pasture, and because of which fact and to prevent the cattle from continually escaping and destroying other parts of his premises he was compelled to confine them in another inclosure. Such damage is not remote and speculative.

267 Mo.]   .   (628)

4. ———: **Participation in Wrong: Acts of Encouragement, Etc.** In order that the owner of a farm may be legally responsible for the acts of his sons in destroying the fence which inclosed plaintiff's land, it was not necessary that such owner should have been personally present participating in the destructive acts of the sons, but if he aided, counselled and encouraged them to do the act, by words or deeds, he is liable; and such participation may be established by circumstantial evidence. And the evidence in this case was sufficient to justify the jury in inferring that the owner of the adjoining farm did advise or encourage his sons in the destruction of the fence.

5. ———: **Excessive Verdict: Destruction of Fences: $7500 Exemplary Damages.** Exemplary damages cannot be accurately measured; but the character and standing of the parties, the malice with which the act was done, and the financial condition of the defendant are elements which should be taken into consideration, and the amount may be such as will serve, by way of example and punishment, to deter the commission of other like acts. It is *held* in this case that a verdict of $510 for actual damages for the destruction of defendant's fences, whereby he lost the grass of an eighty-acre pasture and his cattle escaped into and destroyed his five-acre orchard, was not excessive, but that a judgment of $7500 for exemplary damages is excessive by $6500.

Error to Buchanan Circuit Court.—*Hon. W. K. Amick*, Judge.

AFFIRMED (*conditionally*).

Hewitt & Hewitt and *W. H. Haynes* for plaintiffs in error.

(1) The admission of the testimony as to the value of the Davies County eighty-acre pasture was error. It was not within the issues; such damage was speculative and remote. 13 Cyc. 23; Wynant v. Krouse, 53 L. R. A. 626; Caldwell v. Evans, 85 Ill. 170; Krenger v. Blank, 62 Mich. 70; Loker v. Damon, 17 Pick. 284; Saunders v. Brosius, 52 Mo. 50. (2) There was not any evidence to connect James Hurd with the tearing down of the post and wire fence, charged in the second count of plaintiff's petition;

and the court erred in not sustaining the demurrer to the evidence as to him. Sperry v. Hurd, 151 Mo. App. 579; Sperry v. Hurd, 130 Mo. App. 495. (3) The complainant's prayer for exemplary damages, in the sum of ten thousand dollars, in view of the facts, is suggestive of a joke; but when it received the approval of the trial court, in instructions 8 and 9, viz., "and not exceeding ten thousand dollars exemplary damages," it presents itself stoutly clothed with the solemn garb of the law, which hides all its nakedness from the eye of the layman, however diaphanous such a garb may appear to the sense of justice, carrying with it the inference that the court would approve same for $10,000. It was the poison injected into the minds of the jury that produced the verdict which will shock the conscience of every reasonable person. The *remittitur* in nowise withdrew the poison from the minds of the jury, nor cured the errors committed which caused this most partial and unfair trial, and excessive verdict. Mathew v. Railroad, 26 Mo. App. 88; Doty v. Steinberg, 25 Mo. App. 334; Koeltz v. Bleckman, 46 Mo. 320; Chitty v. Railroad, 148 Mo. 77.

K. B. Randolph and *Hubbell Bros.* for defendant in error.

(1) The plaintiff was deprived of the use of eighty acres of pasture land immediately east of his home forty by reason of the Hurds destroying his fences and knocking boards off of his fences—the destruction of the plaintiff's fences by the defendants being the direct and only cause of the plaintiff losing this pasture. County v. Stout, 91 Pac. 724; County v. Dickens, 40 So. 753; 13 Cyc. 71; Railroad v. McMurrough, 91 S. W. 320; Linn v. Hagan, 92 S. W. 11; Macey v. Carter, 76 Mo. App. 495. (2) The evidence abundantly shows that James Hurd is liable and guilty. (3) The general rule in regard to tres-

passes is that all who direct the commission of a trespass, or wrongfully contribute to its commission, or assent to it after it is committed, are equally liable to the injured person. Holliday v. Jackson, 21 Mo. App. 667; Dyer v. Tyrrell, 127 S. W. 116; McMannus v. Lee, 40 Mo. 206; Cooper v. Johnson, 81 Mo. 485; Reed v. Peck, 163 Mo. 333.. (4) The original verdict as rendered by the jury was not any more than is necessary to properly punish the defendants for trying to perpetuate the methods of the Night Rider and the Ku Klux Klan. The fact that the last verdict is larger than the three previous verdicts is not evidence that the last verdict is excessive—the three previous verdicts were too low. Shohoney v. Railroad, 231 Mo. 141.

WILLIAMS, C.—This is a suit to recover actual and exemplary damages for malicious trespass. The fourth amended petition, upon which the present trial was had, was in two counts. The first count sought to recover $100 actual damages and $10,000 exemplary damages, and was based upon the alleged malicious acts of defendants in destroying a hedge fence belonging to the plaintiff, whereby cattle and horses escaped into one of the plaintiff's enclosures, damaging his orchard, garden and truck patch, in the month of April, 1904. The second count seeks to recover $410 actual damages and $10,000 exemplary damages on account of the alleged malicious acts of defendant in the months of May, June, July, August and September, 1904, in maliciously destroying a portion of plaintiff's fence constructed of wire, boards and posts, whereby certain live stock were permitted to pass into plaintiff's truck patch, orchard, rye field and garden and damaged the same, and further in depriving plaintiff of the use of eighty acres of blue grass pasturage during the months of June, July and August of that year.

Trial was had before a jury, in the circuit court of Buchanan County, which resulted in a verdict in favor of the plaintiff on the first count for $100 actual damages and $7500 exemplary damages, and on the second count for ·$410 actual damages and $7500 exemplary damages. Upon the argument of the motion for a new trial, plaintiff, at the suggestion of the trial court, entered a *remittitur* of one-half of the exemplary damages on each count, and the trial court thereupon overruled the motion for new trial and entered judgment for the plaintiff in the total sum of $8010. Defendants bring the case to this court by writ of error.

This case orginated in the circuit court of De Kalb County, and was first tried upon the first amended petition, containing eleven counts; the first count was in ejectment; the second count for damages, for destruction of a hedge fence in April, 1904; the third count, for damages for destruction of a wire fence in ·May, 1904; the fourth, fifth, sixth, seventh, eighth, ninth and tenth counts were, respectively for the recovery of damages received in June, July, August, September, October, November and December, 1904, as a result of the destruction of the wire fence; the eleventh count asked to have the title determined to a small strip of ground upon which the fence was located. Before the case was submitted to the jury upon the first trial, plaintiff's evidence tends to show that he took a voluntary nonsuit as to counts from four to ten, both inclusive. On that trial the plaintiff recovered judgment on the ejectment count, $20 damages on the second count, and $40 damages on the third count. The trial court granted a new trial with reference to the counts asking for damages.

Plaintiff thereupon filed his second amended petition in six counts, each count being based on the damages accruing in the separate months, beginning with April and ending in August, 1904. The second

trial resulted in a judgment in favor of the plaintiff
in the total sum of $456, based upon a finding in favor
of plaintiff on each count. The trial court thereafter
granted a new trial, and plaintiff appealed the case
to the Kansas City Court of Appeals, where the action
of the trial court was affirmed in the case of Sperry v.
Hurd, 130 Mo. App. 495.

Thereupon, plaintiff took a change of venue to
the circuit court of Buchanan County, where a trial
was had upon a third amended petition, containing
two counts, resulting in a judgment in favor of the
plaintiff in the total sum of $1040. The case was then
taken by defendants, by writ of error, to the Kansas
City Court of Appeals, where the cause was reversed
and remanded, as reported in Sperry v. Hurd, 151 Mo.
App. 579.

When the cause was remanded to the circuit court
of Buchanan County, plaintiff filed a fourth amended
petition, which was the petition upon which the
present trial was had. The fourth amended petition
differed from the third amended petition only in the
amount of exemplary damages asked; the amount of
exemplary damages asked being increased from $1,000
to $10,000 on each count.

The evidence upon the part of the plaintiff tends
to establish the following facts:

The plaintiff and the defendant James Hurd owned adjoining farms. Plaintiff's farm, upon which he
lived, consisted of a forty-acre tract known as the
"home forty" located in the extreme northeast corner of DeKalb County. He also owned eighty acres
of land adjoining him on the east in Davies County.
He bought the home forty in 1873 and had a survey
made, which is referred to as the Williams Survey.
After having the land surveyed, he built a fence along
the south side of his home forty, locating the fence
two feet over on his land. The west third of this
fence was hedge and the east two-thirds was made of

rails. Before this difficulty occurred, the rail fence had been partly supplanted by a wire fence, beginning at the east line of the forty and extending westward to a point about half way of the south boundary, where it joined the end of a fence which ran northward to plaintiff's barn, near the center of the forty. The fence running north to the barn was known as the "barn fence." A large fence post, referred to in the testimony as the "corner post," was located at the junction of the barn fence and the south boundary fence. The space of a few rods, between the east end of the hedge and the "corner post" was not fenced except by the remnants of the decayed rail fence. The barn fence separated plaintiff's pasture land (consisting of about ten acres in this home forty and eighty acres in Davies County), from a small field or truck patch containing about five acres, portions of which were planted in orchard, rye and meadow. A garden containing about one acre joined this orchard or truck patch on the northwest. There was no fence between the garden and the orchard. In April, 1904, there were fifty young cherry trees, forty young apple trees, eighty plum trees, five pear trees and about one hundred and fifty young peach trees growing in the five-acre tract referred to in the testimony as the truck patch. About one and one-half acres of the truck patch was in rye.

Defendant James Hurd bought the forty acres immediately south of plaintiff's home forty in 1878 and, for reasons not disclosed by the evidence, built a fence along the north portion of his forty acres, parallel to the south fence of plaintiff and about six feet distant therefrom, forming between the two fences what was known as a "Devil's Lane."

Sometime in 1903 defendant procured the services of a surveyor and had the surveyor run a line between the adjoining forties. In April, 1904, the defendant James Hurd, and his two sons, codefendants herein, set stakes through on the line made by the surveyor. These stakes were located about a foot and one-half north of plaintiff's south boundary fence.

A short time thereafter defendant James Hurd and his two sons began cutting down the hedge fence belonging to the plaintiff. The defendants brought some guns with them and leaned them against trees near the hedge fence. They cut down about one-half of the hedge fence and made about one hundred fence posts out of the hedge. Defendant also took up his wire fence south of the hedge. The hedge was thirty-six years old and had never been trimmed except on the side facing plaintiff's home for the purpose of fastening wires to the hedge. After the hedge was destroyed in this manner, five cows and five horses, belonging to the defendants, came over on to the premises of the plaintiff and injured his garden, orchard and rye. Plaintiff testified that they would come over on his place at night and that he saw their tracks, twenty-five or thirty different times. The hedge was worth about fifty dollars. The value of the rye destroyed was $15 and the value of the garden destroyed in April and May was $50.

After cutting the hedge, defendants pulled up their wire fence and rebuilt it along the line of the stakes which they had previously set, except that it appears that the wire was run from the east end of the hedge in a straight line to the "corner post" which was about two feet south of the line of stakes. Defendants pulled up the posts holding plaintiff's wire fence for a distance of about sixty yards east from the "corner post," and threw the posts and wire over on plaintiff's premises. Later the defendants pulled up the "corner post" and threw it over on plaintiff's premises. This left a gap of about fourteen feet in the barn fence, and that night about forty head of plaintiff's cattle which were in the Davies County pasture passed into his truck patch and orchard. The next day plaintiff drove the cattle out and with the help of his hired hand went to the woods and cut a large cherry post and placed it in the ground three and one-half feet north of where the original "corner post" stood. He then fastened his barn fence wires and the wires from his east fence to this new corner post. He also located a brace post between the new corner post and defendants' fence and nailed boards across to close the gap of three and one-half feet. The southern end of these boards came within about three inches of defendants' new fence. Sometime during that night, defendants sawed the new corner post off about three inches above the ground and threw it over on plaintiff's land. This permitted plaintiff's barn fence to sag and his cattle to again go into his truck patch. The next day, plaintiff put in another corner post in the same location where the one had been sawed off and again nailed on the boards to close the gap. That night the boards were knocked off by defendants and plaintiff's cattle were permitted to get into his truck patch and orchard. This process of the plaintiff nailing on the boards and the defendants knocking them off was repeated about fifty different times during the summer, permitting the plaintiff's cattle to go into the orchard and truck patch. This resulted in the destruction of plaintiff's orchard of young trees.

In June of that year, plaintiff fenced off thirty acres of timothy meadow and placed his forty head of cattle in that inclosure in order to keep them out of his truck patch, but left his milch cows in the large pasture. He further testified that the eighty-acre pasture was in good blue grass, but there was no water for stock on it; that his cattle, using that pasture, got water from a well on the southeast part of the "home forty" and, for that reason, he could not fence off the Davies County pasture so as to make it available under the circumstances for pasturage. That, by reason of the defendants' repeated acts of destruction, he lost the use of the Davies County pasture during the months of June, July and August of that year; that the pasture was worth forty dollars per month during that time.

There was testimony tending to show that the five acres of orchard and truck patch were worth about $150 per acre before they were damaged by the cattle, and were worth about $75 per acre after the trees, etc., had been destroyed by the cattle.

Plaintiff testified that he did not go down and tell the defendants not to cut the hedge fence, because the defendants "were on the war path" and he thought he would not bother them, but would "go to law." Frequently, during the summer, he saw the two Hurd boys going along the fence carrying their guns, and one time he saw one of the boys holding a gun while the other one knocked the boards off at the corner post.

At one time, when the boys were chopping on his fence, plaintiff took a gun and went down toward the fence and raised up from behind a brush pile as the Hurd boys passed with their guns. The Hurd boys had a shot gun, a target rifle and one pistol. When they saw defendant had a gun, they ran through the brush out of his sight and he heard them fire the shot gun and rifle once and the pistol six times. Plaintiff was sixty-seven years old. The Hurd boys were "grown men." James Hurd's age is not given.

It appears that a short time after the hedge was cut, plaintiff met James Hurd at the southeast corner of his home forty where they had a dispute as to the correct boundary line. Plaintiff claimed that the line was at the place indicated by the Williams Survey, made in 1873, and defendant contending that it was as shown by the recent survey. They parted enemies, and it does not appear that they had any further conversation thereafter.

At one time when the hired hand of the plaintiff was rebuilding the corner post, James Hurd told him not to build any more fence there, because the post was out of line.

There was evidence tending to show that defendant James Hurd was present when the stakes were set for the relocation of his wire fence, but it does not appear that he was present when the plaintiff's wire fence, corner post and boards were torn down. The actual work of destruction was done by his boys. Plaintiff offered in evidence the testimony of defendant James Hurd upon a former trial, which was as follows:

"Q. Did you tell your boys to cut off that corner post? A. No, sir.

"Q. Did you know they were going to cut it? A. No, sir.

"Q. Or that they cut it? A. I didn't know it till afterwards.

"Q. Did you approve of it afterwards? A. Well, I didn't tell them to.

"Q. You didn't object to it? A. No.

"Q. Answer whether you approved of it or not? A. Well, I didn't want anything on my land.

"Q. Well, you approved of it then? A. Yes, sir; it was on my land and I went and told that boy not to put it there."

Plaintiff introduced in evidence the judgment entered on the ejectment count on the first trial and also the writ of restitution. The judgment in ejectment found that the plaintiff was entitled to the possession of the disputed strip of ground, and further found that plaintiff was the owner of all of the land including and north of the original hedge and wire fences of the plaintiff. Plaintiff also introduced evidence tending to show that on the first trial he took a voluntary nonsuit as to counts four, five, six, seven, eight, nine and ten, which counts sought to recover damages, beginning with the month of June, 1904. Neither of the defendants testified in the case. The only evidence offered upon the part of the defendants was the plaintiff's original petition which was in four counts; the verdict of the jury upon the ejectment count, and the verdict on two of the damage counts rendered at the first trial. Defendants also offered in evidence the first amended petition which was in eleven counts.

I. Plaintiffs in error are not now in a position to urge as error the action of the court in overruling their motion to make the petition more definite and certain. This point was waived when they answered over and went to trial upon the merits. [Sauter v. Leveridge, 103 Mo. 615; State ex rel. v. Bank, 160 Mo. 640; Dakan v. Chase & Son Mercantile Co., 197 Mo. 238; Ewing v. Vernon County, 216 Mo. 681.]

Waiver.

In the main opinion in the case of Shohoney v. Railroad, 223 Mo. 649, l. c. 673, an attempt was made to overrule the above cases on the point in question, but since the opinion as to that point did not receive a majority vote the above cited cases are to be considered as announcing the correct rule.

II. It is next contended that the plaintiff's counsel made prejudicial remarks in his opening statement to the jury. This point is not open to appellate review because the plaintiffs in error failed to save an exception to the court's ruling thereon.

Argument to Jury.

III. Plaintiff was permitted to prove, over the objection and exception of the defendants, the rental value of the eighty acres of blue grass pasture during

Speculative Damages. the months of June, July and August, 1904. It is contended that this item of damage was remote and speculative. We are unable to agree with this contention. It appears from the evidence that the defendants repeatedly destroyed a portion of the fence which served as an inclosure to keep plaintiff's cattle upon this pasture. Plaintiff rebuilt the fence many times, but each time it would be destroyed by defendants and the cattle would be permitted to escape. In order to prevent the cattle from continually escaping and destroying other parts of his premises, plaintiff confined the cattle within another inclosure and was deprived of the use of the pasture during those months. This was but a natural and direct consequence of the continued malicious acts of the defendants and was not, therefore, such damages as could properly be termed remote or speculative.

IV. It is contended that there was no evidence connecting the defendant James Hurd with the destruction of the corner post and wire **Participation In Trespass.** fence, and that, therefore, the court erred in refusing to give his instruction in the nature of a demurrer to the evidence under the second count in the petition.

The evidence shows that James Hurd was the owner of the forty acres adjoining the premises of plaintiff on the south; that he had a line surveyed between the two farms and was present personally directing his sons as to the setting of the stakes for the relocation of his fence. These stakes were located north of plaintiff's fence, on plaintiff's land. After this was done, James Hurd was personally present assisting in cutting down the hedge fence of plaintiff, which was on the same line as the wire fence and the corner post. When plaintiff's farm hand was rebuilding the destroyed corner post and wire fence,

James Hurd told him not to build the fence there because the post was out of line. His testimony introduced in evidence was as follows:

"Q. Answer whether you approved of it (the destruction of the corner post) or not? A. Well I didn't want anything on my land. Q. Well you approved of it then? A. Yes sir; it was on my land and I went and told that boy not to put it there."

In order that James Hurd might be held legally responsible for the destructive acts of his sons, it was not necessary that he should be personally present, participating in the acts of destruction, but it was sufficient to establish his liability therefor if he aided, counselled or encouraged, by words or conduct, his sons to do the act. [Allred v. Bray, 41 Mo. 484.] And this. as any other fact, may be proven by circumstantial evidence. [Willi v. Lucas, 110 Mo. 219.]

When this testimony is considered in the light of all the circumstances shown in evidence, we think there was sufficient proof to justify the jury in inferring therefrom that the defendant James Hurd advised or encouraged his sons in the destruction of the wire fence and corner post, and that, therefore, the court acted properly in refusing the demurrer.

V. We are unable to agree with the contention that the instructions given permitted the jury to assess the same damages twice. Plaintiff's instruction
Instructions. number 10 clearly separated and distinguished the different elements of damage which the jury should consider under each count and the instructions were not misleading in this regard. We have carefully read all the numerous instructions given and refused and have failed to find any error therein that would work a reversal of the judgment.

VI. The most important question presented upon the appeal is with regard to the excessiveness of the verdict. There was sufficient evidence, we think, to justify the verdict for the actual damages on each count, but it clearly appears that the amount of exemplary damages allowed, even after the *remittitur* in the trial court, was greatly in excess of what the circumstances and facts in evidence would justify or warrant.

Excessive Verdict.

A review of the many cases awarding exemplary damages discloses that a hard-and-fast rule for the measuring of such damages cannot be declared. Each case turns more or less upon its own peculiar facts. The character and standing of the parties, the malice with which the act was done, and the financial condition of the defendant are elements which should be taken into consideration in awarding damages of this character (Buckley v. Knapp, 48 Mo. 152; 8 R. C. L. 606-608, secs. 151, 152, and cases therein cited; 2 Sutherland on Damages (3 Ed.), p. 1092), and the amount may be such as would by way of punishment and example serve to deter the occurrence of like acts in the future.

There is very little evidence as to the financial condition of these defendants. There is no showing at all with regard to the financial condition of the two sons and the only property of defendant James Hurd which is mentioned in the evidence is the forty acres of land adjoining the premises of the plaintiff. While we do not undertake to say that a man without property should be exempt from the liability of exemplary damages, yet it may be safely said that a man with small means can be sufficiently punished and deterred from malicious action by a sum which would perhaps be wholly inadequate to punish or deter a man of large means.

We have carefully considered the attending circumstances together with all the facts and elements disclosed by the present record and we have reached the conclusion that, upon the present record, exemplary damages should not be permitted in excess of five hundred dollars on each count of the petition and that the judgment is therefore excessive by $6500.

The evidence in the case clearly shows that plaintiff was entitled to a substantial verdict. Four different juries have held the defendants liable for the trespass. In fact, there was very little defense made to the cause of action upon the last trial. There is no evidence of misconduct upon the part of the jury or matters of error which would arouse prejudice and passion upon the part of the jury. It appears that the excessive amount allowed by the jury was more than likely due to a misapprehension of the elements to be considered in allowing exemplary damages than to undue prejudice or passion. The above matters considered, in connection with the fact that this unfortunate controversy, which has now been pending in the courts for more than a decade, should be ended, we think it a proper case in which to exercise the rule which has become established in this State, to-wit, that of ordering an affirmance upon condition of *remittitur* of the excessive portion of the judgment, under the circumstances here present, rather than a reversal of the judgment and a remanding of the cause. [Cook v. Globe Printing Co., 227 Mo. 471, l. c. 547; Moore v. Transit Co., 226 Mo. 689; Clifton v. Railroad, 232 Mo. 708.]

It is therefore ordered that if the defendant in error will, within ten days, enter a *remittitur* of $6500 as of the date of the judgment in the trial court, the judgment will be affirmed in the sum of $1510 with interest at six per cent from the date of the judgment in the trial court; otherwise, the judgment will be reversed and the cause remanded. *Roy, C.*, concurs.

PER CURIAM.—The foregoing opinion by WILLIAMS, C., is adopted as the opinion of the court. All of the judges concur.

MARIE E. BUCK, Executor of STEPHEN B. BUCK, Appellant, v. ST. LOUIS UNION TRUST COMPANY, CARRIE L. BUCK, Executor of RALPH S. BUCK, et al.

Division Two, April 10, 1916.

1. **BILL OF EXCEPTIONS: Bystanders.** Bystanders who may sign a bill of exceptions upon the refusal of the judge to do so, as the word is used in the statute (Sec. 2031, R. S. 1909), mean disinterested spectators, and do not include persons who were not present at the trial.

2. ————: **Wrongfully Signed: Withdrawal.** A bill of exceptions signed by persons who were not bystanders in contemplation of the statute, because they were not present at the trial, is no bill at all; and if filed or deposited with the clerk, may be withdrawn in order that it may be properly signed.

3. ————: **Bystanders: Jurors.** Members of the trial jury, under a reasonable construction of the statute, are bystanders, and may sign the bill of exceptions upon the judge's refusal to approve it.

4. ————: ————: **Affidavits: Part of Record.** Affidavits of bystanders in support of or against the truth of a bill of exceptions which the judge has refused to sign, taken and filed as required by section 2035, Revised Statutes 1909, are a part of the record on appeal and are subject to review in determining the truth of said bill.

5. ————: ————: ————: **Equal Number for Each Side.** Where the judge refused to sign the bill of exceptions because it was untrue, and a number of bystanders made affidavit to its truth and an equal number to the contrary, the trial judge will be upheld on appeal if said affidavits are so nicely balanced in their substantive facts as to present an irreconcilable conflict; but when the affiants in support of the bill, one of whom was the official stenographer, were disinterested and possessed opportunity to acquire full and impartial knowledge, and those in opposition were interested and possessed no such opportunity, the matters preserved in the bill are entitled to review.

6. **REMARKS OF COUNSEL: Will Contest: Attack on Contestant.** In a suit to set aside a will on the sole grounds of the mental incapacity of the testator and of undue influence exercised upon his mind, it is improper to permit counsel for proponents to say in his argument to the jury of and concerning contestant: "He was a spendthrift son. He never did anything for the support

of the family. He took from his mother's estate so far as he could, and his family had to leave the city to get rid of him, or to get rid of his attempts to get the family's money. He was not a success in business life." Whether true or false, the remarks were not relevant to the issues, and therefore unauthorized, and being a personal reflection upon contestant were improper. But they were not reversible error, where there is a preponderance of affirmative evidence that the testator was of sound mind and subject to no undue influence, and little substantial error to the contrary.

7. **WILL CONTEST: Evidence: Will of Testator's Father.** In a suit by a disinherited contestant to set aside his bachelor brother's will, made in 1909 in favor of his mother, sisters and another brother, on the ground of incapacity and undue influence, a will made by the father of testator and of contestant in 1875 is not admissible as having a tendency to disprove testimony offered by proponents and improperly admitted by the court to the effect that contestant was indebted to his mother, the fact being that such indebtedness was by way of an advancement by the mother to contestant on account of his prospective share in his father's estate.

8. **EVIDENCE: Improperly Admitted for One Side: Rebuttal By Other.** The admission of improper testimony on the one side does not authorize the admission of improper testimony in rebuttal on the other.

9. **CONDUCT OF JUDGE: Testy Remarks to Witness.** Frequent testy remarks made by the court to appellant while he was on the witness stand, though seemingly improper in the cold record, will not be held, in the absence of a showing of the conduct and manner of the witness, to be prejudicial error; especially, where the court cautioned the jury not to consider his words and manner towards the witness.

10. **REOPENING CASE: Discretion.** The reopening of the case after both sides have closed and a peremptory instruction has been offered by plaintiff, to permit the introduction of other testimony, is a matter largely within the discretion of the trial court, and does not constitute reversible error unless the discretion has been abused, to the injury of the losing party.

11. **WILL: Contrary to Testator's Understanding.** Where the will was drawn in accordance with the bachelor testator's instructions and he read it over and expressed satisfaction with it, and then was told by his lawyer that in the event the remaindermen survived the life tenant and died without issue the property would go under the statute to his brothers, and thereupon he requested that it be executed, the court cannot peremptorily instruct the jury to find for contestant on the ground

that the will was not testator's will. Besides, it is not necessary that testator have the knowledge of the will's scope and bearing possessed by his legal adviser.

12. ———: ———: Instruction: Contrary to Will Itself. Where the will of the unmarried testator cancels his brothers' debts, gives the property to his mother for life and in remainder to his sisters, and provides that if the mother survives the sisters and they die without issue the property is to be disposed of according to the mother's will, it is not error to refuse to submit to the jury the question whether it was the testator's intention to provide that, if his sisters survived his mother and died without issue, his property should go to his brothers. Such question should not be submitted to the jury, although testator was informed by his lawyer before executing the will that the property, in such contingency, would go to his brothers.

13. REVERSAL OF JUDGMENT: No Material Error. Notwithstanding errors were committed at the trial the judgment will not be reversed unless they materially affect the merits of the case.

Appeal from St. Louis City Circuit Court.—*Hon. Daniel D. Fisher*, Judge.

AFFIRMED.

W. B. Thompson, Ford W. Thompson and *Claud D. Hall* for appellant.

(1) The bill of exceptions which was prepared by the official court stenographer and presented to the court for allowance, was improperly rejected, and the bystanders' bill of exceptions deposited by plaintiff in the clerk's office, in consequence of the court's refusal to sign and allow said bill of exceptions, and permit the same to be filed, is complete and true and a proper bill of exceptions. The truth of said bill of exceptions is to be determined by this court from the affidavits filed in support and against the said bill of exceptions. Secs. 2030, 31, 33, 34, 35, 36, 37, R. S. 1909; State v. Jones, 102 Mo. 307; Simon v. Weipel, 10 Iowa, 505; Rowls v. State, 8 Smed. & M. (Miss.) 599; Dauson v. Louisville E. & R. Co., 6 Ky. L. R. 659; Schneider v. Hesse, 9 Ky. L. R. 814; Smith v.

Railroad, 55 Mo. 601; Blankenship v. Railroad, 48 Mo. 376; State v. Field, 37 Mo. App. 83; Norton v. Dorsey, 65 Mo. 376; State v. Snyder, 98 Mo. 562. (2) The court erred in failing to rebuke defendants' counsel for improper remarks made in his opening statement to the jury, to the effect that plaintiff was a spendthrift son, never supported his family, etc., for the reason that no such issues were in the case. Glover v. Railroad, 129 Mo. App. 575. (3) The court erred in reprimanding witness Stephen B. Buck without cause, just after the witness had been interrogated as to drawing of drafts on the firm, and just after the witness said: "I will ask you what those dates are." State v. Turner, 125 Mo. App. 21; Landers v. Railroad, 134 Mo. App. 80; State ex rel. v. Rubber Co., 149 Mo. 181; Dryfus v. Railroad, 124 Mo. App. 585; Stelte-meyer v. Barrett, 115 Mo. App. 323; Levels v. Rail-road, 196 Mo. 606; Rose v. Kansas City, 125 Mo. App. 231; Bennett v. Harris, 68 N. Y. Misc. 503; McDuff v. Evening Journal Co., 84 Mich. 1. (4) The court erred in not giving to the jury a peremptory instruction, offered by the plaintiff directing the jury to find a verdict in favor of the contestant and that the will offered was not the will of the testator. (a) If in their efforts to prove the due execution of the will, the proponents themselves show that the paper offered is not what the testator was made to believe it was when he signed it, it cannot be adjudged to be his will, even in the absence of an averment to that effect in the petition of the contestants. Cowan v. Shaver, 197 Mo. 212; Bradford v. Blossom, 207 Mo. 225. (b) The evidence of John F. Lee offered by the proponents of the will, conclusively showed that the will as drawn by him for the testator is not what the testator was made to believe it was when he signed it, and the peremptory instruction to the jury, to find that the will offered is not

the will of the testator, should have been given. (c)
In a will contest, where the issue is *devisavit vel non*,
parol evidence is admissible for the purpose of proving or disproving any fact relative to that issue; but
parol evidence is not admissible in a suit to reform a
will, either for the purpose of adding to or explaining
the clear and unequivocal language of a will; the reason therefor being that a will is required to be in
writing, and that a court will not make a will. 1 Jar-
man on Wills (6 Ed.), 484; Earl of Newbury v.
Countess of Newbury, 5 Mad. 364; Fulton v. Andrew,
44 L. J. P. 17.

Charles M. Polk for respondents.

(1) The refusal of the circuit judge to sign appellant's bill of exceptions was proper, as it was untrue and incomplete. (a) Persons not present at the
trial of the cause of action are not bystanders within
the meaning of Sec. 2031, R. S. 1909, and a bill of
exceptions signed by such persons is not a proper bill
of exceptions. Heidenheimer v. Thomas, 63 Tex. 287;
Houston v. Jones, 4 Tex. 172; Williams v. Pitt, 38
Fla. 168. (b) Neither are jurors who participated
in the trial of the cause of action bystanders within
the meaning of our statutes. Oil Co. v. Akins, 140 S.
W. (Ark.) 739; Snyder v. Hesse, 9 Ky. L. R. 814.
(c) After the plaintiff had deposited the bill of exceptions in the circuit court, it could not be added to
without leave of court. (d) As the bill of exceptions
does not correctly set forth the evidence at the trial,
it should not be considered here, and there being no
error in the record proper, the judgment should be
affirmed. State v. Jones, 102 Mo. 308; State v.
Hronek, 94 Mo. 84. (2) Counsel have the right, in
their opening statements, to state in good faith their
claims as to both the law and the facts, in so far as
is necessary to give the jury an understanding of

their theory of the case, and where the remarks concerned facts which the counsel expected to prove and
did prove, which would naturally and did influence
the relationship of the testator to the person who
claimed that he was unfairly deprived of his bounty,
such remarks were proper. Such questions must be
largely left to the sound discretion of the trial court.
It is only when an abuse of the discretion is shown
that the appellate court is justified in interfering.
40 Cyc. 1331; Wilkerson v. McGhee, 153 Mo. App.
355; Mowry v. Norman, 223 Mo. 471; Meier v. Buchter, 197 Mo. 68; Thompson v. Ish, 99 Mo. 172. (3)
The testimony shows conclusively that the testator
was of sound and disposing mind and memory, and
that he was not under the undue influence of any one.
(a) The testimony of the attorney who drew the will
shows conclusively that the will was drawn in accordance with the instructions of the testator. (b)
There is no testimony which shows that the testator
misunderstood the language of the will. (c) The testimony of the attorney who drew the will merely
shows that the testator knew he was not absolutely
excluding his brothers from a share in the *corpus* of
his estate, in the event that a partial intestacy should
occur through the death of the sisters without descendants surviving. (d) No error was committed
by the court in refusing instructions, the effect of
which would have allowed the jury to consider an
alleged mistake about a matter outside of the will.
40 Cyc. 1418, 1942; Hurst v. Von de Veld, 158 Mo.
247; Schneider v. Schneider, 54 Mo. 501; Sec. 544,
R. S. 1909; Couch v. Eastham, 27 W. Va. 796; Bradford v. Blossom, 207 Mo. 226. (e) It is not necessary for the testator to be able to fully understand the
scope and bearing of the will as prepared by his attorney. Couch v. Gentry, 113 Mo. 256; Kishman v.
Scott, 166 Mo. 228; Young v. Ridenbaugh, 67 Mo.
586. (f) The will was executed by a competent testa-

tor not under any undue influence, and was not the
result of any fraud practiced upon the testator, therefore neither a mistake of law or of fact in the mind
of the testator, as to the effect of what he actually and
intentionally did, will avail to set aside the will.
Bradford v. Blossom, 207 Mo. 226; Comstock v. Had-
lyme, 8 Conn. 254; Barker v. Comins, 110 Mass. 488;
Walizi v. Walizi, 55 Pa. St. 242.

WALKER, J.—This was an action instituted in
the circuit court of the city of St. Louis by Stephen
B. Buck to contest the will of his brother, Ralph S.
Buck, on the ground of the mental incapacity of the
latter and that undue influence had been exerted upon
him to induce him to make the will. Upon a trial a
judgment was rendered for defendants, from which
plaintiff appealed. Pending the motion for a new
trial the original plaintiff, Stephen B. Buck, died,
and the suit was revived in the name of the executrix
of his estate, Marie V. Buck, who is the appellant
here.

The judge of the circuit court refused to sign the
bill of exceptions submitted by appellant on the
ground that the same was untrue in that it failed
to insert in the testimony of the contestant, Stephen
B. Buck, an answer alleged by the judge to have been
made by the contestant while on the witness stand,
to this question: "I will ask you what those dates
are?" to which the witness replied "he would not
answer such a fool question." Upon the refusal of the
trial judge to sign the bill, appellant secured the signatures of three bystanders thereto and again submitted same to the judge, who refused to sign it on
the ground that it was untrue, as above stated, and
for the further reason that the so-called bystanders
stated that they were not present at the trial and
did not know what transpired during its progress.
Appellant thereupon secured the signatures of three

of the jurors who had participated in the trial of said cause and had rendered the verdict adverse to appellant and submitted the bill thus signed to the judge for his signature. He refused to sign same on the ground that it was untrue, as before stated, and said bill having been deposited with the clerk as originally signed, that appellant was not authorized in withdrawing same and having other signatures attached thereto; and for the further reason that said jurors were not bystanders within the meaning of the statute (Sec. 2031, R. S. 1909) and hence said bill had not been signed as required by law. Appellant filed said bill signed by said jurors with the clerk of the circuit court and proceeded under the authority of section 2034, Revised Statutes 1909, to procure and file the affidavits of five persons to support the truth of said bill, and respondents procured and filed counter affidavits of five persons against the truth of same.

The testator died in the city of St. Louis, November 11, 1910. His will, made in said city February 27, 1909, omitting formal introductory paragraph, closing testimonial, his signature and the certificate and signatures of attesting witnesses, is as follows:

"Item 1. I desire that all my just debts, should I leave any, shall be paid by my executors hereinafter named as soon as may be practicable after my decease.

"Item 2. I make no provision in this, my will, for my brothers, Stephen B. Buck and Charles H. Buck, but it is my will and I direct that under no circumstances shall any claim be asserted or brought by my estate against them, or either of them, for moneys I have lent to them, or either of them, during my lifetime, and any and all evidences of debt held by me, or my estate against them, or either of them, at the time of my death, shall be cancelled.

"Item 3. I give and bequeath to my mother, if she survives me, or if she predecease me, then to my sister, Carrie L. Buck, all my wearing apparel, watch and other jewelry, all my books, household furniture, plate, glass and chinaware, pictures and bric-a-brac, absolutely.

"Item 4. I give and bequeath to my nephew and namesake, Ralph B. Buck, the sum of two thousand dollars, which I desire my executors shall pay over to the St. Louis Union Trust Company, to be invested, managed and controlled by that company during the minority of my said nephew, and during his said minority the net income or profits arising from said principal sum of two thousand dollars, shall be added to the principal, and the whole amount of principal and accumulated income shall be paid over to my said nephew by said Trust Company when he reaches the age of twenty-one years, to be his absolutely.

"Item 5. I give, devise and bequeath to the said St. Louis Union Trust Company all the rest and remainder of the property, real, personal or mixed, of which I may be possessed, or in which I may have any interest, or over which I may have any power of appointment or disposition at the time of my death, upon trust, however, that the said company will hold, manage, control, invest and reinvest the same in such manner as it may deem best, and after deducting all proper expenses connected with the management and preservation of said trust estate, including a proper commission to said trustee for its services, it shall pay over the net income arising therefrom equally to my dearly beloved mother, Caroline M. Buck, and my said sister, Carrie L. Buck, as long as they shall both live and my said sister, Carrie, is unmarried, and after the death of one of them, or if one of them predeceases me, then from my death until the death of the survivor, all of said net income shall be paid over to such survivor; provided, however, that if my said sister, Carrie, should at any time be married when otherwise under this clause she would be entitled to any income, all of such income shall be payable to my mother so long as she shall live. At any time after my death, when my mother is dead, and my said sister, Carrie, is married, or a widow, I desire that the net income arising under this clause shall be paid equally to my said sister, Carrie, and my sister, Lillie B. Avis, so long as they both shall be alive, and upon the death of one of them, the whole of said net income shall be payable to the survivor until she dies, and upon the death of the survivor, the body of said trust fund shall be divided among the descendants of my said sisters, should they both leave descendants, or among the descendants of the sister leaving descendants if but one leaves descendants, such descendants taking *per stirpes* the share his, her or their parents would have received if then living.

"I desire that there shall be no sale of any property of my estate or reinvestment of the proceeds thereof without the consent of either one or the other of my two friends, John F. Lee, and Dr. Josephus R. Lemen, both of said city of St. Louis, so long as either of them may reside in said city.

"If my mother should survive me and survive my two sisters, I desire that my estate shall be distributed according to the terms of her last will and testament, should she leave one, and all prior clauses in this, my will, are to be construed with reference to this provision.

"I appoint my said sister, Carrie, and the St. Louis Union Trust Company the executors of this, my will, and desire that neither shall be required to give any bond for the performance of her or its duties as executor hereunder, and I authorize my executors during the administration upon my estate to sell, invest and reinvest any portion of my property with the consent of either one of my said friends, as above provided.''

I. Upon the refusal of the trial judge to sign the bill of exceptions on the ground that it was not true, the procuring of the signatures thereto as **Bill of** bystanders of three persons who had not **Exceptions** been present during the trial was not a compliance with the literal meaning or intendment of the statute, which provides that if a judge refuse to sign a bill of exceptions it may be signed by three bystanders who are respectable inhabitants of the State, and the court or judge in vacation shall permit every such bill, if true, to be filed in court or in the clerk's office if ordered in vacation, within the time specified in the order of the court. [Sec. 2031, R. S. 1909.] Bystanders, as used in this statute, mean disinterested spectators (State v. Jones, 102 Mo. 305) and persons not present cannot properly be so classified.

The correctness of this definition is rendered more evident when we seek to ascertain the purpose of the statute. The signing of the bill by the trial judge gives a badge of verity to the proceedings when transmitted to the appellate court; failing to secure this, the law, in its wisdom, does not leave the appellant without remedy in perfecting his appeal, but provides, when reasonably construed, that the truth of the bill may be attested by three disinterested persons who were present during that part of the trial the transcript of the proceedings of which are alleged to be untrue by the trial judge. In the instant case, therefore, the requirement of the statute, whether measured by its words or the purpose it was intended to effect, was not meant by the securing of signatures to the bill of persons unfamiliar with the proceedings of the trial alleged by the judge to be untrue as shown by the transcript. This being true, the ruling of the trial court in this regard was not error.

However, within the time granted for the filing of the bill the appellant withdrew the same from the clerk's office and procured the signatures thereto of three of the jurors who had sat in the trial and had joined in a verdict adverse to the appellant. As stated, the bill thus signed was submitted to the trial judge for his signature. He refused to sign same. We have set forth his reasons therefor in the preliminary statement, but for emphasis repeat them here, as follows: first, because the bill was untrue for the reason heretofore noted; second, that appellant having filed and deposited the bill in the clerk's office as originally signed was without authority to withdraw or in any wise change same; and, third, because jurors are not bystanders within the meaning of the statute.

The ground of the first objection we will discuss later. There is no merit in the second. If the bill was improperly signed, as contended by the trial judge and as we have held, it was no bill and its attempted filing with the clerk had no more binding force than if appellant had deposited and secured the filing of any other memorandum or private paper. Filed without authority, it could be withdrawn at pleasure. It was so withdrawn, and within the time granted by the trial court for the filing of the bill the signatures of the jurors were obtained to same and it was submitted to the judge for his signature with the result stated.

There is a dearth of authority upon the subject of the right of jurors to sign a bill of exceptions as bystanders. One case (Dawson v. L. & N. R. R. Co., 13 Ky. Opin. l. c. 229) from the Kentucky Court of Appeals briefly holds that the affidavits of two members of the jury to a bill of exceptions gotten up in lieu of one signed by the judge who tried the case is sufficient under the statute of that State. A later case in the same court (Schneider v. Hesse, 9 Ky. L.

Rep. 814), while simply holding that the signature of one member of a jury will not suffice to attest a bill of exceptions, intimates by implication that there is a question whether a juror can be regarded as a bystander under the laws of Kentucky. These cases, therefore, throw no light upon the subject and would not be noticed except that they have been cited pro and con by the parties hereto. Here and elsewhere, without burdening this opinion with the citation and discussion of cases, it has been held, under statutes similar in all their material features to that of this State, that an interested party, whether a litigant, an attorney or a witness, cannot be regarded as a bystander. These rulings, even by analogy, afford no aid. We are therefore relegated to the general rules of interpretation to determine this question.

The express requirement of the statute (Section 2031, supra), and it has no other limitation, is that those who sign a bill of exceptions as bystanders shall be respectable inhabitants of the State, and the implied requirement, deduced, as we have shown, from the purpose of the law, is that such bystanders shall be disinterested and possess such a knowledge of the proceedings as will enable them to intelligently certify to the correctness of the bill. If such bystanders are jurors who have sat in the trial of the case, it must have been shown as a prerequisite to their sitting as such that they are disinterested; the nature of their duty necessitates a familiarity with the proceedings of the trial, the truth of which they are consequently enabled to attest as such bystanders. The fact that they have rendered a verdict in the case from which the appellant is seeking to appeal affords no ground of complaint, because such verdict, under their oaths, is a disinterested finding.

Jurors, therefore, under a reasonable construction of the statute, may be said to meet the measure of qualifications necessary to authorize them to sign a bill of exceptions as bystanders.

Further than this,.another matter, of a practical nature, properly influences this construction. A law, when the plain meaning of its words is not misconstrued and its intendment is not perverted, is to be so interpreted as to fully effect the purpose of its enactment. The meaning and the purpose of the statute under review is to aid in the perfecting of appeals. It is a fact well known to every lawyer of general experience that in the trial of cases in the circuit courts of our cities the attendance is more often than otherwise limited to the officers of the court, the litigants, witnesses and jurors. Under this state of facts, if a case arises, as it has here, where the trial judge refuses to sign the bill of exceptions, unless jurors be held qualified to sign same as bystanders, the perfecting of an appeal becomes impossible and the statute is rendered nugatory. Such a condition of affairs was not within the contemplation of the Legislature. The 'law was enacted not that its practical application might be limited to a part but extended to all litigants who come within its provisions; it is remedial in its nature, as are all statutes in regard to appeals (Beechwood v. Railroad, 173 Mo. App. 371; State ex rel. v. Taylor, 134 Mo. App. l. c. 440), and as such should be liberally construed. So construed it authorizes, as we have indicated, the signing of bills of exceptions by jurors as bystanders.

The requirement of the statute (Sec. 2033, R. S. 1909) in regard to the filing of the bill signed by jurors as bystanders was complied with. Upon the refusal of the trial judge to permit the bill of exceptions so signed by jurors to be filed, as evidenced by his certificate thereto attached, the respective parties hereto, in conformity with section 2034, Revised Statutes 1909, procured affidavits, five in number on each side, in support of and against the truth of said bill. Such affidavits, taken and deposited, as required by section 2035, Revised Statutes. 1909, are a part of the record herein and hence properly subject to review in determining the truth of said bill. [State ex rel. v. Taylor, 134 Mo. App. 430.] Equal in number on each side, if said affidavits were so nicely balanced in the substantive facts set forth in each as to present an irreconcilable conflict, we would be inclined, as by precedent authorized (State v. Jones, supra), to hold that the certificate of the trial judge should prevail.

However, we do not find this state of facts to exist. The affidavits in support of the appellant's bill were made by three members of the trial jury, the court stenographer who took the entire notes of the testimony, and an attorney who was present during the trial as a guradian *ad litem* for a minor defendant. The counter affidavits in support of the objections to the bill consisted of one by the attorney who had theretofore filed an affidavit in support of same and one by W. H. Kribben, a witness for the respondents, and three others, one by Carrie L. Buck and another by Lillie B. Avis, respondents, and another by Harry C. Avis, husband of the latter. Discarding, as we are authorized to do, the affidavits of the attorney who, while attesting the correctness of the bill qualified same in his counter affidavit, we have remaining four affidavits on each side. With as little invidious comparison as the nature of the subject will permit or a measuring of the direct statements of one of these sets of affidavits with what is termed in the other as the "best recollections of the affiants," we find that those filed in support of the bill, as submitted by the appellant, are fairly entitled to the greater credence. This finding does not involve any question of veracity in any affiant, but depends for its force upon the nature and substance of the affidavits, the relation which the affiants sustained to the proceeding, their interest or lack of interest in same, and their opportunities, by reason of their relation to obtain a full, free and impartial knowledge of the facts transpiring during the trial. The three jurors found it necessary in the discharge of their duty to give careful heed to what was occurring; and a like duty devolved upon the court stenographer to enable him to carefully preserve a record of the proceeding. He not only testifies generally as to the truth of the bill submitted by appellant, but incorporates in his affidavit, in its own words, the occurrence out of which grew the controversy between the trial judge and the appellant as to the truth of the bill. The record of this occurrence as set forth in said affidavit attests the correctness of the bill as submitted by the appellant, and we feel inclined, under all of the facts, to give it much weight in determining the probative force of these affidavits.

While the presence at the trial of those who made the counter affidavits was not incumbent upon them as a duty but depended wholly upon their inclination and interest, we will presume that they were present during the entire proceeding. The relations they sustained to the case was a sufficient incentive to excite their interest in the matters occurring during the trial and thus induce them to be present; but the very nature of their respective interests tended to prevent them from giving that careful and impartial consideration to the facts as they occurred necessary to enable them to remember such facts clearly. The standard of human testimony is highest when given free from the promptings of personal interest and simply in the discharge of a sworn duty. Much, therefore, as we may be disinclined to hold counter to the conclusion of the trial court in a matter of this nature, we feel impelled, under the facts in this case, to find that the affidavits filed in support of the bill of exceptions, as submitted by the appellant, should be given the greater weight and therefore that the matters preserved in said bill are entitled to a review upon appeal.

II. The trial court, over the objection of the appellant, permitted counsel for respondents in his opening statement to the jury to make these remarks concerning the contestant: "He was a spendthrift son. He never did anything for the support of the family. He took from his mother's estate so far as he could, and his family had to leave the city of St. Louis to get rid of him, or to get rid of his attempts to get the family's money. He was not a success in business life."

Remarks of Counsel.

The issues clearly defined were as to the mental capacity of the testator to make a will and undue influence. While counsel in their opening statements to juries are authorized to state in good faith their claims as to the law and the facts so far as same are necessary to enable the jury to understand the case (40 Cyc. 1331), under no theory of this case, with any proper regard for the rules of evidence, were these remarks permissible. They constitute nothing more than personal reflections upon the character of the contestant, and whether true or false were highly improper. The wide latitude given in the admission of testimony in cases of this character (Mowry v. Norman, 223 Mo. l. c. 470) does not authorize the introduction in evidence of wholly irrelevant matter prejudicial in its nature, and hence the remarks of counsel stating the nature of such proposed testimony are for a like reason unauthorized. As was pertinently said in another jurisdiction (Rickabus v. Gott, 51 Mich. 227), "a trial judge must repress needless scandal and gratuitous attacks upon the character of parties" to proceedings.

III. The offer made by appellant to introduce in evidence the will made in 1875 of Charles H. Buck, the father of the contestant and of the testator, was properly refused. Its submission to the jury **Rulings as to Testimony.** would have served no proper purpose in aiding them to determine the issues presented by the pleadings. Abstruse arguments pro and con as to whether the will of Charles H. Buck created a precatory trust have no place in determining the admissibility of this instrument. To argue that it should have been admitted to show that the contestant had a right to share in his father's estate and to receive money from his mother under a clause which authorized her to distribute the property given her by this will between her children and those of Charles H. Buck, serves no other purpose than to emphasize the fact that the said will is entirely foreign to any matter at issue here, and hence the argument in favor of its admission, when fairly analyzed, carries its own refutation with it; nor will it avail as a reason for the admission of this instrument that its introduction would have tended to disprove testimony offered by respondents and admitted by the court that the contestant was indebted to his mother and that such indebtedness was by way of advancement by her to him on account of his prospective share in his father's estate. While the testimony thus permitted to be introduced by respondents was wholly inadmissible and should have been excluded, the exclusion of testimony offered on the part of the appellant to disprove same was not error. This is true under the rule that the admission of improper testimony on the one side does not authorize the admission of improper testimony in rebuttal on the other. As was tersely said by the Supreme Court of Georgia in discussing this question, "there can be no equation of errors." [Stapleton v. Monroe, 111 Ga. 848.] An examination of the numerous authorities on this subject discloses a marked contrariety of opinion in the different jurisdictions; but, under the particular facts in the instant case, where the appellant duly objected to the improper testimony offered by respondents and his objection was erroneously overruled, he cannot be heard to insist upon the admission of improper testimony in rebuttal, because his objection will save him on appeal and he needs no other protection. [Shaw v. Roberts, 2 Starkie, 455; Stringer v. Young, 3 Pet. (U. S.) l. c. 336; Railroad v. Woodruff, 4 Md. 242, 255; Mitchell v. Sellman, 5 Md. 376, 385; Woolfolk v. State, 81 Ga. 551, 558; Stapleton v. Monroe, supra; Wickenkamp v. Wickenkamp, 77 Ill. 92, 96; Maxwell v. Durkin, 185 Ill. 546, 550.]

The offer of appellant to prove that the business of the manufacturing company of which the testator was the manager at the time the will was made, was so systematized that it required no ability on the part of the testator to manage same, was properly refused. If admitted, the fact would have possessed no probative force. Its truth may be conceded, yet it does not afford proof that the testator was incapable of making a will.

IV. The frequent testy remarks made by the court to the contestant when the latter was on the witness stand seem, in the cold record, to have been improper; it is fair to say, however, in the absence of knowledge of the manner and conduct of the contestant not disclosed except as indicated by the reproof of the court, that a criticism of the court's conduct may be unwarranted. In any event the frank cautionary statement of the court to the jury that they were not to consider the court's words and manner toward the witness in determining the case, as same were not intended in any wise to influence their action but were simply directed to the witness, is sufficient to indicate

Conduct of the Court.

that the jurors could not reasonably have been influenced by the court's conduct.

Complaint is made of the action of the trial court in reopening the case to permit a witness to testify on behalf of respondents after the testimony had been closed on both sides and a peremptory instruction had been asked by appellant. Under our practice the reopening of a case after both sides have closed to permit the introduction of other testimony is a matter largely within the discretion of the trial court, and unless it appears that such discretion has been abused in that injury has resulted therefrom to the party complaining it will not be interfered with. [Joplin W. W. Co. v. Joplin, 177 Mo. l. c. 531; Roe v. Bank of Versailles, 167 Mo. l. c. 426; Drug Co. v. Grocer Co., 179 Mo. App. 676.]

The reopening of the case in this instance was not an abuse of the court's discretion. Especially is this true since it appears that the testimony of the witness was in no material particular different from that given by him when first testifying. The appellant, therefore, has no substantial ground of complaint in this regard.

V. The peremptory instruction requested by appellant and refused by the court directed the jury to find a verdict in favor of the contestant for the reason

Instructions. that the will offered was not the will of testator. This request is based upon the assumption that it had been shown by respondents (the proponents) that the paper offered in evidence as the will was not what the testator was made to believe it was when he signed it, and cannot therefore be adjudged to be his will, despite the absence from the petition of an averment to that effect. The construction placed upon the testimony of John F. Lee, who drew the will, forms the basis for appellant's contention. The substance of this testimony in relation to this matter is as follows:

"I prepared the will and by appointment he (the testator) came to my office, and after he had read the will over he said 'it was satisfactory.' He got up and I hesitated a moment and then said to him: 'Mr. Buck, that's the will as you asked me to draw it. Now I think it is my duty to tell you if you leave it as it is written and your sisters die without children your property will go to your brothers. I don't know whether that is what you want or not, but that is what that will is and I think I ought to call your attention to it.' He put his hand on my desk, by which he was standing, was silent for about five seconds, when he said, 'Let it go.' I then called in the witnesses and the will was executed."

There is not a particle of evidence here to show that the testator did not fully understand the will or that it was in any wise different from the manner in which he directed it to be drawn. He read the will and declared it was satisfactory. Whether he understood before it was explained to him what would be the disposition of his property under the law of descents and distributions in the event of his sisters surviving his mother and dying without issue, the record is silent. This much is clear: when fully informed as to the effect of the will in the event of the contingency mentioned, he reasserted his approval of it in curtly declaring, after listening to Mr. Lee's explanation, "Let it go." This is sufficient to affirmatively show that the testator not only understood, as he doubtless did before the explanation, the terms of the will, but its effect in the event of the death of his sisters without issue. However, if the will expressed his purpose, as it unquestionably did or he would not have approved it, this was all that was necessary. While a testator should have a reasonable understanding as to how he desires his will to take effect, it is not necessary that he should have that knowledge of its scope and bearing possessed by his legal adviser. [Kischman v. Scott, 166 Mo. l. c. 228; Couch v. Gentry, 113 Mo. l. c. 256.] Under the facts the trial court was justified in refusing the peremptory instruction requested by appellant.

The appellant, in two instructions which were refused, asked the court to submit to the jury the question as to whether it was not the intention and purpose of the testator to provide, if his sisters survived his mother and died without issue, that his property should go to his brothers. Much that we have said in support of the action of the trial court in refusing to give the peremptory instruction applies with equal force here. We have shown that the testator read and approved the will and an analysis of same will disclose that it cannot be so construed as to authorize the giving of the instructions in question. As was explained to the testator before he signed the will, its effect in the event of the sisters surviving the mother and dying without issue, was to leave the property subject to the disposition of the statute, in which event the brothers would take by descent and not by devise, as contended by the appellant. [Hurst v. Von De Veld, 158 Mo. l. c. 247; 40 Cyc. 1942.] The incorrectness of appellant's contention that it was the testators purpose to leave the corpus of his estate to his brothers in the event of the contingency mentioned is clearly shown by the terms of the will itself. Item 2 of same cancels the brothers' debts to testator, and Item 5 provides that if his mother survives his sisters the estate is to be disposed of as may be provided by her will. Both by express reference and direct exclusion, therefore, it is shown that the testator did not intend that his brothers should have the corpus of the estate in any event. There is no ambiguity in this will, and the testator's intention may be readily determined therefrom without the aid of extrinsic evidence. Thus determined, it becomes evident that the trial court did not err in refusing the instructions requested.

VI. We have carefully reviewed the facts and do not find that the issues submitted by appellant have been proved; on the contrary there is a preponderance of affirmative evidence that the testator was of sound mind and subject to no undue influence. In fact, there is little substantial evidence to the contrary. This is ample to establish the validity of the will. Under this state of facts the errors we have noticed as having occurred during the trial must be held not of sufficient moment to work a reversal of the judgment of the trial court. [Reynolds v. Reynolds, 234 Mo. 1. c. 153; State v. Vickers, 209 Mo. 1. c. 34; Railroad v. Sloop, 200 Mo. 1. c. 219.]

In Conclusion.

The action of a trial court, as well as the review of same upon appeal, should be to secure to the parties substantial justice. This is what the statute (Sec. 2082, R. S. 1909) means when it admonishes us that we should not reverse a judgment of any court unless we believe that error has been committed which materially affects the merits of the case. Without this statute, which is purely directory, yet nevertheless entitled to observance, we would not be inclined to reverse this case in the absence of any substantial evidence to sustain the contentions of the appellant simply that the errors noted might be rectified. We have all the facts before us. The decree is for the right parties and we will, in the exercise of a wholesome discretion, let it stand. It is so ordered. All concur.

SOCIETY OF THE HELPERS OF THE HOLY SOULS v. ERNEST LAW et al., Appellants.

In Banc, May 15, 1916.

1. **RELIGIOUS CORPORATION: Not to Hold Title, Etc.** Neither the Legislature nor the courts can establish a religious corporation except its charter shows that it is created only to hold title to real estate for church edifices, parsonages and cemeteries; and a corporation organized for purposes other than those alone is not a religious corporation within the meaning of the Missouri Constitution.

   Held, by GRAVES, J., dissenting, that if the circuit court in entering a *pro forma* decree attempted to and did organize a religious corporation, its act was futile, and the chartered company has no standing in a court to recover real estate devised to it; and to determine whether it is a religious corporation resort should be made, first, to its charter, and if that is ambiguous or uncertain in meaning, then, to extraneous proof.

2. ———: **Valid Benevolent Corporation.** *Held*, under the facts stated in the opinion, that the plaintiff is not a religious corporation, but is a valid benevolent corporation under the statutes of Missouri. And that the fact that, in addition to the primary purposes and objects of practical benevolence set forth in its charter, it had the incidental right to impart religious instruction did not prevent this suit for property devised to it, since this particular franchise could only be attacked in a direct suit by the State.

   Held, by GRAVES, J., dissenting, that a corporation whose charter recites that "the purpose and object of said corporation shall be to maintain the establishment now under our charge in said city known as 'The Society of the Helpers of Holy Souls' and also others that we may hereafter establish; and in connection with same, to gratuitously visit the sick poor daily, irrespective of creed or color, rendering them every assistance in our power by nursing them in their homes; to organize our convent, meetings and sewing classes for the working class and poor children and impart religious instruction to same," etc., and which "is composed, exclusively, of members of the religious order of

the Roman Catholic Church known as "The Helpers of the
Holy Souls in Purgatory,'" the purpose of said "religious
order" being an exemplification of the tenets and doctrines
of the church concerning souls in Purgatory, is a religious
corporation, and cannot be held to be a mere benevolent
association.

3. ———: Devise to Unincorporated Society. There is no principle of law which forbids a charitable gift to an unincorporated religious body or any of its orders. Even if an attempted
incorporation must be held to be a religious corporation and
a devise to it of real estate for that reason be invalid, yet
if the unmistakable devise is to a known unincorporated society which has the same name as that of the attempted incorporation, it will be upheld, and the property can be recovered by the society's trustees.

Appeal from St. Louis City Circuit Court.—*Hon.
George C. Hitchcock,* Judge.

AFFIRMED.

*James L. Minnis, Goodbar & Tittmann, Claude
Hardwicke* and *Busby & Withers* for appellants.

(1)   The court erred in finding or holding that
the plaintiff corporation was organized, incorporated
and existed for benevolent and charitable purposes,
and not for religious purposes. It is a religious corporation. Sec. 8, art. 2, Const. 1875; Sec. 3432, R. S.
1909 (Sec. 1394, R. S. 1899); Proctor v. Board of
Trustees, 225 Mo. 56; Klix v. St. Stanislaus Parish,
137 Mo. App. 355; In re St. Louis Institute of Christian Science, 27 Mo. App. 633; Catholic Church v.
Tobbein, 82 Mo. 423; Lilly v. Tobbein, 103 Mo. 477;
State ex rel. v. Board, 175 Mo. 56; Kenrick v. Cole,
Exr., 61 Mo. 577; Boyce v. Christian, 69 Mo. 492;
Schmucker's Estate v. Reel, 61 Mo. 601; Atty.-Gen.

v. St. Cross Hospital, 17 Beavan's Reports (Eng.
Chancery), 465; Pack v. Shanklin, 27 S. E. (W. Va.)
393; St. Peter's Roman Catholic Congregation v.
Germain, 104 Ill. 440. (2) The court erred in divesting the legal title to the real estate out of the heirs
of the deceased and vesting it in the plaintiff. The
attempted devise to the plaintiff, a religious corporation, was void, and did not and could not vest in the
plaintiff. Secs. 7, 8, art. 2, Constitution 1875; Proctor
v. Board of Trustees, 225 Mo. 56; In re McGraw, 111
N. Y. 66, 2 L. R. A. 387; Decamp v. Dobbins, 31 N.
J. Eq. 690; Trustees v. Hilken, 84 Md. 170; Kennett
v. Kidd, 87 Kan. 652, 44 L. R. A. (N. S.) 544; U. S.
v. Utah, 15 Pac. 473; Hansher v. Hansher, 8 L. R. A.
558; 3 Ency. of Ev., p. 635. (3) The heirs of Mrs.
Bailey may contest the right of plaintiff to take the
devise. They do not attack the corporate existence of
plaintiff, or ask a forfeiture of its charter, but simply
contend that as the plaintiff was legally incapable of
taking and holding the property, the attempted devise was void, never took effect, and the property descended to the heirs. Proctor v. Board of Trustees,
225 Mo. 56; 2 Underhill on Wills, sec. 841.

J. L. Hornsby for respondent.

(1) Defendant's charge that plaintiff is a religious corporation, constitutes an attack on the validity
of plaintiff's incorporation, for the reason that in
this State no religious corporation can be created except for the purpose only of holding the title to such
real estate as may be prescribed by law for church
edifices, parsonages and cemeteries. Constitution
1875, art. 2, sec. 8. And if plaintiff's corporate organization was an attempt to create a religious corporation, it not being for any of purposes provided ir
the Constitution, the incorporation was void, and
plaintiff has no corporate existence. Atty.-Genl. v.

Lorman, 59 Mich. 157; Thompson on Corporations,
sec. 171; Note to People v. Water Co., 33 Am. St.
178. The validity of plaintiff's incorporation cannot
be questioned by defendants, but only by the State
in direct proceedings. St. Louis v. Shields, 62 Mo.
252; Catholic Church v. Tobbein, 82 Mo. 418-424;
Church Soc. v. Branch, 120 Mo. 243. (2) Plaintiff is
not a religious corporation. The character of a corporation is to be determined by the objects of its
creation and its purposes as expressed in its charter.
State ex rel. v. Westminster College, 175 Mo. 53-58;
Sherer v. Mendenhall, 23 Minn. 93; Oregon Ry. Co. v.
Oregonian Ry. Co., 130 U. S. 1; Atty.-Genl. v. Lorman, 59 Mich. 157; Hamsher v. Hamsher, 8 L. R. A.
556. The primary objects of a corporation control its
character. State ex rel. v. Westminster, 175 Mo. 52;
Colonization Society v. Hennessy, 11 Mo. App. 555;
In re Institute of Christian Science, 27 Mo. App. 638.
A corporation cannot, by its articles of association,
obtain greater powers than the Constitution or statutes permit. If a lawful purpose is specified, but
the articles also assume for the corporation the existence of a power which it is not permitted to exercise, then this additional and unauthorized assumption may be treated as surplusage and the corporation treated as entitled to exercise the lawful powers
only. Oregon Ry. Co. v. Oregonian Ry. Co., 130 U.
S. 1; Hamsher v. Hamsher, 8 L. R. A. 558; Eastern
P. R. Co. v. Vaughn, 14 N. Y. 546; Beckett v. Union-
town Assn., 88 Pa. St. 211; 1 Thompson, Corporations
(2 Ed.), p. 182; Lighting Co. v. Massey, 56 S. W. 35.
The fact that the persons constituting plaintiff corporation are members of a religious order in the church
does not constitute a corporation which they organize
a religious corporation. Colonization Society v. Hennessy, 11 Mo. App. 555; State ex rel. v. Westminster
College, 175 Mo. 53; Franta v. Bohemian Union, 164
Mo. 304.

I.

BOND, J.—Seven out of seventeen members of a religious order in the Roman Catholic Church, residing in St. Louis, were incorporated under the statutes providing for the formation of benevolent, religious, scientific, fraternal, beneficial and educational corporations by a decree of the circuit court of that city on the nineteenth of October, 1905.

Mrs. Anna Hamilton Bailey, who died the twenty-first of September, 1910 (without any descendants), devised, among a large number of other charities, a lot of ground fifty feet wide on Randolph street to "The Order of the Little Helpers." Plaintiff took possession of this lot and brought the present action against the next of kin of the said testatrix, stating in the petition that the term "Little Helpers" was the name by which the plaintiff was known in St. Louis, and praying a decree vesting title to the lot in the plaintiff corporation.

The answer of defendant, as far as material, averred that plaintiff was organized as a religious corporation in violation of the Constitution of Missouri, article 2, section 8, to-wit:

"Religious corporation may be established for one purpose only. That no religious corporation can be established in this State, except such as may be created under a general law for the purpose only of holding the title to such real estate as may be prescribed by law for church edifices, parsonages and cemeteries."

That plaintiff could not take the real estate devised, and also that the terms of the devise were too uncertain to give it effect, and prayed the court to adjudge defendant as next of kin to be entitled to the property.

The case was submitted to the court upon an agreed statement of facts (subject to objections as to materiality and relevancy of the evidence), which disclosed in substance that the plaintiff corporation was known in St. Louis as "The Little Helpers;" the terms and devises of Mrs. Bailey's will and that she meant and intended by clause 7 thereof to give to the plaintiff corporation the lot described in the petition and that plaintiff was in possession of it. The remaining clauses of the agreed statement were introduced by defendants (plaintiffs objecting to their materiality) and disclosed the kinship of the defendants to Mrs. Bailey; the doctrine of the Roman Catholic Church as to purgatory; that the reason for the adoption by its founders of the name: "The Society of the Helpers of the Holy Souls in Purgatory," was that said Society performed good works, offered prayers to shorten the suffering of the souls in purgatory "and hasten their entrance into heaven." That the Society was organized in France about 1854, and has branches extending throughout the civilized world, including the one established in St. Louis in 1903; that their "main object is, by spiritual and corporeal works of mercy" done for no remuneration whatever and for religious charity, to relieve and deliver the souls in purgatory; that all of the *seventeen* members are engaged in works of charity, especially in nursing the sick poor in their own homes and by such visits alleviating bodily misery and giving spiritual assistance and aid; that the sisters organize meetings for the working class and poor children who then receive familiar instruction, and young women employed during the week in business hours, find protection, amusements and friendly assistance at the convent and have the benefit of a free circulating library. That on July 21, 1905, certain members of said society (the Society of the Helpers of the Holy Souls in Purgatory) filed in the circuit court of the city of

St. Louis a petition, constitution and articles of agreement for a *pro forma* decree of incorporation under the provisions of article 11, chapter 12, of the Revised Statutes of Missouri of 1899, and thereafter on October 19, 1905, a decree was entered purporting to incorporate the plaintiff by the name of "The Society of the Helpers of the Holy Souls."

The agreed statement of facts then recites that a pamphlet attached, entitled "Helpers of the Holy Souls in Purgatory," was published by plaintiff and contained true statements of the objects and duties of that society and that the same are also disclosed in an article by Mrs. Morrison, which also correctly gives information, data and statistics of that society in St. Louis. The constitution and articles of agreement of the plaintiff, the decrees of incorporation, were read in evidence, article 3 of which is as follows, to-wit:

"Article (3): The purpose and object of said corporation shall be to maintain the establishment now under our charge in said city of St. Louis, known as 'The Society of the Helpers of the Holy Souls,' and also others that we may hereafter establish in said city or in the State of Missouri, and in connection with same, to gratuitously visit the sick poor daily, irrespective of creed or color, rendering them every assistance in our power by nursing them in their own homes; to organize in our convent, meetings and sewing classes for the working class and poor children and impart religious instruction to same, and assist said classes and children as best we can; to maintain a free circulating library and perform various other gratuitous works of charity and benevolence."

The trial court rendered a judgment for plaintiff, from which defendant duly appealed.

II.

The plaintiff in this case is not a "religious corporation" in the constitutional sense of those terms (Constitution 1875, art. 2, sec. 8, and art. 10. sec 21);

Religious Corporation.

for neither the Legislature nor the courts can establish a religious corporation except its charter shall show that it is created only to hold title to real estate for church edifices, parsonages and cemeteries. Any other form of "religious incorporation" is a nullity on its face. Hence if the persons who organized the plaintiff corporation designed in so doing to create a "religious corporation," their purpose was not effectuated for the reason that their articles of association or charter do not show that the corporation in question was established "for the purpose only" of taking title to the property specified in the constitution.

The only inquiry, therefore, is not as to its character as a "religious corporation," but whether or no the plaintiff was validly incorporated for "benevolent, scientific or educational purposes." [State ex rel. v. Lesueur, 99 Mo. l. c. 558; R. S. 1899, sec. 1397, now R. S. 1909, sec. 3435.] The determination of this question is decisive of the rights of the parties. The statute regulating this subject, so far as it pertains to the formation of corporations for benevolent purposes, is, to-wit:

"Sec. 3435. *What Associations May Be Incorporated.* Any association formed for benevolent purposes, including any purely charitable society . . . or any association whose object is to promote temperance or other virtue conducive to the well-being of the community and, generally, any association formed to provide for some good in the order of benevolence, that is useful to the public, may become a body corporate and politic under this article; . . . and in general, any association, society, company or organization which tends to the public advantage in relation to any or several of the objects above enumerated, or. whatever is incident to such objects, may be created a body corporate and politic by complying with sections 3432 and 3433. [R. S. 1899, sec. 1397.]''

The corporate powers and purposes of the plaintiff hereinbefore set out are, in brief: the maintenance of the society denoted by the corporate name of the plaintiff in St. Louis and Missouri, and in connection with same (a) ''to gratuitously visit the sick poor daily, irrespective of creed or color, rendering them every assistance in our power by nursing them in their homes;'' (b) ''to organize in our convent meetings and sewing classes for the working class and the poor children and impart religious instruction to same, and assist said classes and children as best we can;'' (c) ''to maintain a free circulating library and perform certain other gratuitous works of charity and benevolence.''

Taking the foregoing alphabetical subdivisions in order, by the first the plaintiff corporation was empowered to maintain an organized society of the same name and in cooperation with it (for that is the meaning of the terms ''in connection with same'') to gratuitously visit the sick poor daily, etc., as indicated in the language of subdivision ''a''; and in the same way to do the things specified under the subdivisions marked ''b'' and ''c,'' with no other reward for any of such acts or deeds than the sense of having done good to others in need, regardless of their faith or race. These specific duties imposed by its charter on the members of the plaintiff corporation are of the essence of practical benevolence. This is indisputable, nor do we conceive this to be gainsaid by counsel for appellant. We gather that their attack upon the charter of the plaintiff is directed, first, to the clause empowering it to maintain an unorganized society in

St. Louis or elsewhere. The answer to this objection is twofold: first, there is no principle of law which forbids a charitable gift to an *unincorporated* religious body or any of its orders, whether it be Protestant or Catholic; second, the fair intendment and signification of the language referring to the maintenance of the religious order to which the incorporators of the plaintiff belong is, that it was to be done in the manner and mode set forth in the remaining clauses of the charter. Now acts of that sort are benevolences, pure and simple, and it could not be held that a charter authorizing them, transcends the power granted by statute to any citizens of whatever church or faith to organize themselves into a body politic for benevolent purposes.

The second objection of appellant relates to the expression under subdivision "b" of the powers given to the plaintiff to provide meetings and sewing classes for the working class and poor children *and impart religious instruction to same,* etc., it being claimed that these underlined words embraced a power which could not have been included in the charter. If, as is inferable from the agreed facts, these underlined terms, considered apart, implied the inculcation of a particular faith by teaching its tenets, then they are not an object for which *a legal* corporation may be exclusively formed under the Constitution of this State, and if the present corporation had been chartered for that purpose alone, or is carried on only for that object, then its franchise would be a nullity or subject to revocation at the suit of the State. [St. Louis v. Shields, 62 Mo. l. c. 252; Haskell v. Worthington, 94 Mo. l. c. 569; Black v. Early, 208 Mo. l. c. 303; Klix v. St. Stanislaus Parish, 137 Mo. App. l. c. 357.] But an inspection and analysis of the powers granted in plaintiff's charter do not sustain the position that it was only created to teach and propogate the Roman Catholic religion, nor that this has been its only employment. The specific powers and active duties prescribed in the charter of plaintiff, as has been shown, provide for the doing *daily* of many acts of diverse nature in helping the helpless and alleviating the sufferings that come from human poverty and want, purely from motives of charity and the sense of duty on the part of the doers of these acts. It is to such services that the corporation seems to have devoted its practical efforts. The fact that another expression in the charter authorizes occasional religious instruction, might in a direct attack by the State afford ground for the annulment or withdrawal of that particular franchise (State ex inf. v. Trust Co., 144 Mo. 562; State ex rel. v. Gas & Oil Co., 153 Ind. 483; State ex rel. v. Railroad, 47 Ohio St. 130; State ex rel. v. Standard Oil Co., 49 Ohio St. 137; Yore v. Superior Court, 108 Cal. 431; State ex rel. v. Topeka, 30 Kan. 653; Commonwealth v. Canal Co., 43 Pa. St. l. c. 301); but it affords no basis in the present action for a judgment, that a charter giving to the corporators many other diverse powers wholly benevolent and strictly within the purview of the law providing for corporations of that nature, should be abrogated or annulled in a suit by the corporation for the enforcement of its property rights against third parties. The record shows that it is admitted that it was the intention of the testatrix in this case to give this little lot of ground to these human helpers engaged in daily work of practical help for the helpless of whatever race or religion *"which tends to the public advantage"* and is done *"for benevolent purposes,"* and is consequently embraced within the very words of the statute on this subject. And if it be that these acts are believed by the doers to be vicariously helpful to souls in purgatory, such a belief does not alter or transform the actual character or nature of the acts themselves, nor deprive them of their essential qualities of unselfish and unpaid kind-

nesses and assistances to the poor and needy, and
hence in the truest sense to be deemed acts of practical benevolence. With the particular faith or
prayers of these charity workers the law is not concerned. In such instances the law gives the fullest
freedom of conscience. But it does commend their
works and deeds and will grant them authority to visit
the sick, the poor and the needy and to relieve their
sufferings, and does not inquire if these good deeds
are done with the expectation, hope, faith and prayer
that their performance will avail the repose of the
dead. In other words, the peculiar religion of the
actors cannot alter the benevolence of their work and
it is but a corollary to this: that the fact that all of
the corporators are members of a particular church
does not affect their right to incorporate for a statutory object. [Franta v. Bohemian Rom. Cath. Cent.
Union, 164 Mo. 1. c. 313; State ex rel. v. Board of
Trustees, 175 Mo. 52; St. Louis Colonization Assn.
v. Hennessy, 11 Mo. App. 1. c. 558.]

III.

Appellant relies upon the case of Proctor v.
Board of Trustees, 225 Mo. 51. In that case there
was a devise *eo nomine* to a religious corporation
chartered in Tennessee, to hold in trust
property for the Methodist Episcopal
Church, South. By the terms of the devise
the Tennessee corporation was to control the property
for the use of the Scarritt Bible and Training School,
a Missouri corporation. It was ruled that both these
corporations fell under the ban of the Constitution
of this State (Art. 3, sec. 8) and that the Tennessee
corporation, the devisee, was not saved by the doctrine of comity, because the observance of that rule
would never be carried to the extent of contravening
the public policy of this State by giving to foreign

Other
Decisions.

corporations any advantage over a similar domestic corporation, and that neither of the corporations could take the devise made to them in their corporate name. In arriving at its conclusions the court considered the charters of the two corporations and concluded therefrom that their "primary object and purpose of organization was for religious purposes." In fact, they seem to have had no other   (Id. pp. 63, 67).

The charter in the instant case discloses "that the primary purpose and object" of the plaintiff corporation are the *daily* duties of its members to. visit and assist the sick poor "irrespective of creed or color," while the imparting of religious instruction is only mentioned as incidental to the occasional meetings of sewing classes and poor children. The present charter is not one void under the Constitution as having been granted only to teach a particular religion, but is one that is valid in so far as it authorizes deeds approved as benevolent by secular as well as Christian standards. Hence, the point ruled in the Proctor case has no bearing on the different charter shown in the present record.

Appellant also relies on the case of Fishing Club v. Kessler, 252 Mo. 424. Nothing ruled in that case bears upon the constitutional validity of the charter presented in the present record. In that case the charter of the plaintiff corporation was assumed to be valid, but it was ruled that the plaintiff corporation could not compel its president to turn over an investment in four hundred and twenty-six acres of land which he had fraudulently taken in his own name while acting on behalf of the plaintiff and which he sought to sell to the corporation at an advance of six dollars per acre, the theory being that the corporation in question was not authorized to acquire that sort of property. Obviously that ruling throws no light on the question of the validity of the plaintiff corpora-

tion in the present case, under the statute providing
for the corporations for benevolent purposes; for if
the present plaintiff was lawfully established under
that statute, it would be entitled to take the devise in
accordance with Mrs. Bailey's will and apply it or
its proceeds to the benevolent purposes specified in its
charter.

IV.

If the plaintiff was not (which it is) a benevolent
corporation, but was an abortive effort to create a
religious corporation and, therefore,
Devise to
Unincorporated
Religious
Society.
claiming to act under a charter void on
account of the prohibition of the Constitution, yet the result would equally
defeat the purpose of the defendants to obtain the title
to the lot in controversy. This, for the reason, that
the langauge of the will of Mrs. Bailey as to this
devise is, viz.:

"Seventh: .I give and bequeath to the order of
the 'Little Helpers' my lot in the city of St. Louis,
State of Missouri, on the north side of Randolph
Street, fronting fifty feet on Randolph Street," etc.

And the attempted incorporation of plaintiff did
not destroy the independent and continued existence
of "The Order of Little Helpers" whose name as a
religious society was used as the corporate name of
plaintiff. This proposition was established in the case
of Catholic Church v. Tobbein, 82 Mo. l. c. 424, where
the facts were that Tobbein devised one-half of his
estate to the Catholic church at Lexington, Missouri,
whereupon that church incorporated itself by that
name and brought suit for the probate of the will and
obtained judgment below, which was reversed on appeal. Said this court: "The Catholic church at Lexington did not lose its existence or organization in
the incorporation of the plaintiff by the same name."

This court then quoted the constitutional provision and held that the plaintiff corporation could not take the property, but added, whether the Catholic church at Lexington as distinguished from the corporation of that name can receive and hold property "can be determined only in a suit instituted by that church." Upon this hint a new suit was brought by the unincorporated body, and, after demurrer, its petition was amended by the substitution of certain members of the church as plaintiffs, from which an appeal was again taken to this court (Lilly v. Tobbein, 103 Mo. l. c. 483), where BLACK, J., held that the church did not lose its existence by its attempted incorporation and that its suit could well be maintained by some of its individual members suing on behalf of themselves and of others, and, as to the rights of the church to recover the devise, added: "But it is well settled law that a charitable devise or bequest will be upheld and enforced, though it is made to a voluntary, unincorporated association," citing Schmidt v. Hess, 60 Mo. 591; 2 Perry on Trusts (3 Ed.), sec. 730.

Now clause 4 of the agreed statement of facts is to-wit:

"(4) The name 'The Little Helpers' is not the name of any corporation, nor of any order or society, and is only the name by which plaintiff and the members of the society of the Helpers of the Holy Souls in Purgatory are commonly known and designated in the City of St. Louis."

This language and that contained in clause 7 of the will, make it certain to a common intent that the testatrix devised this lot either to an order *unincorporated,* or to the plaintiff, since both are known in St. Louis by the name "The Little Helpers." It necessarily follows under the equitable principle which conserves a charitable devise, that the one made by Mrs. Bailey became effective either in the unincorporated society denoted by the terms "Little Helpers" or in the incorporated society equally denoted by the same terms, and if therefore the plaintiff corporation had been held by us to be void under the Constitution, we would have been compelled to hold, further, that the devise in question was valid as to the unincorporated society of the same name. And we would have taken the course in the two cases last cited and would have sent the case back, in order that the individual members of the unincorporated order, on their own behalf and on behalf of all others, might assert its title to the devise, based on the terms of the will giving the lot to a name "Little Helpers," which term designated both the incorporated and the unincorporated order; the one composed of seven members and the other having seventeen. In case of such new suit the unincorporated body would not be prejudiced by any agreements made in this case to which it is not a party.

It follows that the defendants can have no interest in the little lot alleged in their briefs to be assessed at $3500. Other clauses of the will of Mrs. Bailey devised real estate of great value to the Episcopal, Protestant and Catholic charities, and included specific bequests of money and stock to different personal friends, not omitting a thousand dollars given to a faithful colored servant. The names of the defendants in this suit are excluded from any mention in any of the clauses of her will, all of which bears internal evidence of just discrimination and impartiality in the selection of the objects of her bounty. The competency of the testatrix to execute the instrument is incontrovertible. The terms of the gift preclude the possibility of its failure, for one of the two devisees by a common name must take as *against* the defendants.

The judgment in this case is affirmed.

PER CURIAM.—The foregoing opinion of BOND, J., in Division, is adopted by the Court in Banc. All concur except *Graves, J.,* who dissents in separate opinion; *Blair, J.,* not sitting.

GRAVES, J. (dissenting).—I cannot concur in the majority views in this case, and the question involved being one of more than passing interest I feel that my reasons for dissenting should be assigned.

Able counsel for respondent, with commendable frankness (in oral argument), said that if the "Society of the Helpers of the Holy Souls" was in fact an attempted religious corporation, then the judgment *nisi* was wrong. In different language the matter may be thus expressed: If the circuit court in entering the *pro forma* decree attempted to and did organize a religious corporation, when it chartered the respondent, then the act of such court was futile in view of constitutional inhibitions, and respondent has no standing in this case.

Religious Corporation.

To determine the character of a corporation we should go to its charter first. If, however, the language used in the charter is ambiguous and uncertain of meaning, I know of no rule of law which would preclude a court in construing such ambiguous written instrument, from invoking the assistance of extraneous proof in reaching the meaning of the instrument. Nor should we in determining the character of the charter emphasize one portion thereof to the exclusion of other portions. The charter should be read and construed from its four corners. Its real purpose can only be gathered in that way. My learned brother has omitted some of the matters in this charter, which to my mind tend to characterize the corporation, and has emphasized minor matters in discussing the enumerated powers in section three of the charter, and omitted a discussion of the first principal object of the corporation, as in said section 3, stated.

The very first object and purpose of this corporation, as expressed in article 3 of its charter is to *maintain* "the Society of the Helpers of the Holy Souls" in St. Louis, and other similar societies to be thereafter organized in the city of St. Louis and the State. The language of the charter in this respect is:

"The purpose and object of said corporation shall be to maintain the establishment now under our charge in said city of St. Louis known as 'the Society of the Helpers of the Holy Souls,' and also others that we may hereafter establish in said city or in the State of Missouri."

This article cannot be read in full without reaching the conclusion that the maintenance of these societies in the city and the State is the prime object and purpose of the corporation. All other things are, by the very words of the article, made subsidiary thereto. Note the language just following the quotation, supra:

"And in connection with same, to gratuitously visit the sick poor daily, irrespectively of creed or color, rendering them every assistance in our power by nursing them in their homes; to organize in our Convent, meetings and sewing classes for the working class and poor children and impart religious instruction to same, and assist said classes and children as best we can; to maintain a free circulating library and perform various other gratuitous works of charity and benevolence."

There is much significance in the words *"and in connection with same"* as used here. The use of this clause, as it is used, points unerringly to the fact that the prime purpose of the corporation is to maintain these societies, and the other matters mentioned in said article 3, including the imparting of

religious instruction to poor children, are but incidents
to the main purpose. It is well, however, to note that
even these incidental matters authorize the corporation to give religious instruction. At this point, however, we do not desire to further elaborate upon
this matter. Let us get back to the question, that
even by article 3 of the charter the prime purpose
and object of this corporation is to foster and maintain these societies in the city of St. Louis and the
State. No amount of ingenuity can change the plain
reading of this article 3. Said article 3 is very peculiarly worded. It uses the words "purpose and object" in the singular, and not in the plural. Ordinarily
the clause of a corporate charter granting the
powers and specifying the purposes and objects of
the corporation, usually has these words in the plural,
but not so here. This corporation had but one "purpose and object" and that purpose was to maintain
the society already in St. Louis, and such others
of like character as might be thereafter organized
either in the city or the State. All other matters
mentioned are mere subsidiary acts to this one "purpose and object."

The character of the corporation, whether religious or benevolent, is therefore dependent upon
the character of these societies it is chartered to support and maintain. Had the charter said that the
"purpose and object" of the corporation was to
support and maintain the Catholic Church, the
Methodist Church, or the Presbyterian Church, there
would be no question as to the character of the corporation. But isn't this charter just as plain when
it is read from its four corners?

It is declared in the charter that this society,
for the maintenance of which this corporation was
chartered (or rather attempted to be chartered), is
a religious organization. Note the language from
the charter:

"WHEREAS: We, the undersigned *members Professed of a Religious Order of the Roman Catholic Church, known as 'the Society of the Helpers of the Holy Souls,'* and whose Mother House is in Paris, France, 16 Rue de la Baronlilere, do desire to incorporate under the Provisions of article 11, chapter 12, of the Revised Statutes of the State of Missouri, same being an Act for the incorporation of 'Benevolent, Religious, Fraternal, Beneficial, Educational and Miscellaneous Associations,' in order to better perpetuate the usefulness of the Society, we have already for two years successfully conducted in the city of St. Louis, and all others that we may hereafter establish in said city or in the State of Missouri, do hereby by these articles of agreement associate ourselves in writing for said purpose of incorporation."

So, when we take the several portions of this charter, we have (1) this corporation organized for the one "purpose and object" of maintaining societies known and to be known as "The Society of the Helpers of the Holy Souls," and (2) that such societies are religious societies. This much is written in bold English on the face of this charter. From the face of its charter it is clear that there has been a futile attempt to organize a corporation for religious purposes, and this contrary to the Constitution of the State. The judgment of the circuit court granting the *pro forma* decree is void upon its face. Like all other void judgments it can be attacked collaterally in this or any other proceeding.

II. But if it be said that it does not clearly appear from the charter that there was an attempted incorporation of a body for religious purposes, then the ambiguities of the charter may be made plain by extraneous evidence. This was done in this case. The exact character of the societies which the plain-

Religious Corporation: Extraneous Facts.

tiff corporation was chartered to maintain is made to appear from this record. By an agreed statement of facts certain admissions were made, and among them were that a little pamphlet published by the society truly stated its objects, as did also a published report by Mrs. W. K. Morrison. From the agreed statement of facts we gather the following:

"(1) Plaintiff corporation is composed, exclusively, of members of the religious order of the Roman Catholic Church known as 'The Helpers of the Holy Souls in Purgatory.'"

This paragraph of the agreed facts was introduced and read in evidence by the plaintiff (respondent) in this case. They therefore characterize this society which this corporation was formed to maintain, as a "religious order." This is the solemn agreement made in the court *nisi* and it would be hard for this court, in the face of this admission, to say that the society is one for benevolence or charity and not religion. That it is a most worthy society there can be no question. That the world is made better by the teachings and works of those devoted Sisters, there can be no question. But unfortunately for them and for us, these are not the questions involved in this lawsuit. The question here is whether or not there has been a futile attempt to charter a religious corporation. This plaintiff was chartered (more correctly speaking attempted to be chartered) for the one "purpose and object" of maintaining this society and other similar societies. If then this society is a religious order, as is admitted in the agreed facts, then we have a corporation the one "purpose and object" being to maintain a "religious order." We use the expression one purpose advisedly, because the charter uses the words "purpose and object" in the singular, thereby clearly showing that all other things mentioned in the charter, are pure incidents, as will appear more clearly as we reach other admissions in this record.

It will suffice to conclude this paragraph by saying that we have here an attempted corporation for the admitted object and purpose of maintaining a named society, and then we have it admitted in the record that this society is a "religious order." This should be sufficient for a reversal of the judgment *nisi.*

III. In the admissions made in the agreed statement of facts, but introduced by defendants, rather than plaintiff, we have:

"(7) Purgatory, in accordance with the doctrine of the Roman Catholic Church, is a place or condition of temporal punishment for those who, departing this life in God's grace, are not entirely free from venial faults or have not fully paid the satisfaction due to their transgressions.

Extraneous Proof.

"The doctrine of the Catholic Church is that souls in Purgatory are aided by the prayers and works of satisfaction of the living, offered in their behalf.

"The name of the religious societies "The Society of the Helpers of the Holy Souls in Purgatory" was adopted by the founders of this religious society, for the reason that the chief purpose of this society is doing good works and offering prayers as a means of satisfaction as the debt due by the souls in Purgatory on account of their previous wrong doings, and thus to obtain by such prayers and good works, the shortening of the duration of their Purgatorial sufferings and hasten their entrance into Heaven."

We have here the statement of one of the tenets of the Catholic Church, and we refer to it with all due deference. But when we consider this tenet of the church, we can readily see why the society named in the charter of plaintiff corporation is called therein a "religious order." Its very work is an exemplification of this particular religious tenet. It was organized to teach and amplify this tenet of the church. All other things with this society are but incidents of this main work and purpose. It is the living, moving exemplification of this tenet and teachings of the church, and to my mind it is clearly religious in character. If the society is a religious order, and the main purpose and object of this attempted corporation is to foster and maintain the society, no reasoning can make the corporation other than a religious corporation, or a corporation for religious purposes. The society teaches this tenet of the church, and this corporation is the legal guardian and supporter of the society. But going further into this admitted record. It is admitted in the agreed statement of facts that the paper of Mrs. W. K. Morrison truthfully states the facts. Both the pamphlet circulated by plaintiff, and this paper, shows that the prime purpose of the society is to inculcate this religious tenet of the church. In addition, however, we find that Mrs. Morrison reviews the actual work done and gives the statistics of the society in St. Louis. Among other things reported by her, we find:

"Attendance at conferences and cate-
    chism 50,862
Children baptized   22
Adults baptized   89
Confessions 580
First communions .... 484"

We cannot blind ourselves to the facts shown here. The teaching of the "catechism" is religious teaching, this we must know, or the court knows less than the average individual. Likewise we must know that baptizing infants and adults, taking confessions and attending to communions are all church or religious matters. It is therefore apparent that this society was not only organized to exemplify the tenet of purgatory as taught by the Catholic Church, but its actual work is largely along religious lines.

By the charter, the corporation is made the sponsor and supporter of the society. Its purpose is therefore religious, rather than benevolent or charitable. It follows that the action of the circuit court in attempting to charter plaintiff was a void act. Under the agreed facts in the case it is admitted that the testator had in mind this corporation, when she made the bequest. Under these facts the trial court should have found for defendants, rather than for plaintiff. After going through this entire record I have no doubt that the circuit court made a futile attempt to incorporate a religious organization for an object and purpose not permitted by the Constitution, and to the end that all the facts may appear, I make the entire agreed statement of facts and the written instruments referred to therein a part of this dissent, by requesting the reporter to attach the same as an appendix to this opinion. The facts, in unvarnished hues, will then appear for themselves. The judgment *nisi* should be reversed, and the cause remanded.

APPENDIX.

In compliance with the request of GRAVES, J., in the foregoing opinion, the Agreed Statement of Facts and the instruments referred to therein are hereto subjoined.

AGREED STATEMENT OF FACTS.

"It is hereby stipulated and agreed that the following statement of facts may be offered at the trial of this cause and taken by the court as evidence of the facts therein contained, subject, however, to the right of either party, plaintiff or defendant, to object to any statement of fact therein contained on the ground of irrelevancy or immateriality; and subject further to the right of either party, plaintiff or defendant to introduce further testimony or evidence provided that such further testimony or evidence shall not be contradictory to any statement of fact herein agreed upon; and subject further to plaintiff's right to object to the introduction of any evidence by defendants under their answer.

"(1) Plaintiff corporation is composed, exclusively, of members of the religious order of the Roman Catholic Church known as 'The Helpers of the Holy Souls in Purgatory.'

"(2) The said corporation is commonly known in the city of St. Louis as 'The Little Helpers.'

"(3) Anna Hamilton Bailey died in the city of St. Louis on or about the twenty-first day of September, 1910, testate, and seized and possessed, in fee simple, of the following described real estate in said city, to-wit: A lot in City Block 1708, fronting fifty feet on the north side of Randolph street by a depth, northwardly, of equal width between parallel lines of one hundred and twenty feet, two and one-fourth inches to a twenty-foot alley, and being, bounded on the east by a line parallel to and fifty-eight feet east of the east line of Twenty-third street; and that said premises are the same as those described in Clause 7 of the last will of said Anna Hamilton Bailey, as follows: 'My lot in the city of St. Louis, State of Missouri, on the north side of Randolph street, fronting fifty feet on Randolph street, with a depth of one hundred and twenty feet, two and a quarter inches to a twenty-foot alley, being fifty-eight feet east on Twenty-third street, being in City Block 1708.

"(4) The name 'The Little Helpers' is not the name of any corporation, nor of any order or society, and is only the name by which plaintiff and the members of the Society of the Helpers of the Holy Souls in Purgatory are commonly known and designated in the city of St. Louis.

"(5) Anna Hamilton Bailey meant and intended, by her last will and by clause 7 thereof, in naming the order of the Little Helpers as devisee of the real estate in said clause 7 described, to give plaintiff corporation the said parcel of real estate in plaintiff's petition described.

"After the death of Anna Hamilton Bailey, plaintiff took possession of said real estate above described, as devisee thereof under the last will of Anna Hamilton Bailey, deceased, and has continued in possession thereof to the present time.

"(6) Plaintiff admits the truth of the allegations set out in paragraphs three, four, five and six of the second amended answer of defendants, Lawrence K. Kinsey, Ernest Law, Walter A. DeMilly, Augusta Horton Gedney and Arthur L. DeMilly, herein filed.

"(7) Purgatory, in accordance with the doctrine of the Roman Catholic Church, is a place or condition of temporal punishment for those who, departing this life in God's grace, are not entirely free from venial faults or have not fully paid the satisfaction due to their transgressions.

"The doctrine of the Catholic Church is that souls in Purgatory are aided by the prayers and works of satisfaction of the living, offered in their behalf.

"The name of the religious Society 'The Society of the Helpers of the Holy Souls in Purgatory' was adopted by the founders of this religious society, for the reason that the chief purpose of this society is doing good works and offering prayers as a means of satisfaction as the debt due by the souls in Purgatory on account of their previous wrong doings, and thus to obtain, by such prayers and good works, the shortening of the duration of their Purgatorial sufferings and hasten their entrance into Heaven.

"(8) The religious Society of the Helpers of the Holy Souls in Purgatory is a community of religious women which was organized in Paris, France, about the year 1854, and which now has branches or convents in virtually all the civilized countries of the world. The branch or convent of this religious society in the city of St. Louis was established in 1903 by twelve sisters of the order who came here from France at that time, and at present the society here numbers seventeen sisters, their convent being located at 4012 Washington Boulevard, St. Louis. The main object of this community of sisters is the relief and deliverance of the souls in Purgatory by means of spiritual and corporal works of mercy. These works are performed from motives of religious charity and no remuneration, of any kind whatever, is accepted. The society is supported by voluntary offerings, gifts, of benefactors who are interested in the work, and contributions of honorary members. All the seventeen members in this religious community are engaged in works of charity, either at or outside the convent. The sisters are especially active in the nursing of the sick poor, irrespective of creed or nationality, in their own homes. By means of these visits to the homes of the sick and the invalid, the sisters are enabled, not only to alleviate bodily misery, but may assist them spiritually by aiding them to prepare worthily for the sacraments, etc. Both home and abroad, the sisters undertake numerous works· of charity which vary according to the needs of the country and the diocese to which they may be called, but all are consecrated to the same aim—the relief and deliverance of the souls in Purgatory. They visit the sick poor daily, rendering them every assistance in their power and nursing them in their own homes. Out of these visits to the sick and the poor arise many opportunities for doing good.

"In their convents, the sisters organize meetings for the working class and poor children who there receive familiar instruction. Young women employed during the week in business houses find protection, amusements, and friendly assistance at the convent, and have the advantage of a free circulating library.

"One of the works of the Helpers is the preparation of children and adults for the reception of the sacraments and the reception of newly received converts. All the work of the sisters is gratuitous, no other recompense being sought than the consolation of saving the souls of members of the Church and the alleviation of the souls suffering in Purgatory.

"The sisters have the assistance of lay-helpers, Catholic women who aid them in this field of Christian charity, especially on their errands of charity about the city, their visits to poorhouses and hospitals, and in the work of instructing the young in schools, missions, and churches in various parts of the city. These lay-helpers may be enrolled as honorary members. The social side and the recreational features are recognized in the works of the society. Illustrated lectures, musicales, and entertainments are given for the benefit of the children and girls at the meeting in the convent, and for those enrolled in the various sodalities or societies before referred to as 'The Society of the Helpers of the Holy Souls in Purgatory;' that 'The Society of the Holy Souls' mentioned in Article III of said constitution and articles of agreement is the same society hereinbefore mentioned as 'The Society of the Helpers of the Holy Souls in Purgatory;' and at the time of the entering of said decree of incorporation there was not in the city of St. Louis a society known as 'The Society of the

Helpers of the Holy Souls' as distinguished from 'The Society of the Helpers of the Holy Souls in Purgatory' hereinbefore mentioned.

"(10)   It is further agreed that the pamphlet hereto annexed entitled 'Helpers of the Holy Souls in Purgatory' was published by plaintiff and that the statements therein with respect to the object and purposes of the Society of the Helpers of the Holy Souls in Purgatory are true.

"(11)   It is further agreed that the four printed pages hereto annexed, marked 'Exhibit I,' an article written by Mrs. W. K. Morrison, correctly states the object and purposes of the Helpers of the Holy Souls in Purgatory and under the head of 'Information and Data' as amended, correctly states the information there set out in regard to said society; and correctly states under the head of 'Statistics' the items there set out; and correctly states, under 'Division of Works' the facts there set out.''

The contents of the pamphlet entitled "Helpers of the Holy Souls in Purgatory" mentioned in article 10 of the above Agreed Statement of Facts, are as follows:

"HELPERS OF THE HOLY SOULS IN PURGA-TORY.

"The Society of the Helpers of the Holy Souls in Purgatory.

"In a celebrated sermon preached by Bourdaloue, one the 2nd of November, he exclaimed: 'Throughout all time, people have prayed for the dead, but the work of self-sanctification for them was reserved to our generation.' To sanctify themselves, for the souls of Purgatory, is the object that the Religious of the Society of the Helpers of the Holy Souls have in view.

"The Church, ever fruitful, has from time to time raised up many varieties of religious orders to relieve the different miseries of this life; from the

cradle to the grave, she has surrounded her children
who suffer with angels of peace and consolation.
There only remained for her then to extend this same
merciful assistance to the souls of the faithful departed.

"God inspired her to do this at a time when the
powers of hell were endeavoring to consign the dead
to oblivion by relegating to a distance from the abodes
of men the hallowed enclosure where their bodies repose in hope; by often depriving their mortal remains of the priest's blessing; by abolishing the
greater number of those pious foundations instituted
in their behalf by the piety of our ancestors; by drawing the present generation into a vortex of indiffer-
ence for spiritual things; of feverish agitation and
regard for material interests, which, while it leaves
an affectionate remembrance of those who are no
more, deprives them of the efficacious help of the
prayers and suffrages of those by whom they have
been loved. The devil, always hostile to God's glory,
undoubtedly knows how much that glory is augmented
by each soul that enters into its eternal rest, and his
hatred of all who bear our Lord's image, extends
even to these chosen souls whose deliverance the Sacred Heart desires so ardently. To protest against
this selfish forgetfulness of the dead, many pious
associations have been formed, but a religious institution was necessary that would unceasingly raise its
voice, in the name of the Church militant, on behalf
of the Church, suffering in Purgatory, and be in this
unbelieving age, a living witness to our faith in the
realities of the other life. This institution was founded by the good pleasure of God; step by step His
Divine Providence guided her whom He had chosen to
be its Foundress and Mother. Faithful to an inspiration received during a fervent thanksgiving, this soul
did not hesitate to undertake the difficult enterprise
of making a foundation. She was without resources

and lacked all human help, but neither the trials which established her work on the solid foundation of the Cross, nor her natural repugnance, could 'shake her courage. She had placed all her hope in Providence, and it was by the name of this Divine attribute, the object of her life's devotion, that she desired to be henceforth known. (See the life of the Reverend Mother Marie de la Providence, Foundress of the 'Helpers of the Holy Souls,' by the late Lady G. Fullerton. Burns and Oates, Orchard Street, London.) A virile courage lay hid in that woman's breast; in her bosom beat a noble heart full of compassion and tenderness. It was to her that Pere Olivaint applied these words: *'Elle avait une grande ame, et elle savait vouloir.'*

"Sustained internally by grace, and encouraged externally by the representatives of Divine authority, and the blessings with which Providence surrounded her work, she conceived the generous thought of founding a House whence prayer and expiation should without ceasing, rise to Heaven, in behalf of the suffering souls of Purgatory. The Coure' d'Ars became for her one of the interpreters of the Divine Will; and, by his counsels and kindly interest, attached himself to this society from its very birth, defining it as 'A thought of love, coming from the Heart of Jesus.' It was not long before the rule of St. Ignatius, adopted by the rising foundation, conferred on it the benefit of a firm and excellent religious consolidation, and completed the development of a spirit entirely devoted to the interests of our Lord. In fact, the apostolic zeal of the Institution is not confined to the suffering souls of Purgatory. Works of mercy toward the living are one of the most efficacious means that the Church recommends to her children for helping the dead. Providence did not delay to point out this way to the Helpers of the Holy Souls, and the care of the sick-poor in their own homes was undertaken. This work furnishes them with opportunities of abnegation and mortification, of which the lives of the saints offer examples innumerable, and consequently enables them to amass treasures of satisfaction for the captive souls, so dear to them; while at the same time it affords the means of bringing back to the practice of religion souls that have long forgotten their duties, and lived deprived of its consolations.

"To stretch out a helping hand by means of this self-devotion at one and the same time to the most forsaken souls in this world and in the next, was the desire of the Holy Foundress, and her daughters strive to realize it. Both at home and abroad they undertake numerous works of zeal and charity, which vary according to the needs of the country and diocese to which they may be called, but all are consecrated to the same end: 'The relief and deliverance of the Holy Souls.'

"They visit the sick poor daily, rendering them every assistance in their power by nursing them in their own homes. Out of these visits to the sick and the poor arise many opportunities for doing good.

"In their Convents the Helpers organize meetings for the working class and poor children, who receive there familiar instruction. Young women, employed during the week, in business houses, find protection, amusement and friendly assistance at the Convent, and have also the advantage of a free circulating library. One of the most cherished works of the Helpers is the preparation of children and adults for the reception of the Sacraments, and the instruction of newly received converts.

"All these works, however, are gratuitous, for these spouses of our Divine Lord seek no other recompense for their labor and fatigue than the consolation of saving the souls of the Church militant, for the alleviation of the members of the Church suffering.

"An association of expiation ought, above all things, to be an association of prayer, and for this reason, the Society of the 'Helpers of the Holy Souls' attaches great importance to the exercises of interior life, and a great part of each day is devoted to them.

"In addition to the meditations, pious readings, adorations of the Blessed Sacrament obligatory on all, the choir-nuns recite the Office of the Dead. After the example of Blessed Margaret Mary, one of their holy patrons, they have consecrated themselves to a special devotion to the Sacred Heart of our Lord. Every hour they invoke this Sacred Heart, saying the following prayer for the captive souls: 'O My God! we offer for the Holy Souls all the acts of love with which the Sacred Heart of Jesus glorified Thee, during this same hour, when he was upon earth.' The first Friday of every month and the Octave of the Sacred Heart, are observed with special fervor, and the Blessed Sacrament is exposed in the chapel.

"His Holiness the Sovereign Pontiff, Pius IX, honored the Society with two briefs of approbation, and on the 25th of June, 1878, the Religious had the consolation of having their Constitutions approved by his Holiness Leo XIII.

"The Society has now several houses in France, Belgium, England, Italy, America and even China. The Mother house is in Paris, 16 Rue de la Barouilliere.

"But the object of the Helpers is not only to labor themselves for the Holy Souls, but also to diffuse as widely as possible their own spirit and example. With a view, therefore, of augmenting the treasure of merit and satisfaction for the sufferers in purgatory, and of obtaining for them a succession of daily increasing prayers, this Society has added to its ranks Honorary Members, Benefactors, Life-

Members, and Lady Associates, who, upon enrollment enter into a union of prayer and sacrifice with the Helpers, and participate in their privileges.

"HONORARY MEMBERS.

"The Honorary Members conform, as far as they are able, to the motto of the Society of the Religious Helpers of the Holy Souls in Purgatory: 'Pray, Suffer, Work for the Souls in Purgatory.'

"Pray—They recite every day the acts of Faith, Hope and Charity, with the aspiration, 'My Jesus, Mercy!' for their deceased relatives, applying to them the indulgences attached to these prayers.

"Suffer—They offer their daily sufferings and trials for the same intention.

"Work—Alms-giving, being according to the teaching of Holy Church, one of the most efficacious means of helping the Souls in Purgatory, the Honorary members contribute by a yearly offering (usually in the month of November) of a dollar to the support and good works of the Society exclusively devoted to works of mercy for the deliverance of the Souls in Purgatory.

—"Any one unable to contribute a dollar annually, yet desirous of assisting this great work of charity, can become affiliated by giving any small alms according to his means, and by reciting the same prayers as the Honorary Members.

"BENEFACTORS AND LIFE MEMBERS.

"Make a more considerable offering, once for all, or at several times, to support the work. Their names are inscribed in a book specially kept for the purpose.

"All these share in the good works and prayers of the Helpers and in the monthly Masses and Communions of Associated Priests and Religions. In the year 1878, when the last calculation was made, 45,600 communions and 17,280 Masses were received into the spiritual treasury of the Order.

"The deceased relatives of Honorary Members participate in the prayers and good works of the Society of the Helpers of the Holy Souls, and special suffrages are applied to deceased Honorary members.

"A Register is kept, wherein are inscribed the names of deceased persons, for whom suffrages are requested, by Honorary Members.

"LADY ASSOCIATES.

"The Lady-Associates take an active and much greater part in the good works of the Helpers. They can be received only after a due probation, and are bound to lead in the world a truly Christian life, by the constant practice of their religious duties and by great fidelity to the duties of their State.

"There are meetings held especially for them every week at the Convent.

"Besides possessing all the advantages of the Honorary Members, the Associates are thus united in a more intimate manner in prayer, in suffering, and in good works, with the Religious Helpers of the Souls in Purgatory, who admit them during life and after death to a participation in all the privileges, merits, and suffrages of their Society.

"PRIESTS AND RELIGIOUS.

"May become Honorary Members, the former by offering up the Holy Sacrifice once a month, the latter by a monthly Communion according to the intentions of the Society.

"PROMOTERS OF THE ASSOCIATION.

"The Promoters who form bands of Honorary Members are inscribed as Benefactors, and enjoy the same privileges. Thus to the poor and to the rich, to the good and fervent of every condition of life, this pious society addresses a note of invitation. Let us not turn away unheeding while there is one belonging to us numbered among the dead whose love we have not yet forgotten. Let us listen to the voice that cries to us from those realms of suffering holiness: 'Have pity on me, have pity on me, at least you, my friends!' How can we better answer its pleading accents, than by entering into a bond of union with the Order of the Helpers of the Holy Souls? Let us help them with our sympathy. Let us help them with our prayers. Let us help them with our alms to enable them to carry on their work of charity.

"Names for Enrollment and Offerings may be sent to the Convent of the Helpers of the Holy Souls in Purgatory, 4012 Washington Boul., St. Louis, Mo.

"PLENARY INDULGENCES.

Granted by

HIS HOLINESS POPE PIUS IX.

To the

Honorary Members of the Society of the Helpers of the Holy Souls.

"To the humble petition presented to the Holy Father, asking a Plenary Indulgence for all the Honorary Members.

"1. On the day of Enrollment as Honorary Members.

"2. On November 2, All Soul's Day. On November 15, Feast of St. Gertrude. On March 19, Feast of St. Joseph. On March 25, Feast of the Annunciation of the Blessed Virgin. On the first Friday after the Octave of Corpus Christi, Feast of the Sacred Heart. On July 31, Feast of St. Ignatius of Loyola.

"3. At the hour of death, by pronouncing with a contrite heart, or, at least, breathing interiorly the invocation: My Jesus, Mercy!

"His Holiness deigned to make the following reply:

"'St. Peter's. Rome, July 4, 1860.

"'Receiving favorably the petition which has been addressed to us, We grant, IN PERPETUO, by this present Rescript, and without sending out any Brief, the Indulgences asked for, with the power of applying them by way of suffrage to the Holy Souls in Purgatory.—PIUS IX.'"

The article written by Mrs. W. K. Morrison, for the 1912 conference of the Catholic Charities and Social Activities of the city of St. Louis, marked "Exhibit I" mentioned in Article 11 of the above Agreed Statement of Facts, is as follows:

"HELPERS OF THE HOLY SOULS IN PURGATORY.

"The Society of the Helpers of the Holy Souls in Purgatory is a community of religious women, established in St. Louis since the month of May, 1903. Their convent, at present, is· at 4012 Washington Boulevard.

"The main object of this religious community, which was founded in France about fifty years ago, is the relief and deliverance of the souls in purgatory by means of spiritual and corporal works of mercy. These works are always performed from motives of religious charity, and no remuneration, of any kind whatever, is ever accepted. Neither does the society solicit or collect and here this question arises: How is the work supported? By voluntary offerings, gifts of benefactors who are interested in the work, the contributions of Honorary Members, in fine, Trusting to Divine Providence. From the object of their society its members are called Helpers of the Holy Souls in Purgatory.

"There are at present sixteen members in this religious community, all of them engaged in works of charity either at, or outside the convent.

"It may be stated that these sisters are especially active in one phase of charitable work, which, before their location in St. Louis, had not yet been taken up to any large extent by the members of any other religious community of women. This is the nursing of the sick poor, irrespective of creed or nationality, in their own homes. By means of these visits to the homes of the sick and the invalid, the sisters are enabled not only to alleviate bodily misery, but may even assist them spiritually, by aiding them to prepare worthily for the reception of the sacrament, etc.

"Perhaps the one great purpose and aim of the Helpers of the Holy Souls in Purgatory can be shown in no better way than by quoting from a booklet which has been prepared for the benefit of those interested in their work. We read: 'Both at home and abroad the sisters undertake numerous works of zeal and charity, which vary according to the needs of the country and diocese to which they may be called, but all are consecrated to the same end: The relief and deliverance of the holy souls.'

"They visit the sick poor daily, rendering them every assistance in their power by nursing them in their own homes. Out of these visits to the sick and the poor arise many opportunities for doing good.

"In their convents the Helpers organize meetings for the working class and poor children, who there receive familiar instruction. Young women employed during the week in business houses, find protection, amusement and friendly assistance at the convent, and have also the advantage of a free circulating library. One of the most cherished works of the Helpers is the preparation of children and adults for the reception of the sacraments, and the instruction of newly received converts.

"All these works, however, are gratuitous, for no other recompense is sought than the consolation of saving the souls of members of the Church militant, for the alleviation of members of the Church suffering.

"It will be seen, therefore, that the scope of the religious community is wide. The sisters take this opportunity to plead for a large number of lay-helpers—earnest and devoted Catholic women, who may help them in this broad field of Christian charity. They need such assistance, especially on their errands of charity about town, in their visits to poorhouse and hospitals, and also in the work of instructing the young in schools, missions and churches in various parts of the city. There is here large opportunity for our Catholic women to exercise, in behalf of and together with these religious, the Catholic social and religious Apostolate. In fact, without such help the work of the sisters will, to a large extent, prove ineffective or will, at least, not produce those permanent results which a greater participation of Catholic women in this noble work would bring about. Such lay-helpers, may, if they wish, be enrolled as honorary members.

"The social side and the recreational features are not disregarded in the work of the Helpers of the Holy Souls. Illustrated lectures, musicales and entertainments are given for the benefit of the children and girls attending the meetings at the convent and for those enrolled in the various sodalities. (Not less than fourteen Christmas parties, attended by over five hundred guests, took place in their hall last Christmas.)

"In the summer all the young people, as well as their mothers, are given opportunity to enjoy a day in the country, or at an outing home. A circulating library has been started with a good collection of religious books and works of fiction.

"One of the more conspicuous works is the Annual Mission, or Retreat, for the benefit of young women employed during the day, which is generally given in the month of October. This Mission gives the sisters opportunity of becoming acquainted with a number of young women who may stand in need of help, and these persons are invited to call at the convent whenever they may be in need of assistance.

"The work of the Helpers of the Holy Souls is not limited to whites, but special classes for instruction and special meetings have been arranged at the convent for the benefit of colored persons. These are well attended, and several conversions have already resulted from the interest shown by the religious in this part of their work.

INFORMATION AND DATA.

"Name: The Helpers of the Holy Souls in Purgatory.

"Address: 4012 Washington Avenue, St. Louis, Mo.

"In Charge of: The Helpers of the Holy Souls.

"Established: 1903.

"Conducted by: The Helpers of the Holy Souls.

"Purpose: Relief and deliverance of the souls in purgatory by the spiritual and corporal works of Mercy.

"Beneficiaries: Not limited to class, nationality or creed.

"Annual Rent: None—Property, including building, is owned by the religious.

"Sources of maintenance: (a) Donations from benefactors.

"(b) Entertainments and lectures.

"Authorized Public Representative: The Sisterhood of the Helpers of the Holy Souls in Purgatory.

"Salaried Employees Authorized as Collectors or Representatives: None.

"Business Administration: The sisters conduct all business matters, occupying official positions; authorize expenditures, audit accounts and make all payments.

"Employees: Paid employees, giving whole time, none; salaries, none annually. Unpaid assistance, giving part time, ninety-two. Religious, giving whole time, sixteen. Approximate amount of salaries that would be paid for the positions now filled by members of the Order $12,120 annually.

"Annual Report: None published.

"Auxiliary: Ninety-two ladies assist in the works of charity in the Italian sewing schools, the catechism classes and Sunday schools, visits to families of the poor, the hospitals and the quarantine.

STATISTICS.

January 1, 1911, to December 31, 1911.

"Nursing cases 2,223
Errands of charity and helpful visits..........23,711
Particular instructions given................. 1,641
Attendance at conferences and catechism......50,862
Children baptized............................ 22
Adults baptized.............................. 89
Confessions 580
First communions............................ 484
Books issued................................ 7,573
Garments distributed........................ 5,563

DIVISION OF WORKS.
"AT THE CONVENT.

Sodalities for working-girls and children.....Sunday
Sewing for young girls..............................
...............Tuesday and Thursday evenings
Sewing for children................................
..........................Saturday afternoon
Sewing for Christian mothers............Thursday

Sewing for colored mothers......Wednesday evening
Sewing for colored children...............Saturday
    Material for sewing furnished free.

"IN THE PARISHES.

Annunciation: Catechism—Sunday, Wednesday, Friday.

Visits to families. Sodality of the Children of Mary.

Nativity: Sunday-school and catechism. Wednesday.

Visits to families.

St. Paul: Sunday-school.

St. Catherine of Sienna: Sunday-school.

Holy Innocents: Sunday-school.

Our Lady Help of Christians: (Italian Church)

Catechism and sewing for girls...........Saturday

Catechism daily during Lent.

Christian Mothers' meeting...............Thursday

Visits to families.

"VISITING HOSPITALS.

City and Female Hospitals....Wednesday and Friday
City Consumptive Hospital (Quarantine)..Wednesday
Children's Hospital.......................Friday
Skin and Cancer Hospital..................Friday
St. Louis Infirmary (Poor House)......Wednesday."

The Constitution and Articles of Agreement of the plaintiff herein, together with the *pro forma* decree of the circuit court of the city of St. Louis, Missouri, purporting to incorporate the plaintiff, attached to defendants' answer, and marked "Exhibit A," mentioned in Article 9 of the above Agreed Statement of Facts, are as follows:

"CONSTITUTION AND ARTICLES OF AGREEMENT OF

"THE SOCIETY OF THE HELPERS OF THE HOLY SOULS.

"WHEREAS, we the undersigned members Professed of a Religious Order of the Roman Catholic

Church, known as 'The Society of the Helpers of the Holy Souls,' and whose Mother House is in Paris, France, 16 Rue de la Baronillere, do desire to incorporate under the provisions of Article 11, Chapter XII, of the Revised Statutes of the State of Missouri, same being an Act for the incorporation of 'Benevolent, Religious, Fraternal, Beneficial, Educational and Miscellaneous Associations,' in order to better perpetuate the usefulness of the Society, we have already for two years successfully conducted in the city of St. Louis and all others that we may hereafter establish in said city or in the State of Missouri, do here by these articles of agreement associate ourselves in writing, for said purpose of incorporation.

"Article (1): The name and style of said corporation shall be 'The Society of the Helpers of the Holy Souls,' and its main office shall be in the city of St. Louis, Missouri, except that said main office may be removed to any other part of the State of Missouri by a vote of three-fourths of the members of the corporation at any regular or special meeting of the corporation.

"Article (2): The corporate existence of this Society shall be perpetual and shall endure forever, so long as it performs the object for which it is organized.

"Article (3): The purpose and object of said corporation shall be to maintain the establishment now under our charge in said city of St. Louis, known as 'The Society of the Helpers of the Holy Souls,' and also others that we may hereafter establish in said city or in the State of Missouri, and in connection with same, to gratuitously visit the sick poor daily, irrespective of creed or color, rendering them every assistance in our power by nursing them in their own homes; to organize in our Convent, meetings and sewing classes for the working class and poor children and impart religious instructions to same, and assist said classes and children as best we can; to maintain a free circulating library and perform various other gratuitous works of charity and benevolence.

"Article (4): The officers of said corporation shall be a President, Secretary and a Treasurer, and such other officers as may be provided for, by its by-laws.

"Article (5): Said corporation shall enjoy all the privileges in respect to acquiring and holding property for the purposes of the corporation by gift, purchase, devise, or otherwise, as are made and provided for by the general and special statutes of the State of Missouri concerning corporations.

"Article (6): Said corporation shall make and adopt by-laws and rules for its government and support and the management of its property and affairs, and may provide for all things necessary and conducive to the good and successful management of the affairs of said Society. Some to be consistent with the laws of the United States and of Missouri, and with these Articles of Agreement.

"Article (7): These Articles of Agreement may be changed or amended at any regular or special meeting of the corporation by a two-thirds vote of those present, provided said Amendment has been in writing at a meeting of the corporation held at least one month previous to the meeting at which said amendment is adopted, and written notice of said proposed amendment has been given by mail or by personal service to each and every member of the corporation not present in person at said previous meeting when said proposed amendment was presented.

"Witness our hands and seals this 17th day of July, 1905.

Mary Heden George, (SEAL)
Known in Religion as Mary of the Redemption.
Mary Agatha Fitzgerald, (SEAL)
Known in Religion as Mary of St. Magdalene,
Margaret Agnes Chahlan, (SEAL)
Known in Religion as Mary St. Ethelreda,
Bridgett McDermott, (SEAL)
Known in Religion as Sr. of St. Gregory,
Lily Mary Fitzsimmons, (SEAL)
Known in Religion as Mary of Blessed Emanuel
Alvares,
Margaret Pollet, (SEAL)
Known in Religion as Mary of St. Gaeton,
Maria Francois, (SEAL)
Known in Religion as Mary of the V. Joseph
Anchista.

"STATE OF MISSOURI, } ss.
CITY OF ST. LOUIS.

"On this 17th day of July, 1905, before me, a
Notary Public within and for the city of St. Louis,
personally appeared Mary Helen George, Mary Agatha Fitzgerald, Margaret Agnes Chahlan, Bridgett
McDermott, Lily Mary Fitzsimmons, Margaret Pollet
and Maria Francois, known in Religion as: Mary of
the Redemption, Mary of St. Magdalene, Mary of
St. Ethelreda, Mary of St. Gregory, Mary of the
Blessed Emanuel Alvares, Mary of St. Gaeton, and
Mary of Venerable Joseph Anchista respectively, to
me known to be the persons described in and who
executed the foregoing instrument and they severally
acknowledged to me that they executed the same as
their free act and deed, and for the purpose therein
mentioned.

"WITNESS my hand and Notarial seal, this 17th
day of July, 1905,
(SEAL). JOSEPH B. KREIKEMEIR,
Notary Public.

"STATE OF MISSOURI, ⎱
⎰ SS.
CITY OF ST. LOUIS, ⎰

"IN THE CIRCUIT COURT, CITY OF ST. LOUIS, OCTOBER
TERM, 1905.

"Thursday, October 19th, 1905.

"In the matter of ⎱
1875 ⎰
The Society of the ⎰
Helpers of the Holy Souls. ⎰

"And now at this day come Mary Helen George,
as President, Lily Mary Fitzsimmons, as Secretary and
Margaret Pollett, as Treasurer, of the Society of the
Helpers of the Holy Souls, and submit to the court
the articles of agreement of said association, together
with a petition praying for a *pro forma* decree
thereon, in manner provided by law, and it appearing
to the court that said petition has remained on file
in the clerk's office of the court at least three days
since the same was first presented to the court, and
the court having duly examined the articles of agreement, and being duly advised in the premises, doth
now consider, adjudge and determine that such articles of agreement and the purpose of the association
as therein expressed come properly within the purview of article XI, of chapter 12, of the Revised Statutes of the State of Missouri, 1899, entitled 'Benevolent, Religious, Scientific, Fraternal, Beneficial, Educational and miscellaneous associations,' and are not
inconsistent with the Constitution or Laws of the
United States or of the State of Missouri. It is
therefore ordered and decreed that the prayer of the
petition for a *pro forma* decree be and the same is
hereby granted."

AUGALA GRUENDER et al. v. ELIZABETH FRANK et al., Appellants.

Division Two, May 31, 1916.

1. **WILL CONTEST: Pleading: Interest of Plaintiff.** In a suit to set aside a will the petition must allege such facts as show that the contestant has a financial interest in the estate and one which would be benefited by setting the will aside, unless such facts are admitted by the pleadings of the proponents. Otherwise, the petition will not show a cause of action.

2. ———: ———: ———: **Waiver.** A failure to allege in the petition that plaintiff has such a financial interest in the probate of the will as will enable him to institute a suit contesting its validity is not a defect to be classed as a want of "legal capacity to sue," and one that must therefore be raised by demurrer or answer, and if not so raised is to be considered waived. Lack of "legal capacity to sue," as used in the statute, has reference to some legal disability of the plaintiff, such as infancy, idiocy, coverture, and has no reference to the fact that the petition fails to state a cause of action.

3. ———: ———: ———: ———: **General Denial: Demurrer to Evidence.** A petition which fails to state the interest of plaintiff in the probate of the will does not state a cause of action for setting aside the will, and that defect is not waived by failure to make specific objection by demurrer or answer, but a general denial contained in one of the answers is sufficient to raise the issue of fact, and plaintiff is thereby required to prove the existence of such facts as will show him entitled to maintain the suit, and if he fails to do so the court errs in overruling a demurrer to the evidence.

4. ———: ———: **Stating Interest of Heirs.** The body of the petition in a suit to set aside a will should allege facts showing that plaintiffs are heirs of the deceased testator. It is not enough simply to name them in the caption.

Appeal from Cole Circuit Court.—*Hon. John M. Williams*, Judge.

REVERSED AND REMANDED.

Gove & Davidson and *Pope & Lohman* for appellants.

(1) The court erred in not giving the instructions asked by defendants in the nature of a demurrer

to the evidence, for the reason that the petition is fatally defective in failing to allege that plaintiffs were interested in the disposition or devolution of the estate of deceased, and no evidence was given or offered to show such interest. Borland on Wills (Enlarged Ed.), sec. 74; R. S. 1909, sec. 555; State ex rel. v. McQuillin, 246 Mo. 689; Lilly v. Tobbein, 103 Mo. 477; Church v. Tobbein, 82 Mo. 418; Hans v. Holler, 165 Mo. 47; Stowe v. Stowe, 140 Mo. 594; Wells v. Wells, 144 Mo. 198; Kishman v. Scott, 166 Mo. 215; Vaile v. Sprague, 179 Mo. 393; Watson v. Anderson, 146 Mo. 333; Eddy v. Park, 31 Mo. 518; Stewart v. Coshon, 238 Mo. 662; Kelley's Probate Guide (4 Ed.), sec. 86, p. 74, ch. 10. (2) The petition fails to state facts sufficient to constitute a cause of action. Pier v. Heinrichhoffer, 52 Mo. 333; Scott v. Rombard, 67 Mo. 289; Christian v. Ins. Co., 143 Mo. 460; Chitty v. Railroad, 148 Mo. 64; Land v. Live Stock Co., 163 Mo. 342. (3) All interested parties must be before the court in a contested will case, otherwise the case will be dismissed. Eddy v. Park, 31 Mo. 518; Wells v. Wells, 144 Mo. 198; Kishman v. Scott, 166 Mo. 215; Vaile v. Sprague, 179 Mo. 393; Watson v. Anderson, 146 Mo. 333; Scott v. Rombard, 67 Mo. 289; Land v. Live Stock Co., 163 Mo. 342.

Irwin & Peters and *D. F. Calfee* for respondents. ·

(1) Proceedings in reference to contest of a will are proceedings *in rem*. The heirs at law and devisees are made nominal parties, but the proceeding is *ex parte*. Garvin's Admr. v. Williams, 50 Mo. 212; Vaile v. Sprague, 179 Mo. 396. In this suit plaintiffs do not seek to establish any right in themselves. The action is in the nature of a proceeding *in rem* and any question as to the interest or lack of interest of plaintiffs, relates only to their legal capacity, or incapacity,

to sue. Any objection therefore, as to plaintiffs' supposed lack of interest, if such lack of interest appeared on the face of the petition, should have been taken by demurrer; and if it did not appear on the face of the petition, the question should have been raised by answer. Defendants having failed to raise the question by either answer or demurrer, the objection is waived. R. S. 1909, sec. 1804. Appellants contend that plaintiffs' lack of interest (or capacity to maintain the suit), if there was any lack of interest, appeared on the face of the petition; this issue could have been raised only by special demurrer, and appellants having failed to raise it in this manner, the question of plaintiffs' interest was not in issue and it was not necessary for plaintiffs to introduce any evidence as to such interest. Baxter v. Transit Co., 198 Mo. 1. Want of legal capacity to sue and the objection that the action is not brought in the name of the real party in interest is waived where the objection is not urged by demurrer where apparent on the face of the complaint and by answer where not so apparent. 31 Cyc. 737. (2) There was not a total failure to allege plaintiffs' interest; such interest was shown by the petition. The body of the petition states that Rev. Gruender left surviving him, as his heirs, certain persons, naming them. The caption shows that plaintiffs were the heirs at law of three of these persons, and the other one of the four was made a party defendant. A pleading must be construed as an entirety, including the caption. 31 Cyc. 83; McCloskey v. Strickland, 7 Iowa, 259. And especially, after verdict, resort may be had to the caption to show interest, or capacity, on the part of plaintiff, where by reasonable intendment a sufficient cause of action can be made out. State ex rel. v. Crow, 8 Mo. App. 596; 31 Cyc. 82; Goode v. Coal Co., 167 Mo. App. 173. If defendants desired that the averments of plaintiffs' petition should be made more definite and certain, the proper mode of correction was motion before the trial. Pomeroy's Code Remedies, 596. (3) Admitting that the allegation in plaintiffs' petition, as to their interest, was defective, such defect was cured by the verdict. R. S. 1909, sec. 2119. By pleading to the merits, defendants waived all objections to mere formal defects; the only objection they can raise in this court is, that the petition, when taken altogether, fails to state a cause of action; not that a cause of action is defectively stated. Seekinger v. Mfg. Co., 129 Mo. 598; Reineman v. Larkin, 222 Mo. 172. (4) If the question of the pecuniary interest of the petitioners in a proceeding for the revocation of the probate of a will is not raised before the surrogate, it will not be considered on appeal from a judgment revoking such probate. In re Liddington's Will, 4 N. Y. Supp. 648; Thompson v. Farr, 1 Spear's L. (S. C.) 100;   In re Robinson, 106 Cal. 496. (5) Plaintiffs' statement that they were the heirs at law of three of the persons named in the body of the petition as the surviving heirs at law of Rev. Gruender at the time of his death, is a sufficient allegation that plaintiffs would be entitled to share in the distribution of the estate in case of Rev. Gruender's intestacy, and is therefore a sufficient allegation of such interest in plaintiffs as enabled them to maintain this suit. Especially is this true after verdict, the petition being aided by all reasonable inferences and intendments. An heir is one on whom the law casts an estate upon the death of the ancestor. Desloge v. Tucker, 196 Mo. 599; Brown v. Bank, 66 Mo. App. 431. The term "heirs at law," when used with respect to personal property, may properly be regarded as meaning next of kin. Train v. Davis, 98 N. Y. Supp. 820. An heir at law is one who succeeds to the estate of a deceased person. McKinney v. Stewart, 5 Kan. 394; 4 Words and Phrases, 3265.

WILLIAMS, C.—This is a suit to set aside the will of Rev. John Gruender, deceased.

From a verdict and judgment revoking the will, upon trial in the circuit court of Cole County, defendants have duly appealed to this court.

The case was argued and submitted at the April (1915) term of this court, and was then assigned to the late lamented Judge BROWN. His untimely death intervening necessitated a reassignment of the case which was recently done. Hence the delay in delivering an opinion in the case.

The conclusion that we have reached in the case renders it unnecessary that we should burden this opinion with a detailed statement of the facts disclosed by the somewhat voluminous record in the case, but we shall confine the statement to such facts only as shall be necessary to a determination of the case upon this appeal.

That portion of the caption of the petition describing the plaintiffs was as follows:

"Augala Gruender, Henry Behler and Ignatz Gruender, heirs at law of Joseph Gruender, deceased. Ignatz Beller, Frederick Beller, Clara Beller, Joseph Beller, heirs at law of Lissetta Beller, Andrew Amelunsen, Ignatz Amelunsen, Maria Amelunsen, Elizabeth Amelunsen, August Amelunsen, heirs at law of Antoinette Amelunsen, deceased, plaintiffs."

The petition contained the following allegation:

"Plaintiffs for their cause of action say that John Gruender died testate at the county of Cole and State of Missouri on the 20th day of March, 1909, *leaving surviving him as his heirs at law, Joseph Gruender, Lissette Beller, Antoinette Amelunsen and Ignatz Gruender.*"

There was no further allegation in the petition as to the interest of plaintiffs in the estate of the deceased in the event his will should be revoked.

Neither was there any proof offered at the trial to show that the plaintiffs or either of them would share in the distribution of the testator's estate in the event the will should be set aside.

Appellants, seeking a reversal of the judgment below, urge among other grounds the following:

(1) That there was no evidence introduced tending to show that the plaintiffs or any of them would share in the distribution of decedent's estate if the will were revoked and that, therefore, the court erred in overruling the defendant's demurrer to the evidence which was offered at the close of all the evidence.

(2) That the petition fails to state facts sufficient to constitute a cause of action in that the petition does not allege sufficient facts to show that the plaintiffs were interested in the probate of said will.

I. In this State, a suit to contest a will is a statutory proceeding (Sec. 555, R. S. 1909), and the statute requires the contestant to be a person *interested* in the probate of the will. The *interest* required by said statute was defined by Court in Banc in the case of State ex rel. v. McQuillin, 246 Mo. 674, l. c. 691-692, to be "a financial interest in the estate and one which would be benefited by setting the will aside."

Will Contest: Necessary Pleading.

Since it is necessary that the plaintiff have such an interest to enable him to institute the suit to contest the validity of the will, it, necessarily, follows, we think, that such facts must be alleged and proven upon the trial unless admitted by the pleadings of the proponent.

It has long been the rule in this State that in statutory actions "the party suing must bring him-

self strictly within the statutory requirements necessary to confer the right [of action], and this must appear in his petition; otherwise, it shows no cause of
action." [Barker v. Hannibal & St. Joseph Ry. Co.,
91 Mo. 86; Chandler v. Railroad, 251 Mo..592, l. c.
600-601, and cases therein cited.]

Respondents insist that this defect in the proof
relates merely to the want of the plaintiffs' "legal
capacity to sue." That it was, therefore, such a
matter as should have been raised by demurrer if it
appeared upon the face of the petition (Sec. 1800,
R. S. 1909), or by answer if it did not appear upon
the face of the petition (Sec. 1804, R. S. 1909), and
that the defendants having failed to raise it specially, either by demurrer or by answer, thereby waived
the objection (Sec. 1804, supra) and relieved plaintiffs of the necessity of making the proof. *If* the defect is one that relates merely to the "legal capacity"
of the plaintiffs to sue, the position taken by respondents is sound. [Baxter v. St. Louis Transit Co.,
198 Mo. 1; Crowl v. Am. Linseed Co., 255 Mo. 305,
l. c. 327-328, and cases therein cited.]

Was the defect one which involved the "legal
capacity" of the plaintiffs to sue? We think not.

The phrase "that the plaintiff has not *legal capacity* to sue" found in the Code "has reference to
some legal disability of the plaintiff, such as infancy, idiocy, coverture," etc., or that the person
attempting to sue in a representative capacity such
as curator, administrator, etc., "has no title to the
character in which he sues," and has no reference
to the fact that the petition fails to show a right
of action in the plaintiff. [Bliss on Code Pleading
(3 Ed.), secs. 407-8; Ward v. Petrie, 157 N. Y. 301;
McKinney v. Minahan, 119 Wis. 651; Pence v. Aughe,
101 Ind. 317; Brown, Executor, v. Critchell, 110 Ind.
31; Howell v. Iola Portland Cement Co., 86 Kan.

450; Littleton v. Burgess, 16 Wyo. 58; M. K. & T. Ry. Co. v. Lenahan, 39 Okla. 283.]

We are of the opinion that the defect is one which properly falls within. the *sixth* clause of section 1800, Revised Statutes 1909, viz., "that the petition does not state facts sufficient to constitute a cause of action," and hence was a matter that was not waived by virtue of failing to comply with the provisions of section 1804, supra.

"It is elementary that a complaint good in law must not only state a complete cause of action against the defendant, but it must also show a right of action in the plaintiff." [Hunt v. Monroe, 32 Utah, 428.] To the same effect are: Biddle v. Boyce, 13 Mo. 532; State ex rel. v. Dodson, 63 Mo. 451; 31 Cyc. 102, and cases therein cited; Niemi v. Stanley Smith Lumber Co., 149 Pac. 1033, l. c. 1035.

"When the plaintiff is a natural person, under no legal disability to maintain actions, a failure to state a cause. of action in his own favor goes to the sufficiency, in substance, of the petition, not to his legal capacity." [M. K. & T. Ry. Co. v. Lenahan, supra, l. c. 295.]

In the case of Board of Commissioners of Tipton County v. Kimberlin, 108 Ind. 449, l. c. 452-3, it was said:

"It has always been held by this court, that the second statutory cause for demurrer to a complaint, namely, 'that the plaintiff has not legal capacity to sue,' has reference only to some legal disability of the plaintiff, such as infancy, insanity or idiocy, and not the fact, if it be the fact, that the complaint on its face fails to show any cause or right of action in the plaintiff. [Dale v. Thomas, 67 Ind. 570; Dewey v. State ex rel., 91 Ind. 173; Traylor v. Dykins, 91 Ind. 229.]

"But we have often held, and correctly so we think, that a demurrer to a complaint for the fifth statutory cause of demurrer, namely, 'that the complaint does not state facts sufficient to constitute a cause of action,' calls in question not only the sufficiency of the facts stated to constitute a cause of action, but also the right or authority of the particular plaintiff to bring and maintain a suit upon such cause of action. [Pence v. Aughe, 101 Ind. 317; Wilson v. Galey, 103 Ind. 257; Walker v. Heller, 104 Ind. 327; Frazer v. State to use, 106 Ind. 471.]''

Since the matter was such as was not waived by failing to make specific objection either by demurrer or answer, we are of the opinion that the general denial contained in one of the separate answers filed was sufficient to raise the issue of fact and that plaintiffs were thereby required to prove the existence of such facts as would show them entitled to maintain the suit. Having failed to do so, the court erred in overruling the demurrer to the evidence.

II. It is further contended that the petition failed to state facts sufficient to constitute a cause of action in that it failed to allege facts showing that plaintiffs were interested in the probate of the will as required by section 555, Revised Statutes 1909. The body of the petition does not allege facts that would show that plaintiffs were the heirs of the deceased testator, but gives the names of four persons (other than plaintiffs) who are alleged to have been the heirs of the testator. The caption of the petition describes the three groups of plaintiffs as the respective heirs of persons bearing the same names as three of the heirs alleged in the body of the petition and respondents insist that the petition, in this regard, may be aided by the matters contained in the caption. Since the case must be reversed and remanded, it becomes unnecessary to determine whether or not the petition was, in this regard, fatally defective. It is sufficient to say that proper practice would require that matters, of this kind be set forth in the body of the petition. [Sec. 1794, Revised Statutes 1909.] Since the case must be remanded, however, plaintiffs will have an opportunity to amend their petition and thereby avoid the point upon a retrial of the cause.

The judgment is reversed and the cause remanded. *Roy, C.,* concurs.

PER CURIAM.—The foregoing opinion by WILLIAMS, C., is adopted as the opinion of the court. All of the judges concur, except *Revelle, J.,* not sitting.

INDEX.

ABSTRACT.

Transfer from Court of Appeals. When a case reaches the Supreme Court by transfer from a court of appeals, on the ground that a constitutional question is involved, the rule is not to scrutinize too closely the abstract of the record, lest appellant be caught unwittingly between the rules of that court and of this and thereby be pinched out of any appeal at all. Wolf v. Harris, 405.

ACTIONS.

1. **Drainage District: Title of Case.** Prior to a final judgment incorporating a drainage district the title of the case on appeal should run thus: "In re Petition for Incorporation of Mingo Drainage District; George S. Dean et al., Petitioners, Respondents, v. B. F. Wilson et al., Appellants." In re Mingo Drainage Dist., 268.

2. ————: ————: **Right to Sue.** After the decree incorporating a drainage district has been made final it can sue and be sued in its own corporate name. Ib.

3. **Insurance Policy: Foreign Insurance Company: Limitation to Contracts Made in this State.** The statute (Sec. 7042, R. S. 1909) does not limit the right of holders of policies issued by an insurance company licensed to do business in this State to sue in the courts of this State upon contracts made in this State, but gives them the right to sue such a company in the courts of this State upon policies wherever made.

   Held, by GRAVES, J., dissenting, with whom BOND and WALKER, JJ., concur, that the substituted method of service of process provided by the statute is limited to actions arising on contracts made or acts done in this State. Mining Co. v. Ins. Co., 524.

4. **Title: Stating Interest of Heirs.** The body of the petition in a suit to set aside a will should allege facts showing that plaintiffs are heirs of the deceased testator. It is not enough simply to name them in the caption. Gruender v. Frank, 713.

ADMINISTRATION.

1. **Removal Causes: Ascertainment Before Appointment.** Section 50, Revised Statutes 1909, announcing the causes for which letters testamentary or of administration may be revoked, is not to be read into and made a part of section 14, which designates persons who cannot qualify as executor or administrator. The probate court cannot refuse to appoint an executor named in the will on the ground that such person if appointed could be removed for the causes mentioned in section 50. State ex rel. v. Holtcamp, 412.

2. **Executor: Renunciation.** The person named as executor in a will may renounce his right to be appointed, either by an express renunciation, or by acts and conduct *in pais*. Ib.

3. ————: ————: **Determination a Judicial Matter.** The probate court must determine from the facts whether the person nominated executor in the will has renounced his right to be

ADMINISTRATION—Continued.

appointed, and in doing so exercises a judicial function; his act must not be arbitrary, or an abuse of power, or wholly unsupported by facts showing a renunciation; but if such facts are present, the appointment of another cannot be annulled by mandamus brought by the named executor to compel his appointment. State ex rel. v. Holtcamp, 412.

4. **Title of Estate: Domiciliary and Ancillary Executor.** The executor who has duly qualified in the domiciliary jurisdiction succeeds to the title of all testator's estate, wherever situated, and continues to hold such title until an ancillary administrator is appointed, whereupon the title to the estate in the ancillary jurisdiction vests in the latter. Ib.

5. **Executor: Acts of Renunciation: Recall.** Testator died in Ohio, leaving a will which named relator and two women as executors. All qualified in Ohio, but within a few days relator filed his resignation, which was accepted. He did not qualify in the Missouri city in which he lived and where the most of testator's property was situated. He also immediately resigned as director of the corporation in which testator's Missouri assets were principally invested, and avowedly severed all relations with the management and preservation of the estate, and did other things which tended to establish a renunciation *in pais*. Held, that the probate court did not act arbitrarily, in holding relator had renounced his rights under the will and in appointing another administrator with the will annexed; and the renunciation being complete, it could not be recalled, but was lost to relator forever. Ib.

6. **Intention as to Executors.** The rule that the expressed intention of the testator must be the guide in construing a will, applies to every part of it—to the expressed desire that a nominated executor should administer the whole estate, the assets in the State where testator died and those in other States, as well as to other parts of it. Ib.

7. **Executor: Renunciation of Domiciliary Right: Is Renunciation of Ancillary Right.** A resignation in the domiciliary jurisdiction by an executor named in the will who is qualified under the laws of the various jurisdictions in which the estate is located, is a renunciation of his right to administer so much of the estate as is situate in the ancillary jurisdiction in which he resides. So that where relator, a resident of this State, who was named executor in the will of a testator who died in Ohio, qualified in that State and soon afterwards resigned, his resignation, there accepted, operated automatically as a renunciation of his right to administer so much of the estate as was located in this State. Ib.

ADMISSION.

By Pleading. A litigant cannot challenge a finding of facts by the court which stand admitted by his own pleading. Cashion v. Gargus, 68.

ADOPTED CHILDREN.

1. **Right of Heirs to Inherit.** If an adopted child dies during the life of its adopting parent, leaving children, such children inherit as grandchildren upon the death of such adopting parent intestate. Bernero v. Goodwin, 427.

2. ———: **Statute.** Section 1671, Revised Statutes 1909, providing that a person may, by deed, "adopt any child or children as

ADOPTED CHILDREN—Continued.

his or her heir," by the use of the word "heir," and section
332, providing that the estate of an intestate shall descend "to
his children, *or their descendants*," means that the child of an
adopted child who dies during the lifetime of the adopting
parent, inherits from such adopting parent dying intestate. An
adopted child is a child within the meaning of the descent laws,
and the words in section 332 mean the same as if they had read
that the estate shall descend "to his children (either natural-
born or adopted), or their descendants." Ib.

3. ————: **How Determined.** The rights of the natural child of
the adopted child to claim a distributive share in the estate of
the adopting parent is not limited solely to the adoption statutes and the deed of adoption, to the exclusion of all rights
given by the statutes of descents, but those statutes lay down
the general rules of inheritance, and the deed of adoption created the status of the adopted child, or gave to him the status of
an heir. Ib.

APPEALS.

1. **One Law for Innocent and Guilty.** There can be but one law
for the trial of the innocent and guilty; and notwithstanding the
court may be of the opinion that the evidence is sufficient to
warrant a verdict of guilty, a plain statute forbidding the cross-
examination of a defendant concerning matters wholly outside
his examination in chief must be applied to all defendants alike.
The Constitution has not ordained that apparent guilt is the
sole condition of affirmance by the Supreme Court of a verdict
of guilty. State v. Pfeifer, 23.

2. **Specific Assignment: All Law of Case.** An assignment in the
motion for a new trial that the court failed to instruct the jury
as to all the law arising upon the issues in the case, which
does not specify upon what point the court failed to instruct,
does not raise a point for appellate review. State v. Taylor, 41.

3. **Arraignment.** The failure of the record to show either an arraignment or a plea will not, of itself, entitle defendant to a
reversal, the record also failing to show that any objection was
made at any time to a lack of arraignment or plea until the case
reached the appellate court. State v. Allen, 49.

4. **Change of Venue: Trial With Application Pending.** Where the
record fails to show anything on the subject except the bare
fact that an application for a change of venue was filed, it will
not be held on appeal that the case was tried while a formal
and sufficient application was pending. Ib.

5. **Remarks of Court: No Objection.** Unless there is an objection
directed to an objectionable remark made by the trial court, it
cannot be reviewed on appeal. State v. Evans, 163.

6. **Prohibition: Jurisdiction of Appeal.** Jurisdiction to hear and
determine upon appeal the original case out of which the application for a writ of prohibition arose, is not a prerequisite
to the right of the Supreme Court to issue the writ. Ramsey
v. Huck, 333.

7. **Jurisdiction: Derivative.** If the county court had no jurisdiction over the contest for the office of justice of the peace, because notice of contest was not timely served, the circuit court
acquired none by reason of an appeal. Ib.

APPEALS—Continued.

8. **Abstract: Transfer from Court of Appeals.** When a case reaches the Supreme Court by transfer from a court of appeals, on the ground that a constitutional question is involved, the rule is not to scrutinize too closely the abstract of the record, lest appellant be caught unwittingly between the rules of that court and of this and thereby be pinched out of any appeal at all. Wolf v. Harris, 405.

9. **Petition: Cause of Action.** The point that the petition does not state a cause of action may be raised for the first time in the appellate court. Ib.

10. **Sufficiency of Evidence: Judgment of Foreign Court: Raised By Motion for New Trial.** An assignment in the motion for a new trial that "the verdict and judgment is unsupported by any substantial evidence" raises the question of the sufficiency of the evidence, and that proposition necessarily embraces a contention that the judgments against a corporation rendered by a court of another State, which are made the basis of plaintiff's suit against its stockholders for the amount of the unpaid stock issued to them, and introduced in evidence, were insufficient in law to support a finding for plaintiff. Schroeder v. Edwards, 459.

11. **Insufficient Assignment: Striking Out Answer.** An assignment under "Points" that "the portions of defendants' answer stricken out by the court on the motion of the plaintiffs were material to the defense of these defendants, and error was, therefore, committed by the court in such action," with nothing more except the citation of authorities, does not comply with Rule 15, and does not designate any facts from which the court may comprehend what the point is. Ib..

12. **Remanding Cause: Confining Issue.** Where all issues in an equity case except one have on appeal been settled, the court, instead of remanding the cause generally, may remand it with directions that upon a retrial the case be confined to the one issue upon which the evidence at the first trial was insufficient to support a decree for plaintiff. Ib.

13. **Bill of Exceptions: Bystanders.** Bystanders who may sign a bill of exceptions upon the refusal of the judge to do so, as the word is used in the statute (Sec. 2031, R. S. 1909), mean disinterested spectators, and do not include persons who were not present at the trial. Buck v. Buck, 644.

14. ———: **Wrongfully Signed: Withdrawal.** A bill of exceptions signed by persons who were not bystanders in contemplation of the statute, because they were not present at the trial, is no bill at all; and if filed or deposited with the clerk, may be withdrawn that it may be properly signed. Ib.

15. ———: **Bystanders: Jurors.** Members of the trial jury, under a reasonable construction of the statute, are bystanders, and may sign the bill of exceptions upon the judge's refusal to approve it. Ib.

16. ———: ———: **Affidavits: Part of Record.** Affidavits of bystanders in support of or against the truth of a bill of exceptions which the judge has refused to sign, taken and filed as required by section 2035, Revised Statutes 1909, are a part of the record on appeal and are subject to review in determining the truth of said bill. Ib.

ATTORNEYS—Continued.

2. **Partition: Attorney's Fee.** No allowance should be made counsel as general costs for services in contested matters between the parties in a partition suit. But an allowance to plaintiff's attorney should be taxed as costs for such work as counsel would do in an ordinary non-contested partition, although, after new plaintiffs were added, there were brought into the case contested matters between them and defendants because of a denial of the validity of the deeds previously made by some of them. Parrish v. Treadway, 91.

3. **Remarks of Counsel: Preserved for Review.** Where defendant's counsel, in his objection to argument made to the jury by the State's counsel, repeats the statement made by said counsel and states his reason therefor, and the court by his ruling, accepts the repetition as a true reiteration of what had been said, the ruling, being excepted to, is for review on appeal, without any further preservation in the bill of exceptions than the statement and objection of appellant's counsel and the ruling and remarks of the court, and the exception. State v. Evans, 163.

4. ———: **Weak Evidence.** Argument of counsel to the jury, assigned as prejudicial to appellant, is to be examined in the light of the facts of the particular case. Where the evidence of defendant's guilt is weak, the offense charged is one which decent men abhor, and there is no testimony pertaining to a fact which reasonable men would expect to be developed, remarks of counsel for the State, either in their opening statement or in their argument to the jury, by which such lacking testimony is attempted to be supplied, may alone constitute reversible error. Ib.

5. ———: **Seduction: No Request for Fulfillment of Promise to Marry: Supplied by Attorney.** The fact that, after prosecutrix discovered her pregnancy as the result of an admitted sexual relationship, she frequently kept company with defendant in the presence of her and his relatives and requested him to marry her to shield her from its consequences, but at no time suggested or claimed a reparation on account of a promise to marry, there being no legal impediment or other obstacle in the way of such a marriage, tends to impeach her testimony that there had been such a promise, and in view of her unsatisfactory testimony as to the fact of an engagement was a matter of grave importance for the jury in determining whether or not her testimony was true; and remarks made by the State's counsel, in his opening statement that "the young girl who was wronged by this young man has solicited and begged and importuned him to marry her and give this bright little baby a father and a name," and repeated in substance in the argument to the jury, the effect being, whether intended or not, to break the force of the significant omission, and to supply the lack of it, were reversible error.

Held, by REVELLE, J., dissenting, that it is but common knowledge and ordinary human experience that no juror will sit through a trial of a seduction case without the thought that the girl, whose shame and disgrace would be lessened by marriage, was anxious to and did what she could to bring about the marriage, and the statement of counsel could only have hastened the thought; and, in this case, it was not prejudicial, because the jury knew the defendant

ATTORNEYS—Continued.

had not married her, and counsel's statement that she begged him to do so and his refusal, if effective at all, tended only to corroborate his testimony that he had never promised to marry her at any time. Ib.

6. **Argument to Jury: No Exception.** A failure of defendant to save an exception to the court's ruling on his objection that plaintiff's remarks to the jury are prejudicial precludes any consideration of the remarks on appeal. Sperry v. Hurd, 628.

7. **Remarks of Counsel: Will Contest: Attack on Contestant.** In a suit to set aside a will on the sole grounds of the mental incapacity of the testator and of undue influence exercised upon his mind, it is improper to permit counsel for proponents to say in his argument to the jury of and concerning contestant: "He was a spendthrift son. He never did anything for the support of the family. He took from his mother's estate so far as he could, and his family had to leave the city to get rid of him, or to get rid of his attempts to get the family's money. He was not a success in business life." Whether true or false, the remarks were not relevant to the issues, and therefore unauthorized, and being a personal reflection upon contestant were improper. But they were not reversible error, where there is a preponderance of affirmative evidence that the testator was of sound mind and subject to no undue influence and little substantial error to the contrary. Buck v. Buck, 644.

BANKABLE PAPER.

Evidence: Telegraph Money Order. Testimony that a telegraph money order, tendered by the company's agent to an insurance company in payment of a premium note, is bankable paper in the sense that the banks of the town would put it to the credit of the holder and permit him to check out the amount thereof, is competent evidence, where the sufficiency of the tender of such order is the issue in the case. Smith v. Ins. Co., 342.

BANKRUPTCY PROCEEDINGS. See Banks and Banking.

BANKS AND BANKING.

1. **Private Banks: Assets and Rights of Creditors: Power of State Court to Construe Own Laws.** This court has the constitutional power to construe all constitutional provisions and legislative acts of this State applicable to private banks and bankers organized and existing under its laws, and to decide to whom the assets of an insolvent bank belong, and the priority of the rights of creditors thereto. State ex rel. v. Sage, 493.

2. **Natural Person: Right to Engage in Business.** There is no constitutional inhibition against any natural person engaging in any business he may choose which is not *malum in se*. Ib.

3. ———: ———: **Private Banking.** Nor is there any constitutional provision limiting the power of the General Assembly to enact general laws providing for the organization of private banks, authorizing them to engage in a banking business, declaring their legal status, and prescribing the terms and conditions upon which they may carry on that business within this State. Ib.

4. **Private Banks: Corporations Sole.** Since a private bank, though owned by a single individual, is by statute granted powers and privileges not possessed by natural persons or partner-

BANKS AND BANKING—Continued.

ships, and possesses only such powers and privileges as are granted by statute, and cannot exist until it has complied with these statutes, and since the statutes completely segregate the bank's assets and business from its owner's private assets and business, it is a legal entity, a corporation sole, under the pro-provisions of the Constitution (Art. 12, sec. 11) declaring that the term corporation "shall be construed to include all joint stock companies or associations having any powers or privileges not possessed by individuals or partnerships." If owned by more than one person, it is still a separate entity or *quasi*-corporation. [Disapproving Gupton v. Carr, 147 Mo. App. 105.] State ex rel. v. Sage, 493.

5. ———: ———: .Notwithstanding Words of Statute. The words of the statute (Sec. 1116, R. S. 1909) declaring that the owner or owners of a private bank may carry on a banking business "without being incorporated," were used to distinguish private banks from banks incorporated under the general banking laws; they were not intended to declare that a private bank, organized under the statutes and conducted according to their requirements, it not a separate legal entity, or a *quasi*-corporation, or a corporation sole. Ib.

6. ———: ———: Application of Assets. The assets of a private bank, belonging to a single individual, belong to the bank, and upon its insolvency should be used to pay its creditors, and if any surplus remains after they are paid, it should be used in paying the owner's individual creditors, if he too, is insolvent or has been adjudged a bankrupt in the Federal court. Ib.

7. ———: Insolvency: Priority of Jurisdiction of State and Federal Court. The taking possession of a private bank by the Bank Commissioner is the first step in the bringing of a suit for the appointment of a receiver, and that step gives the circuit court jurisdiction of the cause, and a subsequent application for a receiver and the appointment of one cannot be said to be *coram non judice* because of the fact that, before the receiver is appointed, a petition asking that the bank's owner be adjudged a bankrupt is filed in the Federal court. Ib.

8. ———: ———: ———: Bankrupt Proceedings Against Owner. Besides, the filing of a petition in the Federal court, asking that the owner of a private bank be individually adjudged a bankrupt, does not place the assets of his said bank *in custodia legis*—certainly not to the extent of depriving the State court of its jurisdiction to decide whether or not the creditors of the bank are entitled to be paid out of its assets before they can be used to satisfy its owner's individual creditors. Ib.

BENEFIT DISTRICT. See Cities, 3.

BENEVOLENT CORPORATION. See Corporations, 26 to 28.

BEQUESTS, SPECIAL. See Wills, 1 to 4.

BILL OF EXCEPTIONS. See Exceptions.

CAPACITY TO SUE. See Legal Capacity to Sue.

CARNAL KNOWLEDGE.

1. Evidence of Prosecutrix's Age. Where the statute requires the prosecutrix to be under fifteen years of age in order to constitute sexual intercourse with her rape, proof that she was not

CARNAL KNOWLEDGE—Continued.

alleged crime above fifteen years of age and the defendant above seventeen. State v. Allen, 49.

8. **Evidence: Impeachment: Offer to Settle For Money.** Evidence in a prosecution for carnal knowledge of a female under the age of consent that the prosecutrix proposed to defendant or his attorney, to leave the State and not appear at the trial if money were paid to her, and that her uncle after a conference with her and her mother and in pursuance to an understanding with them hunted up defendant and proposed to him, and later proposed to defendant's attorney, that if money were paid to him he would take prosecutrix out of the State and see to it that she did not appear at the trial, is competent for the purpose of impeaching both the prosecutrix and her mother as witnesses to the main fact of sexual intercourse, and the exclusion of such testimony is reversible error. Ib.

CHANGE OF VENUE.

1. **Trial With Application Pending.** Where the record fails to show anything on the subject except the bare fact that an application for a change of venue was filed, it will not be held on appeal that the case was tried while a formal and sufficient application was pending. State v. Allen, 49.

2. ———: **Matter of Exception.** Complaint that the case was tried while an application for a change of venue was pending is a matter of exception, to be saved for review in the bill of exceptions. Ib.

3. **Jurisdiction of Another Judge: Agreement upon Special Judge.** Where the record shows that an application for a change of venue was filed and that a judge of another circuit was called by the regular judge to sit in the case and "was on the bench" and tried the case without objection, it will be presumed, in the absence of a record showing to the contrary, that both the State and defendant waived the privilege of selecting a special judge; and, aided by the presumption of right action on the part of a court of general jurisdiction, it will be *held* that the judge so called in had authority to try the case. Ib.

CHARITIES. See Corporations, 24 to 26.

CITIES.

1. **Public Street: Park Carriage Drive.** A conveyance to a city of a strip of ground fifty feet wide along an established park to be used as a "carriage avenue" of the park "for all such carriages and teams as by regulations and rules governing the park may be allowed to run in same," was a dedication of the strip for highway purposes; and a further clause in the grant subjecting it to the "immediate government of the park commissioners" means such regulation as may be exercised by them in the control of a public street, and nothing more; and being dedicated to street purposes, and being accepted and since uniformly regarded by the city as a street, the strip's status as a street is fixed. Kennard v. Eyermann, 1.

2. ———: ———: **Evidence of Dedication.** The establishment by the city of public improvements on such "carriage avenue," such as pavements, lights, sewers and water mains, constitutes evidence of its permanent public character as a street, as do also the knowledge of and acquiescence in such improvements on the part of the dedicator. Ib.

CITIES—Continued.

has dealt with the subject of the construction and management of property which is held and used by its agents for the highest governmental purposes, no presumption that laws of the character of the charter of the city of St. Louis and ordinances passed in pursuance thereof are applicable to the sovereign, can prevail, for then the power does not rest upon presumption, but upon express legislative declarations. Board of Education v. St. Louis, 356.

10. ———: ———: ———: **Paramount Authority of Statute.** The general charter of the city of St. Louis must yield to the provisions of a law having special application to particular matters and things within the field of its operation; and where there is such a general law, the question of whether the charter and ordinances are impliedly repealed without being mentioned in the general law, is not in the case. Ib.

CITIZENS OF ANOTHER STATE. **See Right to Sue in This State.**

COGNOVIT. **See Judgments, 4.**

CONCURRENT DEPENDENT AGREEMENT. **See Contracts.**

CONSOLIDATED SCHOOL DISTRICT. **See Schools.**

CONSTITUTIONAL LAW.

1. **City Charter.** A municipal charter or a statute of the State will not be held to violate the Constitution if any other rational interpretation can be given it. Pitman v. Drabelle, 78.

2. ———: **Legislative Power of People.** Except as inhibited by the Federal or State Constitution the power of the people of a State to legislate is plenary, and they may exercise that power through the Legislature, or the Initiative, and the same principle applies to municipal corporations, which in their public capacity are but agents of the State. Ib.

3. ———: **Legislation By Initiative: One House Legislature.** The clause of the new charter of St. Louis which provides that, upon the failure of the one house of the municipal legislature to act upon the certification to it of petitions showing the measure which the people request them to adopt, the measure may be enacted into law through the instrumentality of an initiative petition and the vote of the people, does not contravene that clause of the Constitution which declares that the charter of such a city "shall be in harmony with and subject to the Constitution and laws of the State, and shall provide, among other things, for a chief executive and at least one house of legislation to be elected by general ticket." Nor in conditioning initiative legislation upon the inaction of the one house is it so out of harmony with the constitutional amendment of 1908 applicable to the whole State, or with the statutes of 1913 which gave initiative powers to cities of the second and third class, as to render it invalid. Nor does the Constitution require a municipal legislature of more than one house. Ib.

4. ———: **Arrest of Legislation: Election: Injunction.** An election called in pursuance to a provision of the city charter under a valid plan for initiative legislation and proper petitions, cannot be enjoined on the ground that the ordinances as proposed are unconstitutional. During the process of legislation in any mode the work of the lawmakers is not subject to judicial arrest, or control, or even open to judicial inquiry. It is only after the proposed legislation has become an accomplished fact that its constitutionality can be determined by the courts. Ib.

CONSTITUTIONAL LAW—Continued.

5. **Drainage District: Inclusion of Other Lands Not Benefited.** The statutes do not authorize an organized drainage district to so extend its boundaries as to include within the district other lands which do not need reclamation and protection from water. Unless they are beneficially affected and there is some common interest between them and those of the existing district, they cannot be included against the will and protest of their owners. A drainage district can neither go outside the object of its own organization to force upon owners of adjoining land an improvement in which they have no interest, nor improve the land without receiving some benefit to compensate them for the outlay. Drainage Dist. v. Harris, 139.

6. **Natural Person: Right to Engage in Business.** There is no constitutional inhibition against any natural person engaging in any business he may choose which is not *malum in se*. State ex rel. v. Sage, 493.

7. ———: ———: **Private Banking.** Nor is there any constitutional provision limiting the power of the General Assembly to enact general laws providing for the organization of private banks, authorizing them to engage in a banking business, declaring their legal status, and prescribing the terms and conditions upon which they may carry on that business within this State. Ib.

8. **Private Banks: Corporations Sole.** Since a private bank, though owned by a single individual, is by statute granted powers and privileges not possessed by natural persons or partnerships, and possesses only such powers and privileges as are granted by statute, and cannot exist until it has complied with these statutes, and since the statutes segregate the bank's assets and business from its owner's private assets and business, it is a legal entity, a corporation sole, under the provisions of the Constitution (Art. 12, sec. 11) declaring that the term corporation "shall be construed to include all joint stock companies or associations having any powers or privileges not possessed by individuals or partnerships." If owned by more than one person, it is still a separate entity or *quasi*-corporation. [Disapproving Gupton v. Carr, 147 Mo. App. 105.] Ib.

9. **Foreign Insurance Company: Policy Made in Another State: Constitutionality of Statute.** Section 7042, Revised Statutes 1909, designed to authorize service of process against foreign insurance companies doing business in this State in pursuance to a license properly granted, based upon insurance contracts made in another state, by service of summons upon the Superintendent of Insurance appointed as its agent for the purpose of process, is not unconstitutional, either as denying to said companies due process of law, or on the theory that the Legislature has no power to authorize suits to be brought in the courts of this State for a breach of an insurance contract made in another state. Mining Co. v. Ins. Co., 524.

10. ———: ———: ———: ———: ———: **Transitory Action.** In pursuance to broad and specific provisions of the State and Federal Constitution, the Legislature of this State has made ample provision by which a suit on a transitory cause of action—that is, a personal action founded on a violation of rights which, in contemplation of law, have no locality, but follow the person—may be brought in the courts of this State by a citizen of any other State or country, with the same freedom as is accorded to a citizen of this State. The Legislature has enact-

CONSTITUTIONAL LAW—Continued.

ed, and had constitutional authority to enact, laws conferring jurisdiction upon the courts of this State to try and determine actions brought by a citizen of another State or country against a foreign insurance company licensed to do business in this State, upon contracts of fire insurance made in another state or country, whether the property destroyed was located in this State or elsewhere. [GRAVES, BOND and WALKER, JJ., dissenting.] Mining Co. v. Ins. Co., 524.

CONTINUANCE.

1. **Age of Prosecutrix.** Ordinarily in a prosecution for carnal knowledge of a female under fifteen years of age, where her age is a vital issue, an application for a continuance, based on the absence of her grandmother, sick and unable to attend the trial, who, if present, would testify that at the time of the offense she was over fifteen, should not be denied. State v. Arnold, 33.

2. **Contradictory and Insincere Application.** An application for a continuance, which is inconsistent, contradictory, does not import the truth as to defendant's knowledge of what the absent witness would testify and does not show reasonable diligence, should be denied. State v. McWilliams, 437.

3. **Diligence: Deposition.** Where the application states that the defendant had sent to the absent witness money with which to pay her traveling expenses from another State to the place of trial and that she had agreed to attend, the trial court would be justified in granting a continuance, if the allegation therein of defendant's recent knowledge of what her testimony would be bears the impress of truth; but if the facts reveal that he did know what her testimony would be, then proper diligence required him to take her deposition, and having failed to do that the trial court did not abuse its discretion in denying the application. Ib.

CONTRACTS.

1. **Limitation: Written Promise to Pay.** In order to bring an "action upon any writing . . . for the payment of money or property" it must appear in the statement of the cause of action that the money sued for is promised to be paid by the language of the writing. If such promise arises only upon proof of extrinsic facts it is barred by the five-year Statute of Limitations. Parker-Washington Co. v. Dennison, 199.

2. ——: ——: ——: **Bad Faith on Part of Promisor.** The plaintiff being the owner of asphalt used in paving streets in a certain city, and of a plant used in the preparation of asphalt for paving purposes, located in said city, entered into a written contract with defendant whereby defendant agreed to pay plaintiff (1) for the use of said plant, five cents per square yard for all asphalt paving laid under the contract to the extent of forty thousand square yards, and (2) for said asphalt, one-half the amount received for any pavement done by defendant, after deducting all expenses. The defendant was to make bids in good faith to obtain paving contracts from the city. The petition alleged that defendant made no effort in good faith to obtain any such paving contracts, and when he had obtained some such contracts did not perform them and never intended to perform and never shipped any of the asphalt which had been tendered according to contract, and held the plant for a long time; and

CONTRACTS—Continued.

that the gain which would have accrued to plaintiff by the payment of said sum of five cents per square yard for all asphalt agreed to be laid by defendant was two thousand dollars, and one half the profits agreed to be paid and delivered to plaintiff was twenty thousand dollars, for which amounts judgment was asked. The suit was not brought within five years. *Held*, that the contract contained a promise to pay money only on condition that the pavement was laid, and the petition on its face alleges that no paving was laid, and therefore it does not state a promise to pay arising out of the words used in the written contract, but stated only a cause of action upon an implied promise arising in law out of the alleged torts of defendants: that such cause of action is not within the statute and was barred in five years.

Held, by WOODSON, C. J., dissenting, that all written contracts calling for things to be done in the future are conditional and whether they have been performed or not must of necessity be shown by parol testimony; that the contract in suit contained a definite promise in writing to pay two separate sums of money upon its performance; that defendant did not relieve himself from his promise to pay those sums by fraudulently refusing to perform; and that the promise to pay is found in the contract itself, and no evidence *aliunde* is required to show a promise to pay, and hence the five-year Statute of Limitations does not apply. Ib.

3. **Negotiable Note: Notice of Infirmities.** Notes made payable to the maker and indorsed in blank by him become payable to bearer and negotiable by delivery; and a transferee before maturity with actual knowledge of a concurrent dependent agreement, and a transferee after maturity without actual knowledge, take the notes with notice of the agreement and that it makes them non-payable. Simpson v. Van Laningham, 286.

4. ———: **Concurrent Dependent Agreement.** A negotiable promissory note and a concurrent collateral agreement, connected by direct reference or necessary implication, the stipulations of which are mutual and dependent, are to be construed together as one entire contract; and a transferee of the note after maturity, without actual knowledge of the agreement, cannot recover, if the agreement, when so construed, bars a recovery. Ib.

5. ———: ———: **Option to Surrender Stock for Notes.** The maker of negotiable notes received a concurrent written agreement, signed by a corporation and its president, reciting that the maker had purchased one hundred shares of the capital stock of the company, for which he had given his two notes in settlement, due in six months, and guaranteeing that the maker, at their maturity might, at his option, surrender the stock, whereupon the notes would be cancelled and returned to him. The certificates of stock, indorsed in blank, were attached to the notes, and the notes were transferred to a bank, whose cashier had full actual knowledge of the agreement. Shortly afterwards the bank went into the hands of a receiver, who, after the maturity of the notes, sold them to plaintiff. *Held*, that the notes and agreement did not constitute independent contracts, but they are dependent, and the agreement constitutes a

CONTRACTS—Continued.

defense to an action on the notes; and since the payee of the notes, when the agreement was delivered, was the holder, and the holder signed the agreement, the rule is not changed by the fact that another also signed it. Simpson v. Van Laningham, 286.

6. **Guarantee.** The fact that the makers of an agreement "guarantee" certain things does not of itself constitute the agreement a guaranty. The word may be used simply to give emphasis and not to change the plain character of the agreement. Ib.

7. **Negotiable Notes: Conditioned on Return of Stock: Failure to Return as Part of Defense.** Where negotiable notes, given for the purchase of certificates of stock of a corporation, indorsed in blank, attached to the notes and delivered with them to the payee, were accompanied by a concurrent dependent agreement that upon the maturity of the notes the certificates could be surrendered and the notes cancelled, and that agreement is set up as a defense to an action on the notes, the instructions may authorize a finding for defendant without requiring a finding that he returned the stock or relinquished his right to it, since the certificates were already in possession of the holder of the notes, and it was impossible for defendant to tender the physical return of the stock. Ib.

8. ——: ——: **Evidence of Demand for Return of Notes.** And under such circumstances, evidence that the maker demanded from the signers of the concurrent dependent agreement (the corporation and its president) the return of the notes, in accordance with the agreement, and being told they were in possession of a bank as transferee had his attorney to demand them from the bank, was competent to show an effort on defendant's part to comply with the agreement, as far as he could. Ib.

9. ——: ——: **Evidence of Election.** And evidence that, when defendant was approached by the attorney of the corporation on the theory that he was a stockholder, he announced that he had elected to surrender the stock and cancel the notes in accordance with the agreement, could not have prejudiced the rights of a holder of the notes with notice of the agreement. Ib.

CONVERSION.

Embezzlement: Ownership of Check. Where the loan company contracted to loan $3400 to a farmer, to be evidenced by his note. which was to be secured by a deed of trust on his land, and upon the receipt of the note and deed of trust executed by him caused the deed of trust to be recorded, and forwarded a check for the amount of the note less commission, payable to defendant, the agent who had negotiated the loan, the company parted with the title to the check, and the nominal ownership passed to defendant; and it thereafter became his duty to either indorse it to the farmer, or convert it into cash and pay the proceeds to him, or apply it to the discharge of a prior lien for which the money had been borrowed; but as it was indorsed and placed to defendant's credit in the bank, his act became embezzlement of the money when he drew it out and without the farmer's consent converted it to his own use. State v. McWilliams, 437.

CONVEYANCES.

CORPORATIONS.

CORPORATIONS—Continued.

ticles of incorporation without being specifically authorized to do so by the board of directors or by a vote of its stockholders, is not allowed. In re Mingo Dr. Dist., 268.

6. ———: ———: **Attorney in Fact.** Likewise, an objection by other landowners only, that a certain person who held a power of attorney to act generally for a corporation which owned certain lands in the proposed district had no authority to sign the articles, is disallowed. Ib.

7. **Negotiable Note: Notice of Infirmities.** Notes made payable to the maker and indorsed in blank by him become payable to bearer and negotiable by delivery; and a transferee before maturity with actual knowledge of a concurrent dependent agreement, and a transferee after maturity without actual knowledge, take the notes with notice of the agreement and that it makes them non-payable. Simpson v. Van Laningham, 286.

8. ———: **Concurrent Dependent Agreement.** A negotiable promissory note and a concurrent collateral agreement, connected by direct reference or necessary implication, the stipulations of which are mutual and dependent, are to be construed together as one entire contract; and a transferee of the note after maturity, without actual knowledge of the agreement, cannot recover, if the agreement, when so construed, bars a recovery. Ib.

9. ———: ———: **Option to Surrender Stock for Notes.** The maker of negotiable notes received a concurrent written agreement, signed by a corporation and its president, reciting that the maker had purchased one hundred shares of the capital stock of the company, for which he had given his two notes in settlement, due in six months, and guaranteeing that the maker, at their maturity might, at his option, surrender the stock, whereupon the notes would be cancelled and returned to him. The certificates of stock, indorsed in blank, were attached to the notes, and the notes were transferred to a bank, whose cashier had full actual knowledge of the agreement. Shortly afterwards the bank went into the hands of a receiver, who, after the maturity of the notes, sold them to plaintiff. *Held*, that the notes and agreement did not constitute independent contracts, but they are dependent, and the agreement constitutes a defense to an action on the notes; and since the payee of the notes, when the agreement was delivered, was the holder, and the holder signed the agreement, the rule is not changed by the fact that another also signed it. Ib.

10. **Guarantee.** The fact that the makers of an agreement "guarantee" certain things does not of itself constitute the agreement a guaranty. The word may be used simply to give emphasis and not to change the plain character of the agreement. Ib.

11. **Negotiable Notes: Conditioned on Return of Stock: Failure to Return as Part of Defense.** Where negotiable notes, given for the purchase of certificates of stock of a corporation, indorsed in blank, attached to the notes and delivered with them to the payee, were accompanied by a concurrent dependent agreement that upon the maturity of the notes the certificates could be surrendered and the notes cancelled, and that agreement is set up as a defense to an action on the notes, the instructions may authorize a finding for defendant without requiring a finding that he returned the stock or relinquished his right to it,

CORPORATIONS—Continued.

CORPORATIONS—Continued.

prior to the adoption of the Constitution of 1875, and passed by successive mortgages and foreclosure sales to said present company, cannot by a legislative act be deprived thereof, for such right does not pertain to police powers, but is a contract right. State ex rel. v. Roach, 300.

19. ———: **Permission to Do Business: Retroactive Statute.** The Act of 1913, Laws 1913, p. 179, declaring that no railroad corporation, except one incorporated under the laws of this State, shall be permitted to do an intrastate business in this State, does not have a retroactive operation, and does not apply to a foreign corporation which has succeeded to the rights of another railroad company which long prior to the enactment of said statute had been granted by the State the right to own and operate a railroad in this State and to carry on an intrastate railroad business, and the Secretary of State cannot lawfully withhold from said corporation a permit or license to do business in Missouri. That act cannot contravene existing rights lawfully granted by the State. It applies to railroads built subsequently to its enactment, and does not affect those then operating in the State.

Held, by WOODSON, C. J., dissenting, that the Act of 1913 applies simply to intrastate business and railroads, and the Constitution (Art. 12, sec. 18) retained jurisdiction over so much of a consolidated railroad as is in this State. Ib.

20. ———: ———: **Due Process: Impairment of Contract.** To hold that a foreign corporation which by purchase has acquired the railroad of another company and its franchise right to do business in this State, acquired prior to the enactment of the Act of 1913, Laws 1913, p. 179, cannot do a railroad business in this State, would be to take valuable property rights without due process of law, and to impair the obligation of contracts, not only of said company, but of all other foreign corporations now owning and operating railroads under franchises granted prior to its enactment. Ib.

21. **Jurisdiction: Non-Resident Corporation: Service.** For the reasons stated in the minority opinion of the St. Louis Court of Appeals, 175 Mo. App. l. c. 679 et seq., in this case, the judgment is reversed, and the cause remanded, in order to give plaintiff opportunity to obtain valid service on defendant corporation. McMenamy Inv. Co. v. Catering Co., 340.

22. **Payment for Stock: Services Rendered By Financial Agent.** Where nothing was paid in money by its stockholders at the time the Illinois corporation was organized, but the plan of its incorporators was to issue the company's bonds to the full amount of its capitalization and use the money derived from their sale in the construction of the electric light plant, it cannot be held that one of them, who, as the company's financial agent, indorsed its notes upon which money was obtained for the first work of construction, which notes when the bonds were sold were paid out of the proceeds, thereby, as against general creditors of the company, paid for the stock issued to him in services rendered the company. Schroeder v. Edwards, 459.

23. **Unpaid Stock: Creditor Participating In Wrong.** A stockholder who participated in the transaction whereby the services of a financial agent were received and accepted by the corporation in full payment of stock issued to such agent, cannot be heard to say that the stock is not full paid, even though he has loaned

CORPORATIONS—Continued.

money to the company, and cannot hold said agent as a stockholder as for unpaid subscriptions on his stock, to satisfy a judgment against the company in the amount of the money loaned. [Following Meyer v. Min. & Mill. Co., 192 Mo. 162, and distinguishing Gillet v. Chicago Title & Trust Co., 230 Ill. 373.] Ib.

24. **Private Banks: Corporations Sole.** Since a private bank, though owned by a single individual, is by statute granted powers and privileges not possessed by natural persons or partnerships, and possesses only such powers and privileges as are granted by statute, and cannot exist until it has complied with these statutes, and since the statutes completely segregate the bank's assets and business from its owner's private assets and business, it is a legal entity, a corporation sole, under the provisions of the Constitution (Art. 12, sec. '11) declaring that the term corporation "shall be construed to include all joint stock companies or associations having any powers or privileges not possessed by individuals or partnerships." If owned by more than one person, it is still a separate entity or *quasi*-corporation. [Disapproving Gupton v. Carr, 147 Mo. App. 105.] State ex rel. v. Sage, 493.

25. ———: ———: **Notwithstanding Words of Statute.** The words of the statute (Sec. 1116, R. S. 1909) declaring that the owner or owners of a private bank may carry on a banking business "without being incorporated," were used to distinguish private banks from banks incorporated under the general banking laws; they were not intended to declare that a private bank, organized under the statutes and conducted according to their requirements, is not a separate legal entity, or a *quasi*-corporation, or a corporation sole. Ib.

26. **Religious: Not to Hold Title, Etc.** Neither the Legislature nor the courts can establish a religious corporation except its charter shows that it is created only to hold title to real estate for church edifices, parsonages and cemeteries; and a corporation organized for purposes other than those alone is not a religious corporation within the meaning of the Missouri Constitution. ·

Held, by GRAVES, J., dissenting, that if the circuit court in entering a pro forma decree attempted to and did organize a religious corporation, its act was futile, and the chartered company has no standing in a court to recover real estate devised to it; and to determine whether it is a religious corporation resort should be made, first, to its charter, and if that is ambiguous or uncertain in meaning, then, to extraneous proof. Helpers of the Holy Souls v. Law, 667.

27. **Valid Benevolent Corporation.** Held, under the facts stated in the opinion, that the plaintiff is not a religious corporation, but is a valid benevolent corporation under the statutes of Missouri. And that the fact that, in addition to the primary purposes and objects of practical benevolence set forth in its charter, it had the incidental right to impart religious instruction did not prevent this suit for property devised to it, since this particular franchise could only be attacked in a direct suit by the State. *Held*, by GRAVES, J., dissenting, that a corporation whose charter recites that "the purpose and object of said corporation shall be to maintain the establishment now under our charge in said city known as 'The society of the Helpers of Holy Souls' and also others that we may hereafter establish; and in connection with same, to gratuitously visit the

CORPORATIONS—Continued.

sick poor daily, irrespective of creed or color, rendering them every assistance in our power by nursing them in their homes; to organize our convent meetings and sewing classes for the working class and poor children and impart religious instruction to same," etc., and which "is composed, exclusively, of members of the religious order of the Roman Catholic Church known as 'The Helpers of the Holy Souls in Purgatory.' " the purpose of said "religious order" being an exemplification of the tenets and doctrines of the church concerning souls in Purgatory, is a religious corporation, and cannot be held to be a mere benevolent association. Helpers of the Holy Souls v. Law, 667.

28. ———: **Devise to Unincorporated Society.** There is no principle of law which forbids a charitable gift to an unincorporated religious body or any of its orders. Even if an attempted incorporation must be held to be a religious corporation and a devise to it of real estate for that reason be invalid, yet if the unmistakable devise is to a known unincorporated society which has the same name as that of the attempted incorporation, it will be upheld, and the property can be recovered by the society's trustees. Ib.

COURTS.

1. **Remarks: No Objection.** Unless there is an objection directed to an objectionable remark made by the trial court, it cannot be reviewed on appeal. State v. Evans, 163.

2. **Prohibition: Circuit Courts.** The Supreme Court is given authority by the Constitution to prohibit, by its writ of prohibition, circuit courts and other inferior tribunals from exercising jurisdiction which they do not legally have. Ramsey v. Huck, 333.

3. **Administrator: Removal for Cause: Determination a Judicial Matter.** The probate court must determine from the facts whether the person nominated executor in the will has renounced his right to be appointed, and in doing so exercises a judicial function; his act must not be arbitrary, or an abuse of power, or wholly unsupported by facts showing a renunciation; but if such facts are present, the appointment of another cannot be annulled by mandamus brought by the named executor to compel his appointment. State ex rel. v. Holtcamp, 412.

4. **Remanding Cause: Confining Issue.** Where all issues in an equity case except one have on appeal been settled, the court instead of remanding the cause generally, may remand it with directions that upon a retrial the case be confined to the one issue upon which the evidence at the first trial was insufficient to support a decree for plaintiff. Schroeder v. Edwards, 459.

5. **Private Bank: Insolvency: Priority of Jurisdiction of State and Federal Court.** The taking possession of a private bank by the Bank Commissioner is the first step in the bringing of a suit for the appointment of a receiver, and that step gives the circuit court jurisdiction of the cause, and a subsequent application for a receiver and the appointment of one cannot be said to be *coram non judice* because of the fact that, before the receiver is appointed, a petition asking that the bank's owner be adjudged a bankrupt is filed in the Federal court. State ex rel. v. Sage, 493.

6. ———: ———: ———: **Bankrupt Proceedings Against Owner.** Besides, the filing of a petition in the Federal court, asking that

COURTS—Continued.

the owner of a private bank be individually adjudged a bankrupt, does not place the assets of his said bank *in custodia legis* —certainly not to the extent of depriving the State court of its jurisdiction to decide whether or not the creditors of the bank are entitled to be paid out of its assets before they can be used to satisfy its owner's individual creditors. Ib.

7. **Conduct of Judge: Testy Remarks to Witness.** Frequent testy remarks made by the court to appellant while he was on the witness stand, though seemingly improper in the cold record, will not be held, in the absence of a showing of the conduct and manner of the witness, to be prejudicial error; especially, where the court cautioned the jury not to consider his words and manner towards the witness. Buck v. Buck, 644.

8. **Reopening Case: Discretion.** The reopening of the case after both sides have closed and a peremptory instruction has been offered by plaintiff, to permit the introduction of other te..imony, is a matter largely within the discretion of the trial court, and does not constitute reversible error unless the discretion has been abused, to the injury of the losing party. Ib.

See, also, Justice of the Peace.

COURTS OF APPEALS.

1. **Judgment: Finality: Setting Aside at Subsequent Term.** After a final judgment has been rendered at one term, the court, in the absence of a statute to the contrary and of a pending motion or other proper step to carry the case over to the next term, has no jurisdiction, at such next term, to modify or annul that judgment. State ex rel. v. Ellison, 321.

2. ————: ————: **After Motion for Rehearing Overruled.** Where the Court of Appeals affirmed the judgment of the trial court, and a motion for rehearing having been timely filed was overruled on the last day of the term and an order was made on said day giving all parties ten days in which "to file motions in cases ruled on this day," the judgment was a finality, and the Court of Appeals had no power at the next term to sustain a motion filed at said next term to set aside the order overruling the motion for a rehearing, nor did it have any power on the last day of the term to make the order extending the time to the next term in which to file a motion to set aside said order, but all its orders and judgments made at such subsequent term were null and void. Ib.

3. ————: ————: **Certification of Cause to Supreme Court.** The Court of Appeals has no power to certify a cause to the Supreme Court at a subsequent term after its judgment therein has become a finality. The Constitution requires such transfer to be made at "the same term" at which the judgment is rendered "and not afterwards." Ib.

4. **Abstract: Transfer to Supreme Court.** When a case reaches the Supreme Court by transfer from a court of appeals, on the ground that a constitutional question is involved, the rule is not to scrutinize too closely the abstract of the record, lest appellant be caught unwittingly between the rules of that court and of this and thereby be pinched out of any appeal at all. Wolf v. Harris, 405.

CREDITORS. See Debtor and Creditor.

CRIMINAL LAW.

1. **Instructions: No Assignment in Motion.** Whether or not it was error to give an instruction on murder in the second degree, or to fail to give an instruction on involuntary manslaughter in the fourth degree, or to give an instruction concerning the bad feeling existing between defendant's and decedent's families, or to give an instruction on manslaughter in the fourth degree, will not be reviewed on appeal, where none of these matters was assigned as error in the motion for a new trial. State v. Coff, 14.

2. **Accidental Homicide: Instruction Required.** Where the evidence for defendant tended to show that his participation in the combat was merely that of a person defending himself, and that he was, therefore, engaged in a lawful act; that while in the act of defending himself, the deceased grabbed him by the throat, and in order to protect himself he shoved deceased away, causing him to stagger and fall; and that in the fall deceased's head struck the curb-stone and received the fatal wound, the statute (Sec. 4452, R. S. 1909) declaring that homicide shall be excusable when committed "upon sudden combat, without any undue advantage being taken and without any dangerous weapon being used, and not done in a cruel and unusual manner" required the court to give an instruction on accidental homicide; and a failure to do so, where the point was properly raised at the trial and preserved for review, was reversible error. Ib.

3. **Sodomy: Covered by Statutes, Etc.** Notwithstanding section 4725, Revised Statutes 1909, was repealed and re-enacted, with an amendment, in 1911, the crime of sodomy may be committed by a man by inserting his sexual organ in the mouth of a woman. State v. Pfeifer, 23.

4. **Evidence of Other Crimes: Res Gestae.** Where the information charges sodomy *per os* it is not error to admit evidence tending to show sodomy *per anum* where the proof shows both acts were so connected as to show both were parts of the *res gestae*. Ib.

5. ——: ——: **Restricted by Instruction: No Exception.** Nor can an assignment that an instruction should have been given at the trial restricting the evidence of the crime not charged be considered on appeal where no exception was saved to the giving or refusal of any instruction, or to the giving of the whole instructions. Ib.

6. ——: ——: ——: **Not Required.** And where the two crimes are parts of the *res gestae*, and testimony tending to prove that one not charged is therefore admissible, no instruction as to the evidentiary weight of the testimony or the purpose for which it may be considered is required. Ib.

7. **Defendant: Cross-Examination.** In view of the plain wording of the statute. (Sec. 5242, R. S. 1909) forbidding them, questions asked defendant in cross-examination upon matters neither touched upon nor growing out of his examination in chief, are presumed to be prejudicial error, unless the contrary is made to appear; and where he is compelled to state all his movements the night of the crime, his acquaintanceship with two other persons who had committed a crime against the same woman two hours before he and they are charged with having committed a similar crime against her, and whether or not he and they had been companions since their school days

CRIMINAL LAW—Continued.

and frequenters of the same saloon—all matters not touched upon in his examination in chief and brought out for the purpose of corroborating a police officer—the questions were not only unwarranted but were prejudicial. Ib.

8. ———; ———: **One Law for Innocent and Guilty.** There can be but one law for the trial of the innocent and guilty; and notwithstanding the court may be of the opinion that the evidence is sufficient to warrant a verdict of guilty, a plain statute forbidding the cross-examination of a defendant concerning matters wholly outside his examination in chief must be applied to all defendants alike. The Constitution has not ordained that apparent guilt is the sole condition of affirmance by the Supreme Court of a verdict of guilty. Ib.

9. **Carnal Knowledge: Evidence of Prosecutrix's Age** Where the statute requires the prosecutrix to be under fifteen years of age in order to constitute sexual intercourse with her rape, proof that she was not fifteen at the time should be satisfactory and if possible her testimony thereto should be corroborated. State v. Arnold, 33.

10. ———. ———: **Family Record.** Where the prosecutrix has testified that she was at the time of the carnal knowledge under fifteen years of age, and that her knowledge of her age was obtained from her parents and a family record, and the book being produced testified that it had been changed, the record, showing the date of birth of herself and brothers and sisters, should be admitted in evidence, and it was error to reject it, for three reasons: first, it was evidence of her true age; second, it was competent as tending to show that her statement of her age, based as she said, on said record, was false; and, third, it would tend to contradict her statement that the record, which, admittedly, for sometime had been in defendant's possession, had been changed. Ib.

11. ———: **Pregnancy: Year After Offense.** Where the trial for rape occurs more than twelve months after the prosecutrix was fifteen years of age, testimony by her and her physician that at the trial she was pregnant, and by her that her pregnancy was due to sexual intercourse with defendant, is incompetent, and if admitted is reversible error. Ib.

12. ———: **Continuance: Age of Prosecutrix.** Ordinarily in a prosecution for carnal knowledge of a female under fifteen years of age, where her age is a vital issue, an application for a continuance, based on the absence of her grandmother, sick and unable to attend the trial, who, if present, would testify that at the time of the offense she was over fifteen, should not be denied. Ib.

13. **Carnal Knowledge: Evidence of Good Reputation.** In a prosecution for carnal knowledge of a female of previous chaste character, testimony to the effect that her general reputation for chastity in the community in which she lived, prior to the alleged occurrence, was good, is admissible. [Refusing to follow *dictum* in State v. Kelley, 191 Mo. l. c. 691.] State v. Taylor, 41.

14. **Specific Assignment: All Law of Case.** An assignment in the motion for a new trial that the court failed to instruct the jury as to all the law arising upon the issues in the case, which does not specify upon what point the court failed to instruct, does not raise a point for appellate review. Ib.

CRIMINAL LAW—Continued.

15. **Carnal Knowledge: Issuable Matters.** In a prosecution for carnal knowledge of an unmarried female of previous chaste character between the ages of fifteen and eighteen years, the question of whether or not she consented to the acts of sexual intercourse is not material to the issue; and even though her testimony tending to show that she did not consent seems unbelievable, that does not affect a verdict of guilty. The material issues are (a) that she was an unmarried female between the ages of fifteen and eighteen years, that (b) defendant had sexual intercourse with her and (c) that prior to the act charged she was of chaste character. State v. Taylor, 41.

16. **Arraignment: Appeal.** The failure of the record to show either an arraignment or a plea will not, of itself, entitle defendant to a reversal, the record also failing to show that any objection was made at any time to a lack of arraignment or plea until the case reached the appellate court. State v. Allen, 49.

17. **Information: Amendment of Statute After Crime: Substantial Rights of Defendant.** It is error for the information to charge that the age of the prosecutrix was under fifteen years and that of defendant above seventeen years, in the language of the amendment of the statute which raised the age of consent from fourteen to fifteen years and that of defendant from sixteen to seventeen years, where the act of carnal knowledge was committed before the amendment went into effect; but under the Statute of Jeofails the error is not reversible, unless it tends to the prejudice of the substantial rights of the defendant on the merits; and it does not so prejudice those rights, where the evidence clearly establishes that the prosecutrix was at the time of the alleged crime above fifteen years of age and the defendant above seventeen. Ib.

18. **Change of Venue: Trial With Application Pending.** Where the record fails to show anything on the subject except the bare fact that an application for a change of venue was filed, it will not be held on appeal that the case was tried while a formal and sufficient application was pending. Ib.

19. ——: ——: **Matter of Exception.** Complaint that the case was tried while an application for a change of venue was pending is a matter of exception, to be saved for review in the bill of exceptions. Ib.

20. ——: **Jurisdiction of Another Judge: Agreement upon Special Judge.** Where the record shows that an application for a change of venue was filed and that a judge of another circuit was called by the regular judge to sit in the case and "was on the bench," and tried the case without objection, it will be presumed, in the absence of a record showing to the contrary, that both the state and defendant waived the privilege of selecting a special judge; and, aided by the presumption of right action on the part of a court of general jurisdiction, it will be *held* that the judge so called in had authority to try the case. Ib.

21. **Evidence: Impeachment: Carnal Knowledge: Offer to Settle For Money.** Evidence in a prosecution for carnal knowledge of a female under the age of consent that the prosecutrix proposed to defendant or his attorney, to leave the State and not appear at the trial if money were paid her, and that her uncle after a

CRIMINAL LAW—Continued.

conference with her and her mother and in pursuance to an understanding with them hunted up defendant and proposed to him, and later proposed to defendant's attorney, that if money were paid to him he would take prosecutrix out of the State and see to it that she did not appear at the trial, is competent for the purpose of impeaching both the prosecutrix and her mother as witnesses to the main fact of sexual intercourse, and the exclusion of such testimony is reversible error. Ib.

22. **Failure to Support Wife: No Element of Vagrancy.** Section 4789, Revised Statutes 1909, declaring, among other things, that "every able-bodied married man who shall neglect or refuse to provide for the support of his family . . . shall be deemed a vagrant" and upon conviction punished by imprisonment or fine, is a statute defining vagrancy, and cannot be used to enforce a civil liability; nor is a husband who honestly tries to obtain work and is unable to procure sufficiently remunerative employment to properly support his family, a criminal or a vagrant, nor can he be punished under said statute. [Disapproving Marolf v. Marolf, 191 Mo. App. 239, so far, if at all, as it conflicts with this holding.] State v. Burton, 61.

23. ——: ——: **Placing Wife With Sister to Board.** A husband who at a time when he was receiving sixty dollars per month put his wife and child with her sister under an agreement to pay her twenty dollars per month for their board and lodging, and paid the amount regularly for three months, and who having lost his position after two or three weeks' effort to secure employment obtained a position at a hotel at five dollars a week, cannot be convicted for failure during the next three months to pay to his wife or her sister any part of the five dollars, his purpose being to discharge his obligation to his wife's sister as soon as he was able. Ib.

24. ——: ——: **Wife With Money.** The gift of one thousand dollars by the wife to her sister within the time her husband was unable to obtain remunerative employment simply has a tendency to show the wife was not in destitute circumstances. Ib.

25. **Remarks of Counsel: Preserved for Review.** Where defendant's counsel, in his objection to argument made to the jury by the State's counsel, repeats the statement made by said counsel and states his reason therefor, and the court by his ruling, accepts the repetition as a true reiteration of what had been said, the ruling, being excepted to, is for review on appeal, without any further preservation in the bill of exceptions than the statement and objection of appellant's counsel and the ruling and remarks of the court, and the exception. State v. Evans, 163.

26. ——: **Weak Evidence.** Argument of counsel to the jury, assigned as prejudicial to appellant, is to be examined in the light of the facts of the particular case. Where the evidence of defendant's guilt is weak, the offense charged is one which decent men abhor, and there is no testimony pertaining to a fact which reasonable men would expect to be developed, remarks of counsel for the State, either in their opening statement or in their argument to the jury, by which such lacking testimony is attempted to be supplied, may alone constitute reversible error. Ib.

27. ——: **Seduction: No Request for Fulfillment of Promise to Marry: Supplied by Attorney.** The fact that, after prosecutrix

CRIMINAL LAW—Continued.

discovered her pregnancy as the result of an admitted sexual relationship, she frequently kept company with defendant in the presence of her and his relatives and requested him to marry her to shield her from its consequences, but at no time suggested or claimed a reparation on account of a promise to marry, there being no legal impediment or other obstacle in the way of such a marriage, tends to impeach her testimony that there had been such a promise, and in view of her unsatisfactory testimony as to the fact of an engagement was a matter of grave importance for the jury in determining whether or not her testimony was true; and remarks made by the State's counsel, in his opening statement that "the young girl who was wronged by this young man has solicited and begged and importuned him to marry her and give this bright little baby a father and a name," and repeated in substance in the argument to the jury, the effect being, whether intended or not, to break the force of the significant omission, and to supply the lack of it, was reversible error.

Held, by REVELLE, J., dissenting, that it is but common knowledge and ordinary human experience that no juror will sit through a trial of a seduction case without the thought that the girl, whose shame and disgrace would be lessened by marriage, was anxious to and did what she could to bring about the marriage, and the statement of counsel could only have hastened the thought; and, in this case, it was not prejudicial, because the jury knew the defendant had not married her, and counsel's statement that she begged him to do so and his refusal, if effective at all, tended only to corroborate his testimony that he had never promised to marry her at any time. State v. Evans, 163.

28. Seduction: Evidence: Conclusions and Opinions. In a prosecution for seduction under promise of marriage, the father of prosecutrix should not be permitted to state his conclusions and give his opinions as to the relations between her and defendant, such as, "He treated her like a sweetheart," "He seemed to think a good deal of her."

Held, by REVELLE, J., dissenting, that the testimony was not reversible error, since the father's knowledge and information upon which the conclusions were based were completely developed, and the jury were fully capable of determining whether or not the conclusions expressed were warranted. Ib.

29. ——: ——: ——: Estimates of Others. A voluntary conclusion of prosecutrix's father, drawn from a conversation with some neighbors of defendant, that "from the way they talked about him they had no use for him," is not competent evidence.

Held, by REVELLE, J., dissenting, that, as the statement came out in connection with his explanation of certain matters concerning which he had been interrogated on cross-examination and no motion was made to strike it out, the trial court cannot be convicted of error. Ib.

30. ——: ——: ——: ——: No Motion to Strike Out. The usual rule is that a motion to strike out is prerequisite to a review of a conclusion voluntarily injected into the case by a witness; but where the trial court, upon an objection being made, ruled on the point on its merits, without such motion, the point is thereby preserved for review on appeal.

Held, by REVELLE, J., dissenting, that the trial court, on an objection being made by simply directing attorneys to "go

CRIMINAL LAW—Continued.

ahead" did not rule on the merits, and it cannot be anticipated what his ruling would have been had a motion to strike out been made. Ib.

31. ———: **Remarks of Court: No Objection.** Unless there is an objection directed to an objectionable remark made by the trial court, it cannot be reviewed on appeal. Ib.

32. ———: **Admission of Promise: Corroboration.** The promise of marriage must precede seduction; and while testimony of a witness that defendant, eight months after the alleged seduction, admitted that "he did promise to marry" prosecutrix, is competent and is evidence upon which an instruction on corroboration may be based, if the admission refers to a time preceding the alleged seduction, it is neither corroboration nor admissible if the admission fixes no time when the promise was made. Ib.

33. **Instruction: Weight to Be Given Defendant's Testimony.** *Held*, by BLAIR, J., with whom WOODSON, C. J., and GRAVES, J., concur, that, where the usual general instruction pertaining to the credibility of witnesses is given, it is error to give the usual cautionary instruction as to the weight and credibility to be given to defendant's testimony, telling them, among other things, to take into consideration the fact that he is the defendant and on trial, for several reasons: *first*, it is palpable comment on the evidence; *second*, it is violative of the principle that the mere fact that defendant is charged with a crime is no evidence of his guilt; *third*, similar instructions have always been adjudged erroneous in civil cases, and for the reason that liberty or life is more valuable than property, it should be likewise held to be prejudicial in a prosecution for a crime; *fourth*, the statute (Sec. 5242, R. S. 1909) which is supposed to authorize it and which provides that when defendant offers himself as a witness, the fact that he is the defendant "may be shown for the purpose of affecting the credibility of such witness," merely lays down a rule of evidence and cannot be regarded as justifying the giving of an instruction which specifically singles out and designates the credence to be given any particular one among those the statute renders competent as witnesses; and, *fifth*, while there may be cases, such as upon a plea of guilty, in which such an instruction may be considered harmless, in most cases, especially where the State's case upon material issues is inherently weak, it does harm to give it. *Held*, by REVELLE, J., that, while the instruction should never be given, it does not constitute reversible error where there is, as in this case, no doubt of defendant's guilt. *Held*, by FARIS, J., dissenting, that, while conceding some of the reasons given for the impropriety of the instruction to be sound, and that the giving of it subserves no useful purpose, it is nevertheless buttressed by a solemn statute (Sec. 5242, R. S. 1909) and has for more than forty years been held not to be reversible error, and to now hold it to be such would (1) cause much uncertainty in the law, and (2) if it is to be eliminated that should be done by the Legislature; and (3) the instruction but expresses the law as declared by the statute, and it cannot of itself be reversible error to tell the jury by an instruction what the law is. Ib.

34. **Information: Sufficiency of Charge.** In criminal pleadings nothing material can be left to intendment or implication; and where a crime is.created by statute the charge must be such as to specifically bring the accused within its material words. State v. Wade, 249.

CRIMINAL LAW—Continued.

35. ———: ———: Aided by Proof. The State cannot prove
what it has not charged; it cannot by incompetent evidence supply an absent allegation. Even though the evidence establishes
an offense forbidden by the statute, a conviction cannot stand
if the allegations are insufficient to point out any crime denounced by it. State v. Wade, 249.

36. ———: Ejusdem Generis: Gambling Device. When an enumeration of certain specified things in a statute is followed by
general words or phrases, they are deemed to mean things
of the same class and kind as those enumerated, and do not include things wholly different from those specifically mentioned.
Section 4750, Revised Statutes 1909, condemning the setting up
and keeping of certain enumerated gambling devices, or "any
kind of gambling table or gambling device, adapted, devised,
and designed for the purpose of playing any game of chance for
money," is not broad enough to include all gambling devices regardless of their character, but does include all those of a kindred nature and similar kind to those enumerated. Ib.

37. ———: ———: ———: Craps Table: Must Be Described.
A table, duly marked and arranged for the purpose, on which
the game of craps is played by means of dice for money or
property, is within the purview of the statute; but it is not
specifically enumerated therein, and therefore the rule of
ejusdem generis applies, and the information must contain sufficient averments showing it to belong to the enumerated class.
An information simply charging that the defendant set up and
kept "a certain table and gambling device commonly called a
crap table," with no allegation defining a crap table, or of what
it consists, or how designed, or how and by what means the
game of craps is played, is not sufficient to support a conviction, even though the evidence establishes the fact that the
tables which were operated by defendant are of the class forbidden by the statute. Nor is the general allegation that the
crap table was "a gambling device adapted, devised and designed for the purpose of playing games of chance for money
and property" sufficiently descriptive of a crap table to supply
an allegation necessary to show that such table is of a kindred
nature and similar kind to one of those enumerated in the statute. [Overruling on this point State v. Rosenblatt, 185 Mo.
114; State v. Locket, 188 Mo. 415; State v. Holden, 203 Mo.
581; State v. Lee, 228 Mo. 480.] Ib.

38. Gambling Device: Commonly Known: Proof: Variance. Where
the information charges that the gambling table which defendant set up is one "commonly known as a crap table," the State
must show that there is a table commonly so known, and that
it was this particular kind of table that defendant set up and
kept; and where all the witnesses testify that the tables which
defendant maintained and operated were not of the kind which
they commonly knew as crap tables, and that a crap table is of
a radically different design and construction, a conviction cannot stand. Ib.

39. ———: Location: Street Number: Variance. The information
charged that defendant set up a craps table "at 118½ North
Fifth Street." The evidence tended to prove that defendant
set up gambling tables in the basement of premises designated
as 118 North Fifth Street, the sole available entrance thereto
being under a barber shop at said number, from which initial
point a tunnel, equipped with a series of automatic doors, led

CRIMINAL LAW—Continued.

to the room where the tables were; that the premises and entrance were commonly known as 118½ North Fifth Street;
that defendant's mail in accordance with his direction, was addressed to 118½ North Fifth Street; and that when arrested
defendant gave that number as his address.

> Held, by REVELLE, J., with whom FARIS and BLAIR, JJ.,
> concur, that there is no fatal variance between the allega-
> tion and proof; that it was unnecessary to allege the exact
> location, since it did not relate to a constitutive part of
> the offense, and if a variance at all it is cured by Sec. 5114,
> R. S. 1909.

> Held, by GRAVES, J., with whom WOODSON, C. J., concurs,
> that the variance is not cured by the statute, but is fatal
> to the judgment. WALKER and BOND, JJ., do not con-
> cur with either opinion. Ib.

CRIMINAL LAW—Continued.

place of trial and that she had agreed to attend, the trial court would be justified in granting a continuance, if the allegation therein of defendant's recent knowledge of what her testimony would be bears the impress of truth; but if the facts reveal that he did know what her testimony would be, then proper diligence required him to take her deposition, and having failed to do that the trial court did not abuse its discretion in denying the application. State v. McWilliams, 437.

46. **Embezzlement: Agency of Loan Agent.** Where the borrower called at defendant's office to employ him to secure a loan of $3400, and gave him a note for $127.50 for his services in that behalf, and in addition signed an order directed to the loan company in which he requested that the proceeds of the loan be paid to defendant and in which he said he thereby appointed defendant his agent to settle with the company for said loan, and the loan company, after deducting its own commission, sent a check payable to defendant for the balance, the defendant was the agent of the borrower, in all that was necessary to establish the relation of agency, in a prosecution for having embezzled the proceeds of the check. Ib.

47. ——: ——: **Circumstances.** Circumstances arising out of a transaction, even in establishing the fact that defendant, charged with embezzlement, was the borrower's agent, are sometimes as strong in probative force as sworn testimony. Ib.

48. ——: **Ownership of Check.** Where the loan company contracted to loan $3400 to a farmer, to be evidenced by his note, which was to be secured by a deed of trust on his land, and upon the receipt of the note and deed of trust executed by him caused the deed of trust to be recorded, and forwarded a check for the amount of the note less commission, payable to defendant, the agent who had negotiated the loan, the company parted with the title to the check, and the nominal ownership passed to defendant; and it thereafter became his duty to either indorse it to the farmer, or convert it into cash and pay the proceeds to him, or apply it to the discharge of a prior lien for which the money had been borrowed; but as it was indorsed and placed to defendant's credit in the bank, his act became embezzlement of the money when he drew it out and without the farmer's consent converted it to his own use. Ib.

49. ——: **Felonious Intent: Concealment.** A defendant's felonious intent, in a charge of embezzling his principal's money, is to be measured by his acts; and it may be shown by his evasion of his principal, a concealment from him of the fact that he has received the money, and a neglect or refusal to account for it. Ib.

50. ——: ——: **Use of Money.** Where defendant is charged with embezzling money, in that he as the agent of a farmer undertook to borrow for him a sum of money to be used in paying off a farm mortgage, and when the check for the loan was sent to him it was deposited to his own credit in a bank and drawn out for his own personal uses, it is not error to permit an officer of the loan company to testify that defendant had not used the money in paying off the prior lien on the land, nor returned it to the company. Ib.

51. ——: ——: **Depositing Check.** Nor under such circumstances is it error to permit the State to show that the check payable to defendant's order and received by him was indorsed

CRIMINAL LAW—Continued,

and deposited to his credit in a bank, and later checked out by him. Ib.

52. ———: ———: **Other Loans.** Where the defendant was the agent of the borrower in a particular case and was authorized to receive the proceeds of the loan from a certain company, whatever relationship he may have sustained to that company in previous or subsequent like transactions can have no bearing upon the issue of whether he embezzled the money received by him in that case. Ib.

CROPS, DESTRUCTION OF. See Trespass.

DAMAGES.

1. **Trespass: Destruction of Fence: Loss of Pasture: Speculative Damages.** Plaintiff is entitled to the loss of grass in his pasture caused by the repeated destruction of his fence, whereby his cattle passed out of the pasture, and because of which fact and to prevent the cattle from continually escaping and destroying other parts of his premises he was compelled to confine them in another inclosure. Such damage is not remote and speculative. Sperry v. Hurd, 628.

2. ———: **Participation in Wrong: Acts of Encouragement, Etc.** In order that the owner of a farm may be legally responsible for the acts of his sons in destroying the fence which inclosed plaintiff's land, it was not necessary that such owner should have been personally present participating in the destructive acts of the sons, but if he aided, counselled and encouraged them to do the act, by words or deeds, he is liable; and such participation may be established by circumstantial evidence. And the evidence in this case was sufficient to justify the jury in inferring that the owner of the adjoining farm did advise or encourage his sons in the destruction of the fence. Ib.

3. ———: **Excessive Verdict: Destruction of Fences: $7500 Exemplary Damages.** Exemplary damages cannot be accurately measured; but the character and standing of the parties, the malice with which the act was done, and the financial condition of the defendant are elements which should be taken into consideration, and the amount may be such as will serve, by way of example and punishment, to deter the commission of other like acts. It is *held* in this case that a verdict of $510 for actual damages for the destruction of defendant's fences, whereby he lost the grass of an eighty-acre pasture and his cattle escaped into and destroyed his five-acre orchard, was not excessive, but that a judgment of $7500 for exemplary damages is excessive by $6500. Ib.

DEBTOR AND CREDITOR.

1. **Corporation: Unpaid Stock: Creditor Participating in Wrong.** A stockholder who participated in the transaction whereby the services of a financial agent were received and accepted by the corporation in full payment of stock issued to such agent, cannot be heard to say that the stock is not full paid, even though he has loaned money to the company, and cannot hold said agent as a stockholder as for unpaid subscriptions on his stock, to satisfy a judgment against the company in the amount of the money loaned. [Following Meyer v. Min. & Mill. Co., 192 Mo. 162, and distinguishing Gillett v. Chicago Title & Trust Co., 230 Ill. 373.] Schroeder v. Edwards, 459.

DEBTOR AND CREDITOR—Continued.

.2. **Private Banks: Assets and Rights of Creditors: Power of State Court to Construe Own Laws.** This court has the constitutional power to construe all constitutional provisions and legislative acts of this State applicable to private banks and bankers organized and existing under its laws, and to decide to whom the assets of an insolvent bank belong, and the priority of the rights of creditors thereto. State ex rel. v. Sage, 493.

3. ———: ———: **Application of Assets.** The assets of a private bank, belonging to a single individual, belong to the bank, and upon its insolvency should be used to pay its creditors, and if any surplus remains after they are paid, it should be used in paying the owner's individual creditors, if he too, is insolvent or has been adjudged a bankrupt in the Federal court. Ib.

DEDICATION OF STREET. See Cities, 1 to 3.

DEFENDANT.

1. **Cross-Examination.** In view of the plain wording of the statute (Sec. 5242, R. S. 1909) forbidding them, questions asked defendant in cross-examination upon matters neither touched upon nor growing out of his examination in chief, are presumed to be prejudicial error, unless the contrary is made to appear; and where he is compelled to state all his movements the night of the crime, his acquaintanceship with two other persons who had committed a crime against the same woman two hours before he and they are charged with having committed a similar crime against her, and whether or not he and they had been companions since their school days and frequenters of the same saloon—all matters not touched upon in his examination in chief and brought out for the purpose of corroborating a police officer—the questions were not only unwarranted but were prejudicial. State v. Pfeifer, 23.

2. ———: **One Law for Innocent and Guilty.** There can be but one law for trial of the innocent and guilty; and notwithstanding the court may be of the opinion that the evidence is sufficient to warrant a verdict of guilty, a plain statute forbidding the cross-examination of a defendant concerning matters wholly outside his examination in chief must be applied to all defendants alike. The Constitution has not ordained that apparent guilt is the sole condition of affirmance by the Supreme Court of a verdict of guilty. Ib.

DESCENTS AND DISTRIBUTION.

1. **Voluntary Partition: Deed to Husband and Wife.** A deed in voluntary partition by a conduit to a daughter of the deceased owner and her husband, though seemingly a deed by the entirety, did not vest the husband with the title to the land described in the deed; but upon the daughter's death the entire title descended to her children or her other heirs, since in spite of said deed, the entire title to the tract designated had been inherited by the daughter from said deceased owner. Powell v. Powell, 117.

2. **Adopted Child: Right of Heirs to Inherit.** If an adopted child dies during the life of its adopting parent, leaving children, such children inherit as grandchildren upon the death of such adopting parent intestate. Bernero v. Goodwin, 427.

3. ———: ———: **Statute.** Section 1671, Revised Statutes 1909, providing that a person may, by deed, "adopt any child or chil-

DESCENTS AND DISTRIBUTION—Continued.

> dren as his or·her heir," by the use of the word "heir," and section 332, providing that the estate of an intestate shall descend "to his children, *or their descendants*," mean that the child of an adopting child who dies during the lifetime of the adopting parent, inherits from such adopting parent dying intestate. An adopted child is a child within the meaning of the descent laws, and the words in section 332 mean the same as if they had read that the estate shall descend "to his children (either natural-born or adopted), or their descendants." Ib.

4. ———: ———: **How Determined.** The rights of the natural child of the adopted child to claim a distributive share in the estate of the adopting parent is not limited solely to the adoption statutes and the deed of adoption, to the exclusion of all rights given by the statutes of descents, but those statutes lay down the general rules of inheritance, and the deed of adoption created the status of the adopted child,· or gave to him the status of an heir. Ib.

DESTRUCTION OF FENCES AND CROPS. **See Trespass.**

DEVISE TO UNINCORPORATED SOCIETY. **See Lands and Land Titles.**

DISABILITIES. **See Legal Capacity to Sue.**

DRAINAGE DISTRICT.

1. **Care in Procedure.** The statutes providing for the reclamation of waste lands necessarily involve such radical interference with the owner's control of his property and such a liberal exercise of the taxing power, as .to call for the utmost care in their preparation and execution. Elsberry Dr. Dist. v. Harris, 139.

2. **Jurisdiction: Notice: Personal Service.** The jurisdiction of the circuit court to extend the boundary lines of an existing drainage district, under the Act of 1913, is not dependent upon personal service upon resident owners of the land to be included. Neither the Constitution of Missouri nor of the United States requires a uniform method of obtaining jurisdiction of the persons of litigants, in either general or special proceedings. A notice by publication in the language of the statute "to all persons interested," is sufficient. Ib.

3. **Right to extend Boundaries: Must be Shown by Record: Judicial Notice.** The right of a drainage district to extend its boundaries so as to include other lands subject to overflow must be found in the record at the trial. Its mere corporate existence does not prove its cause of action in such case. The court cannot take judicial notice of its original plan of reclamation and all proceedings of the company connected therewith. Ib.

4. **Inclusion of Other Lands Not Benefited.** The statutes do not authorize an organized drainage district to so extend its boundaries as to include within the district other lands which do not need reclamation and protection from water. Unless they are beneficially affected and there is some common interest between them and those of the existing district, they cannot be included against the will and protest of their owners. A drainage district can neither go outside the object of its organization to force upon owners of adjoining land an improvement in which they have no interest, nor compel such owners to improve the land without receiving some benefit to compensate them for the outlay. Ib.

DRAINAGE DISTRICT—Continued.

11. **Inclusion of Hills.** The inclusion of hills and other high lands which do not overflow within the drainage district does not necessarily render the incorporation invalid. If such lands are not benefited and only by their inclusion a competent number of petitioners is obtained, that would have the effect to oust jurisdiction: but it may well be that the drainage of wet, low or swamp lands lying around and about will so far benefit hills and other high land in matters of sanitation and easier egress and ingress as to render it entirely equitable that they should bear a modicum of the cost of draining the low land. Ib.

12. **Petitioner: President of Corporation.** An objection, made only by other landowners, that the president of a corporation owning land in the proposed district had no authority, in the name of the company, to sign the articles of incorporation without being specifically authorized to do so by the board of directors or by a vote of its stockholders, is not allowed. Ib.

13. **———: Attorney in Fact.** Likewise, an objection by other landowners only, that a certain person who held a power of attorney to act generally for a corporation which owned certain lands in the proposed district had no authority to sign the articles, is disallowed. Ib.

14. **———: Holder of Deed in Escrow.** And an objection by the owners of other land only that a certain person who had contracted to buy the land for which he signed the name of the then apparent owner, was not authorized to sign the articles, is disallowed, the fact being that the deed to him was then actually executed and lying in escrow and before the hearing was taken down by him and recorded. Ib.

15. **Title of Case.** Prior to a final judgment incorporating a drainage district the title of the case on appeal should run thus: "In re Petition for Incorporation of Mingo Drainage District; George S. Dean et al., Petitioners, Respondents, v. B. F. Wilson et al., Appellants." Ib.

16. **———: Right to Sue.** After the decree incorporating a drainage district has been made final it can sue and be sued in its own corporate name. Ib.

DUE PROCESS OF LAW.

Railroad Corporation: Denial of Franchise: Impairment of Contract. To hold that a foreign corporation which by purchase has acquired the railroad of another company and its franchise right to do business in this State, acquired prior to the enactment of the Act of 1913, Laws 1913, p. 179, cannot to do a railroad business in this State, would be to take valuable property rights without due process of law, and to impair the obligation of contracts, not only of said company, but of all other foreign corporations now owning and operating railroads under franchises granted prior to its enactment. State ex rel. v. Roach, 300.

ELECTIONS.

1. **Arrest of Legislation: Injunction.** An election called in pursuance to a provision of the city charter under a valid plan for initiative legislation and proper petitions, cannot be enjoined on the ground that the ordinances as proposed are unconstitutional. During the process of legislation in any mode the work of the lawmakers is not subject to judicial arrest, or control, or

ELECTIONS—Continued.

even open to judicial inquiry. It is only after the proposed legislation has become an accomplished fact that its constitutionality can be determined by the courts. Pitman v. Drabelle, 78.

2. **Justice of Peace: Contest: Jurisdiction.** The county court, except in cities of three hundred thousand inhabitants, has jurisdiction to hear and determine a contested election for the office of justice of the peace; but such court is an inferior tribunal, and the grounds of its jurisdiction must appear affirmatively upon the face of the record. Ramsey y. Huck, 333.

3. ———: **Notice of Contest.** The service of notice of contest for the office of justice of the peace, fifteen days before the term of the county court at which the election is to be contested, is, by the statute, made essential to the validity of the proceeding; and where only twelve days notice is given to contestee the court has no jurisdiction, and the proceeding must be dismissed. Ib.

4. ———: ———: **Amendment.** Notice of contest of less than fifteen days cannot be made sufficient by an amendment fixing the time of hearing at fifteen days from the date of service. It is only where jurisdiction has been obtained by proper notice, in the manner pointed out by the statute, that an amendment may be made to a notice of contest. Ib.

5. ———: ———: **Appeal.** If the county court had no jurisdiction over the contest for the office of justice of the peace, because notice of contest was not timely served, the circuit court acquired none by reason of an appeal. Ib.

ELEVATORS.

1. **Negligence: Injury to Child: Care of Parents: Instruction.** In an action by parents for the negligent killing of their child of tender years while riding in the passenger elevator of defendant's office building, an instruction which told the jury that if the failure of either of the child's parents to guard and look after him "contributed in the least degree" to the happening of the "accident" to the child, the finding should be for defendant, was erroneous. Contributory negligence sufficient to prevent recovery must be negligence that entered into and formed the direct, producing and efficient cause of the casualty. Besides, the instruction should not place the burden of guarding the child upon both parents at the same instant. Howard v. Scarritt Est. Co., 398.

2. ———: **Customary Method of Operating Elevator: Instruction.** Where the effect of closing the sliding doors of a passenger elevator with one hand while the operator threw the speed lever with the other was that the accelerated car was six or eight feet above the floor before the doors became closely shut, and plaintiff's child, a passenger thereon, fell through and was killed, an instruction which tells the jury that if they believe from the evidence that the elevator doors were at the time operated "in the usual and customary way that this and other similar elevators and doors in this and other buildings were operated" the defendant was not negligent in the operation thereof, was erroneous. The apparatus is not so intricate as to require expert exposition, or an instruction based thereon. Ib.

EMBEZZLEMENT.

1. **Information: Sufficiency.** Where the statute sets out the specific facts constituting the crime, as does Sec. 4550, R. S. 1909, concerning embezzlement, an information based thereon which is definitely descriptive of the offense as defined therein, is sufficient. State v. McWilliams, 437.

2. ———: ———: **Intent.** Where the embezzlement consists of doing the act itself, that is, where it consists of the fraudulent conversion of money by one to whom it has been intrusted, the information need not allege the intent with which the act was done, since the criminal intent will be inferred from the fraudulent conversion. Ib.

3. ———: **Former Jeopardy: Based on Assumption.** A defendant cannot be put in peril by being placed upon his trial under an invalid amended information upon the assumption that a valid information was then pending undisposed of. To constitute former jeopardy there must have been a valid information or indictment charging the same offense, and in a proceeding under that valid information or indictment a jury must have been impaneled and sworn for defendant's trial. Ib.

4. ———: ———: **Amended Information: Quashed: Former Restored.** An information, in one count, charging defendant with embezzlement, was filed in one county, and after the case was transferred to another county the prosecuting attorney of the first filed an amended information in two counts, the first charging embezzlement of money, and the second embezzlement of a check, and a jury was impaneled and sworn and the trial proceeded, but before a verdict was rendered the court, of its own motion, quashed the amended information and ordered defendant to be held for trial under the original information. *Held*, that by being put upon his trial on the amended information defendant was not, because of its invalidity, put in jeopardy under the original valid information. Ib.

5. **Continuance: Contradictory and Insincere Application.** An application for a continuance, which is inconsistent, contradictory, does not import the truth as to defendant's knowledge of what the absent witness would testify and does not show reasonable diligence, should be denied. Ib.

6. ———: **Diligence: Deposition.** Where the application states that the defendant had sent to the absent witness money with which to pay her traveling expenses from another State to the place of trial and that she had agreed to attend, the trial court would be justified in granting a continuance, if the allegation therein of defendant's recent knowledge of what her testimony would be bears the impress of truth; but if the facts reveal that he did know what her testimony would be, then proper diligence required him to take her deposition, and having failed to do that the trial court did not abuse its discretion in denying the application. Ib.

7. **Agency of Loan Agent.** Where the borrower called at defendant's office to employ him to secure a loan of $3400, and gave him a note for $127.50 for his services in that behalf, and in addition signed an order directed to the loan company in which he requested that the proceeds of the loan be paid to defendant and in which he said he thereby appointed defendant his agent to settle with the company for said loan, and the loan company after deducting its own commission, sent a check payable to defendant for the balance, the defendant was the agent of the bor-

EMBEZZLEMENT—Continued.

rower, in all that was necessary to establish the relation of
agency, in a prosecution for having embezzled the proceeds of
the check. State v. McWilliams, 437.   ..

8. ———: Circumstances. Circumstances arising out of a transaction, even in establishing the fact that defendant, charged
with embezzlement, was the borrower's agent, are sometimes
as strong in probative force as sworn testimony. Ib.

9. Ownership of Check. Where the loan company contracted to
loan $3400 to a farmer, to be evidenced by his note which was to
be secured by a deed of trust on his land, and upon the receipt of the note and deed of trust executed by him caused the
deed of trust to be recorded, and forwarded a check for the
amount of the note less commission, payable to defendant, the
agent who had negotiated the loan, the company parted with the
title to the check, and the nominal ownership passed to defendant; and it thereafter became his duty to either indorse it to the
farmer, or convert it into cash and pay the proceeds to him, or
apply it to the discharge of a prior lien for which the money had
been borrowed; but as it was indorsed and placed to defendant's credit in the bank, his act became embezzlement of the
money when he drew it out and without the farmer's consent
converted it to his own use. Ib.

10. Felonious Intent: Concealment. A defendant's felonious intent,
in a charge of embezzling his principal's money, is to be measured by his acts; and it may be shown by his evasion of his
principal, a concealment from him of the fact that he has received the money, and a neglect or refusal to account for it. Ib.

11. ———: Use of Money. Where defendant is charged with embezzling money, in that he as the agent of a farmer undertook
to borrow for him a sum of money to be used in paying off a
farm mortgage, and when the check for the loan was sent to him
it was deposited to his own credit in a bank and drawn out for
his own personal uses, it is not error to permit an officer of the
loan company to testify that defendant had not used the money
in paying off the prior lien on the land, nor returned it to the
company. Ib.

12. ———: Depositing Check. Nor under such circumstances is it
error to permit the State to show that the check payable to defendant's order and received by him was indorsed and deposited to his credit in a bank, and later checked out by him. Ib.

13. ———: Other Loans. Where the defendant was the agent of
the borrower in a particular case and was authorized to receive the proceeds of the loan from a certain company, whatever relationship he may have sustained to that company in
previous or subsequent like transactions can have no bearing
upon the issue of whether he embezzled the money received by
him in that case. Ib.

EQUALITY OF RIGHT. See Rights of Accused.

EQUITY.

1. Corporation: Unpaid Stock: Creditor Participating in Wrong.
A stockholder who participated in the transaction whereby the
services of a financial agent were received and accepted by the
corporation in full payment of stock issued to such agent, cannot be heard to say that the stock is not full paid, even though
he has loaned money to the company, and cannot hold said

EQUITY—Continued.

agent as a stockholder as for unpaid subscriptions on his stock, to satisfy a judgment against the company in the amount of the money loaned. [Following Meyer v. Min. & Mill. Co., 192 Mo. 162, and distinguishing Gillett v. Chicago Title & Trust Co., 230 Ill. 373.] Schroeder v. Edwards, 459.

2. **Remanding Cause: Confining Issue.** Where all issues in an equity case except one have on appeal been settled, the court, instead of remanding the cause generally, may remand it with directions that upon a retrial the case be confined to the one issue upon which the evidence at the first trial was insufficient to support a decree for plaintiff. Ib.

ESTOPPEL.

1. **Voluntary Partition: Deed to Husband and Wife.** Even though the wife directed that her husband's name be placed in the deed as grantee made in the voluntary partition of land inherited by her and others from her father, and he improved it with her knowledge, neither she, nor her heirs after her death, are estopped to deny that he acquired any title by the partition deed. Powell v. Powell, 117.

2. **Corporation: Unpaid Stock: Creditor Participating in Wrong.** A stockholder who participated in the transaction whereby the services of a financial agent were received and accepted by the corporation in full payment of stock issued to such agent, cannot be heard to say that the stock is not full paid, even though he has loaned money to the company, and cannot hold said agent as a stockholder as for unpaid subscriptions on his stock, to satisfy a judgment against the company in the amount of the money loaned. [Following Meyer v. Min. & Mill. Co., 192 Mo. 162, and distinguishing Gillett v. Chicago Title & Trust Co., 230 Ill. 373.] Schroeder v. Edwards, 459.

3. **Insurance Policy: Forfeiture Clauses: Evidence.** Where the general agents of an insurance company, at the time or subsequent to the issuance of a policy of fire insurance, are informed of the existence of any fact regarding the property which is violative of conditions expressed in the policy (such as vacancy or failure to operate a manufacturing plant for more than thirty days), then the company is estopped to interpose a violation of such conditions of forfeiture as a defense to a suit based on the policy to recover damages sustained; and testimony that the company's agents were informed at the time the policies were issued and subsequently that such conditions were not being kept and the reasons therefor and waived objection thereto, is competent evidence. Mining Co. v. Ins. Co., 524.

EVIDENCE.

1. **Of Other Crimes: Res Gestae.** Where the information charges sodomy *per os* it is not error to admit evidence tending to show sodomy *per anum* where the proof shows both acts were so connected as to show both were parts of the *res gestae*. State v. Pfeifer, 23.

2. **Defendant: Cross-Examination.** In view of the plain wording of the statute (Sec. 5242, R. S. 1909) forbidding them, questions asked defendant in cross-examination upon matters neither touched upon nor growing out of his examination in chief, are presumed to be prejudicial error, unless the contrary is made

EVIDENCE—Continued.

to appear; and where he is compelled to state all his movements the night of the crime, his acquaintanceship with two other persons who had committed a crime against the same woman two hours before he and they are charged with having committed a similar crime against her, and whether or not he and they had been companions since their school days and frequenters of the same saloon—all matters not touched upon in his examination in chief and brought out for the purpose of corroborating a police officer—the questions were not only unwarranted but were prejudicial. State v. Pfeifer, 23.

3. ——: ——: One Law for Innocent and Guilty. There can be but one law for the trial of the innocent and guilty; and notwithstanding the court may be of the opinion that the evidence is sufficient to warrant a verdict of guilty, a plain statute forbidding the cross-examination of a defendant concerning matters wholly outside his examination in chief must be applied to all defendants alike. The Constitution has not ordained that apparent guilt is the sole condition of affirmance by the Supreme Court of a verdict of guilty. Ib.

4. Carnal Knowledge: Evidence of Prosecutrix's Age. Where the statute requires the prosecutrix to be under fifteen years of age in order to constitute sexual intercourse with her rape, proof that she was not fifteen at the time should be satisfactory and if possible her testimony thereto should be corroborated. State v. Arnold, 33.

5. ——: ——: Family Record. Where the prosecutrix has testified that she was at the time of the carnal knowledge under fifteen years of age, and that her knowledge of her age was obtained from her parents and a family record, and the book being produced testified that it had been changed, the record, showing the date of birth of herself and brothers and sisters, should be admitted in evidence, and it was error to reject it, for three reasons; first, it was evidence of her true age; second, it was competent as tending to show that her statement of her age, based as she said, on said record, was false; and, third, it would tend to contradict her statement that the record, which admittedly, for sometime had been in defendant's possession, had been changed. Ib.

6. ——: Pregnancy: Year After Offense. Where the trial for rape occurs more than twelve months after the prosecutrix was fifteen years of age, testimony by her and her physician that at the trial she was pregnant, and by her that her pregnancy was due to sexual intercourse with defendant, is incompetent, and if admitted is reversible error. Ib.

7. ——: Continuance: Age of Prosecutrix. Ordinarily in a prosecution for carnal knowledge of a female under fifteen years of age, where her age is a vital issue, an application for a continuance, based on the absence of her grandmother, sick and unable to attend the trial, who, if present, would testify that at the time of the offense she was over fifteen, should not be denied. Ib.

8. ——: Evidence of Good Reputation. In a prosecution for carnal knowledge of a female of previous chaste character, testimony to the effect that her general reputation for chastity in the community in which she lived, prior to the alleged occurrence, was good, is admissible. [Refusing to follow *dictum* in State v. Kelley, 191 Mo. l. c. 691.] State v. Taylor, 41.

EVIDENCE—Continued.

9. ———: **Issuable Matters.** In a prosecution for carnal knowledge of an unmarried female of previous chaste character between the ages of fifteen and eighteen years, the question of whether or not she consented to the acts of sexual intercourse is not material to the issue, and even though her testimony tending to show that she did not consent seems unbelievable, that does not affect a verdict of guilty. The material issues are (a) that she was an unmarried female between the ages of fifteen and eighteen years, that (b) defendant had sexual intercourse with her and (c) that prior to the act charged she was of chaste character. Ib.

10. **Impeachment: Carnal Knowledge: Offer to Settle for Money.** Evidence in a prosecution for carnal knowledge of a female under the age of consent that the prosecutrix proposed to defendant or his attorney, to leave the State and not appear at the trial if money were paid to her, and that her uncle after a conference with her and her mother and in pursuance to an understanding with them hunted up defendant and proposed to him, and later proposed to defendant's attorney, that if money were paid to him he would take prosecutrix out of the State and see to it that she did not appear at the trial, is competent for the purpose of impeaching both the prosecutrix and her mother as witnesses to the main fact of sexual intercourse, and the exclusion of such testimony is reversible error. State v. Allen, 49.

11. **Will: General Incompetency of Witness: Husband of Legatee.** A will must stand or fall as a whole; and if the husband of the principal devisee is a competent witness for any person in a suit by which the validity of the will is being contested, his testimony would inure to her benefit. Ray v. Westall, 130.

12. ———: **Husband of Legatee: Competency as Witness.** Property, both real and personal, devised to a married woman by a will, is her separate property, and can be sold or mortgaged without reference to her husband; and in a suit contesting the validity of the will, by which she is made the principal legatee and he is given nothing, he is competent to express his opinion, as a non-professional witness, based upon what he observed while in testatrix's presence, as to her sanity. Ib.

13. **Seduction: Conclusions and Opinions.** In a prosecution for seduction under promise of marriage, the father of prosecutrix should not be permitted to state his conclusions and give his opinions as to the relations between her and defendant, such as, "He treated her like a sweetheart," "He seemed to think a good deal of her."

Held, by REVELLE, J., dissenting, that the testimony was not reversible error, since the father's knowledge and information upon which the conclusions were based were completely developed, and the jury were fully capable of determining whether or not the conclusions expressed were warranted. State v. Evans, 163.

14. ———: ———: **Estimates of Others.** A voluntary conclusion of prosecutrix's father drawn from a conversation with some neighbors of defendant, that "from the way they talked about him they had no use for him," is not competent evidence.

Held, by REVELLE, J., dissenting, that as the statement came out in connection with his explanation of certain matters concerning which he had been interrogated on cross-examination and no motion was made to strike it out, the trial court cannot be convicted of error. Ib.

EVIDENCE—Continued.

15. ——: ——: ——: **No Motion to Strike Out.** The usual rule is that a motion to strike out is prerequisite to a review of a conclusion voluntarily injected into the case by a witness; but where the trial court, upon an objection being made, ruled on the point on its merits, without such motion, the point is thereby preserved for review on appeal.

Held, by REVELLE, J., dissenting, that the trial court, on an objection being made by simply directing attorneys to "go ahead" did not rule on the merits, and it cannot be anticipated what his ruling would have been had a motion to strike out been made. State v. Evans, 163.

16. **Admission of Promise: Corroboration.** The promise of marriage must precede seduction; and while testimony of a witness that defendant, eight months after the alleged seduction, admitted that "he did promise to marry" prosecutrix, is competent and is evidence upon which an instruction on corroboration may be based, if the admission refers to a time preceding the alleged seduction, it is neither corroboration nor admissible if the admission fixes no time when the promise was made. Ib.

17. **Gambling Device: Commonly Known: Proof: Variance.** Where the information charges that the gambling table which defendant set up is one "commonly known as a crap table," the State must show that there is a table commonly so known, and that it was this particular kind of table that defendant set up and kept; and where all the witnesses testify that the tables which defendant maintained and operated were not of the kind which they commonly knew as crap tables, and that a crap table is of a radically different design and construction, a conviction cannot stand. State v. Wade, 249.

18. **Negotiable Notes: Conditioned on Return of Stock: Failure to Return as Part of Defense.** Where negotiable notes, given for the purchase of certificates of stock of a corporation, indorsed in blank, attached to the notes and delivered with them to the payee, were accompanied by a concurrent dependent agreement that upon the maturity of the notes the certificates could be surrendered and the notes cancelled, and that agreement is set up as a defense to an action on the notes, the instructions may authorize a finding for defendant without requiring a finding that he returned the stock or relinquished his right to it, since the certificates were already in possession of the holder of the notes, and it was impossible for defendant to tender the physical return of the stock. Simpson v. Van Laningham, 286.

19. ——: ——: **Evidence of Demand for Return of Notes.** And, under such circumstances, evidence that the maker demanded from the signers of the concurrent dependent agreement (the corporation and its president) the return of the notes, in accordance with the agreement, and being told they were in possession of a bank as transferee had his attorney to demand them from the bank, was competent to show an effort on defendant's part to comply with the agreement, as far as he could. Ib.

20. ——: ——: **Evidence of Election.** And evidence that, when defendant was approached by the attorney of the corporation on the theory that he was a stockholder, he announced that he elected to surrender the stock and cancel the notes in accordance with the agreement, could not have prejudiced the rights of a holder of the notes with notice of the agreement. Ib.

FILING.

Papers: Indorsement by Depositary. The petition, notice, plat, proceedings of meeting, etc., required by section 3 of the Consolidated School District Act (Laws 1913, p. 721) need not be indorsed "filed" in order to be filed with the county clerk and county superintendent. Indorsement on the paper of the fact of filing is not a necessary element of filing, unless the statute specifically so says. State ex inf. v. Clardy, 371.

FOREIGN INSURANCE COMPANY. See Insurance.

GAMING AND GAMBLING DEVICE.

1. **Information: Sufficiency of Charge.** In criminal pleadings nothing material can be left to intendment or implication; and where a crime is treated by statute the charge must be such as to specifically bring the accused within its material words. State v. Wade, 249.

2. ————: ————: **Aided by Proof.** The State cannot prove what it has not charged; it cannot by incompetent evidence supply an absent allegation. Even though the evidence establishes an offense forbidden by the statute, a conviction cannot stand if the allegations are insufficient to point out any crime denounced by it. Ib.

3. ————: **Ejusdem Generis.** When an enumeration of certain specified things in a statute is followed by general words or phrases, they are deemed to mean things of the same class and kind as those enumerated, and do not include things wholly different from those specifically mentioned. Section 4750, Revised Statutes 1909, condemning the setting up and keeping of certain enumerated gambling devices, or "any kind of gambling table or gambling device, adapted, devised, and designed for the purpose of playing any game of chance for money," is not broad enough to include all gambling devices regardless of their character, but does include all those of a kindred nature and similar kind to those enumerated. Ib.

4. ————: ————: ————: **Craps Table: Must Be Described.** A table, marked and arranged for the purpose, on which the game of craps is played by means of dice for money or property, is within the purview of the statute; but it is not specifically enumerated therein, and therefore the rule of *ejusdem generis* applies, and the information must contain sufficient averments showing it to belong to the enumerated class. An information simply charging that the defendant set up and kept "a certain table and gambling device commonly called a crap table," with no allegation defining a crap table, or of what it consists, or how designed, or how and by what means the game of craps is played, is not sufficient to support a conviction, even though the evidence establishes the fact that the tables which were operated by defendant are of the class forbidden by the statute. Nor is the general allegation that the crap table was "a gambling device adapted, devised and designed for the purpose of playing games of chance for money and property" sufficiently descriptive of a crap table to supply an allegation necessary to show that such table is of a kindred nature and similar kind to one of those enumerated in the statute. [Overruling on this point State v. Rosenblatt, 185 Mo. 114; State v. Locket, 188 Mo. 415; State v. Holden, 203 Mo. 581; State v. Lee, 228 Mo. 480.] Ib.

HUSBAND AND WIFE—Continued.

agreement to pay her twenty dollars per month for their board and lodging, and paid the amount regularly for three months, and who having lost his position, after two or three weeks' effort to secure employment obtained a position at a hotel at five dollars a week, cannot be convicted for failure during the next three months to pay to his wife or her sister any part of the five dollars, his purpose being to discharge his obligation to his wife's sister as soon as he was able. State v. Burton, 61.

3. ———: ———: **Wife With Money.** The gift of one thousand dollars by the wife to her sister within the time her husband was unable to obtain remunerative employment simply has a tendency to show the wife was not in destitute circumstances. Ib.

4. **Voluntary Partition: Deed to Husband and Wife.** A deed in voluntary partition by a conduit to a daughter of the deceased owner and her husband, though seemingly a deed by the entirety, did not vest the husband with the title to the land described in the deed; but upon the daughter's death the entire title descended to her children or her other heirs, since, in spite of said deed, the entire title to the tract designated had been inherited by the daughter from said deceased owner. Powell v. Powell, 117.

5. ———: ———: **Money Paid to Equalize Interest.** A payment made by the husband of one of the coparceners to another coparcener for the purpose of equalizing the share of his wife, did not convert the deed to him and her into a deed by the entirety; at most it made them tenants in common, but it did not have even that effect if it conveyed only the wife's share, for a deed in voluntary partition does not convey the title, but that was cast upon the wife by descent. Ib.

6. ———: ———: **Estoppel..** Even though the wife directed that her husband's name be placed in the deed as grantee made in the voluntary partition of land inherited by her and others from her father, and he improved it with her knowledge, neither she, nor her heirs after her death, are estopped to deny that he acquired any title by the partition deed. Ib.

7. ———: ———: **Limitations: Husband's Possession: Curtesy.** Prior to the amendment of the Married Woman's Act of 1889, the husband was entitled to the possession of the wife's land, and that amendment did not change his possessory right already accrued. His wife could not maintain an action to oust him of his possession begun prior to 1889, nor could his children after her death, because immediately upon her death he became a tenant by the curtesy for life; but that possession cannot avail to invest title in him by limitations. Ib.

IMPAIRMENT OF CONTRACTS. See **Railroads.**

IN CUSTODIA LEGIS. See **Banks and Banking.**

INDICTMENT AND INFORMATION.

1. **Amendment of Statute After Crime: Substantial Rights of Defendant.** It is error for the information to charge that the age of prosecutrix was under fifteen years and that of defendant above seventeen years, in the language of the amendment of the statute which raised the age of consent from fourteen to fifteen years and that of de-

INDICTMENT AND INFORMATION—Continued.

fendant from sixteen to seventeen years, where the act of carnal knowledge was committed before the amendment went into 'effect; but under the Statute of Jeofails the error is not reversible, unless it tends to the prejudice of the substantial rights of the defendant on the merits; and it does not so prejudice those rights, where the evidence clearly establishes that the prosecutrix was at the time of the alleged crime above fifteen years of age and the defendant above seventeen. State v. Allen, 49.

2. **Sufficiency of Charge.** In criminal pleadings nothing material can be left to intendment or implication; and where a crime is created by statute the charge must be such as to specifically bring the accused within its material words. State v. Wade, 249.

3. ———: **Aided by Proof.** The State cannot prove what it has not charged; it cannot by incompetent evidence supply an absent allegation. Even though the evidence establishes an offense forbidden by the statute, a conviction cannot stand if the allegations are insufficient to point out any crime denounced by it. Ib.

4. **Ejusdem Generis: Gambling Device.** When an enumeration of certain specified things in a statute is followed by general words or phrases, they are deemed to mean things of the same class and kind as those enumerated, and do not include things wholly different from those specifically mentioned. Section 4750, Revised Statutes 1909, condemning the setting up and keeping of certain enumerated gambling devices, or "any kind of gambling table or gambling device, adopted, devised, and designed for the purpose of playing any game of chance for money," is not broad enough to include all gambling devices regardless of their character, but does include all those of a kindred nature and similar kind to those enumerated. Ib.

5. ———: ———: ———: **Craps Table: Must Be Described.** A table, duly marked and arranged for the purpose, on which the game of craps is played by means of dice for money or property, is within the purview of the statute; but it is not specifically enumerated 'therein, and therefore the rule of *ejusdem generis* applies, and the information must contain sufficient averments showing it to belong to the enumerated class. An information simply charging that the defendant set up and kept "a certain table and gambling device commonly called a crap table," with no allegation defining a crap table, or of what it consists, or how designed, or how and by what means the game of craps is played, is not sufficient to support a conviction, even though the evidence establishes 'the fact that the tables which were operated by defendant are of the class forbidden by the statute. Nor is the general allegation that the crap table was "a gambling device adapted, devised and designed for the purpose of playing games of chance for money and property" sufficiently descriptive of a crap table to supply an allegation necessary to show that such table is of a kindred nature and similar kind to one of those enumerated in the statute. [Overruling on this point State v. Rosenblatt, 185 Mo. 114; State v. Locket, 188 Mo. 415; State v. Holden, 203 Mo. 581; State v. Lee, 228 Mo. 480.] Ib.

6. **Sufficiency: Embezzlement.** Where the statute sets out the specific facts constituting the crime, as does Sec. 4550, R. S. 1909, concerning embezzlement, an information based thereon

INDICTMENT AND INFORMATION—Continued.

which is definitively descriptive of the offense as defined therein, is sufficient. State v. McWilliams, 437.

7. ——: ——: Intent. Where the embezzlement consists of doing the act itself, that is, where it consists of the fraudulent conversion of money by one to whom it has been intrusted, the information need not allege the intent with which the act was done, since the criminal intent will be inferred from the fraudulent conversion. Ib.

8. Former Jeopardy: Based on Assumption. A defendant cannot be put in peril by being placed upon his trial under an invalid amended information upon the assumption that a valid information was then pending undisposed of. To constitute former jeopardy there must have been a valid information or indictment charging the same offense, and in a proceeding under that valid information or indictment a jury must have been impaneled and sworn for defendant's trial. Ib.

9. ——: Amended Information: Quashed: Former Restored. An information, in one count, charging defendant with embezzlement, was filed in one county, and after the case was transferred to another county the prosecuting attorney of the first filed an amended information in two counts, the first charging embezzlement of money, and the second embezzlement of a check, and a jury was impaneled and sworn and the trial proceeded, but before a verdict was rendered the court, of its own motion, quashed the amended information and ordered defendant to be held for trial under the original information. Held, that by being put upon his trial on the amended information defendant was not, because of its invalidity, put in jeopardy under the original valid information. Ib.

INITIATIVE LEGISLATION. See Constitutional Law.

INJUNCTION.

1. Arrest of Legislation: Election: Injunction. An election called in pursuance to a provision of the city charter under a valid plan for initiative legislation and proper petitions, cannot be enjoined on the ground that the ordinances as proposed are unconstitutional. During the process of legislation in any mode the work of the lawmakers is not subject to judicial arrest, or control, or even open to judicial inquiry. It is only after the proposed legislation has become an accomplished fact that its constitutionality can be determined by the courts. Pitman v. Drabelle, 78.

2. Publication of Libel. Injunction, when that is the only relief prayed for, will not lie to restrain the threatened publication of either a libel or slander. Wolf v. Harris, 405.

3. ——: Remedy. The issue of libel or no libel is an issue of law and a matter for the jury; and before plaintiff can have an injunction to restrain a further publication of libelous statements, there must be a verdict of the jury finding the statements to be false and libelous. If he goes to a jury with the alleged libel and obtains a judgment, which owing to defendant's insolvency he is unable to collect, further publication of a libel of like or similar import may be enjoined in a separate suit; or he may couple a count for injunction in his petition with a count at law for damages, and having sustained before a jury his law count, the court, upon allegation

INSTRUCTIONS—Continued.

9. ———: **Customary Method of Operating Elevator.** Where the effect of closing the sliding doors of a passenger elevator with one hand while the operator threw the speed lever with the other was that the accelerated car was six or eight feet above the floor before the doors became closely shut, and plaintiff's child, a passenger thereon, fell through and was killed, an instruction which tells the jury that if they believe from the evidence that the elevator doors were at the time operated "in the usual and customary way that this and other similar elevators and doors in this and other buildings were operated" the defendant was not negligent in the operation thereof, was erroneous. The apparatus is not so intricate as to require expert exposition, or an instruction based thereon. Ib.

10. **Will Contest: Contrary to Will Itself.** Where the will of the unmarried testator cancels his brothers' debts, gives the property to his mother for life and in remainder to his sisters, and provides that if the mother survives the sisters and they die without issue the property is to be disposed of according to the mother's will, it is not error to refuse to submit to the jury the question whether it was the testator's intention to provide that, if his sisters survived his mother and died without issue, his property should go to his brothers. Such question should not be submitted to the jury, although testator was informed by his lawyer before executing the will that the property, in such contingency, would go to his brothers. Buck v. Buck, 644.

11. ———: **Contrary to Testator's Understanding.** Where the will was drawn in accordance with the bachelor testator's instructions and he read it over and expressed satisfaction with it, and then was told by his lawyer that in the event the remaindermen survived the life tenant and died without issue the property would go under the statute to his brothers, and thereupon he requested that it be executed, the court cannot peremptorily instruct the jury to find for contestant on the ground that the will was not the testator's will. Besides, it is not necessary that testator have the knowledge of the will's scope and bearing possessed by his legal adviser. Ib.

INSURANCE.

1. **Jurisdiction: Foreign Insurance Company As Defendant: Foreign Plaintiff: Right to Sue In This State.** An Arizona corporation, not licensed to do business in either Colorado or Missouri, can bring and maintain a suit in the circuit court of any county in Missouri, against an insurance company organized under the laws of Pennsylvania and licensed to do insurance business in this State, upon an insurance policy issued and delivered in Colorado, insuring property in that State against loss by fire, by having the summons served by the sheriff of Cole County upon the Superintendent of Insurance, as the statutory agent of said insurance company, in accordance with the provisions of section 7042, Revised Statutes 1909. [GRAVES, BOND and WALKER, JJ., dissenting.] Mining & Milling Co. v. Fire Ins. Co., 524.

2. ———: ———: ———: ———: **Limitation to Contracts Made In this State.** The statute (Sec. 7042, R. S. 1909) does not limit the right of holders of policies issued by an insurance company licensed to do business in this State to sue in the courts of this State upon contracts made in this State, but gives

INSURANCE—Continued.

them the right to sue such a company in the courts of this State upon policies wherever made.

Held, by GRAVES, J., dissenting, with whom BOND and WALKER, JJ., concur that the substituted method of service of process provided by the statute is limited to actions arising on contracts made or acts done in this State. Mining & Milling Co. v. Fire Ins. Co., 524.

3. ——: ——: ——: ——: **So Long as Policies Are Outstanding.** The language of the statute declaring that the authority of the Superintendent of Insurance to accept service of process for an insurance company licensed to do business in this State shall continue "so long as it shall have any policies or liabilities outstanding in this State," is not a limitation upon the authority of the Superintendent to act for such company, and not a limitation upon the character of the actions that may be brought and maintained in the courts of this State, and does not distinguish between contracts made in this State and contracts made elsewhere, but is a mere limitation of the time within which suits may be brought.

Held, by GRAVES, J., dissenting, with whom BOND and WALKER, JJ., concur, that the language of the statute declaring that service of process upon the Superintendent of Insurance shall be valid and binding upon said company "so long as it shall have any policies or liabilities outstanding in this State," does characterize the kind of litigation to which foreign insurance companies can be required to respond in the courts of this State, and fixes a limitation upon the causes over which they can assume jurisdiction; and when read in connection with the preceding clause, which mentions policies issued when the company was in the State, it is apparent that the substituted method of service of process is limited to suits on contracts made within the State, and does not apply to contracts made outside the State. Ib.

4. ——: **Foreign Insurance Company: Licensed to Do Business in State: Process: Application of Statutes.** Neither section 7042 nor section 7044, Revised Statutes 1909, authorizes service of process in suits brought in the courts of this State against a foreign insurance company doing business herein without a license, based upon a policy of insurance issued by it in another state or country. Section 7042 does not apply to suits based on contracts of insurance written in this State by a foreign company having no license to do business herein, but section 7044 applies to such a situation. Section 7042 limits the service of process therein provided to foreign insurance companies doing business in this State under authority from the State duly granted to them; and by section 7044 the process therein mentioned is limited to suits upon policies issued in this State by companies which do not have authority from the State to do business here. Ib.

5. ——: ——: ——: ——: **Constitutionality of Statute.** Section 7042, Revised Statutes 1909, designed to authorize service of process against foreign insurance companies doing business in this State in pursuance to a license properly granted, based upon insurance contracts made in another state, by service of summons upon the Superintendent of Insurance appointed as its agent for the purpose of process, is not unconstitutional, either as denying to said companies due process of law, or on the theory that the Legislature has no power to authorize suits to be brought in the courts of this State for a breach of an insurance contract made in another state. Ib.

INTERSTATE COMMERCE.

Personal Injuries: Jurisdiction of State Court. If the petition
states the facts which, under the statute of this State and the
statute of Congress, constitute a cause of action for personal
injuries due to defendant's negligence, the court should refuse
an instruction directing the jury that if the car which the crew
was attempting to couple at the time plaintiff was injured was
employed in interstate comerce, their verdict must be for defendant; for the State courts have jurisdiction to enforce the
liability created by those statutes for such injuries so inflicted.
Pipes v. Railroad, 385.

INTERVENOR. See Quieting Title.

JEOPARDY. See Indictment and Information, 6 to 9.

JUDGMENTS.

1. Finality: Setting Aside at Subsequent Term. After a final
judgment has been rendered at one term, the court, in the absence of a statute to the contrary and of a pending motion or
other proper step to carry the case over to the next term, has
no jurisdiction, at such next term, to modify or annul that judgment. State ex rel. v. Ellison, 321.

2. ————: After Motion for Rehearing Overruled. Where the
Court of Appeals affirmed the judgment of the trial court, and a
motion for rehearing having been timely filed was overruled on
the last day of the term and an order was made on said day
giving all parties ten days in which "to file motions in cases
ruled on this day," the judgment was a finality, and the Court of
Appeals had no power at the next term to sustain a motion filed
at said next term to set aside the order overruling the motion
for a rehearing, nor did it have any power on the last day of the
term to make the order extending the time to the next term in
which to file a motion to set aside said order, but all its orders
and judgments made at such subsequent term were null and
void. Ib.

3. ————: Court of Appeals: Certification of Cause to Supreme
Court. The Court of Appeals has no power to certify a cause
to the Supreme Court at a subsequent term after its judgment
therein has become a finality. The Constitution requires such
transfer to be made at "the same term" at which the judgment
is rendered "and not afterwards." Ib.

4. Sufficiency of Evidence: Judgment of Foreign Court: Raised by
Motion for New Trial. An assignment in the motion for a new
trial that "the verdict and judgment is unsupported by any substantial evidence" raises the question of the sufficiency of the
evidence, and that proposition necessarily embraces a contention that the judgments against a corporation rendered by a
court of another State, which are made the basis of plaintiff's
suit against its stockholders for the amount of the unpaid stock
issued to them, and introduced in evidence, were insufficient in
law to support a finding for plaintiff. Schroeder v. Edwards,
459.

5. ————: ————: Presumption: Cognovit. Where the plaintiff's
cause of action is bottomed on the judgment of a circuit court
of another State, proof of a judgment entered by the clerk of
that court in vacation is not sufficient, unless there are also introduced in evidence the statutes of that State establishing the
jurisdiction and the authority to do that which was done by the

JUDGMENTS—Continued.

clerk in vacation. In such case the presumption that the judgment so entered was regular and valid cannot be indulged, because such a judgment being unknown to the common law, must depend for its validity upon the statutes authorizing it. Ib.

JUDICIAL NOTICE.

Drainage District: Right to Extend Boundaries: Must be Shown by Record. The right of a drainage district to extend its boundaries so as to include other lands subject to overflow must be found in the record at the trial. Its mere corporate existence does not prove its cause of action in such case. The court cannot take judicial notice of its original plan of reclamation and all proceedings of the company connected therewith. Drainage Dist. v. Harris, 139.

JURISDICTION.

1. Drainage District: Notice: Personal Service. The jurisdiction of the circuit court to extend the boundary lines of an existing drainage district, under the Act of 1913, is not dependent upon personal service upon resident owners of the land to be included. Neither the Constitution of Missouri nor of the United States requires a uniform method of obtaining jurisdiction of the persons of litigants, in either general or special proceedings. A notice by publication in the language of the statute "to all persons interested," is sufficient. Drainage District v. Harris, 139.

2. Prohibition: Circuit Courts. The Supreme Court is given authority by the Constitution to prohibit, by its writ of prohibition, circuit courts and other inferior tribunals from exercising jurisdiction which they do not legally have. Ramsey v. Huck, 333.

3. ———: Justice of Peace: Title to Office. The Constitution gives the Supreme Court exclusive jurisdiction in cases involving title to any office under this State, and the office of a justice of the peace is such an office. Ib.

4. ———: Jurisdiction of Appeal. Jurisdiction to hear and determine upon appeal the original case out of which the application for a writ of prohibition arose, is not a prerequisite to the right of the Supreme Court to issue the writ. Ib.

5. Justice of Peace: Election Contest. The county court, except in cities of three hundred thousand inhabitants, has jurisdiction to hear and determine a contested election for the office of justice of the peace; but such court is an inferior tribunal, and the grounds of its jurisdiction must appear affirmatively upon the face of the record. Ib.

6. ———: Notice of Election Contest. The service of notice of contest for the office of justice of the peace, fifteen days before the term of the county court at which the election is to be contested, is, by the statute, made essential to the validity of the proceedings; and where only twelve days' notice is given to contestee the court has no jurisdiction, and the proceeding must be dismissed. Ib.

7. ———: ———: Amendment. Notice of contest of less than fifteen days cannot be made sufficient by an amendment fixing the time of hearing at fifteen days from the date of service. It is only where jurisdiction has been obtained by proper notice, in

JURISDICTION—Continued.

the manner pointed out by the statute, that an amendment may
be made to a notice of contest. Ramsey v. Huck, 533.

8. ——: ——: Appeal. If the county court had no jurisdiction over the contest for the office of justice of the peace, because notice of contest was not timely served, the circuit court
acquired none by reason of an appeal. Ib.

9. Non-Resident Corporation: Service. For the reasons stated in
the minority opinion of the St. Louis Court of Appeals, 175 Mo.
App. l. c. 679 et seq., in this case, the judgment is reversed, and
the cause remanded, in order to give plaintiff opportunity to
obtain valid service on defendant corporation. McMenamy Inv.
Co. v. Catering Co., 340.

10. Interstate Commerce: Personal Injuries: Jurisdiction of State
Court. If the petition states the facts which, under the statute
of this State and the statute of Congress, constitute a cause of
action for personal injuries due to defendant's negligence, the
court should refuse an instruction directing the jury that if the
car which the crew was attempting to couple at the time plaintiff was injured was employed in interstate commerce, their
verdict must be for defendant; for, the State courts have jurisdiction to enforce the liability created by those statutes for such
injuries so inflicted. Pipes v. Railroad, 385.

11. Private Bank: Insolvency: Priority of Jurisdiction of State and
Federal Court. The taking possession of a private bank by the
Bank Commissioner is the first step in the bringing of a suit
for the appointment of a receiver, and that step gives the
circuit court jurisdiction of the cause, and a subsequent application for a receiver and the appointment of one cannot be said
to be *coram non judice* because of the fact that, before the receiver is appointed, a petition asking that the bank's owner
be adjudged a bankrupt is filed in the Federal court. State ex
rel. v. Sage, 493.

12. ——: ——: ——: Bankrupt Proceedings Against Owner.
Besides, the filing of a petition in the Federal court, asking that
the owner of a private bank be individually adjudged a bankrupt, does not place the assets of his said bank *in custodia legis*
—certainly not to the extent of depriving the State court of its
jurisdiction to decide whether or not the creditors of the bank
are entitled to be paid out of its assets before they can be used
to satisfy its owner's individual creditors. Ib.

13. Foreign Insurance Company As Defendant: Foreign Plaintiff:
Right to Sue In This State. An Arizona corporation, not licensed to do business in either Colorado or Missouri, can bring
and maintain a suit in the circuit court of any county in Missouri, against an insurance company organized under the laws
of Pennsylvania and licensed to do insurance business in this
State, upon an insurance policy issued and delivered in Colorado, insuring property in that State against loss by fire, by
having the summons served by the sheriff of Cole County upon
the Superintendent of Insurance, as the statutory agent of said
insurance company, in accordance with the provisions of section 7042, Revised Statutes 1909. [GRAVES, BOND and
WALKER, JJ., dissenting.] Mining & Milling Co. v. Fire Ins.
Co., 524.

14. ——: ——: ——: Limitation to Contracts Made In this
State. The statute (Sec. 7042, R. S. 1909) does not limit the

JURISDICTION—Continued.

right of holders of policies issued by an insurance company licensed to do business in this State to sue in the courts of this State upon contracts made in this State, but gives them the right to sue such a company in the courts of this State upon policies wherever made.

Held, by GRAVES, J., dissenting, with whom BOND and WALK-ER, JJ., concur, that the substituted method of service of process provided by the statute is limited to actions arising on contracts made or acts done in this State. Ib.

15. ———: ———: ———: **So Long as Policies Are Outstanding.** The language of the statute declaring that the authority of the Superintendent of Insurance to accept service of process for an insurance company licensed to do business in this State shall continue "so long as it shall have any policies or liabilities outstanding in this State," is not a limitation upon the authority of the Superintendent to act for such company, and not a limitation upon the character of the actions that may be brought and maintained in the courts of this State, and does not distinguish between contracts made in this State and contracts made elsewhere, but is a mere limitation of the time within which suits may be brought.

Held, by GRAVES, J., dissenting, with whom BOND and WALK-ER, JJ., concur, that the language of the statute declaring that service of process upon the Superintendent of Insurance shall be valid and binding upon said company "so long as it shall have any policies or liabilities outstanding in this State," does characterize the kind of litigation to which foreign insurance companies can be required to respond in the courts of this State, and fixes a limitation upon the causes over which they can assume jurisdiction; and when read in connection with the preceding clause, which mentions policies issued when the company was in the State, it is apparent that the substituted method of service of process is limited to suits on contracts made within the State, and does not apply to contracts made outside the State. Ib.

16. **Foreign Insurance Company: Licensed to Do Business in State: Process: Application of Statutes.** Neither section 7042 nor section 7044, Revised Statutes 1909, authorizes service of process in suits brought in the courts of this State against a foreign insurance company doing business herein without a license, based upon a policy of insurance issued by it in another state or country. Section 7042 does not apply to suits based on contracts of insurance written in this State by a foreign company having no license to do business herein, but section 7044 applies to such a situation. Section 7042 limits the service of process therein provided to foreign insurance companies doing business in this State under authority from the State duly granted to them; and by section 7044 the process therein mentioned is limited to suits upon policies issued in this State by companies which do not have authority from the State to do business here. Ib.

17. ———: ———: ———: **Constitutionality of Statute.** Section 7042, Revised Statutes 1909, designed to authorize service of process against foreign insurance companies doing business in this State in pursuance to a license properly granted, based upon insurance contracts made in another state, by service of summons upon the Superintendent of Insurance appointed as its agent for the purpose of process, is not unconstitutional, either as denying to said companies due process of law, on the

JURISDICTION—Continued.

theory that the Legislature has no power to authorize suits to be brought in the courts of this State for a breach of an insurance contract made in another state. Mining & Milling Co. v. Fire Ins. Co., 524.

18. ———: ———: ———: ———: **Transitory Action.** In pursuance to broad and specific provisions of the State and Federal Constitution, the Legislature has made ample provision by which a suit on a transitory cause of action—that is, a personal action founded on a violation of rights which, in contemplation of law, have no locality, but follow the person—may be brought in the courts of this State by a citizen of any other State or country, with the same freedom as is accorded to a citizen of this State. The Legislature has enacted, and had constitutional authority to enact, laws conferring jurisdiction upon the courts of this State to try and determine actions brought by a citizen of another State or country against a foreign insurance company licensed to do business in this State, upon contracts of fire insurance made in another state or country, whether the property destroyed was located in this State or elsewhere. [GRAVES, BOND and WALKER, JJ., dissenting.] Ib.

19. **Raised by Answer.** Jurisdiction over the person is a proper subject-matter of a plea in the answer, when the lack of jurisdiction does not appear on the face of the petition, but when such lack so appears, it should be raised by demurrer. [Per GRAVES, J.] Ib.

20. ———: **Waiver By Appearance.** A motion to quash the service of process, which is in effect a demurrer to the jurisdiction of the court over the person of defendant and limited to that purpose, is not an appearance, such as amounts to a waiver of jurisdiction. [Per GRAVES, J.]. Ib.

JUSTICE OF THE PEACE.

1. **Prohibition: Circuit Courts.** The Supreme Court is given authority by the Constitution to prohibit, by its writ of prohibition, circuit courts and other inferior tribunals from exercising jurisdiction which they do not legally have. Ramsey v. Huck, 333.

2. ———: **Title to Office.** The Constitution gives the Supreme Court exclusive jurisdiction in cases involving title to any office under this State, and the office of a justice of the peace is such an office. Ib.

3. ———: **Jurisdiction of Appeal.** Jurisdiction to hear and determine upon appeal the original case out of which the application for a writ of prohibition arose, is not a prerequisite to the right of the Supreme Court to issue the writ. Ib.

4. **Election Contest: Jurisdiction.** The county court, except in cities of three hundred thousand inhabitants, has jurisdiction to hear and determine a contested election for the office of justice of the peace; but such court is an inferior tribunal, and the grounds of its jurisdiction must appear affirmatively upon the face of the record. Ib.

5. **Notice of Election Contest.** The service of notice of contest for the office of justice of the peace, fifteen days before the term of the county court at which the election is to be contested, is, by the statute, made essential to the validity of the proceeding;

JUSTICE OF THE PEACE—Continued.

and where only twelve days' notice is given to contestee the court has no jurisdiction, and the proceeding must be dismissed. Ib.

6. ———: Amendment. Notice of contest of less than fifteen days cannot be made sufficient by an amendment fixing the time of hearing at fifteen days from the date of service. It is only where jurisdiction has been obtained by proper notice, in the manner pointed out by the statute, that an amendment may be made to a notice of contest. Ib.

7. ———: Appeal. If the county court had no jurisdiction over the contest for the office of justice of the peace, because notice of contest was not timely served, the circuit court acquired none by reason of an appeal. Ib.

LANDS AND LAND TITLES.

1. Parties to Action: Suit to Quiet Title: Right of Person in Interest to Intervene. Section 2541, Revised Statutes 1909, is a part of the Act of 1873, Laws 1873, p. 49, relating to the right of persons whose deeds or other evidences of title are lost or destroyed, to have the title adjudged to them and the record title restored to them, and does not apply to proceedings under section 2535, and does not authorize one who claims title by adverse possession to intervene and file an answer in a suit to quiet title. Miller v. Boulware, 487.

2. ———: ———: ———: Section 1733. One who is not united in interest with any other party to the suit to quiet title is not authorized by section 1733, Revised Statutes 1909, to intervene, nor to be joined either as plaintiff or defendant. Ib.

3. ———: ———: ———: Section 1732: Adversary Interests. Section 1732, Revised Statutes 1909, does not authorize one in possession of land and claiming by adverse possession to intervene and to be made a party defendant to a suit to quiet title brought against the record title owner by one who bases his title upon the Statute of Limitations by actual possession and does not ask for possession. Such an intervenor does not (1) have or claim an interest in the controversy adverse to the plaintiff, nor (2) is he a necessary party to a complete determination or settlement of the question involved, nor (3) is such a suit one for possession of the real estate. Ib.

4. Religious Corporation: Not to Hold Title, Etc. Neither the Legislature nor the courts can establish a religious corporation except its charter shows that it is created only to hold title to real estate for church edifices, parsonages and cemeteries; and a corporation organized for purposes other than those alone is not a religious corporation within the meaning of the Missouri Constitution.
Held, by GRAVES, J., dissenting, that if the circuit court in entering a pro forma decree attempted to and did organize a religious corporation, its act was futile, and the chartered company has no standing in a court to recover real estate devised to it; and to determine whether it is a religious corporation resort should be made, first, to its charter, and if that is ambiguous or uncertain in meaning, then, to extraneous proof. Helpers of the Holy Souls v. Law, 667.

5. ———: Valid Benevolent Corporation. Held, under the facts stated in the opinion, that the plaintiff is not a religious cor-

267 Mo.-50.

LANDS AND LAND TITLES—Continued.

poration, but is a valid benevolent corporation under the statutes of Missouri. And that the fact that, in addition to the primary purposes and objects of practical benevolence set forth in its charter, it had the incidental right to impart religious instruction did not prevent this suit for property devised to it, since this particular franchise could only be attacked in a direct suit by the State.

Held, by GRAVES, J., dissenting, that a corporation whose charter recites that "the purpose and object of said corporation shall be to maintain the establishment now under our charge in said city known as 'The Society of the Helpers of Holy Souls' and also others that we may hereafter establish; and in connection with same, to gratuitously visit the sick poor daily, irrespective of creed or color, rendering them every assistance in our power by nursing them in their homes; to organize our convent meetings and sewing classes for the working class and poor children and impart religious instruction to same," etc., and which "is composed, exclusively, of members of the religious order of the Roman Catholic Church known as 'The Helpers of the Holy Souls in Purgatory,'" the purpose of said "religious order" being an exemplification of the tenets and doctrines of the church concerning souls in Purgatory, is a religious corporation, and cannot be held to be a mere benevolent association. Helpers of the Holy Souls v. Law, 667.

6. ———: Devise to Unincorporated Society. There is no principle of law which forbids a charitable gift to an unincorporated religious body or any of its orders. Even if an attempted incorporation must be held to be a religious corporation and a devise to it of real estate for that reason be invalid, yet if the unmistakable devise is to a known unincorporated society which has the same name as that of the attempted incorporation, it will be upheld, and the property can be recovered by the society's trustees. Ib.

LAWS.

1. Pleading: Personal Injuries: Action Given by Statute. It is not necessary that the statute of this State or of Congress which gives to plaintiff his cause of action be pleaded; all that is required is that the facts which bring the case within them be stated in the petition. The laws of Congress are not foreign laws that must be pleaded or proven in this State. Pipes v. Railroad, 385.

2. Statutes of Another State: Proof. In Missouri the statutory law of another State must be proven the same as any other fact in the case. Schroeder v. Edwards, 459.

LEGACIES, SPECIAL. See Wills, 1 to 4.

LEGAL CAPACITY TO SUE.

`Will Contest: Interest of Contestant: Waiver. A failure to allege in the petition that plaintiff has such a financial interest in the probate of the will as will enable him to institute a suit contesting its validity is not a defect to be classed as a want of "legal capacity to sue," and one that must therefore be raised by demurrer or answer, and if not so raised is to be considered waived. Lack of "legal capacity to sue," as used in the statute, has reference to some legal disability of the plaintiff, such as infancy, idiocy, coverture, and has no reference to the fact that the petition fails to state a cause of action. Gruender v. Frank, 713.

LEGAL TENDER MONEY. See Tender.

LIBEL.

1. Injunction: Publication of Libel. Injunction, when that is the only relief prayed for, will not lie to restrain the threatened publication of either a libel or slander. Wolf v. Harris, 405.

2. ———: ———: Remedy. The issue of libel or no libel is an issue of law and a matter for the jury; and before plaintiff can have an injunction to restrain a further publication of libelous statements, there must be a verdict of the jury finding the statements to be false and libelous. If he goes to a jury with the alleged libel and obtains a judgment, which owing to defendant's insolvency he is unable to collect, further publication of a libel of like or similar import may be enjoined in a separate suit; or he may couple a count for injunction in his petition with a count at law for damages, and having sustained before a jury his law count, the court, upon allegation and proof of defendant's insolvency and threatened continuance of the libelous publication, or to avoid a multiplicity of suits, can enjoin a continued publication thereof. Ib.

LICENSE TO DO BUSINESS IN STATE. See Railroads.

LIMITATIONS.

1. Minor: Avoidance of Deed. The deed of a minor conveying his interest in real estate, unless disaffirmed within ten years after he reaches his majority, is valid, and cannot be avoided by him. Parrish v. Treadway, 91.

2. ———: ———: Remainderman. The act of disaffirmance of a conveyance of real estate by a minor goes to the instrument itself, and has no particular reference to the estate conveyed or attempted to be conveyed. If the deed conveyed the contingent reversion of a remainderman while he was yet a minor and while the life tenant was yet living, the remainderman's deed cannot be disaffirmed by him after the expiration of ten years after he reached his majority, it matters not how long the life tenant lived after the deed was executed. Ib.

3. ———: ———: Disability of Coverture. And the deed of a minor who was a married woman at the time it was made, must be disaffirmed within ten years after she first became discovert, having then reached her majority, although she may have soon thereafter married a second time. The disability of a second coverture cannot avail her. And where the only act of disaffirmance is by bringing suit, the petition must be filed within ten years after she first became discovert. Ib.

4. Voluntary Partition: Deed to Husband and Wife: Husband's Possession: Curtesy. Prior to the amendment of the Married Woman's Act of 1889, the husband was entitled to the possession of the wife's land, and that amendment did not change his possessory right already accrued. His wife could not maintain an action to oust him of his possession begun prior to 1889, nor could his children after her death, because immediately upon her death he became a tenant by the curtesy for life; but that possession cannot avail to invest title in him by limitations. Powell v. Powell, 117.

5. Quieting Title: Time to Bring Suit. No limitation is fixed by the statute (Sec. 650, R. S. 1889; Sec. 2535, R. S. 1909) in which a suit to quiet title must be brought. The ten-year Statute of Limitations does not apply. [Following Armor v. Frey, 253 Mo. l. c. 474.]. Ib.

LIMITATIONS—Continued.

6. **Written Promise to Pay.** In order to bring an "action upon any writing . . . . for the payment of money or property" it must appear in the statement of the cause of action that the money sued for is promised to be paid by the language of the writing. If such promise arises only upon proof of extrinsic facts it is barred by the five-year Statute of Limitations. Parker-Washington Co. v. Dennison, 199.

7. ———: ———: ———: **Bad Faith on Part of Promisor.** The plaintiff being the owner of asphalt used in paving streets in a certain city, and of a plant used in the preparation of asphalt for paving purposes, located in said city, entered into a written contract with defendant whereby defendant agreed to pay plaintiff (1) for the use of said plant, five cents per square yard for all asphalt paving laid under the contract to the extent of forty thousand square yards, and (2) for said asphalt, one-half the amount received for any pavement done by defendant, after deducting all expenses. The defendant was to make bids in good faith to obtain paving contracts from the city. The petition alleged that defendant made no effort in good faith to obtain any such paving contracts, and when he had obtained some such contracts did not perform them and never intended to perform, and never shipped any of the asphalt which had been tendered according to contract, and held the plant for a long time; and that the gain which would have accrued to plaintiff by the payment of said sum of five cents per square yard for all asphalt agreed to be laid by defendant was two thousand dollars, and one half the profits agreed to be paid and delivered to plaintiff was twenty thousand dollars, for which amounts judgment was asked. The suit was not brought within five years. *Held*, that the contract contained a promise to pay money only on condition that the pavement was laid, and the petition on its face alleges that no paving was laid, and therefore it does not state a promise to pay arising out of the words used in the written contract, but stated only a cause of action upon an implied promise arising in law out of the alleged torts of defendants: that such cause of action is not within the statute and was barred in five years.

Held, by WOODSON, C. J., dissenting, that all written contracts calling for things to be done in the future are conditional, and whether they have been performed or not must of necessity be shown by parol testimony; that the contract in suit contained a definite promise in writing to pay two separate sums of money upon its performance; that defendant did not relieve himself from his promise to pay those sums by fraudulently refusing to perform; and that the promise to pay is found in the contract itself, and no evidence *aliunde* is required to show a promise to pay, and hence the five-year Statute of Limitations does not apply. Ib.

MINORS.

1. **Amended Petition: Change of Cause of Action: No New Summons.** Although the defendants are minors, if they have been properly brought into court, a guardian *ad litem* appointed and his acceptance filed, the filing thereafter of an amended petition by which an erroneous description of the land contained in the original petition is corrected, is as binding on them as upon adult defendants, and they have no greater right to an additional summons and service; and a judgment against them without such additional summons is not void or voidable. Cashion v. Gargus, 68.

MINORS—Continued.

2. **Conveyance of Real Estate.** The deed of a minor is not void, but only voidable; and to be avoided must be disaffirmed by him after reaching his majority. Parrish v. Treadway, 91.

3. ———: **Limitations.** The deed of a minor conveying his interest in real estate, unless disaffirmed within ten years after he reaches his majority, is valid, and cannot be avoided by him. Ib.

4. ———: ———: **Remainderman.** The act of disaffirmance of a conveyance of real estate by a minor goes to the instrument itself, and has no particular reference to the estate conveyed or attempted to be conveyed. If the deed conveyed the contingent reversion of a remainderman while he was yet a minor and while the life tenant was yet living, the remainderman's deed cannot be disaffirmed by him after the expiration of ten years after he reached his majority, it matters not how long the life tenant lived after the deed was executed. Ib.

5. ———: ———: **Disability of Coverture.** And the deed of a minor who was a married woman at the time it was made, must be disaffirmed within ten years after she first became discovert, having then reached her majority, although she may have soon thereafter married a second time. The disability of a second coverture cannot avail her. And where the only act of disaffirmance is by bringing suit, the petition must be filed within ten years after she first became discovert. Ib.

MONEY ORDER. See **Tender.**

MORTGAGES AND DEEDS OF TRUST.

1. **Corporate Franchise: What Passes by Mortgage Sale.** Both by the laws and Constitution of Missouri and by the general law, all the franchise rights of a railway company except the mere right to be a corporation, including the right to do business within this State, pass to the purchaser at a foreclosure mortgage sale, where the franchise rights have been conveyed by the mortgage. State ex rel. v. Roach, 300.

2. **Validity of Foreclosure Sale: Failure to Name Grantor in Notice.** The omission from the notice of sale under a deed of trust of the name of one of two grantors, all other requirements being met, the grantor whose name was omitted having previously parted with his equity, the representative of the owner of the entire equity being present at the sale, a fair price being obtained for the property, and the balance of the secured note afterwards being paid, so that the grantor whose name was omitted from the notice is no longer liable directly or indirectly for any sum by reason of his signature on the note secured, does not render the sale void, in spite of the statute (Sec. 2843, R. S. 1909) which requires that "such notice shall set forth . . . the grantors." Hassler v. Bank, 365.

3. ———: **Proof of Time of Publication.** Where the recitals in the trustee's deed show a compliance with the statutory requirements and are not contradicted, further proof of the time during which the notice of sale was published is not necessary. Ib.

MOTION FOR JUDGMENT.

Timely Answer:. Must Be Shown by Record. Allegations in a motion for judgment on the pleadings, that defendant failed to file his answer within the time given him by the court, do not prove themselves, but must be established by record entries; and in the absence of any record entries in the abstract tending to show them to be true, the motion cannot be considered on appeal. Cashion v. Gargus, 68.

MOTION FOR NEW TRIAL.

1. **Instructions: No Assignment in Motion.** Whether or not it was error to give an instruction on murder in the second degree, or to fail to give an instruction on involuntary manslaughter in the fourth degree, or to give an instruction concerning the bad feeling existing between defendant's and decedent's families, or to give an instruction on manslaughter in the fourth degree, will not be reviewed on appeal, where none of these matters was assigned as error in the motion for a new trial. State v. Coff, 14.

2. **Specific Assignment: All Law of Case.** An assignment in the motion for a new trial that the court failed to instruct the jury as to all the law arising upon the issues in the case, which does not specify upon what point the court failed to instruct, does not raise a point for appellate review. State v. Arnold, 3S.

S. **Sufficiency of Evidence: Judgment of Foreign Court: Raised by Motion for New Trial.** An assignment in the motion for a new trial that "the verdict and judgment is unsupported by any substantial evidence" raises the question of the sufficiency of the evidence, and that proposition necessarily embraces a contention that the judgments against a corporation rendered by a court of another State, which are made the basis of plaintiff's suit against its stockholders for the amount of the unpaid stock issued to them, and introduced in evidence, were insufficient in law to support a finding for plaintiff. Schroeder v. Edwards, 459.

MOTION TO MAKE DEFINITE.

Petition: Waiver. Defendant by answering over and going to trial on the merits waives any error in the action of the court in overruling his motion to require plaintiff to make his petition more definite and certain, and cannot urge any error in that ruling on appeal. Sperry v. Hurd, 628.

MOTION TO STRIKE OUT.

1. **Waiver.** Any error of the trial court in overruling defendant's motion to strike the amended petition from the files, on the ground that it constituted a departure, is waived by filing an answer to the merits and going to trial. Schroeder v. Edwards, 459.

2. **Appeal: Insufficient Assignment: Striking out Answer.** An assignment under "Points" that "the portions of defendant's answer stricken out by the court on the motion of the plaintiffs were material to the defense of these defendants, and error was, therefore, committed by the court in such action," with nothing more except the citation of authorities, does not comply with Rule 15, and does not designate any facts from which the court may comprehend what the point is. Ib.

NATURAL PERSONS, RIGHTS. See Constitutional Law, 6 and 7.

NEGLIGENCE.

1. **Pleading: Personal Injuries: Action Given by Statute.**
It is not necessary that the statute of this State or of Congress
which gives to plaintiff his cause of action be pleaded; all that
is required is that the facts which bring the case within them
be stated in the petition. The laws of Congress are not foreign
laws that must be pleaded or proven in this State. Pipes v.
Railroad, 385.

2. **Interstate Commerce: Personal Injuries: Jurisdiction of State
Court.** If the petition states the facts which, under the statute
of this State and the statute of Congress, constitute a cause
of action for personal injuries due to defendant's negligence,
the court should refuse an instruction directing the jury that if
the car which the crew was attempting to couple at the time
plaintiff was injured was employed in interstate commerce,
their verdict must be for defendant; for, the State courts have
jurisdiction to enforce the liability created by those statutes
for such injuries so inflicted. Ib.

3. **Evidence: Cause of Stopping Cars.** Where plaintiff fell
from the running board of a car and was injured, when the
drag of sixteen cars, which the crew were attempting to couple
with other loose cars, suddenly stopped, it is error to permit
plaintiff to testify what caused them to stop and deny that
right to defendant—where the cause of the sudden stop is the
vital issue in the case. Ib.

4. **Injury to Child: Care of Parents: Instruction.** In an action
by parents for the negligent killing of their child of
tender years while riding in the passenger elevator of defendant's office building, an instruction which told the jury
that if the failure of either of the child's parents to guard and
look after him "contributed in the least degree" to the happening of the "accident" to the child, the finding should be for defendant, was erroneous. Contributory negligence sufficient to
prevent recovery must be negligence that entered into and
formed the direct, producing and efficient cause of the casualty.
Besides, the instruction should not place the burden of guarding the child upon both parents at the same instant. Howard
v. Scarritt Est. Co., 398.

5. **Customary Method of Operating Elevator: Instruction.** Where
the effect of closing the sliding doors of a passenger
elevator with one hand while the operator threw the
speed lever with the other was that the accelerated car was
six or eight feet above the floor before the doors became
closely shut, and plaintiff's child, a passenger thereon, fell
through and was killed, an instruction which tells the jury that
if they believe from the evidence that the elevator doors were at
the time operated "in the usual and customary way that this and
other similar elevators and doors in this and other buildings
were operated" the defendant was not negligent in the operation thereof was erroneous. The apparatus is not so intricate
as to require expert exposition, or an instruction based thereon.
Ib.

NEGOTIABLE INSTRUMENTS.

1. **Note: Notice of Infirmities.** Notes made payable to the
maker and indorsed in blank by him become payable to bearer and negotiable by delivery; and a transferee before maturity

NEGOTIABLE INSTRUMENTS—Continued.

7. ——: ——: **Evidence of Election.** And evidence that, when defendant was approached by the attorney of the corporation on the theory that he was a stockholder, he announced that he had elected to surrender the stock and cancel the notes in accordance with the agreement, could not have prejudiced the rights of a holder of the notes with notice of the agreement. Ib.

NOTICE.

1. **Drainage District: Jurisdiction: Personal Service.** The jurisdiction of the circuit court to extend the boundary lines of an existing drainage district, under the Act of 1913, is not dependent upon personal service upon resident owners of the land to be included. Neither the Constitution of Missouri nor of the United States requires a uniform method of obtaining jurisdiction of the persons of litigants, in either general or special proceedings. A notice by publication in the language of the statute "to all persons interested," is sufficient. Drainage Dist. v. Harris, 139.

2. **Election Contest.** The service of notice of contest for the office of justice of the peace, fifteen days before the term of the county court at which the election is to be contested, is, by the statute, made essential to the validity of the proceeding; and where only twelve days' notice is given to contestee the court has no jurisdiction, and the proceeding must be dismissed. Ramsey v. Huck, 333.

3. ——: **Amendment.** Notice of contest of less than fifteen days cannot be made sufficient by an amendment fixing the time of hearing at fifteen days from the date of service. It is only where jurisdiction has been obtained by proper notice, in the manner pointed out by the statute, that an amendment may be made to a notice of contest. Ib.

4. **Deed of Trust: Validity of Foreclosure Sale: Failure to Name Grantor in Notice.** The omission from the notice of sale under a deed of trust of the name of one of two grantors, all other requirements being met, the grantor whose name was omitted having previously parted with his equity, the representative of the owner of the entire equity being present at the sale, a fair price being obtained for the proporty, and the balance of the secured note afterwards being paid, so that the grantor whose name was omitted from the notice is no longer liable directly or indirectly for any sum by reason of his signature on the note secured, does not render the sale void, in spite of the statute (Sec. 2843, R. S. 1909) which requires that "such notice shall set forth . . . the grantors." Hassler v. Bank, 365.

5. ——: ——: **Proof of Time of Publication.** Where the recitals in the trustee's deed show a compliance with the statutory requirements and are not contradicted, further proof of the time during which the notice of sale was published is not necessary. Ib.

OBLIGATION OF CONTRACTS. See **Railroads.**

OFFICES.

Justice of Peace: Title to Office: Jurisdiction. The Constitution gives the Supreme Court exclusive jurisdiction in cases involving title to any office under this State, and the office of justice of the peace is such an office. Ramsey v. Huck, 333.

OPTION.

Negotiable Note: Concurrent Dependent Agreement: Option to Surrender Stock for Notes. The maker of negotiable notes received a concurrent written agreement, signed by a corporation and its president, reciting that the maker had purchased one hundred shares of the capital stock of the company, for which he had given his two notes in settlement, due in six months, and guaranteeing that the maker, at their maturity might, at his option, surrender the stock, whereupon the notes would be canceled and returned to him. The certificates of stock, indorsed in blank, were attached to the notes, and the notes were transferred to a bank whose cashier had full actual knowledge of the agreement. Shortly afterwards the bank went into the hands of a receiver, who after the maturity of the notes, sold them to plaintiff. *Held*, that the notes and agreement did not constitute independent contracts, but they are dependent, and the agreement constitutes a defense to an action on the notes; and since the payee of the notes, when the agreement was delivered, was the holder, and the holder signed the agreement, the rule is not changed by the fact that another also signed it. Simpson v. Van Laningham, 286.

ORDER OF PUBLICATION. See Notice.

ORDER TO PAY MONEY. See Tender.

PARENT AND CHILD. See Elevators.

PARK DRIVE. See Cities, 1 to 3.

PARTIES TO ACTIONS.

1. **Suit to Quiet Title: Right of Person in Interest to Intervene.** Section 2541, Revised Statutes 1909, is a part of the Act of 1873, Laws 1873, p. 49, relating to the right of persons whose deeds or other evidences of title are lost or destroyed, to have the title adjudged to them and the record title restored to them, and does not apply to proceedings under section 2535, and does not authorize one who claims title by adverse possession to intervene and file an answer in a suit to quiet title. Miller v. Boulware, 487.

2. ———: ———: **Section 1733.** One who is not united in interest with any other party to the suit to quiet title is not authorized by section 1733, Revised Statutes 1909, to intervene, nor to be joined either as plaintiff or defendant. Ib.

3. ———: ———: **Section 1732: Adversary Interests.** Section 1732, Revised Statutes 1909, does not authorize one in possession of land and claiming by adverse possession to intervene and to be made a party defendant to a suit to quiet title brought against the record title owner by one who bases his title upon the Statute of Limitations by actual possession and does not ask for possession. Such an intervenor does not (1) have or claim an interest in the controversy adverse to the plaintiff, nor (2) is he a necessary party to a complete determination or settlement of the question involved, nor (3) is such a suit one for possession of the real estate. Ib.

PARTITION.

1. **Attorney's Fee.** No allowance should be made counsel as general costs for services in contested matters between the parties in a partition suit. But an allowance to plaintiff's

PARTITION—Continued.

attorney should be taxed as costs for such work as counsel would do in an ordinary non-contested partition, although, after new plaintiffs were added, there were brought into the case contested matters between them and defendants because of a denial of the validity of the deeds previously made by some of them. Parrish v. Treadway, 91.

2. **Voluntary: Through Conduit.** The fact that all the heirs of the owner of land, which they had inherited from him, selected their mother as a mere conduit for the purposes of partition, by deeding it to her, to be by her deeded to them in severalty, did not affect the character of the voluntary partition, nor did the deed from her to them convey any title, but only designated the possessory boundary to the land they already owned. Powell v. Powell, 117.

3. ————: **Deed to Husband and Wife.** And a deed in voluntary partition by a conduit to a daughter of the deceased owner and her husband, though seemingly a deed by the entirety, did not vest the husband with the title to the land described in the deed; but upon the daughter's death the entire title descended to her children or her other heirs, since, in spite of said deed, the entire title to the tract designated had been inherited by the daughter from said deceased owner. Ib.

4. ————: ————: **Money Paid to Equalize Interest.** A payment made by the husband of one of the coparceners to another coparcener for the purpose of equalizing the share of his wife, did not convert the deed to him and her into a deed by the entirety; at most it made them tenants in common, but it did not have even that effect if it conveyed only the wife's share, for a deed in voluntary partition does not convey the title, but that was cast upon the wife by descent. Ib.

5. ————: ————: **Estoppel.** Even though the wife directed that her husband's name be placed in the deed as grantee made in the voluntary partition of land inherited by her and others from her father, and he improved it with her knowledge, neither she, nor her heirs after her death, are estopped to deny that he acquired any title by the partition deed. Ib.

6. ————: ————: **Limitation: Husband's Possession: Curtesy.** Prior to the amendment of the Married Woman's Act of 1889, the husband was entitled to the possession of the wife's land, and that amendment did not change his possessory right already accrued. His wife could not maintain an action to oust him of his possession begun prior to 1889, nor could his children after her death, because immediately upon her death he became a tenant by the curtesy for life; but that possession cannot avail to invest title in him by limitations. Ib.

PASSENGER IN ELEVATOR. See Elevators.

PASTURE, LOSS OF. See Trespass.

PAYMENT. See Tender.

PLEADING.

1. **Admission: By Pleading.** A litigant cannot challenge a finding of facts by the court which stand admitted by his own pleading. Cashion v. Gargus, 68.

PLEADING—Continued.

2. **Timely Answer: Must Be Shown By Record.** Allegations in a motion for judgment on the pleadings, that defendant failed to file his answer within the time given him by the court, do not prove themselves, but must be established by record entries; and in the absence of any record entries in the abstract tending to show them to be true, the motion cannot be considered on appeal. Cashion v. Gargus, 68.

3. **Amended Petition: Departure: Description of Land.** An amendment of a petition in a suit for the specific performance of a contract to purchase land by changing the erroneous description of the land to a correct description, made before judgment, by leave of court, is permissible, and is not such a departure as to change the cause of action. Ib.

4. ———: ———: ———: **Minors: No New Summons.** And although the defendants are minors, if they have been properly brought into court, a guardian *ad litem* appointed and his acceptance filed, the filing thereafter of an amended petition by which an erroneous description of the land contained in the original petition is corrected, is as binding on them as upon adult defendants, and they have no greater right to an additional summons and service; and a judgment against them without additional summons is not void or voidable. Ib.

5. **Drainage District: Specific Objection: Should Be Pleaded.** If certain persons who are not owners of land sign the articles of incorporation for some fraudulent or ulterior motive, the objectors should deny by name that they are owners and upon the hearing break down by evidence their prima-facie showing of ownership; or, at least, deny generally that divers persons who signed the petition were competent signers or owners of land, and destroy the prime-facie case by proof. In re Mingo Dr. Dist., 268.

6. **Consolidated School District: Area.** No consolidated school district can be formed unless it contains an area of at least twelve square miles, or has an enumeration of at least two hundred children of school age; and when its directors are called upon collectively, and directly by the State in a suit in the nature of *quo warranto*, to show a right to exist, their answer unless it states one or the other of these necessary statutory requirements, is insufficient. State ex inf. v. Clardy, 371.

7. ———: ———: ———: **Assumed at Trial.** But if no point was made, either at the trial or in the appellate court, that the answer of the directors, sued by the State in *quo warranto*, to determine the validity of the organization of an alleged consolidated school district, does not contain an allegation that the district contains an area of at least twelve square miles, and if both plaintiff and defendants proved, conclusively, without objection, that the area of said district is more than twelve square miles, the court will assume on appeal that the answer was amended so as to include such necessary allegation. Ib.

8. **Personal Injuries: Action Given by Statute.** It is not necessary that the statute of this state or of Congress which gives to plaintiff his cause of action be pleaded; all that is required is that the facts which bring the case within them be stated in the petition. The laws of Congress are not foreign laws that must be pleaded or proven in this State. Pipes v. Railroad, 385.

PLEADING—Continued.

POLICE REGULATION.

1. **Railroad Corporation: Franchises.** The grant of a right to construct and own a railroad and to do a railroad business within the State is not a right that falls within the police power. The control of common carriers, such as, for instance, the fixing of maximum passenger or freight rates, is an exercise of police power, but that is a totally different question from the right to do business at all. State ex rel. v. Roach, 300.

2. ———: ———: **Violation of Charter Rights.** The Legislature cannot in the exercise of assumed police powers, violate charter contracts and overthrow vested rights. The Wabash Railway Company, being the owner of a franchise right to own and operate a railroad and do a railroad business in this State, granted by the State to the North Missouri Railroad Company prior to the adoption of the Constitution of 1875, and passed by successive mortgages and foreclosure sales to said present company, cannot by a legislative act be deprived thereof, for such right does not pertain to police powers, but is a contract right. Ib.

3. **Water-closets: Conflicting Authority of City and School Board.** The Board of Education of the city of St. Louis is not subject to the ordinances and regulations of the city in respect to the manner of construction of water-closets and vents therefrom in a public school building. Under the statute the Board of Education is specifically "charged with the care of the public school buildings of said city, and with the responsibility for the ventilation and sanitary condition thereof," and under the Constitution that statute makes their authority exclusive. Bd. of Education v. St. Louis, 356.

4. ———: ———: **Presumption of Application to Sovereign: Repeal by Implication.** Where the sovereignty itself has dealt with the subject of the construction and management of property which is held and used by its agents for the highest governmental purposes, no presumption that laws of the character of the charter of the city of St. Louis and ordinances passed in pursuance thereof are applicable to the sovereign, can prevail, for then the power does not rest upon presumption, but upon express legislative declarations. Ib.

5. ———: ———: **Paramount Authority of Statute.** The general charter of the city of St. Louis must yield to the provisions of a law having special application to particular matters and things within the field of its operation; and where there is such a general law, the question of whether the charter and ordinances are impliedly repealed without being mentioned in the general law, is not in the case. Ib.

POWER TO HOLD TITLE TO LAND. See Corporations, 26 to 28.

PRACTICE.

1. **Timely Answer: Must Be Shown by Record.** Allegations in a motion for judgment on the pleadings, that defendant failed to file his answer within the time given him by the court, do not prove themselves, but must be established by record entries; and in the absence of any record entries in the abstract tending to show them to be true, the motion cannot be considered on appeal. Cashion v. Gargus, 68.

2. **Amended Petition: Departure: Description of Land.** An amendment of a petition in a suit for the specific performance of a contract to purchase land by changing the erroneous de-

PRACTICE—Continued.

scription of the land to a correct description, made before judgment, by leave of court, is permissible, and is not such a departure as to change the cause of action. Ib.

3. ———: ———: ———: Minors: No New Summons. And although the defendants are minors, if they have been properly brought into court, a guardian *ad litem* appointed and his acceptance filed, the filing thereafter of an amended petition by which an erroneous description of the land contained in the original petition is corrected, is as binding on them as upon adult defendants, and they have no greater right to an additional summons and service; and a judgment against them without such additional summons is not void or voidable. Ib.

4. Injunction: Publication of Libel: Remedy. The issue of libel or no libel is an issue of law and a matter for the jury; and before plaintiff can have an injunction to restrain a further publication of libelous statements, there must be a verdict of the jury finding the statements to be false and libelous. If he goes to a jury with the alleged libel and obtains a judgment, which owing to defendant's insolvency he is unable to collect, further publication of a libel of like or similar import may be enjoined in a separate suit; or he may couple a count for injunction in his petition with a count at law for damages, and having sustained before a jury his law count, the court, upon allegation and proof of defendant's insolvency and threatened continuance of the libelous publication, or to avoid a multiplicity of suits, can enjoin a continued publication thereof. Wolf v. Harris, 405.

5. Motion to Strike Out: Waiver. Any error of the trial court, in overruling defendant's motion to strike the amended petition from the files, on the ground that it constituted a departure, is waived by filing an answer to the merits and going to trial. Schroeder v. Edwards, 459.

6. Remanding Cause: Confining Issue. Where all issues in an equity case except one have on appeal been settled, the court, instead of remanding the cause generally, may remand it with directions that upon a retrial the case be confined to the one issue upon which the evidence at the first trial was insufficient to support a decree for plaintiff. Ib.

7. Evidence: Improperly Admitted for One Side: Rebuttal By Other. The admission of improper testimony on the one side does not authorize the admission of improper testimony in rebuttal on the other. Buck v. Buck, 644.

8. Reopening Case: Discretion. The reopening of the case after both sides have closed and a peremptory instruction has been offered by plaintiff, to permit the introduction of other testimony, is a matter largely within the discretion of the trial court, and does not constitute reversible error unless the discretion has been abused, to the injury of the losing party. Ib.

9. Reversal of Judgment: No Material Error. Notwithstanding errors were committed at the trial the judgment will not be reversed unless they materially affect the merits of the case. Ib.

10. Will Contest: Pleading: Interest of Contestant: General Denial: Demurrer to Evidence. A petition which fails to state the interest of plaintiff in the probate of the will does not state

PRACTICE—Continued.

a cause of action for setting aside the will, and that defect is not waived by failure to make specific objection by demurrer or answer, but a general denial contained in one of the answers is sufficient to raise the issue of fact, and plaintiff is thereby required to prove the existence of such facts as will show him entitled to maintain the suit, and if he fails to do so the court errs in overruling a demurrer to the evidence. Gruender v. Frank, 713.

11. ———: ———: Stating Interest of Heirs. The body of the petition in a suit to set aside a will should allege facts showing that plaintiffs are heirs of the deceased testator. It is not enough simply to name them in the caption. Ib.

PRINCIPAL AND AGENT.

1. Embezzlement: Agency of Loan Agent. Where the borrower called at defendant's office to employ him to secure a loan of $3400, and gave him a note for $127.50 for his services in that behalf, and in addition signed an order directed to the loan company in which he requested that the proceeds of the loan be paid to defendant and in which he said he thereby appointed defendant his agent to settle with the company for said loan, and the loan company, after deducting its own commission, sent a check payable to defendant for the balance, the defendant was the agent of the borrower, in all that was necessary to establish the relation of agency, in a prosecution for having embezzled the proceeds of the check. State v. McWilliams, 437.

2. Corporation: Payment for Stock: Services Rendered by Financial Agent. Where nothing was paid in money by its stockholders at the time the Illinois corporation was organized, but the plan of its incorporators was to issue the company's bonds to the full amount of its capitalization and use the money derived from their sale in the construction of the electric light plant, it cannot be held that one of them, who, as the company's financial agent, indorsed its notes upon which money was obtained for the first work of construction, which notes when the bonds were sold were paid out of the proceeds, thereby, as against general creditors of the company, paid for the stock issued to him in services rendered the company. Schroeder v. Edwards, 459.

PRIVATE BANKS. See Banks and Banking.

PROCESS.

1. Change of Cause of Action: Minors: No New Summons. Although the defendants are minors, if they have been properly brought into court, a guardian *ad litem* appointed and his acceptance filed, the filing thereafter of an amended petition by which an erroneous description of the land contained in the original petition is corrected, is as binding on them as upon adult defendants, and they have no greater right to an additional summons and service; and a judgment against them without such additional summons is not void or voidable. Cashion v. Gargus, 68.

2. Drainage District: Jurisdiction: Notice: Personal Service. The jurisdiction of the circuit court to extend the boundary lines of an existing drainage district, under the Act of 1913, is not dependent upon personal service upon resident owners of the land to be included. Neither the Constitution of Missouri nor of the United States requires a uniform method of obtaining

PROCESS—Continued.

jurisdiction of the persons of litigants, in either general or special proceedings. A notice by publication in the language of the statute "to all persons interested," is sufficient. Drainage Dist. v. Harris, 139.

3. **Jurisdiction: Non-Resident Corporation: Service.** For the reasons stated in the minority opinion of the St.Louis Court of Appeals, 175 Mo. App. l. c. 679 et seq., in this case, the judgment is reversed, and the cause remanded, in order to give plaintiff opportunity to obtain valid service on defendant corporation. McMenamy Inv. Co. v. Catering Co., 340.

4. ———: **Foreign Insurance Company As Defendant: Foreign Plaintiff: Right to Sue in This State.** An Arizona corporation not licensed to do business in either Colorado or Missouri, can bring and maintain a suit in the circuit court of any county in Missouri, against an insurance company organized under the laws of Pennsylvania and licensed to do insurance business in this State, upon an insurance policy issued and delivered in Colorado, insuring property in that State against loss by fire by having the summons served by the sheriff of Cole County upon the Superintendent of Insurance, as the statutory agent of said insurance company, in accordance with the provisions of section 7042, Revised Statutes 1909. [GRAVES, BOND and WALKER, JJ., dissenting.] Mining & Milling Co. v. Fire Ins. Co., 524.

5. ———: ———: ———: ———: **So Long as Policies Are Outstanding.** The language of the statute declaring that the authority of the Superintendent of' Insurance to accept service of process for an insurance company licensed to do business in this State shall continue "so long as it shall have any policies or liabilities outstanding in this State," is not a limitation upon the authority of the Superintendent to act for such company, and not a limitation upon the character of the actions that may be brought and maintained in the courts of this State, and does not distinguish between contracts made in this State and contracts made elsewhere, but is a mere limitation of the time within which suits may be brought.

Held, by GRAVES, J., dissenting, with whom BOND and WALKER, JJ., concur, that the language of the statute declaring that service of process upon the Superintendent of Insurance shall be valid and binding upon said company "so long as it shall have any policies or liabilities outstanding in this State," does characterize the kind of litigation to which foreign insurance companies can be required to respond in the courts of this State, and fixes a limitation upon the causes over which they can assume jurisdiction; and when read in connection with the preceding clause, which mentions policies issued when the company was in the State, it is apparent that the substituted method of service of process is limited to suits on contracts made within the State, and does not apply to contracts made outside the State. Ib.

PROHIBITION.

1. **Circuit Courts.** The Supreme Court is given authority by the Constitution to prohibit, by its writ of prohibition, circuit courts and other inferior tribunals from exercising jurisdiction which they do not legally have. Ramsey v. Huck, 533.

PROHIBITION—Continued.

2. **Justice of Peace: Title to Office.** The Constitution gives the Supreme Court exclusive jurisdiction in cases involving title to any office under this State, and the office of a justice of the peace is such an office. Ramsey v. Huck, 333.

3. **Jurisdiction of Appeal.** Jurisdiction to hear and determine upon appeal the original case out of which the application for a writ of prohibition arose, is not a prerequisite to the right of the Supreme Court to issue the writ. Ib.

PUBLICATION. See Notice.

PUBLIC SCHOOLS. See Schools.

QUIETING TITLE.

1. **Limitation: Time to Bring Suit.** No limitation is fixed by the statute (Sec. 650, R. S. 1889; Sec. 2535, R. S. 1909) in which a suit to quiet title must be brought. The ten-year Statute of Limitations does not apply. [Following Armor v. Frey, 253 Mo. l. c. 474.] Powell v. Powell, 117.

2. **Parties to Action: Suit to Quiet Title: Right of Person in Interest to Intervene.** Section 2541, Revised Statutes 1909, is a part of the Act of 1873, Laws 1873, p. 49, relating to the right of persons whose deeds or other evidences of title are lost or destroyed, to have the title adjudged to them and the record title restored to them, and does not apply to proceedings under section 2535, and does not authorize one who claims title by adverse possession to intervene and file an answer in a suit to quiet title. Miller v. Boulware, 487.

3. ———: ———: ———: **Section 1733.** One who is not united in interest with any other party to the suit to quiet title is not authorized by section 1753, Revised Statutes 1909, to intervene, nor to be joined either as plaintiff or defendant. Ib.

4. ———: ———: ———: **Section 1732: Adversary Interests.** Section 1732, Revised Statutes 1909, does not authorize one in possession of land and claiming by adverse possession to intervene and to be made a party defendant to a suit to quiet title brought against the record title owner by one who bases his title upon the Statute of Limitations by actual possession and does not ask for possession. Such an intervenor does not (1) have or claim an interest in the controversy adverse to the plaintiff, nor (2) is he a necessary party to a complete determination or settlement of the question involved, nor (3) is such a suit one for possession of the real estate. Ib.

QUO WARRANTO.

1. **Consolidated School District: Area: Pleading.** No consolidated school district can be formed unless it contains an area of at least twelve square miles, or has an enumeration of at least two hundred children of school age; and when its directors are called upon collectively, and directly by the State in a suit in the nature of *quo warranto*, to show a right to exist, their answer unless it states one or the other of these necessary statutory requirements is insufficient. State ex inf. v. Clardy, 571.

2. ———: ———: ———: **Assumed at Trial.** But if no point was made, either at the trial or in the appellate court, that the answer of the directors, sued by the State in *quo warranto* to determine the validity of the organization of an alleged con-

QUO WARRANTO—Continued.

solidated school district, does not contain an allegation that the district contains an area of at least twelve square miles, and if both plaintiff and defendants proved, conclusively, without objection, that the area of said district is more than twelve square miles, the court will assume on appeal that the answer was amended so as to include such necessary allegation. Ib.

RAILROADS.

1. Corporation: Franchises: Sale. The franchises of a rail way company are divisible into two classes: first, the mere right of being a body corporate; and, second, all other powers or privileges granted by the sovereign power. The first is not subject to barter and sale; the second are. State ex rel. v. Roach, 300.

2. ———: ———: What Passes by Mortgage Sale. Both by the laws and Constitution of Missouri and by the general law, all the franchise rights of a railway company except the mere right to be a corporation, including the right to do business within this State, pass to the purchaser at a foreclosure mortgage sale, where the franchise rights have been conveyed by the mortgage. Ib.

3. ———: Wabash Railroad: Right of Purchaser to Do Business. On December 26, 1906, the Wabash Railroad Company, then possessed of the right, privilege and franchise to do a railroad business in this State, mortgaged all those rights, and they passed by foreclosure sale in 1915 to the Wabash Railway Company, a new corporation, organized under the laws of Indiana. Ever since the building of the North Missouri Railroad under the Act of 1851, there has been a State grant of a right to do intrastate business over that railroad and its after-acquired and after-constructed portions, which has successively passed, by statutory authority, to divers successors of the old railroad company, and is now vested, by reason of said foreclosure sale and purchase, in the said Wabash Railway Company. Ib.

4. ———: ———: Police Power. The grant of a right to construct and own a railroad and to do a railroad business within the State is not a right that falls within the police power. The control of common carriers, such as, for instance, the fixing of maximum passenger or freight rates, is an exercise of police power, but that is a totally different question from the right to do business at all. Ib.

5. ———: ———: ———: Violation of Charter Rights. The Legislature cannot, in the exercise of assumed police powers, violate charter contracts and overthrow vested rights. The Wabash Railway Company, being the owner of a franchise right to own and operate a railroad and do a railroad business in this State, granted by the State to the North Missouri Railroad Company prior to the adoption of the Constitution of 1875, and passed by successive mortgages and foreclosure sales to said present company, cannot by a legislative act be deprived thereof, for such right does not pertain to police powers, but is a contract right. Ib.

6. ———: ———: Permission to Do Business: Retroactive Statute. The Act of 1913, Laws 1913, p. 179, declaring that no railroad corporation, except one incorporated under the laws of this State, shall be permitted to do an intrastate business in

RAILROADS—Continued.

this State, does not have a retroactive operation, and does not apply to a foreign corporation which has succeeded to the rights of another railroad company which long prior to the enactment of said statute had been granted by the State the right to own and operate a railroad in this State and to carry on an intrastate railroad business, and the Secretary of State cannot lawfully withhold from said corporation a permit or license to do business in Missouri. That act cannot contravene existing rights lawfully granted by the State. It applies to railroads built subsequently to its enactment, and does not affect those then operating in the State.

Held, by WOODSON, C. J., dissenting, that the Act of 1913 applies simply to intrastate business and railroads, and the Constitution (Art. 12, sec. 18) retained jurisdiction over so much of a consolidated railroad as is in this State. State ex rel. v. Roach, 300.

7. ——— : ——— : **Due Process: Impairment of Contract.** To hold that a foreign corporation which by purchase has acquired the railroad of another company and its franchise right to do business in this State, acquired prior to the enactment of the Act of 1913, Laws 1913, p. 179, cannot do a railroad business in this State, would be to take valuable property rights without due process of law, and to impair the obligation of contracts, not only of said company, but of all other foreign corporations now owning and operating railroads under franchises granted prior to its enactment. Ib.

RECEIVER. See.Banks and Banking.

RELIGIOUS CORPORATION. See Corporations, 26 to 28.

REMARKS OF COUNSEL. See Attorneys.

REMARKS OF COURT. See Courts, 1.

RIGHT TO SUE IN THIS STATE.

1. **Jurisdiction: Foreign Insurance Company As Defendant: Foreign Plaintiff.** An Arizona corporation, not licensed to do business in either Colorado or Missouri, can bring and maintain a suit in the circuit court of any county in Missouri, against in insurance company organized under the laws of Pennsylvania and licensed to do insurance business in this State, upon an insurance policy issued and delivered in Colorado, insuring property in that State against loss by fire, by having the summons served by the sheriff of Cole County upon the Superintendent of Insurance, as the statutory agent of said insurance company, in accordance with the provisions of section 7042, Revised Statutes 1909. [GRAVES, BOND and WALKER, JJ., dissenting.] Mining & Milling Co. v. Fire Ins. Co., 524.

2. ——— : ——— : ——— : **Limitation to Contracts Made in this State.** The statute (Sec. 7042, R. S. 1909) does not limit the right of holders of policies issued by an insurance company licensed to do business in this State to sue in the courts of this State upon contracts made in this State, but gives them the right to sue such a company in the courts of this State upon policies wherever made.

Held, by GRAVES, J., dissenting, with whom BOND and WALKER, JJ., concur, that the substituted method of service of process provided by the statute is limited to actions arising on contracts made or acts done in this state. Ib.

RIGHT TO SUE IN THIS STATE—Continued.

3. ——: ——: ——: So Long as Policies Are Outstanding.
The language of the statute declaring that the authority of the
Superintendent of Insurance to accept service of process for
an insurance company licensed to do business in this State shall
continue "so long as it shall have any policies or liabilities outstanding in this State," is not a limitation upon the authority
of the Superintendent to act for such company, and not a
limitation upon the character of the actions that may be brought
and maintained in the courts of this State, and does not distinguish between contracts made in this State and contracts
made elsewhere, but is a mere limitation of the time within
which suits may be brought.

Held, by GRAVES, J., dissenting, with whom BOND and WAL-
KER, JJ., concur, that the language of the statute declaring
that service of process upon the Superintendent of Insurance shall be valid and binding upon said company "so
long as it shall have any policies or liabilities outstanding
in this State," does characterize the kind of litigation to
which foreign insurance companies can be required to respond in the courts of this State, and fixes a limitation upon the causes over which they can assume jurisdiction; and
when read in connection with the preceding clause, which
mentions policies issued when the company was in the
State, it is apparent that the substituted method of service
of process is limited to suits on contracts made within the
State, and does not apply to contracts made outside the
state. Ib.

RIGHTS OF ACCUSED.

One Law for Innocent and Guilty. There can be but one law for
the trial of the innocent and guilty; and notwithstanding the
court may be of the opinion that the evidence is sufficient to
warrant a verdict of guilty, a plain statute forbidding the cross-
examination of a defendant concerning matters wholly outside
his examination in chief must be applied to all defendants alike.
The Constitution has not ordained that apparent guilt is the
sole condition of affirmance by the Supreme Court of a verdict
of guilty. State v. Pfeifer, 23.

RIGHTS OF NATURAL PERSONS. See Constitutional Law, 6 and
7.

SALES.

Corporation: Franchises. The franchises of a railway company
are divisible into two classes: first, the mere right of being a
body corporate; and, second, all other powers or privileges
granted by the sovereign power. The first is not subject to
barter and sale; the second are. State ex rel v. Roach, 300.

SCHOOLS.

1. Police Regulation: Water-closets: Conflicting Authority of
City and School Board. The Board of Education of the city
of St. Louis is not subject to the ordinances and regulations
of the city in respect to the manner of construction of water-
closets and vents therefrom in a public school building. Under
the statute the Board of Education is specifically "charged
with the care of the public school buildings of said city, and
with the responsibility for the ventilation and sanitary condition thereof," and under the Constitution that statute makes
their authority exclusive. Bd. of Education v. St. Louis, 356.

SCHOOLS—Continued.

2. ———:· ———: ———: **Presumption of Application to Sovereign: Repeal by Implication.** Where the sovereignty itself has dealt with the subject of the construction and management of property which is held and used by its agents for the highest governmental purposes, no presumption that laws of the character of the charter of the city of St. Louis and ordinances passed in pursuance thereof are applicable to the sovereign, can prevail, for then the power does not rest upon presumption, but upon express legislative declarations. Bd. of Education v. St. Louis, 556.

3. ———: ———: ———: **Paramount Authority of Statute.** The general charter of the city of St. Louis must yield to the provisions of a law having special application to particular matters and things within the field of its operation; and where there is such a general law, the question of whether the charter and ordinances are impliedly repealed without being mentioned in the general law, is not in the case. Ib.

4. **Consolidated School District: Area: Pleading.** No consolidated school district can be formed unless it contains an area of at least twelve square miles, or has an enumeration of at least two hundred children of school age; and when its directors are called upon collectively, and directly by the State in a suit in the nature of *quo warranto*, to show a right to exist, their answer unless it states one or the other of these necessary statutory requirements is insufficient. State ex inf. v. Clardy, 371.

5. ———: ———: .———: **Assumed at Trial.** But if no point was made, either at the trial or in the appellate court, that the answer of the directors, sued by the State in *quo warranto* to determine the validity of the organization of an alleged consolidated school district, does not contain an allegation that the district contains an area of at least twelve square miles, and if both plaintiff and defendants proved, conclusively, without objection, that the area of said district is more than twelve square miles, the court will assume on appeal that the answer was amended so as to include such necessary allegation. Ib.

6. ———: **Filing Papers: Indorsement by Depositary.** The petition, notice, plat, proceedings of meeting, etc., required by section 3 of the Consolidated School District Act (Laws 1913, p. 721) need not be indorsed "filed" in order to be filed with the county clerk and county superintendent. Indorsement on the paper of the fact of filing is not a necessary element of filing, unless the statute specifically so says. Ib.

7. ———: **Validity of Organization: Recital in Minutes: Manner of Voting.** If the minutes of the special meeting to organize a consolidated school district state that the vote was taken by ballot and that a certain number of votes were cast, of which a certain number were for consolidation and a less number against it, the organization will not be held invalid on the sole ground that the minutes do not recite that each voter advanced to the front of the chairman and deposited his ballot in a box provided for that purpose, nor because they do not recite that the tellers announced each ballot aloud. The statute (Sec. 10865, R. S. 1909) does not require the minutes to recite the details of each act constituting the statutory requirements of the meeting. Ib.

SEDUCTION.

1. **Remarks of Counsel: Preserved for Review.** Where defendant's counsel, in his objection to argument made to the jury by the State's counsel, repeats the statement made by said counsel and states his reason therefor, and the court by his ruling, accepts the repetition as a true reiteration of what had been said, the ruling, being excepted to, is for review on appeal, without any further preservation in the bill of exceptions than the statement and objection of appellant's counsel and the ruling and remarks of the court, and the exception. State v. Evans, 163.

2. ———: **Weak Evidence.** Argument of counsel to the jury, assigned as prejudicial to appellant, is to be examined in the light of the facts of the particular case. Where the evidence of defendant's guilt is weak, the offense charged is one which decent men abhor, and there is no testimony pertaining to a fact which reasonable men would expect to be developed, remarks of counsel for the State, either in their opening statement or in their argument to the jury, by which such lacking testimony is attempted to be supplied, may alone constitute reversible error. Ib.

3. ———: **No Request for Fulfillment of Promise to Marry: Supplied by Attorney.** The fact, that, after prosecutrix discovered her pregnancy as the result of an admitted sexual relationship, she frequently kept company with defendant in the presence of her and his relatives and requested him to marry her to shield her from its consequences, but at no time suggested or claimed a reparation on account of a promise to marry, there being no legal impediment or other obstacle in the way of such a marriage, tends to impeach her testimony that there had been such a promise, and in view of her unsatisfactory testimony as to the fact of an engagement was a matter of grave importance for the jury in determining whether or not her testimony was true; and remarks made by the State's counsel, in his opening statement that "the young girl who was wronged by this young man has solicited and begged and importuned him to marry her and give this bright little baby a father and a name," and repeated in substance in the argument to the jury, the effect being, whether intended or not, to break the force of the significant omission, and to supply the lack of it, were reversible error.

Held, by REVELLE, J., dissenting, that it is but common knowledge and ordinary human experience that no juror will sit through a trial of a seduction case without the thought that the girl, whose shame and disgrace would be lessened by marriage, was anxious to and did what she could to bring about the marriage, and the statement of counsel could only have hastened the thought; and, in this case, it was not prejudicial, because the jury knew the defendant had not married her, and counsel's statement that she begged him to do so and his refusal, if effective at all, tended only to corroborate his testimony that he had never promised to marry her at any time. Ib.

4. **Evidence: Conclusions and Opinions.** In a prosecution for seduction under promise of marriage, the father of prosecutrix should not be permitted to state his conclusions and give his opinions as to the relations between her and defendant, such as, "He treated her like a sweetheart," "He seemed to think a good deal of her."

SEDUCTION—Continued.

οf such witness," merely lays down a rule of evidence and cannot be regarded as justifying the giving of an instruction which specifically singles out and designates the credence to be given any particular one among those the statute renders competent as witnesses; and, *fifth*, while there may be cases, such as upon a plea of guilty, in which such an instruction may be considered harmless, in most cases, especially where the State's case upon material issues is inherently weak, it does harm to give it. *Held*, by REVELLE, J., that, while the instruction should never be given, it does not constitute reversible error where there is, as in this case, no doubt of defendant's guilt. *Held*, by FARIS, J., dissenting, that, while conceding some of the reasons given for the impropriety of the instruction to be sound, and that the giving of it subserves no useful purpose, it is nevertheless buttressed by a solemn statute (Sec. 5242, R. S. 1909) and has for more than forty years been held not to be reversible error, and to now hold it be such would (1) cause much uncertainty in the law, and (2) if it is to be eliminated that should be done by the Legislature; and (3) the instruction but expresses the law as declared by the statute, and it cannot of itself be reversible error to tell the jury by an instruction what the law is. Ib.

SERVICE OF SUMMONS. See Process.

SODOMY.

1. **Covered by Statutes, Etc.** Notwithstanding section 4725, Revised Statutes 1909, was repealed and re-enacted, with an amendment, in 1911, the crime of sodomy may be committed by a man by inserting his sexual organ in the mouth of a woman. State v. Pfiefer, 23.

2. **Evidence of Other Crimes: Res Gestae.** Where the information charges sodomy *per os* it is not error to admit evidence tending to show sodomy *per anum* where the proof shows both acts were so connected as to show both were parts of the *res gestae*. Ib.

SPECIAL LEGACIES. See Wills, 1 to 4.

SPECIFIC PERFORMANCE.

1. **Amended Petition: Departure: Description of Land.** An amendment of a petition in a suit for the specific performance of a contract to purchase land by changing the erroneous description of the land to a correct description, made before judgment, by leave of court, is permissible, and is not such a departure as to change the cause of action. Cashion v. Gargus, 68.

2. ——: ——: ——: **Minors: No New Summons.** And although the defendants are minors, if they have been properly brought into court, a guardian *ad litem* appointed and his acceptance filed, the filing thereafter of an amended petition by which an erroneous description of the land contained in the original petition is corrected, is as binding on them as upon adult defendants, and they have no greater right to an additional summons and service; and a judgment against them without such additional summons is not void or voidable. Ib.

STATEMENT TO JURORS. See Attorneys.

STATUTES AND STATUTORY CONSTRUCTION.

1. **Defendant: Cross-Examination.** In view of the plain wording of the statute (Sec. 5242, R. S. 1909) forbidding them, questions asked defendant in cross-examination upon matters neither touched upon nor growing out of his examination in chief, are presumed to be prejudicial error, unless the contrary is made to appear; and where he is compelled to state all his movements the night of the crime, his acquaintanceship with two other persons who had committed a crime against the same woman two hours before he and they are charged with having committed a similar crime against her, and whether or not he and they had been companions since their school days and frequenters of the same saloon—all matters not touched upon in his examination in chief and brought out for the purpose of corroborating a police officer—the questions were not only unwarranted but were prejudicial. State v. Pfiefer, 23.

2. **Sodomy: Covered by Statutes, Etc.** Notwithstanding section 4725, Revised Statutes 1909, was repealed and re-enacted, with an amendment, in 1911, the crime of sodomy may be committed by a man by inserting his sexual organ in the mouth of a woman. Ib.

3. **Quieting Title: Limitation: Time to Bring Suit.** No limitation is fixed by the statute (Sec. 650, R. S. 1889; Sec. 2535, R. S. 1909) in which a suit to quiet title must be brought. The ten-year Statute of Limitations does not apply. [Following Armor v. Frey, 253 Mo. l. c. 474.] Powell v. Powell, 117.

4. **Railroad Corporation: Permission to Do Business: Retroactive Statute.** The act of 1913, Laws 1913, p. 179, declaring that no railroad corporation, except one incorporated under the laws of this State, shall be permitted to do an intrastate business in this State, does not have a retroactive operation, and does not apply to a foreign corporation which has succeeded to the rights of another railroad company which long prior to the enactment of said statute had been granted by the State the right to own and operate a railroad in this State and to carry on an intrastate railroad business, and the Secretary of State cannot lawfully withhold from said corporation a permit or license to do business in Missouri. That act cannot contravene existing rights lawfully granted by the State. It applies to railroads built subsequently to its enactment, and does not affect those then operating in the State.

   Held, by WOODSON, C. J., dissenting, that the act of 1913 applies simply to intrastate business and railroads, and the Constitution (Art. 12, sec. 18) retained jurisdiction over so much of a consolidated railroad as is in this State. State ex rel. v. Roach, 300.

5. **Administration: Removal Causes: Ascertainment Before Appointment.** Section 50, Revised Statutes 1909, announcing the causes for which letters testamentary or of administration may be revoked, is not to be read into and made a part of section 14, which designates persons who cannot qualify as executor or administrator. The probate court cannot refuse to appoint an executor named in the will on the ground that such person if appointed could be removed for the causes mentioned in section 50. State ex rel. v. Holtcamp, 412.

6. **Adopted Child: Right of Heirs to Inherit.** Section 1671, Revised Statutes 1909, providing that a person may, by deed, "adopt any child or children as his or her heir," by the use of the word

STATUTES AND STATUTORY CONSTRUCTION—Continued.

"heir," and section 352, providing that the estate of an intestate shall descend "to his children, *or their descendants*," mean that the child of an adopted child who dies during the lifetime of the adopting parent, inherits from such adopting parent dying intestate. An adopted child is a child within the meaning of the descent laws, and the words in section 332 mean the same as if they had read the estate shall descend "to his children (either natural-born or adopted), or their descendants." Bernero v. Goodwin, 427.

7. ———: How Determined. The rights of the natural·child of the adopted child to claim a distributive share in the estate of the adopting parent is not limited solely to the adoption statutes and the deed of adoption, to the exclusion of all rights given by the statutes of descents, but those statutes lay down the general rules of inheritance, and the deed of adoption created the status of the adopted child, or gave to him the status of an heir. Ib.

8. Statutes of Another State: Proof. In Missouri the statutory law of another State must be proven the same as any other fact in the case. Schroeder v. Edwards, 459.

9. Judgment of Another State: Presumption: Cognovit. Where the plaintiff's cause of action is bottomed on the judgment of a circuit court of another State, proof of a judgment entered by the clerk of that court in vacation, is not sufficient, unless there are also introduced in evidence the statutes of that State establishing the jurisdiction and the authority to do that which was done by the clerk in vacation. In such case the presumption that the judgment so entered was regular and valid cannot be indulged, because such a judgment, being unknown to the common law, must depend for its validity upon the statutes authorizing it. Ib.

10. Parties to Action: Suit to Quiet Title: Right of Person in Interest to Intervene. Section 2541, Revised Statutes 1909, is a part of the Act of 1873, Laws 1873, p. 49, relating to the right of persons whose deeds or other evidences of title are lost or destroyed, to have the title adjudged to them and the record title restored to them, and does not apply to proceedings under section 2535, and does not authorize one who claims title by adverse possession to intervene and file an answer in a suit to quiet title. Miller v. Boulware, 487.

11. ———: ———: ———: Section 1733. One who is not united in interest with any other party to the suit to quiet title is not authorized by section 1733, Revised Statutes 1909, to intervene, nor to be joined either as plaintiff of defendant. Ib.

12. ———: ———: ———: Section 1732: Adversary Interests. Section 1732, Revised Statutes 1909, does not authorize one in possession of land and claiming by adverse possession to intervene and to be made a party defendant to a suit to quiet title brought against the record title owner by one who bases his title upon the Statute of Limitations by actual possession and does not ask for possession. Such an intervenor does not (1) have or claim an interest in the controversy adverse to the plaintiff, nor (2) is he a necessary party to a complete determination or settlement of the question involved, nor (3) is such a suit one for possession of the real estate. Ib.

STATUTES AND STATUTORY CONSTRUCTION—Continued.

13. **Private Bank: Corporation: Notwithstanding Words of Statute.**
The words of the statute (Sec. 1116, R. S. 1909) declaring that
the owner or owners of a private bank may carry on a banking
business "without being incorporated," were used to distinguish
private banks from banks incorporated under the general banking laws; they were not intended to declare that a private bank,
organized under the statutes and conducted according to their
requirements, it not a separate legal entity, or a *quasi*-cor-
poration, or a corporation sole. State ex rel. v. Sage, 493.

14. **In the Light of Prior Condition.** There are few guides to the
construction of a statute more useful than that which directs
attention to the prior condition of the law as an aid in determining the meaning of any change therein. Mining Co. v.
Ins. Co., 524.

15. **Jurisdiction: Foreign Insurance Company: Licensed to Do
Business in State: Process: Application of Statutes.** Neither
section 7042 nor section 7044, Revised Statutes 1909, authorizes service of process in suits brought in the courts of this
State against a foreign insurance company doing business
herein without a license, based upon a policy of insurance issued by it in another state or county. Section 7042 does not
apply to suits based on contracts of insurance written in this
State by a foreign company having no license to do business
herein, but section 7044 applies to such a situation. Section
7042 limits the service of process therein provided to foreign
insurance companies doing business in this State under authority from the State duly granted to them; and by section
7044 the process therein mentioned is limited to suits upon
policies issued in this State by companies which do not have
authority from the State to do business here. Ib.

STATUTES CITED AND CONSTRUED.

United States Statutes.

85 Stat. at Large, p. 65, see page 392.

Revised Statutes 1909.

STATUTES CITED AND CONSTRUED—Continued.

Revised Statutes 1899.

Revised Statutes 1889.

Revised Statutes 1879.

General Statutes 1865.

Revised Statutes 1855.

Revised Statutes 1845.

Laws 1913.

STATUTES CITED AND CONSTRUED—Continued.

STREET. See Cities, 1 to 3.

TAXES AND TAXATION.

Drainage District: To Aid Private Enterprises. A drainage district has no power to levy taxes to aid a purely private enterprise. Where the plan of reclamation of land which it is proposed to include in a drainage district by an extension of its boundaries, is the plan agreed upon by a contract between the district engineer and the owner of a part of the land, by which that part was to be admitted to the benefits of the improvement and the cost to be charged against it was to be limited to a designated amount, the balance and principal amount to be charged against the remaining lands to be included against the will of its owners, the extension instituted for the purpose of consummating that contract should not be allowed. Drainage Dist. v. Harris, 159.

TELEGRAPH MONEY ORDER. See Tender.

TENDER.

1. **Evidence: Telegraph Order: Bankable Paper.** Testimony that a telegraph money order, tendered by the company's agent to an insurance company in payment of a premium note, is bankable paper in the sense that the banks of the town would put it to the credit of the holder and permit him to check out the amount thereof, is competent evidence, where the sufficiency of the tender of such order is the issue in the case. Smith v. Ins. Co., 342.

2. **Telegraph Money Order.** A telegraph money order drawn by the cashier of the sendee office of the Postal Telegraph-Cable Company upon its treasurer in New York is equally as satisfactory and trustworthy in the payment of debts as bank drafts or individual checks. Ib.

3. **Submitting Issue to Jury.** The facts stated in the opinion authorized the trial court to submit to the jury the issue of implied waiver of a tender of actual money. Ib.

4. **Draft or Order.** A tender of bank notes, checks or drafts or orders for the payment of money, if not objected to for failure to produce legal tender money, is a legal tender in payment of a private debt. Ib.

5. ———: **Implied Waiver.** The creditor, if he objects to a payment in bank notes or such things as represent money in the marts of trade and commerce, should put his refusal on that ground, and if he suppresses his objection at the time the offer is made, he is estopped from subsequently making the objection, if his later insistence thereon would inflict a loss or damage upon his debtor who in reliance upon his implied waiver failed to produce the kind of money made legal tender by law. Ib.

TITLE OF CASE. See Actions.

TITLE TO OFFICE. See Offices.

TITLE TO REAL ESTATE. See Corporations, 26 to 28.

TORTFEASORS.

Destruction of Fences: Participation in Wrong: Acts of Encouragement, Etc. In order that the owner of a farm may be legally responsible for the acts of his sons in destroying the fence which inclosed plaintiff's land, it was not necessary that such owner should have been personally present participating in the destructive acts of the sons, but if he aided, counselled and encouraged them to do the act, by words or deeds, he is liable; and such participation may be established by circumstantial evidence. And the evidence in this case was sufficient to justify the jury in inferring that the owner of the adjoining farm did advise or encourage his sons in the destruction of the fence. Sperry v. Hurd, 628.

TRESPASS.

1. **Destruction of Fence: Loss of Pasture: Speculative Damages.** Plaintiff is entitled to the loss of grass in his pasture caused by the repeated destruction of his fence, whereby his cattle passed out of the pasture, and because of which fact and to prevent the cattle from continually escaping and destroying other parts of his premises he was compelled to confine them in another inclosure. Such damage is not remote and speculative. Sperry v. Hurd, 628.

TRESPASS—Continued.

2. **Participation in Wrong: Acts of Encouragement, Etc.** In order that the owner of a farm may be legally responsible for the acts of his sons in destroying the fence which inclosed plaintiff's land, it was not necessary that such owner should have been personally present participating in the destructive acts of the sons, but if he aided, counselled and encouraged them to do the act, by words or deeds, he is liable; and such participation may be established by circumstantial evidence. And the evidence in this case was sufficient to justify the jury in inferring that the owner of the adjoining farm did advise or encourage his sons in the destruction of the fence. Sperry v. Hurd, 628.

3. **Excessive Verdict: Destruction of Fences: $7500 Exemplary Damages.** Exemplary damages cannot be accurately measured; but the character and standing of the parties, the malice with which the act was done, and the financial condition of the defendant are elements which should be taken into consideration, and the amount may be such as will serve, by way of example and punishment, to deter the commission of other like acts. It is *held* in this case that a verdict of $510 for actual damages for the destruction of defendant's fences, whereby he lost the grass of an eighty-acre pasture and his cattle escaped into and destroyed his five-acre orchard, was not excessive, but that a judgment of $7500 for exemplary damages is excessive by $6500. Ib.

UNINCORPORATED RELIGIOUS SOCIETY. See **Lands and Land Titles.**

VAGRANCY.

1. **Failure to Support Wife: No Element of Vagrancy.** Section 4789, Revised Statutes 1909, declaring, among other things, that "every able-bodied married man who shall neglect or refuse to provide for the support of his family . . . shall be deemed a vagrant" and upon conviction punished by imprisonment or fine, is a statute defining vagrancy, and cannot be used to enforce a civil liability; nor is a husband who honestly tries to obtain work and is unable to procure sufficiently remunerative employment to properly support his family, a criminal or a vagrant, nor can he be punished under said statute. [Disapproving Marolf v. Marolf, 191 Mo. App. 239, so far, if at all, as it conflicts with this holding.] State v. Burton, 61.

2. ———: ———: **Placing Wife With Sister to Board.** A husband who at a time when he was receiving sixty dollars per month put his wife and child with her sister under an agreement to pay her twenty dollars per month for their board and lodging, and paid the amount regularly for three months, and who having lost his position, after two or three weeks' effort to secure employment obtained a position at a hotel at five dollars a week, cannot be convicted for failure during the next three months to pay to his wife or her sister any part of the five dollars, his purpose being to discharge his obligation to his wife's sister as soon as he was able. Ib.

3. ———: ———: **Wife With Money.** The gift of one thousand dollars by his wife to her sister within the time her husband was unable to obtain remunerative employment simply has a tendency to show the wife was not in destitute circumstances. Ib.

VARIANCE.

1. **Gambling Device: Commonly Known: Proof.** Where the information charges that the gambling table which defendant set up is one "commonly known as a crap table," the State must show that there is a table commonly so known, and that it was this particular kind of table that defendant set up and kept; and where all the witnesses testify that the tables which defendant maintained and operated were not of the kind which they commonly knew as crap tables, and that a crap table is of a radically different design and construction, a conviction cannot stand. State v. Wade, 249.

2. ———: **Location: Street Number.** The information charged that defendant set up a craps table "at 118½ North Fifth ' Street." The evidence tended to prove that defendant set up gambling tables in the basement of premises designated as 118 North Fifth Street, the sole available entrance thereto being under a barber shop at said number, from which initial point a tunnel, equipped with a series of automatic doors, led to the room where the tables were; that the premises and entrance were commonly known as 118½ North Fifth Street; that defendant's mail in accordance with his direction, was addressed to 118½ North Fifth Street; and that when arrested defendant gave that number as his address. *Held*, by RE-VELLE, J., with whom FARIS and BLAIR, JJ., concur, that there is no fatal variance between the allegation and proof; that it was unnecessary to allege the exact location, since it did not relate to a constitutive part of the offense, and if a variance at all it is cured by Sec. 5114, R. S. 1909. *Held*, by GRAVES, J., with whom WOODSON, C. J., concurs, that the variance is not cured by the statute, but is fatal to the judgment. WALKER and BOND, JJ., do not concur with either opinion. Ib.

VERDICT.

1. **Excessive; Destruction of Fences: $7500 Exemplary Damages.** Exemplary damages cannot be accurately measured; but the character and standing of the parties, the malice with which the act was done, and the financial condition of the defendant are elements which should be taken into consideration, and the amount may be such as will serve, by way of example and' punishment, to deter the commission of other like acts. It is *held* in this case that a verdict of $510 for actual damages for the destruction of defendant's fences, whereby he lost the grass of an eighty-acre pasture and his cattle escaped into and destroyed his five-acre orchard, was not excessive, but that a judgment of $7500 for exemplary damages is excessive by $6500. Sperry v. Hurd, 628.

WABASH RAILWAY COMPANY. See **Railroads.**

WAIVER.

1. **Jurisdiction of Another Judge: Agreement upon Special Judge.** Where the record shows that an application for a change of venue was filed and that a judge of another circuit was called by the regular judge to sit in the case and "was on the bench" and tried the case without objection, it will be presumed, in the absence of a record showing to the contrary, that both the State and defendant waived the privilege of selecting a special judge; and, aided by the presumption of right action on the part of a court of general jurisdiction, it will be *held* that the udge so called in had authority to try the case. State v. Allen, 149.

WAIVER—Continued.

2. **Tender: Telegraph Money Order: Implied Waiver.** The creditor, if he objects to a payment in bank notes or such things as represent money in the marts of trade and commerce, should put his refusal on that ground, and if he suppresses his objection at the time the offer is made, he is estopped from subsequently making the objection, if his later insistence thereon would inflict a loss or damage upon his debtor who in reliance upon his implied waiver failed to produce the kind of money made legal tender by law. Smith v. Ins. Co., 342.

3. **Submitting Issues to Jury.** The facts stated in the opinion authorized the trial court to submit to the jury the issue of implied waiver of a tender of actual money. Ib.

4. **Motion to Strike Out.** Any error of the trial court in overruling defendant's motion to strike the amended petition from the files, on the ground that it constituted a departure, is waived by filing an answer to the merits and going to trial. Schroeder v. Edwards, 459.

5. **Insurance Policy: Forfeiture Conditions: Waiver.** The general agent of the insurance company who on its behalf issues a policy is the company's *alter ego*; and his knowledge that a forfeiture condition of the policy is being violated and his assurance of "all right" is a waiver of the condition; and a waiver may be inferred from the conduct and acts of the agent, and need not be proved by express agreement; his failure to express dissent when informed of a breach of the condition, is such evidence of waiver as to carry the question to the jury. Mining Co. v. Ins. Co., 524.

6. ———: ———: ———: **Acceptance of Premium.** Acceptance by the general agent who issued the policy of payment of an unpaid premium after the fire has occurred, with knowledge, is a waiver of the conditions of forfeiture. Ib.

7. ———: **Conspiracy of Agent and Insured: Telling Truth.** Telling the true facts by the agents as to knowledge and waiver of policy conditions is no evidence of a conspiracy or collusion between them and the insured. Ib.

8. ———: **Jurisdiction: By Appearance.** A motion to quash the service of process, which is in effect a demurrer to the jurisdiction of the court over the person of defendant and limited to that purpose, is not an appearance, such as amounts to a waiver of jurisdiction. [Per GRAVES, J.] Ib.

9. **Petition: Motion to Make Definite and Certain.** Defendant by answering over and going to trial on the merits waives any error to the action of the court in overruling his motion to require plaintiff to make his petition more definite and certain, and cannot urge any error in that ruling on appeal. Sperry v. Hurd, 628.

10. **Will Contest: Failure to Plead Interest.** A failure to allege in the petition that plaintiff has such a financial interest in the probate of the will as will enable him to institute a suit contesting its validity is not a defect to be classed as a want of "legal capacity to sue," and one that must therefore be raised by demurrer or answer, and if not so raised is to be considered waived. Lack of "legal capacity to sue," as used in the statute, has reference to some legal disability of the plaintiff, such as infancy, idiocy, coverture, and has no reference to the fact that the petition fails to state a cause of action. Gruender v. Frank, 713.

WILLS.

WILLS—Continued.

8. ——: ——: Incapacity: Monomania. An instruction telling the jury that if they find from the evidence that at the time of making the will, the mind of testatrix "was unsound or impaired in any one or more particulars, yet practically sound and unimpaired in all others, still you will not be warranted in finding that she was thereby mentally incapacitated from making a will," is misleading, since it authorized the jury to sustain the will, even though her mental impairment had gone to the extent of rendering her incapable of understanding the nature and extent of her property. Ray v. Westall, 130.

9. Intention as to Executors. The rule that the expressed intention of the testator must be the guide in construing a will, applies to every part of it—to the expressed desire that a nominated executor should administer the whole estate, the assets in the State where testator died and those in other States, as well as to other parts of it. State ex rel. v. Holtcamp, 412.

10. Executor: Renunciation. The person named as executor in a will may renounce his right to be appointed either by an express renunciation, or by acts and conduct *in pais*. Ib.

11. Contest: Evidence: Will of Testator's Father. In a suit by a disinherited contestant to set aside his bachelor brother's will, made in 1909 in favor of his mother, sisters and another brother, on the ground of incapacity and undue influence, a will made by the father of testator and of contestant in 1875 is not admissible as having a tendency to disprove testimony offered by proponents and improperly admitted by the court to the effect that contestant was indebted to his mother, the fact being that such indebtedness was by way of an advancement by the mother to contestant on account of his prospective share in his father's estate. Buck v. Buck, 644.

12. Contrary to Testator's Understanding. Where the will was drawn in accordance with the bachelor testator's instructions and he read it over and expressed satisfaction with it, and then was told by his lawyer that in the event the remaindermen survived the life tenant and died without issue the property would go under the statute to his brothers, and thereupon he requested that it be executed, the court cannot peremptorily instruct the jury to find for contestant on the ground that the will was not testator's will. Besides, it is not necessary that testator have the knowledge of the will's scope and bearing possessed by his legal adviser. Ib.

13. ——: Instruction: Contrary to Will Itself. Where the will of the unmarried testator cancels his brother's debts, gives the property to his mother for life and in remainder to his sisters, and provides that if the mother survives the sisters and they die without issue the property is to be disposed of according to the mother's will, it is not error to refuse to submit to the jury the question whether it was the testator's intention to provide that, if his sisters survived his mother and died without issue, the property should go to his brothers. Such question should not be submitted to the jury, although testator was informed by his lawyer before executing the will that the property, in such contingency, would go to his brothers. Ib.

14. Remarks of Counsel: Attack on Contestant. In a suit to set aside a will on the sole grounds of the mental incapacity of the testator and of undue influence exercised upon his mind, it is improper to permit counsel for proponents to say in his argu-

WILLS—Continued.

ment to the jury of and concerning contestant: "He was a spendthrift son. He never did anything for the support of the family. He took from his mother's estate so far as he could, and his family had to leave the city to get rid of him, or to get rid of his attempts to get the family's money. He was not a success in business life."' Whether true or false, the remarks were not relevant to the issues, and therefore unauthorized, and being a personal reflection upon contestant were improper. But they were not reversible error, where there is a preponderance of affirmative evidence that the testator was of sound mind and subject to no undue influence, and little substantial error to the contrary. Ib.

15. **Contest: Pleading: Interest of Plaintiff.** In a suit to set aside a will the petition must allege such facts as show that the contestant has a financial interest in the estate and one which would be benefited by setting the will aside, unless such facts are admitted by the pleadings of the proponents. Otherwise, the petition will not show a cause of action. Gruender v. Frank, 713.

16. ———: ———: ———: **Waiver.** A failure to allege in the petition that plaintiff has such a financial interest in the probate of the will as will enable him to institute a suit contesting its validity is not a defect to be classed as a want of "legal capacity to sue," and one that must therefore be raised by demurrer or answer, and if not raised is to be considered waived. Lack of "legal capacity to sue," as used in the statute, has reference to some legal disability of the plaintiff, such as infancy, idiocy, coverture, and has no reference to the fact that the petition fails to state a cause of action. Ib.

17. ———: ———: ———: ———: **General Denial: Demurrer to Evidence.** A petition which fails to state the interest of plaintiff in the probate of the will does not state a cause of action for setting aside the will, and that defect is not waived by failure to make specific objection by demurrer or answer, but a general denial contained in one of the answers is sufficient to raise the issue of fact, and plaintiff is thereby required to prove the existence of such facts as will show him entitled to maintain the suit, and if he fails to do so the court errs in overruling a demurrer to the evidence. Ib.

18. ———: ———: **Stating Interest of Heirs.** The body of the petition in a suit to set aside a will should allege facts showing that plaintiffs are heirs of the deceased testator. It is not enough simply to name them in the caption. Ib.

Rules of the Supreme Court of Missouri

REVISED AND ADOPTED APRIL 10, 1916.

Rule 1.—Chief Justice, Duty. The Chief Justice shall be elected for a term of one and three-sevenths years, and shall superintend matters of order in the courtroom.

Rule 2.—Motions to be Written, etc. All motions shall be in writing, signed by counsel and filed of record. At least twenty-four hours notice of the filing of same, unless herein otherwise provided, shall be given to the adverse party or his attorney.

Rule 3.—Argument of Motions. No motion shall be argued unless by the direction of the court.

Rule 4.—Diminution of Record, Suggestion after Joinder in Error. No suggestion of diminution of record in civil cases will be entertained after joinder in error, except by consent of the parties.

Rule 5.—Application for Certiorari. Whenever *certiorari* is applied for to correct a record, an affidavit shall be made thereto of the defect in the transcript sought to be supplied and at least twenty-four hours notice of such application shall be given to the adverse party or his attorney.

Rule 6.—Reviewing Instructions. To enable this court to review the action of the trial court in giving and refusing instructions it shall not be necessary to set out the evidence in the bill of exceptions; but it shall be sufficient to state that there was evidence tending to prove the particular fact or facts. If the parties disagree as to what fact or facts the evidence tends to prove, then the testimony of the witnesses shall be stated in narrative form, avoiding repetition and omitting immaterial matter.

Rule 7.—Bills of Exceptions in Equity Cases. In equity cases the entire evidence shall be embodied in the bill of exceptions; provided it shall be sufficient to state the legal effect of documentary evidence where there is no dispute as to its admissibility or legal effect; and provided further that parole evidence shall be reduced to a narrative form where this can be done and its full force and effect be preserved.

Rule 8.—Presumptions in Support of Bills of Exceptions. In the absence of a showing to the contrary, it will be presumed as a matter of fact that bills of exceptions contain all the evidence applicable to any particular ruling to which exception is saved.

Rule 9.—Making up Transcripts. Clerks of courts in making out transcripts of the record for the Supreme Court, unless an exception is saved to the regularity of the process or its execution, or to the acquiring by the court of jurisdiction in the cause, shall not set out the original or any subsequent writ or the return thereof, but in lieu of same shall simply note the dates respectively of the issuance and execution of the summons.

If any pleading be amended, the clerk in making out the transcript will only insert therein the last amended pleading and will set out no abandoned pleading or part of the record not called for by the bill of exceptions; nor shall any clerk insert in the transcript any matter touching the organization of the court or any continuance, motion or affidavit not made a part of the bill of exceptions.

Rule 10.—"Appellant" and "Respondent:" What They Include. Whenever the words appellant and respondent appear in these rules they shall be taken to mean and include plaintiff in error and defendant in error and other parties occupying like positions in a case.

Rule 11.—Abstracts In Lieu of Transcript, When Filed and Served. Where the appellant shall, under the provisions of section 2048, Revised Statutes 1909, file a copy of the judgment, order or decree, in lieu of a complete transcript, he shall deliver to the respondent a copy of his abstract at least thirty days before the cause is set for hearing, and in a like time file ten copies thereof with our clerk. If the respondent is not satisfied with such abstract, he shall deliver to the appellant an additional abstract at least fifteen days before the cause is set for hearing, and within like time file ten copies thereof with our clerk. Objections to such additional abstract shall be filed with our clerk within ten days after service of such abstract upon the appellant, and a copy of such objections shall be served upon the respondent in like time.

Rule 12.—Abstracts: When Filed and Served. Where a complete transcript is brought to this court in the first instance, the appellant shall deliver to the respondent a copy of his abstract of the record at least thirty days before the day on which the cause is set for hearing, and file ten copies thereof with our clerk not later than the day preceding the one on which the cause is set for hearing. If the respondent desires to file an additional abstract he shall deliver to the appellant a copy of same at least five days before the cause is set for hearing and file ten copies thereof with our clerk on the day preceding that on which the cause is to be heard.

Rule 13.—Abstracts: What They Shall Contain. The abstracts mentioned in Rules 11 and 12 shall be printed in fair type, be paged and have a complete index at the end thereof, which index shall specifically identify exhibits when there are more than one, and said abstract shall set forth so much of the record as is necessary to a complete understanding of all the questions presented for decision. Where there is no controversy as to the pleadings or as to deeds or other documentary evidence it shall be sufficient to set out the substance of such pleadings or documentary evidence. The evidence of witnesses shall be in narrative form except when the questions and answers are necessary to a complete understanding of the testimony. Pleadings and documentary evidence shall be set forth in full when there is any question as to the former or as to the admissibility or legal effect of the latter; in all other respects the abstract must set for a copy of so much of the record as is necessary to be consulted in the disposition of the assigned errors.

Rule 14.—Printed Transcripts. A printed and indexed transcript duly certified by the clerk of the trial court may be filed instead of a manuscript record, and in all cases ten printed, indexed and uncertified copies of the entire record, filed and served within the time prescribed by the rules for serving abstracts, shall be deemed a full compliance with said rules and dispense with the necessity of any further abstracts.

Rule 15.—Briefs: What to Contain and When Served. The appellant shall deliver to the respondent a copy of his brief thirty days before the day on which the cause is set for hearing, and the respondent shall deliver a copy of his brief to the appellant at least five days before the last named date, and the appellant shall deliver a copy of his reply brief to the respondent not later than the day preceding that on which the cause is set for hearing, and ten copies of each brief shall be filed with the clerk on or before the last named date.

All briefs shall be printed and the brief for appellant shall contain under separate heads: (1) a fair and concise statement of the facts of the case without reiteration, statements of law or argument; (2) a statement, in numerical order, of the points relied upon, with citation of authorities thereunder, and no reference will be permitted at the argument to errors not thus specified; and (3) a printed argument, if such is desired. The respondent in his brief may adopt the statement of appellant; or, if not satisfied therewith, he shall, in a concise statement, correct any errors therein. In other respects the brief of respondent shall follow the order of that required of appellant. No brief or statement which violates this rule will be considered by the court.

In citing authorities counsel shall give the names of the parties in any case cited and the number of the volume and page where the case may be found; and when reference is made to any elementary work or treatise the number of the edition, the volume, section and page where the matter referred to may be found shall be set forth.

Rule 16.—Failure to Comply with Rules 11, 12, 13, and 15. If any appellant in any civil case fail to comply with the rules numbered 11, 12, 13 and 15, the court, when the cause is called for hearing, will dismiss the appeal, or writ of error; or, at the option of the respondent continue the cause at the cost of the party in default.

Rule 17.—Costs: When Allowed for Printing Abstracts and Records. Costs will not be allowed either party for any abstract filed in lieu of a complete transcript under section 2048, R. S. 1909, which fails to make a full presentation of the record necessary to be considered in disposing of all the questions arising in the cause. But in cases brought to this court by a copy of the judgment, order or decree instead of a complete transcript, and in which the appellant shall file a printed copy of the entire record as and for an abstract, costs will be allowed for printing the same.

Where a manuscript record has been or may be filed in this court, a reasonable fee for printing an abstract of the record or the entire record in lieu of an abstract may be taxed as costs upon the written stipulation of both parties to that effect. The affidavit of the printer shall be received in cases where costs may properly be taxed for printing, as prima-facie evidence of the reasonableness thereof; and objections thereto may be filed within ten days after service of notice of the amount of such charge.

Rule 18.—Service of Abtracts and Briefs. Delivery of an abstract or brief to the attorney of record of the opposing party shall be deemed a delivery to such party under the foregoing rules, and the evidence of such delivery must be by the written acknowledgement of such opposing party or his attorney or the affidavit of the person making the service, and such evidence of service must be filed with the abstract or brief.

Rule 19.—Service of Abstracts and Briefs in Criminal Cases. Attorneys for appellants in criminal cases in which transcripts have been filed in the office of the clerk sixty days before the day the cause is docketed for hearing, shall, at least thirty days before the day of hearing, file in the office of the clerk of this court a printed statement containing apt references to the pages of the transcript, with an assignment of errors and brief of points and an argument, and serve a copy thereof upon the.Attorney-General, and thereupon the Attorney-General shall, fifteen days before 'the day of hearing, serve defendant or his counsel wth a copy of his statement and brief.

When a criminal case shall be advanced on the docket the court shall designate the time for filing statements and briefs.

When such transcript has been filed in this court fifteen days before the first day of the term at which such case is set for hearing, the appellant or plaintiff in error shall file his statement, brief and assignments of error five days before the first day of such term, and the Attorney-General shall, on or before the first day of the term, file his brief and statement.

Hereafter no statement or brief shall be filed in a criminal case out of time, nor will counsel who violate this rule be heard in oral argument unless for a good cause shown on motion theretofore filed and ruled on before the day set for the hearing of the case.

When appellants have been allowed to prosecute their appeal as poor persons by the trial court, counsel will be permitted to file typewritten statements and briefs. In cases where the transcript has been filed thirty days before the day on which the cause is docketed, counsel for appellant shall file their statements, briefs and assignments of error fifteen days before the hearing, and the Attorney-General his brief and statement five days before the hearing.

Rule 20.—Taking Record from Clerk's Office. No member of the bar shall be permitted to take a record from the clerk's office.

Rule 21.—Motions for Rehearing. Motions for rehearing must be accompanied by a brief statement of the reasons for a reconsideration of the cause, and must be founded on papers showing clearly that some question decisive of the case, and duly submitted by counsel, has been overlooked by the court, or that the decision is in conflict with an express statute, or with a controlling decision to which the attention of the court was not called through the neglect or inadvertence of counsel; and the question so submitted by counsel and overlooked by the court, or the sta ute with which the decision conflicts, or the controlling decision to which the attention of the court was not called, as the case may be, must be distinctly and particularly set forth in the motion, otherwise the motion will be disregarded. Such motion must be filed within ten days after the opinion of the court shall be delivered, and notice of the filing thereof must be served on the opposite counsel. After a cause has been once reheard and the motion for rehearing overruled either in division or *En Banc* no further motion for rehearing or motion to set aside the order overruling the motion for rehearing, by the same party, will be entertained by the court or filed by the clerk.

Rule 22.—Extension of Time. Hereafter in no case will extension of time for filing statements, abstracts and briefs be granted, except upon affidavit showing satisfactory cause.

Rule 23.—Notice to Adverse Party. A party, in any cause, filing a motion either to dismiss an appeal or writ of error, or to affirm the judgment, shall first notify the adverse party or his attorney of record, at least twenty-four hours before making the motion, by telegram, by letter, or by written notice, and shall on filing such motion, satisfy the court that such notice has been given.

SUPREME COURT RULES.

Rule 24.—Transfers to Court En Banc. A motion to transfer a cause under the provisions of the Constitution from either division to court *En Banc* must be filed within ten days after the final disposition of the cause by the division, and notice of such motion shall be given as provided in Rule 23.

Rule 25.—Return of Original Writs. Original writs or other process issued by either division of the court, or by any judge in vacation, may be made returnable to and disposed of by such division, or the Court *En Banc*, as such division or judge in vacation may order.

Rule 26.—Assignment of Motions in Civil Causes. All motions and matters in civil causes which have not been assigned by the Court *En Banc* to a division for final determination, upon the record, shall be presented to, heard and determined by the Court *En Banc*. All matters in civil causes which have been assigned to a division shall be presented to and heard and determined by such divison.

Rule 27.—Assignment of Criminal Causes. All criminal causes, and matters pertaining thereto, shall be heard and determined by Division Number Two.

Rule 28.—When Appeal Is Returnable: Certificate of Judgment: Transcript. Where appeals shall be taken or writs of error sued out, the appellant shall file a complete transcript or in lieu thereof a certificate of judgment as provided by section 2048, Revised Statutes 1909, within the time provided by said section and the date of the allowance of the appeal and not the time of filing the bill of exceptions after the appeal is granted, shall determine the term to which such appeal is returnable; and when the appellant for any reason cannot or does not file a complete transcript, he shall file within the time allowed by said section 2048 a certificate of judgment, and may thereafter file a complete transcript and an abstract of the record, or simply an abstract of the record. And neither the fact that this court has heretofore held that the return term of the appeal is to be determined by the date of the filing of the bill of exceptions, nor the fact that for any reason a complete transcript could not be filed in time for the return term, shall be taken as an excuse, but in all such cases the appellant shall file a certificate of the judgment as and when required by said section 2048, Revised Statutes 1909.

Rule 29.—Oral Arguments. The time allowed for oral argument and statement shall be an hour and ten minutes for appellant or plaintiff in error, or relator in original proceedings, and fifty minutes for respondent or defendant in error or respondent in original proceedings.

Rule 30.—Letters, etc., to Court. All motions, briefs, letters or communications in any wise relating to a matter pending in this court must be addressed to the clerk, who will lay them before the court in due course. Hereafter any letter or communication relating directly or indirectly to any pending matter, addressed personally or officially to any judge of this court, will be filed with the case and be open to the inspection of the public and opposing parties.

Rule 31.—Record Matters on Appeal. Hereafter an appellant, filing here a certified copy of the order granting an appeal, need not abstract the record entries showing the steps taken below to perfect such appeal. If the abstract state the appeal was duly taken, then absent a record showing to the contrary, by respondent, it will be presumed the proper steps were taken at the proper time and term.

SUPREME COURT RULES.

Hereafter no appellant need abstract record entries evidencing his leave to file, or the filing of, a bill of exceptions. It shall be sufficient if his abstract state the bill of exceptions was duly filed. The burden is then on respondent to produce here the record showing the contrary to be the fact, if he make the point.

Rule 32.—Granting Original Writs. No original remedial writ, except *habeas corpus*, will be issued by this court in any case wherein adequate relief can be afforded by an appeal or writ of error, or by application for such writ to a court having in that behalf concurrent jurisdiction.

Rule 33.—Procedure as to Original Writs. Oral arguments will not be granted on applications for original remedial writs; and before such writs shall issue, the applicant therefor shall give not less than five days' notice thereof to the adverse party, or his attorney. Such notice shall be in writing, accompanied by a copy of the application for the writ, and the suggestions in support of same. The adverse party may file in this court suggestions in opposition to the issuance of the writ, a copy of which he shall, before filing, serve on the applicant. Whenever the required notice would, in the judgment of the court, defeat the purpose of the writ, it may be dispensed with. On final hearing printed abstracts and briefs shall be filed in all respects as is required in appeals and writs of error in ordinary cases. Motions for reconsideration of the court's action in refusing applications for original writs shall not be filed.

Rule 34.—Certiorari to Courts of Appeals. No writ of *certiorari* shall be granted to quash the judgment of a Court of Appeals on the ground that such court has failed or refused to follow the last controlling decision of the Supreme Court, unless the applicant for such writ shall give all parties to be adversely affected, or their attorneys of record, at least five days' notice of such application; and the applicant shall, in a petition of not exceeding five pages, concisely set out the issue presented to the Court of Appeals and show wherein and in what manner the alleged conflicting ruling arose, and shall designate the precise place in our official reports where the controlling decision will be found. Said petition shall be accompanied by a true copy of the opinion of the Court of Appeals complained of, a copy of the motion for rehearing or to transfer the cause to this court, a copy of the ruling of the Court of Appeals on said motion, and suggestions in support of the petition not to exceed six printed typewritten pages.

The notice to the party to be adversely affected shall be printed or typewritten, accompanied by a true copy of the petition and all exhibits and suggestions in regard thereto. The party to be adversely affected may file, on or before the date fixed by the notice, suggestions of not more than five printed or typewritten pages stating the reasons why such writ should not issue.

Rule '
a cause up
to court J
sition of
given as

R
proce
vacat
ion,
ma

tj
t'

Lightning Source UK Ltd.
Milton Keynes UK
UKHW050915041218
333390UK00037B/773/P